W9-BTP-900

Fodor's

SOUTHERN
CALIFORNIA

Welcome to Southern California

Balmy weather, blissful beaches, chic desert resorts, Hollywood glamour—Southern California delivers fun and relaxation year-round. Outdoor enthusiasts revel in the drama of the Mojave Desert and the Big Sur coast. Beachgoers appreciate the state's seemingly endless stretches of sand. In trendy Los Angeles and sunny San Diego, culture vultures enjoy superb restaurants, movie studio tours, and America's preeminent zoo. Note that this book was produced during the COVID-19 pandemic. As you plan your travels, please confirm that places are still open and let us know when we need to make updates at editors@fodors.com.

TOP REASONS TO GO

★ **Cool Cities:** San Diego's bay, Los Angeles's movie lore, Palm Springs' spa resorts.

★ **Beaches:** For swimming, surfing, or tanning, the beaches can't be beat.

★ **Feasts:** Cutting-edge cuisine, food trucks, fusion flavors, farmers' markets.

★ **Theme Parks:** From Disneyland to LEGOLAND, SoCal has some of the biggest and best.

★ **Outdoor Adventures:** Hiking, golfing, and national park excursions are all excellent.

★ **Road Trips:** The Pacific Coast Highway offers spectacular views and thrills aplenty.

Contents

Fodor's Features

Lions and Tigers and Bears 75

MAPS

EXPERIENCE SOUTHERN CALIFORNIA

20 ULTIMATE EXPERIENCES

Southern California offers terrific experiences that should be on every traveler's list. Here are Fodor's top picks for a memorable trip.

1 Hike the Hollywood Sign

The iconic Hollywood sign was originally erected in 1923 and read "Hollywoodland." The easiest path starts from the Griffith Park Observatory. *(Ch. 6)*

2 Find the Weird at Venice Beach

California's counterculture—bodybuilders at Muscle Beach, head shops on the boardwalk—contrasts with multimillion-dollar homes along the Venice Canals. *(Ch. 6)*

3 Catch Waves in Malibu

Surfrider Beach, a stretch of Malibu that includes the Malibu Pier, is popular with surfers and beach bums. On Zuma Beach, surfers share the water with sea lions. *(Ch. 6)*

4 Suspend Disbelief at Universal Studios

Universal has more than just thrill rides. Tours offer a good look at familiar movie sets. The Wizarding World of Harry Potter offers total immersion. *(Ch. 6)*

5 Take the Ferry to Coronado

The 15-minute ferry ride to Coronado provides great views of Downtown San Diego and the Naval Air Station. *(Ch. 4)*

6 Shop and Dine in Seaport Village

San Diego's 14-acre, open-air Seaport Village shopping and dining complex often hosts special events. *(Ch. 4)*

7 Explore Old Town San Diego

California's earliest settlement and San Diego's most storied neighborhood is a hub for historical attractions and cultural celebrations, as well as souvenir shops and Mexican restaurants. *(Ch. 4)*

8 Spend a Day in Balboa Park

This 1,200-acre urban oasis contains museums, performing arts venues, gardens, sculpture, and other attractions like the San Diego Zoo. *(Ch. 4)*

9 Explore the Gaslamp Quarter

A guided walking tour is a great way to experience this bustling, 16-block historic district, which is also a shopping, dining, and nightlife hub. *(Ch. 4)*

10 Experience San Diego's Wild Side

The San Diego Zoo and the San Diego Safari Park showcase wildlife without the claustrophobic animal cages. *(Ch. 4)*

11 Camp in Joshua Tree

Just east of Palm Springs is this national park, named for the yucca trees that Mormons named after the biblical Joshua, who raised his hands into the sky. *(Ch. 8)*

12 Traverse Death Valley

One of the hottest places on Earth sits on the eastern edge of California along the border with Nevada. *(Ch. 10)*

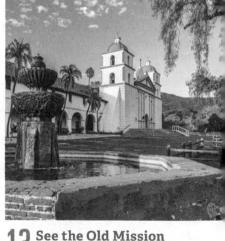

13 See the Old Mission Santa Barbara

The "Queen of Missions"—one of the Central Coast's most photographed structures—also contains superb colonial Spanish/Mexican art. *(Ch. 11)*

14 Seals at La Jolla

Seals and sea lions love the Children's Pool Beach, but keep your distance. For good views from Coast Avenue, walk along the sea cliffs toward the seawall. *(Ch. 4)*

15 Find Your Inner Child at Disneyland

"The Happiest Place on Earth" continues to delight children and all but the most cynical adults. *(Ch. 5)*

16 Go to a Show Taping in L.A.

Dozens of sitcoms, talk shows, and game shows film every day in Los Angeles, and you can get tickets to be an audience member. *(Ch. 6)*

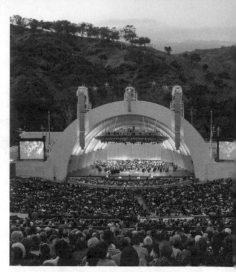

17 See a Concert at the Hollywood Bowl

This live-music amphitheater built into the side of the Hollywood Hills is known for its incredible acoustics. *(Ch. 6)*

18 See Stars on the Walk of Fame

The first stars were revealed in the early 1960s; today, more than 2,600 dot the pavement. *(Ch. 6)*

19 Experience Opulence at the Hearst Castle

At this Roaring '20s celebrity hotspot you can tour the zoo, gold-leaf Roman pool, and priceless art collection. *(Ch. 11)*

20 Get a Bird's-eye View of Palm Springs

Ride the Palm Springs Aerial Tramway—the world's largest rotating tramway. At the top (8,516 feet) are restaurants and hiking trails. *(Ch. 7)*

California Today

"Has the Golden State Lost Its Luster?" "Is the California Dream Dead?" So read the rueful headlines upon the early-2021 announcement of California's first-ever population decline (in 2020) and, based on recent census data, the loss of a congressional seat. These articles and similar pieces detailed the supposedly insurmountable obstacles—most notably the high cost of living (especially housing), but also wildfires, drought, crime, traffic congestion, homelessness, COVID-19, and high taxes—fueling out-of-state migration.

So dire were some of the assessments that one might have assumed there was no reason to stay (or come for a visit). This was despite the fact that everything that has lured settlers and tourists from the get-go—among them breathtaking scenery, abundant natural resources, agricultural bounty, and a hospitable climate—remains well in evidence.

Although California, like the rest of the nation and world, faces daunting challenges, the same gloomy predictions (often bearing precisely the same "lost its luster" and "dream dead" headlines) have appeared before: in the middle of the Great Recession (2009), after the first dot-com implosion (2000), all the way back to the gold and silver busts of the 19th century. And guess what? In every instance, the state bounced back, sometimes brilliantly.

Each allegedly ruinous calamity required reinvention, and each time residents rose to the occasion. Based on the past, there's no reason to think that the Golden State won't regain its luster—if it's even been lost.

POPULATION, POTENTIAL

California's birth rate and the pace of migration may have slowed, but they're hardly stagnant. For perspective, consider that the current population of just under 40 million (an eighth of the U.S. . total) represents a 2.2 million increase between 2010 and 2020, the third-highest after Texas and Florida. While many residents departing California cite the high cost of living, recent transplants tend to perceive the same potential in the state as previous settlers.

HISTORICAL CONTEXT

By most accounts, the ancestors of California's indigenous peoples migrated from Asia, traversing a land bridge across the Bering Strait that formerly joined what's now Russia and Alaska. Some of these trailblazers continued south to California, flourishing for centuries off the fertile land. Many famous place names—Malibu, Napa, Ojai, Shasta, and Sonoma among them—reflect this heritage.

Millennia later, Spanish explorers ventured north from Mexico searching for gold, with converts to Christianity the quest of 18th-century missionaries. Nineteenth-century miners rushed here from the world over also seeking gold—the state achieved statehood two years after the precious metal's 1848 discovery.

During the 20th century, successive, sometimes overlapping, waves of newcomers followed in their footsteps: real-estate speculators, would-be motion-picture actors and producers, Dust Bowl farmers and migrant workers, Asians fleeing poverty or chasing opportunity, sexual and gender pioneers, artists, dot-commers, and venture capitalists.

POLITICS

The result is a population that leans toward idealism (some say utopianism)—without necessarily being as liberal as voter-registration statistics might lead one to think. (Democrats hold a 2–1 registration advantage over Republicans, the latter essentially tied with "no party preference.") This is Ronald Reagan's old stomping ground after all, and Herbert Hoover's, and Richard Nixon was born here. If you wander into some inland counties, you may see signs proposing a breakaway, more conservative 51st State of Jefferson. Many residents in these areas supported 2021 efforts to recall Governor Gavin Newsom, a liberal Democrat. (Early summer polls indicated the special-election race might be tight, but the governor prevailed by a substantial margin.)

DEMOGRAPHICS

As with politics, despite the stereotype of the blue-eyed, blond surfer, California's population isn't homogeneous either. Latino residents outnumber Whites 39%–36%, with Asians (15%) and African Americans (6%) the next-largest groups. Residents here speak more than 220 languages, making California by far the nation's most linguistically diverse state.

ECONOMICS

Back to California's supposedly desperate situation: keep in mind that, in 2021, the Golden State reported a $75 billion budget *surplus*, hardly numbers to prompt despair and proving the Great Recession doomsayers predicting economic catastrophe way off the mark. California, responsible for 14% of gross domestic product, leads all other states in terms of the income generated by agriculture, tourism, entertainment, and industrial activity. With a gross state product of approximately $3 trillion (median household income about $75,000), by many estimates, California would have the world's fifth-largest economy were it an independent nation.

STILL DREAMIN'

In mid-2021, dueling state-of-the-state analyses appeared within days of each other. A historian's *New York Times* opinion piece described the 2020 census numbers and the loss of the seat in Congress as among recent negative "firsts" for California that had "sapped the collective sense of zealous optimism." The historian also predicted "decades of pain" if politicians don't quickly produce solutions to California's pressing problems.

Two days before the *Times* piece ran, the University of California published a study suggesting pretty much the opposite: that the rate of residents moving out of state is not unusual and isn't something to fret over; that residents, by a 2–1 majority, still believe in the California Dream; and that the state attracts more than half the nation's venture-capital investments, a sign that favorable economic conditions persist.

The naysayers may well be right about California's demise, but if history is any indication, the populace will likely shift gears as necessary. And again the next time it's required.

WHAT'S WHERE

1 San Diego. San Diego's Gaslamp Quarter and early California–theme Old Town have a human scale—but big-ticket animal attractions like the San Diego Zoo pull in visitors.

2 Disneyland and Orange County. A diverse destination with premium resorts and restaurants, strollable waterfront communities, and kid-friendly attractions.

3 Los Angeles. Go for the glitz of the entertainment industry, but stay for the rich cultural attributes and communities.

4 Palm Springs and the Desert Resorts. Golf on some of the West's most challenging courses, lounge at fabulous resorts, check out mid-century-modern architectural gems, and trek through primitive desert parks.

5 Joshua Tree National Park. Proximity to major urban areas—as well as world-class rock climbing and nighttime celestial displays—help make this one of the most visited national parks.

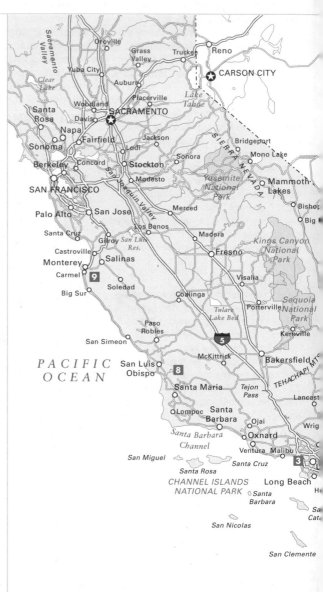

6 Mojave Desert.
Material pleasures are in short supply here, but Mother Nature's stark beauty more than compensates.

7 Death Valley National Park. This vast, beautiful national park is often the hottest place in the country.

8 The Central Coast. Three of the state's top stops—swanky Santa Barbara, Hearst Castle, and Big Sur—sit along the scenic 200-mile route. A quick boat trip away lies scenic Channel Islands National Park.

9 Monterey Bay Area. Postcard-perfect Monterey, Victorian-flavored Pacific Grove, and exclusive Carmel all share this stretch of California coast. To the north, Santa Cruz boasts a boardwalk, a UC campus, ethnic clothing shops, and plenty of surfers.

What to Eat and Drink in Southern California

Avocado toast

CRAFT BEER
Dubbed the "Capital of Craft," San Diego has more than 150 craft breweries, a movement that began with Karl Strauss Brewing Company in 1989. Since then, the San Diego Brewers Guild established the San Diego Beer Week held every November, and a few neighborhoods have become craft brewery destinations in their own right.

L.A. HOT DOGS
While every major city in the country has their own take on street hot dogs, L.A.'s Mexican-inspired version is arguably the best. Wrapped in bacon and topped with grilled onions, bell peppers, ketchup, mustard, mayo, and jalapenos, it's practically a ritual for anyone stumbling home drunk to grab one. Look for street carts in areas with a lot of bars.

KOREAN BBQ TACOS
If you like Korean BBQ and you enjoy street tacos, then you might be ready for Korean BBQ tacos, one of the few culinary creations that originated in La La Land. They're exactly what they sound like—tacos but with Korean BBQ meats— and the best place to get them is from one of Roy Choi's legendary Kogi food trucks. To find a location, go to *kogibbq.com*.

In-N-Out

FISH TACOS
There's a great debate about who makes the best fish tacos in San Diego. Rubio's Coastal Grill is credited with popularizing fish tacos in the U.S.; the original location is still in Pacific Beach. The original tacos have fried pollock, white sauce, salsa, cabbage, and a corn tortilla.

MEZCAL
Mezcal is made from the agave plant, typically in Oaxaca, Mexico, so naturally the best Oaxacan restaurant in L.A. (Guelaguetza) would have a top-shelf selection. Hollywood's Sassafrass Saloon has exquisite craft mezcals.

IN-N-OUT
No California food list is complete without the legendary In-N-Out. "Where's the closest In-N-Out?" is asked by just about every tourist the moment they arrive. In-N-Out burgers and fries are made fresh and made to order, which is why they're so good in the first place.

FRENCH DIP
Not only was the French Dip invented in Los Angeles, two different restaurants claim its origin. Philippe the Original in Downtown opened in 1908 and is a counter-style diner; Cole's, also opened in 1908, is (slightly) more upscale and features a hidden speakeasy in the back of the restaurant.

SEAFOOD FRESH FROM THE OCEAN
You don't have to go far to find a bounty of fresh seafood, most likely sourced from the waters off Southern California. Always check out the day's catch—served shucked and placed on ice or in a sandwich, salad, or other dish.

VEGETARIAN FOOD
Californians are generally known to be health conscious, eating lots of fresh local produce (including adding avocado to everything). There are abundant vegetarian and vegan options throughout most of Southern California.

TIKI COCKTAILS
Tiki culture has obvious parallels to San Diego's tropical, laid-back vacation vibe, so it's no surprise that the concept took root here with rum as the star spirit. Sure bets include The Grass Skirt and False Idol. If you're heading to Palm Springs, check out Bootlegger Tiki, Tonga Hut, or Toucans Tiki Lounge.

10 Best Beaches in San Diego

CORONADO

Often praised for its sparkling sand, the island is home to Hotel del Coronado, a 130-year-old luxury hotel perfect for postbeach snacks; Del Beach, which is open to the public; and Dog Beach where pooches can run free sans leash.

MISSION BEACH

Located near SeaWorld San Diego, Mission Beach is home to a bustling boardwalk that's frequented by walkers, cyclists, and people-watchers. The bay is popular for water sports such as stand-up paddleboarding and Jet Skiing, but the beach is best known for Belmont Park, its oceanfront amusement park.

WINDANSEA BEACH

Seasoned surfers should head to La Jolla's Windansea Beach for powerful waves. Tucked away in a residential area, Windansea's entrance is marked by large rocks that make for a great place to watch or dry out, but recreational swimming is not advised here due to the strong surf.

TORREY PINES STATE BEACH

Situated at the base of a 1,500-acre natural reserve, La Jolla's Torrey Pines State Beach offers a long, narrow stretch of pristine beach framed by picturesque sea cliffs. Beachgoers can add a hike to their itinerary that starts or finishes on the sand, with plenty of lookout areas for great photo ops. Beyond the bluffs, a salt marsh provides seclusion from businesses and their associated street noise.

LA JOLLA SHORES

Pack up the whole family for a beach day in La Jolla Shores, which is known for its calm waves, two parks, and playground. Sea caves and underwater canyons that are part of La Jolla Underwater Park and Ecological Reserve—a marine protected area—attract kayakers and scuba divers.

DEL MAR CITY BEACH

In the upscale coastal neighborhood of Del Mar lie two beach parks that are popular for special events because of their stunning views of the Pacific. Seagrove Park is perched on the hill at the end of 15th Street, with benches for ocean gazing and winding paths along the bluffs. Farther north across the railroad tracks, Powerhouse Park offers easy beach access, a playground area, and a volleyball court.

La Jolla Shores is the best beach in San Diego for water sports.

SWAMI'S STATE BEACH

West of the magnificent Self-Realization Fellowship Temple and Meditation Gardens in Encinitas, this beach draws surfers and yogis in with its Zen vibes, while others treat the steep staircase leading down to the beach as a workout, with a rewarding view of sea cliffs waiting at the bottom. At low tide, shells and other sea creatures are left behind for beachcombers to easily discover.

FLETCHER COVE BEACH PARK

Nestled in the heart of Solana Beach, Fletcher Cove Beach Park doubles as a recreational park and beach access area. Here you'll find a basketball court, playground, lawn area, and picnic tables. A paved ramp leads down to the crescent-shape beach that's flanked by cliffs on both sides. For sweeping views of the ocean, position yourself at one of the lookouts outfitted with seating and/or binoculars—yup, binoculars are waiting for you.

BEACON'S BEACH

Follow the windy dirt path laden with switchbacks down to find Beacon's Beach in Encinitas, a well-known beach spot and favorite locals' hangout; on maps it may be labeled Leucadia State Beach. Since its entrance is hidden below sea cliffs on a one-way residential street, Beacon's Beach has an air of exclusivity. With plenty of space to spread out here, you won't have to infringe on sun-worshipping neighbors.

MOONLIGHT STATE BEACH

Fans of active beach days should head to this Encinitas beach. Volleyball courts, picnic tables, and playgrounds line the beach, with a concession stand, equipment rentals, and free Sunday concerts in high season.

10 Best Celebrity Hangouts in Los Angeles

CAFÉ GRATITUDE LARCHMONT

Round out your L.A. vacation with a plant-based meal at local chain Café Gratitude. For a celeb sighting, head to their Larchmont Boulevard location where Jake Gyllenhaal and Beyoncé obligingly declare what they're grateful for before digging in.

THE HOLLYWOOD ROOSEVELT

The Hollywood Roosevelt, one of L.A.'s oldest hotels, has hosted numerous celebrities and dignitaries in its Spanish Colonial Revival rooms. Set in the heart of Hollywood, it offers a convenient location as well as a number of watering holes, including Tropicana Pool & Café.

PINZ BOWLING CENTER

For a bit of family-friendly fun, head to Pinz in Studio City, where bowling is more than just a game, it's also a neon- and black-light party. Celebrities often pop in here for a bowling night, from A-listers like Vin Diesel and Jessica Alba to performers like Bruno Mars and Missy Elliott.

THE GROVE

L.A. may be strewn with outdoor malls, but it's The Grove that gets the highest billing, not just for its collection of mid- to high-end shops and restaurants, but also for its next-door neighbor, the Farmers Market. It's also one of the best places to see stars like Lena Headey, Zendaya, and Mario Lopez.

NOBU MALIBU

Nobu is a known A-list hot spot that's hosted everyone from Keanu Reeves to Kendall Jenner. Even if you don't spot a star, it's still worth the trip for its impeccable sushi and sashimi. Be warned, though: mingling with A-listers doesn't come cheap.

TOSCANA

Upscale Brentwood is home to many celebrities, and rustic trattoria Toscana is one of their neighborhood haunts. It may not be L.A.'s best Italian restaurant—for that, check out Osteria Mozza—but for star sightings, it's your best bet.

CHATEAU MARMONT

The Chateau Marmont is possibly L.A.'s best-known celebrity haunt. Come for brunch in the garden terrace or drop in at night for the Hollywood-inspired cocktails. Photos are not allowed.

Catch

CRAIG'S

A West Hollywood dining staple with a plain facade, Craig's is a safe haven for the movie industry's most important names and well-known faces like John Legend and Chrissy Teigen. Just keep in mind this joint is always busy, so you might not even get a table. It's a good thing the food is worth the effort.

CATCH

Secure a table at the flora-cluttered Catch in West Hollywood and rub elbows with the likes of David Beckham and the Jenner-Kardashian clan. This eatery is as L.A. as you can get, with its alfresco setting, vegan and gluten-free offerings, and locally and sustainably grown ingredients.

RUNYON CANYON

Out of L.A.'s numerous beautiful hiking spots, Runyon Canyon gets the biggest share of celebrity regulars, probably because it's strategically tucked between the Hollywood Hills, where many stars live, and the Sunset Strip. It's also a great venue for getting some fresh air, not to mention an ideal spot to take panoramic sunset photos.

What to Read and Watch

CHINATOWN
In this 1974 film noir, a young private eye (Jack Nicholson) in Depression-era Los Angeles gets in over his head with a client's case involving her husband's death. It's a tale of corruption and intrigue that incorporates fictionalized details of L.A.'s historic water wars.

FAST TIMES AT RIDGEMONT HIGH
Many don't know that this humorous, coming-of-age, cult classic was based on the journalistic efforts of *Rolling Stone* prodigy Cameron Crowe. He spent a year undercover at San Diego's Clairemont High School, and the resulting book (1981) and movie (1982) are accounts of this wild, adolescent period and its characters.

MULHOLLAND DRIVE
Surreal, psychotic, and artsy, David Lynch's 2001 film paints L.A. as a city of creepy fun house turns and blurs the lines between reality and cuts from a movie. Such dichotomies also exist in the two main characters: Betty, the blond Midwesterner fresh to L.A., and Rita, an amnesiac shrouded in darkness and mystery.

SUNSET BOULEVARD
This classic, 1950s, Billy Wilder movie offers a wild, entertaining glimpse at the film business and its eccentric characters. A has-been star and a young screenwriter hope to use each other in some way. But things get complicated, demonstrating that what happens behind the scenes in Hollywood isn't the same as what appears on the big screen.

ASK THE DUST BY JOHN FANTE
During the Great Depression, an Italian American writer lives in a seedy Los Angeles hotel and struggles with poverty, love, and creativity. Downtown is rendered well, and the character's relationship with Los Angeles is nuanced.

THE GANGSTER WE ARE ALL LOOKING FOR BY LE THI DIEM THUY
The characters of this novel, based on the author's own childhood, are Vietnamese refugees in the late '70s, adjusting to life in crowded bungalows and apartments of Normal Heights, Linda Vista, and east San Diego.

HAM ON RYE BY CHARLES BUKOWSKI
America's favorite degenerate poet writes an off-the-cuff novel about growing up in L.A. during the mid-20th century as the child of German immigrants. Told through Henry Chinaski, the author's alter ego and antihero, the book offers gritty takes on everything from family violence, alcoholism, and school-yard bullying to Model Ts and orange trees.

THE HOUSE OF BROKEN ANGELS BY LUIS ALBERTO AURREA
Focusing on three generations of a Mexican-American family, with a history in the California Territories since World War I, this robust, happy novel teems with big personalities and vivid characters.

THE REVOLT OF THE COCKROACH PEOPLE BY OSCAR ZETA ACOSTA
Grounded in real events, this story outlines aspects of east Los Angeles's Chicano movement through protests, marches, and court cases. The main protagonist is based on the fascinating author, an activist, lawyer/politician, and key player in the movement.

Chapter 2

TRAVEL SMART

Updated by
Daniel Mangin

★ **CAPITAL:**
Sacramento

♟ **POPULATION:**
39.5 million

💬 **LANGUAGE:**
English

$ **CURRENCY:**
U.S. dollar

☎ **COUNTRY CODE:**
1

⚠ **EMERGENCIES:**
911

🚗 **DRIVING:**
On the right

⚡ **ELECTRICITY:**
120–240 v/60 cycles;
plugs have two or three
rectangular prongs

🕐 **TIME:**
Three hours behind
New York

🌐 **WEB RESOURCES:**
www.visitcalifornia.com,
www.parks.ca.gov,
www.dot.ca.gov/cttravel,
www.travel.state.gov

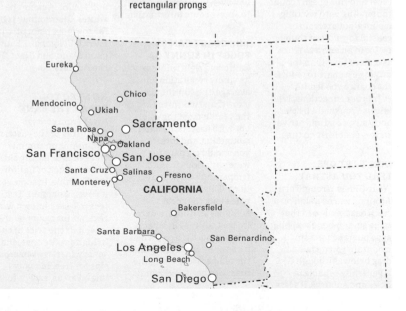

Know Before You Go

To help you prepare for a visit to the vast, diverse, unique state of California, below are tips about driving, destinations, the weather, saving money at restaurants and hotels, wildlife, cannabis tourism, and things to see and do that may save you time or money or increase peace of mind.

ROAD TRIPS TAKE TIME

California has some of the most scenic drives in the world. It's also the third-largest state behind Alaska and Texas and, in square miles, is similar in size to Sweden, Japan, or Paraguay. So, if you want to see all its beaches, deserts, mountains, and forests, you'll need a car—and, perhaps, a bit of patience.

A road trip through even half of the state takes several hours in the best of traffic (frequently not the case), and this doesn't count contending with winding, mountainous terrain or coastal fog. Rule of thumb: factor in an extra 20% or 25% more time than the GPS driving estimate to reduce the chance you'll miss events or connections. Who knows? You might be pleasantly surprised and arrive early—or at least on time.

DON'T LET GPS LEAD YOU ASTRAY

"Your GPS is Wrong: Turn Around," warns a sign on a steep dead-end road that some smartphone mapping apps mistake for a small mountain town's main drag below. Although GPS is generally reliable in cities and suburbs, it's less so in coastal, mountain, and desert areas, including some national and state parks. In addition to referencing the maps in this book, back yourself up with old-school atlases or fold-out paper maps.

If you plot out a trip and begin navigation while your smartphone reception is good, you should still receive turning directions even if you move out of cell range. If you're already out of range when initiating a destination search, however, you won't be able to access route information.

THE COAST CAN BE FOGGY IN SUNNY CA

California rightfully earns its sunny reputation: on average, the sun shines more than two-thirds of the year in most regions, but with deserts, beaches, mountains, and forests, you should prepare for wide variations in both temperature and conditions. This is especially true along the coast and at higher altitudes, where it's best to dress in layers year-round. On a day when it's 85 or 95 degrees inland, the temperature along the coast can be 55 and windy.

In July and August, hot inland temperatures often cause cooler Pacific Ocean air—in the form of fog—to blanket areas nearest the shore. As a rule along the coast: the farther south you go, the drier and hotter the weather tends to be. The farther north, the cooler and wetter you're likely to find it.

"WINE COUNTRY" IS MORE THAN NAPA AND SONOMA

Modern California winemaking got its start in Sonoma County, and Napa Valley wines raised the state's profile worldwide, but with about 4,000 wineries from the Oregon border to San Diego County producing nearly ¾ billion gallons—80-plus percent of the U.S. total—the whole state's pretty much "Wine Country." Tasting rooms abound, even in unlikely places.

The top red-wine grapes include Cabernet Sauvignon, Pinot Noir, Zinfandel, and Merlot. Among the whites, Chardonnay is by far the most planted, with French Colombard, Sauvignon Blanc, and Pinot Gris the runners-up.

NO NEED TO BREAK THE BANK

Away from coastal California or the eastern mountains on summer weekends or during ski season, much of California is affordable. In some cases, it's even a bargain. Tasting fees in lesser-known wine regions, for example, are at least half the price of those in high-profile ones, and some wineries even provide sips for free. In many inland areas, except for the fanciest bed-and-break-fasts, room rates trend way lower than by the shore.

AVOIDING STICKER SHOCK AT RESTAURANTS

Even if you're not dining at temples of haute cuisine, eating out in California can induce sticker shock. There are several ways to avoid this. Have the day's fancy meal at brunch or lunch, when prices tend to be lower. Happy hour, when a restaurant might serve a signature appetizer or smaller version of a famous plate at a lower price, is another option. Even small towns in the interior are likely to have a purveyor or two of gourmet food to go, making picnicking in a park or eating back at your lodging a viable strategy.

AVOIDING STICKER SHOCK AT HOTELS

California's hotels, inns, and resorts are the most expensive from late spring to early fall. The easiest way to avoid sticker shock is to come during winter when, except at ski resorts and a few desert hot spots, prices are the least expensive. Year-round you can save money by traveling midweek, when rates tend to drop. Visiting during the shoulder seasons of mid-to-late spring and mid-to-late fall, when the weather can be nice and the crowds less formidable, can also save you money.

Many travelers cut costs by booking a big-city business hotel on the weekend, when rates trend lower (with Sunday often the cheapest night of the week at such places). Conversely, weekend prices at beach or countryside resorts are generally high but sometimes drop midweek.

MAKERS AND MUSEUMS

The state's early-21st-century DIY types birthed what's come to be known as the maker movement, and throughout California you'll see evidence of this artisanal activity. Blue jeans, lasers, Apple computers, sourdough bread, Popsicles, McDonald's, Barbie Dolls, Hollywood movie glamour, and television all emerged from California. Nearly 3,000 museums (more than any other state) honor such accomplishments and more—if you can think of it, there's probably a museum here that celebrates it.

PLAY BALL

The weather is great year-round, so there's a dynamic sports culture in the Golden State. Spectacular (and often free) recreation areas and parks offer opportunities for surfing, skiing, hiking, and biking, among other activities.

If you're more into spectating, California supports more professional sports teams than any other state, including five MLB, four NBA (plus one WNBA), three NFL and NHL franchises, and several (men's and women's) soccer squads. Any day of the week, you can witness athletic greatness at the highest levels.

CALL OF THE WILDLIFE

Off the coast, creatures from gray and humpback whales to blue whales and orcas might come into view, along with sea lions, elephant seals, dolphins, and the occasional shark. Inland forests contain black bears, mountain lions, bobcats, beavers, and foxes. The desert supplies no end of reptiles, and the entire state is a birder's paradise.

Wild animals generally avoid interacting with humans, but contact is not unheard of. Most state and national parks post advice about steering clear of potentially dangerous encounters and what to do if you find yourself in one.

POT IS LEGAL, BUT...

Marijuana is legal in California for medical and recreational purposes. If you're 21 (or 18 with a doctor's order) and have proof of age or medical status, you can acquire and use marijuana, albeit not always in public. The California Cannabis Portal website maintains a searchable database (⊕ search. cannabis.ca.gov/retailers) of licensed dispensaries, where cannabis might come as flowers, edibles, and concentrates, among other things. The Cannabis Travel Association (⊕ www. cannabistravelassociation. org) promotes "safe and responsible cannabis tourism," and provides general information.

Getting Here and Around

From Los Angeles To:	By Air	By Car
San Diego	55 mins	2 hrs
Death Valley	No flights	5 hrs
San Francisco	1 hr 30 mins	5 hrs 40 mins
Monterey	1 hr 10 mins	5 hrs
Santa Barbara	50 mins	1 hr 40 mins
Big Sur	No flights	5 hrs 40 mins
Sacramento	1 hr 30 mins	6 hrs 15 mins

From Los Angeles To:	Route	Distance
San Diego	I–5 or I–405	127 miles
Las Vegas	I–10 to I–15	270 miles
Death Valley	I–10 to I–15 to Hwy. 127 to Hwy. 190	290 miles
San Francisco	I–5 to I–580 to I–80	382 miles
Monterey	U.S. 101 to Salinas, Hwy. 68 to Hwy. 1	320 miles
Santa Barbara	U.S. 101	95 miles
Big Sur	U.S. 101 to Hwy. 1	349 miles
Sacramento	I–5	391 miles

 Air

Most national and many international airlines fly to California. Flying time to the state is about 6½ hours from New York and 4¾ hours from Chicago. Travel from London to either Los Angeles or San Francisco is 11½ hours and from Sydney approximately 14 hours. Flying between San Francisco and Los Angeles takes about 90 minutes.

 Bus

Greyhound is the primary bus carrier in California. Regional bus service is available in metropolitan areas.

 Car

A car is essential in most of California, the exceptions being parts of its largest cities, where it can be more convenient to use public transportation, taxis, or ride-sharing services. Two main north–south routes run through California: I–5 through the middle of the state, and U.S. 101, a parallel route closer to the coast. Slower but more scenic is Highway 1, which winds along much of the coast.

The state's main east–west routes are I–8, I–10, and I–15 (in the south) and I–80 (in the north). Much of California is mountainous, and you may encounter winding roads and steep mountain grades.

CAR RENTAL

When you reserve a car, ask about cancellation penalties, taxes, drop-off charges (to drop off in another city), and surcharges (for age, additional drivers, or driving across state or country borders).

ROAD CONDITIONS

View current road conditions online or download the easier-to-use Caltrans QuickMap smartphone app. Rainy weather can make driving along the coast or in the mountains treacherous. Some smaller routes over mountain ranges and in the deserts are prone to flash flooding. Many smaller roads over the Sierra Nevada are closed in winter, and if it's snowing, tire chains may be required on routes that are open. Note, though, that most rental-car companies prohibit chain installation on their vehicles. If you disregard this rule, your insurance likely won't cover chains-related damage.

Chains or cables generally cost $30–$75. ■ TIP→ **It's less expensive to purchase chains before you get to the mountains.** On some highways and freeways, uniformed chain installers will apply chains for a fee (around $30), though these installers are not allowed to sell or rent chains. On lesser roads, you're on your own.

RULES OF THE ROAD

All passengers must wear a seat belt at all times. A child must be secured in a federally approved child passenger restraint system and ride in the back seat until at least eight years of age or until the child is at least 4 feet 9 inches tall. Unless indicated, right turns are allowed at red lights after you've come to a full stop. Drivers with a blood-alcohol level higher than 0.08 are subject to arrest.

You must turn on your headlights whenever weather conditions require the use of windshield wipers. Texting on a wireless device is illegal. If using a mobile phone while driving, it must be hands-free and mounted (i.e., it's not legal having it loose on the seat or your lap). For more driving rules, refer to the Department of Motor Vehicles driver's handbook at ⊕ *www.dmv.ca.gov.*

Train

Amtrak provides rail service within California. On some trips, passengers board motor coaches part of the way.

Essentials

Activities

Athletic Californians often boast that it's possible to surf in the morning and ski in the afternoon (or vice versa) in the Golden State. With thousands of hiking, biking, and horse-riding trails and hundreds of lakes, rivers, and streams for fishing, swimming, and boating—not to mention sandy coastal strands for sunning and surfing and other beaches with dunes or rocks to explore—there's no shortage of outdoor fun to be had. One challenge on many a hiker's bucket list is the Pacific Crest Trail, which travels the length of the state. The National Park Service operates numerous parks and sites in California, and the state park system is robust.

🍴 Dining

California has led the pack in bringing natural and organic foods to the forefront of American dining. Though rooted in European cuisine, California cooking sometimes has strong Asian and Latin influences. Wherever you go, you're likely to find that dishes are made with fresh produce and other local ingredients.

The restaurants we list are the cream of the crop in each price category. *Restaurant reviews have been shortened. For full information, visit Fodors.com. For price information, see the Planning sections in each chapter.*

DISCOUNTS AND DEALS
The better grocery and specialty-food stores have grab-and-go sections, with prepared foods on a par with restaurant cooking, perfect for picnicking.

MEALS AND MEALTIMES
Lunch is typically served from 11 or 11:30 to 2:30 or 3, with dinner service starting at 5 or 5:30 and lasting until 9 or later. Restaurants that serve breakfast usually open by 7, sometimes earlier, with some serving breakfast through the lunch hour. Most weekend brunches start at 10 or 11 and go at least until 2.

PAYING
In 2020, most restaurants began taking only credit cards and not cash, though some still don't accept one or the other. In most establishments tipping is the norm, but some include the service in the menu price or add it to the bill. *For guidelines on tipping see the Tipping chart, on page 34.*

RESERVATIONS AND DRESS
It's a good idea to make a reservation when possible. Where reservations are indicated as essential, book a week or more ahead in summer and early fall. Large parties should always call ahead to check the reservations policy. Except as noted in individual listings, dress is informal.

➕ Health/Safety

If you have a medical condition that may require emergency treatment, be aware that many rural and mountain communities have only daytime clinics, not hospitals with 24-hour emergency rooms. Take the usual precautions to protect your person and belongings. In large cities, ask at your lodging about areas to avoid, and lock valuables in a hotel safe when not using them. Car break-ins are common in some larger cities, but it's always a good idea to remove valuables from your car or at least keep them out of sight.

COVID-19
Although COVID-19 brought travel to a virtual standstill for most of 2020 and into 2021, vaccinations have made travel possible and safe again. Remaining requirements and restrictions—including those for non-vaccinated travelers—can, however, vary from one place (or even business) to the next. Check out

the websites of the CDC and the U.S. Department of State, both of which have destination-specific, COVID-19 guidance. Also, in case travel is curtailed abruptly again, consider buying trip insurance. Just be sure to read the fine print: not all travel-insurance policies cover pandemic-related cancellations.

THE OUTDOORS

At beaches, heed warnings about high surf and deadly rogue waves, and don't fly within 24 hours of scuba diving. When hiking, stay on trails, and heed all warning signs about loose cliffs, predatory animals, and poison ivy or oak.

Before heading out into remote areas, let someone know your trip route, destination, and estimated time and date of return. Make sure your vehicle is in good condition and equipped with a first-aid kit, snacks, extra water, jack, spare tire, tools, and a towrope or chain. Mind your gas gauge, keeping the needle at above half if possible and stopping to top off the tank whenever you can.

In arid regions, stay on main roads, and watch out for wildlife, horses, and cattle. Don't enter mine tunnels or shafts. Not only can such structures be unstable, but they might also have hidden dangers such as pockets of bad air. Be mindful of sudden rainstorms, when floodwaters can cover or wash away roads and quickly fill up dry riverbeds and canyons. Never place your hands or feet where you can't see them: rattlesnakes, scorpions, and black widow spiders may be hiding there.

Sunscreen and hats are musts, and layered clothing is best as desert temperatures can fluctuate greatly between dawn and dusk. Drink at least a gallon of water a day (three gallons if you're hiking or otherwise exerting yourself). If you have a headache or feel dizzy or nauseous, you could be suffering from dehydration. Get

out of the sun immediately, dampen your clothing to lower your body temperature, and drink plenty of water.

Although you might not feel thirsty in cooler, mountain climes, it's important to stay hydrated (drinking at least a quart of water during activities) at high altitudes, where the air is thinner, causing you to breathe more heavily. Always bring a fold-up rain poncho to keep you dry and prevent hypothermia. Wear long pants, a hat, and sturdy, closed-toe hiking boots with soles that grip rock. If you're going into the backcountry, bring a signaling device (such as a mirror), emergency whistle, compass, map, energy bars, and water purifier.

🛏 Lodging

With just under 5,600 lodgings, California has inns, motels, hotels, and specialty accommodations to suit every traveler's fancy and finances. Retro motels recalling 1950s roadside culture but with 21st-century amenities are a recent popular trend, but you'll also see traditional motels and hotels, along with luxury resorts and boutique properties. Reservations are a good idea throughout the year but especially so in the summer. On weekends at smaller lodgings, minimum-stay requirements of two or three nights are common, though some places are flexible about this in winter. Some accommodations aren't suitable for children, so ask before you book.

The lodgings we review are the top choices in each price category. *Hotels reviews have been shortened. For full information, visit Fodors.com.* We don't specify whether the facilities cost extra; when pricing accommodations, ask what's included and what costs extra. *For price information, see the Planning sections in each chapter.*

Essentials

APARTMENT AND HOUSE RENTALS

You'll find listings for Airbnb and similar rentals throughout California.

BED-AND-BREAKFASTS

California has more than 1,000 bed-and-breakfasts. You'll find everything from simple homestays to lavish luxury lodgings, many in historic hotels and homes. The California Association of Boutique and Breakfast Inns represents 200 member properties you can locate and book through its website.

HOTELS

Some properties allow you to cancel without a penalty—even if you prepaid to secure a discounted rate—if you cancel at least 24 hours in advance. Others require you to cancel a week in advance or penalize you the cost of one night. Small inns and B&Bs are most likely to require you to cancel far in advance. Most hotels allow children under a certain age to stay in their parents' room at no extra charge, but others charge for them as additional adults; find out the cutoff age for discounts.

 Money

On the coast, you'll pay top dollar for everything from gas and food to lodging and attractions. Aside from desert and ski resorts, inland prices tend to be lower.

TAXES

The base state sales tax is 7.25%, but local taxes can add as much as 3.25%. Exceptions include grocery-store food items and some takeout. Hotel taxes vary from about 8% to 15%.

Tipping Guidelines for California	
Bartender	$1–$3 per drink, or 15%–20% per round
Bellhop	$2–$5 per bag, depending on the level of the hotel
Hotel Concierge	$5–$10 for advice and reservations, more for difficult tasks
Hotel Doorman	$3–$5 for hailing a cab
Valet Parking Attendant	$3–$5 when you get your car
Hotel Maid	$4–$6 per day (either daily or at the end of your stay, in cash)
Waiter	18%–22% (20%–25% is standard in upscale restaurants); nothing additional if a service charge is added to the bill
Skycap at Airport	$2 per bag
Hotel Room-Service Waiter	15%–20% per delivery, even if a service charge was added since that fee goes to the hotel, not the waiter
Tasting-room server	$5–$10 per couple basic tasting, $5–$10 per person hosted seated tasting
Taxi Driver	15%–20%, but round up the fare to the next dollar amount
Tour Guide	15% of the cost of the tour, more depending on quality

▼ Nightlife

The good life in California extends to the evening with skilled mixologists serving up farm-to-bar cocktails in big-city night spots, some of them modeled on speakeasies of yore. Regular ole bartenders provide an additional layer of atmosphere to dives in towns large and small.

📋 Packing

The California lifestyle emphasizes casual wear, and with the generally mild climate you needn't worry about packing cold-weather clothing unless you're going into mountainous areas. Jeans, walking shorts, and T-shirts are acceptable in most situations. Few restaurants require men to wear a jacket or tie, though a collared shirt is the norm at upscale establishments.

Summer evenings can be cool, especially near the coast, where fog often rolls in. Always pack a sweater or light jacket. If you're headed to state or national parks, packing binoculars, clothes that layer, long pants and long-sleeve shirts, sunglasses, and a wide-brimmed hat is wise. Pick up insect repellant, sunscreen, and a first-aid kit once in-state.

🎭 Performing Arts

With about 40 million residents, California supplies a built-in audience for touring and homegrown companies from the worlds of dance, opera, theater, comedy, and music of all types. A-list performers appear at venues large and intimate, and numerous cultural festivals fill the calendar. In all the major cities and some smaller ones you'll find a former movie palace or two (or more) converted into a performance venue. Look also for events sponsored by top-tier museums. Wineries throughout the state host concerts during the summer.

👜 Shopping

California is home to world-class shopping in its big cities, where you'll find major designer labels and fine-jewelry establishments represented. The state was the birthplace of the maker movement, and artisans throughout California craft beautiful soaps, clothing from organic cotton, fashion jewelry from recycled products, and other handmade items.

📅 When to Go

Expect high summer heat in the desert areas and low winter temperatures in the Sierra Nevada and other inland mountain ranges.

HIGH SEASON $$$–$$$$
High season lasts from late May through early September (a little later in wine regions and well into winter in desert resorts and ski areas). Expect higher hotel occupancy rates and prices.

LOW SEASON $$
From December to March, tourist activity slows. Except in the mountainous areas, which may see snowfall and an influx of skiers, winters here are mild and hotels are cheaper.

VALUE SEASON $$–$$$
From April to late May and from late September to mid-November the weather is pleasant and hotel prices are reasonable.

Contacts

Air

AIRLINE SECURITY ISSUES CONTACTS Transportation Security Administration. (*TSA*). ☎ 866/289–9673 ⊕ www.tsa.gov.

AIRLINES CONTACTS Air Canada. ☎ 888/247–2262 ⊕ www.aircanada.com. **Alaska Airlines/Horizon Air.** ☎ 800/252–7522 ⊕ www.alaskaair.com. **American Airlines.** ☎ 800/433–7300 ⊕ www.aa.com. **Delta Airlines.** ☎ 800/221–1212 for U.S. reservations, 800/241–4141 for international reservations ⊕ www.delta.com. **Frontier Airlines.** ☎ 801/401–9000 ⊕ www.flyfrontier.com. **JetBlue.** ☎ 800/538–2583 ⊕ www.jetblue.com. **Southwest Airlines.** ☎ 800/435–9792 ⊕ www.southwest.com. **United Airlines.** ☎ 800/864–8331 ⊕ www.united.com.

AIRPORTS Hollywood Burbank Airport. ☎ 818/840–8840 ⊕ www.hollywoodburbankairport.com. **John Wayne Airport.** ☎ 949/252–5200 ⊕ www.ocair.com. **Long Beach Airport.** ☎ 562/570–2600 ⊕ www.lgb.org. **Los Angeles International Airport.** ☎ 855/463–5252 ⊕ www.flylax.com.

Ontario International Airport. ☎ 909/544–5300 ⊕ www.flyontario.com. **San Diego International Airport.** ☎ 619/400–2400 ⊕ www.san.org.

Bus

CONTACTS Greyhound. ☎ 800/231–2222 ⊕ www.greyhound.com.

Car

INFORMATION Caltrans Current Highway Conditions. ☎ 800/427–7623 ⊕ quickmap.dot.ca.gov. **511 Traffic/Transit Alerts.** ☎ 511.

MAJOR RENTAL AGENCIES Alamo. ☎ 800/462–5266 ⊕ www.alamo.com. **Avis.** ☎ 800/633–3469 ⊕ www.avis.com. **Budget.** ☎ 800/218–7992 ⊕ www.budget.com. **Hertz.** ☎ 800/654–3131 ⊕ www.hertz.com. **National Car Rental.** ☎ 844/382–6875 ⊕ www.nationalcar.com.

ROADSIDE ASSISTANCE American Automobile Association. (*AAA*). ☎ 800/222–4357 ⊕ www.aaa.com.

SPECIALTY CAR AGENCIES Enterprise Exotic Car Rentals. ☎ 866/458–9227 ⊕ exoticcars.enterprise.com.

⊕ Health/Safety

EMERGENCIES Ambulance, fire, police. ☎ 911 emergency.

Reservation Service

CONTACTS California Association of Boutique and Breakfast Inns. (*CABBI*). ☎ 800/373–9251 ⊕ www.cabbi.com.

🚂 Train

CONTACTS Amtrak. ☎ 800/872–7245 ⊕ www.amtrak.com.

Chapter 3

SOUTHERN CALIFORNIA'S BEST ROAD TRIPS

Updated by
Daniel Mangin

A California visit wouldn't be complete without taking a spin through the state's spectacular scenery. However, adding a road trip to your itinerary is not just a romantic idea: it's often a practical one, too—perhaps linking one urban area with another, say, or sampling some of this massive state's remote areas. Whether you have just a few days or longer to spare, these itineraries will help you hit the road.

SoCal for Kids and the Young at Heart, 7 Days

SoCal offers many opportunities to entertain the kids and the young at heart beyond the Magic Kingdom, this trip's last stop. San Diego's LEGOLAND is a blast for kids 12 and under, and the city's diverse attractions include a water park, the zoo, and several historic districts. Oh yes, and well-groomed La Jolla and other beach towns, too. If you can, fly into San Diego and out of Los Angeles to save time (and maybe money).

DAYS 1–2: LEGOLAND

LEGOLAND's hotels are a 35-min drive from the airport.

Arrive at **San Diego** International Airport, pick up your rental car, and settle in at the **LEGOLAND Hotel** or the **Sheraton Carlsbad Resort & Spa**, perhaps taking a dip in the pool. In the late afternoon, drive south along the Pacific Coast Highway (PCH) past popular San Diego County surfing beaches. Stop in Solana Beach or Del Mar for a sunset cocktail, perhaps staying for dinner.

Getting an early start for an action-packed day at **LEGOLAND** is a breeze because both hotels offer direct access to the park. LEGOLAND has a water park and aquarium in addition to LEGO-based rides, shows, and roller coasters. Little ones can live out their fairy-tale fantasies, and bigger ones can spend all day on waterslides, shooting water pistols, driving boats, or water fighting with pirates.

DAY 3: DOWNTOWN SAN DIEGO

Downtown is 35 mins from Carlsbad.

Check out of your LEGOLAND hotel in the late morning, taking the freeway south 35 minutes to **Downtown San Diego**. It'll probably be too early to check in (do it when convenient later in the afternoon), but park your car at your hotel and drop off your bags. Then proceed straight to the city's nautical heart, exploring the restored ships of the **Maritime Museum**

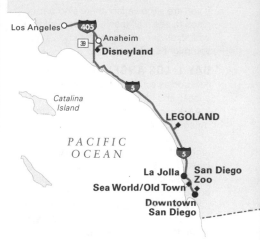

and walking south along the waterfront. Victorian buildings—and plenty of other tourists—surround you on a stroll inland a few blocks to **Gaslamp Quarter,** where you can grab a happy-hour cocktail or mock-tail before dining close to your hotel.

DAY 4: SEA WORLD, OLD TOWN, AND LA JOLLA
SeaWorld is 15 mins from Downtown; Old Town is 10 mins from SeaWorld; La Jolla is 20 mins from Old Town.

Two commercial and touristy sights are on the agenda, with a sunset cocktail the day's-end reward. With its walk-through shark tanks, **SeaWorld** delivers a ton of fun if you surrender to the experience. Also touristy, but with genuine historical significance, **Old Town** drips with Mexican and early Californian heritage. Soak it up in the plaza at **Old Town San Diego State Historic Park,** then browse the stalls and shops at **Fiesta de Reyes** and along San Diego Avenue. As the day winds down, make your way to **La Jolla Cove.** At the **Children's Pool,** look at, but don't go in the water, which is likely to be filled with barking seals. Have a sunset cocktail in La Jolla and dine there or Downtown.

DAY 5: SAN DIEGO ZOO
10 mins by car from Downtown San Diego.

Malayan tapirs in a faux-Asian rain forest, polar bears in an imitation Arctic, and pandas frolicking in the trees—the **San Diego Zoo** maintains a vast and varied collection of creatures in a world-renowned facility comprised of meticulously designed habitats. Come early, and wear comfy shoes. If you have time, explore a little of **Balboa Park,** which contains the zoo. Have dinner in the Hillcrest neighborhood near the park, or dine Downtown.

DAYS 6–7: DISNEYLAND
90 mins by car from San Diego to Disneyland.

As early as you can get moving, hop onto I-5 and drive north. By the time you reach San Clemente, you 'll be in **Orange County** (aka the O.C.). In less than an hour from there, you'll be in **Disneyland!** Skirt the lines at the box office with advance-purchased tickets in hand, and storm the gates of the Magic Kingdom. You can cram the highlights into a single day, but if you get a two-day ticket and stay the night, you can see the end-of-day parade and visit **Downtown Disney** before heading south. The **Grand Californian Hotel** is a top choice for lodging within the Disney Resort.

Hooray for Hollywood, 4 Days

If you are a movie fan, there's no better place to see it all than L.A. Always keep your eyes peeled: you never know when you might spot a celebrity.

DAY 1: LOS ANGELES

As soon as you land at LAX, make like a local, and hit the freeway. Even if L.A.'s top-notch art, history, and science museums don't tempt you, the mélange of art deco, Beaux Arts, and futuristic architecture begs at least a drive-by. Heading east from Santa Monica, Wilshire Boulevard cuts through a historical and cultural cross section of the city. Two stellar sights on its Miracle Mile are the encyclopedic **Los Angeles County Museum of Art** and the fossil-filled **La Brea Tar Pits.** Come evening, the open-air **Farmers Market** and its many eateries hum. Hotels in Beverly Hills or West Hollywood beckon, just a few minutes away.

DAY 2: HOLLYWOOD AND THE MOVIE STUDIOS

Avoid driving to the studios during rush hour. Studio tours vary in length—plan at least a half day for the excursion.

Every L.A. tourist should devote at least one day to the movies and take at least one studio tour in the San Fernando Valley. For fun, choose the special-effects theme park at **Universal Studios Hollywood**; for the nitty-gritty, choose **Warner Bros. Studios.** Nostalgic musts in Hollywood itself include the **Hollywood Walk of Fame** along **Hollywood Boulevard** and the celebrity footprints cast in concrete outside **Grauman's Chinese Theatre** (now known as the TCL Chinese Theater). When evening arrives, the Hollywood scene includes a bevy of trendy restaurants and nightclubs.

DAYS 3–4: BEVERLY HILLS AND SANTA MONICA

15–20 mins by car between destinations, but considerably longer in traffic.

The **Getty Center's** pavilion architecture, hilltop gardens, and frame-worthy L.A. views make it a dazzling destination—and that's before you experience the extensive art collection. From the museum, descend to the sea via Santa Monica Boulevard for lunch along **Third Street Promenade,** followed by a ride on the historic carousel on the pier. The buff and the bizarre meet at Venice Beach's **Ocean Front Walk**—strap on some in-line skates if you want to join them. Over in Beverly Hills, the **Rodeo Drive** shopping district specializes in exhibitionism with a hefty price tag, but voyeurs are still welcome.

Splurge on breakfast or brunch at a posh café in the **Farmers Market,** then stroll through aisles and aisles of gorgeous produce and specialty food before you take a last look at the Pacific Ocean through the camera obscura at **Palisades Park** in Santa Monica.

Palm Springs and the Desert, 5 Days

Many visitors consider the Palm Springs area pure paradise, and not just for the opportunity to get a good tan or play golf on championship courses. Expect fabulous and funky spas, a dog-friendly atmosphere, and sparkling stars at night.

DAY 1: ARRIVE IN PALM SPRINGS

Just over 2 hrs by car from LAX, without traffic.

Somehow in harmony with the harsh environment, mid-century-modern homes and businesses with clean, low-slung lines define the **Palm Springs** style. Although the desert cities—Rancho Mirage, Palm Desert, Indian Wells, Indio, and La Quinta—comprise a trendy

destination with sumptuous hotels, multicultural cuisine, abundant nightlife, and plenty of culture, a quiet atmosphere prevails. Fans of Palm Springs' legendary architecture won't want to miss the home tours, lectures, and other events at the annual Modernism Week held each February or the smaller fall preview event in October. If your visit doesn't coincide with these happenings, swing by the Palm Springs Visitor's Center for information on self-guided architecture tours.

The city seems far away when you hike in hushed **Tahquitz** or **Indian Canyon;** cliffs and palm trees shelter rock art, irrigation works, and other remnants of Agua Caliente culture. If your boots aren't made for walking, you can always practice your golf game or indulge in spa treatments at an area resort instead. Embrace the Palm Springs vibe, and park yourself at the modern-chic **Kimpton Rowan Palm Springs Hotel** or the legendary **Parker Palm Springs.** Alternatively, base yourself at the desert oasis, **La Quinta Resort,** about 40 minutes from downtown Palm Springs.

DAY 2: EXPLORE PALM SPRINGS
The Aerial Tram is 15 mins by car from central Palm Springs. Plan at least a half day for the excursion.

If riding a tram up an 8,516-foot mountain for a stroll or even a snowball fight above the desert sounds like fun, then show up at the **Palm Springs Aerial Tramway** before the first morning tram leaves (later, the line can get discouragingly long). Dress in layers, and wear decent footwear as it can be significantly colder at the top. Afterward, stroll through the **Palm Springs Art Museum,** with its shimmering display of contemporary studio glass, array of Native American baskets, and significant 20th-century sculptures by Henry Moore and others. After all that walking you may be ready for an early dinner. Nearly every restaurant in Palm Springs offers a happy hour, during which you can sip a cocktail and nosh on a light entrée, usually for half price.

DAY 3: JOSHUA TREE NATIONAL PARK
1 hr by car from Palm Springs.

Joshua Tree is among the most accessible of the national parks. You can see most of it in a day, entering the park at the town of Joshua Tree, exploring sites along **Park Boulevard,** and exiting at **Twentynine Palms.** With the signature trees, piles of rocks, glorious spring wildflowers, starlit skies, and colorful pioneer history, the experience is more like the

Wild West than Sahara dunes. Whether planning to take a day hike or a scenic drive, load up on drinking water before entering the park.

DAY 4: ANZA-BORREGO DESERT STATE PARK AND THE SALTON SEA

About 2 hrs by car from Palm Springs.

The **Salton Sea,** about 60 miles southeast of Palm Springs via I–10 and Highway 86S, is one of the largest inland seas on Earth. Formed by the flooding of the Colorado River in 1905, it attracts thousands of migrating birds and bird-watchers every fall. **Anza-Borrego Desert State Park** to the west, California's largest state park, contains 600,000 acres of mostly untouched wilderness. The springtime wildflower displays here rank among the state's best. The park surrounds **Borrego Springs,** a tiny hamlet most notable for its 130 life-size bronze sculptures of animals that roamed this space millions of years ago. The desert is home to an archaeological site, where scientists continue to uncover remnants of prehistoric animals ranging from mastodons to horses. If you have four-wheel drive, a detour down the sandy track to **Font's Point** rewards the intrepid with unforgettable views of the Borrego badlands. However, do not take the challenging road conditions lightly—inquire with park rangers before setting out.

DAY 5: RETURN TO L.A.

LAX is just over 2 hrs by car from Palm Springs without traffic, but the drive often takes significantly more time.

If you intend to depart from LAX, plan for a full day of driving from the desert to the airport. Be prepared for heavy traffic at any time of day or night. If possible, fly out of Palm Springs International Airport or Ontario International Airport instead.

Southern PCH: Sand, Surf, and Sun, 4 Days

This tour along the southern section of the Pacific Coast Highway (PCH) is a beach vacation on wheels, taking in the highlights of the Southern California coast and its surfer-chic vibe. If at any point the drive feels like something out of a movie, that's because it likely is—this is the California of Hollywood legend. And this segment is only the warm-up: after you get to Santa Barbara you can just keep heading north as far up the coast as time permits. Roll the top down on the convertible and let the adventure begin.

DAY 1: LAGUNA BEACH TO NEWPORT BEACH

1 hr by car.

Easily accessed off I–5, the PCH begins near Dana Point, a town famous for its harbor and whale-watching excursions, but you can just as easily start 10 miles north in **Laguna Beach.** Browse the art galleries, and enjoy lunch in the charming downtown before or after walking along the Pacific. Then head north a few miles to **Crystal Cove State Park.** If the tide is low, this is a wonderful spot for tide pooling. Don't miss the historic beach cottages dating as far back as 1935.

From the park, continue north a few more miles to **Newport Beach.** The affluent coastal cities of Orange County (aka the O.C.) are familiar to many thanks to *Arrested Development, The Real Wives of Orange County,* and other TV shows, though the yachts and multimillion-dollar mansions of Newport Beach may still take you by surprise. **Balboa Island,** a quaint, if expensive, getaway, sits in the middle of Newport Harbor. Browse the boutiques along Marine Avenue before hopping in a Duffy

Santa Barbara
Santa Barbara Channel
Ventura
Oxnard
101
Point Mugu State Park
Malibu
Getty Villa Malibu
Santa Monica
Marina Del Ray
Point Dune State Beach
Venice Beach
Santa Cruz
Manhattan Beach
Redondo Beach
Santa Rosa
Santa Barbara
Newport Beach
Laguna Beach
Dana Point
Catalina Island

(electric boat) for a harbor tour. Back on land, enjoy a Balboa Bar—the ice-cream treat is virtually mandatory for all Balboa Island visitors. Spend the night on Balboa Island or elsewhere in Newport Beach.

DAY 2: NEWPORT BEACH TO SANTA MONICA

About 2 hrs by car without traffic, but plan on it.

From Newport Beach, eschew Highway 1, driving north on Highway 55 to the 405 freeway also north. Exit at West 190st Street, following the signs to Redondo Beach, well-known, along with Hermosa and Manhattan beaches to the north, among beach-volleyball enthusiasts. If time permits, follow Highway 1 through Marina del Ray; otherwise skip this section of the PCH in favor of the 405 freeway. (As is always advisable near L.A., check current traffic reports before choosing your route.)

Get settled into a hotel near the **Santa Monica Pier,** then catch some of the action there before grabbing dinner along the **Third Street Promenade** or at Santa Monica Place.

DAY 3: SANTA MONICA TO SANTA BARBARA

About 2 hrs by car via Hwy. 1 and U.S. 101. When the weather's good, though, allow more time for beach stops.

Begin with a morning walk along **Santa Monica State Beach.** Check out of your hotel, but leave your bags there to pick up later. Rent beach cruiser bikes, and pedal south about 3 miles along the bike path to **Venice Beach.** When you've had your fill of skateboarders, bodybuilders, and street performers, head inland a few blocks to Abbott Kinney Boulevard for lunch at **Gjelina** and a browse in the local boutiques. Then head back to Santa Monica, drop off your bikes, and begin the drive north to Santa Barbara. If you plan to visit the **Getty Villa Malibu** and its impressive antiquities collection and jaw-dropping setting overlooking the Pacific, spend less time on the bike ride. And be sure to obtain free timed-entry tickets—the last admission is at 3 pm—online before your arrival.

As you drive from Santa Monica through **Malibu** and beyond, chances are you'll experience déjà vu: mountains on one side, ocean on the other, opulent homes perched on hillsides. You've seen this piece of coast countless times on TV and film. In Malibu proper, affectionately known as "the 'bu," walk out on the **Malibu Pier** for a great photo op, then check out **Surfrider Beach,** with three famous points where perfect waves ignited a worldwide surfing rage in the 1960s. Continuing past Malibu, you'll experience miles of protected, largely unpopulated coastline. Scout for offshore whales at **Point Dume State Beach,** or hike the trails at **Point Mugu State Park.**

On the north side of **Oxnard,** you'll trade Highway 1 for U.S. 101 (aka "the 101" and the Ventura Freeway) into **Ventura.** Approaching Ventura on a clear day, the Channel Islands are visible in the distance. If you haven't been held up in traffic too much, stretch your legs on the **Ventura Oceanfront** with a walk on **San Buenaventura State Beach** or around the picturesque **Ventura Harbor.** Otherwise, continue to **Santa Barbara,** and check into your hotel. Splurge on an overnight stay at the posh **Rosewood Miramar Beach** resort, or book a room at the **Santa Barbara Inn,** whose restaurant, **Convivo,** is a smart spot for dinner.

DAY 4: SANTA BARBARA
45 mins–1 hr by car.

Santa Barbara is a gem. Combining elegance with a laid-back coastal vibe, the city provides a tranquil escape from the congestion of Los Angeles and a dose of sophistication to the largely rural Central Coast.

Start your day at **Old Mission Santa Barbara,** known as the "Queen" of the 21 missions that comprise the California Mission Trail. Plan to spend some time here; if your visit doesn't coincide with one of the 60-minute docent-led tours, self-guided tours are also available. From here, head to the architecturally significant **Santa Barbara County Courthouse.** Don't miss the murals in the ceremonial chambers or, from the tower, the incredible views of downtown's distinctive red-tile-roofed buildings and beyond them the Pacific Ocean.

Next up: the waterfront. Spend some time enjoying vast, sandy **East Beach,** and walk a little of **Stearns Wharf** before having lunch two blocks from the wharf at State Street's **Santo Mezcal** (upscale Mexican) or across the harbor at **Brophy Bros.** (fresh, straightforward seafood with a view).

After lunch, peek into the nearby **Funk Zone**'s art galleries, and indulge in a wine tasting or two. Dine in this area, or head to tony **Montecito** for an elegant meal.

Santa Barbara Wine Country, 2 Days

It's been nearly two decades since the movie *Sideways* brought the Santa Barbara Wine Country to the world's attention, and interest in this area continues to grow. This itinerary, best done from Thursday through Monday when most of the wineries and restaurants are open, makes a perfect add-on to a trip to Los Angeles and for those touring farther north along the coast.

DAY 1: SANTA RITA HILLS, LOMPOC, AND LOS OLIVOS
Without stops, this route takes about 2 hrs by car. Plan to linger at—and detour down side roads to—the wineries.

Take the scenic drive along the coast on the 101 to Buellton, exiting west onto Highway 246. After ½ mile, turn south (left) on Industrial Way. Don't let the **Industrial Way** food-and-drink complex's warehouse setting deter you—the tasting rooms here include well-regarded producers, many of whose grapes come from the Sta. Rita Hills AVA farther west a few miles. With its relatively cooler climate, the appellation excels at Chardonnay and Pinot Noir. **Alma Rosa Winery,** among the first noteworthy operations in these parts, is a good place to start. Consider also **Lafond Winery and Vineyards** and **McClain Cellars.** After or between tastings, walk to **Industrial Eats** for wood-fired pizzas and hearty salads and sandwiches.

Santa Barbara Channel

Back on Highway 101, head north about 6 miles before exiting toward **Los Olivos,** where you can park the car and spend the rest of the day exploring on foot. Tasting rooms, galleries, boutiques, and restaurants have made this former stagecoach town quite wine-country chic. **Blair Fox Cellars** and **Coquelicot Estate Vineyard** are just two of the wineries with tasting rooms in town. If you're staying at **Fess Parker's Wine Country Inn and Spa** or just outside town at the **Ballard Inn,** dine at **Nella,** inside Fess Parker's. Alternatively, slip south a few miles to **Solvang,** check into the **Hotel Corque,** and have dinner in Buellton at the much-heralded **Tavern at Zaca Creek.**

DAY 2: SOLVANG, FOXEN CANYON, AND THE SANTA YNEZ VALLEY

About 1 hr of driving to wineries, plus 45 mins to return to Santa Barbara via Highway 154.

Start the day with pastries in the Danish town of **Solvang,** whose windmills and distinct half-timber architecture are charming, if touristy. Walk a little of Solvang before hitting the road.

Los Olivos, **Santa Ynez,** and Solvang are located just a few minutes apart, with wineries spread between them in an area known as the Santa Ynez Valley. A mile east of tiny Santa Ynez's commercial drag (4¼ miles east of Solvang) lies **Gainey Vineyard,** whose wines impress major critics. Past Los Olivos heading north, the Foxen Canyon Wine Trail (⊕ *www. foxencanyontrail.net* for info and a map) extends to Santa Maria. Expect some backtracking as you venture into the canyon. If it's being offered, the well-conceived tour at **Firestone Vineyard** is a must for those interested in wine making. Farther along, **Foxen Vineyard & Winery** earns plaudits for its Pinot Noirs. Before or after a tasting in **Los Alamos** at **Casa Dumetz** (Rhône-style reds), stop for lunch at **Bob's Well Bread Bakery** (sandwiches, salads, cheese boards) or, on weekends, **Pico** for its farm-to-fork brunch.

Stay another night in the region, or return to Santa Barbara via scenic Highway 154 over the San Marcos Pass

Santa Barbara to Big Sur, 3 Days

This drive is all about the Pacific Coast's jaw-dropping scenery. The human-made treasures include Hearst Castle, newspaper magnate William Randolph Hearst's opulent monument to his fabulousness. Book Big Sur lodgings weeks ahead, the castle at least several days ahead in summer.

DAY 1: SANTA BARBARA TO CAMBRIA

About 3 hrs by car, not counting stops.

Drive north from Santa Barbara on the combined Highway 1 and U.S. 101, exiting the latter when the former forks west (watch for signs to Lompoc and Vandenberg Air Force Base). For this stretch, Highway 1 is also signed as Cabrillo Highway. Stop for a spell at **Guadalupe-Nipomo Dunes Preserve,** where on a sunny day the enormous namesake dunes make for a fantastic photo op. Highway 1 rejoins U.S. 101 at **Pismo Beach.** If you're starving, detour for lunch, though downtown **San Luis Obispo** (aka SLO), 13 miles farther along, offers more variety. **Piadina** restaurant in the **Hotel San Luis Obispo** is a good choice, as are **Luna Red** and **Novo.**

After lunch, explore a little of SLO before, just north of downtown, picking up Highway 1 as it again separates west from the 101. **Morro Bay, Cayucos,** and tiny **Harmony** are among the fun potential stops en route to Cambria, where you'll spend the night at the **White Water Inn** or elsewhere in town (nearby Morro Bay and Cayucos also have affordable options). End the day in Cambria with a walk along **Moonstone Beach** and a French-fusion dinner at **Madeline's.**

DAY 2: HEARST CASTLE TO BIG SUR

About 2 hrs by car. Allow ample time for hiking and stops at vista points and 2 hrs to tour Hearst Castle.

At least a few days ahead (more in summer), make a reservation for one of the mid-morning tours (the Grand Rooms Tour is good for first-timers) of **Hearst Castle,** 9 miles north of Cambria in **San Simeon.** Having traveled the surrounding coastline, you'll appreciate the bird's-eye perspective the castle provides. After the tour, have lunch down the hill at Hearst Ranch Winery, co-owned by one of William Randolph Hearst's great grandsons. On your way north out of San Simeon, don't miss the **Piedras Blancas Elephant Seal Rookery.**

The drive through coastal **Big Sur** is justifiably one of the world's most famous stretches of road. The curves, endless views, and scenic waypoints are the stuff of road-trip legend. Keep your camera handy, fill up the tank, and prepare to be wowed. Traffic can easily back up along the route, and you should be cautious while navigating the road's twists and turns. To fully experience the area, spend at least a night here. If room rates at the legendary **Post Ranch Inn** or **Ventana Big Sur** exceed your budget, seek out one of the more rustic options. If not dining at your lodging, do so at **Nepenthe,** which offers decent food and gorgeous views. Time your reservation (again, made well ahead) to witness the sunset.

DAY 3: BIG SUR

About 1 hr by car, not counting stops for hikes, beach exploration, and photo ops.

Start the morning off with a hike in southern Big Sur at **Julia Pfeiffer Burns State Park,** a draw for **McWay Falls,** which tumbles dramatically into the sea. There's no beach access due to trail erosion, but you can walk ½ mile to an overlook from a lot near the park's entrance. A pullout just to the north, near mile marker 36.2, also affords a view. Check the park's website for other trails open when you visit.

About 7½ miles north of the state park, watch for the odd-angled turnout for (the unmarked) Sycamore Canyon Road, which leads to **Pfeiffer Beach.** Following the road 2¼ miles toward the sea, you may question whether you are lost, but your perseverance will be rewarded when you reach the secluded beach and its signature rocky arch just offshore. Don't miss it!

If you're game for another hike, head into **Pfeiffer Big Sur State Park.** Near the Big Sur Lodge's restaurant are trailheads for a ¼-mile-loop, wheelchair-accessible **self-guided nature walk** and the **Valley View Trail,** a 2-mile moderate-to-strenuous loop past redwoods.

End your day 13 miles north of Big Sur Lodge (10 miles past the cluster of services known as Big Sur Village) at the extremely photogenic **Bixby Creek Bridge.** Pull over on the bridge's north side to get that perfect shot.

Most travelers continue north from here to Carmel-by-the-Sea or Monterey, either stopping there or returning to U.S. 101 via Highway 68 east from Monterey.

Chapter 4

SAN DIEGO

Updated by
Claire Deeks van Der Lee, Marlise Kast-Myers,
Sabrina Medora, Kai Oliver-Kurtin, and Jeff Terich

◉ Sights	🍴 Restaurants	🧳 Hotels	⬤ Shopping	🍸 Nightlife
★★★★★	★★★★★	★★★★★	★★★★☆	★★★☆☆

WELCOME TO SAN DIEGO

TOP REASONS TO GO

★ **Sun and surf:** Legendary beaches and surfing in La Jolla, Coronado, and Point Loma.

★ **Good eats:** Brewpubs, a wide mix of ethnic cuisines, fresh seafood and produce, and modern cafés delight diners.

★ **Great golf:** A concentration of beautiful courses with sweeping ocean views and light breezes.

★ **Stellar shopping:** From hip boutiques and fine Mexican crafts to the upscale Fashion Valley Mall.

★ **Family time:** Fun for all ages at LEGOLAND, Balboa Park, the San Diego Zoo, and more.

★ **Outdoor sports:** A perfect climate for biking, hiking, sailing—anything—outdoors.

1 Downtown. This area is filled with walkable A-list attractions like the Gaslamp Quarter and the waterfront.

2 Balboa Park, Bankers Hill, and San Diego Zoo. San Diego's cultural heart is where you'll find most of the city's museums and its world-famous zoo.

3 Old Town and Uptown. California's first permanent European settlement is now preserved as a state historic park in Old Town. Uptown's neighborhoods offer a unique mix of historical charm and modern urbanity.

4 Mission Bay and the Beaches. With 27 miles of shoreline, this 4,600-acre aquatic park is a monument to sports and fitness.

5 La Jolla. This luxe, bluff-top enclave fittingly means "the jewel" in Spanish. Come here for fantastic upscale shopping and unspoiled stretches of coast.

6 Point Loma Peninsula. Visit the site of the first European landfall on Point Loma.

7 Coronado. Home to the Hotel Del, Coronado's island-like isthmus is a favorite celebrity haunt. .

PACIFIC OCEAN

```
0                    2 mi
|----------|----------|
0          |          2 km
```

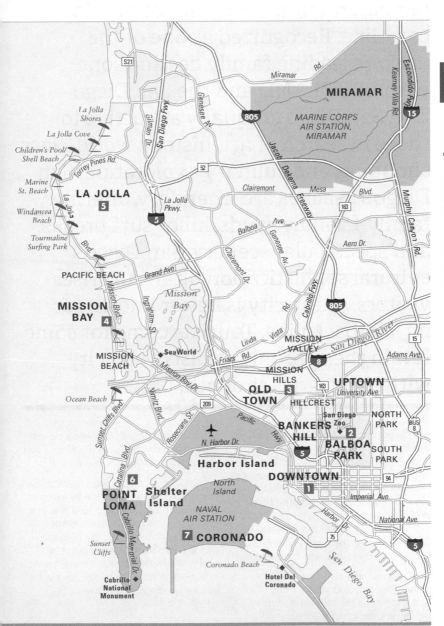

San Diego is a vacationer's paradise, complete with idyllic year-round temperatures and 70 miles of pristine coastline. Recognized as one of the nation's leading family destinations, with LEGOLAND and the San Diego Zoo, San Diego is equally attractive to those in search of art, history, world-class shopping, and culinary exploration. San Diego's beaches are legendary, offering family-friendly sands, killer surf breaks, and spectacular scenery. San Diego's cultural sophistication often surprises visitors, as the city is better known for its laid-back vibe. Tourists come for some fun in the sun, only to discover a city with much greater depth.

San Diego is a big California city—second only to Los Angeles in population—with a small-town feel. San Diego's many neighborhoods offer diverse adventures: from the tony boutiques in La Jolla to the yoga and surf shops of Encinitas; from the subtle sophistication of Little Italy to the flashy nightlife of the Downtown Gaslamp Quarter, each community adds flavor and flair to San Diego's personality.

San Diego County also covers a lot of territory, roughly 400 square miles of land and sea. To the north and south of the city are its famed beaches. Inland, a succession of chaparral-covered mesas is punctuated with deep-cut canyons that step up to forested mountains.

Known as the birthplace of California, San Diego was claimed for Spain by explorer Juan Rodríguez Cabrillo in 1542 and eventually came under Mexican rule. You'll find reminders of San Diego's Spanish and Mexican heritage throughout the region—in architecture and place-names, in distinctive Mexican cuisine, and in the historic buildings of Old Town.

In 1867 developer Alonzo Horton, who called the town's bay front "the prettiest place for a city I ever saw," began building a hotel, a plaza, and prefab homes on 960 Downtown acres. A remarkable number of these buildings are preserved in San Diego's historic Gaslamp Quarter today. The city's fate was sealed in the 1920s when the U.S. Navy, impressed by the city's excellent harbor and temperate climate, decided to build a destroyer base on San Diego Bay. Today, the military operates many bases and installations throughout the county (which, added together, form the largest military base in the world) and continues to be a major contributor to the local economy.

Planning

Getting Here and Around

AIR

The major airport is San Diego International Airport (SAN), formerly called Lindbergh Field. Most airlines depart and arrive at Terminal 2. Southwest, Frontier, and Alaska Airlines are reserved for Terminal 1. Free, color-coded shuttles loop the airport and match the parking lot they serve.

AIRPORT San Diego International Airport. ✉ *3225 N. Harbor Dr., off I–5* ☎ *619/400–2400* ⊕ *www.san.org.*

AIRPORT TRANSFERS San Diego Transit. ☎ *619/233–3004* ⊕ *www.511sd.com.* **SuperShuttle.** ☎ *800/258–3826* ⊕ *www.supershuttle.com.*

CAR

A car is necessary for getting around greater San Diego on the sprawling freeway system and for visiting the North County beaches, mountains, and desert. Driving around San Diego County is pretty simple: most major attractions are within a few miles of the Pacific Ocean. Interstate 5, which stretches

north–south from Oregon to the Mexican border, bisects San Diego. Interstate 8 provides access from Yuma, Arizona, and points east. Drivers coming from the Los Angeles area, Nevada, and the mountain regions beyond can reach San Diego on Interstate 15. During rush hours there are jams on Interstate 5 and on Interstate 15 between Interstate 805 and Escondido.

There are a few border inspection stations along major highways in San Diego County, the largest just north of Oceanside on Interstate 5 near San Clemente. Travel with your driver's license, and passport if you're an international traveler.

PUBLIC TRANSPORTATION

Visit ⊕ *www.511sd.com*, which lists routes and timetables for the Metropolitan Transit System and North County Transit District. Local/urban bus fare is $2.50 one-way, or $6 for an unlimited day pass (exact change only; pay when you board). A one-way ride on the city's iconic red trolleys is $2.50; get your ticket at any trolley vending machine.

Under the umbrella of the Metropolitan Transit System, there are two major transit agencies in the area: San Diego Transit and North County Transit District (NCTD). You will need to buy a $2 compass card, available when you board for the first time, on which are loaded your destinations to use MTS. Day passes, available for 1 to 30 days and starting at $6, give unlimited rides on nonpremium regional buses and the San Diego Trolley. You can buy them from most trolley vending machines, at the Downtown Transit Store, and at Albertsons markets. A $12 Regional Plus Day Pass adds Coaster service and premium bus routes.

The bright-red trolleys of the San Diego Trolley light-rail system operate on three lines that serve Downtown San Diego, Mission Valley, Old Town, South Bay, the U.S. border, and East County. The trolleys operate seven days a week from about 5 am to midnight, depending on the station, at intervals of about 15 minutes. The trolley system connects with San Diego Transit bus routes—connections are posted at each trolley station. Bicycle lockers are available at most stations and bikes are allowed on buses and trolleys though space is limited. Trolleys can get crowded during morning and evening rush hours. Schedules are posted at each stop; on-time performance is excellent.

NCTD bus routes connect with Coaster commuter train routes between Oceanside and the Santa Fe Depot in San Diego. They serve points from Del Mar north to San Clemente, inland to Fallbrook, Pauma Valley, Valley Center, Ramona, and Escondido, with transfer points within the city of San Diego. The Sprinter light rail provides service between Oceanside and Escondido, with buses connecting to popular North County attractions.

San Diego Transit bus fares range from $2.50 to $5; North County Transit District bus fares are $2.50. You must have exact change in coins and/or bills. Pay upon boarding. Transfers are not included; the $6 day pass is the best option for most bus travel and can be purchased onboard.

San Diego Trolley tickets cost $2.50 and are good for two hours, but for one-way travel only. Round-trip tickets are double the one-way fare.

Tickets are dispensed from self-service machines at each stop; exact fare in coins is recommended, although some machines accept bills in $1, $5, $10, and $20 denominations and credit cards. Ticket vending machines will return up to $5 in change. For trips on multiple buses and trolleys, buy a day pass good for unlimited use all day.

FRED (FREE RIDE EVERYWHERE DOWNTOWN)

These open-air electric vehicles offer free rides throughout the Downtown area. Riders can make a pickup request through the FRED app, or simply flag one down. ⊕ *www.thefreeride.com*

CONTACTS North County Transit District. ☎ *760/966–6500* ⊕ *www.gonctd.com.* **San Diego Transit.** ☎ *619/233–3004* ⊕ *www.511sd.com.*

RIDE-SHARING

App-driven ride-sharing services such as Uber and Lyft are popular in San Diego. Drivers are readily available from most in-town destinations and also service the airport.

TRAIN

Amtrak serves Downtown San Diego's Santa Fe Depot with daily trains to and from Los Angeles, Santa Barbara, and San Luis Obispo. Amtrak trains stop in San Diego North County at Solana Beach and Oceanside. Coaster commuter trains, which run between Oceanside and San Diego Monday through Saturday, stop at the same stations as Amtrak as well as others. The frequency is about every half hour during the weekday rush hour, with four trains on Saturday. One-way fares are $5 to $6.50, depending on the distance traveled. The *Sprinter* runs between Oceanside and Escondido, with many stops along the way.

Metrolink operates high-speed rail service ($17) between the Oceanside Transit Center and Union Station in Los Angeles.

CONTACTS Coaster. ☎ *760/966–6500* ⊕ *www.gonctd.com/coaster.* **Metrolink.** ☎ *800/371–5465* ⊕ *www.metrolinktrains.com.*

Activities

San Diego offers bountiful opportunities for bikers, from casual boardwalk cruises to strenuous rides into the hills. The mild climate makes biking in San Diego a year-round delight. Bike culture is respected here, and visitors are often impressed with the miles of designated bike lanes running alongside city streets and coastal roads throughout the county.

If you're a beginner surfer, consider paddling in the waves off Mission Beach, Pacific Beach, Tourmaline Surfing Park, La Jolla Shores, Del Mar, or Oceanside. More experienced surfers usually head for Sunset Cliffs, La Jolla reef breaks, Black's Beach, or Swami's in Encinitas. All necessary equipment is included in the cost of all surfing schools. Beach-area Y's offer surf lessons and surf camp in the summer months and during spring break.

Beaches

San Diego's beaches have a different vibe from their northern counterparts in neighboring Orange County and glitzy Los Angeles farther up the coast. San Diego is more laid-back and less of a scene. Cyclists on cruiser bikes whiz by as surfers saunter toward the waves and sunbathers bronze under the sun, be it July or November.

Even at summer's hottest peak, San Diego's beaches are cool and breezy. Ocean waves are large, and the water will be colder than what you experience at tropical beaches—temperatures range from 55°F to 65°F from October through June, and 65°F to 73°F from July through September.

Finding a parking spot near the ocean can be hard in summer. Del Mar has a pay lot and metered street parking around the 15th Street Beach. La Jolla Shores has free street parking up to two hours. Mission Beach and other large beaches have unmetered parking lots, but space can be limited. Your best bet is to arrive early.

Pay attention to signs listing illegal activities; undercover police often patrol the beaches. Smoking and alcoholic beverages are completely banned on city beaches. Drinking in beach parking lots, on boardwalks, and in landscaped areas is also illegal. Glass containers are not permitted on beaches, cliffs, and walkways, or in park areas and adjacent parking lots. Littering is not tolerated, and skateboarding is prohibited at some beaches. Fires are allowed only in fire rings or elevated barbecue grills. Although it may be tempting to take a sea creature from a tide pool as a souvenir, it may upset the delicate ecological balance, and it's illegal, too.

Year-round, lifeguards are stationed at nine permanent stations from Sunset Cliffs to Black's Beach. All other beaches are covered by roving patrols in the winter, and seasonal towers in the summer. When swimming in the ocean be aware of rip currents, which are common in California shores. For a surf and weather report, call San Diego's Lifeguard Services at ☎ 619/221–8899. Visit ⊕ www.surfline.com for live webcams on surf conditions and water temperature forecasts.

Dining

San Diego is an up-and-coming culinary destination, thanks to its stunning Pacific Ocean setting, proximity to Mexico, diverse population, and the area's extraordinary farming community. Increasingly the city's veteran top chefs are being joined by a new generation of talented chefs and restaurateurs who are adding stylish restaurants with innovative food and drink programs to the dining scene at a record pace. Yes, visitors still are drawn to the San Diego Zoo and miles of beaches, but now they come for memorable dining experiences as well.

The city's culinary scene got a significant boost when San Diego emerged as one of the world's top craft beer destinations, with artisan breweries and gastropubs now in almost every neighborhood. San Diego also was on the cutting edge of the farm-to-table, Slow Food movement. Local sourcing is possible for everything from seafood to just-picked produce from a host of nationally recognized producers like Chino Farms and Carlsbad Aquafarm. The city's ethnically diverse neighborhoods with their modest eateries offering affordable authentic international cuisines add spice to the dining mix.

San Diego's distinct neighborhoods have their own dining personalities with friendly restaurants and bistros catering to every craving in this sun-blessed city. The trendy Gaslamp Quarter delights visitors looking for a broad range of innovative and international dining and nightlife, while bustling Little Italy offers a mix of affordable Italian fare and posh new eateries. Modern restaurants and cafés thrive in East Village, amid the luxury condos near Petco Park.

The Uptown neighborhoods centered on Hillcrest—an urbane district with San Francisco flavor—are a mix of bars and independent restaurants, many of which specialize in ethnic cuisine. North Park, in particular, has a happening restaurant and craft beer scene, with just about every kind of cuisine you can think of, and laid-back prices to boot. And scenic La Jolla offers some of the best fine dining in the city with dramatic water views as an added bonus.

Restaurant reviews have been shortened. For full information, visit Fodors. com. Prices are the average cost of a main course at dinner, or if dinner is not served, at lunch.

What It Costs

	$	$$	$$$	$$$$
RESTAURANTS				
	under $18	$18–$27	$28–$35	over $35

Hotels

In San Diego, you could plan a luxurious vacation at the beach, staying at a resort with panoramic ocean views, private balconies, and a full-service spa. Or you could stay Downtown, steps from the bustling Gaslamp Quarter, in a modern hotel featuring lively rooftop pools, complimentary wine receptions, and high-tech entertainment systems. But with some flexibility—maybe opting for a partial-view room a quick drive from the action—it's possible to experience San Diego at half the price.

Sharing the city's postcard-perfect sunny skies are neighborhoods and coastal communities that offer great diversity; San Diego is no longer the sleepy beach town it once was. In action-packed Downtown, luxury hotels cater to solo business travelers and young couples with trendy restaurants and cabana-encircled pools. Budget-friendly options can be found in smaller neighborhoods just outside the Gaslamp Quarter such as Little Italy and Uptown (Hillcrest, Mission Hills, and North Park).

You'll need a car if you stay outside Downtown, but the beach communities are rich with lodging options. Across the bridge, Coronado's hotels and resorts offer access to a stretch of glistening white sand that's often recognized as one of the best beaches in the country. La Jolla offers many romantic, upscale ocean-view hotels and some of the area's best restaurants and specialty shopping. But it's easy to find a water view in any price range: surfers make themselves at home at the casual inns and budget stays of Pacific Beach and Mission Bay. If you're planning to fish, check out hotels located near the marinas in Shelter Island, Point Loma, or Coronado.

For families, Uptown, Mission Valley, and Old Town are close to SeaWorld and the San Diego Zoo, offering good-value accommodations with extras like sleeper sofas and video games. Mission Valley is ideal for business travelers; there are plenty of well-known chain hotels with conference space, modern business centers, and kitchenettes for extended stays.

When your work (or sightseeing) is done, join the trendsetters flocking to Downtown's Gaslamp Quarter for its eateries, lounges, and multilevel clubs that rival L.A.'s stylish scenes.

PRICES

Note that even in the most expensive areas, you can find affordable rooms. High season is summer, and rates are lowest in fall. If an ocean view is important, request it when booking, but it will cost you.

Hotel reviews have been shortened. For full information, visit Fodors.com. Prices are the lowest cost of a standard double room in high season.

What It Costs			
$	$$	$$$	$$$$
HOTELS			
under $161	$161–$230	$231–$300	over $300

Nightlife

The San Diego nightlife scene is much more diverse and innovative than it was just a decade ago. Back then, options were limited to the pricey singles-heavy dance clubs Downtown, the party-hearty atmosphere of Pacific Beach, and a handful of charmingly musty neighborhood dive bars popular with locals. Today,

options in San Diego have expanded dramatically, boasting more than 150 craft breweries throughout the county, not to mention several stylish cocktail lounges.

The Gaslamp Quarter is still one of the most popular areas to go for a night on the town. Named for actual gaslights that once provided illumination along its once-seedy streets (it housed a number of gambling halls and brothels), the neighborhood bears only a trace of its debauched roots. Between the Gaslamp and nearby East Village, Downtown San Diego mostly comprises chic nightclubs, tourist-heavy pubs, and a handful of live music venues. Even most of the hotels Downtown have a street-level or rooftop bar—so plan on making it a late night if that's where you intend to bunk. On weekends, parking can be tricky; most lots run about $20, and though there is metered parking (free after 6 pm and all day Sunday), motorists don't give up those coveted spots so easily. Some restaurants and clubs offer valet, though that can get pricey.

Hillcrest is a popular area for LGBTQ nightlife and culture, whereas just a little bit east of Hillcrest, ever-expanding North Park features a diverse range of bars and lounges that cater to a twenty- and thirtysomething crowd, bolstering its reputation as the city's hipster capital. Nearby Normal Heights is a slightly less pretentious alternative, though whichever of these neighborhoods strikes your fancy, a cab from Downtown will run about the same price: $15.

Nightlife along the beaches is more of a mixed bag. Where the scene in Pacific Beach might feel like every week is spring break, La Jolla veers toward being more cost-prohibitive. And although Point Loma is often seen as a sleepier neighborhood in terms of nightlife, it's coming into its own with some select destinations.

If your drink involves caffeine and not alcohol, there's no shortage of coffeehouses in San Diego, and some of the better ones in Hillcrest and North Park stay open past midnight. Many of them also serve beer and wine, if the caffeine buzz isn't enough.

Shopping

San Diego's retail landscape has changed radically in recent years with the opening of several new shopping centers—some in historic buildings—that are focused more on locally owned boutiques than national retailers. Where once the Gaslamp was the place to go for urban apparel and unique home decor, many independently owned boutiques have decided to set up shop in the charming neighborhoods east of Balboa Park known as North Park and South Park. Although Downtown is still thriving, any shopping trip to San Diego should include venturing out to the city's diverse and vibrant neighborhoods. Not far from Downtown, Little Italy is the place to find contemporary art, modern furniture, and home accessories.

Old Town is a must for pottery, ceramics, jewelry, and handcrafted baskets. Uptown is known for its mélange of funky bookstores, offbeat gift shops, and nostalgic collectibles and vintage stores. The beach towns offer the best swimwear and sandals. La Jolla's chic boutiques offer a more intimate shopping experience, along with some of the classiest clothes, jewelry, and shoes in the county. The new La Plaza La Jolla is an open-air shopping center with boutiques and galleries in a Spanish-style building overlooking the cove. Point Loma's Liberty Station shopping area in the former Naval Training Center has art galleries, restaurants, and home stores. Trendsetters will have no trouble finding must-have handbags and designer apparel at the world-class Fashion Valley mall in Mission Valley, a haven for luxury brands such as Hermès, Gucci, and Jimmy Choo.

Enjoy near-perfect weather year-round as you explore shops along the scenic waterfront. The Headquarters at Seaport is a new open-air shopping and dining center in the city's former Police Headquarters building. Here there are some big names, but mostly locally owned boutiques selling everything from gourmet cheese to coastal-inspired home accessories. Just next door, Seaport Village is still the place to go for trinkets and souvenirs. If you don't discover what you're looking for in the boutiques, head to Westfield Horton Plaza, the Downtown mall with more than 120 stores. The sprawling mall completed a major restoration project in 2016 to include a new public plaza, amphitheater, and fountains.

Most malls have free parking in a lot or garage, and parking is not usually a problem. Some of the shops in the Gaslamp Quarter offer validated parking or valet parking.

Tours

BOAT TOURS
Visitors to San Diego can get a great overview of the city from the water. Tour companies offer a range of harbor cruises, from one-hour jaunts to dinner and dancing cruises. In season, whale-watching voyages are another popular option.

Flagship Cruises and Events
BOAT TOURS | One- and two-hour tours of the San Diego Harbor loop north or south from the Broadway Pier throughout the day. Other offerings include dinner and dance cruises, brunch cruises, and winter whale-watching tours December–mid-April. ✉ *990 N. Harbor Dr., Embarcadero* ☎ *619/234–4111* ⊕ *www.flagshipsd.com* 🎟 *From $28.*

H&M Landing

BOAT TOURS | From mid-December to mid-March, this outfitter offers three-hour tours to spot migrating gray whales just off the San Diego coast. ✉ *2803 Emerson St.* ☎ *619/222–1144* ⊕ *www. hmlanding.com* ✉ *From $55.*

Hornblower Cruises & Events

BOAT TOURS | Sixty- and 90-minute tours around San Diego Harbor depart from the Embarcadero several times a day and alternate between the northern and southern portion of the bay. If you're hoping to spot some sea lions, take the North Bay route. Dinner and brunch cruises are also offered, as well as whale-watching tours in winter. ✉ *970 N. Harbor Dr.* ☎ *619/686–8700, 888/467-6256* ⊕ *www.hornblower.com* ✉ *From $30.*

San Diego SEAL Tours

BOAT TOURS | This amphibious tour drives along the Embarcadero before splashing into the San Diego Harbor for a cruise. The 90-minute tours depart daily from 10 am to 5 pm from Seaport Village and the Embarcadero. Call for daily departure times and locations. ✉ *500 Kettner Blvd., Embarcadero* ☎ *619/298–8687* ⊕ *www. sealtours.com* ✉ *$42.*

Seaforth Boat Rentals

BOAT TOURS | For those seeking a private tour on the water, this company can provide a skipper along with your boat rental. Options include harbor cruises, whale-watching, and sunset sails. Seaforth has four locations and a diverse fleet of sail and motorboats to choose from. ✉ *1641 Quivira Rd., Mission Bay* ☎ *888/834–2628* ⊕ *www.seaforthboat-rental.com* ✉ *From $160.*

BUS AND TROLLEY TOURS

For those looking to cover a lot of ground in a limited time, narrated trolley tours include everything from Balboa Park to Coronado. To venture farther afield, consider a coach tour to the desert, Los Angeles, or even Baja, Mexico.

DayTripper Tours

BUS TOURS | FAMILY | Single- and multiday trips throughout Southern California, the Southwest, and Baja depart from San Diego year-round. Popular day trips include the Getty Museum, and theater performances in Los Angeles. Call or check the website for pickup locations. ☎ *619/334–3394* ⊕ *www.daytripper.com* ✉ *From $89.*

Five Star Tours

BUS TOURS | Private and group sightseeing bus tour options around San Diego and beyond include everything from the San Diego Zoo and brewery tours to city tours and trips to Baja, Mexico. ✉ *1050 Kettner Blvd.* ☎ *619/232–5040* ⊕ *www. fivestartours.com* ✉ *From $50.*

Old Town Trolley Tours

GUIDED TOURS | FAMILY | Combining points of interest with local history, trivia, and fun anecdotes, this hop-on, hop-off trolley tour provides an entertaining overview of the city and offers easy access to all the highlights. The tour is narrated, and you can get on and off as you please. Stops include Old Town, Seaport Village, the Gaslamp Quarter, Coronado, Little Italy, and Balboa Park. The trolley leaves every 30 minutes, operates daily, and takes two hours to make a full loop. ✉ *San Diego* ☎ *866/754–0966* ⊕ *www. trolleytours.com/san-diego* ✉ *From $42.*

WALKING TOURS

Several fine walking tours are available on weekdays or weekends; upcoming walks are usually listed in the *San Diego Reader.*

Balboa Park Walking Tours

GUIDED TOURS | On Tuesday and Sunday at 11 am, free, hour-long walks start from the Balboa Park Visitor Center. Tuesday tours are led by volunteers from the visitor center and Sunday tours are led by the park rangers. Reservations are not required, but no tours are scheduled between Thanksgiving and the New Year. Private, custom tours are also available for a fee, with proceeds going to the Balboa Park Conservancy. Contact the visitor center for details and to schedule. ✉ *Balboa Park Visitor Center, 1549 El Prado, Balboa Park* ☎ *619/239–0512* ⊕ *www.balboapark.org* 🎟 *Free.*

Coronado Walking Tours

WALKING TOURS | Departing from the Glorietta Bay Inn at 11 am Tuesday, Thursday, and Saturday, this 90-minute stroll through Coronado's historic district takes in the island's mansions, old Tent City, the Hotel del Coronado, and the castles and cottages that line the beautiful beach. Reservations are recommended. ✉ *1630 Glorietta Blvd.* ☎ *619/435–5993* ⊕ *www.coronadowalkingtour.com* 🎟 *$15* ☞ *Cash only.*

Gaslamp Quarter Historical Foundation

WALKING TOURS | Ninety-minute walking tours of the Downtown historic district depart from the William Heath Davis House at 1 pm on Thursday and 11 am on Saturday. ✉ *410 Island Ave.* ☎ *619/233–4692* ⊕ *gaslampfoundation.org* 🎟 *$20.*

Visitor Information

For general information and brochures before you go, contact the San Diego Tourism Authority, which publishes the helpful *San Diego Visitors Planning Guide.* When you arrive, stop by one of the local visitor centers for general information.

When to Go

San Diego's weather is so ideal that most locals shrug off the high cost of living and relatively lower wages as a "sunshine tax." Along the coast, average temperatures range from the mid-60s to the high 70s, with clear skies and low humidity. Annual rainfall is minimal, less than 10 inches per year.

The peak season for sun seekers is July through October. In July and August, the mercury spikes and everyone spills outside. From mid-December to mid-March,

whale-watchers can glimpse migrating gray whales frolicking in the Pacific. In spring and early summer, a marine layer hugs the coastline for much or all of the day (locals call it "June Gloom"), which can be dreary and disappointing for those who were expecting to bask in Southern California sunshine.

Downtown

Nearly written off in the 1970s, today Downtown San Diego is a testament to conservation and urban renewal. Once derelict Victorian storefronts now house the hottest restaurants, and the *Star of India,* the world's oldest active sailing ship, almost lost to scrap, floats regally along the Embarcadero. Like many modern U.S. cities, Downtown San Diego's story is as much about its rebirth as its history. Although many consider Downtown to be the 16½-block Gaslamp Quarter, it's actually comprised of eight neighborhoods, including East Village, Little Italy, and Embarcadero.

Gaslamp Quarter

Considered the liveliest of the Downtown neighborhoods, the Gaslamp Quarter's 4th and 5th avenues are peppered with trendy nightclubs, swanky lounge bars, chic restaurants, and boisterous sports pubs. The Gaslamp has the largest collection of commercial Victorian-style buildings in the country. Despite this, when the move for Downtown redevelopment gained momentum in the 1970s, there was talk of bulldozing them and starting from scratch. In response, concerned history buffs, developers, architects, and artists formed the Gaslamp Quarter Council to clean up and preserve the quarter. The majority of the quarter's landmark buildings are on 4th and 5th avenues, between Island Avenue and Broadway.

Sights

Gaslamp Museum at the Davis-Horton House

HISTORIC SITE | The oldest wooden house in San Diego houses the Gaslamp Quarter Historical Foundation, the district's curator. Before developer Alonzo Horton came to town, Davis, a prominent San Franciscan, had made an unsuccessful attempt to develop the waterfront area. In 1850 he had this prefab saltbox-style house, built in Maine, shipped around Cape Horn and assembled in San Diego (it originally stood at State and Market Streets). Ninety-minute walking tours ($20) of the historic district leave from the house on Thursday at 1 pm (summer only) and Saturday at 11 am (year-round). If you can't time your visit with the tour, a self-guided tour map ($2) is available. ✉ *410 Island Ave., at 4th Ave., Gaslamp Quarter* ☎ *619/233–4692* 🌐 *www.gaslampfoundation.org* 🎫 *$5 self-guided, $10 with audio tour* 🕘 *Closed Mon.*

Restaurants

Breakfast Republic

$ | **AMERICAN** | Just because it's the most important meal of the day doesn't mean it can't also be flashy or innovative. Breakfast Republic adds some hipster flair to typical brunch fare with a menu that combines hearty Southern staples (grits, jambalaya), Mexican food (chilaquiles, breakfast burritos), and over-the-top treats such as Oreo pancakes and s'mores French toast. Come hungry, but come early; the restaurant doesn't accept reservations and the wait can be a bit long. **Known for:** rich, gooey pancakes and French toast; kombucha flights; kitschy decor. [$] *Average main: $12* ✉ *707 G St., Gaslamp Quarter* ☎ *619/501–8280* 🌐 *www.breakfastrepublic.com* 🕘 *No dinner.*

Taka

$$ | **JAPANESE** | Pristine fish imported from around the world and presented creatively attracts crowds nightly to this intimate Gaslamp restaurant. Table service is available inside and outside where an *omakase* (tasting menu) or eight-piece rolls can be shared and savored; take a seat at the bar to watch one of the sushi chefs preparing appetizers. The restaurant is a favorite with Japanese visitors and conventioneers. **Known for:** uni sushi topped with wasabi; omakase tasting menu; upscale sake offerings. [$] *Average main: $18* ✉ *555 5th Ave., Gaslamp Quarter* ☎ *619/338–0555* 🌐 *www.takasushi.com* 🕘 *No lunch.*

Hotels

★ **Hard Rock Hotel**

$$$ | **HOTEL** | Self-billed as a hip playground for rock stars and people who want to party like them, the Hard Rock is near Petco Park overlooking glimmering San Diego Bay. The interior oozes laid-back sophistication, and guest rooms include branded Sleep Like a Rock beds and the option of renting a guitar. **Pros:** central location; energetic scene; luxurious rooms. **Cons:** pricey drinks; some attitude; party scene tends to be loud. [$] *Rooms from: $249* ✉ *207 5th Ave., Gaslamp Quarter* ☎ *619/702–3000, 866/751–7625* 🌐 *www.hardrockhotelsd.com* 🛏 *420 rooms* 🍴 *No meals.*

★ **Pendry San Diego**

$$$$ | **HOTEL** | Opened in early 2017, the Pendry San Diego is the Gaslamp's newest stunner. **Pros:** well situated in Gaslamp Quarter; excellent dining options; complimentary coffee in the mornings. **Cons:** pricey room rates; meals are expensive; not very family-friendly. [$] *Rooms from: $480* ✉ *550 J St., Gaslamp Quarter* ☎ *619/738–7000* 🌐 *www.pendry.com* 🛏 *317 rooms* 🍴 *No meals.*

★ The Sofia Hotel

$$$ | HOTEL | This stylish and centrally located boutique hotel may have small rooms, but it more than compensates with pampering extras like motion-sensor temperature controls, a Zen-like 24-hour yoga studio, an updated lobby, and a brand-new spa suite. **Pros:** upscale amenities; historic building; near shops and restaurants. **Cons:** busy area; small rooms; spotty Wi-Fi. $ *Rooms from: $259 ✉ 150 W. Broadway, Gaslamp Quarter ☎ 619/234–9200, 800/826–0009 ⊕ www.thesofiahotel.com ⮏ 211 rooms* ⦿ *No meals.*

★ The U.S. Grant, a Luxury Collection Hotel

$$$$ | HOTEL | The U.S. Grant may be more than a hundred years old (it first opened in 1910) but thanks to a top-to-bottom renovation in 2017, this grand old dame is now one of the most glamorous hotels in Southern California. **Pros:** sophisticated rooms; great location; near shopping and restaurants. **Cons:** street noise can be heard from the guest rooms; no in-room minibars or coffeemakers; surrounded by many major construction projects Downtown. $ *Rooms from: $304 ✉ 326 Broadway, Gaslamp Quarter ☎ 619/232–3121, 800/325–3589 ⊕ www.marriott.com ⮏ 270 rooms* ⦿ *No meals.*

Nightlife

★ The Grant Grill

BARS/PUBS | Though the Grant Grill—located on the ground floor of the historic U.S. Grant Hotel—is a full-service restaurant, it's built up a reputation in recent years for stepping up San Diego's craft cocktail game. The cocktail menu is updated seasonally with fresh ingredients and themes (one recently featured a mini "Voodoo" doll frozen inside of a large ice cube), all of which are both innovative and palate pleasant. The atmosphere is comfortable and elegant, even on its busiest nights. ✉ *U.S. Grant Hotel, 326 Broadway, Gaslamp Quarter ☎ 619/744–2077 ⊕ www.grantgrill.com.*

★ Vin de Syrah

WINE BARS—NIGHTLIFE | This "spirit and wine cellar" sends you down a rabbit hole (or at least down some stairs) to a whimsical spot straight out of Alice in Wonderland. Behind a hidden door (look for a handle in the grass wall), you'll find visual delights (grapevines suspended from the ceiling, vintage jars with flittering "fireflies," cozy chairs nestled around a faux fireplace and pastoral vista) that rival the culinary ones—the wine list is approachable and the charcuterie boards are exquisitely curated. ■ **TIP→ More than just a wine bar, the cocktails are also worth a try.** ✉ *901 5th Ave., Gaslamp Quarter ☎ 619/234–4166 ⊕ www.syrahwineparlor.com.*

★ Westgate Hotel Plaza Bar

PIANO BARS/LOUNGES | The old-money surroundings, including leather-upholstered seats, marble tabletops, and a grand piano, supply one of the most elegant and romantic settings for a drink in San Diego. ✉ *1055 2nd Ave., Gaslamp Quarter ☎ 619/238–1818 ⊕ www.westgatehotel.com.*

Embarcadero

The Embarcadero cuts a scenic swath along the harbor front and connects today's Downtown San Diego to its maritime routes. The bustle of Embarcadero comes less these days from the activities of fishing folk than from the throngs of tourists, but this waterfront walkway, stretching from the convention center to the Maritime Museum, remains the nautical soul of the city. There are several seafood restaurants here, as well as sea vessels of every variety—cruise ships, ferries, tour boats, and navy destroyers.

A huge revitalization project is under way along the northern Embarcadero. The overhaul seeks to transform the area with large mixed-use development projects, inviting parks, walkways, and public art installations. The redevelopment will eventually head south along the waterfront, with plans under way for a major overhaul of the entire Central Embarcadero and Seaport Village.

Sights

★ Maritime Museum

MARINA | FAMILY | From sailing ships to submarines, the Maritime Museum is a must for anyone with an interest in nautical history. This collection of restored and replica ships affords a fascinating glimpse of San Diego during its heyday as a commercial seaport. The jewel of the collection, the *Star of India,* was built in 1863 and made 21 trips around the world in the late 1800s. Saved from the scrap yard and painstakingly restored, the windjammer is the oldest active iron sailing ship in the world. The newly constructed *San Salvador* is a detailed historic replica of the original ship first sailed into San Diego Bay by explorer Juan Rodriguez Cabrillo back in 1542, and the popular HMS *Surprise* is a replica of an 18th-century British Royal Navy frigate. The museum's headquarters are on the *Berkeley,* an 1898 steam-driven ferryboat, which served the Southern Pacific Railroad in San Francisco until 1958.

Numerous cruises of San Diego Bay are offered, including a daily 45-minute narrated tour aboard a 1914 pilot boat and three-hour weekend sails aboard the topsail schooner the *Californian,* the state's official tall ship, and 75-minute tours aboard a historic swift boat, which highlights the city's military connection. Partnering with the museum, the renowned yacht *America* also offers sails on the bay, and whale-watching excursions are available in winter. ⊠ *1492 N. Harbor Dr., Embarcadero* ☏ *619/234–9153* ⊕ *www. sdmaritime.org* ⊒ *$18.*

★ Museum of Contemporary Art San Diego (MCASD)

MUSEUM | At the Downtown branch of the city's contemporary art museum, explore the works of international and regional artists in a modern, urban space. The Jacobs Building—formerly the baggage building at the historic Santa Fe Depot—features large gallery spaces, high ceilings, and natural lighting, giving artists the flexibility to create large-scale installations. MCASD's collection includes many pop art, minimalist, and conceptual works from the 1950s to the present. The museum showcases both established and emerging artists in temporary exhibitions, and has permanent, site-specific commissions by Jenny Holzer and Richard Serra. ⊠ *1100 and 1001 Kettner Blvd., Downtown* ☏ *858/454–3541* ⊕ *www. mcasd.org* ⊒ *$10; free 3rd Thurs. of the month 5–7* ⊙ *Closed Wed.*

★ The New Children's Museum (NCM)

MUSEUM | FAMILY | The NCM blends contemporary art with unstructured play to create an environment that appeals to children as well as adults. The 50,000-square-foot structure was constructed from recycled building materials, operates on solar energy, and is convection-cooled by an elevator shaft. It also features a nutritious and eco-conscious café. Interactive exhibits include designated areas for toddlers and teens, as well as plenty of activities for the entire family. Several art workshops are offered each day, as well as hands-on studios where visitors are encouraged to create their own art. The studio projects change frequently and the entire museum changes exhibits every 18 to 24 months, so there is always something new to explore. The adjoining 1-acre park and playground is across from the convention center trolley stop. ⊠ *200 W. Island Ave., Embarcadero* ☏ *619/233–8792* ⊕ *www. thinkplaycreate.org* ⊒ *$14* ⊙ *Closed Tues.*

Seaport Village

PEDESTRIAN MALL | FAMILY | You'll find some of the best views of the harbor at Seaport Village, three bustling shopping plazas designed to reflect the New England clapboard and Spanish Mission architectural styles of early California. On a prime stretch of waterfront the dining, shopping, and entertainment complex connects the harbor with hotel towers and the convention center. Specialty shops offer everything from a kite store and swing emporium to a shop devoted to hot sauces. You can dine at snack bars and restaurants, many with harbor views.

Live music can be heard daily from noon to 4 at the main food court. Additional free concerts take place every Sunday from 1 to 4 at the East Plaza Gazebo. The **Seaport Village Carousel** (rides $3) has 54 animals, hand-carved and hand-painted by Charles Looff in 1895. Across the street, the **Headquarters at Seaport Village** converted the historic police headquarters into several trendsetting shops and restaurants. ⊠ *849 W. Harbor Dr., Downtown* ☎ *619/530–0704 office and events hotline* ⊕ *www.seaportvillage.com.*

★ USS *Midway* Museum

MILITARY SITE | FAMILY | After 47 years of worldwide service, the retired USS *Midway* began a new tour of duty on the south side of the Navy pier in 2004. Launched in 1945, the 1,001-foot-long ship was the largest in the world for the first 10 years of its existence. The most visible landmark on the north Embarcadero, it now serves as a floating interactive museum—an appropriate addition to the town that is home to one-third of the Pacific fleet and the birthplace of naval aviation. A free audio tour guides you through the massive ship while offering insight from former sailors. As you clamber through passageways and up and down ladder wells, you'll get a feel for how the *Midway's* 4,500 crew members lived and worked on this "city at sea."

Though the entire tour is impressive, you'll really be wowed when you step out onto the 4-acre flight deck—not only the best place to get an idea of the ship's scale, but also one of the most interesting vantage points for bay and city skyline views. An F-14 Tomcat jet fighter is just one of many vintage aircraft on display. Free guided tours of the bridge and primary flight control, known as "the Island," depart every 10 minutes from the flight deck. Many of the docents stationed throughout the ship served in the Navy, some even on the *Midway*, and they are eager to answer questions or share stories. The museum also offers multiple flight simulators for an additional fee, climb-aboard cockpits, and interactive exhibits focusing on naval aviation. There is a gift shop and a café with pleasant outdoor seating. This is a wildly popular stop, with most visits lasting several hours. ⚠ **Despite efforts to provide accessibility throughout the ship, some areas can only be reached via fairly steep steps; a video tour of these areas is available on the hangar deck.** ⊠ *910 N. Harbor Dr., Embarcadero* ☎ *619/544–9600* ⊕ *www.midway.org* ⊠ *$21.*

 Restaurants

★ Eddie V's Prime Seafood

$$$ | SEAFOOD | Don't be put off by the name, or that it is part of a small chain. This fine-dining restaurant at the Headquarters at Seaport in Downtown has won a devoted following for classic seafood, casual but sophisticated settings, and nightly live jazz. Chilled oysters and other shellfish compete with Maine lobster tacos and kung pao–style calamari to start the meal. The polished staff helps with informed descriptions of almost two-dozen entrées starring fish flown in fresh daily and prime steaks. Sea bass in a savory soy broth and Parmesan-crusted sole are favorites, while the seafood chopped salad is light and sharable. Truffled mac and cheese and au gratin cheddar potatoes are not-to-be-missed sides. Nightly happy hours in the V Lounge offer $8 wines, cocktails, and appetizers. **Known for:** wallet-friendly happy hour deals; indulgent truffled mac and cheese. [$] *Average main: $34* ✉ *789 W. Harbor Dr., Embarcadero* ☎ *619/615–0281* 🌐 *www.eddiev.com* ⏲ *No lunch.*

★ Puesto

$ | **MEXICAN** | Bold graffiti graphics, chandeliers with tangled telephone wires, and beat-heavy music energize this Downtown eatery that celebrates Mexican street food with a modern twist. Settle into one of the interior rooms or the sunny patio under orange umbrellas to sip margaritas and other specialty cocktails, Baja wines, or fruity aguas frescas made daily. Guacamole, ceviche, seafood tostadas, and a festive stack of chili-and-salt-spiced mango whet appetites for tasty street tacos—nine varieties including lobster, mushroom, and striped bass that can be mixed and matched for plates of three. Deep-fried carnitas with a cactus leaf salad, grilled filet mignon, and octopus tacos round out the menu. The original (and smaller) Puesto is in downtown La Jolla. **Known for:** taco trio plates; unique Parmesan guacamole; fruit-infused margaritas made in-house. [$] *Average main: $16* ✉ *789 W. Harbor Dr., Downtown* ☎ *619/233–8880* 🌐 *www.eatpuesto.com.*

Hotels

★ InterContinental San Diego

$$$ | **HOTEL** | A new addition to the waterfront skyline, InterContinental San Diego provides a more luxurious and stylish option for travelers in what's generally an area populated by more family-friendly lodging. **Pros:** stunning waterfront views; excellent dining options at Vistal and Garibaldi; close to both airport and attractions. **Cons:** a bit on the pricier side; pedestrian traffic can be hectic because of nearby shopping/boating areas; entrances and elevators are a bit confusing. [$] *Rooms from: $269* ✉ *901 Bayfront Ct., Embarcadero* ☎ *619/501–9400* 🌐 *ihg.com* 🛏 *400 rooms* 🍴 *No meals.*

Shopping

★ The Headquarters at Seaport

OUTDOOR/FLEA/GREEN MARKETS | This new upscale shopping and dining center is in the city's former police headquarters, a beautiful and historic Mission-style building featuring an open courtyard with fountains. Restaurants and shops, many locally owned, occupy former jail facilities and offices. Pop into **Urban Beach House** for coastal-inspired fashion from popular surf brands for men and women, including accessories and home decor. Swing by **Fair World** for ethically sourced fashion and handmade gifts. **Perfume Gallery** offers more than 1,000 different scents in its extensive collection. **Madison San Diego** offers a great selection of leather goods and accessories, from apparel and handbags to belts and travel accessories. ✉ *789 W. Harbor Dr., Downtown* ☎ *619/235–4013* 🌐 *theheadquarters.com.*

East Village

The most ambitious of the Downtown projects is East Village, not far from the Gaslamp Quarter, and encompassing 130 blocks between the railroad tracks up to J Street, and from 6th Avenue east to around 10th Street. Sparking the rebirth of this former warehouse district was the 2004 construction of the San Diego Padres' baseball stadium, Petco Park. The Urban Art Trail has added pizzazz to drab city thoroughfares by transforming such things as trash cans and traffic controller boxes into works of art. As the city's largest Downtown neighborhood, East Village is continually broadening its boundaries with its urban design of redbrick cafés, spacious galleries, rooftop bars, sleek hotels, and warehouse restaurants.

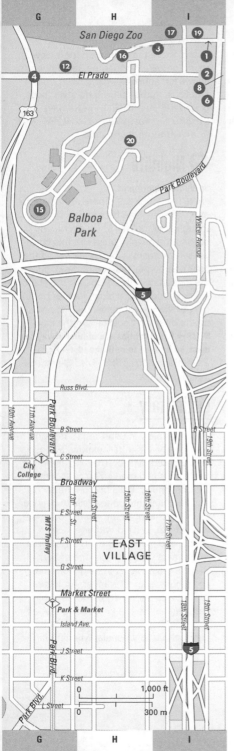

Sights ▼

1 Balboa Park Carousel I1
2 Bea Evenson Fountain ...I1
3 Botanical Building I1
4 Cabrillo Bridge G1
5 Chicano Park............. E9
6 Fleet Science Center.....I1
7 Gaslamp Museum at the Davis-Horton House..... E8
8 Inez Grant Parker Memorial Rose Garden and Desert Garden I1
9 Little Italy Mercato C4
10 Maritime Museum...... A5
11 Museum of Contemporary Art San Diego (MCASD).... B6
12 The Museum of Us G1
13 The New Children's Museum (NCM)......... D8
14 Petco Park................ F9
15 San Diego Air & Space Museum G3
16 San Diego Museum of Art.......... H1
17 San Diego Zoo I1
18 Seaport Village.......... B9
19 Spanish Village Art Center.....................I1
20 Spreckels Organ Pavilion H2
21 USS Midway Museum A7

Restaurants ▼

1 The Blind Burro F9
2 Born and Raised C3
3 Breakfast Republic F8
4 Civico by The Park....... E1
5 The Crack Shack........ B2
6 Las Cuatro Milpas E9
7 Cucina Urbana E1
8 Eddie V's Prime Seafood.................. B8
9 Extraordinary Desserts D5
10 Herb & Wood............ B2
11 Little Italy Food Hall......C4
12 Puesto.................... B8
13 ¡Salud! E9
14 Taka E8

Hotels ▼

1 Hard Rock Hotel E9
2 InterContinental San Diego................ B6
3 Pendry San Diego E8
4 The Sofia Hotel.......... D6
5 The U.S. Grant, a Luxury Collection Hotel...................... E6

Sights

Petco Park

SPORTS VENUE | FAMILY | Petco Park is home to the city's major league baseball team, the San Diego Padres. The ballpark is strategically designed to give fans a view of San Diego Bay, the skyline, and Balboa Park. Reflecting San Diego's beauty, the stadium is clad in sandstone from India to evoke the area's cliffs and beaches; the 42,000 seats are dark blue, reminiscent of the ocean, and the exposed steel is painted white to reflect the sails of harbor boats on the bay. The family-friendly lawnlike berm, "Park at the Park," is a popular and affordable place for fans to view the game. The ballpark underwent a huge effort to improve dining in the park, and local food vendors and craft breweries now dominate the dining options. Behind-the-scenes guided tours of Petco, including the press box and the dugout, are offered throughout the year. ✉ *100 Park Blvd., East Village* ☎ *619/795–5011 tour hotline* 🌐 *sandiego.padres.mlb.com* 🎫 *$20 tour.*

Restaurants

The Blind Burro

$$ | MODERN MEXICAN | FAMILY | East Village families, baseball fans heading to or from Petco Park, and happy-hour-bound singles flock to this airy restaurant with Baja-inspired food and drink. Traditional margaritas get a fresh kick from fruit juices or jalapeño peppers; other libations include sangria and Mexican beers, all perfect pairings for house-made guacamole, ceviche, or salsas with chips. The menu doesn't include enchiladas or burritos, but the well-loved lobster and surf-and-turf tacos and extensive and innovative tortas like an Angus short rib topped with pico de gallo, and side dishes including Mexican-style corn dressed in cotija cheese as well as serrano-spiced pinto beans, more than make up for it. Save room for warm, cinnamon-sugar churros. **Known for:** house margarita with fruit infusions; surf-and-turf Baja-style tacos; gluten-free menu. [$] *Average main: $18* ✉ *639 J St., East Village* ☎ *619/795–7880* 🌐 *www.theblindburro.com.*

Nightlife

★ Noble Experiment

PIANO BARS/LOUNGES | There are a handful of speakeasy-style bars in San Diego, though none deliver so far above and beyond the novelty quite like this cozy-yet-swank cocktail lounge hidden in the back of a burger restaurant. Seek out the hidden door (hint: look for the stack of kegs), tuck into a plush leather booth next to the wall of golden skulls, and sip on the best craft cocktails in the city. **■ TIP→ Reservations are almost always a must, so be sure to call ahead.** ✉ *777 G St., East Village* ☎ *619/888–4713* 🌐 *nobleexperimentsd.com.*

Little Italy

Home to many in San Diego's design community, Little Italy exudes a sense of urban cool while remaining authentic to its roots and marked by old-country charms: church bells ring on the half hour, and Italians gather daily to play bocce in Amici Park. The main thoroughfare, India Street, is filled with lively cafés, chic shops, and many of the city's trendiest restaurants. Little Italy is one of San Diego's most walkable neighborhoods, and a great spot to wander. Art lovers can browse gallery showrooms, while shoppers adore the Fir Street cottages. The neighborhood bustles each Saturday during the wildly popular Mercato farmers' market.

Sights

Little Italy Mercato

MARKET | Each Saturday tourists and residents alike flock to the Little Italy Mercato, one of the most popular farmers' markets in San Diego. More than 150 vendors line Date Street selling everything from paintings and pottery to flowers and farm-fresh eggs. Come hungry, as several booths and food trucks serve prepared foods. Alternatively, the neighborhood's many cafés and restaurants are just steps away. The Mercato is a great opportunity to experience one of San Diego's most exciting urban neighborhoods. ✉ *Date and India Sts., Little Italy* 🌐 *www.littleitalysd.com/events/mercato.*

Restaurants

★ Born and Raised

$$$$ | **STEAKHOUSE** | The name is cheeky if a little morbid; the title refers to the restaurant's speciality—steak. It's a twist on a classic steak house, with a menu full of aged, prime cuts of beef served with a number of sauces, or perhaps try the table-side-prepared steak Diane with flambéed jus. With its large gold doors, intimate booths, and stiff Manhattans, everything about the restaurant feels like old luxury, until you notice the portraits of famous rappers on the walls. **Known for:** table-side Caesar salad; aged New York steak; cheeky, glamorous decor. [$] *Average main: $45* ✉ *1909 India St., Little Italy* ☎ *619/202–4577* 🌐 *www.bornandraisedsteak.com.*

★ The Crack Shack

$ | **AMERICAN** | **FAMILY** | Next to his successful fine-dining restaurant, Juniper and Ivy, celebrity chef Richard Blais has opened this more casual eatery complete with a walk-up counter, picnic-style tables, a boccie court, and a giant rooster—a nod to the egg- and chicken-theme menu. Ingredients are sourced from high-quality vendors and used for sandwiches, of which the fried chicken varieties shine, as well as salads and sides like fluffy minibiscuits with a miso-maple butter and a Mexican spin on poutine. The all-outdoor space feels like a cool playground for foodies, and there's even a slick bar that doles out craft cocktails. **Known for:** Señor Croque fried chicken sandwich with smoked pork belly; biscuits with miso-maple butter; all-outdoor seating with boccie court. [$] *Average main: $12* ✉ *2266 Kettner Blvd., Little Italy* ☎ *619/795–3299* 🌐 *www.crackshack.com.*

★ Extraordinary Desserts

$ | **CAFÉ** | For Paris-perfect cakes and tarts embellished California-style with fresh flowers, head to this sleek, serene branch of Karen Krasne's pastry shop and café. The space with soaring ceilings hosts breakfasts, lunches, and light dinners, accompanied by a wide selection of teas, coffee, organic wines, and craft beers. For those who don't want to start with dessert, there are sandwiches, soups, salads, and artisanal cheeses, plus a kids' menu of grilled cheese or free-range turkey served on local bread. When it's time to satisfy your sweet tooth, try a slice of passion fruit ricotta cake, a mini-banana cream pie, or helping of croissant bread pudding. The original shop near Balboa Park, at 2929 5th Avenue, serves only desserts, coffees, and teas. **Known for:** blueberry coffee cake for breakfast; chocolate dulce de leche cake; house-made dips including onion dip and Parmesan pesto. [$] *Average main: $14* ✉ *1430 Union St., Little Italy* ☎ *619/294–7001* 🌐 *www.extraordinarydesserts.com.*

★ Herb & Wood

$$ | **AMERICAN** | Design lovers will fall for celebrity chef Brian Malarkey's sprawling restaurant, a former art store that has been refashioned into four luxe spaces in one—an entryway lounge, outdoor lounge, fireplace-dotted patio, and the main dining room, which is flanked by beaded chandeliers, lush banquettes, and paintings in rich jewel tones. The menu is heavy on wood-roasted dishes, many of which are apt for sharing, like the roasted baby carrots or hiramasa with crispy quinoa. There are also larger options like an oxtail gnocchi and pizzas with toppings from mushrooms to bone marrow. Stop by the adjacent **Herb & Eatery** for coffee, pastries, prepared foods, and gift items. **Known for:** roasted baby carrots with cashew sesame dukkah; pillow-soft oxtail gnocchi; the secret menu Parker House rolls topped with Maldon sea salt. $ Average main: $20 ⊠ 2210 Kettner Blvd., Little Italy ☎ 619/955–8495 ⊕ www.herbandwood.com ☾ No lunch.

Little Italy Food Hall
$ | FUSION | FAMILY | A recently opened, chic update on the food court, Food Hall brings together a half dozen different innovative food counters to offer quick bites vastly more interesting than mall fare. Among its offerings are the seafood-centric Single Fin Kitchen and Wicked Maine Lobster, and an update on a local delicacy, Not Not Tacos. There's also a bar at the center, so every bite can be paired with a cold beer or cocktail. **Known for:** fusion tacos; bustling crowds of Mercato shoppers; beer/wine cart dispensing refreshments in the outdoor seating area. $ Average main: $10 ⊠ 550 W. Date St., Suite B, Little Italy ☎ 619/269–7187 ⊕ www.littleitalyfoodhall.com.

Nightlife

★ Ballast Point Brewing Co.
BREWPUBS/BEER GARDENS | Until recently, you had to head to the Miramar/Scripps Ranch area for a tasting at Ballast Point, but now there's a spacious (and popular) local taproom in Little Italy. The Sculpin IPA is outstanding, as are the blue cheese duck nachos ⊠ 2215 India St., Little Italy ☎ 619/255–7213 ⊕ www.ballastpoint.com.

★ False Idol
BARS/PUBS | A walk-in refrigerator harbors the secret entrance to this tiki-theme speakeasy, which is attached to Craft & Commerce. Beneath fishing nets full of puffer-fish lights and elaborate tiki-head wall carvings, the knowledgeable staff serves up creative takes on tropical classics with the best selection of rums in town. ■ TIP➜ **The bar fills up quickly, especially on weekends. Make a reservation online a week or more in advance.** ⊠ 675 W. Beech St., Little Italy ⊕ falseidoltiki.com.

Karl Strauss' Brewing Company
BARS/PUBS | San Diego's first microbrewery now has multiple locations, but the original one remains a staple. This locale draws an after-work crowd for pints of Red Trolley Ale and later fills with beer connoisseurs from all walks of life to try Karl's latest concoctions. The German-inspired pub food is above average. ⊠ 1157 Columbia St., Little Italy ☎ 619/234–2739 ⊕ www.karlstrauss.com.

Barrio Logan

San Diego's Mexican-American community is centered in Barrio Logan, under the San Diego–Coronado Bay Bridge on the Downtown side. Chicano Park, spread along National Avenue from Dewey to Crosby streets, is the barrio's recreational hub. It's worth taking a short detour to see the huge murals of Mexican history painted on the bridge supports at National Avenue and Dewey Street; they're among the best examples of folk art in the city. Art enthusiasts will also enjoy the burgeoning gallery scene in the Barrio Logan neighborhood, rapidly becoming a hub for artists in San Diego.

GETTING HERE AND AROUND
Barrio Logan is located right off Interstate 5, at the Cesar E. Chavez Parkway exit. Driving is the easiest way to get there, especially coming from Downtown—in fact, it's only a mile from Petco Park,

and easily accessible via Imperial and Logan avenues. However, the Blue Line trolley also stops in Barrio Logan, and several bus lines also cross through the neighborhood, including the 9, 6, 20, 705, and 923.

When staying Downtown, Barrio Logan is also just a 15-minute walk, but with its somewhat isolated location under a bridge, visitors should exercise caution visiting the Chicano Park murals after dark.

Sights

★ Chicano Park

PUBLIC ART | FAMILY | The cultural center of the Barrio Logan neighborhood, Chicano Park—designated a National Historic Landmark in 2017—was born in 1970 from the activism of local residents who occupied the space after the state rescinded its promise to designate the land a park. Signed into law a year later, the park is now a protected area that brings together families and locals for both public and private events, a welcoming gathering space as well as an outdoor gallery featuring large murals documenting Mexican-American history and Chicano activism. Every year Chicano Park Day is held on April 21, filling the park with the sights and sounds of music, dancers, vintage cars, and food and clothing vendors. ✉ *Logan Ave. and Cesar Chavez Pkwy., Barrio Logan* 🌐 *chicano-park.com; www.chicanoparksandiego.com.*

Restaurants

Las Cuatro Milpas

$ | MEXICAN | One of the oldest restaurants in San Diego, having opened in 1933, Las Cuatro Milpas feels like a closely held secret in Barrio Logan. Open daily until 3 pm, it almost inevitably attracts a big lunchtime rush, though the wait is worth it for the homemade tortillas, beans with chorizo, and rolled tacos. The menu is simple, though everything is delicious, and the interior—with checkered picnic tables—looks like it hasn't changed in 85 years. **Known for:** homemade tortillas; checkered picnic tables; chorizo con huevos. [$] *Average main: $5* ✉ *1857 Logan Ave., Barrio Logan* ☎ *619/234–4460* 🌐 *www.las-cuatro-milpas.com* 🕒 *Closed Sun.* 💳 *No credit cards.*

★ ¡Salud!

$ | MEXICAN | The line that inevitably wraps around the building is indicative of the quality of the tacos and the large selection of local craft beers on tap. Indeed, these are some of the best tacos in all of San Diego, ranging from the classic carne asada and Baja fish tacos to fried-shell beef tacos and Califas, which features French fries inside the tortilla. Just remember—alcohol isn't allowed at the outdoor tables. **Known for:** Baja-style street tacos; Pruno de Piña (beer and fermented pineapple); churros and ice cream. [$] *Average main: $3* ✉ *2196 Logan Ave., Barrio Logan* ☎ *619/255–3856* 🌐 *saludtacos.com.*

Balboa Park, Bankers Hill, and San Diego Zoo

Overlooking Downtown and the Pacific Ocean, 1,200-acre Balboa Park is the cultural heart of San Diego. Ranked as one of the world's best parks by the Project for Public Spaces, it's also where you can find most of the city's museums, art galleries, the Tony Award–winning Old Globe Theatre, and the world-famous San Diego Zoo. Often referred to as the "Smithsonian of the West" for its concentration of museums, Balboa Park is also a series of botanical gardens, performance spaces, and outdoor playrooms endeared to the hearts of residents and visitors alike.

In addition, the captivating architecture of Balboa's buildings, fountains, and courtyards gives the park an enchanted feel. Historic buildings dating from San Diego's

1915 Panama–California International Exposition are strung along the park's main east–west thoroughfare, El Prado, which leads from 6th Avenue eastward over the Cabrillo Bridge (formerly the Laurel Street Bridge), the park's official gateway. If you're a cinema fan, many of the buildings may be familiar—Orson Welles used exteriors of several Balboa Park buildings to represent the Xanadu estate of Charles Foster Kane in his 1941 classic, *Citizen Kane*. Prominent among them was the California Building, whose 200-foot tower, housing a 100-bell carillon that tolls the hour, is El Prado's tallest structure. Missing from the black-and-white film, however, was the magnificent blue of its tiled dome shining in the sun.

Bankers Hill is a small neighborhood west of Balboa Park, with gorgeous views ranging from Balboa Park's greenery in the east to the San Diego Bay in the west. It's become one of San Diego's hottest restaurant destinations.

Sights

★ Balboa Park Carousel

CAROUSEL | FAMILY | Suspended an arm's length away on this antique merry-go-round is the brass ring that could earn you an extra free ride (it's one of the few carousels in the world that continue this bonus tradition). Hand-carved in 1910, the carousel features colorful murals, big-band music, and bobbing animals including zebras, giraffes, and dragons; real horsehair was used for the tails. ⊠ *1889 Zoo Pl., behind zoo parking lot, Balboa Park* ☎ *619/239–0512* ⊕ *www. balboapark.org* ⊠ *$3* ⊙ *Closed weekdays Labor Day–mid-June.*

Bea Evenson Fountain

FOUNTAIN | A favorite of barefoot children, this fountain shoots cool jets of water upwards of 50 feet. Built in 1972 between the Fleet Center and Natural History Museum, the fountain offers plenty of room to sit and watch the crowds go by. ⊠ *Balboa Park* ✛ *East end of El Prado* ⊕ *www.balboapark.org.*

★ Botanical Building

GARDEN | The graceful redwood-lath structure, built for the 1915 Panama–California International Exposition, now houses more than 2,000 types of tropical and subtropical plants plus changing seasonal flower displays. Ceiling-high tree ferns shade fragile orchids and feathery bamboo. There are benches beside miniature waterfalls for resting in the shade. The rectangular pond outside, filled with lotuses and water lilies that bloom in spring and fall, is popular with photographers. ⊠ *1549 El Prado, Balboa Park* ☎ *619/239–0512* ⊕ *www.balboapark.org* ⊠ *Free* ⊙ *Closed Thurs.*

Cabrillo Bridge

BRIDGE/TUNNEL | The official gateway into Balboa Park soars 120 feet above a canyon floor. Pedestrian-friendly, the 1,500-foot bridge provides inspiring views of the California Tower and El Prado beyond. ■TIP→ **This is a great spot for photo-capturing a classic image of the park.** ⊠ *Balboa Park* ✛ *On El Prado, at 6th Ave. park entrance* ⊕ *www.balboapark.org.*

Fleet Science Center

MUSEUM | FAMILY | Interactive exhibits here are artfully educational and for all ages: older kids can get hands-on with inventive projects in Studio X, while the five-and-under set can be easily entertained with interactive play stations like the Ball Wall and Fire Truck in the center's Kid City. The IMAX Dome Theater, which screens exhilarating nature and science films, was the world's first, as was the Fleet's "NanoSeam" (seamless) dome ceiling that doubles as a planetarium. ⊠ *1875 El Prado, Balboa Park* ☎ *619/238–1233* ⊕ *www.rhfleet.org* ⊠ *The Fleet experience includes gallery exhibits and 1 IMAX film $22; additional cost for special exhibits or add-on 2nd IMAX film or planetarium show.*

★ **Inez Grant Parker Memorial Rose Garden and Desert Garden**

GARDEN | These neighboring gardens sit just across the Park Boulevard pedestrian bridge and offer gorgeous views over Florida Canyon. The award-winning formal rose garden contains 1,600 roses representing nearly 130 varieties; peak bloom is usually in April and May but the garden remains beautiful and worthy of a visit year-round. The adjacent Desert Garden provides a striking contrast, with 2½ acres of succulents and desert plants seeming to blend into the landscape of the canyon below. ⊠ *2525 Park Blvd., Balboa Park* ⊕ *www.balboapark.org.*

★ **The Museum of Us**

MUSEUM | FAMILY | Originally known as San Diego Museum of Man, the name was changed in efforts to reflect values of equity, inclusion, and decolonization. If the facade of this building—the landmark California Building—looks familiar, it's because filmmaker Orson Welles used it and its dramatic tower as the principal features of the Xanadu estate in his 1941 classic, *Citizen Kane.* Closed for 80 years, the tower was recently reopened for public tours. An additional timed ticket and a climb up 125 steps is required, but the effort will be rewarded with spectacular 360-degree views of the coast, Downtown, and the inland mountains. Back inside, exhibits at this highly respected anthropological museum focus on Southwestern, Mexican, and South American cultures. Carved monuments from the Mayan city of Quirigua in Guatemala, cast from the originals in 1914, are particularly impressive. Exhibits might include examples of intricate beadwork from across the Americas, the history of Egyptian mummies, or the lifestyles of the Kumeyaay peoples, American Indians who live in the San Diego area. ⊠ *California Bldg., 1350 El Prado, Balboa Park* 🕾 *619/239-2001* ⊕ *www.museumofman. org* 🎫 *$13; special exhibits and private tower tour cost extra* ☞ *Tower tours are timed-entry and can be booked in advance through website or on arrival at museum.*

★ **San Diego Air & Space Museum**

MUSEUM | FAMILY | By day, the streamlined edifice looks like any other structure in the park; at night, outlined in blue neon, the round building appears—appropriately enough—to be a landed UFO. Every available inch of space in the rotunda is filled with exhibits about aviation and aerospace pioneers, including examples of enemy planes from the World Wars. In all, there are more than 60 full-size aircraft on the floor and hanging from the rafters. In addition to exhibits from the dawn of flight to the jet age, the museum displays a growing number of space-age exhibits, including the actual *Apollo 9* command module. To test your own skills, you can ride in a two-seat Max Flight simulator or try out the Talon Racing simulator. Movies in the 3-D/4-D theater are included with admission. ⊠ *2001 Pan American Pl., Balboa Park* 🕾 *619/234-8291* ⊕ *www. sandiegoairandspace.org* 🎫 *$22; max flight simulator $8.*

★ **San Diego Museum of Art**

MUSEUM | Known for its Spanish baroque and Renaissance paintings, including works by El Greco, Goya, Rubens, and van Ruisdael, San Diego's most comprehensive art museum also has strong holdings of South Asian art, Indian miniatures, and contemporary California paintings. The museum's exhibits tend to have broad appeal, and if traveling shows from other cities come to town, you can expect to see them here. Free docent tours are offered throughout the day. An outdoor Sculpture Court and Garden exhibits both traditional and modern pieces. Enjoy the view over a craft beer and some locally sourced food in the adjacent Panama 66 courtyard restaurant. ∎TIP➜ **The museum hosts "Art After Hours" most Friday nights, with discounted admission 5–8 pm.** ⊠ *1450 El Prado, Balboa Park* 🕾 *619/232-7931* ⊕ *www.sdmart.org* 🎫 *$15; sculpture garden is free* ⊘ *Closed Wed.*

★ San Diego Zoo

ZOO | FAMILY | Balboa Park's—and perhaps the city's—most famous attraction is its 100-acre zoo. Nearly 4,000 animals of some 800 diverse species roam in hospitable, expertly crafted habitats that replicate natural environments as closely as possible. The flora in the zoo, including many rare species, is even more dear than the fauna. Walkways wind over bridges and past waterfalls ringed with tropical ferns; elephants in a sandy plateau roam so close you're tempted to pet them.

Exploring the zoo fully requires the stamina of a healthy hiker, but open-air double-decker buses that run throughout the day let you zip through three-quarters of the exhibits on a guided 35- to 40-minute, 3-mile tour. There are also express buses, used for quick transportation, that make five stops around the grounds and include some narration. The Skyfari Aerial Tram, which soars 170 feet above the ground, gives a good overview of the zoo's layout and, on clear days, a panorama of the park, Downtown San Diego, the bay, and the ocean, far beyond the San Diego–Coronado Bridge. **■TIP→ Unless you come early, expect to wait for the regular bus, and especially for the top tier—the line can take more than 45 minutes; if you come at midday on a weekend or school holiday, you'll be doing the in-line shuffle for a while.**

Don't forget the San Diego Safari Park, the zoo's 1,800-acre extension to the north at Escondido. ✉ *2920 Zoo Dr., Balboa Park* ☎ *619/234–3153* 🌐 *www.sandiegozoo.org* 🎟 *$62.*

★ Spanish Village Art Center

MUSEUM | More than 200 local artists, including glassblowers, enamel workers, wood-carvers, sculptors, painters, jewelers, and photographers work and give demonstrations of their craft on a rotating basis within and outside of these red tile–roof studio-galleries that were set up for the 1935–36 exposition in the style of an old Spanish village. The center is a great source for memorable gifts. ✉ *1770 Village Pl., Balboa Park* ☎ *619/233–9050* 🌐 *spanishvillageartcenter.com* 🎟 *Free.*

★ Spreckels Organ Pavilion

ARTS VENUE | The 2,400-bench-seat pavilion, dedicated in 1915 by sugar magnates John D. and Adolph B. Spreckels, holds the 4,518-pipe Spreckels Organ, the largest outdoor pipe organ in the world. You can hear this impressive instrument at one of the year-round, free, 2 pm Sunday concerts, regularly performed by the city's civic organist Raúl Prieto Ramírez and guest artists—a highlight of a visit to Balboa Park. On Monday evenings from late June to mid-August, internationally renowned organists play evening concerts. At Christmastime the park's Christmas tree and life-size Nativity display turn the pavilion into a seasonal wonderland. ✉ *2211 Pan American Rd., Balboa Park* ☎ *619/702–8138* 🌐 *spreckelsorgan.org.*

🍴 Restaurants

★ Civico by the Park

$ | ITALIAN | Dario and Pietro Gallo, the Italian brothers behind the Civico restaurants in Little Italy, have taken their concept into Banker's Hill, bringing with them authentic Italian dishes from the Calabria region of Southern Italy. The menu offers traditional and vegan options, as well as introducing a scratch pizza program in two distinct styles: Pinsa Romana (a healthier style of pizza derived from Ancient Rome) and Calabrian. The restaurant is beautifully done with notes of velvet and marble, and a towering bar standing as the central focus of the space showcases one of the city's largest collections of Amaro and Grappa. **Known for:** cocktails; vegan menu; Pinsa Romana and Calabrian pizza. [$] *Average main: $14* ✉ *2550 5th Ave., Suite 120, Bankers Hill* ☎ *619/310–5669* 🌐 *www.civicobythepark.com.*

Continued on page 80

Polar bear, San Diego Zoo

LIONS AND TIGERS AND BEARS:
The World-Famous San Diego Zoo

From diving polar bears and 6-ton elephants to swinging great apes, San Diego's most famous attraction has it all. Nearly 4,000 animals representing 800 species roam the 100-acre zoo in expertly crafted habitats that replicate the animals' natural environments. The pandas may have gone home (in 2019), but there are plenty of other cool creatures to see here, from teeny-tiny mantella frogs to two-story-tall giraffes. But it's not all just fun and games. Known for its exemplary conservation programs, the zoo educates visitors on how to go green and explains its efforts to protect endangered species.

SAN DIEGO ZOO TOP ATTRACTIONS

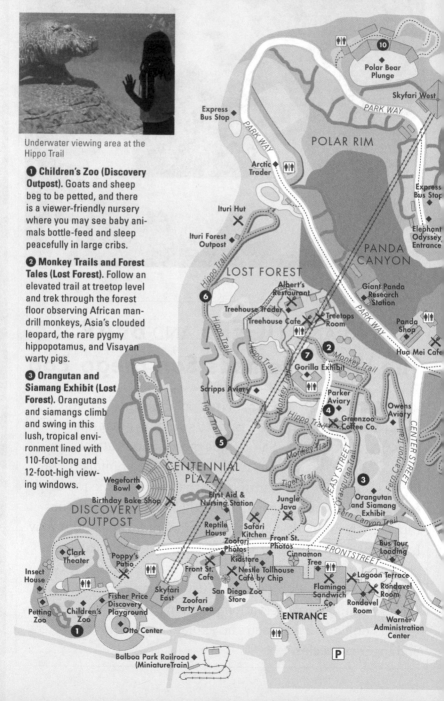

Underwater viewing area at the Hippo Trail

❶ Children's Zoo (Discovery Outpost). Goats and sheep beg to be petted, and there is a viewer-friendly nursery where you may see baby animals bottle-feed and sleep peacefully in large cribs.

❷ Monkey Trails and Forest Tales (Lost Forest). Follow an elevated trail at treetop level and trek through the forest floor observing African mandrill monkeys, Asia's clouded leopard, the rare pygmy hippopotamus, and Visayan warty pigs.

❸ Orangutan and Siamang Exhibit (Lost Forest). Orangutans and siamangs climb and swing in this lush, tropical environment lined with 110-foot-long and 12-foot-high viewing windows.

4 Scripps, Parker, and Owens Aviaries (Lost Forest). Wandering paths climb through the enclosed aviaries where brightly colored tropical birds swoop between branches inches from your face.

5 Tiger Trail (Lost Forest). The mist-shrouded trails of this simulated rainforest wind down a canyon. Tigers, Malayan tapirs, and Argus pheasants wander among the exotic trees and plants.

6 Hippo Trail (Lost Forest). Glimpse huge but surprisingly graceful hippos frolicking in the water through an underwater viewing window and buffalo cavorting with monkeys on dry land.

7 Gorilla Exhibit (Lost Forest). The gorillas live in one of the zoo's bioclimatic zone exhibits modeled on their native habitat with waterfalls, climbing areas, and an open meadow. The sounds of the tropical rain forest emerge from a 144-speaker sound system that plays CDs recorded in Africa.

8 Africa Rocks. This massive exhibit consists of six different rocky habitats designed to showcase the diversity of topography and species on the African continent. Penguins, meerkats, and a band of baboons are just a few of the animals that call this ambitious exhibit home.

Lories at Owen's Aviary

9 Sun Bear Forest (Asian Passage). Playful beasts claw apart the trees and shrubs that serve as a natural playground for climbing, jump-ing, and general merrymaking.

10 Polar Bear Plunge (Polar Rim). Watch polar bears take a chilly dive from the underwater viewing room. There are also Siberian reindeer, white foxes, and other Arctic creatures here. Kids can learn about the Arctic and climate change through interactive exhibits.

11 Elephant Odyssey. Get a glimpse of the animals that roamed Southern California 12,000 years ago and meet their living counterparts. The 7.5-acre, multispecies habitat features elephants, California condors, jaguars, and more.

12 Koala Exhibit (Outback). The San Diego Zoo houses the largest number of koalas outside Australia. Walk through the exhibit for photo ops of these marsupials from Down-Under curled up on their perches or dining on eucalyptus branches.

MUST-SEE ANIMALS

❶ GORILLA

This troop of primates engages visitors with their human-like expressions and behavior. The youngsters are sure to delight, especially when hitching a ride on mom's back. Up-close encounters might involve the gorillas using the glass partition as a backrest while peeling cabbage. By dusk the gorillas head inside to their sleeping quarters, so don't save this for your last stop.

❷ ELEPHANT

Asian and African elephants coexist at the San Diego Zoo. The larger African elephant is distinguished by its big flapping ears—shaped like the continent of Africa—which it uses to keep cool. An elephant's trunk has over 40,000 muscles in it—that's more than humans have in their whole body.

❸ ORANGUTAN

Bornean and Sumatran orangutans have been entertaining San Diego visitors since 1928. The exhibit has rope climbing structures, a man-made "termite mound" that's often filled with treats, rocky caves, and tall "sway poles" that allow the orangutans to swing like they would in trees. Don't be surprised if the orangutans come right up to the glass to observe the humans observing them!

❹ KOALA

While this collection of critters is one of the cutest in the zoo, don't expect a lot of activity from the koala habitat. These guys spend most of their day curled up asleep in the branches of the eucalyptus tree—they can sleep up to 20 hours a day. Although eucalyptus leaves are poisonous to most animals, bacteria in koalas' stomachs allow them to break down the toxins.

❺ POLAR BEAR

The trio of polar bears is one of the San Diego Zoo's star attractions, and their brand-new exhibit gets you up close and personal. Visitors sometimes worry about polar bears living in the warm San Diego climate, but there is no cause for concern. The San Diego-based bears eat a lean diet, thus reducing their layer of blubber and helping them keep cool.

Did You Know?

Red pandas aren't actually pandas, but more like skunks or raccoons in your backyard. With the giant pandas gone from the San Diego Zoo though, the red pandas are an adorable alternative.

★ **Cucina Urbana**

$$ | ITALIAN | Twentysomethings mingle with boomers in this convivial Bankers Hill dining room and bar, one of the most popular restaurants in town. The open kitchen turns out innovative Italian food with a California sensibility including a selection of small plates and family-style pasta dishes alongside traditional entrées. Many dishes are under $20, including crowd-pleasing short-rib pappardelle, fried stuffed squash blossoms, creamy mascarpone polenta, and thin-crust pizzas. At the in-house wine shop, purchase reasonably priced bottles from California and Italy opened table-side for a $9 corkage fee. **Known for:** in-house wine shop with reasonably priced bottles and $9 corkage fee; seasonal polenta with ragu; ricotta-stuffed zucchini blossoms. [$] *Average main: $21* ✉ *505 Laurel St., Bankers Hill* ☎ *619/239–2222* 🌐 *www.cucinaurbana.com* 🕒 *No lunch Sat.–Mon.*

Performing Arts

★ **Globe Theatres**

THEATER | This complex, comprised of the Sheryl and Harvey White Theatre, the Lowell Davies Festival Theatre, and the Old Globe Theatre, offers some of the finest theatrical productions in Southern California. Theater classics such as *Into the Woods* and *Dirty Rotten Scoundrels*, and more recent hits like *Bright Star* and *Meteor Shower*, premiered on these famed stages and went on to perform on Broadway. The Old Globe presents a renowned summer Shakespeare Festival with three to four plays in repertory. The theaters, done in a California version of Tudor style, sit between the sculpture garden of the San Diego Museum of Art and the California Tower. ✉ *1363 Old Globe Way, Balboa Park* ☎ *619/234–5623* 🌐 *www.theoldglobe.org* 🕒 *Box office closed Mon.*

Old Town and Uptown

San Diego's Spanish and Mexican roots are most evident in Old Town and the surrounding hillside of Presidio Park. Visitors can experience settlement life in San Diego from Spanish and Mexican rule to the early days of U.S. statehood. Nearby Uptown is composed of several smaller neighborhoods near Downtown and around Balboa Park: the vibrant neighborhoods of Hillcrest, Mission Hills, North Park, and South Park showcase their unique blend of historical charm and modern urban community.

Sights

★ **Fiesta de Reyes**

HISTORIC SITE | FAMILY | North of San Diego's Old Town Plaza lies the area's unofficial center, built to represent a colonial Mexican plaza. The collection of more than a dozen shops and restaurants around a central courtyard in blossom with magenta bougainvillea, scarlet hibiscus, and other flowers in season reflects what early California might have looked like from 1821 to 1872. Mariachi bands and folklorico dance groups frequently perform on the plaza stage—check the website for times and upcoming special events. **■ TIP→ Casa de Reyes is a great stop for a margarita and some chips and guacamole.** ✉ *4016 Wallace St., Old Town* ☎ *619/297–3100* 🌐 *www.fiestadereyes.com.*

★ **Old Town San Diego State Historic Park**

HISTORIC SITE | FAMILY | The six square blocks on the site of San Diego's original pueblo are the heart of Old Town. Most of the 20 historic buildings preserved or re-created by the park cluster are around **Old Town Plaza,** bounded by Wallace Street on the west, Calhoun Street on the north, Mason Street on the east, and San Diego Avenue on the south. The plaza is a pleasant place to rest, plan your tour of the park, and watch passersby. San Diego Avenue is closed to vehicle traffic here.

Some of Old Town's buildings were destroyed in a fire in 1872, but after the site became a state historic park in 1968, reconstruction and restoration of the remaining structures began. Five of the original adobes are still intact.

Facing Old Town Plaza, the **Robinson-Rose House** was the original commercial center of Old San Diego, housing railroad offices, law offices, and the first newspaper press. The largest and most elaborate of the original adobe homes, the **Casa de Estudillo** was occupied by members of the Estudillo family until 1887 and later gained popularity for its billing as "Ramona's Marriage Place" based on a popular novel of the time. Albert Seeley, a stagecoach entrepreneur, opened the **Cosmopolitan Hotel** in 1869 as a way station for travelers on the daylong trip south from Los Angeles. Next door to the Cosmopolitan Hotel, the **Seeley Stable** served as San Diego's stagecoach stop in 1867 and was the transportation hub of Old Town until 1887, when trains became the favored mode of travel.

Several reconstructed buildings serve as restaurants or as shops purveying wares reminiscent of those that might have been available in the original Old Town. **Racine & Laramie**, a painstakingly reproduced version of San Diego's first cigar store in 1868, is especially interesting.

Pamphlets available at the Robinson-Rose House give details about all the historic houses on the plaza and in its vicinity. Free tours of the historic park are offered daily at 11:30 and 2; they depart from the Robinson-Rose House. **■ TIP→ The covered wagon located near the intersection of Mason and Calhoun Streets provides a great photo op.** ✉ *Visitor center (Robinson-Rose House), 4002 Wallace St., Old Town* ☎ *619/220–5422* 🌐 *www.parks.ca.gov* 🎫 *Free.*

The Whaley House Museum

HISTORIC SITE | A New York entrepreneur, Thomas Whaley came to California during the gold rush. He wanted to provide his East Coast wife with all the comforts of home, so in 1857 he had Southern California's first two-story brick structure built, making it the oldest double-story brick building on the West Coast. The house, which served as the county courthouse and government seat during the 1870s, stands in strong contrast to the Spanish-style adobe residences that surround the nearby historic plaza and marks an early stage of San Diego's "Americanization." A garden out back includes many varieties of prehybrid roses from before 1867. The place is perhaps most famed, however, for the ghosts that are said to inhabit it. You can tour on your own during the day, but must visit by guided tour after 4:30 pm. The evening tours are geared toward the supernatural aspects of the house. Tours start at 6 pm (5 pm on Saturday) and are offered every half hour, with the last tour departing at 9:30 pm. ✉ *2476 San Diego Ave., Old Town* ☎ *619/297–7511* 🌐 *www.whaleyhouse.org* 🎫 *From $10* 🕒 *Closed Sept.–May and Wed.*

🍴 Restaurants

El Agave

$$$ | **MEXICAN** | Not a typical San Diego taco shop, this Mexican eatery is upstairs in a shopping complex in the middle of a tequila museum with some 2,000 bottles dating from the 1930s. The owners are equally serious about food, calling their cuisine Hispanic-Mexican Gastronomy, which means meat and fish dishes with lots of unusual spicy chilies, herbs, spices, and moles. **Known for:** impressive tequila selection and tequila flights; variety of mole dishes; upscale option in generally casual Old Town. [$] *Average main: $32* ✉ *2304 San Diego Ave., Old Town* ☎ *619/220–0692* 🌐 *www.elagave.com.*

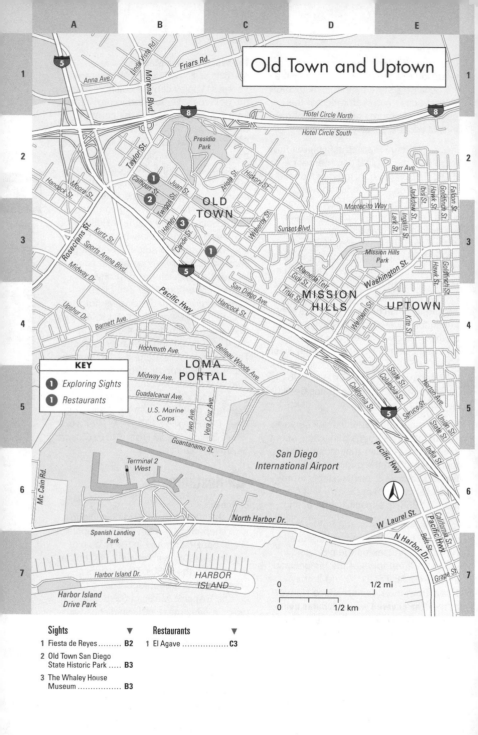

Old Town and Uptown

🛍 Shopping

★ Bazaar del Mundo Shops

SHOPPING CENTERS/MALLS | With a Mexican villa theme, the Bazaar hosts riotously colorful gift shops such as **Ariana,** for ethnic and artsy women's fashions; **Artes de Mexico,** which sells handmade Latin American crafts and Guatemalan weavings; and **The Gallery,** which carries handmade jewelry, American Indian crafts, collectible glass, and original silk-screen prints. The **Laurel Burch Gallerita** carries the complete collection of its namesake artist's signature jewelry, accessories, and totes. ⊠ *4133 Taylor St., at Juan St., Old Town* ☎ *619/296–3161* ⊕ *www.bazaardelmundo.com.*

Mission Bay and the Beaches

Mission Bay and the surrounding beaches are the aquatic playground of San Diego. The choice of activities available is astonishing, and the perfect weather makes you want to get out there and play. If you're craving downtime after all the activity, there are plenty of peaceful spots to relax and simply soak up the sunshine.

Mission Bay welcomes visitors with its protected waters and countless opportunities for fun. The 4,600-acre **Mission Bay Park** is the place for water sports like sailing, stand-up paddleboarding, and waterskiing. With 19 miles of beaches and grassy areas, it's also a great place for a picnic.

Mission Beach is a famous and lively fun zone for families and young people; if it isn't party time at the moment, it will be five minutes from now. The pathways in this area are lined with vacation homes, many for rent by the week or month.

North of Mission Beach is the college-packed party town of Pacific Beach, or "PB" as locals call it. The laid-back vibe of this surfer's mecca draws in free-spirited locals who roam the streets on skateboards and beach cruisers. The energy level peaks during happy hour, when PB's cluster of nightclubs, bars, and 150 restaurants open their doors to those ready to party.

👁 Sights

★ Belmont Park

AMUSEMENT PARK/WATER PARK | **FAMILY**
The once-abandoned amusement park between the bay and Mission Beach boardwalk is now a shopping, dining, and recreation complex. Twinkling lights outline the **Giant Dipper,** an antique wooden roller coaster on which screaming thrill seekers ride more than 2,600 feet of track and 13 hills (riders must be at least 4 feet, 2 inches tall). Created in 1925 and listed on the National Register of Historic Places, this is one of the few old-time roller coasters left in the United States.

Other Belmont Park attractions include miniature golf, a laser maze, video arcade, bumper cars, a tilt-a-whirl, and an antique carousel. The zip line thrills as it soars over the crowds below, while the rock wall challenges both junior climbers and their elders. ⊠ *3146 Mission Blvd., Mission Bay* ☎ *858/488–1549 for rides* ⊕ *www.belmontpark.com* 🎟 *Unlimited ride day package from $32.*

★ Crystal Pier

BEACH—SIGHT | Stretching out into the ocean from the end of Garnet Avenue, Crystal Pier is Pacific Beach's landmark. In the 1920s, it was a classic amusement park complete with ballroom. Today, it's mainly comprised of a series of quaint cottages that are all a part of the Crystal Pier Hotel. Guests have access to fishing, as well as the intersecting Mission Beach boardwalk. For those that aren't hotel guests, you may access the pier through a side gate from 8 am to sunset. ⊠ *Pacific Beach* ✛ *At end of Garnet Ave.*

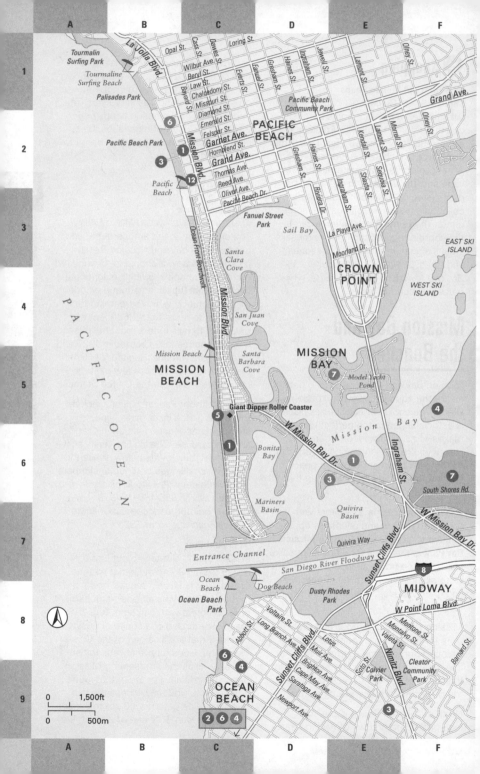

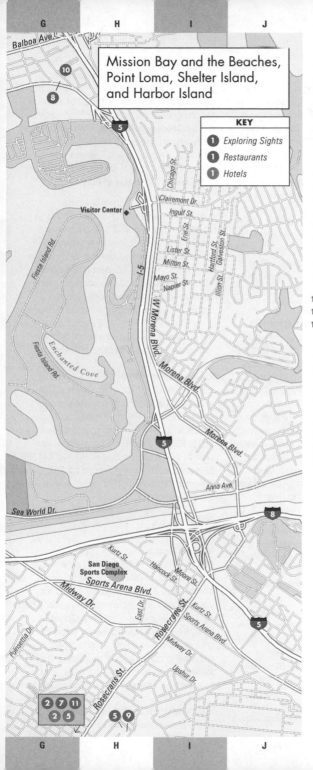

Mission Bay and the Beaches, Point Loma, Shelter Island, and Harbor Island

KEY

1 Exploring Sights
1 Restaurants
1 Hotels

Sights ▼

1 Belmont Park........................C6
2 Cabrillo National Monument......C9
3 Crystal Pier B2
4 Mission Bay Park..................F5
5 Mission Beach Boardwalk........C5
6 Ocean Beach Pier..................C8
7 SeaWorld San Diego...............F6

Restaurants ▼

1 The Baked Bear....................C2
2 Bali Hai...............................G9
3 Cesarina E9
4 Hodad's C9
5 Liberty Public Market.............H9
6 The Little Lion Cafe C9
7 Point Loma Seafoods..............G9
8 Rubio's Coastal Grill G1
9 Stone Brewing World Bistro and Gardens............................H9
10 Sushi Ota G1
11 Tom Ham's Lighthouse G9
12 Waterbar C2

Hotels ▼

1 The Dana on Mission Bay E6
2 Homewood Suites San Diego Airport Liberty Station.....................G9
3 Hyatt Regency Mission Bay Spa and Marina....................E6
4 Inn at Sunset Cliffs C9
5 Kona Kai Resort & Spa... G9
6 Pacific Terrace Hotel..............B2
7 Paradise Point Resort & Spa......E5

★ **Mission Bay Park**

BEACH—SIGHT | San Diego's monument to sports and fitness, this 4,600-acre aquatic park has 27 miles of shoreline including 19 miles of sandy beaches. Playgrounds and picnic areas abound on the beaches and low, grassy hills. On weekday evenings, joggers, bikers, and skaters take over. In the daytime, swimmers, water-skiers, paddleboarders, anglers, and boaters—some in single-person kayaks, others in crowded powerboats—vie for space in the water. ⊠ *2688 E. Mission Bay Dr., Mission Bay* ⊕ *Off I–5 at Exit 22, E. Mission Bay Dr.* ☎ *858/581–7602 park ranger's office* ⊕ *www.sandiego.gov/park-and-recreation* ⊠ *Free.*

★ **Mission Beach Boardwalk**

BEACH—SIGHT | The cement pathway lining the sand from the southern end of Mission Beach north to Pacific Beach is always bustling with activity. Cyclists ping the bells on their beach cruisers to pass walkers out for a stroll alongside the oceanfront homes. Vacationers kick back on their patios, while friends play volleyball in the sand. The activity picks up alongside Belmont Park, where people stop to check out the action at the amusement park and beach bars. ⊠ *Mission Beach* ⊕ *Alongside sand from Mission Beach Park to Pacific Beach.*

SeaWorld San Diego

AMUSEMENT PARK/WATER PARK | **FAMILY** Spread over 189 tropically landscaped bay-front acres, SeaWorld is one of the world's largest marine-life amusement parks. The majority of its exhibits are walk-through marine environments like **Shark Encounter,** where guests walk through a 57-foot acrylic tube and come face-to-face with a variety of sharks that call the 280,000-gallon habitat home. **Turtle Reef** offers an incredible up-close encounter with the green sea turtle, while the moving sidewalk at **Penguin Encounter** whisks you through a colony of nearly 300 penguins. The park also wows

with its adventure rides like the **Electric Eel,** a shocking multilaunch coaster that sends riders twisting forward and backwards 150 feet in the air at speeds reaching 60 mph, and the comparatively milder **Journey to Atlantis,** a water coaster with a heart-stopping 60-foot plunge. Younger children will enjoy the rides, climbing structures, and splash pads at the **Sesame Street Bay of Play**.

SeaWorld is most famous for its large-arena entertainments, but this is an area in transition. The park's latest orca experience features a nature-inspired backdrop and demonstrates orca behaviors in the wild, part of SeaWorld's efforts to refocus its orca program toward education and conservation. Other live-entertainment shows feature dolphins, sea otters, and even household pets. Several upgraded animal encounters are available including the Dolphin Interaction Program, which gives guests the chance to interact with SeaWorld's bottlenose dolphins in the water. The hour-long program (20 minutes in the water), during which visitors can feed, touch, and give behavior signals, costs $215. ⊠ *500 SeaWorld Dr., near west end of I–8, Mission Bay* ☎ *800/257–4268* ⊕ *www.seaworldparks.com* ⊠ *$92; advanced purchase discounts available online; parking $22.*

 Beaches

Mission Beach

BEACH—SIGHT | **FAMILY** | With an amusement park and rows of eclectic local shops, this 2-mile-long beach has a carnival vibe and is the closest thing you'll find to Coney Island on the West Coast. It's lively year-round but draws a huge crowd on hot summer days. A wide boardwalk paralleling the beach is popular with walkers, joggers, skateboarders, and bicyclists. To escape the crowds, head to South Mission Beach. It attracts surfers, swimmers, and volleyball players, who often play competitive pickup games on the courts near the north jetty. The water near the Belmont Park roller coaster can be a bit rough but makes for good bodyboarding and bodysurfing. For free parking, you can try for a spot on the street, but your best bets are the two big lots at Belmont Park. **Amenities:** lifeguards; parking (no fee); showers; toilets. **Best for:** swimming; surfing; walking. ✉ *3000 Mission Blvd., Mission Bay* ✥ *Parking near roller coaster at West Mission Bay Dr.* 🌐 *www.sandiego.gov/lifeguards/beaches/mb.shtml.*

Pacific Beach/North Pacific Beach
BEACH—SIGHT | This beach, known for attracting a young college-age crowd and surfers, runs from the northern end of Mission Beach to Crystal Pier. The scene here is lively on weekends, with nearby restaurants, beach bars, and nightclubs providing a party atmosphere. In PB (as the locals call it) Sundays are known as "Sunday Funday," and pub crawls can last all day. Although drinking is no longer allowed on the beach, it's still likely you'll see people who have had one too many. The mood changes just north of the pier at North Pacific Beach, which attracts families and surfers. Although not quite pillowy, the sand at both beaches is nice and soft, which makes for great sunbathing and sandcastle building. **■ TIP→ Kelp and flies can be a problem on this stretch, so choose your spot wisely.** Parking at Pacific Beach can also be a challenge. A few coveted free angle parking spaces are available along the boardwalk, but you'll most likely have to look for spots in the surrounding neighborhood. **Amenities:** food and drink; lifeguards; parking (no fee); showers, toilets. **Best for:** partiers; swimming; surfing. ✉ *4500 Ocean Blvd., Pacific Beach* 🌐 *www.sandiego.gov/lifeguards/beaches/pb.shtml.*

Tourmaline Surfing Park
BEACH—SIGHT | Offering slow waves and frequent winds, this is one of the most popular beaches for surfers. For windsurfing and kiteboarding, it's only sailable with northwest winds. The 175-space parking lot at the foot of Tourmaline Street normally fills to capacity by midday. Just like Pacific Beach, Tourmaline has soft, tawny-color sand, but when the tide is in the beach becomes quite narrow, making finding a good sunbathing spot a bit of a challenge. Parking will be difficult on evenings and weekends. **Amenities:** seasonal lifeguards; parking (no fee); showers; toilets. **Best for:** windsurfing; surfing. ✉ *600 Tourmaline St., Pacific Beach.*

🍴 Restaurants

★ The Baked Bear
$ | **BAKERY** | **FAMILY** | This build-your-own ice-cream-sandwich shop a block from Pacific Beach is a local favorite thanks to its homemade cookies and diverse array of ice-cream flavors, from birthday cake to peanut butter fudge. Don't miss out on their hot pressed ice-cream sandwiches! **Known for:** Bear Bowls made of cookies; doughnut ice-cream sandwiches; long lines on summer evenings. [$] *Average main: $5* ✉ *4516 Mission Blvd., Suite C, Pacific Beach* ☎ *858/886–7433* 🌐 *www.thebakedbear.com.*

Rubio's Coastal Grill
$ | **SEAFOOD** | Credited with popularizing fish tacos in the United States, Ralph Rubio brought the Mexican staple to San Diego, opening his first restaurant in Pacific Beach where it still stands today. The original beer-battered fish tacos have fried pollock topped with white sauce, salsa, and cabbage atop a corn tortilla. **Known for:** the original fish taco; Taco Tuesday deal—fish taco and a beer for $5; $7 lunch specials. [$] *Average main: $10* ✉ *4504 E. Mission Bay Dr., Pacific Beach* ☎ *858/272–2801* 🌐 *www.rubios.com.*

★ Sushi Ota
$$ | **SUSHI** | One fan called it "a notch above amazing"—an accolade not expected for a Japanese eatery wedged in a strip mall in Pacific Beach. But it's

a destination for lovers of high-quality, superfresh raw fish from around San Diego and abroad; reservations strongly encouraged. **Known for:** velvety hamachi belly; sea urchin specials; chef's omakase tasting menu. [$] *Average main: $25* ✉ *4529 Mission Bay Dr., Pacific Beach* ☎ *858/270–5670* 🌐 *www.sushiota.com* 🕒 *No lunch Sat.–Mon.*

★ Waterbar
$$ | **SEAFOOD** | Occupying a prime oceanfront lot just south of Crystal Pier, the views from the raised dining room are impressive. Throw in an excellent raw bar, a wide selection of shared plates, and a buzzy bar scene and you get Waterbar's "social seafood" concept. **Known for:** late-night "Boardwalk hour" oyster specials; boozy weekend brunch; ocean views. [$] *Average main: $24* ✉ *4325 Ocean Blvd., Pacific Beach* ☎ *858/888–4343* 🌐 *www.waterbarsd.com.*

Hotels

The Dana on Mission Bay
$$$ | **RESORT** | **FAMILY** | This waterfront resort, just down the road from SeaWorld, has an ideal location for active leisure travelers. **Pros:** water views; many outdoor activities; shuttle to SeaWorld. **Cons:** expensive resort fee; popular wedding venue; rooms vary in quality and view. [$] *Rooms from: $289* ✉ *1710 W. Mission Bay Dr., Mission Bay* ☎ *619/222–6440, 800/445–3339* 🌐 *www.thedana.com* 🛏 *271 rooms* 🍴 *No meals.*

Hyatt Regency Mission Bay Spa and Marina
$$$ | **RESORT** | **FAMILY** | This modern property has many desirable amenities, including balconies with excellent views of the garden, bay, ocean, or swimming pool courtyard. **Pros:** proximity to water sports; 120-foot waterslides in pools, plus kiddie slide; several suite configurations good for families. **Cons:** daily resort fee; not centrally located; some areas in need of updates. [$] *Rooms from: $299* ✉ *1441 Quivira Rd., Mission Bay* ☎ *619/224–1234, 800/233–1234* 🌐 *www.hyatt.com* 🛏 *429 rooms* 🍴 *No meals.*

Pacific Terrace Hotel
$$$$ | **RESORT** | Travelers love this terrific beachfront hotel and the ocean views from most rooms; it's a perfect place for watching sunsets over the Pacific. **Pros:** beach views; large rooms; friendly service. **Cons:** busy and sometimes noisy area; expensive in peak season; resort fee. [$] *Rooms from: $569* ✉ *610 Diamond St., Pacific Beach* ☎ *858/581–3500, 800/344–3370* 🌐 *www.pacificterrace.com* 🛏 *73 rooms* 🍴 *No meals.*

Paradise Point Resort & Spa
$$$ | **RESORT** | **FAMILY** | Minutes from SeaWorld but hidden in a quiet part of Mission Bay, the beautiful landscape of this 44-acre resort offers plenty of space for families to play and relax. **Pros:** water views; five pools; good service. **Cons:** not centrally located; motel-thin walls; parking and resort fees. [$] *Rooms from: $296* ✉ *1404 Vacation Rd., Mission Bay* ☎ *858/274–4630, 800/344–2626* 🌐 *www.paradisepoint.com* 🛏 *462 rooms* 🍴 *No meals.*

Nightlife

BARS

★ The Grass Skirt
BARS/PUBS | Accessed through a false freezer door inside Good Time Poke, this speakeasy-styled tiki bar serves a wide selection of rum-based tropical cocktails in delightfully kitsch surroundings. The Polynesian-inspired menu features shareable poke and pupus, but call ahead to reserve a table—this hidden gem is no secret! ✉ *910 Grand Ave., Pacific Beach* ☎ *858/412–5237* 🌐 *www.thegrassskirt.com.*

JRDN
BARS/PUBS | This contemporary lounge (pronounced "Jordan") occupies the ground floor of Pacific Beach's chicest boutique hotel, Tower23, and offers a more sophisticated vibe in what is a very party-happy neighborhood. Sleek walls of windows and

an expansive patio overlook the board-walk. ⊠ *723 Felspar St., Pacific Beach* ☎ *858/270–2323* ⊕ *www.t23hotel.com.*

Activities

DIVING AND SNORKELING

The kelp forests and protected marine areas off the San Diego coast are easily accessible and offer divers ample opportunities to explore. Classes are available for beginners, while experienced divers will appreciate the challenges of local wreck and canyon dives. Water temperatures can be chilly, so check with a local outfitter for the appropriate gear before setting out.

The HMCS *Yukon,* a decommissioned Canadian warship, was intentionally sunk off Mission Beach to create the main diving destination in San Diego. A mishap caused the ship to settle on its side, creating a surreal, M.C. Escher–esque diving environment. This is a technical dive and should be attempted only by experienced divers; even diving instructors have become disoriented inside the wreck, and a few have even died trying to explore it.

SURFING

If you're a beginner, consider paddling in the waves off Mission Beach, Pacific Beach, and Tourmaline Surfing Park. Several outfitters offer year-round surf lessons as well as surf camp in the summer months and during spring break.

WATER SPORTS

Mission Bay Aquatic Center

BOATING | FAMILY | The world's largest instructional waterfront facility offers lessons in wakeboarding, sailing, surfing, waterskiing, rowing, kayaking, and windsurfing. Equipment rental is also available, but the emphasis is on instruction, and most rentals require a minimum two-hour orientation lesson before you can set out on your own. Reservations are recommended, particularly during the summer. Skippered keelboats and boats for waterskiing or wakeboarding can be hired with reservations. Free

parking is available but keep an eye out for signage—not all the parking spots are free or overnight. ⊠ *1001 Santa Clara Pl., Mission Beach* ☎ *858/488–1000* ⊕ *www.mbaquaticcenter.com.*

★ Seaforth Boat Rentals

BOATING | The Mission Bay outpost of this popular rental company offers a wide variety of motorized and nonmotorized craft. Jet Skis, SUPs, kayaks, and fishing skiffs are available alongside sailboats and powerboats of all sizes. For added relaxation, charter a skippered pontoon party boat, some with waterslides for added fun. ⊠ *1641 Quivira Rd., Mission Bay* ☎ *888/834–2628* ⊕ *www.seaforthboatrental.com.*

La Jolla

La Jolla (pronounced La Hoya) means "the jewel" in Spanish and appropriately describes this small, affluent village and its beaches. Some beautiful coastline can be found here, as well as an elegant upscale atmosphere.

◉ Sights

Birch Aquarium at Scripps

ZOO | FAMILY | Affiliated with the world-renowned Scripps Institution of Oceanography, this excellent aquarium sits at the end of a signposted drive leading off North Torrey Pines Road and has sweeping views of La Jolla coast below. More than 60 tanks are filled with colorful saltwater fish, and a 70,000-gallon tank simulates a La Jolla kelp forest. A special exhibit on sea horses features several examples of the species, plus mesmerizing sea dragons and a sea horse nursery. Besides the fish themselves, attractions include interactive educational exhibits based on the institution's ocean-related research and a variety of environmental issues. ⊠ *2300 Expedition Way, La Jolla* ☎ *858/534–3474* ⊕ *www.aquarium.ucsd.edu* ⊠ *$17.*

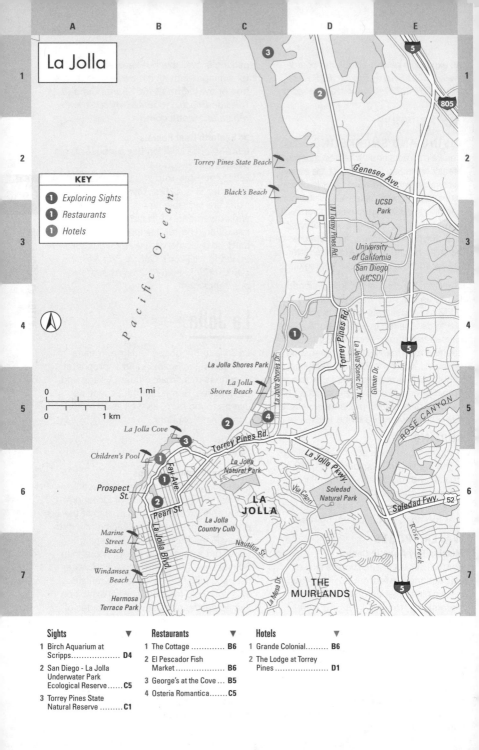

La Jolla

KEY
- **1** Exploring Sights
- **1** Restaurants
- **1** Hotels

Pacific Ocean

Torrey Pines State Beach

Black's Beach

UCSD Park

University of California San Diego (UCSD)

Genesee Ave.

N Torrey Pines Rd.

Torrey Pines Rd.

La Jolla Scenic Dr. N.

Gilman Dr.

ROSE CANYON

La Jolla Shores Park

La Jolla Shores Beach

La Jolla Shores Dr.

La Jolla Cove

Children's Pool

Prospect St.

Pearl St.

Fay Ave.

La Jolla Blvd.

Torrey Pines Rd.

La Jolla Natural Park

LA JOLLA

Via Capri

Soledad Natural Park

La Jolla Pkwy.

Soledad Fwy. 52

Rose Creek

Marine Street Beach

La Jolla Country Culb

Nautilus St.

Windansea Beach

Hermosa Terrace Park

La Mesa Dr.

THE MUIRLANDS

0   1 mi
0   1 km

Sights ▼

1 Birch Aquarium at Scripps.................. **D4**
2 San Diego - La Jolla Underwater Park Ecological Reserve......**C5**
3 Torrey Pines State Natural Reserve **C1**

Restaurants ▼

1 The Cottage **B6**
2 El Pescador Fish Market **B6**
3 George's at the Cove ... **B5**
4 Osteria Romantica.......**C5**

Hotels ▼

1 Grande Colonial.......... **B6**
2 The Lodge at Torrey Pines **D1**

San Diego-La Jolla Underwater Park Ecological Reserve

BODY OF WATER | Four habitats across 6,000 acres make up this underwater park and ecological reserve. When the water is clear, this is a diver's paradise with reefs, kelp beds, sand flats, and a submarine canyon. Plunge deeper to see guitarfish rays, perch, sea bass, anchovies, squid, and hammerhead sharks. Snorkelers, kayakers, and stand-up paddleboarders are likely to spot sea lions, seals, and leopard sharks. The Seven La Jolla Sea Caves, 75-million-year-old sandstone caves, are at the park's edge. ■TIP➔ **While the park can be explored on your own, the best way to view it is with a professional guide.** ✉ *La Jolla ✢ La Jolla Cove.*

★ Torrey Pines State Natural Reserve

NATIONAL/STATE PARK | *Pinus torreyana,* the rarest native pine tree in the United States, enjoys a 1,500-acre sanctuary at the northern edge of La Jolla. About 6,000 of these unusual trees, some as tall as 60 feet, grow on the cliffs here. The park is one of only two places in the world (the other is Santa Rosa Island, off Santa Barbara) where the Torrey pine grows naturally. The reserve has several hiking trails leading to the cliffs, 300 feet above the ocean; trail maps are available at the park station. Wildflowers grow profusely in spring, and the ocean panoramas are always spectacular. From December to March, whales can be spotted from the bluffs. When in this upper part of the park, respect the restrictions. Not permitted: picnicking, smoking, leaving the trails, dogs, alcohol, or collecting plant specimens.

You can unwrap your sandwiches, however, at Torrey Pines State Beach, just below the reserve. When the tide is out, it's possible to walk south all the way past the lifeguard towers to Black's Beach over rocky promontories carved by the waves (avoid the bluffs, however; they're unstable). **Los Peñasquitos Lagoon** at the north end of the reserve is one of the many natural estuaries that flow inland between Del Mar and Oceanside. It's a good place to watch shorebirds. Volunteers lead guided nature walks at 10 and 2 on most weekends and holidays. ✉ *12600 N. Torrey Pines Rd., La Jolla ✢ N. Torrey Pines Rd. exit off I–5 onto Carmel Valley Rd. going west, then turn left (south) on Coast Hwy. 101* ☎ *858/755–2063* ⊕ *www.torreypine.org* ✉ *Parking from $20.*

Beaches

Black's Beach

BEACH—SIGHT | The powerful waves at this beach attract world-class surfers, and the strand's relative isolation appeals to nudist nature lovers (although by law nudity is prohibited) as well as gays and lesbians. Backed by 300-foot-tall cliffs whose colors change with the sun's angle, Black's can be accessed from Torrey Pines State Beach to the north, or by a narrow path descending the cliffs from Torrey Pines Glider Port. Be aware that the city has posted a "do not use" sign there because the cliff trails are unmaintained and highly dangerous, so use at your own risk. If you plan to access Black's from the beaches to the north or south, do so at low tide. High tide and waves can restrict access. Strong rip currents are common—only experienced swimmers should take the plunge. Lifeguards patrol the area only between spring break and mid-October. Also keep your eyes peeled for the hang gliders and paragliders who ascend from atop the cliffs. Parking is available at the Glider Port and Torrey Pines State Beach. **Amenities:** none. **Best for:** solitude; nudists; surfing. ✉ *Between Torrey Pines State Beach and La Jolla Shores, La Jolla ✢ 2 miles south of Torrey Pines State Beach parking lot* ⊕ *www.sandiego.gov/ lifeguards/beaches/blacks.shtml.*

A surfer prepares to head out before sunset at La Jolla's Torrey Pines State Beach and Reserve.

★ La Jolla Cove

BEACH—SIGHT | FAMILY | This shimmering blue-green inlet surrounded by cliffs is what first attracted everyone to La Jolla, from Native Americans to the glitterati. "The Cove," as locals refer to it, beyond where Girard Avenue dead-ends into Coast Boulevard, is marked by towering palms that line a promenade where people strolling in designer clothes are as common as Frisbee throwers. Ellen Browning Scripps Park sits atop cliffs formed by the incessant pounding of the waves and offers a great spot for picnics with a view. The Cove has beautiful white sand that is a bit coarse near the water's edge, but the beach is still a great place for sunbathing and lounging. At low tide, the pools and cliff caves are a destination for explorers. With visibility at 30-plus feet, this is the best place in San Diego for snorkeling, where bright-orange garibaldi fish and other marine life populate the waters of the **San Diego–La Jolla Underwater Park Ecological Reserve.** From above water, it's not uncommon to spot sea lions and birds basking on the rocks, or dolphin fins just offshore. The cove is also a favorite of rough-water swimmers, while the area just north is best for kayakers wanting to explore the Seven La Jolla Sea Caves. **Amenities:** lifeguards; showers; toilets. **Best for:** snorkeling; swimming; walking. ⊠ *1100 Coast Blvd., east of Ellen Browning Scripps Park, La Jolla* ⊕ *www.sandiego.gov/lifeguards/ beaches/cove.*

La Jolla Shores

BEACH—SIGHT | FAMILY | This is one of San Diego's most popular beaches due to its wide sandy shore, gentle waves, and incredible views of La Jolla Peninsula. There's also a large grassy park, and adjacent to La Jolla Shores lies the **San Diego–La Jolla Underwater Park Ecological Reserve,** 6,000 acres of protected ocean bottom and tide lands, bordered by the Seven La Jolla Sea Caves. The white powdery sand at La Jolla Sands is some of San Diego's best, and several surf and scuba schools teach here. Kayaks can also be rented nearby. A concrete boardwalk parallels the beach, and a boat launch for small vessels lies 300 yards south of the lifeguard station at Avenida de Playa. Arrive early to get a parking spot in the lot near Kellogg Park at the foot of Calle Frescota. Street parking is limited to one or two hours. **Amenities:** lifeguards; parking (no fee); showers; toilets. **Best for:** surfing; swimming; walking. ✉ *8200 Camino del Oro, in front of Kellogg Park, La Jolla* ✣ *2 miles north of downtown La Jolla* 🌐 *www.sandiego.gov/lifeguards/beaches/shores.shtml.*

★ Windansea Beach

BEACH—SIGHT | With its rocky shoreline and strong shore break, Windansea stands out among San Diego beaches for its dramatic natural beauty. It's one of the best surf spots in San Diego County. Professional surfers love the unusual A-frame waves the reef break here creates. Although the large sandstone rocks that dot the beach might sound like a hindrance, they actually serve as protective barriers from the wind, making this one of the best beaches in San Diego for sunbathing. The beach's palm-covered surf shack is a protected historical landmark, and a seat here at sunset may just be one of the most romantic spots on the West Coast. The name Windansea comes from a hotel that burned down in the late 1940s. You can usually find nearby street parking. **Amenities:** seasonal lifeguards; toilets. **Best for:** sunset; surfing; solitude. ✉ *Neptune Pl. at Nautilus St., La Jolla* 🌐 *www.sandiego.gov/lifeguards/beaches/windan.shtml.*

🍴 Restaurants

★ The Cottage

$ | **AMERICAN** | **FAMILY** | A cozy beach cottage sets the stage for American comfort food with a California twist at this La Jolla staple. The restaurant serves lunch and dinner, but it's the well-loved daily breakfast that has locals and visitors happily queuing—sometimes up to two hours on weekends. Egg dishes have unique fillings like soy chorizo and pork belly braised beef, and the sizable, shareable stuffed French toast is a can't-miss. Post-surf or hike, keep it healthy with the avocado smash and smoked salmon on rosemary bread. Lunch spans tuna melts and fish tacos, while dinner offers veggie fettuccine, peach BBQ-glazed ribs, and Vietnamese shrimp bowls. The drink menu, with Bloody Marys and hard kombucha, will have you justifying, "it's five o'clock somewhere." It's worth waiting for a patio seat that overlooks a charming stretch of downtown La Jolla. There's usually free coffee cake and coffee for those in line, or you can reserve a table with the "Yelp Waitlist" app. **Known for:** daily breakfast that people line up for; treats for those waiting in line; great patio seating. [$] *Average main: $15* ✉ *7702 Fay Ave., La Jolla* ☎ *858/454–8409* 🌐 *www.cottagelajolla.com* 🕒 *No dinner Sun. and Mon.*

El Pescador Fish Market

$ | **SEAFOOD** | This bustling fish market and café in the heart of La Jolla Village has been popular with locals for its super-fresh fish for more than 30 years. Order the char-grilled, locally caught halibut, swordfish, or yellowtail on a toasted torta roll to enjoy in-house or to go for an oceanfront picnic at nearby La Jolla Cove. Other delicious choices include seafood cocktails, ceviche, Dungeness crab and shrimp salad, and fish and shrimp tacos. **Known for:** clam chowder; bustling on-site fish market; daily-caught cuts to go. [$] *Average main: $15* ✉ *634 Pearl St., La Jolla* ☎ *858/456–2526* 🌐 *www.elpescadorfishmarket.com.*

George's at the Cove

$$$$ | **AMERICAN** | La Jolla's ocean-view destination restaurant includes three distinct levels: California Modern on the bottom floor, the Level2 bar in the middle, and Ocean Terrace on the roof. At the sleek main dining room, open only for dinner, give special consideration to the legendary "fish tacos" and the six-course chef's tasting menu; for a more casual and inexpensive lunch or dinner option, head to the outdoor-only Ocean Terrace for spectacular views; for unique craft cocktails, like the "La Jolla" chilled with seaweed-laced ice cubes, and a seasonal happy hour with small bites, cocktails, beer, and wine, it's the Level2 lounge. **Known for:** beef tartare with 67°F egg; excellent ocean views; attention to detail for special occasion dinners. [$] *Average main: $37* ✉ *1250 Prospect St., La Jolla* ☎ *858/454–4244* 🌐 *www.georgesatthe-cove.com.*

★ Osteria Romantica

$ | ITALIAN | Between music by Pavarotti, the checkered tablecloths, and the sight of homemade pasta and free-flowing vino, you'll swear you've died and gone to Italy. At this cozy La Jolla Shores eatery, northern and southwestern Italian flavors have fused into culinary magic—house-made breads, sauces, gnocchi, and pastas like pappardelle with braised lamb, and linguine with mussels—since 2004. The breaded veal and lobster ravioli are both exceptional. Pork osso buco in port wine sauce is a popular main course that can be enjoyed alfresco on warm summer nights on the dog-friendly patio. Despite its size, the tiramisu with espresso-dipped ladyfingers goes down way too easy. **Known for:** tender lamb pappardelle; cozy Italian vibe; homemade pasta, breads, and sauces. [$] *Average main: $17* ✉ *2151 Av. de la Playa, La Jolla* ☎ *858/551–1221* 🌐 *www.osteriaromantica.com.*

Hotels

★ Grande Colonial

$$$$ | HOTEL | This white-wedding-cake-style hotel in the heart of La Jolla Village has ocean views and charming European details that include chandeliers, mahogany railings, a wooden elevator, crystal doorknobs, and French doors. **Pros:** the Village's only four-diamond hotel; superb restaurant; hospitality extras included in rate. **Cons:** small pool; no fitness center; valet parking only. [$] *Rooms from: $369* ✉ *910 Prospect St., La Jolla* ☎ *888/828–5498* 🌐 *www.thegrandecolonial.com* 🛏 *93 rooms* 🍴 *No meals.*

The Lodge at Torrey Pines

$$$$ | RESORT | Best known for its two 18-hole championship golf courses, this beautiful Craftsman-style lodge sits on a bluff between La Jolla and Del Mar with commanding coastal views, excellent service, a blissful spa, and the upscale A. R. Valentien restaurant, which serves farm-to-table California cuisine. **Pros:** spacious upscale rooms; remarkable service; adjacent to the famed Torrey Pines Golf Course; warm decor with Craftsman accents and hardwoods. **Cons:** not centrally located; expensive; $30 daily parking fee. [$] *Rooms from: $452* ✉ *11480 N. Torrey Pines Rd., La Jolla* ☎ *858/453–4420, 888/826–0224* 🌐 *www.lodgetorreypines.com* ⛳ *Two 18-hole championship golf courses* 🛏 *170 rooms* 🍴 *No meals.*

Activities

DIVING

Scuba San Diego

SCUBA DIVING | This center is well regarded for its top-notch instruction and certification programs, as well as for guided dive tours. Scuba Adventure classes for non-certified divers are held daily in Mission Bay, meeting near Mission Point. Trips for certified divers depart from La Jolla and include dives to kelp reefs in La Jolla Cove, and night diving at La Jolla Canyon. They also have snorkeling tours to La Jolla's Sea Caves. ✉ *8008 Girard St., La Jolla* ☎ *619/260–1880* 🌐 *www.scubasandiego.com* 🎟 *From $70* ☞ *Scuba Adventure meeting point is 2615 Bayside La. in South Mission Bay, near Mission Point.*

GOLF

★ Torrey Pines Golf Course

GOLF | Due to its cliff-top location overlooking the Pacific and its classic championship holes, Torrey Pines is one of the best public golf courses in the United States. The course was the site of the 2008 and 2021 U.S. Open and has been the home of the Farmers Insurance Open since 1968. The par-72 South Course, redesigned by Rees Jones in 2001, receives rave reviews from touring pros; it is longer, more challenging, and more expensive than the North Course. Tee times may be booked from 4 to 90 days in advance (☎ 858/552–1662) and are subject to an advance booking fee ($45). ✉ 11480 N. Torrey Pines Rd., La Jolla ☎ 858/452–3226, 800/985–4653 ⊕ www.torreypinesgolfcourse.com ⚑ South: from $202. North: from $128; $40 for golf cart ⚐. South: 18 holes, 7707 yards, par 72. North: 18 holes, 7258 yards, par 72.

HIKING
Los Peñasquitos Canyon Preserve
HIKING/WALKING | Twelve miles of trails at this inland park north of Mira Mesa accommodate equestrians, runners, walkers, and cyclists as well as leashed dogs. Look at maps for trails specific to bikes and horses. The trail parallels Los Peñasquitos and is marked by a small waterfall at the 3.5 mile marker. Hikers can cross the creek and loop back among large rock boulders—it's an unexpected oasis amid the arid valley landscape. ✉ 12020 Black Mountain Rd., Rancho Peñasquitos ⊹ From I–15, exit Mercy Rd., and head west to Black Mountain Rd.; turn right then left at first light; follow road to Ranch House parking lot ☎ 858/484–7504 ⊕ www.sdparks.org.

Torrey Pines State Reserve
HIKING/WALKING | FAMILY | Hikers and runners will appreciate this park's many winning features: switchback trails that descend to the sea, an unparalleled view of the Pacific, and a chance to see the Torrey pine tree, one of the rarest pine breeds in the United States. The reserve hosts guided nature walks as well. Dogs and food are prohibited at the reserve. Parking is $20–$25, depending on day and season. ✉ 12600 N. Torrey Pines Rd., La Jolla ⊹ Exit I–5 at Carmel Valley Rd. and head west toward Coast Hwy. 101

until you reach N. Torrey Pines Rd.; turn left. ☎ 858/755–2063 ⊕ www.torreypine.org ⚑ Parking from $20.

KAYAKING
Hike Bike Kayak Adventures
KAYAKING | This shop offers several kayak tours, from easy excursions in La Jolla Cove that are well suited to families and beginners to more advanced jaunts. Tours include kayaking the caves off La Jolla coast, and whale-watching (from a safe distance) December through March. Tours last 90 minutes to two hours and require a minimum of four people. ✉ 2222 Av. de la Playa, La Jolla ☎ 858/551–9510 ⊕ www.hikebikekayak.com ⚑ From $50.

SURFING
★ Surf Diva Surf School
SURFING | Check out clinics, surf camps, and private lessons especially formulated for girls and women. Most clinics and trips are for women only, but there are some coed options. Guys can also book group or private lessons from the nationally recognized staff. Surf Diva is also home to a boutique that sells surf and stand-up paddleboard equipment. They also offer surf retreats in Costa Rica. ✉ 2160 Ave. de la Playa, La Jolla ☎ 858/454–8273 ⊕ www.surfdiva.com ⚑ Group lessons $69; private lessons $95.

Point Loma

The hilly peninsula of Point Loma curves west and south into the Pacific and provides protection for San Diego Bay. Its high elevations and sandy cliffs provide incredible views, and make Point Loma a visible local landmark. Its maritime roots are evident, from its longtime ties to the U.S. Navy to its bustling sportfishing and sailing marinas. The funky community of Ocean Beach coexists alongside the stately homes of Sunset Cliffs and the honored graves at Fort Rosecrans National Cemetery.

Sights

★ Cabrillo National Monument

LIGHTHOUSE | FAMILY | This 166-acre preserve marks the site of the first European visit to San Diego, made by 16th-century Spanish explorer Juan Rodríguez Cabrillo when he landed at this spot on September 15, 1542. Today the site, with its rugged cliffs and shores and outstanding overlooks, is one of the most frequently visited of all the national monuments. There's a good visitor center and useful interpretive stations along the cliff-side walkways. Highlights include the moderately difficult Bayside Trail, the Old Point Loma Lighthouse, and the tide pools. There's also a sheltered viewing station where you can watch the gray whales' yearly migration from Baja California to Alaska (including high-powered telescopes). ✉ *1800 Cabrillo Memorial Dr., Point Loma* ☎ *619/ 523–4285* 🌐 *www.nps.gov/cabr* 🎫 *$20 per car, $10 per person on foot/bicycle, entry good for 7 days.*

Ocean Beach Pier

MARINA | This T-shape pier is a popular fishing spot and home to the Ocean Beach Pier Café and a small tackle shop. Constructed in 1966, it is the longest concrete pier on the West Coast and a perfect place to take in views of the harbor, ocean, and Point Loma Peninsula. Surfers flock to the waves that break just below. ✉ *1950 Abbott St., Ocean Beach.*

Beaches

Sunset Cliffs

BEACH—SIGHT | As the name would suggest, this natural park near Point Loma Nazerene University is one of the best places in San Diego to watch the sunset thanks to its cliff-top location and expansive ocean views. Some limited beach access is accessible via an extremely steep stairway at the foot of Ladera Street. Beware of the treacherous cliff trails and pay attention to warning signs since the cliffs are very unstable. If you're going to make your way to the narrow beach below, it's best to go at low tide when the southern end, near Cabrillo Point, reveals tide pools teeming with small sea creatures. Farther north the waves lure surfers, and Osprey Point offers good fishing off the rocks. Keep your eyes peeled for migrating California gray whales during the winter months. Check WaveCast (🌐 *www.wavecast.com/tides*) for tide schedules. **Amenities:** parking (no fee). **Best for:** solitude; sunset; surfing. ✉ *Sunset Cliffs Blvd., between Ladera St. and Adair St., Point Loma* 🌐 *www.sunsetcliffs.info.*

Restaurants

★ Cesarina

$$ | ITALIAN | A wall of mason jars with pickled vegetables and brined olives transports you to an Italian market in Rome where the owner's mother perfected generations of recipes that have made their way into this Point Loma eatery. Since its 2019 opening, customers have lined up for homemade Italian staples including pasta, gnocchi, meatballs, sausage, bread, and decadent desserts. Portions are generous and flavors are as authentic as they get. The tagliere cutting board is piled high with prosciutto, burrata, green olives, artichoke hearts, and marinated vegetables beckoning a dunk of focaccia with every bite, while the risotto and tagliata are cooked to perfection and the spaghetti with mussels and clams will have you reenacting *Lady and the Tramp*. For the finale, bite into the chocolate cannoli and then be sure to check yourself in the mirror as the homemade cannoli shells are flaky. **Known for:** nearly everything made from scratch; authentic Italian cuisine; excellent vegan options. [$] *Average main: $20* ✉ *4161 Voltaire St., Point Loma* ☎ *619/226–6222* 🌐 *www.cesarinarestaurant.com.*

★ Hodad's

$ | **BURGER** | **FAMILY** | Surfers with big appetites, and fans of Food Network's *Diners, Drive-ins and Dives,* chow down on huge, messy burgers, fries, onion rings, and shakes at this funky, hippie beach joint adorned with beat-up surfboards and license plates from almost every state. Don't be put off by lines out the door—they move quickly and the wait is worth it, especially now that they have their own microbrewery with six draft beers including a hazy IPA and a Mexican lager. A miniburger is a less-filling option, and there are veggie and chicken patty options for the red-meat averse. Newer outposts—as family-friendly as the original '60s joint—are Downtown and at Petco Park. **Known for:** legendary bacon cheeseburgers and thick-cut onion rings; surf-shack vibe; a little sass with your burger. $ *Average main: $10* ⊠ *5010 Newport Ave., Ocean Beach* ☎ *619/224–4623* ⊕ *www.hodadies.com.*

★ Liberty Public Market

$ | **INTERNATIONAL** | **FAMILY** | The city's former Naval Training Center is home to more than 30 vendors so even the pickiest of diners will be pleased. Options include tacos and quesadillas at Cecilia's Taqueria; fried rice, pad Thai, and curries at Mama Made Thai; lavender lattes from Westbean Coffee Roasters; fried chicken and fries from Fluster Cluck; sweet and savory crepes from Ooh La La; more than a dozen Argentinean empanadas at Paraná; and croissants, éclairs, and macarons at Le Parfait Paris. There are a few communal tables indoors, but the best seating is the kid- and dog-friendly outdoor patio, outfitted with Adirondack chairs and market lights. **Known for:** cuisines from around the world; lively kid- and dog-friendly patio; the best regional foods under one roof. $ *Average main: $10* ⊠ *2820 Historic Decatur Rd., Liberty Station* ☎ *619/487–9346* ⊕ *www.liberty-publicmarket.com.*

★ The Little Lion Cafe

$$ | **MODERN AMERICAN** | Amid surf shacks and hippie beach bars, this restaurant perched on stunning Sunset Cliffs feels like a hidden European bistro. The sisters who run the show come from a long line of successful local restaurateurs and have brought their passed-down expertise to the simple, healthy menu and thoughtful service. Entrées include plant-based tacos, Baja shrimp in garlic butter, and grilled cheese with honey, Dijon, and Brie. Their morning menu features chia seed puddings and baked eggs, which are a welcome contrast to the typical indulgent brunch fare. **Known for:** eggs Benedict; cozy bistro setting; flash-fried cauliflower. $ *Average main: $20* ⊠ *1424 Sunset Cliffs Blvd., Ocean Beach* ☎ *619/756–6921* ⊕ *www.thelittle-lioncafe.com* ☽ *Closed Mon. No dinner Tues., Wed., and Sun.*

Point Loma Seafoods

$ | **SEAFOOD** | **FAMILY** | When fishing boats unload their catch on-site, a seafood restaurant and market earns the right to boast that they offer "the freshest thing in town." In the early 1960s, mostly sportfishermen came here, but word got out about the just-caught fried fish on San Francisco–style sourdough bread, and now locals and visitors come to enjoy bay views, sunshine, and a greatly expanded menu of seafood dishes. A friendly, efficient crew takes orders for food and drinks at the counter, keeping the wait down even on the busiest days. In addition to sandwiches, favorites include fish tacos, seafood cocktails, sushi, salads, and fried platters of fish, shrimp, and scallops. **Known for:** San Francisco–style seafood on sourdough; dockside bay views; hickory-wood smoked fish. $ *Average main: $15* ⊠ *2805 Emerson St., Point Loma* ☎ *619/223–1109* ⊕ *www.pointlomaseafoods.com.*

Stone Brewing World Bistro and Gardens
$$ | **ECLECTIC** | **FAMILY** | This 50,000-square-foot monument to beer and good food is a crowd-pleaser, especially for fans of San Diego's nationally known craft beer scene. The global menu features dishes like the Bavarian pretzel and Brewmaster's Brisket Dip that pair perfectly with on-tap and bottled beers from around the world and Stone's famous IPAs. Dine indoors in high-ceiling rooms guarded by etched-metal gargoyles and lit by beer-bottle chandeliers. Or, relax outdoors where parents often unwind as their kids enjoy the patio. Before leaving, browse the company store for hip logo wear like hats, hoodies, and bomber jackets. **Known for:** massive outdoor patio; brew-friendly eats; artisanal burgers. [$] *Average main: $22* ✉ *2816 Historic Decatur Rd., Liberty Station* ☎ *619/269–2100* 🌐 *www.stonelibertystation.com.*

Hotels

★ Homewood Suites San Diego Airport Liberty Station
$$$ | **HOTEL** | **FAMILY** | With amenities like kitchens and a business center, most guests stay at least five nights, turning this all-suites hotel into a home. **Pros:** outstanding central location near attractions; close to paths for joggers and bikers; complimentary airport shuttle. **Cons:** breakfast area can get crowded; far from nightlife. [$] *Rooms from: $249* ✉ *2576 Laning Rd., Point Loma* ☎ *619/222–0500* 🌐 *www.homewoodsuites.com* 🛏 *150 suites* 🍴 *Free breakfast.*

Inn at Sunset Cliffs
$$$$ | **HOTEL** | At this U-shape beachfront property, every room gets a glimpse of the ocean, meaning you can fall asleep to the sound of the crashing waves and wake up to the sight of surfers paddling at Pescadero break just in front of the hotel. **Pros:** midweek rates from $175; rooms remodeled in 2018; Rooms 201 and 214 have full ocean views. **Cons:** standard rooms are tiny; no elevator; thin walls. [$] *Rooms from: $315* ✉ *1370 Sunset Cliffs Blvd., Ocean Beach* ☎ *619/222–7901, 866/786–2543* 🌐 *www.innatsunsetcliffs.com* 🛏 *28 rooms* 🍴 *No meals.*

Activities

★ Bayside Trail at Cabrillo National Monument
HIKING/WALKING | Driving here is a treat in itself, as a vast view of the Pacific unfolds before you. The view is equally enjoyable on Bayside Trail (2 miles round-trip), which is home to the same coastal sagebrush that Juan Rodriguez Cabrillo saw when he first discovered the California coast in the 16th century. After the hike, you can explore nearby tide pools, the monument statue, and the Old Point Loma Lighthouse. Don't worry if you don't see everything on your first visit; your entrance receipt ($20 per car) is good for seven days. ✉ *1800 Cabrillo Memorial Dr., Point Loma* ✣ *From I–5, take Rosecrans exit and turn right on Canon St. then left on Catalina Blvd. (also known as Cabrillo Memorial Dr.); follow until end* ☎ *619/523–4285* 🌐 *www.nps.gov/cabr* 🅿 *Parking $20.*

Shelter Island

In 1950 San Diego's port director decided to raise the shoal that lay off the eastern shore of Point Loma above sea level with the sand and mud dredged up during the course of deepening a ship channel in the 1930s and '40s. The resulting peninsula, **Shelter Island,** became home to several marinas and resorts, many with Polynesian details that still exist today, giving them a retro flair. This reclaimed peninsula now supports towering palms and resorts, restaurants, and side-by-side marinas. A long sidewalk runs past boat brokerages to the hotels and marinas that line the inner shore, facing Point Loma. On the bay side, fishermen launch their boats and families relax at picnic tables along the grass, where there are fire rings and permanent barbeque grills.

Restaurants

Bali Hai

$$ | HAWAIIAN | For more than 50 years, generations of San Diegans and visitors have enjoyed this Polynesian-themed icon with its stunning bay and city skyline views. The menu is a fusion of Hawaiian and Asian cuisines with standouts like the Hawaiian tuna poke, Mongolian lamb with pad Thai, and wok-fried bass. **Known for:** potent Bali Hai mai tais; Sunday brunch buffet with a DIY sundae bar; Hawaiian and Asian-themed menu. $ *Average main: $25* ✉ *2230 Shelter Island Dr., Shelter Island* ☎ *619/222–1181* ⊕ *www.balihairestaurant.com* ⊙ *No lunch Sun.*

Hotels

★ Kona Kai Resort & Spa

$$$ | RESORT | A $30 million renovation took this Shelter Island resort up a notch, with remodeled rooms, a new pool, spa, gym, and lobby—making the marina view an added bonus rather than the main focus. **Pros:** private beach with firepits; near marina with water view; on-site sports rental equipment. **Cons:** not centrally located; resort fees; popular for business meetings and weddings. $ *Rooms from: $269* ✉ *1551 Shelter Island Dr., Shelter Island* ☎ *619/221–8000, 800/566–2524* ⊕ *www.resortkonakai.com* ➠ *170 rooms* ⦿ *No meals.*

Harbor Island

Following the successful creation of Shelter Island, in 1961 the U.S. Navy used the residue from digging berths deep enough to accommodate aircraft carriers to build **Harbor Island**. Restaurants and high-rise hotels dot the inner shore of this 1½-mile-long peninsula adjacent to the airport. Restaurants and high-rise hotels

dot the inner shore while the bay's shore is lined with pathways, gardens, and scenic picnic spots. On the west point, the restaurant Tom Ham's Lighthouse has a U.S. Coast Guard–approved beacon shining from its tower and a sweeping view of San Diego's bay front.

Restaurants

Tom Ham's Lighthouse

$$$ | SEAFOOD | It's hard to top this long-time Harbor Island restaurant's incredible views across San Diego Bay to the Downtown skyline and Coronado Bridge. Now a new alfresco dining deck and a contemporary seafood-focused menu ensure the dining experience at this working lighthouse doesn't take a back seat to the scenery. Sample the iced shellfish platter before moving on to traditional lobster bouillabaisse and paella or grilled prawns with spicy grits. The family-owned institution also serves a popular Sunday brunch that stars crab legs, peel-and-eat shrimp, smoked salmon, and oysters along with bottomless orange or pineapple mimosas. Prefer beer? Choose from a long list of on-tap and bottled craft brews. **Known for:** bottomless mimosa Sunday brunch; alfresco dining deck with skyline and Coronado bridge views; fresh seafood and beer-battered cod. $ *Average main: $30* ✉ *2150 Harbor Island Dr., Harbor Island* ☎ *619/291–9110* ⊕ *www.tomhamslighthouse.com* ⊙ *No lunch Sun.*

Coronado

As if freeze-framed in the 1950s, Coronado's quaint appeal is captured in its old-fashioned storefronts, well-manicured gardens, and charming **Ferry Landing Marketplace.** The streets of Coronado are wide, quiet, and friendly, and many of today's residents live in grand Victorian homes handed down for generations. Naval Air Station North Island was established in 1911 on Coronado's north end,

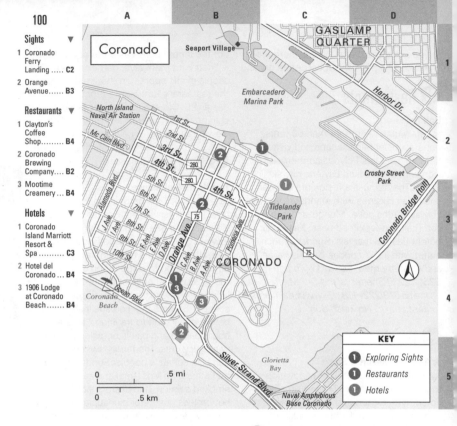

across from Point Loma, and was the site of Charles Lindbergh's departure on the transcontinental flight that preceded his famous solo flight across the Atlantic. Coronado's long relationship with the U.S. Navy and its desirable real estate have made it an enclave for military personnel; it's said to have more retired admirals per capita than anywhere else in the United States.

Coronado is accessible via the arching blue 2.2-mile-long San Diego–Coronado Bay Bridge, which offers breathtaking views of the harbor and Downtown. Alternatively, pedestrians and bikes can reach Coronado via the popular ferry service. Bus 904 meets the ferry and travels as far as Silver Strand State Beach. Bus 901 runs daily between the Gaslamp Quarter and Coronado.

◉ Sights

Coronado Ferry Landing

STORE/MALL | **FAMILY** | This collection of shops at Ferry Landing is on a smaller scale than the Embarcadero's Seaport Village, but you do get a great view of the Downtown San Diego skyline. The little bay-side shops and restaurants resemble the gingerbread domes of the Hotel del Coronado. ⊠ *1201 1st St., at B Ave., Coronado* ⊕ *www.coronadoferrylanding.com.*

★ Orange Avenue

NEIGHBORHOOD | Comprising Coronado's business district and its village-like heart, this avenue is surely one of the most charming spots in Southern California. Slow-paced and very "local" (the city fights against chain stores), it's a blast from the past, although entirely up-to-date in other respects. The military presence—Coronado is home to the U.S. Navy Sea, Air, and Land (SEAL) forces—is reflected in shops selling military gear and places like **McP's Irish Pub,** at No. 1107. A family-friendly stop for a good, all-American meal, it's the unofficial SEALs headquarters. Many clothing boutiques, home-furnishings stores, and upscale restaurants cater to visitors with deep pockets, but you can buy plumbing supplies, too, or get a genuine military haircut at **Crown Barber Shop,** at No. 947. If you need a break, stop for a latte at the sidewalk café of **Bay Books,** San Diego's largest independent bookstore, at No. 1029. ✉ *Orange Ave., near 9th St., Coronado.*

Beaches

★ Coronado Beach

BEACH—SIGHT | FAMILY | This wide beach is one of San Diego's most picturesque thanks to its soft white sand and sparkly blue water. The historic Hotel del Coronado serves as a backdrop, and it's perfect for sunbathing, people-watching, and Frisbee tossing. The beach has limited surf, but it's great for bodyboarding and swimming. Exercisers might include Navy SEAL teams or other military units that conduct training runs on beaches in and around Coronado. There are picnic tables, grills, and popular fire rings, but don't bring lacquered wood or pallets. Only natural wood is allowed for burning. There's also a dog beach on the north end. There's free parking along Ocean Boulevard, though it's often hard to snag a space. **Amenities:** food and drink; lifeguards; showers; toilets. **Best for:** walking; swimming. ✉ *Ocean Blvd., between S. O St. and Orange Ave., Coronado* ✥ *From San Diego–Coronado bridge, turn left on Orange Ave. and follow signs.*

Silver Strand State Beach

BEACH—SIGHT | FAMILY | This quiet beach on a narrow sand spit allows visitors a unique opportunity to experience both the Pacific Ocean and the San Diego Bay. The 2½ miles of ocean side is great for surfing and other water sports while the bay side, accessible via foot tunnel under Highway 75, has calmer, warmer water and great views of the San Diego skyline. Lifeguards and rangers are on duty year-round, and there are places for biking, volleyball, and fishing. Picnic tables, grills, and firepits are available in summer, and the Silver Strand Beach Cafe is open Memorial Day through Labor Day. The beach is close to Loews Coronado Bay Resort and the Coronado Cays, an exclusive community popular with yacht owners. You can reserve RV sites ($65 beach; $50 inland) online (🌐 *www.reserveamerica.com*). Three day-use parking lots provide room for 800 cars. **Amenities:** food and drink; lifeguards; parking (fee); showers; toilets. **Best for:** walking; swimming; surfing. ✉ *5000 Hwy. 75, Coronado* ✥ *4½ miles south of city of Coronado* ☎ *619/435–5184* 🌐 *www.parks.ca.gov/silverstrand* 🎟 *Parking $10, motor home $30.*

Restaurants

Clayton's Coffee Shop

$ | AMERICAN | FAMILY | A classic diner with bar seating in a circle, Clayton's is a great lunch or breakfast spot with a menu that ranges from classic American fare to Mexican-inspired dishes like the popular breakfast burrito. Just don't forget dessert! **Known for:** bottomless coffee; breakfast burrito; gooey cinnamon roll sundae. [$] *Average main: $10* ✉ *979 Orange Ave., Coronado* ☎ *619/435–5425* 🌐 *www.claytonscoffeeshop.com.*

Coronado Brewing Company

$ | AMERICAN | FAMILY | Perfect for beer lovers with kids, this popular, laid-back Coronado brewpub offers a menu that features large portions of basic bar food like burgers, sandwiches, pizza, and salads. Enjoy a brew at a pair of sidewalk terraces or belly up to the bar and a new batch being made such as the Islander Pale Ale (IPA) or Mermaid's Red Ale. **Known for:** a good selection of house-crafted beers;

kids' menu; more strollers than bar stools. $ *Average main: $12* ⊠ *170 Orange Ave., Coronado* ☎ *619/437–4452* ⊕ *www.coronadobrewing.com.*

Mootime Creamery

$ | CAFÉ | FAMILY | For a deliciously sweet pick-me-up, check out the rich ice cream, frozen yogurt, and sorbet made fresh daily on the premises. Dessert nachos made from waffle-cone chips are an unusual addition to an extensive sundae menu. Just look for the statue of Elvis on the sidewalk in front. **Known for:** daily house-made ice cream, yogurt, and sorbet; dessert nachos; "moopies" sandwiches, with ice cream between two cereal bars. $ *Average main: $5* ⊠ *1025 Orange Ave., Coronado* ☎ *619/435–2422* ⊕ *www.mootime.com.*

 ## Hotels

★ Coronado Island Marriott Resort & Spa

$$$$ | RESORT | FAMILY | Near San Diego Bay, this snazzy hotel has rooms with great Downtown skyline views. **Pros:** spectacular views; on-site spa; close to water taxis. **Cons:** not in downtown Coronado; resort fee; expensive self-parking. $ *Rooms from: $329* ⊠ *2000 2nd St., Coronado* ☎ *619/435–3000* ⊕ *www.marriott.com/hotels/travel/sanci-coronado-island-marriott-resort-and-spa* ⇨ *300 rooms* ❤️ *No meals.*

★ Hotel del Coronado

$$$$ | RESORT | FAMILY | As much of a draw today as it was when it opened in 1888, the Victorian-style "Hotel Del" is always alive with activity, as guests—including U.S. presidents and celebrities—and tourists marvel at the fanciful architecture and ocean views. **Pros:** 17 on-site shops; on the beach; well-rounded spa. **Cons:** some rooms are small; expensive dining; hectic public areas. $ *Rooms from: $425* ⊠ *1500 Orange Ave., Coronado* ☎ *800/468–3533, 619/435–6611* ⊕ *www.hoteldel.com* ⇨ *757 rooms* ❤️ *No meals.*

★ 1906 Lodge at Coronado Beach

$$$$ | B&B/INN | Smaller but no less luxurious than the sprawling beach resorts of Coronado, this lodge—whose name alludes to the main building's former life as a boardinghouse built in 1906—welcomes couples for romantic retreats two blocks from the ocean. **Pros:** most suites feature Jacuzzi tubs, fireplaces, and porches; historic property; free underground parking. **Cons:** too quiet for families; no pool; limited on-site dining options. $ *Rooms from: $329* ⊠ *1060 Adella Ave., Coronado* ☎ *619/437–1900, 866/435–1906* ⊕ *www.1906lodge.com* ⇨ *17 rooms* ❤️ *Free breakfast.*

 ## Activities

BIKING
Holland's Bicycles

BICYCLING | This is a great bike rental source on Coronado Island, so you can ride the Silver Strand Bike Path on an electric bike, beach cruiser, road bike, or tandem. ⊠ *977 Orange Ave., Coronado* ☎ *619/435–3153* ⊕ *www.hollandsbicycles.com* 🚲 *From $8.*

DISNEYLAND AND ORANGE COUNTY

WITH KNOTT'S BERRY FARM AND CATALINA ISLAND

Updated by
Jill Weinlein

👁 Sights	🍴 Restaurants	🛏 Hotels	🛍 Shopping	🍸 Nightlife
★★★★★	★★★★☆	★★★★★	★☆☆☆☆	★☆☆☆☆

WELCOME TO DISNEYLAND AND ORANGE COUNTY

TOP REASONS TO GO

★ **Disneyland:** Walking down Main Street, U.S.A., with Sleeping Beauty Castle straight ahead, you really will feel like you're in one of the happiest places on Earth.

★ **Beautiful beaches:** Surf, swim, kayak, paddleboard, or just relax on some of the state's most breathtaking stretches of coastline. Calm coves offer clear water for snorkeling and scuba diving.

★ **Santa Catalina Island:** Just 22 miles from the mainland, Santa Catalina Island is the only inhabited island of the Channel Islands chain. A fast and easy cruise away on a high-speed catamaran, once there you can explore the Mediterranean-inspired small town of Avalon, dive or snorkel through the state's first underwater park, or explore the unspoiled beauty of the island's wild interior.

★ **Family fun:** Ride roller coasters, eat ice cream and frozen chocolate-dipped bananas, bike on oceanfront paths, fish off ocean piers, or rent a Duffy boat and cruise around the calm harbors.

1 Disneyland Resort. Southern California's top draw is now a megaresort, with more attractions spilling over into Disney's California Adventure.

2 Knott's Berry Farm. Amusement park lovers will enjoy this Buena Park attraction, with thrill rides, the *Peanuts* gang, and lots of fried chicken and boysenberry pie.

3 Huntington Beach. This resort destination is often referred to as Surf City U.S.A.

4 Newport Beach. There's something for every taste here, from glamorous boutiques to simple snack huts.

5 Corona del Mar. No matter your preferred outdoor activity, you'll find it on one of the beaches here.

6 Laguna Beach. With 30 beaches and coves to explore, there's plenty to keep visitors busy.

7 San Juan Capistrano. Take a trip back in time among the historic missions.

8 Catalina Island. This island paradise—with its pocket-size town, Avalon, and large nature preserve—is just off the Orange County coast.

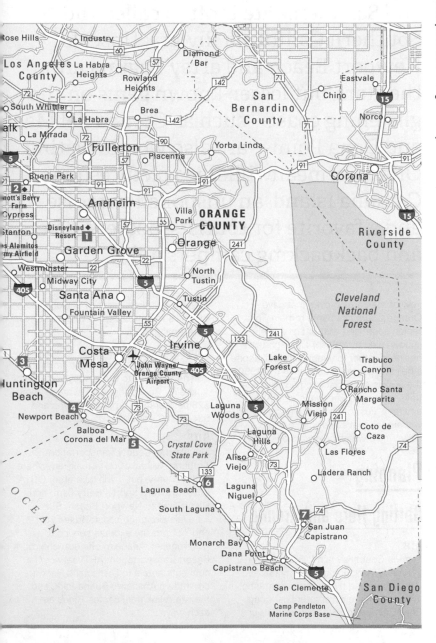

With its tropical flowers and palm trees, the stretch of coast between Seal Beach and San Clemente is often called the Southern California Riviera. Upscale Newport Beach and artsy Laguna are the stars, but lesser-known gems on the glistening coast—such as Corona del Mar and Dana Point—are also worth visiting. Offshore, meanwhile, lies picturesque Catalina Island, an unspoiled paradise and a favorite for tourists, boaters, divers, and backpacking campers alike.

Few of the citrus groves that gave Orange County its name remain. This region south and east of Los Angeles is now ruled by tourism and high-tech business rather than agriculture. Despite a building boom that began in the 1990s, the area is still a place to find wilderness trails, canyons, greenbelts, and natural environs. Just offshore is a deep-water wilderness that's possible to explore via daily whale-watching excursions.

Planning

Getting Here and Around

AIR

Orange County's main facility is John Wayne Airport Orange County (SNA), which is served by six major domestic airlines and one commuter line. Long Beach Airport (LGB) is served by four airlines, including its major player, Jet-Blue. It's roughly 20 to 30 minutes by car from Anaheim.

Super Shuttle and Prime Time Airport Shuttle provide transportation from John Wayne and LAX to the Disneyland area of Anaheim. Round-trip fares average about $28 per person from John Wayne and $34 to $80 from LAX.

BUS

The Orange County Transportation Authority will take you virtually anywhere in the county, but it will take time; OCTA buses go from Knott's Berry Farm and Disneyland to Newport Beach. Bus 1 travels along the coast; Buses 701 and 721 provide express service to Los Angeles. Anaheim offers Anaheim Resort Transportation (ART) service that connects hotels to Disneyland Resort, downtown Anaheim, Buena Park, and the Metrolink train center. Rides are $3 each way.

CONTACTS Anaheim Resort Transportation.
✉ 2099 S. State College Blvd., Suite 600,
Anaheim ☎ 714/563–5287 ⊕ rideart.org.
Orange County Transportation Authority.
☎ 714/636–7433 ⊕ www.octa.net.

CAR

The San Diego Freeway (Interstate 405),
the coastal route, and the Santa Ana
Freeway (Interstate 5), the inland route,
run north–south through Orange County.
South of Laguna, Interstate 405 merges
into Interstate 5 (called the San Diego
Freeway south from this point). A toll
road, Highway 73, runs 15 miles from
Newport Beach to San Juan Capistrano;
it costs $6.22–$8.48 (lower rates are for
weekends and off-peak hours) and is usually less jammed than the regular freeways. Do your best to avoid all Orange
County freeways during rush hours (6–9
am and 3:30–6:30 pm). Highway 55 leads
to Newport Beach. The Pacific Coast
Highway (Highway 1) allows easy access
to beach communities and is the most
scenic route but expect it to be crowded,
especially on summer weekends and
holidays.

FERRY

There are two ferries that service
Catalina Island; Catalina Express runs
multiple departures daily from San Pedro,
Long Beach, and Dana Point. From
each port, it takes about 90 minutes to
reach the island. The Catalina Flyer runs
from Newport Beach to Avalon in about
75 minutes. Reservations are strongly
advised for summer months and weekends. During the winter months, ferry
crossings are not as frequent.

TRAIN

Amtrak makes daily stops in Orange
County at all major towns. Metrolink is a
weekday commuter train that runs to and
from Los Angeles and Orange County.

CONTACTS Metrolink. ✉ 800 N. Alameda St., Los Angeles ☎ 800/371–5465
⊕ www.metrolinktrains.com.

Restaurants

Guests dining at restaurants in Orange
County generally wear beach casual,
although at top resorts and fine dining
venues, guests usually choose to dress
up. Of course, there's also a swath of
casual places along the beachfronts—
seafood takeout, taquerias, burger
joints—that won't mind if you wear
shorts and flip-flops. Reservations are
recommended for the nicest restaurants.

Many places don't serve past 11 pm, and
locals tend to eat early. Remember that
according to California law, smoking is
prohibited in all enclosed areas.

Hotels

Along the coast there are remarkable
luxury resorts; if you can't afford a stay,
pop in for the view at Laguna Beach's
Montage Mosiac Tile pool or the always
welcoming Ritz-Carlton at Dana Point. For
a taste of the O.C. glam life, the Resort
at Pelican Hills is an idyllic place for
lunch, brunch or dinner at its Coliseum
Grill overlooking the world's largest
circular pool and the ocean beyond. For a
nautical experience, enjoy lunch or dinner
next to multimillion-dollar yachts secured
in Newport Bay at the Balboa Bay Resort.

As a rule, lodging prices tend to rise the
closer the hotels are to the beach. If
you're looking for value, consider a hotel
that's inland along the Interstate 405
freeway corridor.

In most cases, you can take advantage
of some of the facilities of the high-end
resorts, such as restaurants and spas,
even if you aren't an overnight guest.

*Restaurant and hotel reviews have
been shortened. For full information,
visit Fodors.com. Prices in the restaurant reviews are the average cost of
a main course at dinner or, if dinner is
not served, at lunch. Prices in the hotel*

reviews are the lowest cost of a standard double room in high season.

What It Costs

$	$$	$$$	$$$$
RESTAURANTS			
under $20	$20–$30	$31–$40	over $40
HOTELS			
under $200	$200–$300	$301–$400	over $400

Visitor Information

Visit Anaheim is an excellent resource for both leisure and business travelers and can provide materials on many area attractions. Kiosks at the Anaheim Convention Center act as a digital concierge and allow visitors to plan itineraries and buy tickets to area attractions.

The Orange County Visitors Association's website is also a useful source of information.

CONTACTS Orange County Visitors Association. ⊕ *www.travelcostamesa. com/visittheoc.* **Visit Anaheim.** ✉ *2099 S. State College Blvd., Suite 600, Anaheim* ☎ *714/765–2800* ⊕ *www.visitanaheim. org.*

Disneyland Resort

26 miles southeast of Los Angeles, via I–5.

The snowcapped Matterhorn, the centerpiece of Disneyland, punctuates the skyline of Anaheim. Since 1955, when Walt Disney chose this once-quiet farming community for the site of his first amusement park, Disneyland has attracted more than 650 million visitors and tens of thousands of workers, and Anaheim has been their host. Today, there are more than 60 attractions and adventures in the park's nine themed lands: Fantasyland, Adventureland, Tomorrowland, Frontierland, Main Street U.S.A., New Orleans Square, Critter Country, Mickey's Toontown, and Star Wars: Galaxy's Edge.

The resort is a sprawling complex that includes Disney's two amusement parks (Disneyland and Disney's California Adventure); three hotels; and Downtown Disney, a shopping, dining, and entertainment promenade. Anaheim's tourist center includes Angel Stadium of Anaheim, home of baseball's Los Angeles Angels of Anaheim; the Honda Center (formerly the Arrowhead Pond), which hosts concerts and the Anaheim Ducks hockey team; and the enormous Anaheim Convention Center.

GETTING THERE

Disney is about a 30-mile drive from either LAX or Downtown. From LAX, follow Sepulveda Boulevard south to the Interstate 105 freeway and drive east 16 miles to the Interstate 605 north exit. Exit at the Santa Ana Freeway (Interstate 5) and continue south for 12 miles to the Disneyland Drive exit. Follow signs to the resort. From Downtown, follow Interstate 5 south 28 miles and exit at Disneyland Drive. **Disneyland Resort Express** (☎ *800/828–6699*) offers daily nonstop bus service between LAX, John Wayne Airport, and Anaheim. Reservations are not required. The cost is $30 one-way from LAX, and $20 from John Wayne Airport.

SAVING TIME AND MONEY

If you plan to visit for more than a day, you can save money by buying multiday Park Hopper tickets that grant same-day "hopping" privileges between Disneyland and Disney's California Adventure. You get a discount on the multiple-day passes if you buy online through the Disneyland website.

Single-day admission prices vary by date. A one-day Park Hopper pass costs $147–$185 for anyone 10 or older, $141–$177 for kids ages three to nine. Admission to either park (but not both) is $97–$135 for adults or $91–$127 for kids three to nine; kids two and under are free.

In addition to tickets, parking is $20–$35 (unless your hotel has a shuttle or is within walking distance), and meals in the parks and at Downtown Disney range from $15 to $75 per person.

Disneyland

★ **Disneyland**
AMUSEMENT PARK/WATER PARK | FAMILY
An imaginative original, Disneyland was an unproven concept when it opened in 1955, but Walt Disney himself could never have predicted the park's success and its beloved place in the hearts of Southern Californians. It is the only one of the parks to have been overseen by Walt himself, has a genuine historic feel, and occupies a unique place in the Disney legend. Expertly run, with perfectly maintained grounds and a helpful staff ("cast members" in the Disney lexicon), the park offers plenty of fun experiences that you won't find anywhere else: you can visit a galaxy far, far away in the Star Wars land; cruise to a world of pirates in search of Jack Sparrow from the *Pirates of the Caribbean* series; and take a ride to Storybook Land, with its miniature replicas of animated Disney scenes from classics such as *Frozen* and *Alice in Wonderland*. Beloved Disney characters appear for autographs and photos throughout the day; times and places are posted at the entrances and on the Disneyland mobile app. Live shows, parades, strolling musicians, fireworks (on weekends and during the summer and holidays), and endless creative snack choices add to the carnival atmosphere. You can also meet some of the animated icons at one of the character meals served at the three Disney hotels (open to the public, but reservations are needed). Belongings can be stored in lockers

just off Main Street while stroller rentals, wheelchairs, and Electric Conveyance Vehicles (ECV) are at the entrance gate as convenient options for families with mobility challenges. The park's popularity means there are always crowds, especially during the holidays and summer months, so take advantage of the Disney FastPass Service to spend less time waiting in lines. Also be sure to make dining reservations at least three weeks before your visit to guarantee a table without a wait. ⊠ *Disneyland Park, 1313 S. Disneyland Dr., between Ball Rd. and Katella Ave., Anaheim* ☎ *714/781–4636 guest information* ⊕ *disneyland.disney. go.com* 💲 *From $97; parking $20.*

PARK NEIGHBORHOODS
Neighborhoods for Disneyland are arranged in geographic order.

MAIN STREET, U.S.A.
Walt's hometown of Marceline, Missouri, was the inspiration behind this romanticized image of small-town America, circa 1900. The sidewalks are lined with a penny arcade and shops that sell everything from tradeable pins to Disney-themed clothing, an endless supply of sugar confections, and a photo shop that offers souvenirs created via Disney's PhotoPass (on-site photographers capture memorable moments digitally—you can access them in person or online via the Disneyland app). Main Street opens half an hour before the rest of the park, so it's a good place to explore if you're getting an early start to beat the crowds (it's also open an hour after the other attractions close, so you may want to save your shopping for the end of the day).

Step into city hall to receive a complimentary button showcasing whatever you're celebrating (your first visit, a birthday, a marriage, or just Disney in general); throughout the day, Disney cast members will congratulate you with friendly smiles and well wishes. **Main Street Cinema** offers a cool respite from the crowds and six classic Disney

animated shorts, including *Steamboat Willie*. There's rarely a wait to enter. Grab a cappuccino and fresh-made pastry at the Jolly Holiday bakery to jump-start your visit. Board the **Disneyland Railroad,** an authentic steam-powered train located at the entrance that makes stops in the park's different lands. Or the 18-minute scenic round-trip will also give you unique views of Star Wars: Galaxy's Edge, Autopia, Splash Mountain, the Grand Canyon, and Rivers of America.

NEW ORLEANS SQUARE

This minireplica of the French Quarter in New Orleans, with narrow streets, hidden courtyards, and live street performances, is home to two iconic attractions and the Cajun-inspired Blue Bayou restaurant. The **Pirates of the Caribbean** ride now features Jack Sparrow and the cursed Captain Barbossa of the blockbuster series, plus enhanced special effects and battle scenes (complete with cannonball explosions). Nearby **Haunted Mansion** continues to spook guests with its stretching walls and "doombuggy" rides (there's now an expanded storyline for the beating-heart bride). The *Nightmare Before Christmas* holiday overlay is an annual tradition that starts in the fall and extends throughout the holidays. This is a good area to eat; you can get a nonalcoholic mint julep and Mickey Mouse–shaped beignets; a Monte Cristo sandwich at Cafe Orleans; or corn chowder in a sourdough bread bowl, po-boy sandwiches, and jambalaya at the French Market Restaurant. Food carts offer everything from just-popped popcorn to churros and even fresh fruit.

FRONTIERLAND

Between Adventureland and Fantasyland, Frontierland transports you to the wild, wild West with its rustic buildings, shooting gallery, foot-stompin' dance hall, and singing birds in the Enchanted Tiki Room. The marquee attraction, **Big Thunder Mountain Railroad,** is a relatively tame roller coaster ride (no steep descents) that takes the form of a runaway mine car as it rumbles and turns through desert canyons and an old mining town. Tour the Rivers of America on the 19th-century **Mark Twain Riverboat,** which takes you on a 14-minute paddleboat cruise around Tom Sawyer Island, or the **Sailing Ship Columbia,** a full-scale replica of a merchant ship that once sailed the globe (usually limited to weekends). From here, you can also ride a motorized raft over to Pirate's Lair on **Tom Sawyer Island,** where you can explore pirate-themed caves, go on a treasure hunt, and climb a fort. Dine outside at the River Belle Terrace for Southern culinary favorites including Mickey Mouse pancakes for breakfast, barbecued ribs and fried chicken sandwich for lunch, and a healthier barbecued tofu for dinner. Or take a seat on the festive Mexican terrace at Rancho del Zocalo for a trio of street tacos, fire-grilled citrus-marinated chicken, and creamy flan for dessert.

CRITTER COUNTRY

Iconic Splash Mountain is the biggest draw to this down-home country-themed area, but you can also take a peek through Winnie the Pooh's Hundred-Acre Wood and paddle the Rivers of America on Davy Crockett's Explorer Canoes. The patio of the popular Hungry Bear Restaurant has great views of Tom Sawyer's Island, and beyond is a galaxy far, far away: the Star Wars: Galaxy's Edge section of the park.

STAR WARS: GALAXY'S EDGE

This 14-acre expansive land has guests step into the planet Batuu, designed from architectural locations in Morocco, Turkey, and Israel. At the **Star Wars: Rise of the Resistance** ride, you will accept a mission from the Resistance to fight against the First Order; to ride, guests need to obtain a timed boarding group on the Disneyland app or at the park's main entrance. You can also take a thrilling interactive ride on **Millennium Falcon: Smugglers Run,** where you will soar into hyperspace and be

Best Tips for Disneyland

Download the Disneyland mobile app. You can do a lot with this app so it's a no-brainer to download if you have a smartphone. It provides a ticket barcode to skip long ticket lines; you can view maps of both parks and get access to FastPass tickets via the digital MAXPASS; learn about shows and attraction wait times, character visits, and parade times; view restaurant menus and make dining reservations; preorder and pay for contactless pickup at both parks; and download and share Disney PhotoPass photos.

Buy entry tickets in advance. Lines at ticket booths can take more than an hour on busy days. Save time by buying in advance. Nearby hotels sell park admission tickets; you can also buy them through Disney's website and the Disneyland app. Seek out package deals offered through AAA and discount Disneyland Park Hopper tickets at Costco.

Come midweek. Weekends (especially during the summer, Halloween, and winter holidays) are often the busiest times to visit. A rainy winter weekday is often the least crowded time to check out the parks.

Plan your times to hit the most popular rides. Get to the park as early as possible, even before the gates open, and make a beeline for the top rides before the crowds reach a critical mass. Later in the evening the parks thin out and you can catch a special show or parade. Save the quieter attractions for midafternoon.

Use FastPass. These passes allow you to reserve your place in line at some of the most popular attractions (only one at a time). Distribution machines are posted near the entrances of each attraction. Show the barcode on your Disneyland app or feed in your park admission ticket, and you'll receive a pass with a printed time frame (up to one to four hours later) during which you can return to wait in a much shorter line or walk right onto the ride.

Avoid peak mealtime crowds. Outside food and beverages in nonglass containers are allowed inside the parks, but dining at one of the park's many theme restaurants can be an experience to remember. For any sit-down establishment, be sure to make dining reservations in advance or wait until after 2 pm to avoid a long wait. If you just need a quick recharge, Disney carts offer creative snacks including popcorn in souvenir buckets, Mickey Mouse–shaped pretzels, Rice Crispies treats, cake pops, and ice cream.

If you want to eat at the **Blue Bayou** in Disneyland's New Orleans Square or Carthay Circle at Disney California Adventure, you can make a reservation up to 60 days in advance of your visit online or via the Disneyland app. It's always a good idea to bring water, juice boxes, and snacks for little ones.

Check the daily events schedule online, on the Disneyland app, or at the park entrance. During parades, fireworks, and other special events, sections of the parks are filled with crowds. This distraction can work in your favor to take advantage of shorter lines at dining venues and rides. It also can work against you in maneuvering around a section of the park so plan ahead.

assigned to be a pilot, engineer, or gunner on a smuggling mission.

The Build-a-Droid Workshop is stocked with colorful parts, chips, and tech items. Starting at $99.99, you will receive a basket and blueprint to build your droid. Another treasure to purchase and take home is a hand-built lightsaber at Savi's Workshop.

For dining, popular Oga's Cantina is good for coffee, all-day light snacks, and unique cocktails for grown-ups. Galactic food and drink options can be found at the Milk Stand, where guests can sample Batuu's legendary blue and green beverages, similar to what Luke Skywalker drank in the movies.

ADVENTURELAND
Modeled after the lands of Africa, Polynesia, and Arabia, this tiny tropical paradise is worth braving the crowds that flock here for the ambience and better-than-average food. Sing along with the animatronic birds and tiki gods in the **Enchanted Tiki Room,** sail the rivers of the world with joke-cracking skippers on **Jungle Cruise,** and climb the Disneyodendron semperflorens (the always-blooming Disney tree) to **Tarzan's Treehouse,** where you can walk through scenes, some interactive, from the 1999 animated film. Cap off the visit with a wild jeep ride at **Indiana Jones Adventure,** where the special effects and decipherable hieroglyphics distract you while you're waiting in line. There's a single-rider option for a quicker ride. The skewers (some vegetarian options available) at Bengal Barbecue and pineapple whip at Tiki Juice Bar are some of the best fast-food options in the park.

FANTASYLAND
Sleeping Beauty Castle marks the entrance to Fantasyland, a visual wonderland of princesses, spinning teacups, flying elephants, and other classic storybook characters. Rides, and shops such as the princess-themed Bibbidi Bobbidi Boutique, take precedence over restaurants in this area of the park, but outdoor carts sell everything from churros to turkey legs. Tots love the **King Arthur Carousel, Casey Jr. Circus Train,** and **Storybook Land Canal Boats.** This is also home to **Mr. Toad's Wild Ride, Peter Pan's Flight, Snow White's Enchanted Wish,** and **Pinocchio's Daring Journey,** all classic movie-theater-dark rides that immerse riders in Disney fairy tales. Keep an eye out for the Abominable Snowman when he pops up on the **Matterhorn Bobsleds,** a roller coaster that twists and turns up and around on a made-to-scale model of the real Swiss mountain. Anchoring the east end of Fantasyland is **It's a Small World,** a smorgasbord of dancing animatronic dolls, cuckoo clock–covered walls, and variations of the song everyone knows, or soon will know, by heart. Beloved Disney characters like Ariel from The Little Mermaid are also part of the mix. Fantasy Faire is a fairy tale–style village that collects all the Disney princesses together. Each has her own reception nook in the Royal Hall. Condensed retellings of Tangled and Beauty and the Beast take place at the Royal Theatre.

MICKEY'S TOONTOWN
Geared toward small kids, this lopsided cartoonlike downtown, complete with cars and trolleys that invite interactive exploring, is where Mickey, Donald, Goofy, and other classic Disney characters hang their hats. One of the most popular attractions is **Roger Rabbit's Car Toon Spin,** a twisting, turning cab ride through the Toontown of Who Framed Roger Rabbit? You can also walk through **Mickey's House** to meet and be photographed with the famous mouse, take a low-key ride on **Gadget's Go Coaster,** or bounce around the fenced-in playground in front of **Goofy's Playhouse.** For food, you can enjoy pizza at Daisy's Diner, hot dogs at Pluto's Dog House, and sweet treats at Clarabelle's.

Did You Know?

The plain purple teacup in Disneyland's Mad Tea Party ride spins the fastest—though no one knows why.

TOMORROWLAND

This popular section of the park continues to tinker with its future, adding and enhancing rides regularly. *Star Wars*–themed attractions can't be missed, like the immersive, 3-D **Star Tours—The Adventures Continue,** where you can join the Rebellion in a galaxy far, far away. **Finding Nemo's Submarine Voyage** updates the old Submarine Voyage ride with the exploits of Nemo, Dory, Marlin, and other characters from the Disney-Pixar film. Try to visit this popular ride early in the day if you can, and be prepared for a wait. The interactive **Buzz Lightyear Astro Blasters** lets you zap your neighbors with laser beams and compete for the highest score. Hurtle through the cosmos on **Space Mountain** or check out mainstays like the futuristic **Astro Orbiter** rockets, **Star Wars Launch Bay,** which showcases costumes, models, and props from the franchise, and **Star Wars, Path of the Jedi,** which catches viewers up on all the movies with a quick 12-minute film. Put the pedal to the metal while driving a flashy coupe through winding roads at **Autotopia,** powered by Honda. Disneyland Monorail and Disneyland Railroad both have stations here. There's also a video arcade and dancing water fountain that makes a perfect playground for kids on hot summer days. The Jedi Training Academy spotlights future Luke Skywalkers in the crowd.

Besides the nine lands, the daily live-action shows and parades are always crowd pleasers. ■**TIP→ Arrive early to secure a good view; if there are two shows scheduled for the day, the second one tends to be less crowded. A fireworks display lights up weekends and most summer evenings.** Brochures with maps, available at the entrance, list show and parade times.

Disney California Adventure

★ **Disney California Adventure**
AMUSEMENT PARK/WATER PARK | FAMILY | The sprawling Disney California Adventure, adjacent to Disneyland (their entrances face each other), pays tribute to the Golden State with multiple theme areas that re-create vintage architectural styles and embrace several hit Pixar films via engaging attractions. Visitors enter through the art deco–style Buena Vista Street, past shops and a helpful information booth that advises wait times on attractions. The 12-acre Cars Land features Radiator Springs Racers, a speedy trip in six-passenger speedsters through scenes featured in the blockbuster hit. (FastPass tickets for the ride run out early most days, but there is a single rider line to experience the thrills quicker). Other popular attractions include the World of Color, a nighttime water-effects show and Toy Story Midway Mania!, an interactive adventure ride hosted by Woody and Buzz Lightyear. At night the park takes on neon hues as glowing signs light up Route 66 in Cars Land and Pixar Pal-A-Round, a giant Ferris wheel on the Pixar Pier. Cocktails, beer, and wine are available; craft beers and premium wines from California are poured. Live nightly entertainment also features a 1930s jazz troupe that arrives in a vintage jalopy. Some rides have a minimum height limit of 40 inches. Opened in 2021, the Avengers Campus is a land for a new generation of superheroes, focusing on the characters of the Marvel Cinematic Universe. On Web-Slingers: A Spider-man Adventure, guests of all ages can help wrangle Spider-bots while wearing 3-D glasses; the free-falling Guardians of the Galaxy—Mission: BREAKOUT! is more for teens and adults. ⊠ *1313 S. Disneyland Dr., between Ball Rd. and Katella Ave., Anaheim* ☎ *714/781–4636* ⊕ *disneyland.disney.go.com* ⊠ *From $97; parking $20.*

PARK NEIGHBORHOODS
BUENA VISTA STREET

California Adventure's grand entryway re-creates the lost 1920s Los Angeles that Walt Disney encountered when he moved to the Golden State. There's a **Red Car trolley** (modeled after Los Angeles's bygone streetcar line); hop on for the brief ride to Hollywood Land. Buena Vista Street is also home to a Starbucks outlet—within the Fiddler, Fifer and Practical Café—and the upscale Carthay Circle Restaurant and Lounge, which serves modern craft cocktails and beer. The comfy booths of the Carthay Circle restaurant on the second floor feel like a relaxing world away from the theme park outside. Keep an eye out for Officer Blue; he is known to give guests a citation to take home as a unique souvenir.

GRIZZLY PEAK

This woodsy land celebrates the great outdoors. Test your skills on the **Redwood Creek Challenge Trail,** a challenging trek across net ladders and suspension bridges. **Grizzly River Run** mimics the river rapids of the Sierra Nevadas; be prepared to get soaked.

Soarin' Around the World is a spectacular simulated hang-gliding ride over internationally known landmarks like Switzerland's Matterhorn and India's Taj Mahal.

HOLLYWOOD LAND

With a main street modeled after Hollywood Boulevard, a fake sky backdrop, and real soundstages, this area celebrates California's film industry. **Disney Animation** gives you an insider's look at how animators create characters. **Turtle Talk with Crush** lets kids have an unscripted chat with a computer-animated Crush, the sea turtle from *Finding Nemo.* The Hyperion Theater hosts **Frozen,** a 45-minute live performance from a Broadway-size cast with terrific visual effects. ■TIP➔ **Plan on getting in line about half an hour in advance; the show is worth the wait.** On the film-inspired ride **Monsters, Inc. Mike & Sulley to the Rescue,** visitors climb into taxis and travel the streets of Monstropolis on a mission to safely return Boo to her bedroom.

CARS LAND

Amble down Route 66, the main thoroughfare of Cars Land, and discover a pitch-perfect re-creation of the vintage highway. Quick eats are found at the Cozy Cone Motel (in a teepee-shaped motor court) while Flo's V8 café serves hearty comfort food. Start your day at Radiator Springs Racers, the park's most popular attraction, where waits can be two hours or longer. Strap into a nifty sports car and meet the characters of Pixar's *Cars*; the ride ends in a speedy auto race through the red rocks and desert of Radiator Springs. ■TIP➔ **To bypass the line, there's a single-rider option for Radiator Springs Racers.**

PACIFIC WHARF

In the midst of the California Adventure you'll find 10 different dining options, from light snacks to full-service restaurants. The Wine Country Trattoria is a great place for Italian specialties; relax outside on the restaurant's terrace for a casual bite while sipping a California-made craft beer or wine. Mexican cuisine and potent margaritas are available at the Cocina Cucamonga Mexican Grill and Rita's Baja Blenders, and Lucky Fortune Cookery serves Chinese stir-fry dishes.

PARADISE GARDENS PARK

The far corner of California Adventure is a mix of floating, zigzagging, and flying rides: soar via the **Silly Symphony Swings**; **Goofy's Sky School** rollicks and rolls through a cartoon-inspired landscape; and the sleek retro-style gondolas of the **Golden Zephyr** mimic 1920s movies and their sci-fi adventures. Journey through Ariel's colorful world on **The Little Mermaid—Ariel's Undersea Adventure.** The best views of the nighttime music, water, and light show, **World of Color,** are from the paths along Paradise Bay. FastPass tickets are available. Or for a guaranteed spot, book dinner at the Wine Country Trattoria that includes a ticket to a viewing area to catch all the show's stunning visuals.

PIXAR PIER

This section re-creates the glory days of California's seaside piers, themed with Pixar film characters. If you're looking for thrills, join The Incredibles family on the **Incredicoaster** as the fast-moving roller coaster takes its riders from 0 to 55 mph in about four seconds and proceeds through scream tunnels, steeply angled drops, and a 360-degree loop. **Pixar Pal-A-Round,** a giant Ferris wheel, provides a good view of the grounds, though some cars spin and sway for more kicks. There are also carnival games, an aquatic-themed carousel, and **Toy Story Midway Mania!,** an interactive ride where you can take aim at a series of cartoon targets. Soft-serve ice cream, turkey legs, hot dogs, and churros are readily available for quick snacking. At the **Lamplight Lounge** adults can chill out and overlook the action while sipping on craft cocktails.

OTHER ATTRACTIONS

Anaheim GardenWalk

PROMENADE | FAMILY | This popular dining, shopping, and entertainment outdoor complex offers 10 eateries, a bowling lounge, an escape room, and an Art on the Walk showcasing local artists and nonprofit organizations. Monthly and seasonal pop-up events are displayed on the website. ⊠ *400 W. Disney Way, Anaheim* ☎ *562/695–1513* ⊕ *www.anaheimgardenwalk.com.*

Downtown Disney District

AMUSEMENT PARK/WATER PARK | FAMILY | The Downtown Disney District is a 20-acre promenade of dining, shopping, and entertainment that connects the resort's hotels and theme parks. Get refreshed at the bar or dining room at **Splitsville**, a mid-century modern–style bowling alley serving American comfort food. At **Ralph Brennan's Jazz Kitchen** you can dig into New Orleans–style food and music. Enjoy a cold beer at Ballast Point Brewery and gourmet burger at Black Tap Craft

Burgers. Save room for sweets: **Salt and Straw** has gourmet ice cream while **Sprinkles** offers ultrarich cupcakes. Disney merchandise and artwork is showcased at the brightly lit **World of Disney** store. Deck your home and garden with Disney decorative items at **HOME;** they even have a Disney Tails & Pet Collection for your four-legged friends. At the megasize **LEGO Store** there are bigger than life LEGO creations, hands-on demonstrations and space to play with the latest LEGO creations. All visitors must pass through a security checkpoint and metal detectors before entering. ⊠ *1580 Disneyland Dr., Anaheim* ☎ *714/781–4565* ⊕ *disneyland.disney.go.com/downtown-disney* ⊠ *Free.*

🍴 Restaurants

Anaheim White House

$$$$ | ITALIAN | FAMILY | Although a massive fire gutted the Anaheim White House in 2017, owner and executive chef Bruno Serato rebuilt and expanded the local landmark known for its specialty pastas. The 1909-built original mansion was the inspiration for the complete renovation, and Serato added olive trees and a courtyard outside and Italian frescoes and mosaics inside. **Known for:** classic Mediterranean cuisine; popular salmon chocolat (salmon with white chocolate mashed potatoes); friendly chef who is a pillar of the community. $ *Average main: $40* ⊠ *887 S. Anaheim Blvd., Anaheim* ☎ *714/772–1381* ⊕ *www.anaheimwhitehouse.com* ☾ *Closed Mon. and Tues.*

Catal Restaurant and Uva Bar and Cafe

$$ | MEDITERRANEAN | This relaxed bi-level Mediterranean spot offers more than 30 wines by the glass, craft beers, and craft cocktails that pair well with the Spanish-influenced dishes. Upstairs, Catal's menu has tapas, a variety of flavorful paellas, and charcuterie. **Known for:** gourmet burgers; good happy hour; outdoor terrace with Disneyland fireworks views. $ *Average main: $30* ⊠ *Downtown*

Disney District, 1580 S. Disneyland Dr., Suite 103, Anaheim ☎ *714/774–4442* 🌐 *www.patinagroup.com.*

Napa Rose

$$$$ | AMERICAN | Done up in a handsome Craftsman style, Napa Rose's rich seasonal cuisine is matched with an extensive wine list, with 1,500 labels and 80 available by the glass. For a look into the open kitchen, sit at the counter and watch the chefs as they whip up such signature dishes as grilled diver scallops and chanterelles, and lamb pot roast topped with a pomegranate mint glaze. **Known for:** excellent wine list; kid-friendly options; gorgeous dining room. [$] *Average main: $50* ✉ *Disney's Grand Californian Hotel, 1600 S. Disneyland Dr., Anaheim* ☎ *714/300–7170, 714/781–3463 reservations* 🌐 *disneyland.disney.go.com/grand-californian-hotel/napa-rose.*

🛏 Hotels

Anaheim Fairfield Inn by Marriott

$$ | HOTEL | FAMILY | Attentive service and a great location just across the street from Disneyland's entrance makes this high-rise hotel a big draw for families. **Pros:** across the street from Disneyland; Disney-themed guest rooms; reasonable rates for the area. **Cons:** some rooms have just parking lot views; lack of green space; can be noisy when guests return from parks. [$] *Rooms from: $225* ✉ *1460 S. Harbor Blvd., Anaheim* ☎ *714/772–6777* 🌐 *www.marriott.com* 🛏 *467 rooms* 🍴 *No meals.*

Anaheim Marriott

$ | RESORT | This busy two-tower hotel is well equipped for business travelers, and has nice amenities for vacationers. **Pros:** balconies in all rooms; large pool and deck area; offers shuttle to Disneyland. **Cons:** most rooms only have a shower; popular with conventioneers who often take over the place; no Disney-themed guest rooms. [$] *Rooms from: $159* ✉ *700 W. Convention Way, Anaheim* ☎ *714/750–8000, 888/236–2427* 🌐 *www.marriott.com* 🛏 *1030 rooms* 🍴 *No meals.*

Desert Palms Hotel and Suites

$ | HOTEL | FAMILY | This hotel midway between Disneyland and the Anaheim Convention Center is a great value, with some one-bedroom suites that can accommodate groups of six or more. **Pros:** large lobby that welcomes with Disney decor; variety of special rates; free Wi-Fi. **Cons:** drab exterior fronts busy Katella Avenue; small pool gets limited sun; some noise issues. [$] *Rooms from: $125* ✉ *631 W. Katella Ave., Anaheim* ☎ *714/535–1133, 888/521–6420* 🌐 *www.desertpalmshotel.com* 🛏 *195 rooms* 🍴 *No meals.*

★ Disney's Grand Californian Hotel and Spa

$$$$ | RESORT | FAMILY | The most opulent of Disneyland's three hotels, the Craftsman-style Grand Californian offers views of Disney California Adventure and Downtown Disney. **Pros:** gorgeous lobby; family-friendly with three beautiful pools; direct access to California Adventure. **Cons:** very expensive; standard rooms are on the small side; waits to dine at on-site restaurants. [$] *Rooms from: $625* ✉ *1600 S. Disneyland Dr., Anaheim* ☎ *714/635–2300* 🌐 *disneyland.disney.go.com/grand-californian-hotel* 🛏 *1019 rooms* 🍴 *No meals.*

Doubletree Suites by Hilton Hotel Anaheim Resort-Convention Center

$ | HOTEL | This busy hotel near the Anaheim Convention Center and a 20-minute walk from Disneyland caters to business travelers and vacationers alike. **Pros:** huge suites; walking distance to a variety of restaurants; chocolate chip cookies at check-in. **Cons:** a bit far from Disneyland; pool area is small; daily parking fee. [$] *Rooms from: $153* ✉ *2085 S. Harbor Blvd., Anaheim* ☎ *714/750–3000, 800/215–7316* 🌐 *doubletreeanaheim.com* 🛏 *252 rooms* 🍴 *No meals.*

Hilton Anaheim

$ | **HOTEL** | **FAMILY** | Next to the Anaheim Convention Center, this busy Hilton is the third-largest hotel in Southern California, with a restaurant and food court, hopping lobby lounge with communal tables, a full-service gym, and its own Starbucks. **Pros:** 15-minute walk to Disneyland; fast-casual dining options; some rooms have views of the park fireworks. **Cons:** huge size can be daunting; fee to use health club; megasize parking lot. $ *Rooms from: $159* ✉ *777 Convention Way, Anaheim* ☎ *714/750–4321, 800/445–8667* ⊕ *www.hiltonanaheimhotel.com* ⟳ *1572 rooms* ⦿ *No meals.*

Hyatt Regency Orange County

$ | **HOTEL** | **FAMILY** | This Disney-friendly hotel sells park tickets in the lobby and offers a free shuttle to Disneyland. **Pros:** large suites for families; modern rooms in coastal colors; two pools, one kid-friendly and one with adult-only hours. **Cons:** North Tower rooms are dated in decor and furniture; parking is $28 a day; a little more than 1 mile from Disneyland Parks. $ *Rooms from: $199* ✉ *11199 Harbor Blvd., Anaheim* ☎ *714/750–1234* ⊕ *www.hyatt.com* ⟳ *653 rooms* ⦿ *No meals.*

★ JW Marriott, Anaheim Resort

$$ | **RESORT** | **FAMILY** | The first luxury hotel in the area to open outside the Disneyland Resorts and the first JW Marriott in Orange County, this resort pays homage to the agricultural history of the region with unique architectural elements. **Pros:** gorgeous artwork throughout; great fireworks views; luxury amenities. **Cons:** popular event space for conventions and big gatherings; no Disneyland-themed rooms; valet parking only ($40 a day). $ *Rooms from: $225* ✉ *1775 S. Clementine St., Anaheim* ☎ *714/294–7800* ⊕ *www.marriott.com* ⟳ *468 rooms* ⦿ *No meals.*

Majestic Garden Hotel

$ | **HOTEL** | **FAMILY** | If you're hoping to escape from the commercial atmosphere of the hotels near Disneyland and California Adventure, consider this sprawling replica of an English Tudor estate. **Pros:** large, attractive lobby; spacious rooms with comfortable beds; shuttle to the theme parks. **Cons:** confusing layout; hotel sits close to a busy freeway; small bathrooms. $ *Rooms from: $150* ✉ *900 S. Disneyland Dr., Anaheim* ☎ *714/778–1700, 844/227–8535* ⊕ *www.majesticgardenhotel.com* ⟳ *489 rooms* ⦿ *No meals.*

🏃 Activities

Anaheim Ducks

HOCKEY | **FAMILY** | The National Hockey League's Anaheim Ducks, winners of the 2007 Stanley Cup, play at Honda Center. ✉ *Honda Center, 2695 E. Katella Ave., Anaheim* ☎ *877/945–3946* ⊕ *nhl.com/ducks.*

Los Angeles Angels of Anaheim

BASEBALL/SOFTBALL | **FAMILY** | Professional baseball's Los Angeles Angels of Anaheim have called Anaheim and Angel Stadium home since 1966. An "Outfield Extravaganza" celebrates great plays on the field, with fireworks and a geyser exploding over a model evoking the California coast. ✉ *Angel Stadium, 2000 E. Gene Autry Way, Anaheim* ☎ *714/420–4357* ⊕ *www.angels.com* Ⓜ *Metrolink Angels Express.*

Knott's Berry Farm

25 miles south of Los Angeles, via I–5, in Buena Park.

Once an actual farm, Knott's Berry Farm now offers a non-Disney theme park option for anyone with a love of roller coasters and boysenberries.

Knott's Berry Farm

AMUSEMENT PARK/WATER PARK | FAMILY | The land where the boysenberry was invented (by crossing raspberry, blackberry, and loganberry bushes) is now occupied by a popular amusement park. In 1934, Cordelia Knott began serving chicken dinners on her wedding china to supplement her family's income. The dinners and her boysenberry pies proved more profitable than her husband Walter's farm, so the two moved first into the restaurant business and then into the entertainment business. The park is now a 160-acre complex with close to 40 rides, dozens of restaurants and shops, arcade games, live shows, and a brick-by-brick replica of Philadelphia's Independence Hall. Take a step back into the 1880s while walking through Knott's Old West Ghost Town. Ride on a horse-drawn stagecoach or board a steam engine to start your journey into the park; just keep your valuables close to you, as bandits might enter your train car and put on quite a show. Camp Snoopy has plenty to keep small children occupied as they explore 15 kid-friendly attractions. The park is also known for its awesome thrill rides in the Boardwalk area, including the zooming HangTime that pauses dramatically then drops nearly 15 stories, and the Xcelerator that goes from zero to 80 mph in 2.3 seconds.

And, yes you can still get that boysenberry pie, as well as boysenberry soft serve ice cream, jam, juice, you name it. There's even a Boysenberry Food Festival once a year. In the fall, part of the park is turned into Knott's Scary Farm, a popular activity for teens and adults. Buy adult tickets online for a discount; FastLane wristbands give you quicker access to the most popular rides. Nearby Knott's Soak City is open during the summer for guests who want to float on the lazy river, go down waterslides, and swim in the wave pool. ⊠ 8039 Beach Blvd., Buena Park ✛ Between La Palma Ave. and Crescent St., 2 blocks south of Hwy. 91 ☎ 714/220–5200 ⊕ www.knotts.com ⊠ $82.

Park Neighborhoods

THE BOARDWALK

Not-for-the-squeamish thrill rides and skill-based games dominate the scene at the **Boardwalk.** Roller coasters—Coast Rider, Surfside Glider, and Pacific Scrambler—surround a pond that keeps things cooler on hot days. **HangTime** towers 150 feet above the boardwalk as coaster cars hang, invert and drop the equivalent of 15 stories. The boardwalk is also home to a string of test-your-skill games that are fun to watch whether you're playing or not, and Johnny Rockets, the park's all-American diner.

CAMP SNOOPY

It can be gridlock on weekends, but kids love this miniature High Sierra wonderland where the *Peanuts* gang hangs out. Tykes can push and pump their own mini-mining cars on **Huff and Puff,** soar around via **Charlie Brown's Kite Flyer,** and hop aboard **Woodstock's Airmail,** a kids' version of the park's Supreme Scream ride. Most of the rides here are geared toward kids only, leaving parents to cheer them on from the sidelines. **Sierra Sidewinder,** a roller coaster near the entrance of Camp Snoopy, is aimed at older children, with spinning saucer-type vehicles that go a maximum speed of 37 mph.

FIESTA VILLAGE

Over in **Fiesta Village** are two more musts for adrenaline junkies: **Montezooma's Revenge,** a roller coaster that goes from 0 to 55 mph in less than five seconds, and **Jaguar!,** a three-minute long coaster, which simulates the motions of a cat stalking its prey, twisting, spiraling, and speeding up and slowing down as it takes you on its stomach-dropping course through a Mayan temple. There's also **Hat Dance,** a version of the spinning teacups but with sombreros, and a 100-year-old **Dentzel carousel,** complete with an antique organ and menagerie of hand-carved animals. In a nod to history, there are restored scale models of the California Missions at Fiesta Village's southern entrance.

GHOST TOWN

Clusters of authentic old buildings relocated from their original mining-town sites mark this section of the park. You can stroll down the street, stop and chat with a blacksmith, pan for gold (for a fee), crack open a geode, check out the chalkboard of a circa-1879 one-room schoolhouse, and ride an original Butterfield stagecoach. Looming over it all is **GhostRider,** Orange County's first wooden roller coaster. Traveling up to 56 mph and reaching 118 feet at its highest point, the park's biggest attraction is riddled with sudden dips and curves, subjecting riders to forces up to three times that of gravity. On the Western-themed **Silver Bullet,** riders are sent to a height of 146 feet and then back down 109 feet. Riders spiral, corkscrew, fly into a cobra roll, and experience overbanked curves. The **Calico Mine** ride descends into a replica of a working gold mine complete with 50 animatronic figures. The **Timber Mountain Log Ride** is a visitor favorite: the flume ride tours through pioneer scenes before splashing down. Also found here is the **Pony Express,** a roller coaster that lets riders saddle up on packs of "horses" tethered to platforms that take off on a series of hairpin turns and travel up to 38 mph. Take a step inside the **Western Trails Museum,** a dusty old gem full of Old West memorabilia and rural Americana, plus menus from the original chicken restaurant and an impressive antique button collection. **Calico Railroad** departs regularly from Ghost Town station for a round-trip tour of the park (bandit holdups notwithstanding). You can order a boysenberry soft-serve ice-cream cone nearby afterward.

This section is also home to **Big Foot Rapids,** a splash-fest of white-water river rafting over towering cliffs, cascading waterfalls, and wild rapids. Don't miss the visually stunning show at **Mystery Lodge,** which tells the story of Native Americans in the Pacific Northwest with lights, music, and special effects.

INDIAN TRAILS

Celebrate Native American traditions through interactive exhibits like tepees and daily dance and storytelling performances.

Knott's Soak City Waterpark is directly across from the main park on 13 acres next to Independence Hall. It has a dozen major water rides; **Pacific Spin** is an oversize waterslide that drops riders 75 feet into a catch pool. There's also a children's pool, a 750,000-gallon wave pool, and a fun house. Soak City's season runs mid-May to mid-September. It's open daily after Memorial Day, weekends only after Labor Day, and then closes for the season.

🍴 Restaurants

★ Mrs. Knott's Chicken Dinner Restaurant
$$ | **AMERICAN** | **FAMILY** | Cordelia Knott's fried chicken and boysenberry pies drew crowds so big that Knott's Berry Farm was built to keep the hungry customers occupied while they waited. The restaurant's current incarnation (outside the park's entrance) still serves crispy fried chicken, along with fluffy handmade biscuits, mashed potatoes, and Mrs. Knott's signature chilled cherry-rhubarb compote. **Known for:** famous fried chicken; long waits especially on weekends; pies and desserts. [$] *Average main: $22* ✉ *Knott's Berry Farm Marketplace, 8039 Beach Blvd., Buena Park* ☎ *714/220–5200* 🌐 *www.knotts.com/california-marketplace/mrs-knott-s-chicken-dinner-restaurant.*

🛏 Hotels

Knott's Berry Farm Hotel
$ | **HOTEL** | **FAMILY** | This convenient low-rise hotel is run by the park and sits right on park grounds surrounded by graceful palm trees. **Pros:** easy access to Knott's Berry Farm; tennis court; decent on-site dining. **Cons:** lobby and hallways can be noisy; can hear the nearby roller coaster;

dated room decor. $ *Rooms from: $129* ✉ *7675 Crescent Ave., Buena Park* ☎ *714/995–1111, 866/752–2444* ⊕ *www. knotts.com/knotts-berry-farm-hotel* ⤳ *320 rooms* ❘○❘ *No meals.*

Huntington Beach

40 miles southeast of Los Angeles.

Once a sleepy residential town with little more than a string of rugged surf shops, Huntington Beach has transformed itself into a resort destination, commonly referred to as Surf City U.S.A. The town's appeal is its broad white-sand beaches with often-towering waves, complemented by a lively pier, shops, and restaurants on Main Street, and a growing collection of resort hotels.

A draw for sports fans and partiers of all stripes is the U.S. Open professional surf competition, which brings a festive atmosphere to town annually in late July. There's even a Surfing Walk of Fame, with plaques set in the sidewalk around the intersection of PCH and Main Street.

ESSENTIALS
VISITOR INFORMATION Visit Huntington Beach. ✉ *301 Main St., Suite 212* ☎ *714/969–3492, 800/729–6232* ⊕ *www. surfcityusa.com.*

 Sights

Bolsa Chica Ecological Reserve
NATURE PRESERVE | FAMILY | Wildlife lovers and bird-watchers flock to Bolsa Chica Ecological Reserve, which has a 1,445-acre salt marsh where 302 bird species—including great blue herons, snowy and great egrets, and brown pelicans—have been spotted. Throughout the reserve are trails for bird-watching, including a comfortable 1½-mile loop. There are two entrances off the Pacific Coast Highway: one close to the Interpretive Center and a second one 1 mile south on Warner Avenue, opposite Bolsa Chica State Beach.

Each parking lot connects to 4 miles of walking and hiking trails with scenic overlooks. ✉ *Bolsa Chica Wetlands Interpretive Center, 3842 Warner Ave.* ☎ *714/846–1114* ⊕ *www.bolsachica.org* ✉ *Free.*

Bolsa Chica State Beach
BEACH—SIGHT | FAMILY | In the northern section of the city, Bolsa Chica State Beach is usually less crowded than its southern neighbors. The sand is somewhat gritty and not the cleanest, but swells make it a hot surfing spot. Picnic sites can be reserved in advance. Fire pits attract beachgoers most nights. **Amenities:** food and drink; lifeguards; parking; showers; toilets. **Best for:** sunset; surfing; swimming; walking; RV camping. ✉ *Pacific Coast Hwy., between Seapoint St. and Warner Ave.* ☎ *714/846–3460* ⊕ *www.parks.ca.gov* ✉ *$15 parking.*

Huntington Beach Pier
MARINA | FAMILY | This municipal pier stretches 1,856 feet out to sea, past the powerful waves that gave Huntington Beach the title of "Surf City U.S.A." Well above the waves, it's a prime vantage point to watch the dozens of surfers in the water below. On the pier you'll find a snack shop and a shop where you can buy fishing rod rentals, tackle, and bait to fish off the pier. ✉ *Pacific Coast Hwy.* ⊕ *www.surfcityusa.com.*

Huntington City Beach
BEACH—SIGHT | FAMILY | Stretching for 3½ miles from Bolsa Chica State Beach to Huntington State Beach, Huntington City Beach is most crowded around the pier; amateur and professional surfers brave the waves daily. Fire pits, numerous concession stands, an area for dogs, and well-raked white sand make this a popular beach come summertime. **Amenities:** food and drink; lifeguards; parking; showers; toilets. **Best for:** sunset; surfing; swimming; walking. ✉ *Pacific Coast Hwy., from Beach Blvd. to Seapoint St.* ☎ *714/536–5281, 714/536–9303 surf report* ⊕ *www. huntingtonbeachca.gov/residents/beach_info* ✉ *Parking from $15.*

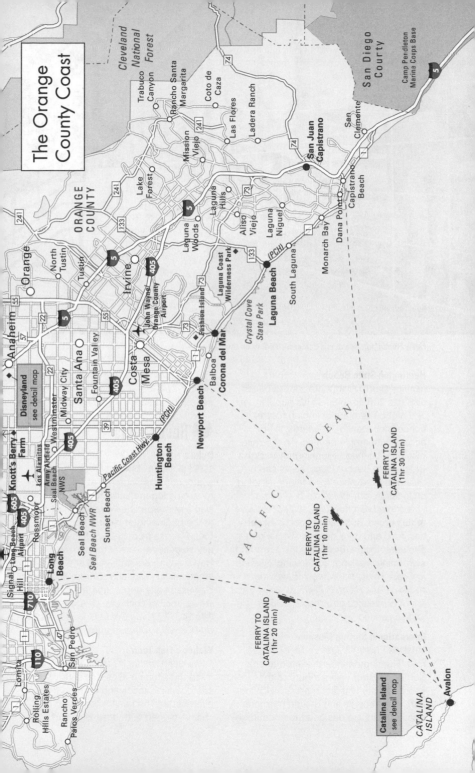

Lively Huntington Beach is a center for surfing on the coast.

Huntington State Beach

BEACH—SIGHT | **FAMILY** | This state beach also has 200 fire pits, so it's popular day and night. There are changing rooms, concession stands, lifeguards, Wi-Fi access, and ample parking. An 8.5-mile bike path connects Hunnington to Bolsa Chica State Beach. Picnic areas can be reserved in advance for a fee depending on location; otherwise it's first come, first served. On hot days, expect crowds at this broad, soft sandy beach. **Amenities:** food and drink; lifeguards; parking; showers; toilets. **Best for:** sunset; surfing; swimming; walking; surf fishing. ✉ *Pacific Coast Hwy., from Beach Blvd. south to Santa Ana River* ☎ *714/536–1454* 🌐 *www.parks.ca.gov/?page_id=643* 🎟 *$15 parking.*

International Surfing Museum

MUSEUM | **FAMILY** | Just up Main Street from Huntington Pier, the International Surfing Museum pays tribute to the sport's greats with an impressive collection of surfboards and related memorabilia. Exhibits are designed to encourage kids to study and to surf. ✉ *411 Olive Ave.* ☎ *714/465–4350* 🌐 *www.surfingmuseum.org* 🎟 *$3* 🕒 *Closed Mon.*

🍴 Restaurants

Duke's

$$$$ | **SEAFOOD** | **FAMILY** | Freshly caught seafood reigns supreme at this homage to surfing legend Duke Kahanamoku; it's also a prime people-watching spot right at the beginning of Huntington Beach Pier. Choose from several fish-of-the-day selections—many topped with Hawaiian ingredients—and shellfish like lobster, king crab, and shrimp. **Known for:** Hawaiian-style decor; gorgeous sunset views; mai tai cocktails. [$] *Average main: $45* ✉ *317 Pacific Coast Hwy.* ☎ *714/374–6446* 🌐 *www.dukeshuntington.com.*

Wahoo's Fish Taco

$ | **MEXICAN FUSION** | **FAMILY** | Proximity to the ocean makes this eatery's seafood-filled tacos and burritos taste even better. The healthy fast-food chain—tagged with dozens of surf stickers—brought Baja's fish tacos north of the border to quick success. **Known for:** organic ingredients; Hawaiian onion ring burrito; casual beachy ambience. $ *Average main: $12* ✉ *120 Main St.* ☎ *714/536–2050* ⊕ *www.wahoos.com.*

 ## Hotels

Hyatt Regency Huntington Beach Resort and Spa

$$$ | **RESORT** | **FAMILY** | The Spanish design of this sprawling property incorporates arched courtyards, beautiful tiled fountains, and fire pits, all a nod to California's Mission period. **Pros:** close to beach; variety of pool areas; family-friendly vibe. **Cons:** some partial ocean-view rooms; resort and daily valet fees; some rooms can hear the traffic on PCH. $ *Rooms from: $360* ✉ *21500 Pacific Coast Hwy.* ☎ *714/698–1234* ⊕ *www.hyatt.com* ⬲ *517 rooms* ⦿ *No meals.*

Kimpton Shorebreak Resort

$$ | **HOTEL** | **FAMILY** | This surfer-style Kimpton hotel is not only across the street from the beach, but it's the closest hotel to the Huntington Beach Pier and Main Street. **Pros:** proximity to beach and shops; free surfboard storage; quiet rooms despite central location. **Cons:** $35 valet parking fee; courtyard rooms have uninspiring alley views; additional resort fee to receive best perks. $ *Rooms from: $250* ✉ *500 Pacific Coast Hwy.* ☎ *714/861–4470, 877/212–8597* ⊕ *www.shorebreakhotel.com* ⬲ *157 rooms* ⦿ *No meals.*

Pasea Hotel & Spa

$$$ | **RESORT** | **FAMILY** | Painted in shades of sea blue, the contemporary-styled Pasea is a rarity along the O.C. coast: at eight stories, almost every room has an ocean view and all have balconies to take in the fresh breezes. **Pros:** excellent ocean views; beach butlers to provide everything for a beach day; supercomfortable beds. **Cons:** pool can

get crowded; $40 valet parking fee; noise issues from nearby bars at Pacific City. $ *Rooms from: $350* ✉ *21080 Pacific Coast Hwy.* ☎ *866/478–9702* ⊕ *www.meritagecollection.com/pasea-hotel* ⬲ *250 rooms* ⦿ *No meals.*

The Waterfront Beach Resort, a Hilton Hotel

$$ | **RESORT** | **FAMILY** | This two-tower resort offers a variety of amenities for families, couples, and business travelers alike. **Pros:** quick walk to beach and pier; fun surf decor; oceanfront views from rooms. **Cons:** different towers have different vibes; valet parking only for $42; crowded pool and deck during summer. $ *Rooms from: $239* ✉ *21100 Pacific Coast Hwy.* ☎ *714/845–8000, 855/271–3617* ⊕ *www.waterfrontresort.com* ⬲ *437 rooms* ⦿ *No meals.*

 ## Shopping

HSS Main St

SPORTING GOODS | **FAMILY** | The largest surf-gear source in town is Huntington Surf and Sport, right across from Huntington Pier. Staffed by true surf enthusiasts, it's also one of the only surf shops with a coffee counter inside. Surfboard rentals are $15 an hour or $50 all day while soft top boards are $18 per hour or $30 a day. They also rent bodyboards and wetsuits. ✉ *300 Pacific Coast Hwy.* ☎ *714/841–4000* ⊕ *www.hsssurf.com.*

 ## Activities

SURFING
Corky Carroll's Surf School

SURFING | **FAMILY** | This surf school organizes lessons, weeklong workshops, and international surf camps at Bolsa Chica State Beach. They also provide hard and soft top boards and wetsuits to rent during your lesson. ✉ *Bolsa Chica State Beach, Lifeguard Tower 18* ☎ *714/969–3959* ⊕ *www.surfschool.net.*

Dwight's Beach Concession

BICYCLING | FAMILY | You can rent surrey or cruiser bikes, wet suits, surfboards, bodyboards, umbrellas, and beach chairs at Dwight's, one block south of Huntington Pier. They also serve casual beach food, including their world-famous cheese strips. ✉ *201 Pacific Coast Hwy.* ☎ *714/536–8083* ⊕ *www.dwightsbeach-concession.com.*

Zack's HB

BICYCLING | FAMILY | This place offers beach equipment, surfing lessons and boards, wet suits, and bicycles. Food like hamburgers, corn dogs, fish-and-chips, grilled mahimahi, and Mexican favorites are sold here, too. ✉ *405 Pacific Coast Hwy., at Main St.* ☎ *714/536–0215* ⊕ *www.zackssurfcity.com.*

Newport Beach

6 miles south of Huntington Beach.

Newport Beach has evolved from a simple seaside village to an icon of chic coastal living. Its ritzy reputation comes from megayachts bobbing in the harbor, boutiques that rival those in Beverly Hills, and spectacular homes overlooking the ocean.

The city boasts some of the cleanest beaches in Southern California; inland Newport Beach's concentration of high-rise office buildings, shopping centers, and luxury hotels drives the economy. But on the city's Balboa Peninsula, you can still catch a glimpse of a more humble, down-to-earth town scattered with taco spots, tackle shops, and sailor bars.

VISITOR INFORMATION Visit Newport Beach Concierge. ✉ *Atrium Court at Fashion Island, 1600 Newport Center Dr.* ☎ *949/719–6100* ⊕ *www.newport-beachandco.com.*

 Sights

★ Balboa Island

BEACH—SIGHT | FAMILY | This sliver of terra firma in Newport Harbor boasts quaint streets tightly packed with impossibly charming multimillion-dollar cottages. The island's main drag, Marine Avenue, is lined with equally picturesque cafés, frozen chocolate banana shops, and apparel stores. Rent a bike and pedal around on the car-free bike path and boardwalk encircling much of the island for an easy and scenic ramble. Be sure to visit the free Balboa Island Museum, too.

To get here, you can either park your car on the mainland side of the PCH in Newport Beach and walk or bike over the bridge onto Marine Avenue, or take the Balboa Island Ferry, the country's longest-running auto ferry. The one-way fare is $1.25 for an adult pedestrian; $1.50 for an adult with a bike; and $2.25 to take your car on board. ✉ *Marine Ave.* ☎ *949/719–6100* ⊕ *www.visitnewport-beach.com.*

Balboa Peninsula

BEACH—SIGHT | FAMILY | Newport's best beaches are on Balboa Peninsula, where many jetties pave the way to ideal swimming areas. The most intense spot for bodysurfing in Orange County, and arguably on the West Coast, known as the **Wedge,** is at the south end of the peninsula. It was created by accident in the 1930s when the Federal Works Progress Administration built a jetty to protect Newport Harbor. ⚠ **Rip currents and punishing waves mean it's strictly for the pros—but it sure is fun to watch an experienced local ride it.** ✉ *Newport Beach* ⊕ *www.visitnewportbeach.com/beaches-and-parks/the-wedge.*

Newport Beach Pier

BEACH—SIGHT | FAMILY | Jutting out into the ocean near 21st Street, Newport Pier is a popular fishing spot. Below is 5 miles of sandy beach for sunbathing, surfing, and walking along the beach. Street

Newport Beach is another popular place in the O.C. to catch waves.

parking is difficult, so grab the first space you find and be prepared to walk. Early on Wednesday–Sunday morning you're likely to encounter dory fishermen hawking their predawn catches, as they've done for generations. On weekends the area is alive with kids of all ages on in-line skates, skateboards, and bikes dodging pedestrians and whizzing past fast-food joints and classic dive bars. Skate, bike, and surfboard rental shops are nearby. ✉ *70 Newport Pier* ☎ *949/644–3309* 🌐 *www.visitnewportbeach.com.*

★ Newport Harbor

BEACH—SIGHT | **FAMILY** | Sheltering nearly 16,000 small boats, Newport Harbor may seduce even those who don't own a yacht. Spend an afternoon exploring the charming avenues and surrounding alleys or take California's longest-running auto ferry across to Balboa Island, popular with pedestrians, bicyclists, and automobiles. Several grassy areas on the primarily residential Lido Isle have views of the water. To truly experience the harbor, rent a kayak or an electric Duffy boat for a pleasant picnic cruise or try stand-up paddleboarding to explore the sheltered waters. ✉ *Pacific Coast Hwy.* 🌐 *www.balboaislandferry.com.*

Sculpture Exhibition in Civic Center Park

PUBLIC ART | **FAMILY** | This outdoor museum is a favorite walking spot for locals and visitors. Look for the array of meaningful and whimsical public art sculptures on a hillside looking out toward the Pacific Ocean. Families love "Bunnyhenge," a collection of 14 white bunny statues arranged in a circle. ✉ *1000 Avocado Ave.* ☎ *949/717–3802* 🌐 *www.newportbeachca.gov.*

🍴 Restaurants

Basilic Restaurant

$$$ | **BRASSERIE** | This intimate French-Swiss bistro adds a touch of old-world elegance to Balboa Island with its white linen and flower-topped tables. Chef Bernard Althaus grows the herbs used in his classic French dishes. **Known for:** French classics; fine wine; old-school ambience. [$] *Average main: $32* ✉ *217 Marine Ave., Balboa*

Island ☎ *949/673–0570* ⊕ *www.basilicres-taurant.com* ⊗ *Closed Sun. and Mon.*

★ Bear Flag Fish Co.

$ | SEAFOOD | FAMILY | Expect long lines in summer at this indoor/outdoor dining spot serving up the freshest local fish (swordfish, sea bass, halibut, and tuna) and a wide range of creative seafood dishes (the Hawaiian-style *poke* salad with ahi tuna is a local favorite). Order at the counter, which doubles as a seafood market, and sit inside the airy dining room or outside on a grand patio. **Known for:** freshest seafood thanks to restaurant's own fishing boat; fish tacos with homemade hot sauce; craft beers. $ *Average main: $15* ⊠ *Newport Peninsula, 3421 Via Lido* ☎ *949/673–3474* ⊕ *www.bearflagfishco.com.*

Bluewater Grill

$$$ | SEAFOOD | FAMILY | On the site of an old sportfishing dock, this popular spot offers a variety of seafood, from Idaho trout amandine and lemon pepper mahimahi to lobster, pan-seared scallops, and chipotle-blackened swordfish. There's a tranquil bay view from either the dining room, which is adorned with early-1900s fishing photos, or the waterfront patio. **Known for:** boat and harbor views; happy hour specials; daily-changing menu of fresh fish. $ *Average main: $35* ⊠ *Lido Peninsula, 630 Lido Park Dr.* ☎ *949/675–3474* ⊕ *www.bluewatergrill.com.*

The Cannery

$$$ | SEAFOOD | This 1920s cannery building still teems with fish, but now they go into dishes on the eclectic Pacific Rim menu rather than being packed into crates. Settle in at the sushi bar, in the dining room, or on the patio before choosing between sashimi, freshly shucked oysters, or cilantro-marinated fish tacos. **Known for:** waterfront views; seafood specialties; craft cocktails. $ *Average main: $37* ⊠ *3010 Lafayette Rd.* ☎ *949/566–0060* ⊕ *www.cannerynewport.com* ⊗ *Closed Mon. and Tues.*

Gulfstream

$$$ | SEAFOOD | FAMILY | Established in 1999, this on-trend restaurant has an open kitchen, comfortable booths, and outdoor seating. The patio is a fantastic place to hang out to enjoy a shrimp cocktail and glass of wine. **Known for:** oysters on the half shell; local hangout; outdoor patio. $ *Average main: $35* ⊠ *850 Avocado Ave.* ☎ *949/718–0188* ⊕ *www.gulfstreamrestaurant.com.*

Hotels

Balboa Bay Resort

$$$ | RESORT | FAMILY | Sharing the same frontage as the private Balboa Bay Club that long ago hosted Humphrey Bogart, Lauren Bacall, and Ronald Reagan, this waterfront resort has one of the best bay views around, especially at its lively gastropub. **Pros:** exquisite bayfront views; comfortable beds; two popular restaurants for locals and visitors. **Cons:** swimming pool in the middle of the resort has no views; $35 nightly hospitality fee; some rooms don't face the bay. $ *Rooms from: $339* ⊠ *1221 W. Coast Hwy.* ☎ *949/645–5000* ⊕ *www.balboabayresort.com* ⊅ *159 rooms* ⚄ *No meals.*

Fashion Island Hotel

$$ | RESORT | FAMILY | Across a palm tree–lined boulevard from stylish Fashion Island, this 20-story tower caters to business types during the week and leisure travelers on weekends. **Pros:** lively lounge scene; large tropical heated pool; great location. **Cons:** steep valet parking prices; some rooms have views of mall parking; destination fee added to price. $ *Rooms from: $295* ⊠ *690 Newport Center Dr.* ☎ *949/759–0808, 877/591–9145* ⊕ *www.fashionislandhotel.com* ⊅ *295 rooms* ⚄ *No meals.*

Hyatt Regency Newport Beach

$$ | RESORT | FAMILY | The best aspect of this beloved resort-style Newport hotel is its lushly landscaped acres: 26 of them, all overlooking the Back Bay. The casually elegant architecture, spread over the generous grounds, will appeal to travelers weary of high-rise hotels. **Pros:** high-quality linens; centrally located for shopping; numerous sport activities offered. **Cons:** $30 self-parking is far from main property; 10-minute drive to beach; $30 daily resort fee. [$] *Rooms from: $235* ✉ *1107 Jamboree Rd.* ☎ *949/729–1234* 🌐 *www.hyatt.com* 🛏 *410 rooms* 🍴 *No meals.*

★Lido House, Autograph Collection
$$$ | RESORT | FAMILY | This Marriott Autograph Collection resort is located at the gateway of the exclusive Lido Island and three blocks from the beach. **Pros:** large hot tub and pool deck; lively hotel bar; free bikes to cruise the nearby boardwalk. **Cons:** pricey restaurant; $35 resort fee; $43 valet parking. [$] *Rooms from: $325* ✉ *3300 Newport Blvd., Balboa Island* ☎ *949/524–8500* 🌐 *www.lidohousehotel.com* 🛏 *130 rooms, 5 cottages* 🍴 *No meals.*

Newport Beach Hotel
$$$$ | B&B/INN | FAMILY | At this charming boutique hotel just steps from the beach and Newport Beach Pier, some of the coastal-themed guest rooms have ocean views, all have complimentary Wi-Fi, and most offer a whirlpool bathtub and shower. **Pros:** beach and oceanview guest rooms; in a lively area near restaurants; steps to the pier and beach. **Cons:** some rooms are small; not all rooms have views; parking is $25 a day. [$] *Rooms from: $425* ✉ *2306 W. Oceanfront* ☎ *949/673–7030* 🌐 *www.thenewportbeachhotel.com* 🛏 *15 rooms* 🍴 *Free breakfast.*

Newport Beach Marriott Hotel and Spa
$$ | RESORT | FAMILY | This centrally located property is across the street from the popular Fashion Island shopping and dining complex. **Pros:** million-dollar views of Orange County and beyond; large spa; central location across from Fashion Island. **Cons:** sprawling floor plan; smaller bathrooms; valet parking $36 a day. [$] *Rooms from: $229* ✉ *900 Newport Center Dr.* ☎ *949/640–4000* 🌐 *www.marriott.com* 🛏 *523 rooms* 🍴 *No meals.*

Shopping

★Fashion Island
STORE/MALL | Shake the sand out of your shoes to head inland to the ritzy Fashion Island outdoor mall, a cluster of archways and courtyards complete with koi pond, fountains, and a mix of high-end shopping and chain dining. It has the luxe department stores Neiman Marcus, Nordstrom, and Bloomingdale's, plus expensive boutiques like Trina Turk, Kate Spade, and Michael Stars. ✉ *401 Newport Center Dr., between Jamboree and MacArthur Blvds., off PCH* ☎ *949/721–2000, 855/658–8527* 🌐 *www.fashionisland.com.*

Activities

BOAT RENTALS

Balboa Boat Rentals
BOATING | FAMILY | You can tour the waterways surrounding Lido and Balboa isles on six-person power motorboats ($85 an hour), and electric Duffy boats ($95 to $115 an hour for 8 to 12 people) at Balboa Boat Rentals. ✉ *510 E. Edgewater Ave., Balboa Island* ☎ *855/690–0794* 🌐 *www.boats4rent.com.*

BOAT TOURS

Catalina Flyer
TOUR—SPORTS | FAMILY | At Balboa Pavilion, the *Catalina Flyer* operates a 90-minute round-trip passage daily to Catalina Island for $70. Reservations are required; check the schedule for times, as crossings may be rescheduled due to weather or annual maintenance. All day parking is $27 a day in a nearby Newport Beach lot. Payment is made at self-serve pay stations. ✉ *400 Main St., Balboa Island* ☎ *949/673–5245* 🌐 *www.catalinainfo.com.*

A whimbrel hunts for mussels at Crystal Cove State Park.

Hornblower Cruises and Events

TOUR—SPORTS | This operator books two-hour harbor cruises, Sunday brunch cruises, and three-hour weekend dinner cruises with dancing. The trips traverse the mostly placid and scenic waters of Newport Harbor. ✉ *2431 W. Coast Hwy.* ☎ *949/646–0155* ⊕ *www.hornblower. com.*

FISHING

Davey's Locker

FISHING | **FAMILY** | In addition to a complete tackle shop, Davey's Locker offers two-hour whale-watching cruises starting at $28, half-day sportfishing trips starting at $34; and overnight fishing excursions starting at $149. ✉ *Balboa Pavilion, 400 Main St., Balboa Island* ☎ *949/673–1434* ⊕ *www.daveyslocker.com.*

Corona del Mar

2 miles south of Newport Beach.

A small jewel on the Pacific Coast, Corona del Mar (known by locals as "CDM") has exceptional beaches that some say resemble their majestic Northern California counterparts. South of CDM is an area referred to as the Newport Coast or Crystal Cove—whatever you call it, it's another dazzling spot on the California Riviera.

Sights

Corona del Mar State Beach

BEACH—SIGHT | **FAMILY** | This beach is actually made up of two beaches, Little Corona and Big Corona, separated by a cliff. Both have soft, golden-hue sand. Facilities include fire pits and volleyball courts. Two colorful reefs (and the fact that it's off-limits to boats) make Corona del Mar great for snorkelers and beachcombers. Parking in the lot is pricey, but you can often find a spot on the street on weekdays. **Amenities:** lifeguards; parking; showers; toilets. **Best for:** snorkeling; sunset; swimming. ✉ *3100 Ocean Blvd., Corona del Mar* ☎ *949/644–3151* 🌐 *www.parks.ca.gov.*

★ Crystal Cove State Park

BEACH—SIGHT | **FAMILY** | Midway between Corona del Mar and Laguna, Crystal Cove State Park is a favorite of local beachgoers and wilderness trekkers. It encompasses a 3.2-mile stretch of unspoiled beach and has some of the best tide-pooling in Southern California. Here you can see starfish, crabs, and sea anemones near the rocks. The park's 2,400 acres of backcountry are ideal for hiking and mountain biking, but stay on the trails to preserve the beauty. The Moro Campground offers campsites with picnic tables, including spots designated for RVs and trailers. The Crystal Cove Historic District holds a collection of historic cottages (24 of which are available for overnight rental), decorated and furnished to reflect the 1935 to 1955 beach culture that flourished here. On the sand above the high tide line and on a bluff above the beach, the cottages offer a funky look at beach life in times past. ✉ *8471 N. Coast Hwy., Laguna Beach* ☎ *949/494–3539* 🌐 *www.crystalcovestatepark.org* 🎟 *$15 parking.*

Roger's Gardens

GARDEN | **FAMILY** | One of the largest retail gardens in Southern California, Roger's showcases some of the best holiday decorations during Halloween and Christmas. An on-site Farmhouse at Roger's Gardens restaurant is popular with visitors and locals, who enjoy the locally sourced menu items while overlooking the bucolic gardens. ✉ *2301 San Joaquin Hills Rd.* ☎ *949/640–5800* 🌐 *www.rogersgardens.com.*

Sherman Library and Gardens

GARDEN | **FAMILY** | This 2½-acre botanical garden and library specializes in the history of the Pacific Southwest. You can wander among cactus gardens, rose gardens, a cool fern garden, and a tropical conservatory. There's a good gift shop, too. Café Jardin serves lunch on weekdays and Sunday brunch. ✉ *2647 E. Pacific Coast Hwy.* ☎ *949/673–2261* 🌐 *www.thesherman.org* 🎟 *$5.*

Store

HISTORIC SITE | Located among the Crystal Cove Cottages in the area's Historic District, Store carries fine art works by local plein air artists, as well as seaglass and ocean-themed jewelry, children's toys, snacks, and beach apparel. ✉ *State Park Historic District, Newport Coast* ☎ *949/376–6200* 🌐 *www.crystalcove.org/visit/things-to-do/store-gallery.*

🍴 Restaurants

The Beachcomber Cafe at Crystal Cove

$$ | **SEAFOOD** | Beach culture flourishes in this Crystal Cove Historic District's restaurant, thanks to its umbrella-laden deck just a few steps above the white sand. This is where you can sip a really good mai tai at the Bootlegger Bar, while waiting for your chance to sample ahi tacos, Maine lobster pasta, or blue crab–stuffed salmon. **Known for:** beachside cocktails; fresh seafood; big crowds and long waits (try to make a reservation in advance). [$] *Average main: $25* ✉ *15 Crystal Cove* ☎ *949/376–6900* 🌐 *www.thebeachcombercafe.com.*

Shake Shack at Crystal Cove

$ | **DINER** | **FAMILY** | This Southern California landmark sitting on a bluff off the PCH is the perfect spot to get a quick breakfast or to sample a tasty Cove burger with a side of fries or cole slaw for lunch or dinner. The menu also includes a vegan Impossible burger, hot dogs, and fish-and-chips. **Known for:** over 30 different shake flavors; casual ocean-view dining;

small parking lot with 30 minute limit. $ *Average main: $15* ✉ *7703 E. Coast Hwy., Newport Coast* ☎ *949/464–0100* 🌐 *www.crystalcoveshakeshack.com.*

Hotels

The Resort at Pelican Hill

$$$$ | RESORT | FAMILY | Built on a protected coastal enclave across the PCH and Crystal Cove State Park, this upscale Italian Renaissance–style resort has a dramatic domed rotunda, antique olive jars, and Tuscan columns and pilasters in the lobby. **Pros:** ocean-view paradise for golfers; spectacular swimming pool (the largest of its kind in the world); great spa and dining options. **Cons:** one of the most expensive resorts in Orange County; swimming pool can get very crowded during the holidays; pricey resort fee. $ *Rooms from: $795* ✉ *22701 Pelican Hill Rd. S, Newport Coast* ☎ *949/612–0332, 888/507–6427* 🌐 *www.pelicanhill.com* 🛏 *204 rooms, 128 villas* 🍴 *No meals.*

Shopping

Crystal Cove Promenade

STORE/MALL | FAMILY | Adding to Orange County's overwhelming supply of high-end shopping and dining is Crystal Cove Promenade, which might be described as the toniest strip mall in America. The mix of well-known storefronts, unique boutiques, and popular restaurants of this Mediterranean-inspired center are lined up across the street from Crystal Cove State Park, with the shimmering Pacific waters in plain view. ✉ *7845–8085 E. Coast Hwy., Newport Beach* ☎ *949/494–1239* 🌐 *www.shopirvinecompany.com.*

Laguna Beach

10 miles south of Newport Beach on PCH, 60 miles south of Los Angeles, I–5 south to Hwy. 133, which turns into Laguna Canyon Rd.

Driving in along Laguna Canyon Road from the Interstate 405 freeway gives you the chance to cruise through a gorgeous coastal canyon, large stretches of which remain undeveloped, before arriving at a glistening wedge of ocean. There are 30 coves and beaches to visit, all with some of the cleanest water in Southern California. During the summer, there's a convenient and free trolley service through town that cruises from North Laguna to Main Beach and all the way to the Ritz Carlton Laguna Niguel.

Laguna's welcome mat is legendary. On the corner of Forest and Park avenues is a gate proclaiming, "This gate hangs well and hinders none, refresh and rest, then travel on." A gay community has long been established here; art galleries dot the village streets, and there's usually someone daubing up a plein air on the bluff in Heisler Park. Along the Pacific Coast Highway you'll find dozens of clothing boutiques, jewelry stores, and cafés.

VISITOR INFORMATION Visit Laguna Beach Visitors Center. ✉ *381 Forest Ave.* ☎ *949/497–9229, 800/877–1115* 🌐 *www.visitlagunabeach.com.*

Sights

Festival of Arts and Pageant of the Masters

FESTIVAL | An outdoor amphitheater near the mouth of the canyon hosts the annual Pageant of the Masters, Laguna's signature event. Local participants arrange tableaux vivants, in which live models and carefully orchestrated backgrounds merge in striking mimicry of classical and contemporary paintings. The pageant is part of the **Festival of Arts,** held in July and August; tickets are in high demand, so plan ahead. ✉ *650 Laguna Canyon Rd.* 🕿 *949/497–6582, 800/487–3378* ⊕ *www. foapom.com.*

Heisler Park

CITY PARK | **FAMILY** | One of the most picturesque parks in Laguna Beach, Heisler Park offers plenty of chances for fun and relaxation. Picnic Beach has picnic tables overlooking palm trees and panoramic ocean views while stairs lead down to Diver's Cove for snorkeling, scuba diving, and tidepool exploring. Take the paved walking path along the cliff all the way to Laguna's Main Beach. There are public restrooms and outdoor showers. This is also a popular area for plein-air artists to set up an easel and chair and paint for hours. ✉ *400 Cliff Dr.* ⊕ *www.visitlagunabeach.com.*

Laguna Art Museum

MUSEUM | This museum displays work by California artists from all time periods, representing scenery in Laguna, and life and history of the Golden State in general. Special exhibits change quarterly. ✉ *307 Cliff Dr.* 🕿 *949/494–8971* ⊕ *www. lagunaartmuseum.org* 🗝 *$7* ☉ *Closed Wed.*

Laguna Coast Wilderness Park

HIKING/WALKING | **FAMILY** | With easy, moderate, and difficult trails spread over 7,000 acres of canyon to coastal territory, Laguna Coast Wilderness Park is a hiker's paradise. The 40 miles of trails offer expansive views and are also popular with mountain bikers. Trails open daily at 7 am and stay open until sunset, weather permitting. No dogs are allowed in the park. ✉ *18751 Laguna Canyon Rd.* 🕿 *949/923–2235* ⊕ *www.ocparks.com/ parks/lagunac* 🗝 *$3 parking.*

⊙ Beaches

★ Main Beach Park

BEACH—SIGHT | **FAMILY** | Centrally located in the main town of Laguna Beach near multiple dining venues, art galleries, and shops, Main Beach Park has a fitting name. Walk along this soft-sand beach to Bird Rock and explore nearby tide pools or sit on one of the benches and watch people bodysurfing, playing beach volleyball, or scrambling around two half-basketball courts. The beach also has a children's play area with climbing equipment. Most of Laguna's hotels are within a short (but hilly) walk. **Amenities:** lifeguards; toilets; showers. **Best for:** sunrise, sunset; swimming. ✉ *Broadway at S. Coast Hwy.* ⊕ *www.visitlagunabeach.com.*

1,000 Steps Beach

BEACH—SIGHT | **FAMILY** | Off South Coast Highway at 9th Street, 1,000 Steps Beach isn't too hard to find and actually only has 207 steps. It's one of the many coves in Laguna Beach offering a long stretch of soft sand, waves, and dramatic rock formations. Sea caves and tide pools enhance the already beautiful natural spot. Walking back up to your car, you will feel like you got a good workout. **Amenities:** showers. **Best for:** snorkeling; surfing; swimming. ✉ *S. Coast Hwy., at 9th St.* ⊕ *www.visitlagunabeach.com.*

Wood's Cove

BEACH—SIGHT | **FAMILY** | Off South Coast Highway, Wood's Cove is especially quiet during the week. Big rock formations hide lurking crabs. This is a prime scuba-diving spot, and at high tide much of the beach is underwater. Climbing the steps to leave, you can see a Tudor-style mansion that was once home to Bette Davis. Street parking is free yet limited. **Amenities:** none. **Best for:** snorkeling; scuba diving; sunset. ✉ *Diamond St. and Ocean Way* ⊕ *www.visitlagunabeach.com.*

Looking for shells on Laguna Beach, one of the nicest stretches of sand in Southern California.

🍴 Restaurants

The Cliff

$$$ | **SEAFOOD** | **FAMILY** | Walk through the quaint Laguna Beach artist village to get to the Cliff and its 180-degree views of Main Beach and the Pacific coastline. The multilevel dining patios serve hearty breakfasts and coastal seafood for lunch and dinner. **Known for:** some of Laguna Beach's best ocean-view dining; reservations necessary; splurge-worthy seafood towers. $ *Average main: $35 ⊠ 577 S. Coast Hwy.* ☎ *949/494–1956* ⊕ *www. thecliffrestaurant.com.*

Gelato Paradiso

$ | **EUROPEAN** | Each morning this gelato shop makes fresh small batches of artisanal gelatos and dairy-free sorbettos in a variety of appealing flavors. Located in back of the charming Peppertree Lane shopping center, there is a small outdoor patio where people gather to enjoy the authentic Italian gelato after a day at the beach or to cap off an evening. **Known for:** authentic Italian gelato; fruit flavors; patio gathering spot. $ *Average main: $6 ⊠ Peppertree La. , 448 S. Coast Hwy.* ☎ *949/464–9255* ⊕ *www.gelatoparadiso.com.*

★ Las Brisas

$$ | **MEXICAN FUSION** | **FAMILY** | Located in what used to be the Victor Hugo Inn, Las Brisas is now a Laguna Beach landmark restaurant. Sit on the expansive patio to take in the spectacular coastline views while enjoying signature margaritas and coastal Mexican cuisine with a California twist. **Known for:** fresh seafood; panoramic coastal views; reservations a must. $ *Average main: $30 ⊠ 361 Cliff Dr.* ☎ *949/497–5434* ⊕ *www.lasbrisaslagunabeach.com.*

The Rooftop Lounge

$$ | **AMERICAN** | Another popular sunset cocktail and light dinner venue in South Laguna for its views. Located at the top of La Casa del Camino, be sure to make a reservation to sit at a front row table to watch the sun lower behind Catalina Island. **Known for:** spectacular sunset views; craft cocktails; burgers, pasta, salads and sandwiches. $ *Average main:*

$30 ⊠ 1289 S. Coast Hwy. ☎ 949/497–2446 ⊕ www.rooftoplagunabeach.com.

Sapphire
$$ | INTERNATIONAL | FAMILY | This Laguna Beach establishment set in a historic Craftsman-style building is part gourmet pantry (a must-stop for your every picnic need) and part global dining adventure. Enjoy comfort cuisine from around the world paired with an eclectic wine and beer list. **Known for:** sapphire salad; weekend brunch; pet-friendly patio. $ *Average main: $30 ⊠ The Old Pottery Place, 1200 S. Coast Hwy. ☎ 949/715–9888 ⊕ www.sapphirelagunabeach.com.*

★ Studio
$$$$ | MODERN AMERICAN | In a nod to Laguna's art history, Studio has house-made specialties that entice the eye as well as the palate. The restaurant occupies its own Craftsman-style bungalow, atop a 50-foot bluff overlooking Treasure Island Park and the Pacific coastline. **Known for:** chef's creative tasting menu; great spot for special occasions; California coastal dishes with a French flair. $ *Average main: $75 ⊠ 30801 S. Coast Hwy. ☎ 949/715–6030 ⊕ www.studiolagunabeach.com ⊙ No lunch.*

Taco Loco
$ | MEXICAN | FAMILY | This may look like a fast-food taco stand, and the hemp blackened burgers and brownies on the menu may make you think the kitchen's *really* laid-back, but the quality of the food here equals that in many higher-price restaurants. Some Mexican standards get a seafood twist, like swordfish, calamari, and shrimp tacos. **Known for:** vegetarian tacos; sidewalk seating; surfer clientele. $ *Average main: $16 ⊠ 640 S. Coast Hwy. ☎ 949/497–1635 ⊕ www.lagunabeachmexicanfood.com.*

Urth Caffe
$$ | BAKERY | FAMILY | A local favorite for organic heirloom coffee and hand-blended fine organic teas, Urth is also the place to go for health-conscious breakfast dishes like an egg white and spinach breakfast panini. Sit outside on the charming garden patio looking out toward the Laguna Art Museum across the street. **Known for:** health-conscious cuisine; organic coffee and tea; long lines on the patio during peak hours and weekends. $ *Average main: $20 ⊠ 308 N. Pacific Coast Hwy. ☎ 949/376–8888 ⊕ www.urthcaffe.com/laguna-beach.*

Zinc Café and Market
$ | AMERICAN | FAMILY | Families flock to this small Laguna Beach institution for reasonably priced breakfast and lunch options. Try the signature quiches in the morning, or poached egg dishes later in the day for healthy salads, homemade soups, quesadillas, or pizzettes. **Known for:** gourmet pastries, some gluten-free; avocado toast; busy outdoor patio. $ *Average main: $18 ⊠ 350 Ocean Ave. ☎ 949/494–6302 ⊕ www.zinccafe.com ⊙ No dinner Nov.–Apr.*

Hotels

Inn at Laguna Beach
$$$ | HOTEL | FAMILY | This golden local landmark is stacked neatly on the hillside at the north end of Laguna's Main Beach and it's one of the few hotels in the area set almost on the sand. **Pros:** rooftop with fabulous ocean views; beach essentials provided; beachfront location. **Cons:** ocean-view rooms are pricey; tiny hot tub; some rooms are dark and small. $ *Rooms from: $379 ⊠ 211 N. Coast Hwy. ☎ 949/497–9722, 800/544–4479 ⊕ www.innatlagunabeach.com ⥾ 70 rooms* ⫶◯⫶ *No meals.*

La Casa del Camino
$$ | HOTEL | The look is Old California at the 1929-built La Casa del Camino, with dark woods, arched doors, wrought iron, and a beautiful tiled fireplace in the lobby. **Pros:** breathtaking views from rooftop lounge; modern decor; steps to the beach. **Cons:** some rooms face

the highway; pipes can be noisy; some rooms are small. $ *Rooms from: $225* ✉ *1289 S. Coast Hwy.* ☎ *949/497–6029, 855/634–5736* ⊕ *www.lacasadelcamino. com* ⇨ *36 rooms* ⏀ *Free breakfast.*

★Montage Laguna Beach

$$$$ | **RESORT** | **FAMILY** | Built on a picturesque coastal bluff above the Pacific Ocean and Treasure Island Beach, this elegant Craftsmen-style resort features 30 acres of grassy lawns, soft sand beaches, and a marine sanctuary. **Pros:** picturesque coastal location; stunning tiled mosaic swimming pool; residential style villas with sweeping ocean views. **Cons:** one of the area's priciest resorts, especially during holidays or summer weekends; $60 valet parking; $42 daily resort fee. $ *Rooms from: $895* ✉ *30801 S. Coast Hwy.* ☎ *949/715–6000, 866/271–6953* ⊕ *www.montagehotels. com/lagunabeach* ⇨ *258 rooms* ⏀ *No meals.*

★Surf and Sand Resort

$$$$ | **RESORT** | **FAMILY** | One mile south of downtown, on an exquisite stretch of beach with thundering waves and gorgeous rocks, this is a getaway for those who want a boutique hotel experience without all the formalities. **Pros:** easy sandy beach access; intimate boutique resort; good restaurant with wonderful views. **Cons:** pricey valet parking; surf can be loud; no air-conditioning (but overhead fans help). $ *Rooms from: $450* ✉ *1555 S. Coast Hwy.* ☎ *877/741–5908* ⊕ *www. surfandsandresort.com* ⇨ *167 rooms* ⏀ *No meals.*

Shopping

Coast Highway, Forest and Ocean avenues, and Glenneyre Street are full of art galleries, fine jewelry stores, souvenir shops, and clothing boutiques.

Adam Neeley Fine Art Jewelry

JEWELRY/ACCESSORIES | Be prepared to be dazzled at Adam Neeley Fine Art Jewelry, where artisan proprietor Adam Neeley creates one-of-a-kind modern pieces. ✉ *352 N. Coast Hwy.* ☎ *949/715–0953* ⊕ *www.adamneeley.com.*

Art for the Soul

CRAFTS | A riot of color, Art for the Soul has hand-painted furniture, crafts, and unusual whimsical gifts. ✉ *272 Forest Ave.* ☎ *949/675–1791* ⊕ *www.ra4ts.com.*

Candy Baron

FOOD/CANDY | **FAMILY** | Get your sugar fix at the time-warped Candy Baron, filled with old-fashioned goodies like gumdrops, licorice, bull's-eyes, sugar-free candies, and more than 50 flavors of saltwater taffy. ✉ *231 Forest Ave.* ☎ *949/497–7508* ⊕ *www.thecandybaron.com.*

La Rue du Chocolat

FOOD/CANDY | Located off the PCH in the quaint Peppertree Lane boutique shopping center, this sophisticated chocolate and truffle shop sells handcrafted seasonal chocolates, chocolate-covered strawberries, and creative holiday treats. ✉ *Peppertree La., 448 S. Coast Hwy., Suite B* ☎ *949/494–2372* ⊕ *www.larueduchocolat.com.*

San Juan Capistrano

5 miles north of Dana Point, 60 miles north of San Diego.

San Juan Capistrano is best known for its historic mission, where the swallows traditionally return each year, migrating from their winter haven in Argentina, but these days they are more likely to choose other local sites for nesting. St. Joseph's Day, March 19, launches a week of fowl festivities. Charming antiques stores, which range from pricey to cheap, line Camino Capistrano.

Mission San Juan Capistrano was founded in 1776.

GETTING HERE AND AROUND

If you arrive by train, which is far more romantic and restful than battling freeway traffic, you'll be dropped off across from the mission at the San Juan Capistrano depot. With its appealing brick café and preserved Santa Fe cars, the depot retains much of the magic of early American railroads. If driving, park near Ortega and Camino Capistrano, the city's main streets.

 Sights

★ Los Rios Historic District

NEIGHBORHOOD | FAMILY | Take a walk back in time on the oldest residential street in Southern California, where houses date back to 1790. The Silvas Adobe is a typical example of the dozen or more one-room adobes in the area. Mission San Juan Capistrano was the first Californian mission to allow workers to live outside the mission grounds. On the street you'll also find the Historical Society Museum and the ZOOMARS petting zoo for families. Shopping and dining

options abound. ✉ *31831 Los Rios St.* ☎ *949/493–8444* ⊕ *www.nps.gov.*

★ Mission San Juan Capistrano

RELIGIOUS SITE | FAMILY | Founded in 1776 by Father Junípero Serra (consecrated as St. Serra), Mission San Juan Capistrano was one of two Roman Catholic outposts between Los Angeles and San Diego. The Great Stone Church, begun in 1797, is the largest structure created by the Spanish in California. After extensive retrofitting, the golden-hued interiors are open to visitors who may feel they are touring among ruins in Italy rather than the O.C. Many of the mission's adobe buildings have been restored to illustrate mission life, with exhibits of an olive millstone, tallow ovens, tanning vats, metalworking furnaces, and the padres' living quarters. The beautiful gardens, with their fountains and koi pond, are a lovely spot in which to wander. The bougainvillea-covered Serra Chapel is believed to be the oldest church still standing in California and is the only building remaining in which St. Serra actually led Mass. Enter via a small gift shop in the gatehouse. ✉ *26801 Ortega Hwy.* ☎ *949/234–1300* 🌐 *www.missionsjc.com* 🎟 *$14.*

San Juan Capistrano Library

LIBRARY | **FAMILY** | Near Mission San Juan Capistrano is the San Juan Capistrano Library, a postmodern structure built in 1983. Architect Michael Graves combined classical and Mission styles to striking effect. Its courtyard has secluded places for reading. ✉ *31495 El Camino Real* ☎ *949/493–1752* 🌐 *ocpl.org/libloc/sjc* 🕒 *Closed Sun. and Mon.*

🍴 Restaurants

Cedar Creek Inn

$$ | **AMERICAN** | **FAMILY** | Just across the street from Mission San Juan Capistrano, this restaurant has a patio that's perfect for a late lunch or a romantic dinner. The menu is fairly straightforward, dishes are tasty, and portions are substantial—try the Cobb salad or a burger at lunch, or splurge on the prime rib for dinner. **Known for:** gluten-free and vegetarian options; rich desserts; comfortable seating. [$] *Average main: $30* ✉ *26860 Ortega Hwy.* ☎ *949/240–2229* 🌐 *www.cedarcreekinn.com.*

L'Hirondelle

$$$ | **FRENCH** | Locals have romanced at cozy tables for decades at this delightful restaurant directly across from the San Juan Capistrano Mission. Such classic dishes as beef bourguignon and a New York strip in a black-peppercorn-and-brandy sauce are the hallmarks of this French and Belgian restaurant, whose name means "the little swallow." The extensive wine list is matched by an impressive selection of Belgian beers. **Known for:** popular Sunday brunch; traditional French and Belgian cuisine; good Belgian beer selection. [$] *Average main: $39* ✉ *31631 Camino Capistrano* ☎ *949/661–0425* 🌐 *www.lhirondellesjc.com* 🕒 *Closed Mon.*

The Ramos House Cafe

$$$ | **AMERICAN** | It may be worth hopping the Amtrak to San Juan Capistrano just for the chance to have breakfast or lunch at one of Orange County's most beloved restaurants, located in a historic board-and-batten home dating back to 1881. This café sits practically on the railroad tracks across from the depot—nab a table on the patio and dig into a hearty breakfast featuring seasonal items, such as the smoked bacon scramble with wilted rocket and apple fried potatoes. **Known for:** Southern specialties; weekend brunch; historic setting. [$] *Average main: $35* ✉ *31752 Los Rios St.* ☎ *949/443–1342* 🌐 *www.ramoshouse.com* 🕒 *Closed Wed. No dinner.*

🛏 Hotels

★ Inn at the Mission San Juan Capistrano

$$$ | **HOTEL** | **FAMILY** | This family-friendly hacienda-style boutique hotel is located across the street from the famed San Juan Capistrano Mission, and the property incorporates this history by featuring glass mission bell lighting fixtures and equestrian decor and art. **Pros:** great location next to the mission; terrific culinary program; luxury rooms and suites. **Cons:** guests may hear freeway noise; beach is just less than 3 miles away; expensive parking. [$] *Rooms from: $350* ✉ *31692 El Camino Real* ☎ *949/503–5700* 🌐 *www.marriott.com* 🚪 *135 rooms* 🍴 *No meals.*

★ Ritz-Carlton, Laguna Niguel

$$$$ | **RESORT** | **FAMILY** | Combine the Ritz-Carlton's top-tier level of service with an unparalleled view of the Pacific, and you're in the lap of luxury at this resort. **Pros:** beautiful grounds and views; luxurious bedding; sophisticated service. **Cons:** some rooms are small for the price; in-house dining prices are high; $50 resort fee. [$] *Rooms from: $685* ✉ *1 Ritz-Carlton Dr., Dana Point* ☎ *949/240–2000, 800/542–8680* 🌐 *www.ritzcarlton.com/en/hotels/california/laguna-niguel* 🚪 *396 rooms* 🍴 *No meals.*

⚓ Nightlife

Swallow's Inn

BARS/PUBS | Across the way from Mission San Juan Capistrano you may spot a line of Harleys in front of the down-home and downright funky Swallow's Inn. Despite a somewhat tough look, it attracts all kinds—bikers, surfers, modern-day cowboys, grandparents—for a drink, a casual bite, karaoke nights, and some rowdy live country music. ✉ *31786 Camino Capistrano* ☎ *949/493–3188* ⊕ *www. swallowsinn.com.*

Catalina Island

Just 22 miles out from the L.A. coastline, across from Newport Beach and Long Beach, Catalina has virtually unspoiled mountains, canyons, coves, and beaches; best of all, it gives you a glimpse of what undeveloped Southern California once looked like.

Water sports are a big draw, as divers and snorkelers come for the exceptionally clear water surrounding the island. Kayakers are attracted to the calm cove waters and thrill seekers book the eco-themed zip line that traverses a wooded canyon. The main town, Avalon, is a charming, old-fashioned beach community, where yachts and pleasure boats bob in the crescent bay. Wander beyond the main drag and find brightly painted little bungalows fronting the sidewalks; golf carts are the preferred mode of transport.

In 1919, William Wrigley Jr., the chewing-gum magnate, purchased a controlling interest in the company developing Catalina Island, whose most famous landmark, the Casino, was built in 1929 under his orders. Because he owned the Chicago Cubs baseball team, Wrigley made Catalina the team's spring training site, an arrangement that lasted until 1951.

In 1975, the Catalina Island Conservancy, a nonprofit foundation, acquired about 88% of the island to help preserve the area's natural flora and fauna, including the bald eagle and the Catalina Island fox. These days the conservancy is restoring the rugged interior country with plantings of native grasses and trees. The organization helps oversee the interior's 50 miles of bike trails and 165 miles of hiking trails and helps protect the island's 60 endemic species. Along the coast you might spot oddities like electric perch, saltwater goldfish, and flying fish.

GETTING HERE AND AROUND

FERRY

Two companies offer ferry service to Catalina Island. The boats have both indoor and outdoor seating and snack bars. Excessive baggage is not allowed, and there are extra fees for bicycles and surfboards. The waters around Catalina can get rough, so if you're prone to seasickness, come prepared. Winter, holiday, and weekend schedules vary, so reservations are strongly recommended.

Catalina Express makes an hour-long run from Long Beach or San Pedro to Avalon and a 90-minute run from Dana Point to Avalon with some stops at Two Harbors. Round-trip fares begin at $73.50, with discounts for seniors and kids. On busy days, a $15 upgrade to the Commodore Lounge, when available, is worth it. Service from Newport Beach to Avalon is available through the *Catalina Flyer.* The boat leaves from Balboa Pavilion at 9 am (in season), takes 75 minutes to reach the island, and costs $70 round-trip. The return boat leaves Catalina at 4:30 pm. Reservations are required for the *Catalina Flyer* and recommended for all weekend and summer trips.

■ **TIP→ Keep an eye out for dolphins, which sometimes swim alongside the ferries.**

FERRY CONTACTS Catalina Express. ✉ *320 Golden Shore, Long Beach* ☎ *562/485–3200* ⊕ *www.catalinaexpress.com.* **Catalina Flyer.** ✉ *Balboa Pier, 400 Main St., Newport Beach* ☎ *949/673–5245* ⊕ *www.catalinainfo.com.*

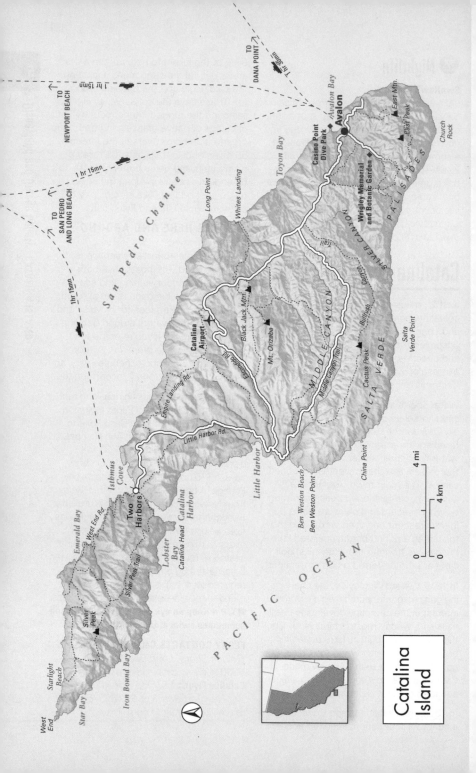

GOLF CARTS

Golf carts constitute the island's main form of transportation for sightseeing in the area; however, some parts of town are off-limits, as is the island's interior. Drivers 21 and over with valid driver's license can rent them along Avalon's Crescent Avenue and Pebbly Beach Road for about $50 per hour with a $50 deposit, payable via cash only.

GOLF CART RENTALS Island Rentals. ⊠ *125 Pebbly Beach Rd., Avalon* ☎ *310/510–1456* ⊕ *www.catalinagolfcartrentals.com.*

TIMING

Although Catalina can be seen in one thrilling day, several inviting hotels make it worth extending your stay for one or more nights. A short itinerary might include breakfast on the pier, a tour of the interior, a snorkeling excursion at Casino Point, or beach day at the Descanso Beach Club and a romantic waterfront dinner in Avalon.

After late October, rooms are much easier to find on short notice, rates drop dramatically, and many hotels offer packages that include transportation from the mainland and/or sightseeing tours. January to March you have a good chance of spotting migrating gray whales on the ferry crossing.

TOURS

Santa Catalina Island Company runs both land tours and ocean tours, including the *Flying Fish* boat trip (summer evenings only); a comprehensive inland motor tour; a tour of Skyline Drive; several Casino tours; a scenic tour of Avalon; a glass-bottom-boat tour; an undersea tour on a semisubmersible vessel; an eco-themed zip line tour that traverses a scenic canyon; a speedy Ocean Runner expedition that searches for all manner of sea creatures and a fast Cyclone boat tour that takes you to the less populated center of the island, Two Harbors. Reservations are highly recommended for the inland tours. Tours cost $22 to $130. There are ticket booths on the Green Pleasure Pier, in the plaza, and at the boat landing. Catalina Adventure Tours, which has booths at the boat landing and on the pier, also arranges excursions at comparable prices.

The Catalina Island Conservancy organizes custom ecotours and hikes of the interior. Naturalist guides drive open jeeps through some gorgeously untrammeled parts of the island. Tours start at $70 per person for a two-hour trip (two-person minimum). The tours run year-round.

CONTACTS Catalina Adventure Tours. ⊠ *302 Pebbly Beach Rd., Avalon* ☎ *562/432–8828* ⊕ *www.catalinaadventuretours.com.* **Catalina Island Conservancy.** ⊠ *708 Crescent Ave., Avalon* ☎ *310/510–2595* ⊕ *www.catalinaconservancy.org.* **Santa Catalina Island Company.** ☎ *877/778–8322* ⊕ *www.visitcatalinaisland.com.*

Avalon

A 1- to 2-hour ferry ride from Long Beach, Newport Beach, or San Pedro.

Avalon, Catalina's only real town, extends from the shore of its natural harbor to the surrounding hillsides. Its resident population is about 3,800, but it swells with tourists on summer weekends. Most of the city's activity, however, is centered on the pedestrian mall on Crescent Avenue, and most sights are easily reached on foot. Private cars are restricted and rental cars aren't allowed, but taxis, trams, and shuttles can take you anywhere you need to go. Bicycles, electric bikes, and golf carts can be rented from shops along Crescent Avenue.

👁 Sights

★ Casino

BUILDING | Built in 1929, this circular white structure is one of the finest examples of art-deco architecture anywhere. Its Spanish-inspired floors and murals gleam with brilliant marine blue and sea foam green Catalina tiles. In this case, *casino,* the Italian word for "gathering place," has nothing to do with gambling. The circular ballroom once famously hosted 1940s big bands and is still used for gala events. The Santa Catalina Island Company leads two narrated walking tours of the Casino. ✉ *1 Casino Way* ☎ *310/510–0179* ⊕ *www.visitcatalinaisland.com.*

Casino Point Dive Park

BEACH—SIGHT | **FAMILY** | In front of the Casino are the crystal clear waters of the Casino Point Dive Park, a protected marine preserve where moray eels, bat rays, spiny lobsters, harbor seals, and the bright orange Garibaldi (California's state marine fish) cruise around kelp forests and along the sandy bottom. No need to don a wet suit: the brilliantly orange Garibaldi, can sometimes be viewed from the seawall. It's a terrific site for scuba diving, with some shallow areas suitable for snorkeling. Equipment can be rented on and near the pier. The shallow waters of Lover's Cove, east of the boat landing, are also good for snorkeling. ✉ *1 Casino Way* ⊕ *www.divingcatalina.com.*

Catalina Island Museum

MUSEUM | **FAMILY** | The exterior of the Catalina Island Museum is a nod to Catalina Island's developer William Wrigley Jr.—it's modeled after Wrigley Field in Chicago. Inside the interactive museum visitors can learn about the island's history from the native Chumash people to its role in Hollywood history and beyond. Two galleries host traveling exhibitions. The view from the outside terrace takes in lovely Avalon and its picturesque harbor. A small gift shop offers Catalina-themed souvenirs and reproductions

Catalina's Bison 👁

Zane Grey, the writer who put the Western novel on the map, spent a lot of time on Catalina, and his influence is still evident in a peculiar way. As the story goes, when the movie version of Grey's book *The Vanishing American* was filmed here in 1924, American bison were ferried across from the mainland to give the land that western plains look. After the crew packed up and left, the buffalo stayed, and a small herd of about 150 still remains, grazing the interior.

of the island's signature colorful Catalina pottery tiles. ✉ *217 Metropole Ave.* ☎ *310/510–2414* ⊕ *www.catalinamuseum.org* 🎟 *$17* 🕙 *Closed Mon. and Tues.*

Green Pleasure Pier

LOCAL INTEREST | **FAMILY** | Head to the Green Pleasure Pier for a good vantage point of Avalon. On the pier you can find the visitor information, snack stands, and scads of squawking seagulls. It's also the landing where visiting cruise-ship passengers catch tenders back out to their ship. ✉ *1 Green Pleasure Pier* ⊕ *www.lovecatalina.com.*

Wrigley Memorial and Botanic Garden

GARDEN | **FAMILY** | Two miles south of the bay is Wrigley Memorial and Botanic Garden, home to many plants native only to Southern California and the Channel Islands. Today there are five different sections where you can see Catalina ironwood, wild tomato, and rare Catalina mahogany. The Wrigley family commissioned the garden as well as the monument, which has a grand staircase and a Spanish-style mausoleum inlaid with colorful Catalina tile. Wrigley Jr. was once buried here but his remains were moved to Glendale, CA, during World War ll. ✉ *Avalon Canyon Rd.* ☎ *310/510–2897* 🌐 *www.catalinaconservancy.org* 🎟 *$8.*

🍴 Restaurants

Bluewater Grill
$$ | **SEAFOOD** | **FAMILY** | Overlooking the ferry landing and the entire harbor, the open-to-the-salt-air Bluewater Grill offers freshly caught fish, savory chowders, and all manner of shellfish. If they're on the menu, don't miss the swordfish steak, the lobster roll, or the sand dabs. **Known for:** fresh local fish; handcrafted cocktails; overwater harbor views. [$] *Average main: $30* ✉ *306 Crescent Ave.* ☎ *310/510–3474* 🌐 *www.bluewatergrill.com.*

Descanso Beach Club
$ | **AMERICAN** | **FAMILY** | Set on an expansive deck overlooking the water, Descanso Beach Club serves a wide range of favorites: grilled burgers, street tacos, clam chowder, salads, and layered nachos are all part of the selection. Watch the harbor seals frolic just offshore while sipping the island's supersweet signature cocktail, the Buffalo Milk, a mix of fruit liqueurs, vodka, and whipped cream. **Known for:** tropical beach vibe; scenic views; chic cabana rentals. [$] *Average main: $12* ✉ *Descanso Beach, 1 Descanso Ave.* ☎ *310/510–7410* 🌐 *www.visitcatalinaisland.com.*

★ **Eric's on the Pier**
$ | **AMERICAN** | This little snack bar has been an Avalon family–run institution since the 1920s. It's a good place to people-watch while drinking a draft beer and munching on a breakfast burrito, fish-and-chips, or signature buffalo burger. **Known for:** comfort foods; quick eats; beachside location. [$] *Average main: $15* ✉ *2 Green Pier* ☎ *310/510–0894* 🌐 *www.lovecatalina.com/listing/erics-on-the-pier/23.*

The Lobster Trap
$$ | **SEAFOOD** | Seafood rules at the Lobster Trap—the restaurant's owner has his own boat and fishes for the catch of the day and, in season, spiny lobster. Ceviche is a great starter, always fresh and brightly flavored. **Known for:** locally caught seafood; convivial atmosphere; locals' hangout. [$] *Average main: $25* ✉ *128 Catalina St.* ☎ *310/510–8585* 🌐 *catalinalobstertrap.com.*

Steve's Steakhouse and Seafood
$$$ | **STEAKHOUSE** | **FAMILY** | Within spitting distance of the bay, this second-floor restaurant keeps hungry diners happy with sizzling steaks and slow-cooked baby back ribs. There's also ample seafood, such as locally caught swordfish and shrimp. **Known for:** friendly staff; water views; steak and seafood dinners. [$] *Average main: $32* ✉ *417 Crescent Ave.* ☎ *310/510–0333* 🌐 *www.stevessteakhouse.com.*

🛏 Hotels

Aurora Hotel
$$ | **HOTEL** | In a town dominated by historic properties, the Aurora is refreshingly contemporary, with a hip attitude and sleek furnishings. **Pros:** trendy design; quiet location off main drag; close to restaurants. **Cons:** standard rooms are small; no elevator; two-night minimum stay required. [$] *Rooms from: $279* ✉ *137 Marilla Ave.* ☎ *310/510–0454* 🌐 *www.auroracatalina.com* 🛏 *18 rooms* 🍴 *Free breakfast.*

Bellanca Hotel
$$ | **HOTEL** | One of the closest boutique hotels to the Catalina Casino, this European-style hotel creates an intimate feel with brick courtyards and serene suites. **Pros:** romantic setting; close to beach; expansive sundeck with comfortable lounge furniture. **Cons:** ground-floor rooms can hear golf carts drive by; some rooms are on the small side; no elevator. [$] *Rooms from: $299* ✉ *111 Crescent Ave.* ☎ *310/510–0555, 888/510–0555* 🌐 *www.bellancahotel.com* 🛏 *35 rooms* 🍴 *No meals.*

★ Hotel Atwater

$$ | HOTEL | FAMILY | Just one block from the beach in the center of Avalon, Hotel Atwater originally opened in 1920 and was recently redesigned to honor Helen Atwater's (daugher-in-law of famed local William Wrigley) impeccable sense of style and deep love for Catalina Island. **Pros:** unique and historical decor; central location; nice amenities. **Cons:** some rooms have street noise; certain rooms on the small side; not on the beach. $ *Rooms from: $269* ✉ *125 Sumner Ave.* ☎ *310/510–1789* ⊕ *www.visitcatalinais-land.com* ⇨ *95 rooms* ¶◎¶ *No meals.*

Hotel Mac Rae

$ | HOTEL | Family-owned for more than a century, the fourth generation now operates this boutique hotel right on Crescent Avenue, with a few rooms overlooking the beach and Avalon Bay. One of the best-priced hotels next to the beach, guests receive a complimentary continental breakfast; beach towels; Internet access; and after checkout luggage storage and shower facility to use after spending a day at the beach and before boarding a return boat home. **Pros:** great value for location; spectacular beachfront views; free breakfast. **Cons:** no elevator and hotel is on the second floor; basic rooms and furniture; restaurants and bars below can mean noise in the evening. $ *Rooms from: $150* ✉ *409 Crescent Ave.* ☎ *310/510–0246* ⊕ *www.HotelMac-Rae.com* ⇨ *26 rooms* ¶◎¶ *Free breakfast.*

Hotel Metropole and Market Place

$$ | HOTEL | FAMILY | Set over a bustling maze of shops, this hotel offers urban style in a quaint setting. **Pros:** family-friendly vibe; outdoor hot tub and sundeck; convenient location. **Cons:** some rooms on small side; soundproofing issues; no hotel shuttle to dock. $ *Rooms from: $250* ✉ *205 Crescent Ave.* ☎ *310/510–1884, 800/541–8528* ⊕ *www.hotel-metropole.com* ⇨ *53 rooms* ¶◎¶ *No meals.*

Hotel Vista del Mar

$$ | HOTEL | FAMILY | On the bay-facing Crescent Avenue, this third-floor property is steps from the beach, where complimentary towels, chairs, and umbrellas await guests. **Pros:** comfortable beds; central location; in-room fireplace. **Cons:** no restaurant or spa facilities; few rooms with ocean views; no elevator. $ *Rooms from: $235* ✉ *417 Crescent Ave.* ☎ *310/510–1452, 800/601–3836* ⊕ *www.hotel-vistadelmar.com* ⇨ *14 rooms* ¶◎¶ *Free breakfast.*

Mt. Ada

$$$$ | B&B/INN | If you stay in the 1921 mansion where Wrigley Jr. once lived, you can enjoy all the comforts of a millionaire's home—at a millionaire's prices. **Pros:** a step back in timeless charm; all-inclusive services, including complimentary shuttle from ferry dock; incredible canyon, bay, and ocean views. **Cons:** some rooms and bathrooms are small; a far walk into town; expensive. $ *Rooms from: $600* ✉ *398 Wrigley Rd.* ☎ *310/510–7330* ⊕ *www.visitcatalinais-land.com* ⇨ *6 rooms* ¶◎¶ *All-inclusive.*

Pavilion Hotel

$$ | HOTEL | FAMILY | This mid-century modern–style hotel is Avalon's most citified spot, though just a few steps from the sand. **Pros:** steps from the beach and harbor; plush bedding; chic decor. **Cons:** no pool; rooms near stairs can be noisy; no elevator. $ *Rooms from: $275* ✉ *513 Crescent Ave.* ☎ *310/510–1788* ⊕ *www.visitcatalinaisland.com* ⇨ *71 rooms* ¶◎¶ *No meals.*

★ Zane Grey Pueblo

$$$$ | HOTEL | The prolific best-selling Western novelist Zane Grey built his home as a retreat to take in the views of Avalon while writing over 100 books; his home was turned into this quaint boutique hotel in 1939. **Pros:** breathtaking views; complimentary continental breakfast; heated swimming pool with ocean views. **Cons:** three-story addition has no elevator; a hike up a hill from town; bell

tower chimes can be loud for some people. $ *Rooms from: $400* ✉ *199 Chimes Tower Rd.* ☎ *310/510–0966* ⊕ *www. zanegreyhotel.com* ⤴ *17 rooms* ⦿ *Free breakfast.*

Activities

BICYCLING
Brown's Bikes
BICYCLING | FAMILY | Look for rentals on Crescent Avenue and Pebbly Beach Road, where Brown's Bikes is located. Beach cruisers start at $25 per day, mountain bikes are $30 per day, and electric bikes are $50 for a day rental, and a good choice for Catalina's hills. ✉ *107 Pebbly Beach Rd.* ☎ *310/510–0986* ⊕ *www.catalinabiking.com.*

DIVING AND SNORKELING
The Casino Point Underwater Park, with its handful of wrecks and ample sea life, is best suited for diving. Lover's Cove is better for snorkeling (but you'll share the area with glass-bottom boats). Both are protected marine preserves.

Catalina Divers Supply
SCUBA DIVING | Head to Catalina Divers Supply to rent equipment, sign up for guided scuba and snorkel tours, and attend certification classes. It also has an outpost at the Dive Park at Casino Point and one on the Green Pleasure Pier. Both offer gear rental and tank air fills. ✉ *1 Casino Way* ☎ *310/510–0330* ⊕ *www. catalinadiverssupply.com.*

HIKING
Catalina Island Conservancy
HIKING/WALKING | FAMILY | Permits from the Catalina Island Conservancy are required for hiking into Santa Catalina Island's rugged interior, where there are more than 165 miles of trails of all levels to explore. If you plan to backpack overnight, you'll need a camping reservation. The interior is dry and desertlike; bring plenty of water, sunblock, a hat, and all necessary supplies. The permits are free or you can make a donation to the Conservancy. You don't need a permit for shorter hikes, such as the 20-minute one from Avalon to the Wrigley Botanical Garden. It's also possible to hike between Avalon and Two Harbors, starting at the Hogsback Gate, above Avalon, but the 28-mile journey has an elevation gain of 3,000 feet and is not for the weak. ■**TIP→ For a pleasant 4-mile hike out of Avalon, take Avalon Canyon Road to the Wrigley Botanical Garden and follow the trail to Lone Pine. At the top there's an amazing view of the Palisades cliffs and, beyond them, the sea.** ✉ *708 Crescent Ave.* ☎ *310/510–2595* ⊕ *www.catalinaconservancy.org.*

Chapter 6

LOS ANGELES

Updated by
Paul Feinstein, Michelle Rae Uy,
and Candice Yacono

◉ Sights	⑪ Restaurants	🛏 Hotels	💼 Shopping	🍸 Nightlife
★★★★★	★★★★★	★★★★★	★★★★★	★★★★☆

WELCOME TO LOS ANGELES

TOP REASONS TO GO

★ **Seeing stars:** Both through the telescope atop Griffith Park and among the residents of Beverly Hills.

★ **Good eats:** From food trucks to fine dining, an unparalleled meal awaits your palate.

★ **Beaches and boardwalks:** The dream of '80s Venice is alive in California.

★ **Shopping:** Peruse eclectic boutiques or window-shop on Rodeo Drive.

★ **Architecture:** Art-deco wonders to Frank Gehry masterpieces abound.

★ **Scenic drives:** You haven't seen the sunset until you've seen it from a winding L.A. road.

1 Santa Monica and Venice. Expect a lively beach scene and a raffish mix of artists, beach punks, and yuppies.

2 Beverly Hills. The glamour here includes Rodeo Drive's excesses—both wretched and ravishing.

3 West Hollywood and Fairfax. West Hollywood is all about shopping, dining, and nightlife.

4 Hollywood and the Studios. Glitzy and tarnished, good and bad—Hollywood mirrors the entertainment business.

5 Mid-Wilshire and Koreatown. Mid-Wilshire has art-deco high-rises and Museum Row. Koreatown has great bars and restaurants.

6 Downtown Los Angeles. This older district shows off spectacular modern architecture.

7 Los Feliz, Silver Lake, and the Eastside. Head east for everything young, cool, and hip.

8 Pasadena. Arts and Crafts homes and two exceptional museums mark this genteel area.

9 Malibu and the Beaches. En route to chichi Malibu, stop at a white-sand beach to spy on sea lions or migrating whales.

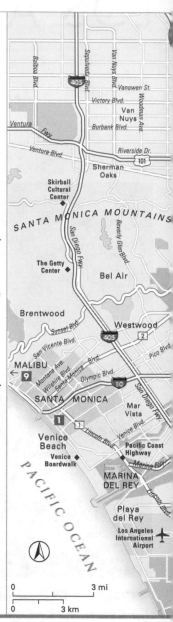

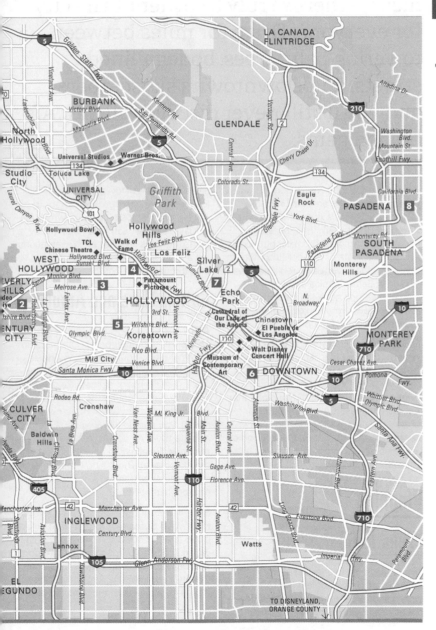

Los Angeles is a polarizing place, but those who hate it just haven't found their niche—there's truly a corner of the city for everyone. Drive for miles between towering palm trees, bodega-lined streets, and Downtown's skyscrapers, and you'll still never discover all of L.A.'s hidden gems.

Yes, you'll encounter traffic-clogged freeways, but there are also walkable pockets like Venice's Abbot Kinney. You'll drive past Beverly Hills mansions and spy palaces perched atop hills, but you'll also see the roots of mid-century modern architecture in Silver Lake. You'll soak up the sun in Santa Monica and then find yourself barhopping in the city's revitalized Downtown while enjoying scrumptious fish tacos along the way.

You might think that you'll have to spend most of your visit in a car, but that's not the case. In fact, exploring by foot is the only way to really get to know the various fringe neighborhoods and mini-cities that make up the vast L.A. area. But no single locale—whether it's Malibu, Downtown, Beverly Hills, or Burbank—fully embodies Los Angeles. It's in the mix that you'll discover the city's character.

Planning

When to Go

Almost any time of the year is the right time to go to Los Angeles; the climate is mild and pleasant year-round. Winter brings crisp, sunny, unusually smogless days from about November to May (expect brief rains from December to April). Los Angeles summers, which are virtually rainless, can lead to air-quality alerts. Prices skyrocket and reservations are a must when tourism peaks from July through early October.

Getting Here and Around

AIR

The fourth-largest airport in the world in terms of passenger traffic, Los Angeles International Airport (LAX) is served by more than 65 major airlines. Because of heavy traffic around the airport (not to mention the city's extended rush hours), you should allow yourself plenty of extra time. All departures are from the upper level, while arrivals are on the lower level. There's no Metro in or out of the airport, but it's coming in the not-too-distant-future.

Several secondary airports serve the city. Hollywood Burbank Airport in Burbank is close to Downtown L.A., so it's definitely worth checking out. Long Beach Airport is equally convenient. Flights to Orange County's John Wayne Airport are often more expensive than those to the other secondary airports. Also check out L.A./Ontario International Airport.

Driving times from LAX to different parts of the city vary considerably: it will take you 20 minutes to get to Santa Monica, 30 minutes to Beverly Hills, and at least 45 minutes to Downtown L.A. In heavy traffic it can take much longer. From Hollywood Burbank Airport, it's 30 minutes to Downtown. Plan on at least 45 minutes for the drive from Long Beach Airport, and an hour from John Wayne Airport or L.A./Ontario International Airport.

AIRPORTS Hollywood Burbank Airport.
(*BUR*) ⊠ *2627 N. Hollywood Way, near I–5 and U.S. 101, Burbank* ☎ *818/840–8840* ⊕ *www.hollywoodburbankairport.com.* **John Wayne Airport.** (*SNA*) ⊠ *18601 Airport Way, Santa Ana* ☎ *949/252–5200* ⊕ *www.ocair.com.* **L.A./Ontario International Airport.** (*ONT*) ⊠ *2500 E. Airport Dr., off I–10, Ontario* ☎ *909/544–5300* ⊕ *www.flyontario.com.* **Long Beach Airport.** (*LGB*) ⊠ *4100 Donald Douglas Dr., Long Beach* ☎ *562/570–2600* ⊕ *www.lgb.org.* **Los Angeles International Airport.** (*LAX*) ⊠ *1 World Way, off Hwy. 1* ☎ *855/463–5252* ⊕ *www.flylax.com.*

SHUTTLES FlyAway.
☎ *714/507–1170* ⊕ *www.flylax.com/en/flyaway-bus.* **Super-Shuttle.** ☎ *323/775–6600, 800/258–3826* ⊕ *www.supershuttle.com.*

BUS
Inadequate public transportation has plagued L.A. for decades. That said, many local trips can be made, with time and patience, by buses run by the Los Angeles County Metropolitan Transit Authority. In certain cases—visiting the Getty Center, for instance, or Universal Studios—buses may be your best option. There's a special Dodger Stadium Express that shuttles passengers between Union Station and the world-famous ballpark for home games. It's free if you have a ticket in hand and saves you parking-related stress.

Metro Buses cost $1.75, plus 50¢ for each transfer to another bus or to the subway. A one-day pass costs $7, and a weekly pass is $25 for unlimited travel on all buses and trains. Passes are valid from Sunday through Saturday. For the fastest service, look for the red-and-white Metro Rapid buses; these stop less frequently and are able to extend green lights. There are 25 Metro Rapid routes, including along Wilshire and Vermont boulevards.

Other bus services make it possible to explore the entire metropolitan area. DASH minibuses cover six different circular routes in Hollywood, Mid-Wilshire, and Downtown. You pay 50¢ every time you get on. The Santa Monica Municipal Bus Line, also known as the Big Blue Bus, is a pleasant and inexpensive way to move around the Westside. Trips cost $1.

You can pay your fare in cash on MTA, Santa Monica, and Culver City buses, but you must have exact change. You can buy MTA TAP cards at Metro Rail stations, customer centers throughout the city, and some convenience and grocery stores.

CONTACTS Culver CityBus.
☎ *310/253–6510* ⊕ *www.culvercitybus.com.* **DASH.** ☎ *310/808–2273* ⊕ *www.ladottransit.com.* **Los Angeles County Metropolitan Transit Authority.** ☎ *323/466–3876* ⊕ *www.metro.net.* **Santa Monica Municipal Bus Line.** ☎ *310/451–5444* ⊕ *www.bigbluebus.com.*

CAR
If you're used to urban driving, you shouldn't have too much trouble navigating the streets of Los Angeles. If not, L.A. can be unnerving. However, the city has evolved with drivers in mind. Streets are wide and parking garages abound, so it's more car-friendly than many older big cities.

If you get discombobulated while on the freeway, remember this rule of thumb: even-numbered freeways run east and west, odd-numbered freeways run north and south.

There are plenty of identical or similarly named streets in L.A. (Beverly Boulevard and Beverly Drive, for example), so be as specific as you can when asking directions or inputting into a map app. Expect sudden changes in addresses as streets pass through neighborhoods, then incorporated cities, then back into neighborhoods. This can be most bewildering on Robertson Boulevard, an otherwise useful north–south artery that, by crossing through L.A., West Hollywood, and Beverly Hills, dips in and out of several such numbering shifts in a matter of miles.

METRO/PUBLIC TRANSPORT

Metro Rail covers only a small part of L.A.'s vast expanse, but it's convenient, frequent, and inexpensive. Most popular with visitors is the underground Red Line, which runs from Downtown's Union Station through Mid-Wilshire, Hollywood, and Universal City on its way to North Hollywood, stopping at the most popular tourist destinations along the way.

The light-rail Green Line stretches from Redondo Beach to Norwalk, while the partially underground Blue Line travels from Downtown to the South Bay. The monorail-like Gold Line extends from Union Station to Pasadena and out to the deep San Gabriel Valley and Azusa. The Orange Line, a 14-mile bus corridor, connects the North Hollywood subway station with the western San Fernando Valley.

Most recently extended was the Expo Line, which connects Downtown to the Westside, and terminates in Santa Monica, two blocks from the Pacific Ocean.

Daily service is offered from about 4:30 am to 12:30 am, with departures every 5 to 15 minutes. On weekends trains run until 2 am. Buy tickets from station vending machines; fares are $1.75, or $7 for an all-day pass. Bicycles are allowed on Metro Rail trains at all times.

CONTACTS Los Angeles County Metropolitan Transit Authority. ☎ *323/466–3876* ⊕ *www.metro.net.*

RIDE-SHARING AND TAXI

Request a ride using apps like Lyft or Uber, and a driver will usually arrive within minutes. Fares increase during busy times, but it's often the most affordable option, especially for the convenience.

Instead of trying to hail a taxi on the street, phone one of the many taxi companies. The Curb Taxi app allows for online hailing of L.A. taxis. The metered rate is $2.70 per mile, plus a $2.85 per-fare charge and an additional $2 curb fee. Taxi rides from LAX have an additional $4 surcharge. Be aware that distances are greater than they might appear on the map so fares add up quickly.

CONTACTS Beverly Hills Cab Co. ☎ *800/273–6611* ⊕ *www.beverlyhillscab-co.com.* **Independent Cab Co.** ☎ *800/521–8294* ⊕ *www.lataxi.com/new.* **LA Checker Cab.** ☎ *800/300–5007* ⊕ *www.ineedtaxi. com.* **United Independent Taxi.** ☎ *800/822–8294, 323/653–5050 text to order taxi* ⊕ *www.unitedtaxi.com.* **Yellow Cab Los Angeles.** ☎ *424/222–2222* ⊕ *www.layellowcab.com.*

TRAIN

Downtown's Union Station is one of the great American railroad terminals. The interior includes comfortable seating, restaurants, and several bars. As the city's rail hub, it's the place to catch an Amtrak, Metrolink commuter train, or the Red, Gold, or Purple lines. Among Amtrak's Southern California routes are 11 daily trips to San Diego and 6 to Santa Barbara. Amtrak's luxury *Coast Starlight* travels along the spectacular coastline from Seattle to Los Angeles in just a day and a half (though it's often a little late). The *Sunset Limited* arrives from New Orleans, and the *Southwest Chief* comes from Chicago.

CONTACTS Metrolink. ☎ *800/371–5465* ⊕ *www.metrolinktrains.com.* **Union Station.** ✉ *800 N. Alameda St., Downtown* ☎ *213/683–6979* ⊕ *www.unionstationla. com* Ⓜ *Union Station.*

Restaurants

Los Angeles may be known for its beach living and celebrity-infused backdrop, but it was once a farm town. The hillsides were covered in citrus orchards and dairy farms, and agriculture was a major industry. Today, even as L.A. is urbanized, the city's culinary landscape has reembraced a local, sustainable, and seasonal philosophy at many levels—from fine dining to street snacks.

With a growing interest in farm-to-fork, the city's farmers' market scene has exploded, becoming popular at big-name restaurants and small eateries alike. In Hollywood and Santa Monica you can often find high-profile chefs scouring farm stands for fresh produce.

The status of the celebrity chef carries weight around this town. People follow the culinary zeitgeist with the same fervor as celebrity gossip. You can queue up with the hungry hordes at Nancy Silverton's **Mozza,** or try and snag a reservation at Ludo Lefebvre's ever-popular **Petit Trois** or David Chang's L.A. outpost, **Majordomo.**

International eats continue to be a backbone of the L.A. dining scene. People head to Koreatown for epic Korean cooking and late-night coffeehouses and to West L.A. for phenomenal sushi. Latin food is well represented in the city, making it tough to choose between Guatemalan eateries, Peruvian restaurants, nouveau Mexican bistros, and Tijuana-style taco trucks. With so many dining options, sometimes the best strategy is simply to drive and explore.

Hotels

When it comes to finding a place to stay, travelers have never been more spoiled for choice than in today's Los Angeles. From luxurious digs in Beverly Hills and along the coast to budget boutiques in Hollywood, hotels are stepping up service, upgrading amenities, and trying all-new concepts, like upscale hostels and retro-chic motels. Hotels in Los Angeles today are more than just a place to rest your head; they're a key part of the experience.

Restaurant and hotel reviews have been shortened. For full information, visit Fodors.com. Restaurant prices are the average cost of a main course at dinner or, if dinner is not served, at lunch. Hotel prices are for the lowest cost of a standard double room in high season.

What It Costs			
$	$$	$$$	$$$$
RESTAURANTS			
under $14	$14–$22	$23–$31	over $31
HOTELS			
under $200	$200–$300	$301–$400	over $400

Nightlife

Los Angeles is not the city that never sleeps—instead it parties until 2 am (save for the secret after-hours parties at private clubs, Hollywood Hills mansions, and warehouses) and wakes up to imbibe green juices and breakfast burritos as hangover cures or to sweat it out in a yoga class. Whether you plan to test your limit at historic establishments Downtown or take advantage of a cheap happy hour at a Hollywood dive, this city's nightlife has something for you.

A night out in Los Angeles can simultaneously surprise and impress. Seeing an unscheduled set by an A-list comedian at a comedy club, being talked into singing karaoke at the diviest place you've ever seen, dancing at a bar with no dance floor because, well, the DJ is just too good at his job—going out isn't always what you expect, but it certainly is never boring.

The focus of nightlife once centered on the Sunset Strip, with its multitude of bars, rock clubs, and dance spots, but more neighborhoods are competing with each other and forcing the nightlife scene to evolve. Although the Strip can be a worthwhile trip, other areas of the city are catching people's attention. Downtown Los Angeles, for instance, is a destination in its own right. Other areas foster more of a neighborhood vibe. Silver Lake and Los Feliz have both cultivated a relaxed environment.

Performing Arts

The arts scene in Los Angeles extends beyond the screen and onto the stage. A place of artistic innovation and history, one can discover new and challenging theatrical works across L.A. stages, while the city still maintains a respect for tradition with its restored theaters and classic plays. See live music at impeccably designed amphitheaters like the Hollywood Bowl or listen in on captivating lectures by authors and directors at various intimate spaces. In homage to the city's roots as a filmmaking mecca, there are also retrospectives and rare screenings in movie theaters all over the city, often followed by Q&As with the cast.

Visitor Information

Discover Los Angeles, the official tourism site, has an annually updated general information packet that includes suggestions for entertainment, lodging, and dining and a list of special events. There are two visitor information centers, both accessible to Metro stops: the Hollywood & Highland Center and Union Station.

CONTACTS Discover Los Angeles.
☏ 213/624–7300 ⊕ www.discover-losangeles.com.

Santa Monica and Venice

Santa Monica and Venice are two of the region's most iconic destinations, but while Santa Monica has its eyes firmly on the future, Venice enjoys indulging a bit in its past.

Silicon Beach, Southern California's tech hub, is centered on the Santa Monica area, which means employees from hundreds of companies like Activision, Hulu, and Snap (of Snapchat fame) flood the area and influence the flavor of its shops and restaurants. (Silicon Beach's influence also impacts many hotel amenity lists, to your benefit.) The Santa Monica Pier, with its Ferris wheel and roller coaster, is the scene of a thousand movie and television show filmings, from *Forrest Gump* to *Iron Man*, while Venice Beach has conjured images of greased-up bodybuilders, boho hippies, and boardwalk palm readers for generations.

Santa Monica

◉ Sights

★ Santa Monica Pier
CAROUSEL | FAMILY | Souvenir shops, carnival games, arcades, eateries, an outdoor trapeze school, a small amusement park, and an aquarium all contribute to the festive atmosphere of this truncated pier at the foot of Colorado Boulevard below Palisades Park. The pier's trademark 46-horse Looff Carousel, built in 1922, has appeared in several films, including *The Sting*. The Soda Jerks ice-cream fountain (named for the motion the attendant makes when pulling the machine's

Santa Monica Pier's West Coaster and Pacific Wheel provide incredible ocean views.

arm) inside the carousel building is a pier staple. Free concerts are held on the pier in the summer. ⊠ *Colorado Ave., Santa Monica* ☎ *310/458–8901* ⊕ *www.santamonicapier.org.*

Santa Monica State Beach

BEACH—SIGHT | The first beach you'll hit after the Santa Monica Freeway (Interstate 10) runs into the Pacific Coast Highway, wide and sandy Santa Monica is *the* place for sunning and socializing. The Strand, which runs across the beach and for 22 miles in total, is popular among walkers, joggers, and bicyclists. Be prepared for a mob scene on summer weekends, when parking becomes an expensive ordeal. Swimming is fine (with the usual poststorm-pollution caveat); for surfing, go elsewhere. For a memorable view, climb up the stairway over PCH to Palisades Park, at the top of the bluffs. Free summer concerts are held on the pier on Thursday evening. **Amenities:** parking; lifeguards; toilets; food and drink; showers; water sports. **Best for:** partiers; sunset; surfing; swimming; walking.

⊠ *1642 Promenade, PCH at California Incline, Santa Monica* ☎ *310/458–8573* ⊕ *www.smgov.net/portals/beach* ⌫ *Parking from $7.*

★ Third Street Promenade and Santa Monica Place

COMMERCIAL CENTER | Stretch your legs along this pedestrian-only, three-block stretch of 3rd Street, close to the Pacific, lined with jacaranda trees, ivy-topiary dinosaur fountains, strings of lights, and branches of nearly every major U.S. retail chain; indeed, it always seems to house the most-coveted brands for each generation of teens. Outdoor cafés, street vendors, movie theaters, and a rich nightlife make this a main gathering spot for locals, visitors, street artists and musicians, and performance artists. Plan a night just to take it all in or take an afternoon for a long people-watching stroll. There's plenty of parking in city structures on the streets flanking the promenade. **Santa Monica Place,** at the south end of the promenade, is a sleek outdoor mall and foodie haven. Its three

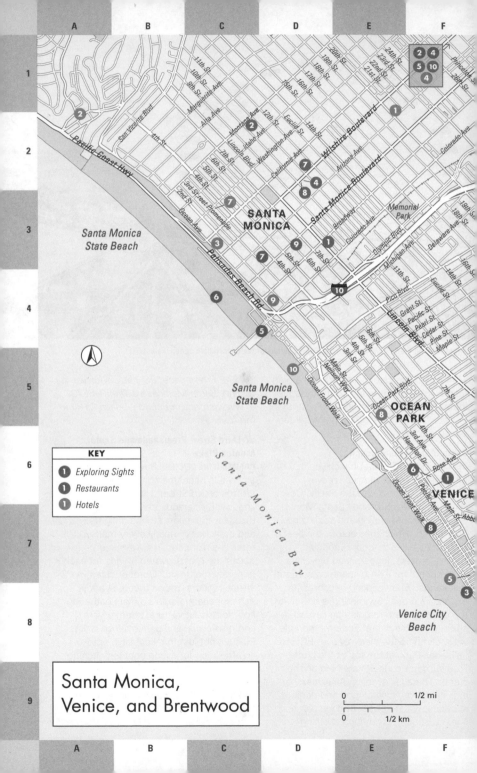

Santa Monica, Venice, and Brentwood

KEY
- ① Exploring Sights
- ① Restaurants
- ① Hotels

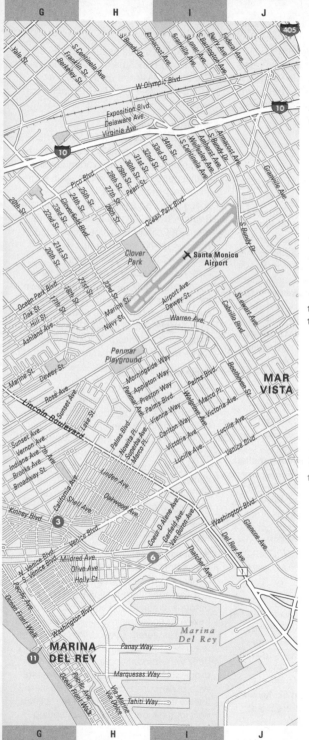

Sights ▼

Restaurants ▼

Hotels ▼

stories are home to Nordstrom, Louis Vuitton, Coach, and other upscale retailers. Don't miss the ocean views from the rooftop food court. ✉ *3rd St., between Colorado and Wilshire Blvds., Santa Monica* 🌐 *www.downtownsm.com.*

🍴 Restaurants

★ Bay Cities Italian Deli

$ | **DELI** | Part deli, part market, Bay Cities has been home to incredible Italian subs since 1925. This renowned counter-service spot is always crowded (best to order ahead), but monster subs run the gamut from the mighty meatball to the signature Godmother, made with prosciutto, ham, capicola, mortadella, Genoa salami, and provolone. **Known for:** market with rare imports; old-school, deli-style service; huge sandwiches. [$] *Average main: $10* ✉ *1517 Lincoln Blvd., Santa Monica* ☎ *310/395–8279* 🌐 *www.baycitiesitaliandeli.com* 🕒 *Closed Mon.*

Father's Office

$$ | **AMERICAN** | Distinguished by its vintage neon sign, this gastropub is famous for handcrafted beers and a brilliant signature burger. Topped with Gruyère and Maytag blue cheeses, arugula, caramelized onions, and applewood-smoked bacon compote, the Office Burger is a guilty pleasure worth waiting in line for, which is usually required. **Known for:** addictive sweet potato fries; strict no-substitutions policy; 36 craft beers on tap. [$] *Average main: $15* ✉ *1018 Montana Ave., Santa Monica* ☎ *310/736–2224* 🌐 *www.fathersoffice.com* 🕒 *No lunch weekdays.*

Huckleberry Bakery and Cafe

$$ | **AMERICANAMERICAN** | **FAMILY** | Founded by Santa Monica natives, Huckleberry brings together the best ingredients from local farmers and growers to craft diner-style comfort food with a chic twist. Everything is made on-site, even the hot sauce and almond milk. **Known for:** from-scratch diner-style breakfast options; delectable pastries; green eggs and Niman Ranch ham. [$] *Average main: $14* ✉ *1014 Wilshire Blvd., Santa Monica* ☎ *310/451–2311* 🌐 *www.huckleberrycafe.com.*

★ Rustic Canyon

$$$$ | **MODERN AMERICAN** | A Santa Monica mainstay, the seasonally changing menu at this farm-to-table restaurant consistently upends norms and has even earned a Michelin star. The homey, minimalist space offers sweeping views of Wilshire Boulevard, and on any given night the menu of California cuisine may include Channel Island rockfish with shelling beans and Sun Gold tomatoes, or buttered ricotta dumplings with golden chanterelles and Coolea cheese. **Known for:** never-ending wine list; knowledgeable staff; everything is made in-house. [$] *Average main: $35* ✉ *1119 Wilshire Blvd., Santa Monica* ☎ *310/393–7050* 🌐 *www.rusticcanyonrestaurant.com.*

Santa Monica Seafood

$$ | **SEAFOOD** | **FAMILY** | A Southern California favorite that seems like a tourist trap at first blush but decidedly isn't, this Italian seafood haven has been serving up fresh fish since 1939. This freshness comes from its pedigree as the largest seafood distributor in the Southwest. **Known for:** deliciously seasoned rainbow trout; oyster bar; historic fish market. [$] *Average main: $20* ✉ *1000 Wilshire Blvd., Santa Monica* ☎ *310/393–5244* 🌐 *www.santamonicaseafood.com.*

★ Tar and Roses

$$$ | **MODERN AMERICAN** | This small and dimly lit romantic spot in Santa Monica is full of adventurous global options, like octopus skewers and venison loin. The new American cuisine, which is centered on the restaurant's wood-fired oven, also features standouts like braised lamb belly with minted apple chutney and drool-worthy strawberry ricotta crostata with honeycomb ice cream for dessert. **Known for:** phenomenal oxtail dumplings; delicious hanger steak; ever-changing

menu. $ *Average main: $30 ⊠ 602 Santa Monica Blvd., Santa Monica* ☎ *310/587–0700* ⊕ *www.tarandroses.com.*

 ## Hotels

The Ambrose

$$$ | **HOTEL** | Tranquillity pervades the airy, California Craftsman–style, four-story Ambrose, which blends right into its mostly residential Santa Monica neighborhood. **Pros:** "green" practices like nontoxic cleaners and recycling bins; partial ocean views; nice amenities (like car service and wine reception) for a $25 extra fee. **Cons:** quiet, residential area of Santa Monica; parking fee ($27); not walking distance to beach. $ *Rooms from: $359 ⊠ 1255 20th St., Santa Monica* ☎ *310/315–1555, 877/262–7673* ⊕ *www.ambrosehotel.com* ⤷ *77 rooms* ⦿ *Free breakfast.*

★ Channel Road Inn

$$ | **B&B/INN** | A quaint surprise in Southern California, the Channel Road Inn is every bit the country retreat bed-and-breakfast lovers adore, with four-poster beds, fluffy duvets, and a cozy living room with a fireplace. **Pros:** free wine and cheese "minipicnic" each afternoon; home-cooked breakfast included; meditative rose garden on-site. **Cons:** no pool; need a car (or Uber) to get around; decidedly non-L.A. decor not for everyone. $ *Rooms from: $225 ⊠ 219 W. Channel Rd., Santa Monica* ☎ *310/459–1920* ⊕ *www.channelroadinn.com* ⤷ *15 rooms* ⦿ *Free breakfast.*

Fairmont Miramar Hotel and Bungalows Santa Monica

$$$$ | **HOTEL** | A mammoth Moreton Bay fig tree dwarfs the main entrance of the 5-acre, beach-adjacent Santa Monica wellness retreat and lends its name to the inviting on-site Mediterranean-inspired restaurant, FIG, which focuses on local ingredients and frequently refreshes its menu. **Pros:** guests can play games on the heated patio; swanky open-air cocktail spot, the Bungalow, on-site; retrofitted '20s and '40s bungalows. **Cons:** all this luxury comes at a big price; standard rooms are on the small side; breakfast not included. $ *Rooms from: $599 ⊠ 101 Wilshire Blvd., Santa Monica* ☎ *310/576–7777, 866/540–4470* ⊕ *www.fairmont.com/santamonica* ⤷ *334 rooms* ⦿ *No meals.*

Palihouse Santa Monica

$$$ | **HOTEL** | Tucked in a posh residential area three blocks from the sea and lively Third Street Promenade, Palihouse Santa Monica caters to design-minded world travelers, with spacious rooms and suites decked out in whimsical antiques. **Pros:** Apple TV in rooms; walking distance to Santa Monica attractions; fully equipped kitchens. **Cons:** no pool; decor might not appeal to more traditional travelers; parking fee ($45). $ *Rooms from: $355 ⊠ 1001 3rd St., Santa Monica* ☎ *310/394–1279* ⊕ *www.palihousesantamonica.com* ⤷ *38 rooms* ⦿ *No meals.*

Sea Shore Motel

$ | **HOTEL** | On Santa Monica's busy Main Street, the Sea Shore (family-owned for almost 50 years) is a charming throwback to Route 66 and to '60s-style roadside motels in an ultratrendy neighborhood. **Pros:** close to beach and restaurants; free Wi-Fi, parking, and use of beach equipment; popular rooftop deck. **Cons:** street noise; motel-style decor and beds; not the Santa Monica style a lot of people are looking for. $ *Rooms from: $159 ⊠ 2637 Main St., Santa Monica* ☎ *310/392–2787* ⊕ *www.seashoremotel.com* ⤷ *25 rooms* ⦿ *No meals.*

Shore Hotel

$$$$ | **HOTEL** | With views of the Santa Monica Pier, this hotel with a friendly staff offers eco-minded travelers stylish rooms with a modern design, just steps from the sand and sea. **Pros:** near beach and Third Street Promenade; rainfall showerheads; solar-heated pool and hot tub. **Cons:** expensive rooms and parking fees; fronting busy Ocean Avenue;

some sharing a room may be wary of the see-through shower. [$] *Rooms from: $432* ✉ *1515 Ocean Ave., Santa Monica* ☎ *310/458–1515* 🌐 *shorehotel.com* 🛏 *164 rooms* 🍴 *No meals.*

★Shutters on the Beach
$$$$ | HOTEL | FAMILY | Set right on the sand, this inn has become synonymous with staycations, with the beachfront location and show-house decor making it one of SoCal's most popular luxury hotels. **Pros:** built-in cabinets filled with art books and curios; rooms designed by Michael Smith; bathrooms come with whirlpool tubs. **Cons:** have to pay for extras like beach chairs; very expensive; breakfast not included. [$] *Rooms from: $675* ✉ *1 Pico Blvd., Santa Monica* ☎ *310/458–0030, 800/334–9000* 🌐 *www.shuttersonthebeach.com* 🛏 *198 rooms* 🍴 *No meals.*

Nightlife

★Chez Jay
BARS/PUBS | Around since 1959, this dive bar continues to be a well-loved place in Santa Monica. Everyone from the young to the old (including families) frequents this historical landmark. It's a charming place, from the well-worn booths with their red checkered tablecloths to the ship's wheel near the door. The backyard lounge is perfect for warm low-key days. ✉ *1657 Ocean Ave., Santa Monica* ☎ *310/395–1741* 🌐 *www.chezjays.com.*

The Galley
BARS/PUBS | Nostalgia reigns at this true neighborhood fixture, which has had the same owner for more than 30 years. As Santa Monica's oldest restaurant and bar, the Galley has a consistent nautical theme inside and out: the boatlike exterior features wavy blue neon lights and porthole windows; inside, fishing nets and anchors adorn the walls, and the whole place is aglow with colorful string lights. Most patrons tend to crowd the center bar, with the more dinner-oriented folks frequenting the booths. Prices are a good deal during "most hours" and a steal during "happy hours." And strangely enough, the secret-recipe salad dressing is justifiably famous. ✉ *2442 Main St., Santa Monica* ☎ *310/452–1934.*

Shopping

The Acorn Store
TOYS | FAMILY | Remember when toys didn't require computer programming? This old-fashioned shop (for ages 10 and under) sparks children's imaginations with dress-up clothes, picture books, and hand-painted wooden toys by brands like Poan and Haba. ✉ *1220 5th St., near Wilshire Blvd., Santa Monica* ☎ *310/451–5845* 🌐 *www.theacornstore.com.*

Limonaia
GIFTS/SOUVENIRS | This charming and cozy neighborhood boutique has something for every kind of gift recipient. Ben's Garden goods (pillows, coasters, trays, etc.) decorated with inspirational words, lovely cards for all occasions, beaded jewelry, cookbooks, and an extensive puzzle selection are just a few things shoppers can find here. ✉ *1325 Montana Ave., Santa Monica* ☎ *310/458–1858* 🌐 *www.shoplimonaia.com.*

Third Street Promenade
SHOPPING CENTERS/MALLS | There is no shortage of spots to shop everything from sporting goods to trendy fashions on this pedestrian-friendly strip. Outposts here are mainly of the chain variety, and in between splurging on books, clothing, sneakers, and more, shoppers can pop into one of the many eateries to stay satiated or even catch a movie at one of the theaters. Additionally, the chef-approved Farmers Market takes over twice a week, and with the beach just a few steps away, the destination is a quintessential California stop. ✉ *3rd St., between Broadway and Wilshire Blvd., Santa Monica.*

Venice

Sights

Binoculars Building

BUILDING | Frank Gehry is known around the world for his architectural master-pieces. In L.A. alone he's responsible for multiple houses and buildings like the Gehry Residence, Loyola Law School, and Walt Disney Hall. But one of his most interesting creations is the Binoculars Building, a quirky Venice spot that is exactly as advertised—a giant set of binoculars. The project was originally designed for the Chiat/Day advertising agency and today is home to one of Google's Silicon Beach offices. While you can't tour the building, you can take a clever Instagram shot out front. ⊠ *340 Main St., Venice.*

Muscle Beach

LOCAL INTEREST | Bronzed young men bench-pressing five girls at once, weightlifters doing tricks on the sand—the Muscle Beach facility fired up the country's imagination from the get-go. There are actually two spots known as Muscle Beach. The original Muscle Beach, just south of the Santa Monica Pier, is where bodybuilders Jack LaLanne and Vic and Armand Tanny used to work out in the 1950s. When it was closed in 1959, the bodybuilders moved south along the beach to Venice, to a city-run facility known as "the Pen," and the Venice Beach spot inherited the Muscle Beach moniker. The spot is probably best known now as a place where a young Arnold Schwarzenegger first came to flex his muscles in the late '60s and began his rise to fame. The area now hosts a variety of sports and gymnastics events and the occasional "beach babe" beauty contests that always draw a crowd. But stop by any time during daylight for an eye-popping array of beefcakes (and would-be beefcakes). ⊠ *1800 Ocean Front Walk, Venice* ⊕ *www. musclebeach.net.*

★ Venice Beach Boardwalk

PROMENADE | The surf and sand of Venice are fine, but the main attraction here is the boardwalk scene, which is a cosmos all its own. Go on weekend afternoons for the best people-watching experience. You can also swim, fish, surf, and skateboard, or play racquetball, handball, shuffleboard, and basketball (the boardwalk is the site of hotly contested pickup games). Or you can rent a bike or in-line skates and hit the Strand bike path, then pull up a seat at a sidewalk café and watch the action unfold. ⊠ *1800 Ocean Front Walk, west of Pacific Ave., Venice* ☎ *310/392–4687* ⊕ *www. venicebeach.com.*

🍴 Restaurants

★ Gjelina

$$ | **AMERICAN** | This spot comes alive the moment you walk through the rustic wooden door and into a softly lit dining room with long communal tables. The menu is seasonal, with outstanding small plates, charcuterie, pastas, and pizza. **Known for:** lively crowd on the patio; late-night menu; Michelin-approved dishes like crispy duck leg confit. $ *Average main: $22* ⊠ *1429 Abbot Kinney Blvd., Venice* ☎ *310/450–1429* ⊕ *www.gjelina.com.*

Rose Cafe

$$$ | **MODERN AMERICAN** | **FAMILY** | This indoor-outdoor restaurant has served Venice for decades but constantly reinvents itself, serving mouthwatering California cuisines with multiple patios, a full bar, and a bakery. Creative types loiter under the macramé chandeliers for the Wi-Fi and sip espressos, while young families gather out back to snack on smoked radiatore carbonara and crispy brussels sprouts. **Known for:** sophisticated but unpretentious vibe; location in the heart of Venice; lively patio seating. $ *Average main: $25* ⊠ *220 Rose Ave., Venice* ☎ *310/399– 0711* ⊕ *www.rosecafevenice.com.*

Venice Whaler

$$ | AMERICAN | This beachfront bar that's been the local watering hole for musicians like the Doors and the Beach Boys since 1944 boasts an amazing view and serves tasty California pub food like fish tacos, pulled-pork sliders, and avocado toast with a basic selection of beers. The Whaler Double Burger is an institution in itself. **Known for:** rock-n-roll history; great pub food; fun brunch. ⓢ *Average main: $15* ✉ *10 W. Washington Blvd., Venice* ☎ *310/821–8737* ⊕ *www.venicewhaler.com.*

 ## Hotels

Hotel Erwin

$$$ | HOTEL | A boutique hotel a block off the Venice Beach Boardwalk, the Erwin will make you feel like a hipper version of yourself. **Pros:** dining emphasizing fresh ingredients; playful design in guest rooms; free Wi-Fi and use of hotel bikes. **Cons:** some rooms face a noisy alley; no pool; breakfast not included. ⓢ *Rooms from: $369* ✉ *1697 Pacific Ave., Venice* ☎ *310/452–1111, 800/786–7789* ⊕ *www.hotelerwin.com* ⇲ *119 rooms* ⦿ *No meals.*

★ The Kinney

$$ | HOTEL | Walking distance to Venice Beach and Abbot Kinney's artsy commercial strip, this playful hotel announces itself boldly with wall murals by Melissa Scrivner before you even enter the lobby. **Pros:** affordable, artistic rooms; Ping-Pong area; Jacuzzi bar. **Cons:** valet parking is a must ($15); hotel can get loud; some hipper-than-thou vibes. ⓢ *Rooms from: $239* ✉ *737 Washington Blvd., Venice* ☎ *310/821–4455* ⊕ *www.thekinneyvenicebeach.com* ⇲ *68 rooms* ⦿ *No meals.*

ⓨ Nightlife

The Brig

BARS/PUBS | This charming bar has its pluses (interesting drinks, talented DJs) and minuses (ugh, parking) but is worth a look if you're in the area. There's always a food truck around, and the bar's fine with you bringing in outside food. ✉ *1515 Abbot Kinney Blvd., Venice* ☎ *310/399–7537* ⊕ *www.thebrig.com.*

 ## Shopping

General Store

GIFTS/SOUVENIRS | Right at home in the beachy, bohemian neighborhood, this well-curated shop is a decidedly contemporary take on the concept of general stores. The very definition of "California cool," General Store offers beauty and bath products loaded with organic natural ingredients, handmade ceramics, linen tea towels, and a spot-on selection of art books. Featuring an impressive number of local makers and designers, the boutique also sells modern, minimal clothing and has a kids' section that will wow even the hippest moms and dads. ✉ *1801 Lincoln Blvd., Venice* ☎ *310/751–6393* ⊕ *www.shop-generalstore.com.*

Heist

CLOTHING | Owner Nilou Ghodsi has admitted that she stocks her Westside shop like an extension of her own closet, which in her case means keeping the focus on floaty, modern-yet-classic pieces as opposed to trendy ones. The airy boutique offers elegantly edgy separates from American designers like Nili Lotan and Ulla Johnson, as well as from hard-to-find French and Italian designers like Pas de Calais. ✉ *1100 Abbot Kinney Blvd., Venice* ☎ *310/450–6531* ⊕ *www.shopheist.com.*

Strange Invisible Perfumes

PERFUME/COSMETICS | Finding your signature fragrance at this sleek Abbot Kinney boutique won't come cheap, but perfumer Alexandra Balahoutis takes creating her scents as seriously as a seasoned winemaker—and they're just as nuanced as a well-balanced glass of vino. Essences for the perfumes are organic, wild crafted, biodynamic, and bottled locally. Highlights from SI's core collection include the cacao-spiked Dimanche and leathery Black Rosette. ✉ *1138 Abbot Kinney Blvd., Venice* ☎ *310/314–1505* 🌐 *www.siperfumes.com.*

Brentwood

Sights

★ The Getty Center

MUSEUM | FAMILY | Architect Richard Meier's Getty Center features stunning design, uncommon gardens, and fascinating art collections. The complex's rough-cut travertine marble skin seems to soak up the light on a sunny day. From the underground parking structure, walk or take a smooth, computer-driven tram up the steep slope, checking out the Bel Air estates across the 405 freeway. From the courtyard, plazas, and walkways, you can survey the city from the San Gabriel Mountains to the ocean. In a ravine separating the museum and the Getty Research Institute, artist Robert Irwin created the Central Garden in stark contrast to Meier's geometrical designs. Though the two sniped at each other during construction (Irwin stirred the pot with every loose twist his garden path took), the result is a refreshing garden walk whose focal point is an azalea maze—some insist the Mickey Mouse shape is on purpose—in a reflecting pool. Inside the pavilions are permanent collections of European paintings, drawings, sculpture, illuminated manuscripts, and decorative arts, as well as world-class temporary exhibitions and photographs gathered internationally. The collection of French furniture and decorative arts, especially from the early years of Louis XIV to the end of the reign of Louis XVI, is renowned for its quality and condition. You'll also find works by Rembrandt, Van Gogh, Monet, and James Ensor. The brochure in the entrance hall guides you to collection highlights, or you can opt for the instructive audio tour (free, but you have to leave your ID). The Getty also presents lectures, films, concerts, and programs for kids and families. Dining options include the upscale restaurant and the cafeteria with panoramic window views, plus outdoor coffee carts. ■ **TIP→ On-site parking is subject to availability and can fill up by midday on holidays and in the summer, so try to come early in the day or after lunch.** A tram takes you from the street-level entrance to the top of the hill. Public buses (Metro Rapid Line 734) also serve the center and link to the Expo Rail extension. ✉ *1200 Getty Center Dr., Brentwood* ☎ *310/440–7300* 🌐 *www.getty.edu* 🎟 *Free; parking $15* 🕓 *Closed Mon.*

Pierce Brothers Westwood Village Memorial Park and Mortuary

CEMETERY | The who's who of the dearly departed can all be found at this peaceful, though unremarkable, cemetery. Notable residents include Marilyn Monroe and Joe DiMaggio; authors Truman Capote, Ray Bradbury, and Jackie Collins; actors Natalie Wood, Rodney Dangerfield, Farrah Fawcett, Jack Lemmon, and Dean Martin; and directors Billy Wilder and John Cassavetes. ✉ *1218 Glendon Ave., Westwood* ☎ *310/474–1579* 🌐 *www.dignitymemorial.com.*

Restaurants

Lady Chocolatt

$ | BELGIAN | The purveyor of the finest Belgian chocolate in all of Los Angeles, Lady Chocolatt is the perfect answer to the age-old question of what to gift on any special occasion. The ornate display case is filled with dark chocolate truffles, hazelnut pralines, Grand Marnier ganaches, and so much more. **Known for:** Belgian chocolate; Italian espresso; tasty sandwiches. [$] *Average main: $5* ✉ *12008 Wilshire Blvd.* ☎ *310/442–2245* 🌐 *www.chocolatt.com.*

Toscana

$$$$ | ITALIAN | This rustic trattoria along San Vicente is a favorite celebrity haunt. Expect elevated sensory offerings, from its cozy atmosphere to its mouthwatering Tuscan fare and excellent wine list. **Known for:** excellent wine list; seasonal menu items like truffle sliders; great celeb-spotting. [$] *Average main: $35* ✉ *11633 San Vicente Blvd., Brentwood* ☎ *310/820–2448* 🌐 *www.toscanabrentwood.com.*

Hotels

★ Hotel Bel-Air

$$$$ | HOTEL | This Spanish Mission–style icon has been a discreet hillside retreat for celebrities and society types since 1946 and was given a face-lift by star designers Alexandra Champalimaud and David Rockwell. **Pros:** shuttle available within 3 mile radius of hotel; perfect for the privacy minded; alfresco dining at Wolfgang Puck restaurant. **Cons:** not walking distance to restaurants or shops; hefty price tag; controversial ownership by the Sultan of Brunei. [$] *Rooms from: $645* ✉ *701 Stone Canyon Rd., Bel Air* ☎ *310/472–1211* 🌐 *www.dorchestercollection.com/en/los-angeles/hotel-bel-air* 🛏 *103 rooms* 🍴 *No meals.*

Beverly Hills

The rumors are true: Beverly Hills delivers on a dramatic, cinematic scale of wealth and excess. A known celebrity haunt, come here to daydream or to live like the rich and famous for a day. Window-shop or splurge at tony stores, and keep an eye out for filming locales; just walking around here will make you feel like you're on a movie set.

Sights

Museum of Tolerance

MUSEUM | FAMILY | A museum that unflinchingly confronts bigotry and racism, one of its most affecting sections covers the Holocaust, with film footage of deportations and concentration camps. Upon entering, you are issued a "passport" bearing the name of a child whose life was dramatically changed by the Nazis; as you go through the exhibit, you learn the fate of that child. Another exhibit called *Anne: The Life and Legacy of Anne Frank* brings her story to life through immersive environments, multimedia presentations, and interesting artifacts, while Simon Wiesenthal's Vienna office is set exactly as the famous "Nazi hunter" had it while conducting his research that brought more than 1,000 war criminals to justice.

Interactive exhibits include the Millennium Machine, which engages visitors in finding solutions to human rights abuses around the world; Globalhate.com, which examines hate on the Internet by exposing problematic sites via touch-screen computer terminals; and the Point of View Diner, a re-creation of a 1950s diner that "serves" a menu of controversial topics on video jukeboxes. **■ TIP→ Plan to spend at least three hours touring the museum; making a reservation is especially recommended for Friday, Sunday, and holiday visits.** ✉ *9786 W. Pico Blvd., south of Beverly Hills* ☎ *310/772–2505 for reservations* 🌐 *www.museumoftolerance.com* 🎟 *From $16* 🕓 *Closed Sat.*

★ Rodeo Drive

NEIGHBORHOOD | The ultimate shopping indulgence, Rodeo Drive is one of L.A.'s bona fide tourist attractions. The art of window-shopping (and reenacting your *Pretty Woman* fantasies) is prime among the retail elite: Tiffany & Co., Gucci, Jimmy Choo, Valentino, Harry Winston, Prada—you get the picture. Near the southern end of Rodeo Drive is Via Rodeo, a curvy cobblestone street designed to resemble a European shopping area and the perfect backdrop to pose for your Instagram feed. To give your feet a rest, free trolley tours depart from the southeast corner of Rodeo Drive and Dayton Way from 11:30 to 4:30. They're a terrific way to get an overview of the neighborhood. ✉ *Rodeo Dr., Beverly Hills* 🌐 *www.rodeodrive-bh.com.*

★ Spadena House

BUILDING | Otherwise known as the Witch's House in Beverly Hills, the Spadena House has an interesting history. First built on the Willat Studios lot in 1920, the house was physically moved to its current ritzy location in 1924. The house is not open for tourists, but the fairy-tale-like appearance is viewable from the street for onlookers to snap pics. Movie buffs will also recognize it from a background shot in the film *Clueless.* ✉ *516 Walden Dr., Beverly Hills.*

🍴 Restaurants

Crustacean

$$$$ | **VIETNAMESE** | A Euro-Vietnamese fusion gem in the heart of Beverly Hills, Crustacean allows you to walk on water above exotic fish and see the kitchen preparing your perfect garlic noodles through a glass window. Standouts (besides the noodles) include Dungeness crab, A5 Wagyu beef, tuna cigars, and hearts-of-palm crab cakes. **Known for:** sake-simmered dishes; no-grease garlic noodles; unique cocktails like artichoke old-fashioneds. [$] *Average main: $36* ✉ *468 N. Bedford Dr., Beverly Hills* ☎ *310/205–8990* 🌐 *crustaceanbh.com* 🕒 *Closed Mon.*

★ Gucci Osteria da Massimo Bottura

$$$$ | **ITALIAN** | Legendary Italian chef Massimo Bottura opened this spot, his first L.A. eatery, to loads of fanfare and celebrity sightings. The restaurant mirrors the Florence, Italy, location of the same name with a menu filled with favorites like a mouthwatering tortellini in brodo. **Known for:** excellent pastas; great people-watching; avant-garde design. [$] *Average main: $80* ✉ *347 N. Rodeo Dr., Beverly Hills* ☎ *424/600–7490* 🌐 *www.gucci.com/us/en/st/capsule/gucci-osteria-beverly-hills.*

Nate 'n' Al's

$$ | **DELI** | A longtime refuge from California's lean cuisine, Nate 'n' Al's serves up steaming pastrami, matzo ball soup, and potato latkes. Big time media and entertainment insiders are often seen kibbitzing at this old-time East Coast–style establishment. **Known for:** matzo ball soup; killer pastrami; long waits. [$] *Average main: $15* ✉ *414 N. Beverly Dr., Beverly Hills* ☎ *310/274–0101* 🌐 *www.natenals.com.*

Polo Lounge

$$$$ | **AMERICAN** | Nothing says Beverly Hills quite like the Polo Lounge inside the Beverly Hills Hotel. This classic, monied spot is home to Hollywood royalty and entertainment luminaries noshing on lobster Nicoise or the famed Wagyu burger during power lunches. **Known for:** celebrity sightings; mouthwatering Wagyu burgers; dress code of no ripped jeans or baseball caps. [$] *Average main: $35* ✉ *The Beverly Hills Hotel, 9641 Sunset Blvd., Beverly Hills* ☎ *310/887–2777* 🌐 *www.dorchestercollection.com/en/los-angeles/the-beverly-hills-hotel/restaurants-bars/the-polo-lounge.*

★ Spago Beverly Hills

$$$$ | **MODERN AMERICAN** | Wolfgang Puck's flagship restaurant is a modern L.A. classic. Spago centers on a buzzing redbrick outdoor courtyard (with retractable roof) shaded by 100-year-old olive trees, and a daily-changing menu that offers dishes like smoked salmon pizza or off-menu schnitzel. **Known for:** great people-watching; off-menu schnitzel; sizzling smoked salmon pizza. [$] *Average main: $35* ✉ *176 N. Canon Dr., Beverly Hills* ☎ *310/385–0880* 🌐 *www.wolfgangpuck.com* 🕒 *Closed Mon. and Tues.*

Hotels

Beverly Wilshire, a Four Seasons Hotel
$$$$ | **HOTEL** | Built in 1928, this Rodeo Drive–adjacent hotel is part Italian Renaissance (with elegant details like crystal chandeliers) and part contemporary. **Pros:** complimentary car service; Wolfgang Puck restaurant on-site; first-rate spa. **Cons:** small lobby; valet parking is expensive; might be too sceney for some. [$] *Rooms from: $545* ✉ *9500 Wilshire Blvd., Beverly Hills* ☎ *310/275–5200, 800/427–4354* 🌐 *www.fourseasons.com/beverlywilshire* 🛏 *395 rooms* 🍴 *No meals.*

The Crescent Beverly Hills
$$ | **HOTEL** | Built in 1927 as a dorm for silent-film actors, the Crescent is now a fanciful boutique hotel with a great location—within the Beverly Hills shopping triangle—and with an even better price (for the area). **Pros:** indoor/outdoor fireplace; lively on-site restaurant, Crescent Bar and Terrace; economic room available for $148. **Cons:** $30 resort fee is not optional; no elevator; rooms on the small side. [$] *Rooms from: $245* ✉ *403 N. Crescent Dr., Beverly Hills* ☎ *310/247–0505* 🌐 *www.crescentbh.com* 🛏 *35 rooms* 🍴 *Free breakfast.*

★ **The Maybourne Beverly Hills**
$$$$ | **HOTEL** | The nine-story, Mediterranean-style palazzo is dedicated to welcoming those who relish luxury, providing classic style and exemplary service. **Pros:** secret whiskey bar tucked upstairs; obliging, highly trained staff; lots of activities and amenities for kids. **Cons:** hefty tab for all this finery; not all rooms have balconies; pricey valet parking. [$] *Rooms from: $550* ✉ *225 N. Canon Dr., Beverly Hills* ☎ *310/860–7800* 🌐 *www.maybournebeverlyhills.com* 🛏 *201 rooms* 🍴 *No meals.*

★ **Peninsula Beverly Hills**
$$$$ | **HOTEL** | This French Riviera–style palace overflowing with antiques and art is a favorite of boldface names, but visitors consistently describe a stay here as near perfect. **Pros:** 24-hour check-in/check-out policy; sunny pool area with cabanas; complimentary Rolls-Royce takes you to nearby Beverly Hills. **Cons:** very expensive; room decor might feel too ornate for some; exclusive vibe can be intimidating. [$] *Rooms from: $600* ✉ *9882 S. Santa Monica Blvd., Beverly Hills* ☎ *310/551–2888, 800/462–7899* 🌐 *www.peninsula.com/en/beverly-hills/5-star-luxury-hotel-beverly-hills* 🛏 *195 rooms* 🍴 *No meals.*

SLS Hotel Beverly Hills
$$$ | **HOTEL** | From the sleek, Philippe Starck–designed lobby and lounge with fireplaces, hidden nooks, and a communal table to luxurious poolside cabanas, this hotel offers a cushy, dreamlike stay. **Pros:** great cocktails at lobby bar; complimentary house car for use within 3-mile radius; dreamy Ciel spa. **Cons:** standard rooms are compact; pricey dining and parking; on a busy intersection outside Beverly Hills. [$] *Rooms from: $365* ✉ *465 S. La Cienega Blvd., Beverly Hills* ☎ *310/247–0400* 🌐 *slshotels.com/beverlyhills* 🛏 *297 rooms* 🍴 *No meals.*

★ **Viceroy L'Ermitage Beverly Hills**
$$$$ | **HOTEL** | This all-suite hotel is the picture of luxury: French doors open to a mini-balcony with views of the Hollywood sign; inside the very large rooms you'll find soaking tubs and oversize bath towels. **Pros:** traditional French cuisine at Avec Nous on-site; free shuttle service within 2-mile radius; all rooms are large suites. **Cons:** small spa and pool; very expensive; a bit of a trek to Beverly Hills shopping. [$] *Rooms from: $495* ✉ *9291 Burton Way, Beverly Hills* ☎ *310/278–3344* 🌐 *www.viceroyhotelsandresorts.com/beverly-hills* 🛏 *116 rooms* 🍴 *No meals.*

🛍 Shopping

Cartier

JEWELRY/ACCESSORIES | Cartier has a bridal collection to sigh for in its chandeliered and respectfully hushed showroom, along with more playful pieces (chunky, diamond-encrusted panther cocktail rings, for example), watches, and accessories. The shop itself feels like the ultimate playground for A-list clientele, complete with a red-carpeted spiral staircase. ✉ *370 N. Rodeo Dr., Beverly Hills* ☎ *310/275–4272* ⊕ *www.cartier.com.*

Céline

CLOTHING | Under designer Hedi Slimane's creative direction, the Parisian brand has entered a new chapter. At the Beverly Hills brick-and-mortar, fashion lovers looking for French Cool Girl clothing will love the selection of the label's leather handbags, heels, and chic ready-to-wear clothing. ✉ *456 N. Rodeo Dr., Beverly Hills* ☎ *310/888–0120* ⊕ *www.celine. com.*

Gearys of Beverly Hills

GIFTS/SOUVENIRS | Since 1930, this has been the ultimate destination for those seeking the most exquisite fine china, crystal, silver, and jewelry, mostly from classic sources like Christofle, Baccarat, and Waterford. No wonder it's a favorite for registries of the rich and famous. ✉ *351 N. Beverly Dr., Beverly Hills* ☎ *310/273–4741* ⊕ *www.gearys.com.*

Harry Winston

JEWELRY/ACCESSORIES | Perhaps the most locally famous jeweler is Harry Winston, *the* source for Oscar-night jewelry. The three-level space, with a bronze sculptural facade, velvet-panel walls, private salons, and a rooftop patio, is as glamorous as the gems. ✉ *310 N. Rodeo Dr., Beverly Hills* ☎ *310/271–8554* ⊕ *www. harrywinston.com.*

Neiman Marcus

DEPARTMENT STORES | Luxury shopping at its finest, this couture salon frequently trots out designer trunk shows, and most locals go right for the shoe department, which features high-end footwear favorites like Giuseppe Zanotti and Christian Louboutin. A café on the third floor keeps your blood sugar high during multiple wardrobe changes, while a bar on the fourth is for celebrating those perfect finds with a glass of champagne. ✉ *9700 Wilshire Blvd., Beverly Hills* ☎ *310/550–5900* ⊕ *www.neimanmarcus.com.*

Taschen

BOOKS/STATIONERY | Philippe Starck designed the Taschen space to evoke a cool 1920s Parisian salon—a perfect showcase for the publisher's design-forward coffee-table books about architecture, travel, culture, and photography. A suspended glass cube gallery in back hosts art exhibits and features limited-edition books. ✉ *354 N. Beverly Dr., Beverly Hills* ☎ *310/274–4300* ⊕ *www.taschen.com.*

Tory Burch

CLOTHING | Preppy, stylish, and colorful clothes appropriate for a road trip to Palm Springs or a flight to Palm Beach fill this flagship boutique. ✉ *142 S. Robertson Blvd., Beverly Hills* ☎ *310/248–2612* ⊕ *www.toryburch.com.*

West Hollywood and Fairfax

West Hollywood is not a place to see things (like museums or movie studios) as much as it is a place to do things—like go to a nightclub, eat at a world-famous restaurant, or attend an art gallery opening. Since the end of Prohibition, the Sunset Strip has been Hollywood's nighttime playground, where stars headed to such glamorous nightclubs as the Trocadero, the Mocambo, and Ciro's.

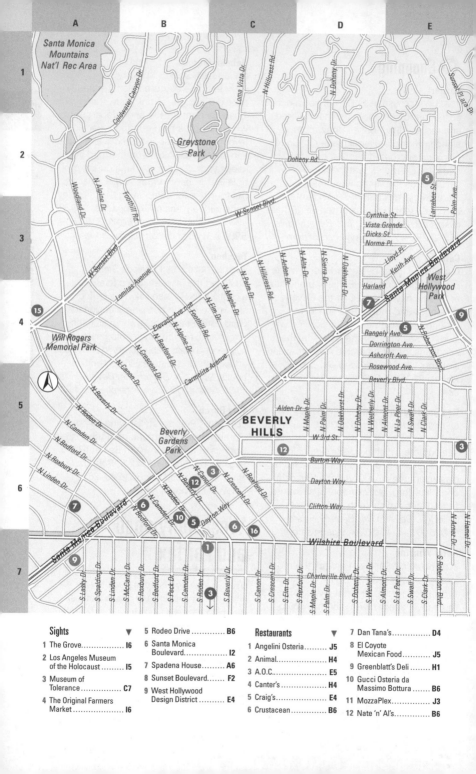

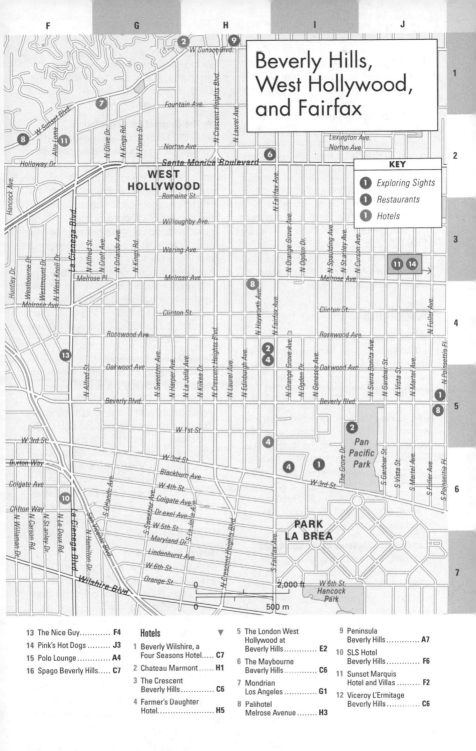

It's still going strong, with crowds still filing into well-established spots like Whisky A Go Go and paparazzi staking out the members-only Soho House. But hedonism isn't all that drives West Hollywood. Also thriving is an important interior design and art gallery trade exemplified by the Cesar Pelli–designed Pacific Design Center.

West Hollywood has also emerged as one of the most progressive cities in Southern California. It's one of the most gay-friendly cities anywhere, with a large LGBTQ+ community. Its annual Gay Pride Parade is one of the largest in the nation, drawing tens of thousands of participants each June.

Sights

★ The Grove

STORE/MALL | Come to this popular outdoor mall for familiar names like Apple, Nike, and Nordstrom; stay for the central fountain with "dancing" water and light shows, people-watching from the trolley, and, during the holiday season, artificial snowfall and a winter wonderland. Feel-good pop blasting over the loudspeakers aims to boost your mood while you spend, and a giant cineplex gives shoppers a needed break with the latest box office blockbusters. ⊠ *189 The Grove Dr., Fairfax District* ☎ *323/900–8080* ⊕ *www. thegrovela.com.*

Los Angeles Museum of the Holocaust

MUSEUM | A museum dedicated solely to the Holocaust, it uses its extensive collections of photos and artifacts as well as award-winning audio tours and interactive tools to evoke European Jewish life in the 20th century. The mission is to commemorate the lives of those who perished and those who survived the Holocaust. The building is itself a marvel, having won two awards from the American Institute of Architects. Every Sunday, the museum hosts talks given by Holocaust survivors, while other events include a lecture series, educational programs, and concerts. ⊠ *100 The Grove Dr.* ☎ *323/651–3704* ⊕ *www.holocaustmuseumla.org* ☜ *Free.*

★ The Original Farmers Market

MARKET | FAMILY | Called the Original Farmers Market for a reason, this special piece of land brought out farmers to sell their wares starting in 1934. Today, the market has more permanent residences, but fresh produce still abounds among the dozens of vendors. Some purveyor standouts include gourmet market Monsieur Marcel, Bob's Coffee & Doughnuts, and Patsy D'Amore's Pizzeria, which has been serving slices since 1949. The market is adjacent to The Grove shopping center, and locals and tourists flock to both in droves. ⊠ *6333 W. 3rd St., Fairfax District* ☎ *323/933–9211* ⊕ *www.farmersmarketla.com.*

Santa Monica Boulevard

NEIGHBORHOOD | From Fairfax Avenue in the east to Doheny Drive in the west, Santa Monica Boulevard is the commercial core of West Hollywood's gay community, with restaurants and cafés, bars and clubs, bookstores and galleries, and other establishments catering largely to the LGBTQ scene. Twice a year—during June's L.A. Pride and on Halloween—the boulevard becomes an open-air festival. ⊠ *Santa Monica Blvd. between Fairfax Ave. and Doheny Dr., West Hollywood* ☎ *323/848-6400* ⊕ *weho.org.*

Sunset Boulevard

NEIGHBORHOOD | One of the most fabled avenues in the world, Sunset Boulevard began humbly enough in the 18th century as a route from El Pueblo de Los Angeles to the Pacific Ocean. Today, as it passes through West Hollywood, it becomes the sexy and seductive Sunset Strip, where rock and roll had its heyday and cocktail bars charge a premium for the views. It slips quietly into the tony environs of Beverly Hills and Bel-Air, twisting and winding past gated estates

From celebrity mansions to rock 'n' roll lore, Sunset Boulevard is a drive through Hollywood history.

and undulating vistas. ✉ *Sunset Blvd., West Hollywood* 🌐 *www.weho.org.*

West Hollywood Design District

STORE/MALL | More than 200 businesses—art galleries, antiques shops, fashion outlets (including Rag & Bone and James Perse), and interior design stores—are found in the design district. There are also about 30 restaurants, including the famous paparazzi magnet, the Ivy. All are clustered within walking distance of each other—rare for L.A. ✉ *Melrose Ave. and Robertson and Beverly Blvds., West Hollywood* ☎ *310/289–2534* 🌐 *westhollywooddesigndistrict.com.*

🍴 Restaurants

★ Angelini Osteria

$$$$ | ITALIAN | Despite its modest, rather congested dining room, this is one of L.A.'s most celebrated Italian restaurants. The keys are chef-owner Gino Angelini's consistently impressive dishes, like whole branzino, *tagliolini al limone,* veal chop *alla* Milanese, as well as lasagna oozing with *besciamella* (Italian béchamel sauce). **Known for:** large Italian wine selection; bold flavors; savory pastas. [$] *Average main: $40* ✉ *7313 Beverly Blvd., Beverly–La Brea* ☎ *323/297–0070* 🌐 *www.angelinirestaurantgroup.com.*

Animal

$$$ | AMERICAN | Owned by Jon Shook and Vinny Dotolo of *Iron Chef* fame, this oft-packed James Beard Award–winning restaurant offers shareable plates with a focus on meat. Highlights include barbecue pork belly sandwiches, poutine with oxtail gravy, and braised rabbit legs with mushrooms. **Known for:** bacon-chocolate crunch bar for dessert; reputation as a must for foodies; menu that is carnivore heaven. [$] *Average main: $30* ✉ *435 N. Fairfax Ave., Fairfax District* ☎ *323/782–9225* 🌐 *www.animalrestaurant.com* ⏲ *No lunch.*

A.O.C.

$$$ | MEDITERRANEAN | Not to be confused with the congresswoman from New York, the acronym here stands for Appellation d'Origine Contrôlée, the regulatory system that ensures the quality of local wines and cheeses in France. Fittingly, A.O.C. upholds this standard of excellence in its shared plates and perfect wine pairings in the stunning exposed-brick and vine-laden courtyard. **Known for:** amazing cocktail hour; quaint outdoor courtyard; charming indoor fireplaces. $ *Average main: $25* ✉ *8700 W. 3rd St., West Hollywood* ☎ *310/859–9859* ⊕ *www.aocwinebar.com.*

Canter's

$ | DELI | FAMILY | This granddaddy of L.A. delicatessens (it opened in 1931) cures its own corned beef and pastrami and features delectable desserts from the in-house bakery. It's not the best (or friendliest) deli in town, but it's a classic. **Known for:** location adjacent to Kibitz Room bar; plenty of seating and short wait times; open 24 hours. $ *Average main: $12* ✉ *419 N. Fairfax Ave., Fairfax District* ☎ *323/651–2030* ⊕ *www.canters-deli.com.*

Craig's

$$$$ | AMERICAN | Behind the unremarkable facade is an übertrendy—yet decidedly old-school—den of American cuisine that doubles as a safe haven for the movie industry's most important names and well-known faces. Be aware that this joint is always busy so you might not even get a table and reservations are hard to come by. **Known for:** lots of celebrities; delicious chicken Parm; strong drinks. $ *Average main: $32* ✉ *8826 Melrose Ave., West Hollywood* ☎ *310/276–1900* ⊕ *craigs.la.*

Dan Tana's

$$$$ | ITALIAN | If you're looking for an Italian vibe straight out of *Goodfellas*, your search ends here. Checkered tablecloths cover the tightly packed tables as Hollywood players dine on the city's

best chicken and veal Parm, and down Scotches by the finger. **Known for:** elbow-room-only bar; lively atmosphere; celeb spotting. $ *Average main: $35* ✉ *9071 Santa Monica Blvd., West Hollywood* ☎ *310/275–9444* ⊕ *www.dantanasrestaurant.com.*

★ El Coyote Mexican Food

$$ | MEXICAN | FAMILY | Open since 1931, this landmark spot is perfect for those on a budget or anyone after an authentic Mexican meal. The traditional fare is decadent and delicious while the margaritas are sweetened to perfection. **Known for:** affordable, quality cuisine; festive atmosphere; being an L.A. staple. $ *Average main: $14* ✉ *7312 Beverly Blvd., Beverly–La Brea* ☎ *323/939–2255* ⊕ *www.elcoyotecafe.com* ⊘ *Closed Mon. and Tues.*

Greenblatt's Deli

$$ | DELI | In 1926, Herman Greenblatt opened his eponymous deli, which serves Jewish deli food, wine, and spirits. The restaurant claims to have the rarest roast beef in town—and they're probably right. **Known for:** matzo ball soup; pastrami sandwiches; old-school vibe. $ *Average main: $18* ✉ *8017 Sunset Blvd., West Hollywood* ☎ *323/656–0606* ⊕ *www.greenblattsdeli.com.*

★ MozzaPlex

$$$ | ITALIAN | A trio of restaurants by star chef Nancy Silverton, MozzaPlex consists of Pizzeria Mozza, a casual pizza and wine spot; Osteria Mozza, an upscale Italian restaurant with incredible pastas; and chi SPACCA, an Italian steak house with succulent cuts of steak. The restaurant complex is one of the most beloved in the whole city and if you're craving any kind of Italian food, you'll want to get yourself inside. **Known for:** great pizzas; intimate atmosphere; the chi SPACCA burger. $ *Average main: $25* ✉ *641 N. Highland Ave., Beverly–La Brea* ☎ *323/297–1130* ⊕ *www.mozzarestaurantgroup.com.*

The Nice Guy

$$$ | ITALIAN | This dark and brooding Italian restaurant sits discretely on La Cienega Boulevard and hides one of the cooler scenes in L.A. A favorite among privacy-minded celebs (there's a no-photo policy), the Nice Guy is known for its cavatelli *alla* vodka and mouthwatering chicken Parm. **Known for:** mouthwatering pastas; see-and-be-seen crowd; live piano music. $ *Average main: $25* ⊠ *401 N. La Cienega Blvd., West Hollywood* ☎ *310/360–9500* ⊕ *www.theniceguyla.com.*

★ Pink's Hot Dogs

$ | HOT DOG | FAMILY | Since 1939, Angelenos and tourists alike have been lining up at this roadside hot dog stand. But Pink's is more than just an institution, it's a beloved family-run joint that serves a damn good hot dog. **Known for:** the famous Brando Dog; late-night dining; chili fries. $ *Average main: $6* ⊠ *709 N. La Brea Ave., Hollywood* ☎ *323/931–4223* ⊕ *www.pinkshollywood.com.*

Hotels

Chateau Marmont

$$$$ | HOTEL | Built in 1929 as a luxury apartment complex, the Chateau is now one of the most unique see-and-be-seen hotel hot spots in all of L.A. A remarkably good-looking, young, and super-creative crowd of artists, writers, actors, and photographers roams about this historic haunt. **Pros:** private and exclusive vibe; famous history; beautiful pool. **Cons:** some may find it pretentious; service can be spotty; some of the rooms are underwhelming. $ *Rooms from: $450* ⊠ *8221 Sunset Blvd., West Hollywood* ☎ *323/656–1010* ⊕ *www.chateaumarmont.com* ⇌ *63 rooms* ⦿ *No meals.*

★ Farmer's Daughter Hotel

$$ | HOTEL | A favorite of *Price Is Right* and *Dancing with the Stars* hopefuls (both TV shows tape at the CBS studios nearby), this hotel has a tongue-in-cheek country style with a hopping Sunday brunch and a little pool accented by giant rubber duckies and a living wall. **Pros:** bikes for rent; fun brunch restaurant; book lending library. **Cons:** shaded pool; no bathtubs; restaurant food is just okay. $ *Rooms from: $200* ⊠ *115 S. Fairfax Ave., Fairfax District* ☎ *323/937–3930, 800/334–1658* ⊕ *www.farmersdaughterhotel.com* ⇌ *65 rooms* ⦿ *No meals.*

★ The London West Hollywood at Beverly Hills

$$$ | HOTEL | Cosmopolitan and chic, the London West Hollywood is known for its large suites, rooftop pool with citywide views, and luxury touches throughout. **Pros:** state-of-the-art fitness center; chef Anthony Keene oversees dining program; 110-seat screening room. **Cons:** too refined for kids to be comfortable; lower floors have mundane views; spa and restaurant are pricey. $ *Rooms from: $350* ⊠ *1020 N. San Vicente Blvd., West Hollywood* ☎ *310/854–1111* ⊕ *www.the-londonwesthollywood.com* ⇌ *226 suites* ⦿ *No meals.*

Mondrian Los Angeles

$$$ | HOTEL | The Mondrian has a city club feel; socializing begins in the lobby bar and lounge and extends from the restaurant to the scenic patio and pool, where you can listen to music underwater, and the lively Skybar. **Pros:** acclaimed Skybar on property; flirty social scene; double-paned windows keep out noise. **Cons:** pricey valet parking; late-night party scene not for everyone; *Alice in Wonderland* theme might be too much for some. $ *Rooms from: $300* ⊠ *8440 Sunset Blvd., West Hollywood* ☎ *323/650–8999, 800/606–6090* ⊕ *www.mondrianhotel.com* ⇌ *236 rooms* ⦿ *No meals.*

Palihotel Melrose Avenue

$$ | HOTEL | A mostly young and creative clientele flocks here, to one of the only boutique hotels on Melrose Avenue. **Pros:** great decor; walking distance to Melrose shops and restaurants; cheap bike rentals ($20/day). **Cons:** no gym, spa, or pool; neighborhood can be sketchy at night;

need to request alarm clocks and phones from front desk. $ *Rooms from: $200* ✉ *7950 Melrose Ave., West Hollywood* ☎ *323/272–4588* ⊕ *www.pali-hotel.com* ⌨ *33 rooms* ⦿*No meals.*

★ Sunset Marquis Hotel and Villas

$$$ | HOTEL | If you're in town to cut your new hit single, you'll appreciate this near-the-Strip hidden retreat in the heart of WeHo, with two on-site recording studios. **Pros:** favorite among rock stars; 53 villas with lavish extras like completely soundproof rooms; exclusive Bar 1200. **Cons:** rooms can feel dark; small balconies; vibe can feel too exclusive. $ *Rooms from: $365* ✉ *1200 N. Alta Loma Rd., West Hollywood* ☎ *310/657–1333, 800/858–9758* ⊕ *www.sunsetmarquis.com* ⌨ *152 rooms* ⦿*No meals.*

Nightlife

★ The Abbey

BARS/PUBS | The Abbey in West Hollywood is one of the most famous gay bars in the world. And rightfully so. Seven days a week, a mixed and very good-looking crowd comes to eat, drink, dance, and flirt. Creative cocktails are whipped up by buff bartenders with a bevy of theme nights and parties each day. ✉ *692 N. Robertson Blvd., West Hollywood* ☎ *310/289–8410* ⊕ *www.theabbeyweho.com.*

Comedy Store

COMEDY CLUBS | Three stages give seasoned and unseasoned comedians a place to perform and try out new material, with big-name performers dropping by just for fun. The front bar along Sunset Boulevard is a popular hangout after or between shows, oftentimes with that night's comedians mingling with fans. ✉ *8433 Sunset Blvd., West Hollywood* ☎ *323/650–6268* ⊕ *www.thecomedystore.com.*

Delilah

THEMED ENTERTAINMENT | Reservations are definitely required for this swanky, New York–style space in West Hollywood. Waiters in white coats serve a mix of upscale American cuisine, but the true reason to come happens a little later when live jazz and burlesque dancers turn the night into a sultry singles scene that's visited by the who's who of Hollywood celebrity royalty. ✉ *7969 Santa Monica Blvd., West Hollywood* ☎ *323/745–0600* ⊕ *www.delilahla.com.*

Employees Only

BARS/PUBS | If you're looking for the best cocktail program in L.A., you'll find it at Employees Only. This very chic spot is a sister of the New York original and is consistently awarded worldwide for its delicious drinks. At this iteration, there are various themed nights with burlesque on Saturday and sporadic live music. In the back is a speakeasy called Harry's, which is a more intimate space where you can get up close and personal with the master barkeeps to tailor you the perfect drink. ✉ *7953 Santa Monica Blvd., West Hollywood* ☎ *323/536–9045* ⊕ *www.employeesonlyla.com.*

Jones

BARS/PUBS | Italian food and serious cocktails are the mainstays at Jones. Whiskey is a popular choice for the classic cocktails, but the bartenders also do up martinis properly (read: strong). The Beggar's Banquet is their version of happy hour (10 pm to 2 am, Sunday through Thursday), with specials on drinks and pizza. ✉ *7205 Santa Monica Blvd., West Hollywood* ☎ *323/850–1726* ⊕ *www.joneshollywood.com.*

Laugh Factory

COMEDY CLUBS | Top stand-up comics regularly appear at this Sunset Boulevard mainstay, often working out the kinks in new material in advance of national tours. Stars such as Tiffany Haddish and Kevin Nealon sometimes drop by unannounced, and theme nights like Midnight Madness and Chocolate Sundaes are extremely popular, with comics performing more daring sets. ⌧ *8001 W. Sunset Blvd., West Hollywood* ☎ *323/656–1336* ⊕ *www. laughfactory.com.*

Rainbow Bar and Grill

BARS/PUBS | Its location next door to a long-running music venue, the Roxy, helped cement this bar and restaurant's status as a legendary watering hole for musicians (as well as their entourages and groupies). The Who, Guns N' Roses, Poison, Kiss, and many others have all passed through the doors. Expect a $5–$10 cover, but you'll get the money back in drink tickets or a food discount. ⌧ *9015 W. Sunset Blvd., West Hollywood* ☎ *310/278–4232* ⊕ *www.rainbowbarand-grill.com.*

★ The Troubadour

MUSIC CLUBS | The intimate vibe of the Troubadour helps make this club a favorite with music fans. Around since 1957, this venue has a storied past where legends like Elton John and James Taylor have graced the stage. These days, the eclectic lineup is still attracting crowds, with the focus mostly on rock, indie, and folk music. Those looking for drinks can imbibe to their heart's content at the adjacent bar. ⌧ *9081 Santa Monica Blvd., West Hollywood* ⊕ *www.troubadour. com.*

Whisky A Go Go

MUSIC CLUBS | The hard-core metal and rock scene is alive and well at the legendary Whisky A Go Go (the full name includes the prefix "World Famous"), where Janis Joplin, Led Zeppelin, Alice Cooper, Van Halen, the Doors (they were the house band for a short stint), and Frank Zappa have all played. On the Strip for more than five decades, the club books both underground acts and huge names in rock. ⌧ *8901 W. Sunset Blvd., West Hollywood* ☎ *310/652–4202* ⊕ *www.whiskyagogo.com.*

🛍 Shopping

★ American Rag Cie

CLOTHING | Half the store features new clothing from established and emerging labels, while the other side is stocked with well-preserved vintage clothing organized by color and style. You'll also find plenty of shoes and accessories being picked over by the hippest of Angelenos. ⌧ *150 S. La Brea Ave., West Hollywood* ☎ *323/935–3154* ⊕ *american-rag.com.*

Beverly Center

SHOPPING CENTERS/MALLS | This eight-level shopping center is home to luxury retailers like Gucci, Louis Vuitton, and Salvatore Ferragamo but also offers plenty of outposts for more affordable brands including Aldo, H&M, and Uniqlo. Don't miss the bevy of great dining options like Eggslut, an extraordinarily popular breakfast joint; Tocaya Organica, a modern Mexican concept with vegan, vegetarian, and gluten-free options; and Yardbird, a fried-chicken lovers' favorite, plus many, many more. ⌧ *8500 Beverly Blvd., West Hollywood* ☎ *310/854–0070* ⊕ *www.beverlycenter.com.*

Book Soup

BOOKS/STATIONERY | One of the best independent bookstores in the country, Book Soup has been serving Angelenos since 1975. Given its Hollywood pedigree, it's especially deep in books about film, music, art, and photography. Fringe benefits include an international newsstand, a bargain-book section, and author readings several times a week. ⌧ *8818 Sunset Blvd., West Hollywood* ☎ *310/659–3110* ⊕ *www.booksoup.com.*

★ Fred Segal

CLOTHING | One of the most well-known boutiques in all of Los Angeles, Fred Segal is a fashion design mecca that has been clothing the rich, famous, and their acolytes since the 1960s. Since moving from its original location on Melrose, the flagship store sits atop Sunset Boulevard with more than 21,000 square feet of space that showcases innovative brands and high-end threads. Inside is also Fred Segal Café and Bakery, which offers fashionistas some fast casual fare as they peruse the merchandise. ⊠ *8500 Sunset Blvd., West Hollywood* ☎ *310/432–0560* ⊕ *www.fredsegal.com.*

★ Maxfield

CLOTHING | This modern concrete structure is one of L.A.'s most desirable destinations for ultimate high fashion. The space is stocked with sleek offerings from Givenchy, Saint Laurent, Valentino, and Rick Owens, plus occasional pop-ups by fashion's labels-of-the-moment. For serious shoppers (or gawkers) only. ⊠ *8825 Melrose Ave., West Hollywood* ☎ *310/274–8800* ⊕ *www.maxfieldla.com.*

★ Melrose Trading Post

OUTDOOR/FLEA/GREEN MARKETS | Hollywood denizens love this hip market, where you're likely to find recycled rock T-shirts or some vinyl to complete your collection in addition to antique furniture and quirky arts and crafts. Live music and fresh munchies entertain vintage hunters and collectors. The market is held 9 to 5 every Sunday—rain or shine—in Fairfax High School's parking lot and admission is $5. ⊠ *Fairfax Ave. and Melrose Ave., Fairfax District* ☎ *323/655–7679* ⊕ *www. melrosetradingpost.org.*

Paul Smith

CLOTHING | You can't miss the massive, minimalist pink box that houses Paul Smith's fantastical collection of clothing, boots, hats, luggage, and objets d'art (seriously, there will be hordes of Instagrammers shooting selfies in front of the bright facade). Photos and art line the walls above shelves of books on pop culture, art, and Hollywood. As for the clothing here, expect the British brand's signature playfully preppy style, with vibrant colors and whimsical patterns mixed in with well-tailored closet staples. ⊠ *8221 Melrose Ave., West Hollywood* ☎ *323/951–4800* ⊕ *www.paulsmith. com/uk.*

The Way We Wore

CLOTHING | Beyond the over-the-top vintage store furnishings, you'll find one of the city's best selections of well-cared-for and one-of-a-kind items, with a focus on sequins and beads. Upstairs, couture from Halston, Dior, and Chanel can cost up to $20,000. ⊠ *334 S. La Brea Ave., Beverly–La Brea* ☎ *323/937–0878* ⊕ *www.thewaywewore.com.*

Hollywood and the Studios

The Tinseltown mythology of Los Angeles was born in Hollywood, still one of the city's largest and most vibrant neighborhoods. In the Hollywood Hills to the north of Franklin Avenue sit some of the most marvelous mansions the moguls ever built; in the flats below Sunset and Santa Monica boulevards are the classic Hollywood bungalows where studio workers once resided.

Reputation aside, though, it's mostly a workaday neighborhood without the glitz and glamour of places like Beverly Hills. The only major studio still located in Hollywood is Paramount; Warner Bros., Disney, and Universal Studios Hollywood are to the north in Burbank and Universal City.

Of course, the notion of Hollywood as a center of the entertainment industry can be expanded to include more than one neighborhood: to the north is Studio City, a thriving strip at the base of the Hollywood Hills, which is home to many smaller film companies; Universal City, where you'll find Universal Studios Hollywood; and Burbank, home to several major studios.

The San Fernando Valley is only a couple of miles north of the Hollywood Bowl, yet some say it's worlds away. Over the hill from the notably trendier areas of Downtown and Hollywood, "the Valley" gets a bad rap. But all snickering aside, this area is home to many of the places that have made Los Angeles famous: **Disney Studios, Warner Bros. Studios,** and **Universal Studios Hollywood.**

Hollywood

 Sights

Dolby Theatre
ARTS VENUE | More than just a prominent fixture on Hollywood Boulevard, the Dolby Theatre has a few accolades under its belt as well, most notably as home to the Academy Awards. The theater is the blend of the traditional and the modern, where an exquisite classical design inspired by the grand opera houses of Europe meets a state-of-the-art sound and technical system for an immersive, theatrical experience. Watch a concert or a show here to experience it fully, but before you do, take a tour for an informative, behind-the-scenes look and to step into the VIP lounge where celebrities rub elbows on the big night. ⊠ *6801 Hollywood Blvd., Hollywood* ☎ *323/308–6300* ⊕ *www.dolbytheatre.com* ⊠ *Tour $25.*

★ Hollywood Bowl
ARTS VENUE | For those seeking a quintessential Los Angeles experience, a concert on a summer night at the Bowl, the city's iconic outdoor venue, is unsurpassed. The Bowl has presented world-class performers since it opened in 1920. The L.A. Philharmonic plays here from June to September; its performances and other events draw large crowds. Parking is limited near the venue, but there are additional remote parking locations serviced by shuttles. You can bring food and drink to any event, which Angelenos often do, though you can only bring alcohol when the L.A. Phil is performing. (Bars sell alcohol at all events, and there are dining options.) It's wise to bring a jacket even if daytime temperatures have been warm—the Bowl can get quite chilly at night. ■**TIP**➜ **Visitors can sometimes watch the L.A. Phil practice for free, usually on a weekday; call ahead for times.** ⊠ *2301 Highland Ave., Hollywood* ☎ *323/850–2000* ⊕ *www.hollywoodbowl.com.*

★ Hollywood Forever Cemetery
CEMETERY | One of the many things that makes this cemetery in the middle of Hollywood so fascinating is that it's the final resting place of many of the Hollywood greats, from directors like Cecil B. DeMille and actors like Douglas Fairbanks and Judy Garland to musicians like Johnny Ramone. Beyond its famous residents, however, the Hollywood Forever Cemetery is also frequented for its serene grounds peppered with intricately designed tombstones, not to mention by cinephiles in the summer and fall months for the outdoor movie screenings that take place under the stars on the Fairbanks Lawn. If you're looking for both tourist and local experiences while in town, this sight lets you tick off both in one visit. ⊠ *6000 Santa Monica Blvd., Hollywood* ☎ *323/706–4826* ⊕ *www.hollywoodforever.com* ⊠ *Free; check online for film screenings.*

★ Hollywood Museum
MUSEUM | Don't let its kitschy facade turn you off: the Hollywood Museum, nestled at the busy intersection of Hollywood and Highland, is worth it, especially for film aficionados. A museum deserving of its name, it boasts an impressive collection of exhibits from the moviemaking world, spanning several film genres and eras. Start in its pink, art deco lobby where the Max Factor exhibit pays tribute to the cosmetics company's pivotal role in Hollywood, make your way to the dark basement, where the industry's penchant for the macabre is on full display, and wrap up your visit by admiring Hollywood's most famous costumes and set props on the top floor. ⊠ *1660 N. Highland Ave., at Hollywood Blvd., Hollywood* ☎ *323/464–7776* ⊕ *www.thehollywoodmuseum.com* ⊠ *$15* ⊗ *Closed Mon. and Tues.*

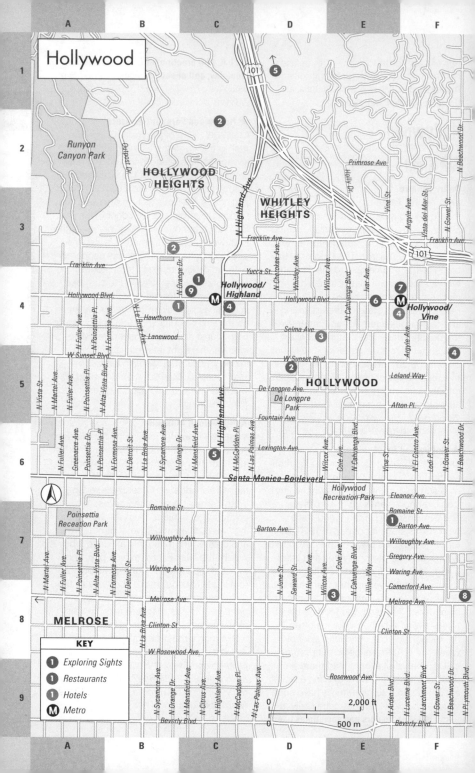

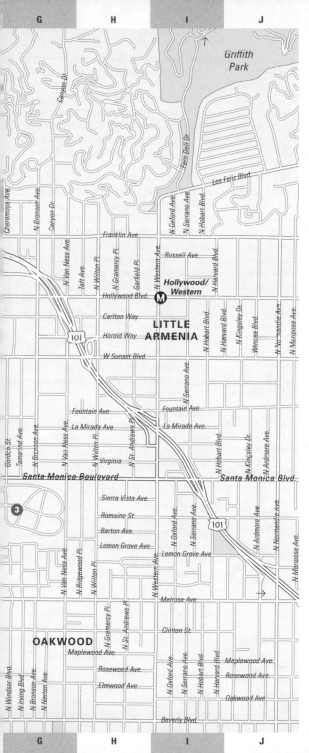

Sights ▼

1 Dolby Theatre **C4**
2 Hollywood Bowl **C2**
3 Hollywood Forever Cemetery **G7**
4 Hollywood Museum **C4**
5 Hollywood Sign **D1**
6 Hollywood Walk of Fame **E4**
7 Pantages Theatre **F4**
8 Paramount Pictures **F8**
9 TCL Chinese Theatre **C4**

Restaurants ▼

1 Cactus Taquerias #1 .... **E7**
2 Gwen **D5**
3 Providence **E8**
4 Roscoe's House of
   Chicken & Waffles **F5**
5 Salt's Cure **C6**

Hotels ▼

1 Hollywood Roosevelt Hotel **C4**
2 Magic Castle Hotel **B3**
3 Mama Shelter **D4**
4 W Hollywood **E4**

★ Hollywood Sign

LOCAL INTEREST | With letters 50 feet tall, Hollywood's trademark sign can be spotted from miles away. The icon, which originally read "Hollywoodland," was erected in the Hollywood Hills in 1923 to advertise a segregated housing development and was outfitted with 4,000 light bulbs. In 1949 the "land" portion of the sign was taken down. By 1973 the sign had earned landmark status, but because the letters were made of wood, its longevity came into question. A makeover project was launched and the letters were auctioned off (rocker Alice Cooper bought an "O" and singing cowboy Gene Autry sponsored an "L") to make way for a new sign made of sheet metal. Inevitably, the sign has drawn pranksters who have altered it over the years, albeit temporarily, to spell out "Hollyweed" (in the 1970s, to push for more lenient marijuana laws), "Go Navy" (before a Rose Bowl game), and "Perotwood" (during businessman Ross Perot's 1992 presidential bid). A fence and surveillance equipment have since been installed to deter intruders, but another vandal managed to pull the "Hollyweed" prank once again in 2017 after Californians voted to make recreational use of marijuana legal statewide. And while it's still very illegal to get anywhere near the sign, several area hikes will get you as close as possible for some photo ops; you can hike just over 6 miles up behind the sign via the Brush Canyon trail for epic views, especially at sunset. ⚠ **Use caution if driving up to the sign on residential streets; many cars speed around the blind corners.** ⊠ *Griffith Park, Mt. Lee Dr., Hollywood* ⊕ *www.hollywoodsign.org.*

Hollywood Walk of Fame

LOCAL INTEREST | Along Hollywood Boulevard (and part of Vine Street) runs a trail of affirmations for entertainment-industry overachievers. On this mile-long stretch of sidewalk, inspired by the concrete handprints in front of TCL Chinese Theatre, names are embossed in brass, each at the center of a pink star embedded in dark gray terrazzo. They're not all screen deities; many stars commemorate people who worked in a technical field, such as sound or lighting. The first eight stars were unveiled in 1960 at the northwest corner of Highland Avenue and Hollywood Boulevard: Olive Borden, Ronald Colman, Louise Fazenda, Preston Foster, Burt Lancaster, Edward Sedgwick, Ernest Torrence, and Joanne Woodward (some of these names have stood the test of time better than others). Since then, more than 2,000 others have been immortalized, though that honor doesn't come cheap—upon selection by a special committee, the personality in question (or more likely his or her movie studio or record company) pays about $30,000 for the privilege. To aid you in spotting celebrities you're looking for, stars are identified by one of five icons: a motion-picture camera, a radio microphone, a television set, a record, or a theatrical mask. ⊠ *Hollywood Blvd. and Vine St., Hollywood* ⊕ *www.walkoffame.com.*

Pantages Theatre

ARTS VENUE | Besides being home to the Academy Awards for a decade in the '50s, this stunning art deco–style theater near Hollywood and Vine has been playing host to many of the musical theater world's biggest and greatest productions, from the classics like *Cats*, *West Side Story*, and *Phantom of the Opera* to modern hits like *Hamilton* and *Wicked*. During your Los Angeles jaunt, see a show or two in order to really experience its splendor. While guided tours are not being offered to the public, an annual open house is available to season pass holders for an exclusive and informative tour of the theater and its history. ⊠ *6233 Hollywood Blvd., Hollywood* ☎ *323/468–1770* ⊕ *www.broadwayinhollywood.com.*

★ Paramount Pictures

FILM STUDIO | With a history dating to the early 1920s, the Paramount lot was home to some of Hollywood's most luminous stars, including Mary Pickford, Rudolph Valentino, Mae West, Marlene Dietrich, and Bing Crosby. Director Cecil B. DeMille's base of operations for decades, Paramount offers probably the most authentic studio tour, giving you a real sense of the film industry's history. This is the only major studio from film's golden age left in Hollywood—all the others are now in Burbank, Universal City, or Culver City.

Memorable movies and TV shows with scenes shot here include *Sunset Boulevard, Forrest Gump,* and *Titanic.* Many of the *Star Trek* movies and TV series were shot entirely or in part here, and several seasons of *I Love Lucy* were shot on the portion of the lot Paramount acquired in 1967 from Lucille Ball. You can take a 2-hour studio tour or a 4½-hour VIP tour, led by guides who walk and trolley you around the back lots. As well as gleaning some gossipy history, you'll spot the sets of TV and film shoots in progress. Reserve ahead for tours, which are for those ages 10 and up. **■ TIP→ You can be part of the audience for live TV tapings (tickets are free), but you must book ahead.** ✉ *5515 Melrose Ave., Hollywood* ☎ *323/956–1777* 🌐 *www.paramountstudiotour.com* 🎫 *$60.*

TCL Chinese Theatre

ARTS VENUE | The stylized Chinese pagodas and temples of the former Grauman's Chinese Theatre have become a shrine both to stardom and the combination of glamour and flamboyance that inspire the phrase "only in Hollywood." Although you have to buy a movie ticket to appreciate the interior trappings, the courtyard is open to the public. The main theater itself is worth visiting, if only to see a film in the same setting as hundreds of celebrities who have attended big premieres here.

And then, of course, outside in front are the oh-so-famous cement hand- and footprints. This tradition is said to have begun at the theater's opening in 1927, with the premiere of Cecil B. DeMille's *King of Kings,* when actress Norma Talmadge just happened to step in wet cement. Now more than 160 celebrities have contributed imprints for posterity, including some oddball specimens, such as casts of Whoopi Goldberg's dreadlocks. ✉ *6925 Hollywood Blvd., Hollywood* ☎ *323/461–3331* 🌐 *www.tclchinesetheatres.com* 🎫 *Tour $20.*

🍴 Restaurants

Cactus Taqueria #1

$ | **MEXICAN** | **FAMILY** | A humble taco shack on the side of the road, Cactus offers up $3 tacos with all types of meat you could imagine, even beef tongue. They also have carne asada and chicken for the less adventurous. **Known for:** California burritos; delicious fries; excellent street-style tacos. [$] *Average main: $11* ✉ *950 Vine St., Hollywood* ☎ *323/464–5865* 🌐 *www.cactustaqueriainc.com.*

★ Gwen

$$$ | **STEAKHOUSE** | A heaven for upscale carnivores, this fine-dining restaurant serves impossibly exquisite dishes in a copper-and-marble setting. Cooking meat is more than an unceremonious, übermasculine endeavor here—it's an intricate, delicate art form. **Known for:** perfect steak; duck fat potatoes; strong cocktails. [$] *Average main: $25* ✉ *6600 Sunset Blvd., Hollywood* ☎ *323/946–7513* 🌐 *www.gwenla.com.*

★ Providence

$$$$ | **SEAFOOD** | This is widely considered one of the best seafood restaurants in the country, and chef-owner Michael Cimarusti elevates sustainably driven fine dining to an art form. The elegant space is the perfect spot to sample exquisite seafood with the chef's signature application of French technique, traditional American themes, and Asian accents. **Known for:** fresh seafood; superb chef tasting menu; exquisite dessert options. [$] *Average main: $150* ✉ *5955 Melrose Ave., Hollywood* ☎ *323/460–4170*

A concert at the Hollywood Bowl is a summertime tradition for Angelenos.

🌐 *www.providencela.com* 🕓 *Closed Sun. and Mon. No lunch Tues.–Thurs. and Sat.*

★ Roscoe's House of Chicken and Waffles
$$ | SOUTHERN | FAMILY | Roscoe's is *the* place for down-home Southern cooking in Southern California. Just ask the patrons who drive from all over L.A. for bargain-priced fried chicken and waffles. The name of this casual eatery honors a late-night combo popularized in Harlem jazz clubs. **Known for:** simple yet famous chicken and waffles; classic soul food dishes; eggs with cheese and onions. [$] *Average main: $15* ✉ *1514 N. Gower St., Hollywood* ☎ *323/466–7453* 🌐 *www.roscoeschickenandwaffles.com.*

Salt's Cure
$$ | AMERICAN | FAMILY | Not only a part of the California gastronomy scene, Salt's Cure celebrates it by keeping all its ingredients locally sourced and homegrown. The former WeHo spot comes to Hollywood to prove that despite appearances, Californians love traditional meat-based staples just as much as they love their kale salads and smoothies. **Known for:** oatmeal griddle cakes; hearty sandwiches; all California-grown ingredients. [$] *Average main: $15* ✉ *1155 N. Highland Ave., Hollywood* ☎ *323/465–7258* 🌐 *www.saltscure.com* 🕓 *Closed Mon. and Tues.*

Hotels

★ Hollywood Roosevelt Hotel
$$$$ | HOTEL | Poolside cabana rooms are adorned with cow-skin rugs and marble bathrooms, while rooms in the main building accentuate the property's history at this party-centric hotel in the heart of Hollywood. **Pros:** Spare Room bowling alley on-site; pool is a popular weekend hangout; great burgers at the on-site 25 Degrees restaurant. **Cons:** reports of noise and staff attitude; stiff parking fees ($45); decor is dated in places. [$] *Rooms from: $419* ✉ *7000 Hollywood Blvd., Hollywood* ☎ *323/466–7000* 🌐 *www.hollywoodroosevelt.com* 🛏 *353 rooms* 🍴 *No meals.*

Local Chains Worth Stopping For 🍴

It's said that the drive-in burger joint was invented in L.A., probably to meet the demands of an ever-mobile car culture. Burger aficionados line up at all hours outside **In-N-Out Burger** (🌐 *www.in-n-out.com, multiple locations*), still a family-owned operation whose terrific made-to-order burgers are revered by Angelenos. Visitors may recognize the chain as the infamous spot where Paris Hilton got nabbed for drunk driving, but locals are more concerned with getting their burger fix off the "secret" menu, with variations like "Animal Style" (mustard-grilled patty with grilled onions and extra spread), a "4 x 4" (four burger patties and four cheese slices, for big eaters) or the bun-less "Protein Style" that comes wrapped in a bib of lettuce. Go online for a list of every "secret" menu item.

Tommy's is best known for their delightfully sloppy chili burger. Visit their no-frills original location (✉ *2575 Beverly Blvd., Los Angeles* ☎ *213/389–9060*)—a culinary landmark. For rotisserie chicken that will make you forget the Colonel altogether, head to **Zankou Chicken** (✉ *5065 Sunset Blvd., Hollywood* ☎ *323/665–7845* 🌐 *www.zankouchicken.com*), a small chain noted for its golden crispy-skinned birds, potent garlic sauce, and Armenian specialties. One-of-a-kind-sausage lovers will appreciate **Wurstküche** (✉ *800 E. 3rd St., Downtown* ☎ *213/687–4444* 🌐 *www.jerrysfamousdeli.com*), where the menu includes items like rattlesnake and rabbit or pheasant with Herbs de Provence. With a lively bar scene, the occasional celebrity sighting, and a spot directly across from the beach, **BOA Steakhouse** (✉ *101 Santa Monica Blvd., Santa Monica* ☎ *310/899–4466* 🌐 *www.hillstone.com*) is a popular hangout, while **Lemonade** (✉ *9001 Beverly Blvd., West Hollywood* ☎ *310/247–2500* 🌐 *www.senorfish.net*) is known for its healthy seasonally driven menu, pulled straight from L.A.'s farmers' markets.

★ Magic Castle Hotel
$$ | **HOTEL** | **FAMILY** | Guests at the hotel can secure advance dinner reservations and attend magic shows at the Magic Castle, a private club in a 1908 mansion next door for magicians and their admirers. **Pros:** heated pool and lush patio; central location near Hollywood & Highland; access to fun Magic Castle shows. **Cons:** strict dress code; no elevator; highly trafficked street. [$] *Rooms from: $250* ✉ *7025 Franklin Ave., Hollywood* ☎ *323/851–0800, 800/741–4915* 🌐 *magiccastlehotel.com* 🛏 *43 rooms* 🍴 *Free breakfast.*

★ Mama Shelter
$ | **HOTEL** | Even locals adore Mama Shelter, one of Hollywood's sexiest boutique hotels, thanks to the rooftop bar populated with beautiful people lounging on love seats, simple affordable rooms with quirky amenities like Bert and Ernie masks, and a down-home lobby restaurant that serves a mean Korean-style burrito. **Pros:** delicious food and cocktails on the property; affordable rooms that don't skimp on style; foosball in lobby. **Cons:** rooms on the small side; creaky elevators; bar and restaurant often get crowded. [$] *Rooms from: $159* ✉ *6500 Selma Ave., Hollywood* ☎ *323/785–6600* 🌐 *www.mamashelter.com/en/los-angeles* 🛏 *70 rooms* 🍴 *No meals.*

W Hollywood

$$$$ | **HOTEL** | This centrally located, ultra-modernly lit location is outfitted for the wired traveler and features a rooftop pool deck and popular on-site bars, like the Station Hollywood and the mod Living Room lobby bar. **Pros:** Metro stop outside the front door; comes with in-room party necessities, from ice to cocktail glasses; comfy beds with petal-soft duvets. **Cons:** small pool; pricey dining and valet parking; location in noisy part of Hollywood. [$] *Rooms from: $500* ✉ *6250 Hollywood Blvd., Hollywood* ☎ *323/798–1300, 888/625–4955* 🌐 *www.whotels.com/hollywood* 🛏 *305 rooms* 🍴 *No meals.*

Nightlife

Birds

BARS/PUBS | They call it your neighborhood bar, because even if you don't live in the neighborhood you'll feel at home at this Alfred Hitchcock–themed eatery. Located in Franklin Village, a block-long stretch of bars, cafés, and bookstores, come here for pub food or a cheap poultry-centric dinner. Weekend nights mean cheap beer and well drinks, crowds spilling onto the streets, and a few rounds of oversize Jenga. ✉ *5925 Franklin Ave., Hollywood* ☎ *323/465–0175* 🌐 *www.birdshollywood.com.*

Burgundy Room

BARS/PUBS | Around since 1919, Burgundy Room attracts a fiercely loyal crowd of locals, as well as the occasional wandering tourist. The bar is supposedly haunted (check out the Ouija boards toward the back), but that just adds to its charm. Its rock-and-roll vibe, strong drinks, and people-watching opportunities make this a worthy detour on any night out on the town. ✉ *1621 N. Cahuenga Blvd., Hollywood* ☎ *323/465–7530.*

★ Dirty Laundry

BARS/PUBS | Tucked away in a basement on the quiet Hudson Avenue, Dirty Laundry is a former speakeasy turned proper cocktail bar with live music and DJs spinning both fresh and throwback music. There's beer on hand, but here, cocktails are king. ✉ *1725 Hudson Ave., Hollywood* ☎ *323/462–6531.*

★ Good Times at Davey Wayne's

BARS/PUBS | It's a fridge; it's a door; it's the entrance to Davey Wayne's, a bar and lounge that pulls out all the stops to transport you back in time to the '70s. The interior is your living room; the outside is an ongoing backyard barbecue with all your friends. Come early to beat the crowds or be prepared to get up close and personal with your neighbors. ✉ *1611 N. El Centro Ave., Hollywood* ☎ *323/498–0859* 🌐 *www.goodtimesatdaveywaynes.com.*

Hotel Cafe

MUSIC CLUBS | This intimate venue caters to fans of folk, indie rock, and music on the softer side. With red velvet backdrops, hardwood furnishings, and the occasional celebrity surprise performance—notably John Mayer—music lovers will not only be very happy but will receive a respite from the ordinary Hollywood experience. ✉ *1623½ N. Cahuenga Blvd., Hollywood* ☎ *323/461–2040* 🌐 *www.hotelcafe.com.*

★ Musso and Frank Grill

BARS/PUBS | **FAMILY** | The prim and proper vibe of this old-school steak house won't appeal to those looking for a raucous night out; instead, its appeal lies in its history and sturdy drinks. Established over a century ago, its dark wood decor, red tuxedo–clad waiters, and highly skilled bartenders can easily shuttle you back to its Hollywood heyday when Marilyn Monroe, F. Scott Fitzgerald, and Greta Garbo once hung around and sipped martinis. ✉ *6667 Hollywood Blvd.,*

Hollywood ☎ 323/467–7788 ⊕ www.
mussoandfrank.com.

No Vacancy

BARS/PUBS | Though at first glance, No
Vacancy might boast an air of exclusivity
and pretentiousness, its relaxed interiors
and welcoming staff will almost instantly
make you feel like you're at a house
party. You know, the kind with burlesque
shows, tightrope performances, a speakeasy secret entrance, and mixologists
who can pretty much whip up any drink
your heart desires. ✉ 1727 N. Hudson
Ave., Hollywood ☎ 323/465–1902
⊕ www.novacancyla.com.

Sassafras Saloon

BARS/PUBS | Put on your dancing shoes
(or your cowboy boots) and step back
in time. The Sassafras boasts not only
an oddly cozy, Western atmosphere
but plenty of opportunities to strut your
moves on the dance floor. Indulge in
exquisite craft mezcal, whiskey, and
tequila cocktails for some liquid courage
before you salsa the night away. ✉ 1233
N. Vine St., Hollywood ☎ 323/467–2800
⊕ www.sassafrassaloon.com.

Three Clubs

BARS/PUBS | Cocktail bars are a dime
a dozen in Hollywood, but there's
something about this Vine Street joint
that makes patrons keep coming back
for more. Maybe it's the down-to-earth
attitude, delicious no-frills cocktails, and
the fact that a taco stand serving greasy
grub is right next door. Come to see
one of the burlesque or comedy shows
for a full experience. ✉ 1123 Vine St.,
Hollywood ☎ 323/462–6441 ⊕ www.
threeclubs.com.

🛍 Shopping

★ Amoeba Records

MUSIC STORES | Touted as the "World's
Largest Independent Record Store,"
Amoeba is a playground for music lovers,
with a knowledgeable staff and a focus
on local artists. Catch free in-store

appearances and signings by artists and
bands that play sold-out shows at venues
down the road. There's a massive and
eclectic collection of vinyl records, CDs,
and cassette tapes, not to mention VHS
tapes, DVDs, and Blu-Ray discs. It's a
paradise for both music and movie lovers. ✉ 6200 Hollywood Blvd., Hollywood
☎ 323/245–6400 ⊕ www.amoeba.com.

Hollywood & Highland Center

SHOPPING CENTERS/MALLS | If you're on the
hunt for unique boutiques, look elsewhere. However, if you prefer the biggest
mall retail chains America has to offer,
Hollywood & Highland is a great spot for
a shopping spree. The design of the complex pays tribute to the city's film legacy,
with a grand staircase leading up to a pair
of three-story-tall stucco elephants, a nod
to the 1916 movie Intolerance. Pause at
the entrance arch, called Babylon Court,
which frames a picture-perfect view of
the Hollywood sign. This place is a huge
tourist magnet, so don't expect to mingle
with the locals. ✉ 6801 Hollywood Blvd.,
at Highland Ave., Hollywood ⊕ www.
hollywoodandhighland.com.

Larry Edmunds Bookshop

BOOKS/STATIONERY | Cinephiles have long
descended upon this iconic 70-plus-year-
old shop that in addition to stocking tons
of texts about motion picture history offers
film fans the opportunity to pick up scripts,
posters, and photographs from Hollywood's golden era to the present. ✉ 6644
Hollywood Blvd., Hollywood ☎ 323/463–
3273 ⊕ www.larryedmunds.com.

The Record Parlour

MUSIC STORES | Vinyl records and music
memorabilia abound in this hip yet modest
record store–slash–music lover magnet
that also touts vintage audio gear and retro jukeboxes. A visit here is usually a mul-
tihour affair, one that involves more than
just browsing through display cases, digging through wooden carts of used vinyls,
and playing your picks at the listening
station. ✉ 6408 Selma Ave., Hollywood
☎ 323/464–7757 ⊕ therecordparlour.com.

Activities

★ Runyon Canyon Trail and Park
HIKING/WALKING | Is Runyon Canyon the city's most famous trail? To the world, it just might be, what with so many A-listers frequenting it. Many folks visiting L.A. take the trail specifically for celebrity spotting. But, if that's not something you're into, this accessible trail right in the middle of Hollywood is also a good place to hike, run, see the Hollywood sign, photograph the city skyline, or simply get a bit of fresh air. If you just happen to run into a famous face, well that's just the cherry on the cake. ✉ *2000 N. Fuller Ave., Hollywood* ☎ *805/370–2301* 🌐 *www.nps.gov/samo/planyourvisit/runyoncanyon.htm.*

Studio City

Restaurants

Asanebo
$$$ | **JAPANESE** | One of L.A.'s finest sushi restaurants, Asanebo is an inviting, no-frills establishment serving top-quality sushi and a wealth of innovative dishes to an A-list clientele. The affable chefs will regale you with memorable specialties such as a caviar-topped lobster, succulent seared *toro* (tuna belly), or just simple morsels of pristine fish dusted with sea salt. **Known for:** omakase (chef's choice) dinners; halibut truffle; excellent sushi. [$] *Average main: $30* ✉ *11941 Ventura Blvd., Studio City* ☎ *818/760–3348* 🌐 *www.asanebo-restaurant.com/* 🕒 *Closed Mon. No lunch weekends.*

Good Neighbor Restaurant
$ | **DINER** | Its walls may be heavy with framed photographs of film and TV stars, and folks from the biz might regularly grace its tables, but this Studio City diner is every bit as down-to-earth as your next-door neighbor, even after 40-some years. It gets pretty busy, but a plateful of that home cooking is worth the wait; or if you're in a mad dash, grab a caffeine or fruit smoothie fix from the Neighbarista. **Known for:** craft-your-own omelet; cottage fries; excellent breakfast food. [$] *Average main: $13* ✉ *3701 Cahuenga Blvd., Studio City* ☎ *818/761–4627* 🌐 *goodneighborrestaurant.com.*

Hotels

Sportsmen's Lodge
$$ | **HOTEL** | **FAMILY** | This sprawling five-story hotel, a San Fernando Valley landmark just a short jaunt over the Hollywood Hills, has an updated contemporary look highlighted by the Olympic-size pool and summer patio with an outdoor bar. **Pros:** close to Ventura Boulevard restaurants; free shuttle to Universal Hollywood; quiet garden-view rooms worth asking for. **Cons:** pricey daily self-parking fee ($25); not centrally located to other Los Angeles sights; a bit pricey for the area. [$] *Rooms from: $249* ✉ *12825 Ventura Blvd., Studio City* ☎ *818/769–4700, 800/821–8511* 🌐 *www.sportsmenslodge.com* 🛏 *190 rooms* 🍴 *No meals.*

Nightlife

Baked Potato
MUSIC CLUBS | Baked Potato might be a strange name to give a world-famous jazz club that's been holding performances of well-known acts (Allan Holdsworth and Michael Landau) under its roof since the '70s, but it only takes a quick peek at the menu to understand. Twenty-four different types of baked potatoes dominate its otherwise short menu, each of which come with sour cream, butter, and salad to offset all that carb intake. ✉ *3787 Cahuenga Blvd., Studio City* ☎ *818/980–1615* 🌐 *www.thebakedpotato.com.*

★ Pinz Bowling Alley
BOWLING | "Bowl. Eat. Drink. Repeat" might be this bowling alley's motto, but thanks to its neon-slash-backlit lanes—each fully equipped with a touch-screen food and drink ordering system—and its

very own arcade, Pinz is more than just your typical bowling experience. A few A-list names are among its loyal clientele, but you don't visit for celebrity sightings; all bells and whistles aside, it's a proper bowling alley and you come here to bowl. ✉ *12655 Ventura Blvd., Studio City* ☎ *818/769–7600* 🌐 *pinzla.com.*

Universal City

👁 Sights

★ Universal Studios Hollywood
AMUSEMENT PARK/WATER PARK | FAMILY | A theme park with classic attractions like roller coasters and thrill rides, Universal Studios also provides a tour of some beloved television and movie sets. A favorite attraction is the tram tour, during which you can duck from King Kong; see the airplane wreckage of *War of the Worlds*; ride along with the cast of the *Fast and the Furious*; and get chills looking at the house from *Psycho*. ■ **TIP→ The tram ride is usually the best place to begin your visit, because the lines become longer as the day goes on.**

Most attractions are designed to give you a thrill in one form or another, including *Jurassic World*—The Ride and Revenge of the Mummy along with immersive rides like the 4D Simpsons Ride, where you can actually smell Maggie Simpson's baby powder. The Wizarding World of Harry Potter, however, is the crown jewel of the park, featuring magical rides, pints of frozen butterbeer, and enough merchandise to drain you wallet faster than you can shout "Expecto Patronum." If you're in town in October, stop by for Halloween Horror Nights, featuring mazes full of monsters, murderers, and jump scares.

Geared more toward adults, CityWalk is a separate venue run by Universal Studios, where you'll find shops, restaurants, nightclubs, and movie theaters. ✉ *100 Universal City Plaza, Universal City* ☎ *800/864–8377* 🌐 *www.universalstudioshollywood.com* 🎟 *$139.*

🍴 Restaurants

Café Sierra
$$$ | SEAFOOD | FAMILY | Don't let the fact that this airy Californian and pan-Asian spot is located inside a Hilton Hotel scare you; Café Sierra has a drool-worthy seafood and prime rib buffet. Lunching here can be a splurge, but it's worth every penny. **Known for:** champagne brunch; Alaskan king crab; live jazz music. [$] *Average main: $30* ✉ *555 Universal Hollywood Dr., Universal City* ☎ *818/509–2030* 🌐 *www.cafesierrahilton.com.*

Dongpo
$$ | SICHUAN | FAMILY | Upmarket regional Chinese cuisine chain Meizhou Dongpo tries its hand at bringing its modern take on authentic Sichuanese cuisine to the area with Dongpo Kitchen, and it's exactly what the CityWalk needed to up its dining game. This bright, contemporary-meets-traditional Chinese restaurant serves delightful, affordable fare right in the middle of a sea of tourists. **Known for:** Dongpo roast duck; Sichuan dumplings; kung pao chicken. [$] *Average main: $20* ✉ *1000 Universal Studios Blvd. V103, Universal City* ☎ *818/358–3272* 🌐 *www.citywalkhollywood.com.*

🛏 Hotels

Sheraton Universal
$$ | HOTEL | FAMILY | With large meeting spaces and a knowledgeable staff, this Sheraton buzzes year-round with business travelers and families, providing easy access to the free shuttle that takes guests to adjacent Universal Studios and CityWalk. **Pros:** pool area with cabanas and bar; oversize desks and office chairs in rooms; good for families and visitors to Universal Studios. **Cons:** average in-house restaurant; tourist crowd; chain hotel feel. [$] *Rooms from: $250* ✉ *333 Universal Hollywood Dr., Universal City*

☎ 818/980–1212, 888/627–7184 🌐 *www.sheratonuniversal.com* 🛏 *461 rooms* 🍴 *No meals.*

Burbank

Sights

★ Warner Bros. Studios

FILM STUDIO | You don't need to be a big film nerd to appreciate a visit to the Warner Bros. Studios, where you can pretend to be your favorite TV or movie characters, whether at a working replica of Central Perk from *Friends* or via a Sorting Hat ceremony from the Harry Potter movies. You'll also visit backlots and soundstages to see how the magic is made.

If you're looking for an authentic behind-the-scenes look at how films and TV shows are made, head to this major studio center, one of the world's busiest. After a short film on the studio's movies and TV shows, hop aboard a tram for a ride through the sets and soundstages of such favorites as *Casablanca* and *Rebel Without a Cause*. You'll see the bungalows where Marlon Brando, Bette Davis, and other icons relaxed between shots, and the current production offices for Clint Eastwood and George Clooney. You might even spot a celeb or see a shoot in action—tours change from day to day depending on the productions taking place on the lot. ✉ *3400 W. Riverside Dr., Burbank* ☎ *818/977–8687* 🌐 *www.wbstudiotour.com* 🎟 *From $69.*

Restaurants

Bea Bea's

$ | **DINER** | Just because Bea Bea's is a no-nonsense kind of place, it doesn't mean the food isn't special. This diner serves breakfast food that is about as close to extraordinary as the most important meal of the day can be. **Known for:** pancakes and French toast; friendly staff; classic diner grub. [$] *Average main: $13* ✉ *353 N. Pass Ave., Burbank* ☎ *818/846–2327* 🌐 *www.beabeas.com.*

Centanni Trattoria

$$ | **ITALIAN** | In a city full of adventurous restaurants touting new takes on traditional dishes and swanking about with bells and whistles and stunning interiors, a run-of-the-mill-looking place like Centanni Trattoria might never make it onto the radar. But what this authentic Italian spot lacks in swagger, it more than makes up for in delicious home cooking. **Known for:** pappardelle with white truffle oil; risotto di funghi; great appetizers. [$] *Average main: $20* ✉ *117 N. Victory Blvd., Burbank* ☎ *818/561–4643* 🌐 *www.centannila.com.*

Los Amigos

$$ | **MEXICAN** | **FAMILY** | If you're in the mood for good old-fashioned fun coupled with hearty Mexican fare and delicious margaritas, then you'll want to consider Los Amigos, whose legendary fruity margaritas alone are worth the drive. Pair those with something from the Platillos Mexicanos menu on karaoke night, and you're guaranteed a good time until the wee hours of the night. **Known for:** classic Mexican food; massive portions; casual dining. [$] *Average main: $18* ✉ *2825 W. Olive Ave., Burbank* ☎ *818/842–3700* 🌐 *www.losamigosbarandgrill.com.*

Porto's Bakery

$ | **CUBAN** | **FAMILY** | Waiting in line at Porto's is as much a part of the experience as is indulging in one of its roasted pork sandwiches or chocolate-dipped croissants. This Cuban bakery and café has been an L.A. staple for more than 50 years, often drawing crowds during lunch. **Known for:** famous potato balls; must-try desserts; fast-moving counter service. [$] *Average main: $8* ✉ *3614 W. Magnolia Blvd., Burbank* ☎ *818/846–9100* 🌐 *www.portosbakery.com.*

🛏 Hotels

Hotel Amarano Burbank

$$ | HOTEL | Close to Burbank's TV and movie studios, the smartly designed Amarano feels like a Beverly Hills boutique hotel, complete with 24-hour room service, a homey on-site restaurant and lounge, and lovely rooms. **Pros:** saltwater pool; complimentary bike rentals; comfortable beds. **Cons:** street noise; away from most of the city's action; breakfast not included. $ *Rooms from: $269* ✉ *322 N. Pass Ave., Burbank* ☎ *818/842–8887, 888/956–1900* ⊕ *www.hotelamarano. com* ⇨ *132 rooms* ⦿ *No meals.*

🍸 Nightlife

Flappers Comedy Club

COMEDY CLUBS | Even though this live comedy club doesn't exactly have as long a history as others in town (it opened in 2010), it's attracted an impressive list of big names like Jerry Seinfeld, Maria Bamford, and Adam Sandler thanks to its Celebrity Drop-In Tuesdays. The food and drinks are good though not great, but you're here for the laughs not the grub. ✉ *102 E. Magnolia Blvd., Burbank* ☎ *818/845–9721* ⊕ *www. flapperscomedy.com.*

👜 Shopping

Magnolia Park Vintage

SHOPPING NEIGHBORHOODS | Melrose Avenue might be Los Angeles's most well-known vintage shopping destination, but to many locals, especially those on the Eastside, Burbank's Magnolia Park is, in many ways, better. Spanning several blocks around Magnolia Avenue, this revitalized area blends vintage, thrift, and antique shopping opportunities with the laid-back small-town vibe that Melrose lacks. Great dining spots and modern coffee shops abound, as well as foot and nail spas for a bit of pampering. ✉ *W. Magnolia Blvd., between N. Niagara and N. Avon St., Burbank* ⊕ *www.visitmagnoliapark.com.*

Mid-Wilshire and Koreatown

While they're two distinctly different neighborhoods, Mid-Wilshire and Koreatown sit side by side and offer Angelenos some of the most interesting sights, sounds, and bites in the city.

Mid-Wilshire is broadly known for its wide variety of museums, but there's also a strip called Little Ethiopia, where you can find incredible cuisine. Koreatown, meanwhile, is a haven for Seoul food (pun intended) but also an area with multiethnic dining nuggets that hit the top of many restaurant lists. Once your stomach is sated, check out a Korean spa, where scrubbing and pampering can close out a perfectly long day.

Mid-Wilshire

👁 Sights

★ Academy Museum of Motion Pictures

MUSEUM | FAMILY | The long-waited Academy Museum of Motion Pictures sits on the corner of Wilshire and Fairfax, and is highlighted by a giant spherical dome that features a 1,000-seat theater and stunning terrace with views of the Hollywood Hills. Inside, the museum has seven floors of exhibition space that delves into the history of cinema with interactive exhibits, features on award-winning story tellers, multiple theaters, and immersive experiences. Dedicated to the art and science of movies, the Academy Museum is the premier center that is a must-stop for film buffs and casual moviegoers alike. ✉ *6067 Wilshire Blvd., Mid-Wilshire* ☎ *323/930–3000* ⊕ *www.academymuseum.org* ⤳ *$25.*

La Brea Tar Pits Museum

ARCHAEOLOGICAL SITE | FAMILY | Show your kids where Ice Age fossils come from by taking them to the stickiest park in town. The area formed when deposits of oil rose to the earth's surface, collected in shallow pools, and coagulated into asphalt. In the early 20th century geologists discovered that all that goo contained the largest collection of Pleistocene (Ice Age) fossils ever found at one location: more than 600 species of birds, mammals, plants, reptiles, and insects. Roughly 100 tons of fossil bones have been removed in excavations during the last 100 years, making this one of the world's most famous fossil sites. You can see most of the pits through chain link fences, and the new Excavator Tour gets you as close as possible to the action.

Pit 91 and Project 23 are ongoing excavation projects; tours are offered, and you can volunteer to help with the excavations in the summer. Several pits are scattered around Hancock Park and the surrounding neighborhood; construction in the area has often had to accommodate them, and in nearby streets and along sidewalks, little bits of tar occasionally ooze up. The museum displays fossils from the tar pits and has a glass-walled laboratory that allows visitors to view paleontologists and volunteers as they work on specimens. ■ TIP➜ Museum admission is free for L.A. County residents weekdays 3–5 pm. ⊠ 5801 Wilshire Blvd., Miracle Mile ☎ 323/934–7243 ⊕ www. tarpits.org ⊠ $15; free 1st Tues. of every month (except July and Aug.) and every Tues. in Sept.

★ Los Angeles County Museum of Art (LACMA)

MUSEUM | Los Angeles has a truly fabulous museum culture and everything that it stands for can be epitomized by the massive, eclectic, and ever-changing Los Angeles County Museum of Art. Opened at its current location in 1965, today the museum boasts the largest collection of art in the western United States with more than 135,000 pieces from 6,000 years of history across multiple buildings atop over 20 acres. Highlights include the

Urban Light sculpture by Chris Burden (an Instagram favorite), *Levitated Mass* by Michael Heizer, and prominent works by Frida Kahlo, Wassily Kandinsky, Henri Matisse, and Claude Monet. With an illustrative permanent collection to go along with an ever-rotating array of temporary exhibits, film screenings, educational programs, and more, the museum is a beacon of culture that stands alone in the middle of the city. ■ TIP➜ Temporary exhibitions sometimes require tickets purchased in advance. ⊠ 5905 Wilshire Blvd., Miracle Mile ☎ 323/857–6000 ⊕ www. lacma.org ⊠ $20 ⊗ Closed Wed.

Petersen Automotive Museum

MUSEUM | FAMILY | L.A. is a mecca for car lovers, which explains the popularity of this museum with a collection of more than 300 automobiles and other motorized vehicles. But you don't have to be a gearhead to appreciate the Petersen; there's plenty of fascinating history here for all to enjoy. Learn how Los Angeles grew up around its freeways, how cars evolve from the design phase to the production line, and how automobiles have influenced film and television. To see how the vehicles, many of them quite rare, are preserved and maintained, take the 90-minute tour of the basement-level Vault (young kids aren't permitted in the Vault, but they'll find plenty to keep them occupied throughout the museum). ⊠ 6060 Wilshire Blvd., Mid-Wilshire ☎ 323/964–6331 ⊕ www.petersen.org ⊠ From $17.

🍴 Restaurants

★ Meals by Genet

$$ | ETHIOPIAN | In a tucked-away stretch along Fairfax Avenue is Little Ethiopia, where Angelenos of all stripes flock for the African country's signatures like *tibs*, *wat*, and *kitfo*. And while there is a plethora of Ethiopian options, no one does the cuisine justice quite like Meals by Genet. **Known for:** authentic Ethiopian cuisine; jovial atmosphere; unreal tibs.

$ *Average main: $20* ✉ *1053 S. Fairfax Ave., Mid-Wilshire* ☎ *323/938–9304* 🌐 *www.mealsbygenetla.com* 🕒 *Closed Mon.–Wed.*

★ République

$$$$ | FRENCH | FAMILY | This stunning expansive space, originally built for Charlie Chaplin back in the 1920s, serves French delicacies for breakfast, lunch, and dinner every day of the week. The scent of homemade croissants wafts through the building in the morning; steak frites can be enjoyed at night. **Known for:** French classics like escargot; unbeatable pastries; nice bar menu. $ *Average main: $35* ✉ *624 S. La Brea Ave., Beverly–La Brea* ☎ *310/362–6115* 🌐 *www.republiquela.com.*

Sky's Gourmet Tacos

$ | MEXICAN | If you're searching for some of the spiciest and most succulent tacos in L.A., look no further than Sky's. This quaint taco joint offers up beef, chicken, turkey, seafood, and vegan options that will leave your mouth on fire and your belly full in all the best ways possible. **Known for:** amazing tacos with a variety of fillings (including breakfast tacos); lots of spices; jovial atmosphere. $ *Average main: $10* ✉ *5303 W. Pico Blvd., Mid-Wilshire* ☎ *833/759–8226* 🌐 *www.skysgourmettacos.com.*

Koreatown

🍴 Restaurants

The Boiling Crab

$$ | SEAFOOD | FAMILY | Put on your bib and prepare to get messy, because this crab shack is not for stodgy eaters. Choices of blue, Dungeness, snow, king, and southern king, are brought out in plastic bags where you can rip, tear, twist, and yank the meaty goodness out of their shells. **Known for:** giant crab legs; unfussy environment; long lines. $ *Average main: $20* ✉ *3377 Wilshire Blvd., Suite 115, Koreatown* ☎ *213/389–2722* 🌐 *www.theboilingcrab.com* [M] *Wilshire/Normandie Station.*

Guelaguetza

$$ | MEXICAN | FAMILY | A classic L.A. Mexican eatery, Guelaguetza serves the complex but not overpoweringly spicy cooking of Oaxaca, one of Mexico's most renowned culinary capitals. Inside, you'll find a largely Spanish-speaking clientele bobbing their heads to nightly jazz and marimba while wolfing down the restaurant's specialty: the moles. **Known for:** salsa-covered chorizo; chili-marinated pork; family-owned restaurant. $ *Average main: $15* ✉ *3014 W. Olympic Blvd., Koreatown* ☎ *213/427–0608* 🌐 *www.ilovemole.com* 🕒 *Closed Mon.*

★ Kobawoo House

$$ | KOREAN | FAMILY | Nestled into a dingy strip mall, this Korean powerhouse is given away by the lines of locals waiting outside. Once inside, scents of grilled meats and kimchi immediately fill your nostrils, and soon enough, your table will be littered with sides, *kalbi* beef, *dolsot* bibimbap, *wang bosam* (cabbage wraps with boiled pork), and tall bottles of Hite beer. **Known for:** perfect kalbi beef; long lines; cheap eats. $ *Average main: $17* ✉ *698 S. Vermont Ave., Suite 109, Koreatown* ☎ *213/389–7300* 🌐 *www.kobawoohouse.com* [M] *Wilshire/Vermont.*

🛏 Hotels

Hotel Normandie

$ | HOTEL | Originally built in 1926, this Renaissance Revival gem has been renovated to today's standards and is now a hip and not-so-pricey spot to post up in the ever-booming center of Koreatown. **Pros:** Michelin-starred French restaurant; complimentary breakfast; cheap prices. **Cons:** feels dated; tiny bathrooms; restaurant is pricey. $ *Rooms from: $190* ✉ *605 Normandie Ave., Koreatown* ☎ *213/388–8138* 🌐 *www.hotelnormandiela.com* 🛏 *92 rooms* [M] *Wilshire/Normandie.*

The Line

$$ | HOTEL | This boutique hotel pays homage to its Koreatown address with dynamic dining concepts and a hidden karaoke speakeasy. **Pros:** on-site bikes to explore the area; unique decor; fun bars on-site (ask about the speakeasy). **Cons:** expensive parking; lobby bar crowds public spaces; far from parts of the city you may want to explore. $ *Rooms from: $250* ✉ *3515 Wilshire Blvd., Koreatown* ☎ *213/381–7411* ⊕ *www.thelinehotel. com* ⊃ *384 rooms* ⦿ *No meals* Ⓜ *Wilshire/Normandie Station.*

Nightlife

Dan Sung Sa

BARS/PUBS | Step through the curtained entrance and back in time to 1970s Korea at Dan Sung Sa, which gained wider popularity after Anthony Bourdain paid a visit. At this quirky time-capsule bar, woodblock menus feature roughly 100 small eats. You'll see much that looks familiar, but fortune favors the bold. Take a chance on corn cheese, or try the *makgeolli*: a boozy Korean rice drink you sip from a bowl. It pairs perfectly with good conversation and snacking all night long. ✉ *3317 W. 6th St., Koreatown* ☎ *213/487–9100* Ⓜ *Wilshire/Vermont.*

★ HMS Bounty

BARS/PUBS | This super-kitschy nautical-theme bar in the heart of Koreatown offers drink specials and food at prices that will make you swoon. Come for the wings, all-day breakfast specials, cheap drinks, and very eclectic crowds. ✉ *3357 Wilshire Blvd., Koreatown* ☎ *213/385–7275* ⊕ *www.thehmsbounty. com* Ⓜ *Wilshire/Normandie.*

The Prince

BARS/PUBS | *Mad Men* and *New Girl* both had multiple scenes filmed in this Old Hollywood relic, which dates back to the early 1900s. The Prince is trimmed with vintage fabric wallpaper and bedecked with a stately mahogany bar; the grand piano waits in the wings. Squire lamps punctuate red-leather booths where you can enjoy Korean fare and standard cocktails, wine, and beer. Whatever you do, get the deep-fried chicken. ✉ *3198 W. 7th St., Koreatown* ☎ *213/389–1586* Ⓜ *Wilshire/Vermont Station.*

Activities

Aroma Spa & Sports

FITNESS/HEALTH CLUBS | It's not difficult to find amazing spa experiences throughout Koreatown. Most places will offer up standard scrubs, hot and cold baths, dry and wet saunas, and more. Aroma takes things to another level as the spa is just the centerpiece of an entire entertainment complex. Spa services include all the traditional treatments, but when you're done getting pampered, the rest of the facility includes a gym, a swimming pool, restaurants, and a state-of-the-art golf driving range. ✉ *3680 Wilshire Blvd., Koreatown* ☎ *213/387–2111* ⊕ *www.aromaresort.com* Ⓜ *Wilshire/Western.*

Wi Spa

FITNESS/HEALTH CLUBS | Koreatown is filled with endless spa experiences, but there are a few that rise above the rest. Wi Spa is a 24/7 wonderland of treatments that includes hot and cold baths, unique sauna rooms, and floors for men, women, or co-ed family spa fun. Signature sauna rooms vary from intense 231-degree thermotherapy to salt-enriched stations and specialty clay imported from Korea. Just remember, Korean spas are not for the shy at heart—you will be nude, you will get scrubbed, and you will feel like a million bucks after. ✉ *2700 Wilshire Blvd., Koreatown* ☎ *213/487–2700* ⊕ *www.wispausa.com* Ⓜ *Wilshire/Vermont.*

Downtown Los Angeles

If there's one thing Angelenos love, it's a makeover, and city planners have put the wheels in motion for a dramatic revitalization of this area in recent years. Downtown is both glamorous and gritty and is an example of Los Angeles's complexity as a whole. There's a dizzying variety of experiences not to be missed here if you're curious about the artistic, historic, ethnic, or sports-loving sides of L.A.

Downtown Los Angeles isn't just one neighborhood: it's a cluster of pedestrian-friendly enclaves where you can sample an eclectic mix of flavors, wander through world-class museums, and enjoy great live performances or sports events.

Sights

★ Angels Flight Railway

TRANSPORTATION SITE (AIRPORT/BUS/FERRY/TRAIN) | The turn-of-the-20th-century funicular, dubbed "the shortest railway in the world," operated between 1901 and 1969, when it was dismantled to make room for an urban renewal project. Almost 30 years later, Angels Flight returned with its original orange-and-black wooden cable cars hauling travelers up a 298-foot incline from Hill Street to the fountain-filled Watercourt at California Plaza. Your reward is a stellar view of the neighborhood. Tickets are $1 each way, but you can buy a souvenir round-trip ticket for $2 if you want something to take home with you. ⊠ *351 S. Hill St., between 3rd and 4th Sts., Downtown* ☎ *213/626–1901* ⊕ *www.angelsflight.org.*

Bradbury Building

BUILDING | Stunning wrought-iron railings, ornate plaster moldings, pink marble staircases, a birdcage elevator, and a skylighted atrium that rises almost 50 feet—it's easy to see why the Bradbury Building leaves visitors awestruck. Designed in 1893 by a novice architect who drew his inspiration from a science-fiction story and a conversation with his dead brother via a Ouija board, the office building was originally the site of turn-of-the-20th-century sweatshops, but now it houses a variety of businesses. Scenes from *Blade Runner*, *Chinatown*, and *500 Days of Summer* were filmed here, which means there's often a barrage of tourists snapping photos. Visits are limited to the lobby and the first-floor landing. ■**TIP→** **Historic Downtown walking tours hosted by the L.A. Conservancy cost $15 and include the Bradbury Building.** ⊠ *304 S. Broadway, Downtown* ☎ *213/626–1893* ⊕ *www.laconservancy.org/locations/bradbury-building* Ⓜ *Pershing Square Station.*

★ The Broad Museum

MUSEUM | The talk of Los Angeles's art world when it opened in 2015, this museum in an intriguing, honeycomb-looking building was created by philanthropists Eli and Edythe Broad (rhymes with "road") to showcase their stunning private collection of contemporary art, amassed over five decades and still growing. With upward of 2,000 pieces by more than 200 artists, the collection has in-depth representations of the work of such prominent names as Jean Michel Basquiat, Jeff Koons, Ed Ruscha, Cindy Sherman, Cy Twombly, Kara Walker, and Christopher Wool. The "veil and vault" design of the main building integrates gallery space and storage space (visitors can glimpse the latter through a window in the stairwell): the veil refers to the fiberglass, concrete, and steel exterior; the vault is the concrete base. Temporary exhibits and works from the permanent collection are arranged in the small first-floor rooms and in the more expansive third floor of the museum, so you can explore everything in a few hours. Next door to the Broad is a small plaza with olive trees and seating, as well as the museum restaurant, Otium. Admission to the museum is free, but book timed tickets in advance to guarantee entry. ⊠ *221 S. Grand Ave., Downtown* ☎ *213/232–6200* ⊕ *www.thebroad.org*

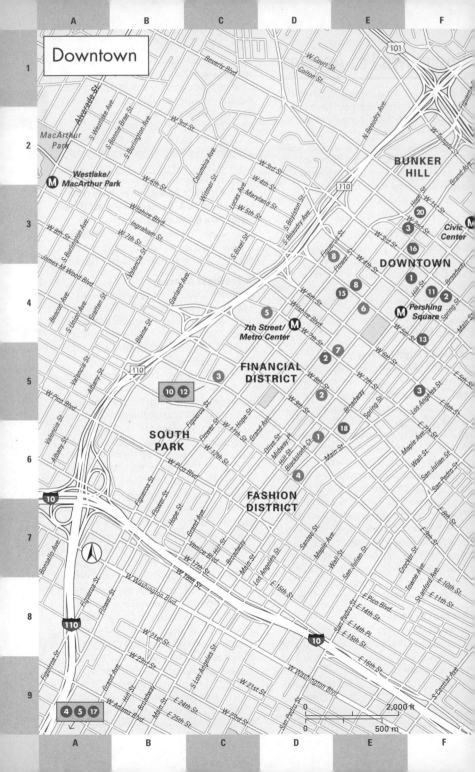

CHINATOWN

MISSION JUNCTION

LITTLE TOKYO

SKID ROW

ARTS DISTRICT

Union Station

KEY

1 Exploring Sights

1 Restaurants

1 Hotels

Metro

Free ⊙ Closed Mon. Ⓜ *Civic Center/ Grand Park Station.*

California African American Museum

MUSEUM | With more than 4,500 historical artifacts, this museum showcases contemporary art of the African diaspora. Artists represented here include Betye Saar, Charles Haywood, and June Edmonds. The museum has a research library with more than 6,000 books available for public use. ∎TIP→ **If possible, visit on a Sunday, when there's almost always a diverse lineup of speakers and performances.** ✉ *600 State Dr., Exposition Park* 🖼 *213/744–7432* ⊕ *www.caamuseum. org* 🎫 *Free; parking $12* ⊙ *Closed Mon.* Ⓜ *Expo/Vermont Station.*

California Science Center

MUSEUM | FAMILY | You're bound to see excited kids running up to the dozens of interactive exhibits here that illustrate the prevalence of science in everyday life. Clustered in different "worlds," the center keeps young guests busy for hours. They can design their own buildings and learn how to make them earthquake-proof; watch Tess, the dramatic 50-foot animatronic star of the exhibit *Body Works,* demonstrate how the body's organs work together; and ride a bike across a trapeze wire three stories high in the air. One of the exhibits in the Air and Space section shows how astronauts Pete Conrad and Dick Gordon made it to outer space in the Gemini 11 capsule in 1966; also here is NASA's massive space shuttle *Endeavor,* located in the Samuel Oschin Pavilion, for which a timed ticket is needed to visit. The IMAX theater screens science-related large-format films. ✉ *700 Exposition Park Dr., Exposition Park* 🖼 *323/724–3623* ⊕ *www. californiasciencecenter.org* 🎫 *Permanent exhibits free; fees for some attractions, special exhibits, and IMAX screenings vary; parking $12* Ⓜ *Expo/Vermont.*

Cathedral of Our Lady of the Angels

RELIGIOUS SITE | A half block from Frank Gehry's curvaceous Walt Disney Concert Hall sits the austere Cathedral of Our Lady of the Angels—a spiritual draw as well as an architectural attraction. Controversy surrounded Spanish architect José Rafael Moneo's unconventional design for the seat of the Archdiocese of Los Angeles. But judging from the swarms of visitors and the standing-room-only holiday masses, the church has carved out a niche for itself in Downtown L.A.

The plaza in front is glaringly bright on sunny days, though a children's play garden with bronze animals mitigates the starkness somewhat. Head underground to wander the mausoleum's mazelike white-marble corridors. Free guided tours start at the entrance fountain at 1 pm on weekdays. ∎TIP→ **There's plenty of underground visitors parking; the vehicle entrance is on Hill Street.** ✉ *555 W. Temple St., Downtown* 🖼 *213/680–5200* ⊕ *www.olacathedral.org* 🎫 *Free* Ⓜ *Civic Center/Grand Park.*

Chinatown

NEIGHBORHOOD | Smaller than San Francisco's Chinatown, this neighborhood near Union Station still represents a slice of East Asian life. Sidewalks are usually jammed with tourists, locals, and residents hustling from shop to shop picking up goods, spices, and trinkets from small shops and miniplazas that line the street. Although some longtime establishments have closed in recent years, the area still pulses with its founding culture. During Chinese New Year, giant dragons snake down the street. And, of course, there are the many restaurants and quick-bite cafés specializing in Chinese feasts. In recent years, a slew of hip eateries like Howlin' Ray's and Majordomo have injected the area with vibrancy.

An influx of local artists has added a spark to the neighborhood by taking up empty spaces and opening galleries along Chung

King Road, a faded pedestrian passage behind the West Plaza shopping center between Hill and Yale. Also look for galleries along a little side street called Gin Ling Way on the east side of Broadway. Chinatown has its main action on North Broadway. There are several garages available for parking here that range from $5 to $10 per day. ⊠ *Bordered by the 110, 101, and 5 freeways, Downtown* ⊕ *chinatown-la.com* Ⓜ *Union Station.*

★ El Pueblo de Los Angeles

NEIGHBORHOOD | The oldest section of the city, known as El Pueblo de Los Angeles, represents the rich Mexican heritage of L.A. It had a close shave with disintegration in the early 20th century, but key buildings were preserved, and eventually **Olvera Street,** the district's heart, was transformed into a Mexican American marketplace. Today vendors still sell puppets, leather goods, sandals, and woolen shawls from stalls lining the narrow street. You can find everything from salt and pepper shakers shaped like donkeys to gorgeous glassware and pottery.

At the beginning of Olvera Street is the Plaza, a Mexican-style park with plenty of benches and walkways shaded by a huge Moreton Bay fig tree. On weekends, mariachi bands and folkloric dance groups perform. Nearby places worth investigating include the historic Avila Adobe, the Chinese American Museum, the Plaza Firehouse Museum, and the America Tropical Interpretive Center. Exhibits at the Italian American Museum of Los Angeles chronicle the area's formerly heavy Italian presence. ⊠ *Avila Adobe/Olvera Street Visitors Center, 125 Paseo De La Plaza, Downtown* ☎ *213/485–6855* ⊕ *elpueblo.lacity.org* ⊠ *Free for Olvera St. and guided tours; fees at some museums.*

Geffen Contemporary at MOCA

MUSEUM | The Geffen Contemporary is one of architect Frank Gehry's boldest creations. One of three MOCA branches, the 40,000 square feet of exhibition space was once used as a police car warehouse. The museum's permanent collection includes works from artists like Willem de Kooning, Franz Kline, Jackson Pollock, Mark Rothko, and Cindy Sherman. ■ **TIP→ Present your TAP metro card to get two-for-one admission.** ⊠ *152 N. Central Ave., Downtown* ☎ *213/626–6222* ⊕ *www.moca.org/visit/geffen-contemporary* ⊠ *Free; special exhibitions $18 or free every Thurs. 5–8; parking $9.*

GRAMMY Museum

MUSEUM | The GRAMMY Museum brings the music industry to life. Throughout four floors and 30,000 square feet of space, the museum showcases rare footage of GRAMMY performances, plus rotating and interactive exhibits on award-winning musicians and the history of music. A 200-seat theater is great for live events that include screenings, lectures, interviews, and intimate music performances. ⊠ *800 W. Olympic Blvd., Downtown* ☎ *213/765–6800* ⊕ *www.grammymuseum.org* ⊠ *$15* ⊙ *Closed Tues.* Ⓜ *Pico.*

★ Grand Central Market

MARKET | With options that include handmade white-corn tamales, warm olive bread, dried figs, Mexican fruit drinks, and much more, this mouthwatering gathering place is the city's largest and most active food market. The spot bustles nonstop with locals and visitors surveying the butcher shop's display of everything from lambs' heads to pigs' tails. Produce stalls are piled high with locally grown avocados and heirloom tomatoes. Stop by **Chiles Secos** at stall C-12 for a remarkable selection of rare chilis and spices; **Ramen Hood** at C-2, for sumptuous vegan noodles and broth; or **Sticky Rice** at stall C-5, for fantastic Thai-style chicken. Even if you don't plan on buying anything, it's a great place to browse and people-watch. ⊠ *317 S. Broadway, Downtown* ☎ *213/624–2378* ⊕ *www.grandcentralmarket.com* ⊠ *Free* Ⓜ *Pershing Square.*

L.A. Live

ARTS VENUE | The mammoth L.A. Live entertainment complex was opened in 2007 when there was little to do or see in this section of Downtown. Since its inception, this once creepy ghost town has become a major hub for sports, concerts, award shows, and more. The first things you'll notice as you emerge from the parking lot are the giant LED screens and sparkling lights, and the buzz of crowds as they head out to dinner before or after a Lakers game, movie, or live show at the Microsoft Theater. There are dozens of restaurants and eateries here, including Los Angeles favorite Katsuya, the spot for sizzling Kobe beef platters and excellent sushi (the crab rolls are not to be missed). ■ TIP➔ **Park for free on weekdays from 11 am to 2 pm if you eat at one of the dozen or so restaurants here.** ⊠ *800 W. Olympic Blvd., Downtown* ☎ *213/763–5483* ⊕ *www.lalive.com* Ⓜ *Pico.*

★ The Last Bookstore

STORE/MALL | California's largest used and new book and record shop is a favorite for both book lovers and fans of a good photo op, thanks to elements like an archway created from curving towers of books, a peephole carved into the stacks, and an in-store vault devoted to horror texts. Aside from the awesome aesthetics, shoppers will love to get lost in the store's collection of affordable books, art, and music. ⊠ *453 S. Spring St., ground fl., Downtown* ☎ *213/488–0599* ⊕ *www. lastbookstorela.com* Ⓜ *Pershing Square.*

★ Little Tokyo

NEIGHBORHOOD | One of three official Japantowns in the country—all of which are in California—Little Tokyo is blossoming again thanks to the next generation of Japanese Americans setting up small businesses. Besides dozens of sushi bars, tempura restaurants, and karaoke bars, there's a lovely garden at the Japanese American Cultural and Community Center and a renovated 1925 Buddhist temple with an ornate entrance at the Japanese American National Museum.

On 1st Street you'll find a strip of buildings from the early 1900s. Look down when you get near San Pedro Street to see the art installation called *Omoide no Shoto-kyo* ("Remembering Old Little Tokyo"). Embedded in the sidewalk are brass inscriptions naming the original businesses, quoted reminiscences from residents, and steel time lines of Japanese American history up to World War II. Nisei Week (a *nisei* is a second-generation Japanese American) is celebrated every August with traditional drums, dancing, a carnival, and a huge parade. ■ TIP➔ **Docent-led walking tours are available the last Saturday of every month starting at 10:15 am. The cost is $15 and includes entry to the Japanese American National Museum.** ⊠ *Bounded by 1st and 3rd Sts., the 101 and 110 freeways, and LA River, Downtown* ☎ *213/880–6875* ⊕ *www.visitlittletokyo.com* Ⓜ *Civic Center/Grand Park Station.*

Los Angeles Central Library

LIBRARY | The nation's third-largest public library, the handsome Los Angeles Central Library was designed in 1926 by Bertram Goodhue. Restored to their pristine condition, a pyramid tower and a torch symbolizing the "light of learning" crown the building. The Cook rotunda on the second floor features murals by Dean Cornwell depicting the history of California, and the Tom Bradley Wing, named for a famed L.A. mayor, has a soaring eight-story atrium.

The library offers frequent special exhibits, plus a small café where you can refuel. Don't ignore the gift shop, which is loaded with unique items for readers and writers. Free docent walking tours are offered Monday through Friday at 12:30, Saturday at 11 and 2, and Sunday at 2. An Art-in-the-Garden tour is on Saturday at 12:30 pm. A self-guided tour map is also available on the library's website. ⊠ *630 W. 5th St., Downtown* ☎ *213/228–7000* ⊕ *www.lapl. org* ⌦ *Free* Ⓜ *Pershing Square.*

MOCA Grand Avenue

MUSEUM | The main branch of the Museum of Contemporary Art, designed by Arata Isozaki, contains underground galleries and presents elegant exhibitions. A huge Nancy Rubins sculpture fashioned from used airplane parts graces the museum's front plaza. The museum gift shop offers apothecary items, modernist ceramics, and even toys and games for children to appease any art lover. ■ TIP→ Take advantage of the free audio tour. ✉ 250 S. Grand Ave., Downtown ☎ 213/626–6222 ⊕ www.moca.org 🎫 General admission free; special exhibitions $18 or free Thurs. 5–8 ⊗ Closed Tues. Ⓜ Civic Center/Grand Park.

Natural History Museum of Los Angeles County

MUSEUM | FAMILY | The hot ticket at this beaux arts–style museum completed in 1913 is the Dinosaur Hall, whose more than 300 fossils include adult, juvenile, and baby skeletons of the fearsome *Tyrannosaurus rex*. The Discovery Center lets kids and curious grown-ups touch real animal pelts, and the Insect Zoo gets everyone up close and personal with the white-eyed assassin bug and other creepy crawlers. A massive hall displays dioramas of animals in their natural habitats. Also look for pre-Columbian artifacts and crafts from the South Pacific, or priceless stones in the Gem and Mineral Hall. Outdoors, the 3½-acre Nature Gardens shelter native plant and insect species and contain an expansive edible garden. ■ TIP→ Don't miss out on the Dino lab, where you can watch paleontologists unearth and clean real fossils. ✉ 900 W. Exposition Blvd., Exposition Park ☎ 213/763–3466 ⊕ www.nhm.org 🎫 $15; free on 1st Tues. of month Ⓜ Expo/Vermont.

Orpheum Theatre

ARTS VENUE | Opened in 1926, the opulent Orpheum Theatre played host to live attractions including classic comedians, burlesque dancers, jazz greats like Lena Horne, Ella Fitzgerald, and Duke Ellington, and later on rock-and-roll performers such as Little Richard. After extensive restorations, the Orpheum once again revealed a stunning white-marble lobby, majestic auditorium with fleur-de-lis panels, and two dazzling chandeliers. A thick red velvet and gold-trimmed curtain opens at showtime, and a white Wurlitzer pipe organ (one of the last remaining organs of its kind from the silent movie era) is at the ready. The original 1926 rooftop neon sign again shines brightly, signaling a new era for this theater. Today the theater plays host to live concerts, comedy shows, and movie screenings. ✉ 842 S. Broadway, Downtown ☎ 877/677–4386 ⊕ www.laorpheum.com/events.

Union Station

HISTORIC SITE | Even if you don't plan on traveling by train anywhere, head here to soak up the ambience of a great rail station. Envisioned by John and Donald Parkinson, the architects who also designed the grand City Hall, the 1939 masterpiece combines Spanish Colonial Revival and art deco elements that have retained their classic warmth and quality. The waiting hall's commanding scale and enormous chandeliers have provided the backdrop for countless scenes in films, TV shows, and music videos. Recently added to the majesty are the Imperial Western Beer Company and the Streamliner, two bars that pay homage to the station's original architecture while serving homemade brews and inventive classic cocktails. ■ TIP→ Walking tours of Union Station are on Saturday at 10 and cost $15. ✉ 800 N. Alameda St., Downtown ⊕ www.unionstationla.com Ⓜ Union Station.

★ Walt Disney Concert Hall

CONCERTS | One of the architectural wonders of Los Angeles, the 2,265-seat hall is a sculptural monument of gleaming, curved steel designed by Frank Gehry. It's part of a complex that includes a public park, gardens, shops, and two outdoor amphitheaters, one of them atop the concert hall. The acoustically superlative venue is the home of the city's premier orchestra, the Los Angeles Philharmonic, whose music director, Gustavo Dudamel, is an international celebrity in his own right. The orchestra's season runs from late September to early June, before it heads to the Hollywood Bowl for the summer. ■ TIP➔ **Free 60-minute guided tours are offered on most days, and there are self-guided audio tours.** ✉ *111 S. Grand Ave., Downtown* ☎ *323/850–2000* ⊕ *www.laphil.org* 🎫 *Tours free* Ⓜ *Civic Center/Grand Park.*

🍽 Restaurants

★ Bavel

$$$$ | **MIDDLE EASTERN** | Fans of Bestia have been lining up for stellar Mediterranean cuisine at this Arts District hot spot, which is owned by the same restaurateurs. Rose gold stools give way to marble tabletops as the open kitchen bangs out hummus and baba ghanoush spreads, along with flatbreads and lamb-neck shawarma. **Known for:** delicious Mediterranean cuisine; sceney atmosphere; great vibes. Ⓢ *Average main: $40* ✉ *500 Mateo St., Downtown* ☎ *213/232–4966* ⊕ *baveldtla.com.*

Bottega Louie

$$$ | **ITALIAN** | A Downtown dining staple, this lively Italian restaurant and gourmet market features open spaces, stark white walls, and majestic floor-to-ceiling windows. If the wait is too long at this no-reservations eatery, you can sip on Prosecco and nibble on pastries at the bar. **Known for:** mouthwatering chicken Parm; one-of-a-kind portobello fries; tartufo pizzas with black truffle mushrooms. Ⓢ *Average main: $25* ✉ *700 S. Grand Ave., Downtown* ☎ *213/802–1470* ⊕ *www.bottegalouie.com* Ⓜ *7th Street/ Metro Center.*

★ Cole's French Dip

$ | **AMERICAN** | There's a fight in Los Angeles over who created the French dip sandwich. The first contender is Cole's, whose sign on the door says it's the originator of the salty, juicy, melt-in-your-mouth meats. **Known for:** historic L.A. dining; one of the top contenders for best French dip sandwich in the country; secret speakeasy in back. Ⓢ *Average main: $10* ✉ *118 E. 6th St., Downtown* ☎ *213/622–4090* ⊕ *www.pouringwith-heart.com/coles.*

★ Guerrilla Tacos

$ | **MEXICAN FUSION** | What started as a food truck serving gourmet tacos has turned into a brick-and-mortar space that also has an excellent (and cheap) bar. Chefs fire up some of the most inventive tacos in the city—think sweet potato with almond chili and feta or the Baja fried cod with chipotle crema. **Known for:** gourmet tacos; cheap drinks; long lines. Ⓢ *Average main: $11* ✉ *2000 E. 7th St., Downtown* ☎ *213/375–3300* ⊕ *www. guerrillatacos.com.*

★ Howlin' Ray's

$$ | **SOUTHERN** | **FAMILY** | Don't let the hour-long waits deter you—if you want the best Nashville fried chicken in L.A., Howlin' Ray's is worth the effort. Right in the middle of Chinatown, this tiny chicken joint consists of a few bar seats, a few side tables, and a kitchen that sizzles as staff yell out "yes, chef" with each incoming order. **Known for:** spicy fried chicken; classic Southern sides; long waits. Ⓢ *Average main: $15* ✉ *727 N. Broadway, Suite 128, Downtown* ☎ *213/935–8399* ⊕ *www.howlinrays. com* ◷ *Closed Sun. and Mon.* Ⓜ *Union Station.*

★ Majordomo

$$$$ | **ECLECTIC** | You would never just stumble upon this out-of-the-way spot in Chinatown, but world-famous celeb chef David Chang likes it that way. The beautifully designed minimal space with spacious patio, an exposed-duct ceiling, and elongated wood bar has a cuisine style that defies any singular category. **Known for:** chuck short rib with raclette; rice-based drinks; hard-to-get reservations (try to eat at the bar). [$] *Average main: $40* ✉ *1725 Naud St., Downtown* ☎ *323/545–4880* 🌐 *www.majordomo.la* 🕒 *Closed Mon. and Tues.*

★ Philippe the Original

$ | **AMERICAN** | **FAMILY** | First opened in 1908, Philippe's is one of L.A.'s oldest restaurants and claims to be the originator of the French dip sandwich. While the debate continues around the city, one thing is certain: the dips made with beef, pork, ham, lamb, or turkey on a freshly baked roll stand the test of time. **Known for:** 50¢ coffee; communal tables; post–Dodgers game eats. [$] *Average main: $8* ✉ *1001 N. Alameda St., Downtown* ☎ *213/628–3781* 🌐 *www.philippes.com* [M] *Union Station.*

71Above

$$$$ | **ECLECTIC** | As its name suggests, this sky-high dining den sits on the 71st floor, 950 feet above ground level. With that elevation comes the most stunning views of any restaurant in L.A., and the food is close to matching it. **Known for:** sky-high views; fine dining with a seafood focus; classy atmosphere and loosely enforced dress code (no shorts or flip-flops). [$] *Average main: $39* ✉ *633 W. 5th St., 71st fl., Downtown* ☎ *213/712–2683* 🌐 *www.71above.com* [M] *Pershing Square Station.*

Sushi Gen

$$ | **JAPANESE** | Consistently rated one of the top sushi spots in L.A., Sushi Gen continues to dole out the freshest and tastiest fish in town. Sit at the elongated bar and get to know the sushi masters while they prepare your lunch. **Known for:** chef-recommended sushi selections; limited seating; great lunch specials. [$] *Average main: $20* ✉ *422 E. 2nd St., Downtown* ☎ *213/617–0552* 🌐 *www.sushigen-dtla.com* 🕒 *Closed Sun. and Mon. No lunch Sat.*

Hotels

★ Ace Hotel Downtown Los Angeles

$$ | **HOTEL** | The L.A. edition of this bohemian-chic hipster haven is at once a hotel, theater, and poolside bar (called Upstairs), housed in the gorgeous Spanish Gothic–style United Artists building in the heart of Downtown. **Pros:** lively rooftop lounge/pool area; gorgeous building and views; location in the heart of Downtown. **Cons:** expensive parking rates compared to nightly rates ($36); some kinks in the service; compact rooms. [$] *Rooms from: $239* ✉ *929 S. Broadway, Downtown* ☎ *213/623–3233* 🌐 *www.acehotel.com/losangeles* 🛏 *183 rooms* 🍴 *No meals.*

★ Freehand Los Angeles

$ | **HOTEL** | Part hotel, part shared accommodation space, the Freehand is one of the newest hotels in Downtown Los Angeles and also one of the coolest. **Pros:** range of affordable rooms from lofts to bunk beds; active social scene; great rooftop pool and bar. **Cons:** sketchy area at night around the hotel; free lobby Wi-Fi attracts nonhotel guests; most affordable rooms are shared. [$] *Rooms from: $100* ✉ *416 W. 8th St., Downtown* ☎ *213/612–0021* 🌐 *freehandhotels.com/los-angeles* 🛏 *59 shared rooms, 167 private rooms* 🍴 *No meals* [M] *Pershing Square.*

Hotel Figueroa

$$ | **HOTEL** | The 12-story Hotel Figueroa was originally built in 1926, and touches of that originality are still seen throughout with original skylights, wood beams, and tiles. **Pros:** a short walk to L.A. Live and the convention center; great poolside bar; in-room iPads and complimentary minibar snacks. **Cons:** the area can be sketchy at night; expensive parking ($40/night); smallish pool. [$] *Rooms from: $200* ✉ *939 S. Figueroa St., Downtown* ☎ *866/734–6018* 🌐 *www.hotelfigueroa.com* 🛏 *268 rooms* 🍴 *No meals* [M] *Olympic/Figueroa.*

The Hoxton

$ | **HOTEL** | Now one of the chicest hotels in Downtown L.A., the Hoxton is an open-house hotel where the lobby is the hub of activity and thoughtful design touches permeate throughout. The historic building was once the headquarters of the L.A. Railway and now sits in an up-and-coming part of the city filled with restaurants and apartments. **Pros:** stellar restaurant; monthly event calendar; great rooftop pool. **Cons:** area can be dodgy at night; no gym; some rooms on the small side. [$] *Rooms from: $160* ✉ *1060 S. Broadway, Downtown* ☎ *213/725–5900* 🌐 *www.thehoxton.com/downtown-la* 🛏 *174 rooms* 🍴 *No meals.*

InterContinental Los Angeles Downtown

$$ | **HOTEL** | This five-star addition to the Downtown L.A. scene impresses with views, an enormous gym, dining, and an outdoor pool. **Pros:** best views in the city; incredible restaurants and bars; top-rate service. **Cons:** too big and impersonal; busy and tricky intersection; parking is $46/night. [$] *Rooms from: $300* ✉ *900 Wilshire Blvd., Downtown* ☎ *213/688–7777* 🌐 *dtla.intercontinental.com* 🛏 *889 rooms* 🍴 *No meals* [M] *7th Street/Metro Center.*

Millennium Biltmore Hotel

$ | **HOTEL** | As the local headquarters of John F. Kennedy's 1960 presidential campaign and the location of some of the earliest Academy Awards ceremonies, this Downtown treasure, with its gilded 1923 beaux arts design, exudes ambience and history. **Pros:** 24-hour business center; tiled indoor pool and steam room; impressive history. **Cons:** pricey valet parking; standard rooms are compact; some decor is dated. [$] *Rooms from: $200* ✉ *506 S. Grand Ave., Downtown* ☎ *213/624–1011, 866/866–8086* 🌐 *www.millenniumhotels.com* 🛏 *683 rooms* 🍴 *No meals* [M] *Pershing Square.*

The NoMad Hotel

$$ | **HOTEL** | This stunningly refurbished property used to house the Bank of Italy and touches of the old bank can still be seen throughout—most notably in the lobby bathrooms that are cut out of the original vault. **Pros:** freestanding tubs; individually sourced artwork throughout; 24-hour gym. **Cons:** sketchy area at night; expensive parking ($48/night); some rooms are small. [$] *Rooms from: $250* ✉ *649 S. Olive St., Downtown* ☎ *213/358–0000* 🌐 *www.thenomadhotel.com/los-angeles* 🛏 *241 rooms* 🍴 *No meals* [M] *7th Street/Metro Center.*

Westin Bonaventure Hotel and Suites

$$ | **HOTEL** | **FAMILY** | Step inside the futuristic lobby of L.A.'s largest hotel to be greeted by fountains, an indoor lake and track, and 12 glass elevators leading up to the historic rooms of this 35-story property. Color-coded hotel floors help newcomers navigate the hotel, which takes up an entire city block. **Pros:** spa with shiatsu massage; revolving rooftop lounge; many on-site restaurants. **Cons:** massive hotel might feel too corporate; mazelike lobby and public areas; standard rooms are on the small side. [$] *Rooms from: $250* ✉ *404 S. Figueroa St., Downtown* ☎ *213/624–1000* 🌐 *westin.marriott.com* 🛏 *1358 rooms* 🍴 *No meals* [M] *7th Street/Metro Center.*

Nightlife

Broadway Bar

BARS/PUBS | This watering-hole-meets-dive sits in a flourishing section of Broadway (neighbors include the swank Ace Hotel). Bartenders mix creative cocktails while DJs spin tunes nightly. The two-story space includes a smoking balcony overlooking the street. The crowd is often dressed to impress. ✉ *830 S. Broadway, Downtown* ☎ *213/614–9909* 🌐 *www.broadwaybarla.com.*

★ The Edison

BARS/PUBS | The glitz and glam of the Roaring '20s is alive and well in the Edison, where the decor serves as tribute to the power plant that once occupied these premises. Black-and-white silent films are projected onto the walls, and tasty nibbles and artisanal cocktails are served (in a private room, if you prefer). There's live entertainment many nights, from jazz bands to burlesque shows to magic. A dress code means no shorts, jerseys, hoodies, flip-flops, tennis shoes, or collarless shirts. ⊠ 108 W. 2nd St., Downtown ☎ 213/613–0000 ⊕ www. theneverlands.com/edison.

★ Golden Gopher

BARS/PUBS | Craft cocktails, beers on tap, an outdoor smoking patio, and retro video games—this bar in the heart of Downtown is not to be missed. With one of the oldest liquor licenses in Los Angeles (issued in 1905), the Golden Gopher is the only bar in Los Angeles with an on-site liquor store for to-go orders—just in case you want to buy another bottle before you head home. ⊠ 417 W. 8th St., Downtown ☎ 213/614–8001 ⊕ www. pouringwithheart.com/golden-gopher Ⓜ 7th Street/Metro Center.

La Cita

BARS/PUBS | This dive bar may not look like much, but it more than makes up for it with an interesting mix of barflies, urban hipsters, and reasonable drink prices. Friday and Saturday night, DJs mix Top 40 hits and a tiny dance floor packs in the crowd. For those more interested in drinking and socializing, head to the back patio where a TV plays local sports. Every day has a differently themed happy hour—hip-hop happy hour on Wednesday or rockabilly happy hour on Thursday. Specials vary from $3 Tecates to free pizza. ⊠ 336 S. Hill St., Downtown ☎ 213/687–7111 ⊕ www.lacitabar.com Ⓜ Pershing Square Station.

The Love Song Bar

BARS/PUBS | Lovers of T. S. Eliot and vinyl will find themselves instantly at home inside this cozy establishment named after Eliot's "The Love Song of J. Alfred Prufrock." When not pouring drinks, bartenders often act as DJs, playing records (the best of the '60s through the '80s) in their entirety. As it's housed inside the Regent Theater, the cozy nature of the place can be disrupted when there's a concert scheduled. For those with an appetite, fantastic food can be ordered from the pizza parlor next door—naturally, it's called Prufrock's. ⊠ 450 S. Main St., Downtown ☎ 323/284–5728 ⊕ www.spacelandpresents.com/events/ the-love-song.

Redwood Bar & Grill

BARS/PUBS | If you're looking for a place with potent drinks and a good burger, this kitschy bar fits the bill perfectly. Known today as the "pirate bar" because of its nautical decor, the place dates back to the 1940s, when it was rumored to attract mobsters, politicians, and journalists due to its proximity to city hall, the Hall of Justice, and the original location of the Los Angeles Times. There's nightly music from local rock bands, though it comes with a cover charge. ⊠ 316 W. 2nd St., Downtown ☎ 213/680–2600 ⊕ www.theredwoodbar.com Ⓜ Civic Center/Grand Park.

★ Resident

MUSIC CLUBS | Catch a lineup of indie tastemakers inside this converted industrial space, or hang outdoors in the beer garden while trying bites from on-site food truck KTCHN (on cooler evenings you can congregate around the fire pits). A wide variety of draft beers and a specially curated cocktail program are available inside at the bar or at the trailer bar outside. ⊠ 428 S. Hewitt St., Downtown ☎ 213/628–7503 ⊕ www. residentdtla.com.

★ Seven Grand

BARS/PUBS | The hunting lodge vibe makes you feel like you need a whiskey in hand—luckily, this Downtown establishment stocks more than 700 of them. Attracting whiskey novices and connoisseurs, the bartenders here are more than willing to help you make a selection. Live jazz and blues bands play every night, so even if you're not a big drinker, there's still some appeal (although you're definitely missing out). For a more intimate setting, try the on-site **Bar Jackalope,** a bar within a bar, which has a "whiskey tasting library" specializing in Japanese varieties and seats only 18. ✉ *515 W. 7th St., 2nd fl., Downtown* ☎ *213/614–0736* ⊕ *www.sevengrandbars.com* Ⓜ *7th Street/Metro Center.*

The Varnish

BARS/PUBS | Beeline through the dining room of Cole's to find an unassuming door that leads to this small, dimly lit bar within a bar. Wooden booths line the walls, candles flicker, and live jazz is performed Sunday through Wednesday. The bartenders take their calling to heart and shake and stir some of the finest cocktails in the city. Those who don't have a drink of choice can list their wants ("gin-based and sweet," "strong whiskey and herbaceous") and be served a custom cocktail. Be warned: patrons requiring quick drinks will want to go elsewhere—perfection takes time. ✉ *118 E. 6th St., Downtown* ☎ *213/265–7089* ⊕ *www. pouringwithheart.com/the-varnish.*

🎭 Performing Arts

Ahmanson Theatre

THEATER | The largest of L.A.'s Center Group's three theaters, the 2,100-seat Ahmanson Theatre presents larger-scale classic revivals, dramas, musicals, and comedies like *Into the Woods,* which are either going to or coming from Broadway and the West End. The ambience is a theater lover's delight. ✉ *135 N. Grand Ave., Downtown* ☎ *213/972–7211* ⊕ *www.musiccenter.org/visit/Our-Venues/ahmanson-theatre* Ⓜ *Civic Center/ Grand Park Station.*

★ Dorothy Chandler Pavilion

CONCERTS | Though half a century old, this theater maintains the glamour of its early years, richly decorated with crystal chandeliers, classical theatrical drapes, and a 24-karat gold dome. Part of the Los Angeles Music Center, this pavilion is home to the L.A. Opera though a large portion of programming is made up of dance and ballet performances as well. Ticket holders can attend free talks that take place an hour before opera performances. ■**TIP➜ Reservations for the talks aren't required, but it's wise to arrive early, as space is limited.** ✉ *135 N. Grand Ave., Downtown* ☎ *213/972–0711* ⊕ *www. musiccenter.org/visit/Our-Venues/dorothy-chandler-pavilion* Ⓜ *Civic Center/ Grand Park.*

Microsoft Theater

CONCERTS | The Microsoft Theater is host to a variety of concerts and big-name awards shows—the Emmys, American Music Awards, BET Awards, and the ESPYs. This theater and the surrounding L.A. Live complex are a draw for those looking for a fun night out. The building's emphasis on acoustics and versatile seating arrangements means that all 7,100 seats are good, whether you're at an intimate acoustic concert or the People's Choice Awards. Outside, the L.A. Live complex hosts restaurants and attractions, including the GRAMMY Museum, to keep patrons entertained before and after shows (though it's open whether or not there's a performance). ✉ *777 Chick Hearn Ct., Downtown* ☎ *213/763–6030* ⊕ *www.microsofttheater.com* Ⓜ *Pico.*

Shrine Auditorium

CONCERTS | Since opening in 1926, the auditorium has hosted nearly every major awards show at one point or another, including the Emmys and the GRAMMYs. Today, the venue and adjacent Expo Hall hosts concerts, film premieres, award shows, pageants, and special events. The Shrine's Moorish Revival–style architecture is a spectacle all its own. ⊠ *665 W. Jefferson Blvd., Downtown* ☎ *213/748–5116* ⊕ *www.shrineauditorium.com.*

Los Feliz, Silver Lake, and the Eastside

The neighborhoods in L.A.'s Eastside are talked about with the same oh-my-god-it's-so-cool reverence by Angelenos as Brooklyn is by New Yorkers. These streets are dripping with trendiness—which will delight some and enrage others. Almost 20 years ago, Los Feliz was the first of these rediscovered, reinvented neighborhoods, then came Silver Lake, then Echo Park. As each one became more expensive, the cool kids relocated, leaving behind their style and influence. Now Highland Park is the center of the oh-so-hip universe. But, the epicenter is constantly shifting. No doubt, by the next edition of this guide, it'll be someplace else.

Los Feliz

 Sights

Barnsdall Art Park

CITY PARK | FAMILY | The panoramic view of Hollywood alone is worth a trip to this hilltop cultural center. On the grounds you'll find the 1921 **Hollyhock House,** a masterpiece of modern design by architect Frank Lloyd Wright. It was commissioned by philanthropist Aline Barnsdall to be the centerpiece of an arts community. While Barnsdall's project didn't turn out the way she planned, the park now hosts the L.A. Municipal Art Gallery and Theatre, which provides exhibition space for visual and performance artists.

Wright dubbed this style "California Romanza" (*romanza* is a musical term meaning "to make one's own form"). Stylized depictions of Barnsdall's favorite flower, the hollyhock, appear throughout the house in its cement columns, roof line, and furnishings. The leaded-glass windows are expertly placed to make the most of both the surrounding gardens and the city views. On summer weekends, there are wildly popular wine tastings and outdoor movie screenings. Self-guided tours are available Thursday through Sunday from 11 to 4. ⊠ *4800 Hollywood Blvd., Los Feliz* ☎ *No phone* ⊕ *www.barnsdall.org* ⊠ *Free; house tours $7* ⊗ *House closed Mon.*

★ Griffith Observatory

OBSERVATORY | Most visitors barely skim the surface of this gorgeous spot in the Santa Monica Mountains, but those in the know will tell you there's more to the Griffith Observatory than its sweeping views and stunning Greek Revival architecture. To start, this free-to-the-public mountaintop observatory is home to the Samuel Oschin Planetarium, a state-of-the-art theater with an aluminum dome and a Zeiss star projector that plays a number of ticketed shows. Those spectacular shows are complemented by a couple of space-related exhibits, and several telescopes (naturally), as well as theater programs and events at the Leonard Nimoy Event Horizon Theater. For visitors who are looking to get up close and personal with the cosmos, monthly star-viewing parties with local amateur astronomers are also on hand. ■TIP→**For a fantastic view, come at sunset to watch the sky turn fiery shades of red with the city's skyline silhouetted.** ⊠ *2800 E. Observatory Ave., Los Feliz* ☎ *213/473–0800* ⊕ *www.griffithobservatory.org* ⊗ *Closed Mon.* ☞ *Observatory grounds and parking are open daily.*

★ **Griffith Park**

CITY PARK | FAMILY | The country's largest municipal park, the 4,310-acre Griffith Park is a must for nature lovers, the perfect spot for respite from the hustle and bustle of the surrounding urban areas. Plants and animals native to Southern California can be found within the park's borders, including deer, coyotes, and even a reclusive mountain lion. Bronson Canyon (where the Batcave from the 1960s *Batman* TV series is located) and Crystal Springs are favorite picnic spots.

The park is named after Colonel Griffith J. Griffith, a mining tycoon who donated 3,000 acres to the city in 1896. As you might expect, the park has been used as a film and television location for at least a century. Here you'll find the Griffith Observatory, the Los Angeles Zoo, the Greek Theater, two golf courses, hiking and bridle trails, a swimming pool, a merry-go-round, and an outdoor train museum. ✉ *4730 Crystal Springs Dr., Los Feliz* ☎ *323/644–2050* 🌐 *www.laparks.org/dos/parks/griffithpk* 🎟 *Free; attractions inside park have separate admission fees.*

🍴 Restaurants

★ **The Best Fish Taco in Ensenada**

$ | MEXICAN | FAMILY | In mirroring the taco stands of Ensenada, Mexico—simple, cheap, and unceremonious, with a selection of spicy homemade salsas—this little local treasure has achieved what many restaurants serving Baja tacos haven't: an authentic (and delicious) experience. **Known for:** fish-and-shrimp tacos; mango salsa; seafood shack atmosphere. [$] *Average main: $6* ✉ *1650 Hillhurst Ave., Los Feliz* ☎ *323/466–5552* 🌐 *www.bestfishtacoinensenada.com.*

Kismet

$$ | MEDITERRANEAN | You may feel like you're about to walk into a sauna rather than a restaurant because of its minimalist light-color wood on white paint interior, but you'll find nothing but colorful gorgeous Middle Eastern dishes here at Kismet. This James Beard nominee perfectly blends comforting Middle Eastern and Israeli cuisine with Californian flavors and plant-based flair, all served in a modern space. **Known for:** Persian crispy rice; tasty lamb meatballs; Middle Eastern classics with a Cali twist. [$] *Average main: $18* ✉ *4648 Hollywood Blvd., Los Feliz* ☎ *323/409–0404* 🌐 *www.kismetla.com.*

Little Dom's

$$ | ITALIAN | With a vintage bar and dapper barkeep who mixes up seasonally inspired retro cocktails, an attached Italian deli where you can pick up a pork-cheek sub, and an $18 Monday-night supper, it's not surprising that Little Dom's is a neighborhood gem. Cozy and inviting, with big leather booths you can sink into for the night, the restaurant puts a modern spin on classic Italian dishes such as *burrata* agnolotti and meatballs. **Known for:** ricotta cheese and fresh blueberry pancakes; excellent pizza margherita; fun weekend brunch. [$] *Average main: $20* ✉ *2128 Hillhurst Ave., Los Feliz* ☎ *323/661–0055* 🌐 *www.littledoms.com.*

🍸 Nightlife

Covell

WINE BARS—NIGHTLIFE | This laid-back spot is the embodiment of what every unpretentious wine drinker wishes a wine bar should be. It's thankfully lacking in staff who might turn up their noses should you forget to swirl the glass. But what else would you expect from a spot with repurposed furnishings and a vintage motorcycle mounted to the wall? ✉ *4628 Hollywood Blvd., Los Feliz* ☎ *323/660–4400* 🌐 *www.barcovell.com.*

Dresden Room

PIANO BARS/LOUNGES | This bar's 1940s lounge decor makes it a favorite with folks in Los Angeles. The long-running house band, Marty and Elayne, has entertained patrons for more than three decades. (They found a new generation of fans, thanks to the film *Swingers*.) Other than the entertainment, perhaps the best reason to wander in is to sip on a Blood and Sand cocktail, self-proclaimed to be "the world's most tantalizing drink." ⊠ *1760 N. Vermont Ave., Los Feliz* ☎ *323/665–4294* ⊕ *www. thedresden.com.*

Performing Arts

★ Greek Theatre

CONCERTS | With a robust lineup from May through November, acts such as Bruce Springsteen, John Legend, and Aretha Franklin (RIP) have all graced the stage at this scenic outdoor venue. Located at the base of Griffith Park, there's usually slow preshow traffic on concert nights, but that'll give you a chance to take in the beautiful park foliage and homes in the Hollywood Hills. Paid lots are available for parking, but wear comfortable shoes and expect to walk as some lots are fairly far from the theater. Or you can park and enjoy cocktails in trendy and chic Los Feliz before a show, then walk up to the venue. ⊠ *2700 N. Vermont Ave., Los Feliz* ☎ *844/524–7335* ⊕ *www.lagreektheatre. com.*

👛 Shopping

Skylight Books

BOOKS/STATIONERY | A neighborhood bookstore through and through, Skylight has excellent sections devoted to kids, fiction, travel, and food; it even has a live-in cat. The space also hosts book discussion groups, panels, and author readings with hip literati. Art lovers can peruse texts on design and photography, graphic novels, and indie magazines at Skylight's annex a few doors down. ⊠ *1818 N. Vermont Ave., Los Feliz* ☎ *323/660–1175* ⊕ *www.skylightbooks.com.*

Soap Plant/Wacko

GIFTS/SOUVENIRS | This pop-culture supermarket offers a wide range of items, including rows of books on art and design. But it's the novelty stock that makes the biggest impression, with ant farms, X-ray specs, and anime figurines for sale. An adjacent gallery space, La Luz de Jesus, focuses on underground art. ⊠ *4633 Hollywood Blvd., Los Feliz* ☎ *323/663–0122* ⊕ *www.soapplant.com.*

Vamp Shoes

CLOTHING | From well-known designers to up-and-coming handcrafters who make their shoes in small batches, boutique store Vamp Shoes has a solid collection of footwear for anyone who appreciates (and who's not afraid to invest in) gorgeous, excellent-quality soles. Inventory here also includes cool bags, hosiery, jewelry, and handcrafted ceramics. ⊠ *1951 Hillhurst Ave., Los Feliz* ☎ *323/662–1150* ⊕ *www. vampshoeshop.com.*

🏃 Activities

Bronson Canyon

HIKING/WALKING | Bronson Canyon—or more popularly, Bronson Caves—is one of L.A.'s most famous filming locations, especially for western and sci-fi flicks. This section of Griffith Park, easily accessible through a trail that's less than half a mile, is a great place to visit whether you're a film buff or an exercise junkie. ⊠ *3200 Canyon Dr., Hollywood.*

Silver Lake

 Restaurants

★ Alimento

$$$ | **ITALIAN** | There's little surprise that chef Zach Pollack's soulful Italian masterpiece in Silver Lake features a lot of influences and inspirations that span the globe; the true-blue Angeleno, after all, grew up in a melting pot. Alimento's dishes are modern takes on traditional Italian cuisine, using locally sourced ingredients and varying in influences—from your classic American to Chinese and Mexican. **Known for:** chicken liver crostone; radiatori with braised pork sugo; surprising takes on Italian classics. $ *Average main: $25* ✉ *1710 Silver Lake Blvd., Silver Lake* ☎ *323/928–2888* 🌐 *www.alimentola.com* 🕑 *Closed Mon. No lunch.*

LaMill Coffee
$$ | CAFÉ | These folks take their coffee seriously, sourcing estate-grown beans that are prepared in a variety of ways (French press or Clover, to name but two) and offering an inventive list of espresso-based drinks. To go along with the requisite coffee is a breakfast-all-day menu, as well as a proper, if select, tea selection for those who take their leaves seriously. **Known for:** Japanese iced coffee; Varlhona mocha; breakfast items served all day. $ *Average main: $14* ✉ *1636 Silver Lake Blvd., Silver Lake* ☎ *323/663–4441* 🌐 *www.lamillcoffee.com.*

★ Night + Market Song
$$ | THAI | There are a lot of Thai restaurants in Los Angeles, but none have quite reached the level of cult status of Night + Market Song. Tucked between a free clinic, a small clothing store, and a tax office, this second rendition of chef Kris Yenbamroong's popular WeHo restaurant might be easy to miss, but keep an eye out, as its authentic (and properly spicy) Thai dishes are practically mandatory when you're in the neighborhood. **Known for:** startled pig; khao soi; long weekend lines. $ *Average main: $15* ✉ *3322 W. Sunset Blvd., Silver Lake* ☎ *323/665–5899* 🌐 *www.nightmarketsong.com* 🕑 *Closed Tues.*

Pine and Crane
$ | TAIWANESE | FAMILY | This is not the typical Chinese restaurant you might expect; it's a fast casual, often locally sourced Taiwanese restaurant housed in a modern setting. The menu changes based on season, the wine and beer list updates constantly, and the tea menu is carefully curated. **Known for:** dan dan noodles; traditional panfried omelet; friendly staff. $ *Average main: $12* ✉ *1521 Griffith Park Blvd., Silver Lake* ☎ *323/668–1128* 🌐 *www.pineandcrane.com* 🕑 *Closed Tues.*

Sawyer
$$$ | SEAFOOD | Simply put, Sawyer is a stunner with its restored brick walls, beautiful hardwood floor, and tiled patio, flourished with mid-century modern furniture; it's exactly the kind of bright and airy place you'd want to start off your day in. Yet most patrons come here less for the ambience and more for the food, with a menu that leans on the healthy side but isn't afraid to indulge in the hearty stuff, touting an assortment of traditional and modern American fare. **Known for:** seafood boil; lobster roll; weekend brunch. $ *Average main: $23* ✉ *3709 Sunset Blvd., Silver Lake* ☎ *323/641–3709* 🕑 *No brunch weekdays.*

Silverlake Ramen
$$ | RAMEN | Now a franchise with several locations around Los Angeles (and a random one in Concord, NC), it's this original spot in the heart of the city's hipsterville that's still the best. The go-to ramen joint for Silverlake and Echo Park denizens is just the ticket if you're in dire need of some comfort food while also partaking in L.A.'s multicultural food scene. **Known for:** The Blaze, a spicy Tonkotsu ramen; crispy rice with spicy tuna; hearty Japanese fare. $ *Average main: $14* ✉ *2927 Sunset Blvd., Silver Lake* ☎ *323/660–8100* 🌐 *www.silverlakeramen.com.*

🍸 Nightlife

Akbar
BARS/PUBS | This bar's welcoming feel is one of the reasons many people consider it their neighborhood bar, even if they don't live in the neighborhood. The crowd is friendly and inviting, and theme nights attract all sorts of folks, gay or straight.

The comedy nights are favorites, as are weekends, when DJs get everyone on the dance floor. ⊠ *4356 W. Sunset Blvd., Silver Lake* ☎ *323/665–6810* ⊕ *www. akbarsilverlake.com.*

Cha Cha Lounge

BARS/PUBS | If chaos and the assortment of ill-matched furnishings and decor is something you can forgive—or revel in—then this import from Seattle is a Silver Lake staple you should check out. Grab your (cheap) poison then meander through the Mexican fiesta-theme bar. Foosball tables, a photo booth, and a vending machine will give you plenty to occupy your time. ⊠ *2375 Glendale Blvd., Silver Lake* ☎ *323/660–7595* ⊕ *www. chachalounge.com.*

★ 4100

BARS/PUBS | With swaths of fabric draped from the ceiling, this low-lit bar with a bohemian vibe makes it perfect for dates. Groups of locals also come through for the night, making the crowd a plentiful mix of people. The bartenders know how to pour drinks that are both tasty and potent. There's plenty of seating at the tables and stools along the central bar, which gets crowded on the weekends. ⊠ *1087 Manzanita St., Silver Lake* ☎ *323/666–4460* ⊕ *www.pouringwith-heart.com/4100-bar.*

Silverlake Lounge

MUSIC CLUBS | Rock bands, burlesque performances, comedy sets, and even open-mike nights all have a home at the cross section of Sunset and Silver Lake at a little dive bar called the Silverlake Lounge. This small club with the yellow awning is a neighborhood spot—cash only, by the way—in the best way possible, with cheap drinks and local talent deserving of their time in the limelight. ⊠ *2906 W. Sunset Blvd., Silver Lake* ☎ *323/663–9636* ⊕ *www.thesilverlake-lounge.com.*

Thirsty Crow

BARS/PUBS | This whiskey bar serves up seasonal cocktails in a fun, rustic environ-ment. Though small, it manages to find space for live musicians and an open-mike night on Saturday. Part of the same hospitality group as Bigfoot Lodge and Highland Park Bowl, it has a locals-only feel. As local L.A. musician Father John Misty once said, "nothing good ever happens at the goddamn Thirsty Crow," but we think you should go and see for yourself. ⊠ *2939 W. Sunset Blvd., Silver Lake* ☎ *323/661–6007* ⊕ *www. thirstycrowbar.com.*

🛍 Shopping

Mohawk General Store

CLOTHING | Filled with a brilliant combina-tion of indie and established designers, this upscale boutique is a mainstay for the modern minimalist. Pick up the wares of local favorites Cathy Callahan and Knotwork, as well as internationally loved labels like Acne Studios, Issey Miyake, and Levi's. The Sunset Boulevard store stocks goods for men and women as well as children, plus accessories and some home goods. ⊠ *4011 W. Sunset Blvd., Silver Lake* ☎ *323/669–1601* ⊕ *www.mohawkgeneralstore.com.*

Secret Headquarters

BOOKS/STATIONERY | This could be the cool-est comic-book store on the planet, with a selection to satisfy both the geekiest of collectors and those more interested in artistic and literary finds. Rich wood floors and a leather chair near the front window of this intimate space mark the sophisticated setting, which features wall displays neatly organized with new com-ics and filing cabinets marked DC and Marvel. ⊠ *3817 W. Sunset Blvd., Silver Lake* ☎ *323/666–2228* ⊕ *www.thesecret-headquarters.com.*

Silver Lake Wine
WINE/SPIRITS | Boutique wineries from around the world provide this shop with the vintage bottles that fill the floor-to-ceiling racks. Looking relaxed and unassuming in jeans and T-shirts, the knowledgeable staff can steer you to the right wine or spirits for any occasion. Those who prefer to enjoy their wine in the privacy of their vacation rental or hotel will be pleased to know they also do deliveries around Silver Lake and the neighboring areas. ✉ *2395 Glendale Blvd., Silver Lake* ☎ *323/662–9024* 🌐 *www.silverlakewine.com.*

Echo Park

👁 Sights

★ Dodger Stadium
SPORTS VENUE | **FAMILY** | Home of the Dodgers since 1962, Dodger Stadium is the third-oldest baseball stadium still in use and has had quite the history in baseball, including Sandy Koufax's perfect game in 1965 and Kirk Gibson's 1988 World Series home run. Not only has it played host to the Dodgers' ups and downs and World Series runs, it's also been the venue for some of the biggest performers in the world, including the Beatles, Madonna, and Beyoncé. The stadium can be tough to get into on game day, so consider getting dropped off in the park and walking up. Alternately, you can arrive early, as locals tend not to roll up until the third inning. If you have the opportunity to take in a Friday night game, make sure to stick around for the fireworks show that follows—if you're patient, you can even wait in line and watch it from the field. ✉ *1000 Vin Scully Ave., Echo Park* ☎ *866/363–4377* 🌐 *dodgers.mlb.com/la/ballpark.*

Elysian Park
HIKING/WALKING | **FAMILY** | Though not Los Angeles's biggest park—that honor belongs to Griffith Park—Elysian comes in second, and also has the honor of being the city's oldest. It's also home to one of L.A.'s busiest and most beloved attractions, Dodger Stadium, the home field to the Los Angeles Dodgers. For this reason, baseball fans flock to this 600-acre park for tailgate parties. The rest of the time, however, Elysian Park serves as the Echo Park residents' backyard, thanks to its network of hiking trails, picnic spaces, and public playgrounds. ✉ *929 Academy Rd., Echo Park* 🌐 *www.laparks.org/park/elysian.*

🍴 Restaurants

Masa of Echo Park
$$ | **PIZZA** | **FAMILY** | While Masa of Echo Park does do excellent "bistro pizzas," as the restaurant calls them, it's mostly known for the delectable deep-dish pies that may just be the best you'll find this side of Chicago. Be prepared though—it can take a while to get seated and up to 45 minutes to get that deep dish you ordered, so it might be best to call ahead. **Known for:** vegan menu options; family-style dining; Italian classics. [$] *Average main: $20* ✉ *1800 W. Sunset Blvd., Echo Park* ☎ *213/989–1558* 🌐 *www.masaofechopark.com.*

Spoon and Pork
$$ | **PHILIPPINE** | In a city where food trucks can be successful enough to have their own brick-and-mortar spaces, and where Filipino food has quickly become a craze, it's no surprise that Spoon and Pork has found its rightful place in the neighborhood. With a name that cleverly plays on the traditional Filipino way of eating (using both spoon and fork), this modern Filipino food spot is the perfect introduction to the cuisine. **Known for:** adobo pork belly; lechon kawali; Filipino comfort food. [$] *Average main: $14* ✉ *3131 W. Sunset Blvd., Echo Park* ☎ *323/922–6061* 🌐 *www.spoonandpork.com* 🕑 *Closed Mon.*

Nightlife

★ The Echo

MUSIC CLUBS | Echo Park is peppered with music venues, but if you want to be in the heart of the neighborhood's live music scene, you should head to the Echo. With a full bar and recurring theme nights, the spot hosts cutting-edge music from both up-and-coming local and touring acts as well as well-known bands. ☒ *1822 Sunset Blvd., Echoplex entrance at 1154 Glendale Blvd., Echo Park* ☎ *No phone* ⊕ *www.spacelandpresents.com.*

★ Mohawk Bend

BARS/PUBS | There are plenty of reasons to stop by Mohawk Bend: 72 craft beers on tap, a wide range of California-only liquor, a vegetarian and vegan-friendly menu that includes tailored-to-your-wants pizza, and a buffalo cauliflower that—rumor has it—started the whole trend. There might be a long line to get into this 100-year-old former theater in the evenings, but it's worth it. ☒ *2141 Sunset Blvd., Echo Park* ☎ *213/483–2337* ⊕ *mohawk.la.*

★ 1642

BARS/PUBS | This romantically lit hole-in-the-wall is easy to miss, but you should aim to check it out if you're a discerning wine connoisseur or looking to experience the best of California's micro-breweries. Perfect for first dates, come here to experiment with craft beers or to warm up with wine while listening to some live old-time fiddle tunes. ☒ *1642 W. Temple St., Echo Park* ☎ *213/989–6836* ⊕ *www.1642bar.com.*

Shopping

Esqueleto

JEWELRY/ACCESSORIES | There's a touch of the macabre on display at Esqueleto, but what do you expect from a jewelry boutique with a name that means "skeleton" in Spanish? That doesn't mean the light, airy, contemporary shop is stereotypically Goth in style. Both its design and the inventory it stocks are perfectly polished and selected with a discerningly artistic eye. With a mix of excellent vintage finds and emerging designers, the shop has become a go-to destination for alternative brides' engagement rings and wedding bands. ☒ *1928 W. Sunset Blvd., Echo Park* ☎ *213/947–3508* ⊕ *www.shopesqueleto.com.*

Stories Books and Café

BOOKS/STATIONERY | With an off-the-beaten-path collection of new and used literature, a café catering to freelancers and free thinkers, and a back patio that showcases singer-songwriters, Stories Books and Café is an authentic reflection of Echo Park. Readings, signings, and other events are a regular occurrence. ☒ *1716 Sunset Blvd., Echo Park* ☎ *213/413–3733* ⊕ *www.storiesla.com.*

Time Travel Mart

SPECIALTY STORES | **FAMILY** | You probably won't find anything useful in the Time Travel Mart and that's exactly the point. From dinosaur eggs to robot milk, this is a store that touts the absurdly hilarious—all of which should bring back memories of your childhood and maybe a little bit of joy. That's because the store holds a secret: it's really a fundraiser for the nonprofit 826LA, which tutors neighborhood kids in the back section. So even when you're buying something unnecessary but absolutely wonderful, remember it's for a noble and worthy cause. ☒ *1714 W.*

Sunset Blvd., Echo Park ☎ 213/413–3388 ⊕ 826la.org/store.

Highland Park

👁 Sights

Heritage Square Museum

MUSEUM | Looking like a prop street set up by a film studio, Heritage Square resembles a row of bright dollhouses in the modest Highland Park neighborhood. Five 19th-century residences, a train station, a church, a carriage barn, and a 1909 boxcar that was originally part of the Southern Pacific Railroad, all built between the Civil War and World War I, were moved to this small park from various locations in Southern California to save them from the wrecking ball. The latest addition, a re-creation of a World War I–era drugstore, has a vintage soda fountain and traditional products. Docents dressed in period costume lead visitors through the lavish homes, giving an informative picture of Los Angeles in the early 1900s. Don't miss the unique 1893 Octagon House, one of just a handful of its kind built in California. ⊠ 3800 Homer St., Highland Park ☎ 323/225–2700 ⊕ www.heritagesquare. org ⊠ $10 ⊘ Closed Tues.–Thurs. and federal holiday Mon.

🍴 Restaurants

Cafe Birdie

$$ | **MEDITERRANEAN** | This spacious 1920s-style spot along a quickly revitalizing stretch of Figueroa has established itself as a neighborhood bistro frequented by Highland Park residents, as well as folks from nearby neighborhoods. The eclectic menu skillfully blends elements of European, Southern, and Japanese cuisines, tying them together with a fresh California flair and a gorgeous interior inspired by a fictional meeting-of-two-souls narrative. **Known for:** square pies; seasonal cocktails; modern, airy spot.

$ Average main: $19 ⊠ 5631 N. Figueroa St., Highland Park ☎ 323/739–6928 ⊕ www.cafebirdiela.com.

★ Donut Friend

$ | **BAKERY** | When this music-influenced doughnut shop first opened on York Boulevard in the early days of Highland Park's renaissance, there wasn't much there, and its arrival helped shape the now bustling strip and its vegan inclinations. Donut Friend had evolved into a destination in its own right, touting both a signature and limited menu of purely vegan doughnuts—which also happen to be inspired by the pop punk and emo music scene. **Known for:** fun flavors like Green Teagan and Sara (with matcha tea glaze); all vegan ingredients; make-your-own doughnut option. $ Average main: $4 ⊠ 5107 York Blvd., Highland Park ☎ 213/908–2745 ⊕ www.donutfriend. com.

El Huarache Azteca

$ | **MEXICAN** | **FAMILY** | While you definitely should try the flat shoe-shaped dish El Huarache Azteca is named after—think somewhere between a flatbread and a tostada—you cannot go wrong with any of the other options at this family restaurant that's been a fixture in the area for the last couple of decades. Just be aware there's often a wait for the food to come out. **Known for:** no-frills Mexican dishes; agua fresca; super huarache. $ Average main: $10 ⊠ 5225 York Blvd., Highland Park ☎ 323/478–9572 ⊕ elhuaracheazte-calive.com.

★ Knowrealitypie

$ | **BAKERY** | The award-winning Knowrealitypie, hidden in a shop the size of a large walk-in closet, serves homemade pies every Friday through Saturday and only stays open until it sells out, which it often does. So hurry on down to partake in a rotating menu of seasonal savory and sweet pies, turnovers, and other pastries while supplies last. **Known for:** triple cherry Cabernet pie; caramel mango passion pie; small space that only stays open until they sell out. $ *Average main: $6* ⊠ *5106 Townsend Ave., Highland Park* ☎ *916/799–5772* ⊕ *www.knowrealitypie. com* ⊗ *Closed Mon.–Thurs.*

Polka Polish Cuisine
$$ | POLISH | There's a coziness in Polka Polish Cuisine that can only be matched by a grandmother's living room. The food here, traditional Polish fare, also has that same comfort. **Known for:** hearty Polish comfort food; traditional pierogi and kielbasa; mom-and-pop ambience. $ *Average main: $20* ⊠ *4112 Verdugo Rd., Highland Park* ☎ *323/255–7887* ⊕ *www. polkarestaurant.com* ⊗ *Closed Mon. and Tues.*

 ## Nightlife

The Hermosillo
BARS/PUBS | This is the kind of laid-back pub every neighborhood should have, with an excellent selection of locally focused draft beer on tap, a rotating wine list, and mouthwatering food. To add to its allure, award-winning Highland Park Brewery got its start in the pub's back storage room and is still featured prominently on the menu. ⊠ *5125 York Blvd., Highland Park* ☎ *323/739–6459* ⊕ *thehermosillo.com.*

★ Highland Park Bowl
BARS/PUBS | FAMILY | Once an ambitious restoration project, Highland Park Bowl now serves as a massive throwback to its Prohibition Era roots as an alcohol-prescribing doctor's office and drugstore with its own bowling alley. That bowling alley remains, complete with the original pin machine. The hooch-pushing doctor and druggist, however, are long gone. But now there's an Italian restaurant that serves excellent pizza made from scratch using a mother dough brought all the way from Italy. ⊠ *5621 N. Figueroa St., Highland Park* ☎ *323/257–2695* ⊕ *www. highlandparkbowl.com.*

The York
BARS/PUBS | Since 2007, before Highland Park became trendy, the York has been holding its own as the ultimate neighborhood bar. It's not just that the aesthetic gives off that neighborhood vibe (think exposed brick and chalkboard menus), but the craft beers on tap are great, and the pub food is delicious—the cheddar burger and the fish-and-chips are favorites. ⊠ *5018 York Blvd., Highland Park* ☎ *323/255–9675* ⊕ *www.they-orkonyork.com.*

 ## Shopping

Galco's Soda Pop Stop
FOOD/CANDY | FAMILY | A local fixture in Highland Park for decades, Galco's is in some ways a trip down memory lane, carrying more than 600 sodas—most of which harken back to the days when soda was a regional affair—and options from all over the world. They also have a collection of retro candies, a soda creation station with more than 100 syrups to choose from, and a selection of alcohol that would put most liquor stores to shame. ⊠ *5702 York Blvd., Highland Park* ☎ *323/255–7115* ⊕ *sodapopstop.com.*

Permanent Records
MUSIC STORES | Part of the vinyl resurgence since 2013, Permanent Records stocks new and used vinyl for every musical taste and does it without any snobbery. The record store, which often has in-store performances, also runs its own label that focuses on local bands, limited-edition runs, and reissues. ⊠ *1906 Cypress Ave., Highland Park* ☎ *323/332–2312* ⊕ *www.permanentrecordsla.com.*

Pasadena

Although seemingly absorbed into the general Los Angeles sprawl, Pasadena is a separate and distinct city. It's best known for the Tournament of Roses, or more commonly, the Rose Bowl, seen around the world every New Year's Day. But the city has sites worth seeing year-round—from gorgeous Craftsman homes to exceptional museums, particularly the Norton Simon and the Huntington Library, Art Museum, and Botanical Gardens. Note that the Huntington and the Old Mill reside in San Marino, a well-heeled, 4-square-mile residential area just over the Pasadena line.

Sights

The Gamble House

HOUSE | Built by Charles and Henry Greene in 1908, this American Arts and Crafts bungalow illustrates the incredible craftsmanship that went into early L.A. architecture. The term "bungalow" can be misleading, since the Gamble House is a huge three-story home. To wealthy Easterners such as the Gambles (as in Procter & Gamble), this type of vacation home seemed informal compared with their mansions back home. Admirers swoon over the teak staircase and cabinetry, the Greene and Greene–designed furniture, and an Emil Lange glass door. The dark exterior has broad eaves, with sleeping porches on the second floor. An hour-long, docent-led tour of the Gamble's interior will draw your eye to the exquisite details. For those who want to see more of the Greene and Greene homes, there are guided walks around the historic Arroyo Terrace neighborhood. Advance tickets are highly recommended. ■TIP➔ Film buffs might recognize this as Doc Brown's house from *Back to the Future*. ⊠ 4 Westmoreland Pl., Pasadena ☎ 626/793–3334 ⊕ gamblehouse.org ⊠ $15 ⊗ Closed Mon.

★ Huntington Library, Art Museum, and Botanical Gardens

MUSEUM | If you have time for just one stop in the Pasadena area, be sure to see this sprawling estate built for railroad tycoon Henry E. Huntington in the early 1900s. Henry and his wife, Arabella (who was also his aunt by marriage), voraciously collected rare books and manuscripts, botanical specimens, and 18th-century British art. The institution they established became one of the most extraordinary cultural complexes in the world.

The library contains more than 700,000 books and 4 million manuscripts, including one of the world's biggest history of science collections and a Gutenberg Bible.

Don't resist being lured outside into the 130-acre Botanical Gardens, which extend out from the main building. The 10-acre Desert Garden has one of the world's largest groups of mature cacti and other succulents (visit on a cool morning or late afternoon). The Shakespeare Garden, meanwhile, blooms with plants mentioned in Shakespeare's works. The Japanese Garden features an authentic ceremonial teahouse built in Kyoto in the 1960s. A waterfall flows from the teahouse to the ponds below. In the Rose Garden Tea Room, afternoon tea is served (reserve in advance). The Chinese Garden, which is among the largest outside China, sinews around waveless pools.

The Bing Children's Garden lets tiny tots explore the ancient elements of water, fire, air, and earth. A 1¼-hour guided tour of the Botanical Gardens is led by docents at posted times, and a free brochure with a map and property highlights is available in the entrance pavilion. Tickets for the monthly free admission day are snapped up within minutes, so plan carefully. ⊠ 1151 Oxford Rd., San Marino ☎ 626/405–2100 ⊕ www.huntington.org ⊠ From $25; free admission 1st Thurs. of every month with advance ticket ⊗ Closed Tues.

★ Norton Simon Museum

MUSEUM | As seen in the New Year's Day Tournament of Roses Parade, this low-profile brown building is one of the finest midsize museums anywhere, with a collection that spans more than 2,000 years of Western and Asian art. It all began in the 1950s when Norton Simon (Hunt-Wesson Foods, McCalls Corporation, and Canada Dry) started collecting works by Degas, Renoir, Gauguin, and Cézanne. His collection grew to include works by old masters and impressionists, modern works from Europe, and Indian and Southeast Asian art. Today the museum is richest in works by Rembrandt, Picasso, and, most of all, Degas.

Head down to the bottom floor to see temporary exhibits and phenomenal Southeast Asian and Indian sculptures and artifacts, where pieces like a Ban Chiang blackware vessel date back to well before 1000 BC. Don't miss a living artwork outdoors: the garden, conceived by noted Southern California landscape designer Nancy Goslee Power. The tranquil pond was inspired by Monet's gardens at Giverny. ⊠ *411 W. Colorado Blvd., Pasadena* ☎ *626/449–6840* ⊕ *www.nortonsimon.org* ⊠ *$15; free 1st Fri. of month 5–8* ⊘ *Closed Tues.*

The Old Mill (El Molino Viejo)

BUILDING | Built in 1816 as a gristmill for the San Gabriel Mission, the mill is the state's oldest commercial building and one of the last remaining examples in Southern California of Spanish Mission architecture. The thick adobe walls and textured ceiling rafters give the interior a sense of quiet strength. Be sure to step into the back room, now a gallery with rotating quarterly exhibits. Outside, a chipped section of the mill's exterior reveals the layers of brick, ground seashell paste, and ox blood used to hold the structure together. The surrounding gardens are reason enough to visit, with a flower-decked arbor and old sycamores and oaks. In summer the Capitol Ensemble performs in the garden. ⊠ *1120 Old Mill Rd., San Marino* ☎ *626/449–5458* ⊕ *www.old-mill. org* ⊠ *Free* ⊘ *Closed Mon.*

Old Town Pasadena

NEIGHBORHOOD | This 22-block historic district contains a vibrant mix of restored 19th-century brick buildings interspersed with contemporary architecture. Chain stores have muscled in, but there are still some homegrown shops, plenty of tempting cafés and restaurants, and a bustling beer scene. In recent years, a vibrant Asian food scene has popped up in the vicinity as well. In the evening and on weekends, the streets are packed with people. Old Town's main action takes place on Colorado Boulevard between Pasadena Avenue and Arroyo Parkway. ⊠ *Pasadena* ☎ *626/356–9725* ⊕ *www.oldpasadena.org.*

★ Rose Bowl and Flea Market

MARKET | With an enormous rose on its exterior, this 90,000-plus-seat stadium is home to the UCLA Bruins and the annual Rose Bowl Game on New Year's Day, and also regularly sees performances from the biggest recording artists in the world. Set at the bottom of a wide arroyo in Brookside Park, the facility is closed except during games, concerts, and special events like its famed Flea Market, a Southern California institution. The massively popular and eclectic event, which happens the second Sunday of each month (rain or shine), deservedly draws crowds that come to find deals from more than 2,500 vendors on goods including mid-century and antique furniture, vintage clothing, pop culture collectibles, books, and music. Food and drink options are on hand to keep shoppers satiated, parking is free, and general admission is just $9, but VIP/early-bird options are available for a little extra. Crowds tend to peak mid-day. Bring cash to avoid an inevitable line at the ATM, and feel free to try your hand at haggling. ⊠ *1001 Rose Bowl Dr., Pasadena* ☎ *626/577–3100* ⊕ *www.rosebowlstadium.com.*

🍴 Restaurants

Pie 'n Burger

$$ | **DINER** | Since 1963, this small and charming diner has done two things really well—pies and burgers. Most seats are counter-style, with a griddle searing up patties. **Known for:** simple burgers; enormous pie slices; retro-style decor. [$] *Average main: $14* ✉ *913 E. California Blvd., Pasadena* ☎ *626/795–1123* 🌐 *pienburger.com.*

The Raymond 1886

$$$ | **MODERN AMERICAN** | The coolest kid on the Pasadena block, the Raymond 1886 is carved out of an old cottage, and has an expansive patio with long wooden tables and hanging lights. Chefs dish out everything from a burrata-and-pear pairing to pork loin Milanese and tots with eel sauce. **Known for:** solid happy hour; great bar food; expansive patio. [$] *Average main: $30* ✉ *1250 S. Fair Oaks Ave., Pasadena* ☎ *626/441–3136* 🌐 *theraymond.com* 🕒 *Closed Mon.*

🛍 Shopping

Vroman's Bookstore

BOOKS/STATIONERY | Southern California's oldest and largest independent bookseller is justly famous for its great service. A newsstand, café, and stationery store add to the appeal, and it's a favorite with locals for its on-trend, eclectic gift selection. A regular rotation of events including trivia night, kids' story time, author meet-and-greets, crafting sessions, discussions, and more get the community actively involved. ✉ *695 E. Colorado Blvd., Pasadena* ☎ *626/449–5320* 🌐 *www.vromansbookstore.com.*

Malibu and the Beaches

The beaches and coastal areas of Los Angeles are an iconic symbol of the region's casual friendliness and endless optimism, and the local love for them is as much a trope as it is a reality. Angelenos are known for working hard and playing hard, and the coast is where they come to play. Getting some sand on the floor of your car is a rite of passage here. Like its most ardent fans, this stretch of the Pacific is best known for its beauty: cosmetically enhanced in some areas and ruggedly pristine in others. From the hillside mansions of Malibu, where even the air is rarified, to the cultural dynamism of Long Beach, the gently arching coastline tells an L.A. story all its own as it transitions from ultrarich to bohemian to working class. Through it all, the sand remains the center of the action.

Malibu

👁 Sights

★ Getty Villa Malibu

HOUSE | Feeding off the cultures of ancient Rome, Greece, and Etruria, the villa exhibits astounding antiquities, though on a first visit even they take a backseat to their environment. This megamansion sits on some of the most valuable coastal property in the world. Modeled after the Villa dei Papiri in Herculaneum, a Roman estate owned by Julius Caesar's father-in-law that was covered in ash when Mt. Vesuvius erupted, the Getty Villa includes beautifully manicured gardens, reflecting pools, and statuary. The structures blend thoughtfully into the rolling terrain and significantly improve the public spaces, such as the outdoor amphitheater, gift store, café, and entry arcade. Talks, concerts, and educational programs are offered at an indoor theater. ■TIP➔ **An advance timed entry ticket is required for admission. Tickets are free and may be ordered from the museum's website or by phone.** ✉ *17985 Pacific Coast Hwy., Pacific Palisades* ☎ *310/440–7300* ⊕ *www.getty. edu* ✆ *Free, tickets required; parking $20* ⊗ *Closed Tues.*

Malibu Lagoon State Beach

BEACH—SIGHT | Bird-watchers, take note: in this 5-acre marshy area near Malibu Beach Inn you can spot egrets, blue herons, avocets, and gulls. (You need to stay on the boardwalks so as not to disturb their habitats.) The path leads out to a rocky stretch of Surfrider Beach and makes for a pleasant stroll. The sand is soft, clean, and white, and you're also likely to spot a variety of marine life. Look for the signs to help identify these sometimes exotic-looking creatures. The lagoon is particularly enjoyable in the early morning and at sunset—and even more so now, thanks to a restoration effort that improved the lagoon's scent. The parking lot has limited hours, but street-side parking is usually available at off-peak times. An on-site museum reveals local history, and close by are shops and a theater. **Amenities:** parking (fee); lifeguards; toilets; showers. **Best for:** sunset; walking. ✉ *23200 Pacific Coast Hwy., Malibu* ☎ *310/457–8143* ⊕ *www. parks.ca.gov/?page_id=835* ✆ *Parking $12.*

Malibu Pier

MARINA | FAMILY | This rustically chic 780-foot fishing dock is a great place to drink in the sunset, take in some coastal views, or watch local fishermen reel up a catch. Some tours also leave from here. A pier has jutted out on this spot since the early 1900s; storms destroyed the last one in 1995, and it was rebuilt in 2001. Over the years, private developers have worked with the state to refurbish the pier, which now yields a gift shop, water-sport rentals, a jeweler housed in a vintage Airstream trailer, and a wonderful farm-to-table restaurant with stunning views and locations at both ends of the pier. ✉ *Pacific Coast Hwy. at Cross Creek Rd., Malibu* ⊕ *www.malibupier.com.*

Westward Beach–Point Dume

BEACH—SIGHT | This famed promontory is a Malibu pilgrimage for any visitor to the area. Go tide pooling, fishing, snorkeling, or bird-watching (prime time is late winter to early spring). Hike to the top of the sandstone cliffs at Point Dume to whale-watch—their migrations can be seen between December and April—and take in dramatic coastal views. Westward is a favorite surfing beach, but the steep surf isn't for novices. The Sunset restaurant is between Westward and Point Dume (at 6800 Westward Beach Road). Otherwise, bring your own food, since the nearest concession is a long hike away. **Amenities:** parking (fee); lifeguards; toilets; food and drink; showers. **Best for:** surfing; walking. ✉ *71030 Westward Beach Rd., Malibu* ☎ *310/305–9503* ✆ *Parking $14.*

Zuma Beach Park

BEACH—SIGHT | This 2-mile stretch of white sand, usually dotted with tanning teenagers, has it all, from fishing and kitesurfing to swings and volleyball courts. Beachgoers looking for quiet or privacy should head elsewhere. Stay alert in the water: the surf is rough and inconsistent and riptides can surprise even experienced swimmers. **Amenities:** parking; lifeguards; toilets; food and drink; showers. **Best for:** partiers; sunset; swimming; walking. ✉ *30000 Pacific Coast Hwy., Malibu* ☎ *310/305–9522* ⊕ *www.zuma-beach.com* ✆ *Parking $10.*

🍴 Restaurants

Nobu Malibu

$$$$ | JAPANESE | At famous chef-restaurateur Nobu Matsuhisa's coastal outpost, super-chic clientele sails in for morsels of the world's finest fish. It's hard not to be seduced by the oceanfront property, and stellar sushi and ingenious specialties match the upscale setting. **Known for:** exotic fish; A-list celebrity chef; bento box Valrhona chocolate soufflé. [$] *Average main: $35* ✉ *22706 Pacific Coast Hwy., Malibu* ☎ *310/317–9140* 🌐 *www.noburestaurants.com.*

Reel Inn

$$ | SEAFOOD | FAMILY | Escape the glitz and glamour at this decades-old, down-home Malibu institution. Long wooden tables and booths are often filled with fish-loving families chowing down on mahimahi sandwiches and freshly caught swordfish. **Known for:** easy-to-miss spot on the PCH; fresh catches; dog-friendly patio. [$] *Average main: $17* ✉ *18661 Pacific Coast Hwy., Malibu* ☎ *310/456–8221* 🌐 *www.reelinnmalibu.com.*

🛏 Hotels

Malibu Beach Inn

$$$$ | B&B/INN | Set right on exclusive Carbon Beach in a stretch known as Billionaire's Beach, Malibu's hideaway for the super-rich remains the room to nab along the coast, with an ultrachic look thanks to designer Waldo Fernandez and an upscale restaurant and wine bar perched over the Pacific. **Pros:** views of the ocean from your private balcony; world-class chocolate chip cookies at reception; ultimate beachside luxury. **Cons:** millionaire's travel budget required; some in-room noise from PCH; no pool, gym, or hot tub. [$] *Rooms from: $749* ✉ *22878 Pacific Coast Hwy., Malibu* ☎ *310/456–6444* 🌐 *www.malibubeachinn.com* 🔑 *47 rooms* 🍽 *No meals.*

🍸 Nightlife

Duke's Barefoot Bar

BARS/PUBS | FAMILY | With a clear view of the horizon from almost everywhere, a sunset drink at Duke's Barefoot Bar is how many beachgoers like to end their day. The entertainment is in keeping with the bar's theme, with Hawaiian dancers as well as live music on Friday night by Hawaiian artists. The menu features island favorites like *poke* tacos, macadamia-crusted fish, and kalua pork and a Sunday brunch buffet from 10 to 2. Just don't expect beach-bum prices, unless you stop by the happy hour weekday events like Taco Tuesday (bargain-priced fish, kalua pork, or grilled chicken tacos and beers). ✉ *21150 Pacific Coast Hwy., Malibu* ☎ *310/317–0777* 🌐 *www.dukesmalibu.com.*

Moonshadows

BARS/PUBS | This outdoor lounge attracts customers with its modern look and views of the ocean. Think dark woods, cabana-style draperies, and ambient lighting in the Blue Lounge, open late on weekends. DJs are constantly spinning lounge music in the background, and there's never a cover charge. Sunday afternoons perfectly blend the laid-back ambience with good vibes. Try a sunset dinner or the lobster roll and dessert lineup. ✉ *20356 Pacific Coast Hwy., Malibu* ☎ *310/456–3010* 🌐 *www.moonshadowsmalibu.com.*

🛍 Shopping

★ Malibu Country Mart

SHOPPING CENTERS/MALLS | Stop by this outdoor outpost for the ultimate Malibu lifestyle experience, complete with browsing designer clothing (Rubin & Chapelle, Ron Herman, or Madison) and eclectic California housewares and gifts (Malibu Colony Company), picking up body-boosting wellness goodies at SunLife Organics, and finishing the day off with dinner at long-standing eatery

Tra di Noi, reputed to be a favorite of Barbra Streisand. If you can squeeze in a workout, there's a Pure Barre and a 5 Point Yoga to choose from, plus tarot readings at metaphysical outpost Malibu Shaman. Then reward yourself for your good health habits by stopping at K Chocolatier by Diane Krön for some of her famed truffles, derived from a Hungarian family recipe. ⊠ *3835 Cross Creek Rd., Malibu* ☎ *310/456–7300* ⊕ *www.malibucountrymart.com.*

Manhattan Beach, Redondo Beach, and Long Beach

 Sights

★ Aquarium of the Pacific

ZOO | FAMILY | Sea lions, zebra sharks, and penguins—this aquarium focuses on creatures of the Pacific Ocean and is home to more than 12,000 animals. The main exhibits include large tanks of sharks, stingrays, and ethereal sea dragons, which the aquarium has successfully bred in captivity. The museum's first major expansion in years, Pacific Visions, features a 29,000-square-foot multisensory experience in which attendees can immerse themselves in humankind's relationship with the natural world through video projections, soundscapes, tactile exhibits, a touchscreen wall, interactive game tables, rumbling theater seats, and more. For a nonaquatic experience, head to Lorikeet Forest, a walk-in aviary full of the friendliest parrots from Australia. Buy a cup of nectar and smile as you become a human bird perch. If you're a true animal lover, book an up-close-and-personal Animal Encounters Tour (extra fee) to learn about and assist in the care and feeding of sharks, penguins, and other aquarium residents; or find out how the aquarium functions with the extensive Behind the Scenes Tour (extra fee). Certified divers can book a supervised dive in the aquarium's Tropical

Reef Habitat (extra fee) and kids go wild for frequent overnight camp experiences in the aquarium. Twice-daily whale-watching trips on Harbor Breeze Cruises depart from the dock adjacent to the aquarium; summer sightings of blue whales are an unforgettable thrill. ⊠ *100 Aquarium Way, Long Beach* ☎ *562/590–3100* ⊕ *www. aquariumofpacific.org* ⊠ *$30.*

Manhattan Beach

BEACH—SIGHT | A wide, sandy strip with good swimming and rows of volleyball courts, Manhattan Beach is the preferred destination of fit, tanned young professionals. There are also such amenities as a bike path, a playground, a bait shop, fishing equipment for rent, and a sizable fishing pier. It's also the perfect place to unwind during a long layover at LAX. **Amenities:** parking (fee); lifeguards; toilets; food and drink; showers. **Best for:** swimming; walking. ⊠ *Manhattan Beach Blvd. at N. Ocean Dr., Manhattan Beach* ☎ *310/372–2166* ⊕ *beaches.lacounty.gov/ manhattan-beach* ⊠ *Metered parking; long- and short-term lots.*

★ Queen Mary

HISTORIC SITE | FAMILY | Though berthed, the *Queen Mary* is an impressive example of 20th-century cruise ship opulence and sadly the last of its kind. The beautifully preserved art deco–style ocean liner was launched in 1936 and made 1,001 transatlantic crossings before finally berthing in Long Beach in 1967.

Take one of several daily themed tours such as the informative Glory Days historical walk, a traipse into the boiler rooms on the Steam and Steel Tour, or the downright spooky Haunted Encounters tour. (Spirits have reportedly been spotted in the pool and engine room.) You can add ongoing theatrical performances by illusionist Aiden Sinclair, a Winston Churchill exhibit, a 4-D documentary experience, a wine tasting room, and a daily British-style high tea. Holidays and special events are celebrated onboard as well, from a haunted Halloween experience to an annual Scottish festival. Stay for dinner at one of the ship's restaurants, listen to live jazz or order a cocktail in the Observation Bar (the sumptuous original first-class lounge), or even spend the night in one of the 347 wood-paneled cabins. The ship's neighbor, a geodesic dome originally built to house Howard Hughes's *Spruce Goose* aircraft, now serves as a terminal for Carnival Cruise Lines, making the *Queen Mary* the perfect pit stop before or after a cruise. Anchored next to the *Queen* is the *Scorpion,* a Russian submarine you can tour for a look at Cold War history. ⊠ *1126 Queens Hwy., Long Beach* ☎ *877/342–0738* ⊕ *www.queenmary. com* ⊘ *Tours from $16.*

Redondo Beach

BEACH—SIGHT | The pier here marks the starting point of this wide, busy beach along a heavily developed shoreline community. Restaurants and shops flourish along the pier, excursion boats and privately owned crafts depart from launching ramps, and a reef formed by a sunken ship creates prime fishing and snorkeling conditions. If you're adventurous, you might try to kayak out to the buoys and hobnob with pelicans and sea lions. A series of free rock and jazz concerts takes place at the pier every summer. **Amenities:** parking; lifeguards; food and drink; toilets; showers; water sports. **Best for:** snorkeling; sunset; swimming; walking. ⊠ *Torrance Blvd. at Catalina Ave., Redondo Beach* ☎ *310/372–2166* ⊕ *www.redondopier.com.*

Updated by
Cheryl Crabtree

👁 **Sights**
★★★★★

🍴 **Restaurants**
★★★★☆

🛏 **Hotels**
★★★★★

🛍 **Shopping**
★★☆☆☆

🍸 **Nightlife**
★★☆☆☆

WELCOME TO PALM SPRINGS

TOP REASONS TO GO

★ **Year-round sunshine:** The Palm Springs area has more than 300 days of sun each year, and the weather is usually ideal for playing one of the area's more than 100 golf courses.

★ **Spa under the stars:** Many resorts and small hotels now offer after-dark spa services, including outdoor soaks and treatments you can savor while sipping wine under the clear, starry sky.

★ **Personal pampering:** The resorts here have it all, beautifully appointed rooms packed with amenities, professional staffs, sublime spas, and delicious dining options.

★ **Divine desert scenery:** You'll probably spend a lot of time taking in the gorgeous 360-degree natural panorama, a flat desert floor surrounded by 10,000-foot mountains rising into a brilliant blue sky.

★ **The Hollywood connection:** The Palm Springs area has more celebrity ties than any other resort community. So keep your eyes open for your favorite star.

1 Palm Springs. A mid-century modern vibe and many restaurants, bars, and galleries line the avenues of Palm Springs. Hiking trails and an aerial tramway lead from the desert floor up to the San Jacinto mountain peaks.

2 Rancho Mirage. An elegant, upscale residential community, Rancho Mirage has resorts, golf courses and gated estates. A main draw here is Annenberg Retreat at Sunnylands, a grand garden estate open to the public for tours.

3 Palm Desert. The mile-long El Paseo shopping and restaurant district is the heart of Palm Desert, a peaceful community also known for its challenging golf courses and the Living Desert Zoo and Gardens.

4 Indian Wells. Exclusive Indian Wells hosts national tennis and pickleball championships at posh resorts, where spas and upscale restaurants pamper players and spectators alike.

5 La Quinta. Coachella Valley's first golf course opened at La Quinta in 1920 and morphed into a quaint town alongside a sprawling resort and club with multiple courses.

6 Indio. The date capital of the nation, Indio lures visitors with date shakes and date palm fields.

7 Borrego Springs. Superb wildflower viewing and numerous nature trails are among the draws at Borrego Springs within Anza-Borrego Desert State Park.

8 Salton Sea. Nature lovers retreat to the shores of the Salton Sea, a haven for birdwatching and lakefront activities.

9 Desert Hot Springs. To the north of Palm Springs, a concentrated network of hot springs flows through this community, where visitors come to soak in soothing mineral waters and rejuvenate mind and body.

10 Yucca Valley. A laid-back roadside city, Yucca Valley is a convenient stop on the way north to Joshua Tree National Park. In nearby Pioneertown, Pappy and Harriet's Pioneertown Palace serves classic Western food and big-name musical entertainment.

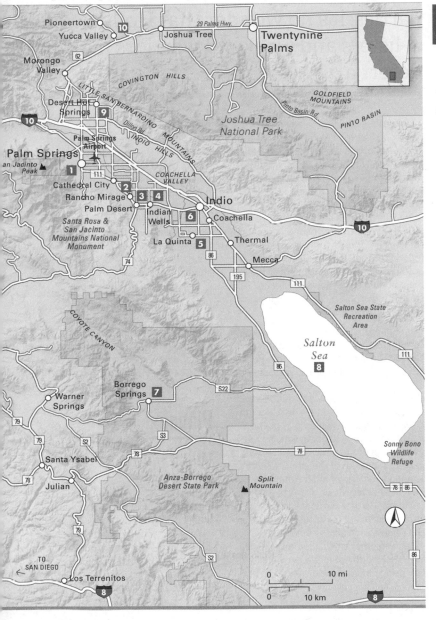

Pioneertown
Yucca Valley
10
29 Palms Hwy.
Joshua Tree
Twentynine
Palms
62
COVINGTON HILLS
GOLDFIELD
MOUNTAINS
Morongo
Valley
Pinto Basin Rd.
PINTO BASIN
Desert Hot
Springs
9
Joshua Tree
National Park
LITTLE SAN BERNARDINO MOUNTAINS
Dillon Rd.
INDIO HILLS
10
Palm Springs
Airport
Palm Springs
1
an Jacinto
Peak
111
COACHELLA
VALLEY
Cathedral City
2
Rancho Mirage
3
4
Indio
10
Palm Desert
6
Coachella
Indian
Wells
Santa Rosa &
San Jacinto
Mountains National
Monument
La Quinta
5
Thermal
74
86
Mecca
195
111
Salton Sea State
Recreation
Area
COYOTE CANYON
Salton
Sea
8
86
Borrego
Springs
7
S22
Warner
Springs
111
Sonny Bono
Wildlife
Refuge
79
S2
S3
78
78
Santa Ysabel
78
Julian
Anza-Borrego
Desert State Park
Split
Mountain
78 86
79
86
TO
SAN DIEGO
S2
Los Terrenitos
8
0   10 mi
0   10 km
8

With the Palm Springs area's year-round sunshine, luxurious spas, chef-driven restaurants, and see-and-be-seen pool parties, it's no wonder that Hollywood A-listers and weekend warriors make the desert a getaway.

The Palm Springs area has long been a playground for the celebrity elite. In the 1920s Al Capone opened the Two Bunch Palms Hotel in Desert Hot Springs (with multiple tunnels to help him avoid the police); Marilyn Monroe was discovered poolside in the late 1940s at a downtown Palm Springs tennis club; Elvis and Priscilla Presley honeymooned here—the list goes on. There's a similar desert resort feel (replete with luxury lodgings, golf courses, and shopping enclaves) in the communities of Rancho Mirage, Palm Desert, Indian Wells, La Quinta, Indio, and Desert Hot Springs.

Palm Springs is laden with urban-chic contemporary artwork (check out Palm Canyon Drive in downtown or the Backstreet Arts District in the southeast end of town). Winter events celebrate the city's modernist design aesthetic as well as its connections with the film industry. Over the years, the desert arts scene has blossomed as spectacularly as the wildflowers of Anza-Borrego Desert State Park, to the south of the city. Each April, attention centers on Indio, where the Coachella Valley Music and Arts Festival, California's largest outdoor concert, attracts droves of rock music lovers from Los Angeles and across the globe. Yucca Valley and other artistic communities all have noteworthy galleries, art installations, and natural scenic views.

MAJOR REGIONS

Palm Springs and the Southern Desert Resorts. The city of Palm Springs is within the Colorado Desert, on the western edge of Coachella Valley and at the northwestern end of Highway 111. From there, the highway travels southeast, providing access to a string of desert resorts, including Rancho Mirage, Palm Desert, Indian Wells, La Quinta, and Indio. Farther south are the Salton Sea and Borrego Springs.

Desert Hot Springs to Twentynine Palms Highway. Northwest of Palm Springs, off I–10 and Scenic California Highway 62, is the resort of Desert Hot Springs, after which Highway 62 becomes Twentynine Palms Highway and travels northeast to Yucca Valley en route to Joshua Tree National Park and its gateway towns.

Planning

When to Go

January through April is the height of the visitor season: the desert weather is best during this time, and it's when major events such as the Palm Springs International Film Festival (mid-January), Modernism Week (mid-February), and Coachella (two weekends in April) are held. Big-time LGBTQ+ fests also happen during this time, including The Dinah (⊕ *thedinah.*

com), a rollicking lesbian party in late March, and White Party Palm Springs (⊕ *jeffreysanker.com*), a spring break extravaganza that draws tens of thousands of gay men from around the world.

The fall months are nearly as lovely, but less crowded and less expensive (although autumn draws many conventions). In summer, a popular time with European visitors, daytime temperatures may rise above 110°F, though evenings cool to the mid-70s. Some attractions and restaurants close or reduce their hours in this season, though.

FESTIVALS AND EVENTS

ANA Inspiration Championship. The best female golfers in the world compete in this late-March or early-April event held in Rancho Mirage. ⊕ *www.anainspiration.com*

BNP Paribas Open. Drawing 200 of the world's top players, this tennis tournament takes place at Indian Wells Tennis Garden for two weeks in March. ⊕ *www.bnpparibasopen.com*

La Quinta Arts Festival. More than 200 painters, sculptors, ceramacists, and other artists participate each March in a four-day juried show that's considered one of the best in the West. ⊕ *www.lqaf.com*

National Date Festival and Riverside County Fair. Indio celebrates its raison d'être in mid-February with exhibits of local dates, camel and ostrich races, a nightly musical pageant, a rodeo, a demolition derby, and monster truck shows. ⊕ *www.datefest.org*

Getting Here and Around

AIR

Palm Springs International Airport serves California's desert communities. Air Canada, Alaska, Allegiant, American, Delta, Flair, Frontier, JetBlue, Southwest, Sun Country, United, and WestJet all fly to Palm Springs, some only seasonally. Yellow Cab of the Desert and Desert City Cab serve the airport, which is about 3 miles from downtown. The fare is $4 to enter the cab and about $3.12 per mile.

AIRPORT INFORMATION Palm Springs International Airport. ⊠ *3200 E. Tahquitz Canyon Way, Palm Springs* ☎ *760/318–3800 general information* ⊕ *www.palmspringsairport.com.*

AIRPORT TRANSFERS Desert City Cab. ⊠ *3465 E. La Campana Way, Palm Springs* ☎ *760/328–3000* ⊕ *desertcitycab.com.* **Yellow Cab of the Desert.** ⊠ *75150 St. Charles Pl., Palm Desert* ☎ *760/340–8294* ⊕ *www.yellowcabofthedesert.com.*

BUS

Greyhound provides service to Palm Springs from many cities. SunBus, operated by the SunLine Transit Agency, serves the entire Coachella Valley, from Desert Hot Springs to Mecca.

BUS CONTACTS SunLine Transit Agency. ☎ *760/343–3451* ⊕ *www.sunline.org.*

CAR

The desert resort communities occupy a 20-mile stretch between I–10 to the east and Palm Canyon Drive (Highway 111) to the west. The region is about a two-hour drive (up to a four-hour drive on spring and winter weekends when traffic is heavy) east of Los Angeles and a three-hour drive northeast of San Diego. From Los Angeles take the San Bernardino Freeway (I–10) east to Highway 111. From San Diego, I–15 north connects with the Pomona Freeway (Highway 60), leading to the San Bernardino Freeway east.

To reach Borrego Springs from Los Angeles, take I–10 east past the desert resorts area to Highway 86 south to the Borrego Salton Seaway (Highway S22) west. You can reach the Borrego area from San Diego via I–8 to Highway 79 through Cuyamaca State Park and to Highway 78 in Julian, which you follow east to Yaqui Pass Road (S3) into Borrego Springs.

TAXI

Yellow Cab of the Desert and Desert City Cab serve the entire Coachella Valley. The fare is $4 to enter a cab and about $3.12 per mile.

TRAIN

The Amtrak *Sunset Limited*, which runs between Florida and Los Angeles, and *Texas Eagle* (Chicago to Los Angeles) stop in Palm Springs. Amtrak buses also meet Pacific Surfliner trains in Fullerton to ferry passengers to the Palm Springs region.

Restaurants

The meat-and-potatoes crowd still has plenty of options, but an influx of talented chefs has also made it possible to find fresh, superbly prepared seafood, as well as contemporary Californian, Asian, Indian, and vegetarian cuisine. Mexican food abounds. Most restaurants have early-evening happy hours, with discounted drinks and small-plate menus. Although some restaurants close or offer limited service in July and August, those that remain open often discount deeply.

Hotels

In general, Palm Springs has the widest choice of lodgings, from tiny bed-and-breakfasts and chain motels to business and resort hotels. Massive resort properties predominate in down-valley communities, such as Palm Desert and Rancho Mirage. You can stay in the desert for as little as $100, or splurge for luxury digs at more than $1,000 a night. Rates vary widely by season and expected occupancy—a $200 room midweek can jump in price to $450 on Saturday.

Hotel and resort prices are frequently 50% cheaper in summer and fall than in winter and early spring. From January through May prices soar, and lodgings fill up far in advance. Book well ahead for stays during events such as Modernism Week or the Coachella music festival.

Most resort hotels charge a daily fee of up to $40 that is not included in the room rate; be sure to ask about extra fees when you book. Many hotels are pet-friendly and offer special services, though these also come with additional fees. Small boutique hotels and B&Bs have plenty of character and are popular with hipsters and artsy types; discounts are sometimes given for extended stays. Casino hotels often offer good deals on lodging. Take care, though, when considering budget lodgings; other than reliable chains, they may not be up to par.

Restaurant and hotel reviews have been shortened. For full information, visit Fodors.com. Restaurant prices are the average cost of a main course at dinner, or if dinner is not served, at lunch. Hotel prices are the lowest cost of a standard double room in high season.

What It Costs			
$	$$	$$$	$$$$
RESTAURANTS			
under $17	$17–$26	$27–$36	over $36
HOTELS			
under $150	$150–$250	$251–$350	over $350

Tours

Best of the Best Tours

GUIDED TOURS | One of the valley's largest outfits leads tours into Andreas Canyon, along the celebrity circuit, or to view windmills up close. ☎ 760/320–1365 ⊕ *www.thebestofthebesttours.com* ✉ *From $45.*

Big Wheel Bike Tours

BICYCLING | This outfit delivers rental mountain, three-speed, and tandem bikes to area hotels. The company also conducts full- and half-day escorted on- and off-road bike tours, and also offers hiking and jeep tours to Joshua Tree National Park and the San Andreas Fault. Guides are first-rate. ✉ *Palm Springs* ☎ *760/779–1837 Palm Desert, 760/548–0500 Palm Springs* ⊕ *www.bwbtours.com* ✆ *$119 per person.*

Desert Adventures

SPECIAL-INTEREST | This outfit's three- to six-hour jeep, SUV, or van tours explore Joshua Tree National Park, Indian Canyon, Mecca Hills Painted Canyons, and the San Andreas Fault. The groups are small and the guides are knowledgeable. Departures are from Palm Desert and/or Palm Springs; hotel pickups are available. ☎ *760/477–4290* ⊕ *www.red-jeep.com* ✆ *From $135.*

Palm Springs

A tourist destination since the late 19th century, Palm Springs evolved into an ideal hideaway for early Hollywood celebrities who slipped into town to play tennis, lounge poolside, attend a party or two, and, unless things got out of hand, steer clear of gossip columnists. But the area blossomed in the 1930s, after actors Charlie Farrell and Ralph Bellamy bought 200 acres of land for $30 an acre and opened the Palm Springs Racquet Club, which soon listed Ginger Rogers, Humphrey Bogart, and Clark Gable among its members.

Today, Palm Springs is embracing its glory days. Owners of resorts, B&Bs, and galleries have renovated mid-century modern buildings, luring a new crop of celebs and high-powered executives. LGBTQ+ travelers, twentysomethings, and families also sojourn here. Pleasantly touristy Palm Canyon Drive is packed with alfresco restaurants, along with indoor cafés and semi-chic shops. Farther west is the Uptown Design District, the area's shopping and dining destination. Continuing east on Palm Canyon Drive, just outside downtown lie resorts and boutique hotels that host lively pool parties and house exclusive dining establishments and trendy bars.

GETTING HERE AND AROUND

Palm Springs is 90 miles southeast of Los Angeles on I–10. Most visitors arrive in the area by car from Los Angeles or San Diego area via this freeway, which intersects with Highway 111 north of Palm Springs. Tahquitz Canyon Way marks the division between north and south on major streets (e.g., North and South Palm Canyon Drive).

ESSENTIALS

VISITOR INFORMATION Greater Palm Springs Convention & Visitors Bureau. ✉ *Visitor Center, 70–100 Hwy. 111, at Via Florencia, Rancho Mirage* ☎ *760/770–9000, 800/967–3767* ⊕ *www.visitgreaterpalmsprings.com.* **Palm Springs Visitors Center.** ✉ *2901 N. Palm Canyon Dr.* ☎ *760/778–8418, 800/347–7746* ⊕ *www.visitpalmsprings.com.*

 ## Sights

Backstreet Art District

MUSEUM | Galleries and live–work studios just off East Canyon Drive showcase the works of a number of highly acclaimed artists. Painter and ceramicist Linda Maxson, innovative digital photographer Taylor Mickle, and new and emerging artists at Galleria Marconi are among the stars here. ■**TIP**➔ **On the first Wednesday evening of the month, the galleries are open from 5 to 8.** ✉ *2600 S. Cherokee Way* ⊕ *www.backstreetartdistrict.com* ✆ *Free* ⊗ *Most galleries closed Mon. and Tues.*

★ Indian Canyons

CANYON | **FAMILY** | The Indian Canyons are the ancestral home of the Agua Caliente, part of the Cahuilla people. You can see remnants of their ancient life, including rock art, house pits and foundations, irrigation ditches, bedrock mortars, pictographs, and stone houses and

Palm Springs

Did You Know?

The Palm Springs Art Museum exemplifies the city's mid-century modern aesthetic, and its collections highlight architecture, design, photography, and sculpture—indoors and out.

shelters atop cliff walls. Short easy walks through the canyons reveal palm oases, waterfalls, and, in spring, wildflowers. Tree-shaded picnic areas are abundant. The attraction includes three canyons open for touring: Palm Canyon, noted for its stand of Washingtonia palms; Murray Canyon, home of Peninsula bighorn sheep; and Andreas Canyon, where a stand of fan palms contrasts with sharp rock formations. Ranger-led hikes to Palm and Andreas canyons are offered Friday–Sunday for an additional charge (no dogs allowed). The trading post at the entrance to Palm Canyon has hiking maps and refreshments, as well as Native American art, jewelry, and weaving. ⊠ *38520 S. Palm Canyon Dr., south of Acanto Dr.* ☎ *760/323–6018* ⊕ *www.indian-canyons. com* ⊠ *$9, ranger hikes $3* ☉ *Closed Mon.–Thurs. July–Sept.*

Moorten Botanical Garden
GARDEN | In 1938, Chester "Cactus Slim" Moorten and his wife Patricia opened this showpiece for desert plants—now numbering in the thousands—that include an ocotillo, a massive elephant tree, a boojum tree, and vine cacti. Their son Clark now operates the garden. ■ TIP➜ **Take a stroll through the Cactarium to spot rare finds such as the welwitschia, which originated in the Namib Desert in southwestern Africa.** ⊠ *1701 S. Palm Canyon Dr.* ☎ *760/327–6555* ⊕ *www.moortengarden. com* ⊠ *$5* ☉ *Closed Wed.*

★ Palm Springs Aerial Tramway
VIEWPOINT | FAMILY | A trip on the tramway provides a 360-degree view of the desert through the picture windows of rotating cars. The 2½-mile ascent through Chino Canyon, the steepest vertical cable ride in the United States, brings you to an elevation of 8,516 feet in less than 20 minutes. On clear days, which are common, the view stretches 75 miles—from the peak of Mt. San Gorgonio in the north to the Salton Sea in the southeast. Stepping out into the snow at the summit is a winter treat. At the top, a bit

below the summit of Mt. San Jacinto, are several diversions. Mountain Station has an observation deck, two restaurants, a cocktail lounge, apparel and gift shops, picnic facilities, a small wildlife exhibit, and a theater that screens movies on the history of the tramway and the adjacent Mount San Jacinto State Park and Wilderness. Take advantage of free guided and self-guided nature walks through the state park, or if there's snow on the ground, rent skis, snowshoes, or snow tubes. The tramway generally closes for maintenance in mid-September. ■ TIP➜ **Ride-and-dine packages are available in late afternoon. The tram is a popular attraction; to avoid a two-hour or longer wait, arrive before the first car leaves in the morning.** ⊠ *1 Tramway Rd., off N. Palm Canyon Dr. (Hwy. 111)* ☎ *888/515–8726* ⊕ *www.pstramway.com* ⊠ *From $27* ☉ *Closed 2 wks in Sept. for maintenance.*

★ Palm Springs Air Museum
MUSEUM | FAMILY | This museum's impressive collection of World War II, Vietnam, and Korea aircraft includes a B-17 Flying Fortress bomber, a Bell P-63 King Cobra, and a Grumman TBF Avenger. Among the cool exhibits are model warships, a Pearl Harbor diorama, and a Mohawk into which kids can crawl. Photos, artifacts, memorabilia, and uniforms are also on display; educational programs take place on Saturday; and flight demonstrations are scheduled regularly. Rides in vintage warbirds are also available, including a T-28 Trojan, PT-17 Stearman, T-33 Shooting Star Jet, and P-51D Mustang. ⊠ *745 N. Gene Autry Trail* ☎ *760/778–6262* ⊕ *palmspringsairmuseum.org* ⊠ *$19.*

Palm Springs Art Museum
MUSEUM | This world-class art museum focuses on photography, modern architecture, and the traditional arts of the Americas. Outside, you're greeted by the 26-foot, 34,000-pound *Forever Marilyn* statue, designed by Seward Johnson, which depicts the actress in

the iconic, billowing-skirt pose from her movie *The Seven Year Itch*. Inside the museum, bright, open galleries contain shimmering, permanent-collection works in glass by Dale Chihuly, Ginny Ruffner, and William Morris; handcrafted furniture by the late actor George Montgomery; mid-century modern architectural photos by Julius Shulman; enormous Native American baskets; and pieces by artists like Allen Houser, Arlo Namingha, and Fritz Scholder. Significant 20th-century sculptors whose works are displayed here include Henry Moore, Marino Marina, Deborah Butterfield, and Mark Di Suvero. The Annenberg Theater presents plays, concerts, lectures, operas, and other cultural events. The museum also has a separate Architecture and Design Center at 300 South Palm Canyon Drive. ✉ *101 Museum Dr., off W. Tahquitz Canyon Dr.* ☎ *760/322–4800* 🌐 *www.psmuseum.org* 🎟 *$14, free Thurs. 5–7 and 2nd Sun. each month* 🕑 *Closed Mon.–Wed.*

Palm Springs Walk of Stars

NEIGHBORHOOD | Along the walk, more than 300 bronze stars are embedded in the sidewalk (à la Hollywood Walk of Fame) to honor celebrities with a Palm Springs connection. Frank, Elvis, Marilyn, Dinah, Lucy, Ginger, Liz, and Liberace have all received their due. Those still around to walk the Walk and see their stars include Nancy Sinatra and Kathy Griffin. ✉ *Palm Canyon Dr., around Tahquitz Canyon Way, and Tahquitz Canyon Way, between Palm Canyon and Indian Canyon Drs.* ☎ *760/325–1577* 🌐 *www.palmsprings.com/walk-of-stars.*

Tahquitz Canyon

CANYON | On ranger-led tours of this secluded canyon on the Agua Caliente Reservation you can view a spectacular 60-foot waterfall, rock art, ancient irrigation systems, and native wildlife and plants. Tours are conducted several times daily; participants must be able to navigate 100 steep rock steps. (You can also take a self-guided tour of the 1.8-mile trail.) At the visitor center at the canyon entrance, watch a short video, look at artifacts, and pick up a map. ✉ *500 W. Mesquite Ave., west of S. Palm Canyon Dr.* ☎ *760/416–7044* 🌐 *www.tahquitzcanyon.com* 🎟 *$13* 🕑 *Closed Mon.–Thurs. July–Sept.*

🍴 Restaurants

★ Cheeky's

$ | **AMERICAN** | The artisanal bacon bar and hangover-halting mimosas attract legions to this breakfast and lunch joint, but brioche French toast and other favorites also contribute to the epic wait on weekends (no reservations accepted). Huevos rancheros, a gem salad with green goddess dressing, and other farmcentric dishes entice the foodie crowd. **Known for:** homemade pastries and sausages; local organic ingredients; grass-fed burger topped with house bacon. [$] *Average main: $13* ✉ *622 N. Palm Canyon Dr., at E. Granvia Valmonte* ☎ *760/327–7595* 🌐 *www.cheekysps.com* 🕑 *Closed Tues. No dinner.*

Copley's on Palm Canyon

$$$ | **MODERN AMERICAN** | Chef Manion Copley prepares innovative cuisine in a setting that's straight out of Hollywood—a hacienda once owned by Cary Grant. Dine in the clubby house or under the stars in the garden. **Known for:** romantic patio dining; fresh seafood and meats with innovative flavors; sweet and savory herb ice creams. [$] *Average main: $34* ✉ *621 N. Palm Canyon Dr., at E. Granvia Valmonte* ☎ *760/327–9555* 🌐 *www.copleyspalmsprings.com* 🕑 *Closed July and Aug. No lunch.*

★ EIGHT4NINE

$$$ | **AMERICAN** | The dazzling interior design and eclectic Pacific Coast dishes made from scratch lure locals and visitors alike to this swank yet casual restaurant and lounge in the Uptown Design District. Sink into white patent leather chairs or comfy sofas in the lounge where you can gaze at historic celebrity photos, or choose a table in a grand corridor with a collection of private rooms, or in the outdoor patio with mountain views. **Known for:** nearly everything made from scratch; four-course chef's menu; all-day happy hour in lounge. $ *Average main: $28* ⊠ *849 N. Palm Canyon Dr.* ☎ *760/325–8490* ⊕ *eight4nine.com.*

El Mirasol at Los Arboles

$$ | **MODERN MEXICAN** | Chef Felipe Castañeda owns two Mexican restaurants in Palm Springs—this one, part of Los Arboles Hotel, is outside on a charming patio set amid flower gardens and shaded by red umbrellas. Castañeda prepares classic combinations of tacos, tamales, and enchiladas, along with specialties such as double-cooked pork and *pollo en pipián* (chicken with a pre-Columbian sauce made of ground roasted pumpkin seeds and dry chilies). **Known for:** classic Mexican dishes; great vegetarian options; garden setting. $ *Average main: $22* ⊠ *266 Via Altamira, off N. Indian Canyon Dr.* ☎ *760/459–3136* ⊕ *www.elmirasolrestaurants.com.*

★ Farm Palm Springs

$ | **FRENCH** | Farm-fresh, locally sourced ingredients and authentic, made-from-scratch, Provençal-style dishes elicit rave reviews of this cozy eatery in downtown's historic La Plaza. Feast on sweet and savory crepes, omelets, or brioche French toast for breakfast; a croque-monsieur or duck confit salad for lunch; and a five-course, seasonal, prix-fixe dinner in the evening. **Known for:** outdoor seating in a flower-filled courtyard; house-made jams, pressed coffee, loose-leaf teas; creative cocktails. $ *Average main: $16* ⊠ *6 La Plaza* ☎ *760/322–2724* ⊕ *www.farmpalmsprings.com* ☉ *No dinner Wed. and Thurs.* ☞ *No reservations except for dinner.*

★ 4 Saints

$$$$ | **CONTEMPORARY** | Perched on the seventh-floor rooftop of the Kimpton Rowan Palm Springs, where stunning views unfold from nearly every table, 4 Saints serves inventive farm-to-table dishes in a slick, hipster dining room and outdoor patio. The eclectic, globally inspired menu focuses on small plates and main dishes made with locally sourced ingredients (e.g., seafood, duck, and short ribs) intended for sharing. **Known for:** creative and classic cocktails; lively social vibe; stellar seafood. $ *Average main: $43* ⊠ *100 W. Tahquitz Cyn. Way* ☎ *760/392–2020* ⊕ *www.4saintspalmsprings.com.*

Le Vallauris

$$$ | **FRENCH** | A longtime favorite that occupies the historic Roberson House, Le Vallauris is popular with ladies who lunch, all of whom get a hug from the maître d'. The Belgian-French-inspired menu changes daily, and each day it's handwritten on a white board. **Known for:** prix-fixe menus for lunch and dinner; lovely tree-shaded garden; romantic setting. $ *Average main: $36* ⊠ *385 W. Tahquitz Canyon Way, west of Palm Canyon Dr.* ☎ *760/325–5059* ⊕ *www.levallauris. com* ☉ *Closed July and Aug.*

LULU California Bistro

$$ | **MODERN AMERICAN** | LULU oozes hipness from morning to night, both within its spacious, mid-century modern dining room and outside on its well-situated terrace with prime Palm Canyon people-watching opportunities. The lengthy menu (the longest in Palm Springs) includes just about anything to please any type of palette, from an avocado-tuna tower to sandwiches, soups, and burgers to osso buco for two—there's even cotton candy. **Known for:** special all-day, vegetarian/vegan or treats-for-two menus; three-course, prix-fixe weekend brunch ($20); hip hangout at night. $ *Average main: $23* ⊠ *200 S. Palm Canyon Dr.*

☎ *760/327–5858* 🌐 *www.lulupalmsprings.com* ⏲ *No breakfast weekdays.*

Spencer's Restaurant

$$$ | **MODERN AMERICAN** | This swank dining space occupies a historic mid-century modern structure at the Palm Springs Tennis Club Resort. Crab cakes, kung pao calamari, and crispy flash-fried oysters are favorite starters. **Known for:** French–Pacific Rim influences; romantic patio; elegant dining room. [$] *Average main: $35* ✉ *701 W. Baristo Rd.* ☎ *760/327–3446* 🌐 *www.spencersrestaurant.com.*

★ Tac/Quila

$$ | **MODERN MEXICAN** | From the lush, flower-laden, "living" walls and vibrant, mid-century modern, Mexico City furnishings to the extensive seafood-focused menu, Tac/Quila celebrates the culture and flavors of Mexico. Ingredients from the greater Palm Springs region help to give the ceviches, fajitas, street tacos, and tamales—made using traditional recipes from Jalisco and beyond—a fresh, California take. **Known for:** craft cocktails, more than 50 specialty tequilas and mezcals, beer and margarita flights; ceviche, taco, and other sampler platters; nightly live music. [$] *Average main: $22* ✉ *415 N. Palm Canyon Dr.* ☎ *760/417–4471* 🌐 *www.tacquila.com.*

Trio

$$ | **MODERN AMERICAN** | The owners of this high-energy Uptown Design District restaurant claim that it's "where Palm Springs eats," and it certainly seems so on nights when the lines to get in run deep. The menu includes home-style staples such as Yankee pot roast, crawfish pie, and other dishes, along with veggie burgers and other vegetarian and gluten-free items. **Known for:** local artwork; inventive desserts; ample vegetarian and gluten-free options. [$] *Average main: $22* ✉ *707 N. Palm Canyon Dr.* ☎ *760/864–8746* 🌐 *www.triopalmsprings.com.*

The Tropicale

$$$ | **INTERNATIONAL** | Tucked onto a side-street corner, the Tropicale is a mid-century-style watering hole with a contemporary vibe. The bar and main dining room hold cozy leather booths; flowers and water features brighten the outdoor area. **Known for:** globe-trotting menu; happy hour (all night on Wednesday); weekly specials. [$] *Average main: $30* ✉ *330 E. Amado Rd., at N. Calle Encilia* ☎ *760/866–1952* 🌐 *www.thetropicale.com* ⏲ *No lunch.*

★ Tyler's Burgers

$ | **AMERICAN** | **FAMILY** | Families, singles, and couples head to Tyler's for simple lunch fare that appeals to carnivores and vegetarians alike. Expect mid-20th-century America's greatest hits: heaping burgers, stacks of fries, root-beer floats, milk shakes; on weekends, be prepared to wait with the masses. **Known for:** house-made cole slaw and potato salad; excellent burgers and fries; delicious shakes. [$] *Average main: $12* ✉ *149 S. Indian Canyon Dr., at La Plaza* ☎ *760/325–2990* 🌐 *www.tylersburgers.com* ⏲ *Closed Sun. late May–mid-Feb. Closed mid-July–early Sept.*

Workshop Kitchen + Bar

$$$ | **AMERICAN** | Chef Michael Beckman's Uptown Design District hot spot pairs high-quality California cuisine with creative cocktails in a sleek, almost utilitarian setting. The outdoor patio lures the oversize sunglasses Sunday brunch crowd, who slurp cava mimosas and artisanal cocktails; inside, the sleek concrete booths are topped with black leather cushions. **Known for:** most ingredients sourced from within a 100-mile radius; artisanal cocktails; communal seating options. [$] *Average main: $32* ✉ *800 N. Palm Canyon Dr., at E. Tamarisk Rd.* ☎ *760/459–3451* 🌐 *www.workshoppalmsprings.com* ⏲ *No lunch.*

Hotels

Ace Hotel and Swim Club
$$ | **RESORT** | With the hotel's vintage feel and hippie-chic decor, it would be no surprise to find guests gathered around cozy communal fire pits enjoying feel-good music. **Pros:** Amigo Room has late-night dining; poolside stargazing deck; weekend DJ scene at the pool. **Cons:** party atmosphere not for everyone; limited amenities; casual staff and service. [$] *Rooms from: $189* ✉ *701 E. Palm Canyon Dr.* ☎ *760/325–9900* 🌐 *www.acehotel.com/palmsprings* 🛏 *188 rooms* 🍴 *No meals.*

Alcazar Palm Springs
$$ | **HOTEL** | Tucked at the border of the Uptown Design District and an area known as the Movie Colony, the hip, modern, and affordable Alcazar features ample, blazing-white guest rooms that wrap around a sparkling pool; some rooms have Jacuzzis, and many have private patios or fireplaces. **Pros:** walking distance of downtown; parking on-site; bikes available. **Cons:** limited service; wall air-conditioners; resort fee. [$] *Rooms from: $180* ✉ *622 N. Indian Canyon Dr.* ☎ *760/318–9850* 🌐 *www.alcazarpalmsprings.com* 🛏 *34 rooms* 🍴 *No meals.*

★ ARRIVE
$$$ | **HOTEL** | By day, sip cocktails at the indoor–outdoor bar (which doubles as the reception desk), lounge in the pool on an inflatable seahorse, or dance to a live DJ; at night, relax in the outdoor hot tub, socialize around communal firepits (half of the rooms also have private patios and fireplaces), or cozy up in your king-size bed amid tasteful modern furnishings. **Pros:** private cabanas with misting systems; great restaurant, artisanal ice-cream shop, and local coffee shop on-site; easy access to Uptown Design District shops, restaurants, galleries. **Cons:** only king rooms available; shower offers little privacy; party scene may not suit everyone. [$] *Rooms from: $329* ✉ *1551 N. Palm Canyon Dr.* ☎ *760/507–1650* 🌐 *www.arrivehotels.com* 🛏 *32 rooms* 🍴 *No meals.*

Avalon Hotel Palm Springs
$$$$ | **RESORT** | With three pools and a spa spread over 4 acres of gardens, the upscale Avalon Hotel Palm Springs calls back to 1960s swanky, with private bungalows, lush gardens, and an emphasis on style. **Pros:** poolside cabanas; complimentary fitness classes; luxurious on-site Estrella Spa and stylish restaurant Chi Chi. **Cons:** popular wedding site; some rooms and facilities need updating; noise travels through thin walls. [$] *Rooms from: $400* ✉ *415 S. Belardo Rd.* ☎ *760/318–3012* 🌐 *www.avalon-hotel.com/palm-springs* 🛏 *79 rooms* 🍴 *No meals.*

★ Hotel California
$$ | **HOTEL** | Expect homey accommodations for all budgets at this delightful hotel that's decked out in rustic Mexican furniture. **Pros:** comfortable design; friendly hosts; free off-street parking. **Cons:** far from downtown; property needs updating; fronts a busy road. [$] *Rooms from: $225* ✉ *424 E. Palm Canyon Dr.* ☎ *760/322–8855* 🌐 *www.palmspringshotelcalifornia.com* 🛏 *14 rooms* 🍴 *No meals.*

The Hyatt Palm Springs
$$ | **HOTEL** | The best-situated downtown hotel in Palm Springs, the Hyatt has spacious suites where you can watch the sun rise over the city, or set behind the mountains from your bedroom's balcony. **Pros:** underground parking; restaurant plus two outdoor bar-lounges; daily sunset hour with free wine, beer, and appetizers. **Cons:** lots of business travelers; some street noise; valet parking only. [$] *Rooms from: $199* ✉ *285 N. Palm Canyon Dr.* ☎ *760/322–9000* 🌐 *palmsprings.hyatt.com* 🛏 *197 suites* 🍴 *No meals.*

★ Kimpton Rowan Palm Springs Hotel

$$$ | **HOTEL** | The Rowan Palm Springs dazzles locals and guests (especially the under-40 set) with stunning views from myriad picture windows and a rooftop deck, as well as an unpretentious vibe that puts people of any age at ease. **Pros:** friendly, attentive service; stunning mountain and valley views; in the heart of downtown. **Cons:** rooftop pool area can get crowded; valet parking only; $35 resort fee. [$] *Rooms from: $259* ✉ *100 W. Tahquitz Canyon Way* ☎ *760/904–5015, 800/532–7320* 🌐 *www.rowanpalmsprings.com* 🛏 *153 rooms* 🍴 *No meals.*

★ Korakia Pensione

$$$$ | **B&B/INN** | The painter Gordon Coutts, best known for desert landscapes, constructed this Moroccan villa in 1924 as an artist's studio, and these days creative types gather in the main house and nearby Mediterranean-style villas, spread across 1½ acres on both sides of the street, to soak up the spirit of that era. **Pros:** two pools; lunch and dinner available on request (fee); yoga on weekends. **Cons:** might not appeal to those who prefer standard resorts; no TVs or phones in rooms; no children under 13. [$] *Rooms from: $379* ✉ *257 S. Patencio Rd.* ☎ *760/864–6411* 🌐 *www.korakia.com* 🛏 *28 rooms* 🍴 *Free breakfast.*

La Maison

$$$ | **B&B/INN** | Offering all the comforts of home, this small B&B contains large rooms that surround the terra-cotta–tiled and very comfortable pool area, where you can spend quiet time soaking up the sun or taking a dip. **Pros:** restaurants nearby; quiet; genial hosts. **Cons:** on busy Highway 111; rooms open directly onto pool deck; some rooms on the small side. [$] *Rooms from: $289* ✉ *1600 E. Palm Canyon Dr.* ☎ *760/325–1600* 🌐 *www.lamaisonpalmsprings.com* 🛏 *13 rooms* 🍴 *Free breakfast.*

Movie Colony Hotel

$$ | **B&B/INN** | Designed in 1935 by Albert Frey, this intimate hotel evokes a mid-century minimalist ambience throughout its gleaming-white, two-story buildings—flanked with balconies—and its SoCal desert–style rooms, which are elegantly appointed and have bright mid-century color accents. **Pros:** architectural icon; in the midtown Design District; property-wide remodel in 2019. **Cons:** close quarters; basic breakfast; staff not available 24 hours. [$] *Rooms from: $169* ✉ *726 N. Indian Canyon Dr.* ☎ *760/320–6340, 888/953–5700* 🌐 *www.moviecolonyhotel.com* 🛏 *19 rooms* 🍴 *Free breakfast.*

★ Orbit In Hotel

$$ | **B&B/INN** | The exterior architectural style—nearly flat roofs, wide overhangs, glass everywhere—of this hip inn on a quiet backstreet dates from its 1955 opening, and the period feel continues inside. **Pros:** saltwater pool; Orbitini cocktail hour; free breakfast served poolside. **Cons:** best for couples; style not to everyone's taste; staff not available 24 hours. [$] *Rooms from: $169* ✉ *562 W. Arenas Rd.* ☎ *760/323–3585, 877/996–7248* 🌐 *www.orbitin.com* 🛏 *9 rooms* 🍴 *Free breakfast.*

★ The Parker Palm Springs

$$$$ | **RESORT** | A cacophony of color and over-the-top contemporary art assembled by New York City–based designer Jonathan Adler mixes well with the brilliant desert garden, three pools (two outdoor), firepits, and expansive spa of this hip hotel that attracts a stylish, worldly clientele. **Pros:** celebrity clientele; on-site restaurants, bars, and spa; design-centric. **Cons:** pricey drinks and wine; a bit of a drive from downtown; resort fee ($35). [$] *Rooms from: $399* ✉ *4200 E. Palm Canyon Dr.* ☎ *760/770–5000, 800/543–4300* 🌐 *www.theparkerpalmsprings.com* 🛏 *144 rooms* 🍴 *No meals.*

★ The Saguaro

$$ | **HOTEL** | A startling, rainbow-hued oasis—the brainchild of Manhattan-based architects Peter Stamberg and Paul Aferiat—the Saguaro caters to young, hip, pet-toting partygoers who appreciate its lively pool-party scene. **Pros:** lively pool scene with weekend DJ parties; daily yoga, on-site spa, 24-hour fitness center, beach cruisers; shuttle service to downtown. **Cons:** a few miles from downtown; pool area can be noisy and crowded; $33 resort fee. [$] *Rooms from: $169* ✉ *1800 E. Palm Canyon Dr.* ☎ *760/323–1711* 🌐 *thesaguaro.com* 🛏 *244 rooms* 🍴 *No meals.*

Smoke Tree Ranch

$$$$ | **RESORT** | **FAMILY** | A laid-back genteel retreat since the mid-1930s for some of the world's foremost families, including Walt Disney's, the area's most under-the-radar resort complex occupies 385 pristine desert acres surrounded by mountains and unspoiled vistas, and still provides an experience reminiscent of the Old West. **Pros:** priceless privacy; simple luxury; recreational activities like horseback riding and more. **Cons:** no glitz; limited entertainment options; family atmosphere not for everyone. [$] *Rooms from: $410* ✉ *1850 Smoke Tree La.* ☎ *760/327–1221, 800/787–3922* 🌐 *www.smoketreeranch.com* 🕒 *Closed Apr.–late Oct.* 🛏 *49 units* 🍴 *All-inclusive.*

Sparrows Lodge

$$$$ | **B&B/INN** | Rustic earthiness meets haute design at the adult-centered Sparrows, just off Palm Springs's main drag. **Pros:** unique design; intimate property; private patios. **Cons:** not family-oriented, minimum age 21; daily resort fee; no TVs or phones in rooms. [$] *Rooms from: $399* ✉ *1330 E. Palm Canyon Dr.* ☎ *760/327–2300* 🌐 *www.sparrowshotel.com* 🛏 *20 rooms* 🍴 *Free breakfast.*

★ Willows Historic Palm Springs Inn

$$$$ | **B&B/INN** | Set in two adjacent, opulent, Mediterranean-style mansions built in the 1920s to host the rich and famous, this luxurious hillside B&B has gleaming hardwood and slate floors, stone fireplaces, frescoed ceilings, hand-painted tiles, iron balconies, antiques throughout, and a 50-foot waterfall that splashes into a pool outside the dining room. **Pros:** short walk to art museum, restaurants, shops; pool; expansive breakfast and afternoon wine hour. **Cons:** closed from June to September; pricey; some rooms on the small side. [$] *Rooms from: $425* ✉ *412 W. Tahquitz Canyon Way* ☎ *760/320–0771* 🌐 *www.thewillowspalmsprings.com* 🛏 *17 rooms* 🍴 *Free breakfast.*

🍸 Nightlife

BARS AND PUBS

Bootlegger Tiki

BARS/PUBS | Palm Springs tiki-drink traditions, especially during the two daily happy hours (4 to 6 pm and midnight to 2 am), draw loyal patrons to Bootlegger, which occupies the same space as Don the Beachcomber in the 1950s. ✉ *1101 N. Palm Canyon Dr.* ☎ *760/318–4154* 🌐 *www.bootleggertiki.com.*

Tonga Hut

BARS/PUBS | The younger sibling of L.A.'s oldest tiki hut (opened in 1958 in North Hollywood), Tonga Hut Palm Springs transports guests to Polynesia with an authentic tiki vibe, pupu platters, and tropical drinks. It's on the second floor of a building in the heart of the downtown strip—try to nab a table on the lanai where you can experience the action from above. The bar and dining area are also fun and lively spaces; ask about the telephone booth that leads to a secret room, available for private parties. ✉ *254 N. Palm Canyon Dr.* ☎ *760/322–4449* 🌐 *www.tongahut.com.*

Palm Springs Modernism

Some of the world's most forward-looking architects designed and constructed buildings around Palm Springs between 1940 and 1970. Described these days as mid-century modern—you'll also see the term "desert modernism" used—these structures, also popular elsewhere in California in the years after World War II, are ideal for desert living because they minimize the separation between indoors and outdoors. Houses with glass exterior walls are common, as are oversize flat roofs that provide shade from the sun. The style is also notable for elegant informality, simple landscaping, and clean lines that often mirror the shapes of surrounding topography.

Noteworthy examples include three buildings that are part of the Palm Springs Aerial Tramway complex, built in the 1960s. Albert Frey, a Swiss-born architect, designed the soaring A-frame Tramway Gas Station, visually echoing the pointed peaks behind it. Frey also created the glass-walled Valley Station, from which you get your initial view of the Coachella Valley before you board the tram to the Mountain Station, designed by E. Stewart Williams.

Frey, a Palm Springs resident for more than 60 years, also designed the indoor-outdoor City Hall, Fire Station No. 1, and numerous houses.

His second home, atop stilts on a hill above the Palm Springs Art Museum, affords a sweeping Coachella Valley view through glass walls. The classy Movie Colony Hotel, one of Frey's first desert designs, might seem like a typical 1950s motel, with rooms surrounding a swimming pool, but when it was built in 1935, it was years ahead of its time.

Donald Wexler, who honed his vision with Los Angeles architect Richard Neutra, brought new ideas about the use of materials to the desert, where he teamed up with William Cody on projects such as the terminal at the Palm Springs Airport. Wexler also experimented with steel framing back in 1961, but the metal proved too expensive. Seven of his steel-frame houses can be seen in a neighborhood off Indian Canyon and Frances drives.

The Palm Springs Modern Committee website has lots of information and resources, including a downloadable app (⊕ *psmodcom.org/mid-century-modern-tour-app*) that guides you to the most interesting buildings. Note, too, that the desert communities celebrate the Palm Springs "look" during mid-February's Modernism Week (⊕ *modernismweek.com*), an 11-day event featuring lectures, films, and home and garden tours. A shorter preview week happens in October.

★ The Village

BARS/PUBS | With live entertainment, DJs, and friendly service, this popular bar caters to a young crowd. Happy hour is fantastic. On weekend days there is live music as well. ⊠ *266 S. Palm Canyon Dr., at Baristo Rd.* ☎ *760/323–3265* ⊕ *thevillagepalmsprings.com.*

CASINOS
Casino Morongo

CASINOS | A 20-minute drive west of Palm Springs, this casino has 2,600 slot machines, video games, the Vibe nightclub, plus Vegas-style shows. ⊠ *49500 Seminole Dr., off I–10, Cabazon*

☎ *800/252–4499, 951/849–3080* ⊕ *www.morongocasinoresort.com.*

Spa Resort Casino

CASINOS | This resort holds 1,000 slot machines, blackjack tables, a high-limit room, four restaurants, two bars, and the Cascade Lounge for entertainment. ✉ *401 E. Amado Rd., at N. Calle Encilia* ☎ *888/999–1995* ⊕ *www.sparesortcasino.com.*

GAY AND LESBIAN

Chill Bar Palm Springs

DANCE CLUBS | Dance, drink, and dine at this wildly popular nightclub in the heart of the gay-centric Arenas Road district. Socialize in the somewhat quieter front bar, where floor-to-ceiling windows let in scenes of the mountains, or the rowdier back bar, where DJs and other performers entice patrons to kick up their heels on the city's largest dance floor. ✉ *217 E. Arenas Rd.* ☎ *760/696–9493* ⊕ *www.chillbarpalmsprings.com.*

Hunter's Palm Springs

DANCE CLUBS | Drawing a young gay and straight crowd, Hunter's is a club-scene mainstay. ✉ *302 E. Arenas Rd., at Calle Encilia* ☎ *760/323–0700* ⊕ *hunterspalmsprings.com.*

Streetbar Palm Springs

BARS/PUBS | The first gay bar in town, laid-back Streetbar and its full slate of live performers (plus twice-weekly karaoke nights) continue to draw loyal patrons to casual digs in the heart of the Arenas neighborhood. ✉ *224 E. Arenas Rd.* ☎ *760/320–1266* ⊕ *www.psstreetbar.com.*

★ Toucans Tiki Lounge

BARS/PUBS | A friendly place with a tropical–rain forest setting, Toucans serves festive drinks and hosts live entertainment and theme nights. On Sunday it seems as though all of Palm Springs has turned out for drag night. ✉ *2100 N. Palm Canyon Dr., at W. Via Escuela* ☎ *760/416–7584* ⊕ *www.toucanstikilounge.com* ☽ *Closed Tues.*

THEMED ENTERTAINMENT

★ Ace Hotel and Swim Club

THEMED ENTERTAINMENT | Events are held here nearly every night, including film screenings, full moon parties, live concerts, DJs, and dancing. Many are free, and some are family friendly. The poolside venue makes most events fun and casual. ✉ *701 E. Palm Canyon Dr., at Calle Palo Fierro* ☎ *760/325–9900* ⊕ *www.acehotel.com.*

🎭 Performing Arts

FILM

Palm Springs International Film Festival

FILM | In mid-January this 12-day festival brings stars and nearly 200 feature films from several dozen countries, plus panel discussions, short films, and documentaries, to various venues. The weeklong "Shortfest," celebrating more than 300 short films, takes place in June. ✉ *Palm Springs* ☎ *760/322–2930, 800/898–7256* ⊕ *www.psfilmfest.org.*

🛍 Shopping

Hadley's Fruit Orchards

FOOD/CANDY | At the Cabazon exit of Interstate 10, Hadley's sells dried fruit, nuts, wine, and their famous date shakes made with caramel-tasting Deglet Noor dates grown in California. The Hadleys developed the recipe for trail mix in the 1950s. In addition to the dried fruit, you can get candy and old-fashioned sodas here. There's also a snack bar. ✉ *47993 Morongo Trail, Cabazon* ☎ *951/849–5255* ⊕ *www.hadleyfruitorchards.com.*

BOUTIQUES

★ Just Fabulous

LOCAL SPECIALTIES | Find everything from original photography and art, coffee table books, greeting cards, designer home decor, candles, and many other eclectic items at this fun gift shop that celebrates the area's retro-modern lifestyle and desert dolce vita. ✉ *515 N. Palm Canyon Dr.* ☎ *760/864–1300* ⊕ *bjustfabulous.com.*

★ Trina Turk Boutique

CLOTHING | Celebrity designer Trina Turk's empire takes up a city block in the Uptown Design District. Turk, famous for men's and women's outdoor wear, reached out to another celebrity, interior designer Kelly Wearstler, to create adjoining clothing and residential boutiques. Lively fabrics brighten up the many chairs and couches for sale at the residential store, which also carries bowls, paintings, and other fun pieces to spiff up your home. ⊠ *891 N. Palm Canyon Dr.* ☎ *760/416–2856* ⊕ *www.trinaturk.com.*

OUTLET MALLS

★ Desert Hills Premium Outlets

OUTLET/DISCOUNT STORES | About 20 miles west of Palm Springs lies one of California's largest outlet centers. The 180 brand-name discount fashion shops include Jimmy Choo, Neiman Marcus, Versace, Saint Laurent, J. Crew, Armani, Gucci, and Prada. ⊠ *48400 Seminole Rd., off I–10, Cabazon* ☎ *951/849–5018* ⊕ *www.premiumoutlets.com.*

SHOPPING DISTRICTS

★ Uptown Design District

SHOPPING NEIGHBORHOODS | A loose-knit collection of consignment and second-hand shops, galleries, and lively restaurants extends north of Palm Springs's downtown. The theme here is decidedly retro. Many businesses sell mid-century modern furniture and decorator items, and others carry clothing and estate jewelry. One spot definitely worth a peek is **The Shag Store,** the gallery of fine art painter Josh Agle. If you dig the mid-mod aesthetic, breeze through the furnishings at **Towne Palm Springs.** ⊠ *N. Palm Canyon Dr., between Amado Rd. and Vista Chino.*

 Activities

GOLF

Indian Canyons Golf Resort

GOLF | Operated by the Aqua Caliente tribe, this spot at the base of the mountains includes two 18-hole courses open to the public. In the 1960s this was *the* place to play for celebrities visiting the desert, including presidents Dwight Eisenhower and Lyndon Johnson. The North Course, designed by William F. Bell, is adjacent to property once owned by Walt Disney and has six water hazards. The South Course, redesigned in 2004 by Casey O'Callaghan with input from the LPGA player Amy Alcott, has four ponds, hundreds of palm trees, and five par-5 holes. ⊠ *1097 E. Murray Canyon Dr., at Kings Rd. E* ☎ *.760/833–8724* ⊕ *www.indiancanyonsgolf.com* 🏌 *North Course, $99; South Course, $125* 🏌 *North Course: 18 holes, 6943 yards, par 72; South Course: 18 holes, 6582 yards, par 72.*

Tahquitz Creek Golf Resort

GOLF | Conveniently located in Palm Springs near Cathedral City, the resort has two popular courses open to the public. Golfers have been walking the Legend course for more than 50 years—the back nine here are challenging, particularly the greens. The newer Resort course, designed by Ted Robinson, offers sweeping mountain views and scenic waterscapes. ⊠ *1885 Golf Club Dr., at 34th Ave.* ☎ *760/328–1005* ⊕ *www.tahquitzgolfresort.com* 🏌 *Legend Course, $69; Resort Course, $89* 🏌 *Legend Course: 18 holes, 6815 yards, par 71; Resort Course: 18 holes, 6705 yards, par 72.*

HORSEBACK RIDING

Smoke Tree Stables

HORSEBACK RIDING | At these stables you can explore desert canyons on horseback like the earliest pioneers. One-hour tours depart on the hour and take riders along the base of the Santa Rosa Mountains. Two-hour tours depart four times daily for trips that take in the Aqua Caliente Indian Reservation. ⊠ *2500 S. Toledo Ave.* ☎ *760/327–1372* ⊕ *www.smoketreestables.com* 🏌 *From $80.*

Palm Springs is a golfer's paradise: the area is home to more than 125 courses.

SPAS

★ Estrella Spa at the Avalon Hotel Palm Springs

FITNESS/HEALTH CLUBS | This spa earns top honors each year for the indoor/outdoor experience it offers with a touch of Old Hollywood ambience. You can enjoy your massage in one of four outdoor treatment cabanas in a garden, experience a sugar or salt scrub, get a facial or pedicure fireside, or receive a full-body treatment with a honey-sugar blend. Whatever the treatment, you can use the spa's private pool, take a break for lunch, and order a drink from the hotel's bar. ⊠ *Avalon Hotel Palm Springs, 415 S. Belardo Rd.* ☏ *760/318–3000* ⊕ *www.avalonpalmsprings.com* ☞ *Salon. Services: facials, specialty massages, prenatal massages, outdoor treatments, wellness classes. $175, 60-min massage or facial.*

Feel Good Spa at the Ace Hotel

FITNESS/HEALTH CLUBS | The Feel Good Spa within its own dedicated facility at the Ace Hotel has five treatment rooms. The estheticians use local clay, mud, sea algae, and other natural ingredients, which you can purchase at the on-site shop. ⊠ *701 E. Palm Canyon Dr.* ☏ *760/866–6188* ⊕ *www.acehotel.com/palmsprings* ☞ *Fully equipped gym. Services: wraps and scrubs, massage, facials, in-room treatments, salon, wellness classes, yoga. $115, 60-min massage.*

Palm Springs Yacht Club

FITNESS/HEALTH CLUBS | It's all about fun at this nautical-theme spa with 15 treatment rooms on the grounds of the Parker estate. Guests receive a complimentary cucumber-infused cocktail while lounging in a poolside tent. Before spa treatments, you can choose music from a playlist and the staff will stream it to your room. Treatments might feature local clay or stones, or a Thai massage. ⊠ *4200 E. Palm Canyon Dr.* ☏ *760/321–4606* ⊕ *www.theparkerpalmsprings.com/spa* ☞ *Sauna, steam room, indoor pool. Services: scrubs and wraps, massage, facials, manicures, pedicures, waxing, salon, fitness center with TechnoGym* *equipment, dining and cocktails. $195, 50-min massage.*

Rancho Mirage

12 miles southeast of Palm Springs.

The rich and famous of Rancho Mirage live in beautiful estates and patronize elegant resorts and expensive restaurants. Although many mansions here are concealed behind the walls of gated communities and country clubs, the grandest of them all, Sunnylands, the Annenberg residence, is open to the public. The city's golf courses host many high-profile tournaments. You'll also find some of the desert's fanciest resorts—as well as plenty of peace and quiet.

GETTING HERE AND AROUND

Rancho Mirage stretches from Ramon Road in the north to the hills south of Highway 111. The western border is Da Vall Drive, the eastern one Monterey Avenue. Major east–west cross streets are Frank Sinatra Drive and Country Club Drive. Most shopping and dining spots are on Highway 111.

👁 Sights

Rancho Mirage Library and Observatory

OBSERVATORY | FAMILY | Gaze at planets, star clusters, and galaxies, and learn about extraterrestrial life at this city-owned observatory next to the public library. The complex includes five high-powered telescopes—four on the deck and a main telescope in the 360-degree observatory dome that's designed to look like a comet. Regular tours and stargazing parties are scheduled every month. ✉ *71–100 Hwy. 111* ☎ *760/341–7323* 🌐 *www.ranchomiragelibrary.org* 🎫 *Free* 🕒 *Closed Sun. and Mon.*

★ Sunnylands Center & Gardens

HOUSE | The stunning, 25,000-square-foot winter home and retreat of the late Ambassador Walter H. Annenberg and his wife, Leonore, opened to the public in 2012. You can spend a whole day enjoying the 15 glorious acres of gardens, and there are guided walks, landscape tours, classes, and other programs. The history made here is as captivating as the surroundings, given that eight U.S. presidents—from Dwight Eisenhower to Barack Obama—and their First Ladies have visited Sunnylands. Britain's Queen Elizabeth and Prince Philip also relaxed here, as did Princess Grace of Monaco and Japanese Prime Minister Toshiki Kaifu. Photos, art, letters, journals, and mementos provide insight. ✉ *37–977 Bob Hope Dr., south of Gerald Ford Dr.* ☎ *760/202–2222* 🌐 *www.sunnylands.org* 🎫 *Historic walking tour $25; guided bird tour $39; open-air shuttle tour of grounds, $125 per shuttle (up to 6 persons); visitor center and gardens free* 🕒 *Closed Mon. and Tues. Closed June–mid-Sept. and during retreats.*

🍴 Restaurants

Catalan

$$$ | MEDITERRANEAN | At this restaurant, known for its beautifully prepared Mediterranean cuisine, you can dine inside or under the stars in the atrium. The service here is attentive, and the menu roams Spain, Italy, California, and beyond. **Known for:** two-course, prix-fixe menu; delicious paella with clams; happy hour with inventive cocktails. [$] *Average main: $28* ✉ *70026 Hwy. 111* ☎ *760/770–9508* 🌐 *www.catalanrestaurant.com* 🕒 *Closed Mon.*

Las Casuelas Nuevas

$ | MEXICAN | FAMILY | Hundreds of artifacts from Guadalajara, Mexico, lend festive charm to this casual restaurant, which has an expansive garden patio. Tamales and shellfish dishes are among the specialties—expect more traditional Mexican fare, rather than California-influenced creations. **Known for:** vast tequila menu; weekend live entertainment; lively happy hour. $ *Average main: $16 ⊠ 70–050 Hwy. 111 ☎ 760/328–8844 ⊕ www. lascasuelasnuevas.com.*

 Hotels

Agua Caliente Casino, Resort, Spa

$$ | RESORT | As in Las Vegas, the Agua Caliente casino is in the lobby, but once you get into the resort's spacious, beautifully appointed guest rooms, all of the cacophony at the entrance is forgotten. **Pros:** poolside cabanas outfitted with TV and Wi-Fi; package deals include access to Indian Canyons Golf Course; on-site Sunstone Spa. **Cons:** casino ambience; not appropriate for kids; some live performances draw huge crowds. $ *Rooms from: $250 ⊠ 32–250 Bob Hope Dr. ☎ 888/999–1995 ⊕ www.hotwatercasino. com ⬑ 366 rooms ❐ No meals.*

Omni Rancho Las Palmas Resort & Spa

$$$ | RESORT | FAMILY | The desert's most family-friendly resort, this large venue holds Splashtopia, a huge water-play zone. **Pros:** rooms come with private balconies or patios; trails for hiking and jogging; nightly entertainment. **Cons:** second-floor rooms accessed by very steep stairs; golf course surrounds rooms; resort hosts conventions. $ *Rooms from: $299 ⊠ 41-000 Bob Hope Dr. ☎ 760/568–2727 ⊕ www.rancholaspalmas.com ⬑ 444 rooms ❐ No meals.*

★ The Ritz Carlton, Rancho Mirage

$$$$ | RESORT | FAMILY | On a hilltop perch overlooking the Coachella Valley, this luxury resort spoils guests with exemplary service and comforts that include a trio of pools, access to the desert's finest spa, and private outdoor sitting areas for each room. **Pros:** firepit overlooking Coachella Valley; access to Mission Hills golf courses and tennis; spa that's a destination in itself. **Cons:** hefty rates; some airport noise; resort and parking fees ($40 each). $ *Rooms from: $430 ⊠ 68900 Frank Sinatra Dr. ☎ 760/321–8282 ⊕ www.ritz-carlton.com ⬑ 244 rooms ❐ No meals.*

The Westin Mission Hills Golf Resort & Spa

$$$$ | RESORT | FAMILY | A sprawling resort on 360 acres, the Westin offers a slew of activities for all ages and is surrounded by fairways and putting greens, two family-friendly pools (one lagoon-style with a 75-foot waterslide) and an adults-only pool. **Pros:** gorgeous grounds; first-class golf facilities; daily activity programs for kids and adults. **Cons:** rooms are spread out; some buildings seem dated; far from town. $ *Rooms from: $369 ⊠ 71333 Dinah Shore Dr. ☎ 760/328–5955, 877/253–0041 ⊕ www.westinmission-hills.com ⬑ 552 rooms ❐ No meals.*

 Nightlife

Agua Caliente Casino

CASINOS | This elegant and surprisingly quiet casino contains 1,300 slot machines, 36 table games, an 18-table poker room, a high-limit room, a no-smoking area, and six restaurants. The Show, the resort's concert theater, presents acts such as The Moody Blues, Joe Bonamassa, Toni Braxton, and Theresa Caputo, as well as live sporting events. *⊠ 32–250 Bob Hope Dr., at E. Ramon Rd. ☎ 888/999–1995 ⊕ www.hotwatercasino.com.*

 Shopping

MALL

The River at Rancho Mirage

SHOPPING CENTERS/MALLS | This shopping-dining-entertainment complex holds 20 high-end shops, all fronting a faux river with cascading waterfalls. Also here are a 12-screen cinema, an outdoor amphitheater, and many restaurants including Acqua (sister to the popular LULU in Palm Springs) and Babe's Bar-B-Que and Brewhouse. *⊠ 71–800 Hwy. 111, at Bob Hope Dr. ☎ 760/341–2711 ⊕ www. theriveratranchomirage.com.*

Activities

GOLF

★ Westin Mission Hills Resort Golf Club

GOLF | Golfers at the Westin Mission Hills have two courses to choose from, the Pete Dye and the Gary Player Signature. They're both great, with amazing mountain views and wide fairways, but if you've only got time to play one, choose the Dye. The club is a member of the Troon Golf Institute, and has several teaching facilities, including the Westin Mission Hills Resort Golf Academy and the *Golf Digest* Golf School. ■TIP➜ The resort's Best Available Rate program guarantees golfers (with a few conditions) the best Internet rate possible. ✉ *71333 Dinah Shore Dr.* ☎ *760/328–3198* ⊕ *www. playmissionhills.com* ⊠ *Gary Player, from $74; Pete Dye, from $114* ⅀. *Pete Dye Resort: 18 holes, 5525 yards, par 72; Gary Player Signature: 18 holes, 5327 yards, par 70.*

SPAS

★ The Ritz Carlton Spa, Rancho Mirage

FITNESS/HEALTH CLUBS | Two hundred–plus suspended quartz crystals guard the entrance of the desert's premier spa. With private men's and women's areas, a co-ed outdoor soaking tub, food service, and some of the kindest spa technicians around, guests can expect pampering par excellence. The signature Spirit of the Mountains treatment, which starts with a full-body exfoliation, includes a massage, and ends with a body wrap and a scalp massage with lavender oil, is a blissful experience. The gym, equipped with state-of-the-art machines, is open 24/7. Private trainers are available to guide your workout; wellness classes are also available. ✉ *68900 Frank Sinatra Dr.* ☎ *760/202–6170* ⊕ *www.ritzcarlton.com* ⊂ *Fully equipped gym. Salon. Services: body wraps, body scrubs, facials, mineral baths, specialty massages, outdoor treatments, waxing, wellness classes. $185, 50-min massage; $345, signature package.*

The Spa at Mission Hills

FITNESS/HEALTH CLUBS | The emphasis at this spa in a quiet corner of the Westin Mission Hills Resort is on comfort rather than glitz and glamour. Attentive therapists incorporate coconut lemon balm, thyme, lavender, hydrating honey, and other botanicals into their treatments. Yoga and other wellness classes are also available. ✉ *71333 Dinah Shore Dr.* ☎ *760/770–2180* ⊕ *www.spaatmissionhills.com* ⊂ *Steam room. Gym with: machines, cardio, pool. Services: rubs and scrubs, massages, facials, nail services. $170, 50-min massage.*

Palm Desert

2 miles southeast of Rancho Mirage.

Palm Desert is a thriving retail and business community with popular restaurants, private and public golf courses, and premium shopping along its main commercial drag, El Paseo. Each October, the Palm Desert Golf Cart Parade launches "the season" with a procession of 80 golf carts decked out as floats buzzing up and down El Paseo. The town's stellar sight to see is the Living Desert complex.

GETTING HERE AND AROUND

Palm Desert stretches from north of I–10 to the hills south of Highway 111. West–east cross streets north to south are Frank Sinatra Drive, Country Club Drive (lined on both sides with gated golfing communities), and Fred Waring Drive. Monterey Avenue marks the western boundary, and Washington Street forms the eastern edge.

TOURS

Art in Public Places

SELF-GUIDED | Several self-guided tours cover the works in Palm Desert's 150-piece Art in Public Places collection. Each tour is walkable or drivable. Maps and information about guided tours (one Saturday each month) are available at the

The Desert
Resources

Palm Springs
see detail
map

---

city's visitor center and online. ✉ *Palm Desert Visitor Center, 73510 Fred Waring Dr.* ☎ *760/568–1441* ⊕ *www.palm-desert. org/arts-entertainment/public-art* 🖾 *Free.*

👁 Sights

★ El Paseo

PEDESTRIAN MALL | West of and parallel to Highway 111, this mile-long, Mediterranean-style shopper's paradise is lined with fountains, courtyards, and upscale boutiques. You'll find shoe salons, jewelry stores, and children's shops, as well as two dozen restaurants and nearly as many art galleries. The strip is a pleasant place to stroll, window-shop, people-watch, and exercise your credit cards. ■**TIP**➔ **In winter and spring, a free, bright-yellow shuttle ferries shoppers from store to store and back to their cars.**

✉ *Between Monterey and Portola Aves.* ☎ *760/674–9012* ⊕ *www.elpaseo.com.*

Faye Sarkowski Sculpture Garden

MUSEUM | This 4-acre desert garden at the west entrance to El Paseo holds 14 cutting-edge works by contemporary sculptors, including Donald Judd, Betty Gold, Yehiel Shemi, Felipe Castañeda, Jesús Bautista Moroles, Dan Namingha, Giò Pomodoro, and Dave McGary. ✉ *72–567 Hwy. 111* ☎ *760/346–5600* ⊕ *www.psmuseum.org/visit/faye-sarkowsky-sculpture-garden* 🖾 *Free.*

★ The Living Desert Zoo and Gardens

ZOO | FAMILY | Come eye-to-eye with wolves, coyotes, mountain lions, cheetahs, bighorn sheep, golden eagles, warthogs, and owls at the Living Desert, which showcases the flora and fauna of the world's arid landscapes. Easy to challenging scenic trails traverse terrain populated with plants of the Mojave, Colorado, and Sonoran deserts. In the 3-acre African WaTuTu village you'll find a traditional marketplace, as well as camels, leopards, hyenas, and other African animals. Children can pet domesticated African creatures, including Nigerian dwarf goats, in a "petting kraal." Gecko Gulch is a playground with crawl-through underground tunnels, climb-on snake sculptures, a carousel, and a Discovery Center that holds ancient Pleistocene animal bones. Wallabies, emus, and kookaburras interact with visitors in the immersive Australian Adventures experience, and a cool model train travels through miniatures of historic California towns. **■ TIP→ Time your visit to begin in the early morning to beat the heat and feed the giraffes.** ✉ *47900 Portola Ave., south from Hwy. 111* ☎ *760/346–5694* 🌐 *www.livingdesert.org* 🎫 *$25.*

Santa Rosa and San Jacinto Mountains National Monument
NATURE PRESERVE | Administered by the U.S. Bureau of Land Management, this monument protects Peninsula bighorn sheep and other wildlife on 280,000 acres of desert habitat. Stop by the visitor center for an introduction to the site and information about the natural history of the desert. A landscaped garden displays native plants and frames an impressive view. The well-informed staff can recommend hiking trails that show off the beauties of the desert. **■ TIP→ Free guided hikes are offered on Thursday and Saturday.** ✉ *51–500 Hwy. 74* ☎ *760/862–9984* 🌐 *www.blm.gov* 🎫 *Free.*

Restaurants

★ Bouchee Café & Deli
$ | **AMERICAN** | Devotees of this La Quinta favorite come here for farm-to-table Euro-style meals and deli items. Order the salads or gorgeous sandwiches—the salmon salad is to die for—at the counter, then retire to the French-inspired dining area or the shaded outdoor terrace. **Known for:** premade dinner to go; gourmet wine and cheese shop; locally sourced ingredients. [$] *Average main: $15* ✉ *72–785 Hwy. 111* ✥ *Off Plaza Way near El Paseo* ☎ *442/666–3296* 🕐 *No dinner.*

Pacifica Seafood
$$$$ | **SEAFOOD** | Choice seafood and rooftop dining draw locals and visitors to this busy restaurant on the second floor of the Gardens of El Paseo. Seafood that arrives daily from San Diego shines in dishes such as twin lobster tails, grilled Pacific swordfish, and barbecued sugar-spiced salmon. **Known for:** inventive sauces and glazes; craft cocktails and bourbon; lower-price sunset menu from 3 to 5:30. [$] *Average main: $38* ✉ *73505 El Paseo* ☎ *760/674–8666* 🌐 *www.pacificaseafoodrestaurant.com* 🕐 *No lunch June–Aug.*

Hotels

Desert Springs J. W. Marriott Resort and Spa
$$$ | **RESORT** | **FAMILY** | With a dramatic U-shape design, this sprawling hotel, which attract business travelers, couples, and families alike, is set on 450 landscaped acres and wraps around the desert's largest private lake.
Pros: gondola rides on the lake to restaurants; popular lobby bar; wonderful spa.
Cons: crowded in-season; high resort fee; long walk from lobby to rooms. [$] *Rooms from: $269* ✉ *74–855 Country Club Dr.* ☎ *760/341–2211, 888/538–9459* 🌐 *www.desertspringsresort.com* 🛏 *884 rooms* 🍴 *No meals.*

Hotel Paseo
$$$ | **HOTEL** | **FAMILY** | A half block from El Paseo, this hip luxury hotel, which is a member of Marriott's Autograph Collection, reflects the mid-century modern history and upscale, yet casual lifestyle of the desert. **Pros:** on-site restaurant; full-service spa; walk to El Paseo restaurants, shops, attractions. **Cons:** some rooms on the small side; pool area can

seem small and crowded; street parking unless you pay for valet. $ *Rooms from: $289* ⊠ *45400 Larkspur La.* ☎ *760/340–9001* ⊕ *www.hotelpaseo.com* ⟿ *149 rooms* ⦿ *No meals.*

 Performing Arts

McCallum Theatre

THEATER | The principal cultural venue in the desert, this theater hosts productions from fall through spring. *The Phantom of the Opera* has played here; Lily Tomlin and Willie Nelson have performed; and Shen Yun dancers have twirled across the stage. ⊠ *73–000 Fred Waring Dr.* ☎ *760/340–2787* ⊕ *www.mccallumtheatre.com.*

Activities

BALLOONING
Fantasy Balloon Flights

BALLOONING | Sunrise excursions over the southern end of the Coachella Valley lift off at 6 am and take from 60 to 90 minutes; a traditional champagne toast follows the landing. Afternoon excursions are timed to touch down at sunset. ⊠ *Palm Desert* ☎ *760/568–0997* ⊕ *www.fantasyballoonflight.com* ⟐ *$195.*

GOLF
Desert Willow Golf Resort

GOLF | Praised for its environmentally smart design, this top-rated, public golf resort planted water-thrifty turf grasses and doesn't use pesticides. The Mountain View course has four configurations; Firecliff is tournament quality with five configurations. ⊠ *38–995 Desert Willow Dr., off Country Club Dr.* ☎ *760/346–0015* ⊕ *www.desertwillow.com* ⟐ *Mountain View from $120, Firecliff from $120* ⚐ *Mountain View: 18 holes, 7079 yards, par 72; Firecliff: 18 holes, 7056 yards, par 72.*

Indian Wells

5 miles east of Palm Desert.

For the most part a quiet and exclusive residential enclave, Indian Wells hosts major tennis tournaments throughout the year, including the BNP Paribas Open. Three hotels share access to championship golf and tennis facilities, and there are several noteworthy resort spas and restaurants.

GETTING HERE AND AROUND

Indian Wells lies between Palm Desert and La Quinta, with most resorts, restaurants, and shopping set back from Highway 111.

 Restaurants

Vue Grille and Bar at the Indian Wells Golf Resort

$$$ | **AMERICAN** | This not-so-private restaurant at the Indian Wells Golf Resort offers a glimpse of how the country-club set lives. The service is impeccable, and the outdoor tables provide views of mountain peaks that seem close enough to touch. **Known for:** farm-to-table cuisine; grilled steaks and seafood; flatbreads and burgers. $ *Average main: $36* ⊠ *44–500 Indian Wells La.* ☎ *760/834–3800* ⊕ *www.vuegrilleandbar.com.*

Hotels

★ Hyatt Regency Indian Wells Resort & Spa

$$$$ | **RESORT** | **FAMILY** | This stark-white resort adjacent to the Golf Resort at Indian Wells is one of the grandest in the desert, with seven pools (one adults-only and several with slides in the HyTides waterpark), an outdoor game area and kids club, and a spa. **Pros:** excellent business services; butler service in some rooms; very pet-friendly. **Cons:** big and impersonal; spread out over 45 acres; noisy public areas. $ *Rooms from: $370* ⊠ *44–600 Indian Wells La.* ☎ *760/776–1234* ⊕ *indianwells.regency.hyatt.com* ⟿ *520 rooms* ⦿ *No meals.*

Miramonte Resort & Spa

$$$ | RESORT | Guest rooms at the most intimate of the Indian Wells hotels are in red-roof villas on 11 acres of bougainvillea-filled gardens against a backdrop of the Santa Rosa Mountains. **Pros:** three swimming pools (one adults-only); on-site farm-to-fork restaurant and lounge; one of the desert's best spas. **Cons:** extra resort fee; limited resort facilities on-site; long walk to lobby from some rooms. $ Rooms from: $299 ⊠ 45000 Indian Wells La. ☎ 760/341–2200 ⊕ www. miramonteresort.com ⇄ 215 rooms ❑ No meals.

Renaissance Esmeralda Resort & Spa, Indian Wells

$$$ | RESORT | FAMILY | The centerpiece of this luxurious resort, adjacent to the Golf Resort at Indian Wells, is an eight-story atrium lobby, onto which most rooms open. **Pros:** adjacent to golf-tennis complex; kids club; bicycles available. **Cons:** higher noise level in rooms surrounding pool; somewhat impersonal ambience; service sometimes under par in off-season. $ Rooms from: $289 ⊠ 44–400 Indian Wells La. ☎ 760/773–4444 ⊕ www. renaissancehotels.com ⇄ 560 rooms ❑ No meals.

 Activities

GOLF
★ **Indian Wells Golf Resort**

GOLF | Adjacent to the Hyatt Regency Indian Wells, this complex includes the Celebrity Course, designed by Clive Clark and twice a host to the PGA's Skins game (lots of water here, including streams, lakes, and waterfalls), and the Players Course, designed by John Fought to incorporate views of the surrounding mountain ranges. Both courses consistently rank among the best public courses in California. ■TIP➔ **It's a good idea to book tee times well in advance, up to 60 days.** ⊠ 44–500 Indian Wells La. ☎ 760/346–4653 ⊕ www.indianwells-golfresort.com ⛳ Both courses from

$79 ⛳. Celebrity Course: 18 holes, 7050 yards, par 72; Players Course: 18 holes, 7376 yards, par 72.

SPAS
★ **The Well Spa**

FITNESS/HEALTH CLUBS | A luxurious, 12,000-square-foot facility, The Well draws on international treatments and ingredients to indulge the senses and relax the body. Hot-stone, Himalayan-salt, and full-body massages and table yoga are well worth the splurge. Sugar or salt exfoliating scrubs may well restore the soul in addition to the skin. ⊠ Miramonte Resort, 45–000 Indian Wells La. ☎ 442/305–4505 ⊕ www.miramonteresort.com ⛳ Services: facials, nail care, solo and couple's massages, scrubs, and other body therapies. $175, 50-min massage.

La Quinta

4 miles south of Indian Wells.

The desert became a Hollywood hideout in the 1920s, when La Quinta Hotel (now La Quinta Resort and Club) opened, introducing the Coachella Valley's first golf course. Old Town La Quinta is a draw, with eateries, shops, and galleries.

GETTING HERE AND AROUND
Most of La Quinta lies south of Highway 111. The main drag through town is Washington Street.

 Restaurants

Arnold Palmer's

$$$ | AMERICAN | From the photos on the walls to the trophy-filled display cases, Arnie's essence infuses this restaurant. Families gather in the spacious dining room for birthdays and Sunday dinners, and the service is always attentive. **Known for:** homemade meat loaf, double-cut pork chops, mac and cheese; top-notch wine list; entertainment most nights. $ Average main: $34 ⊠ 78164 Ave. 52, near

Desert Club Dr. ☎ *760/771–4653* 🌐 *www.arnoldpalmersrestaurant.com.*

Cork & Fork

$$ | **MODERN AMERICAN** | A casual wine bar, restaurant, and popular local hangout in a cozy, contemporary, indoor–outdoor space near Lake La Quinta, Cork and Fork focuses on matching wines with an array of small and large dishes—all designed to share. The globe-trotting menu changes with the seasons, but you might feast on street tacos stuffed with filet mignon or tequila lime shrimp, Neapolitan-style pizzas, salads, or lobster penne in a creamy pink-vodka sauce. **Known for:** daily happy hour; eclectic list of affordable, food-friendly wines by the glass and bottle; special vegan menu (and much of the menu is gluten-free). [$] *Average main: $17* ✉ *47875 Caleo Bay Dr., #A106* ☎ *760/777–7555* 🌐 *www.corkandforkwinebar.com* 🕒 *No lunch.*

★ Lavender Bistro

$$$$ | **BISTRO** | This romantic bistro with a spacious outdoor atrium decked out with flowers, fountains, and twinkling lights makes diners feel like they've been transported to southern France. Choices on the lengthy menu include crispy coastal calamari, a honey-brine pork chop, and lobster ravioli; for dessert, you can't go wrong with the baked apple tart or the warm chocolate lava cake. **Known for:** live music on the patio and in the fireside lounge; organic ingredients; extensive locavore menu. [$] *Average main: $38* ✉ *78073 Calle Barcelona* ☎ *760/564–5353* 🌐 *www.lavenderbistro.com* 🕒 *Closed June–Sept.*

Hotels

The Chateau at Lake La Quinta

$$ | **HOTEL** | Old-world French design, contemporary style, and luxe creature comforts make this lakeside inn a good choice for those who want intimate, upscale lodgings near La Quinta's main attractions. **Pros:** idyllic lakeside setting; on-site restaurant serves breakfast, lunch, and dinner; outdoor pool, deck with firepits. **Cons:** two-story building with no elevator; some rooms not as posh as others; adults-oriented, not ideal for families with children. [$] *Rooms from: $189* ✉ *78–120 Caleo Bay Dr.* ☎ *760/564–7332, 888/226–4546* 🌐 *www.thechateau.com* 🛏 *26 rooms* 🍴 *No meals.*

La Quinta Resort and Club

$$$ | **RESORT** | **FAMILY** | Opened in 1926 and now a member of the Waldorf-Astoria Collection, the desert's oldest resort is a 45-acre oasis with myriad rooms and villas, 23 tennis courts, and 41 pools. **Pros:** some rooms have private pools; gorgeous gardens; pet and family friendly. **Cons:** a party atmosphere sometimes prevails; spotty housekeeping/maintenance; swimming pools can be crowded. [$] *Rooms from: $329* ✉ *49499 Eisenhower Dr.* ☎ *760/564–4111* 🌐 *www.laquintaresort.com* 🛏 *796 units* 🍴 *No meals.*

Activities

GOLF

★ PGA West

GOLF | A world-class golf destination where Phil Mickelson and Jack Nicklaus play, this facility includes five resort courses and four private ones. Courses meander through indigenous desert landscapes, water features, and bunkers. The Norman, Nick Tournament, and TPC Stadium courses are "shot-makers" courses made for pros. TPC highlights include its two lakes, "San Andreas Fault" bunker, and island green called "Alcatraz." The Norman course has tight fairways and small greens. ✉ *49–499 Eisenhower Dr.* ☎ *760/564–5729 for tee times* 🌐 *www.pgawest.com* 🎫 *Mountain Course, from $159; Dunes, from $119; Greg Norman, from $159; TPC Stadium, from $189; Jack Nicklaus Tournament, from $159* 🏌 *Mountain Course: 18 holes, 6732 yards, par 72; Dunes: 18 holes, 6712 yards, par 72; Greg Norman: 18 holes, 7156 yards, par 72; TPC Stadium:*

18 holes, 7300 yards, par 72; Jack Nicklaus Tournament: 18 holes, 7204 yards, par 72.

SPAS

Spa La Quinta

FITNESS/HEALTH CLUBS | The gorgeous Spa La Quinta may be the grandest spa in the entire desert. At this huge standalone facility you'll find everything from massages to facials to salon services and classes, plus a beautiful garden setting with a large fountain, flowers galore, plenty of nooks where you can hide out and enjoy the sanctuary, and a Jacuzzi with a waterfall. ✉ *49499 Eisenhower Dr.* ☎ *760/777–4800* 🌐 *www.laquintaresort.com* ☞ *Fitness center with cardio. Services: aromatherapy, body wraps and scrubs, massage, skin care, salon services, water therapies. $170, 50-min massage; $295, 50-min HydraFacial.*

Indio

5 miles east of Indian Wells.

Indio is the home of the renowned date shake: an extremely thick and sweet milkshake made with dates. The city and surrounding countryside generate 95% of the dates grown and harvested in the United States. If you take a hot-air balloon ride, you will likely drift over the tops of date palm trees.

GETTING HERE AND AROUND

Indio is east of Indian Wells and north of La Quinta. Highway 111 runs right through Indio, and I–10 skirts it to the north.

Sights

Coachella Valley Preserve

NATURE PRESERVE | **FAMILY** | For a glimpse of how the desert appeared before development, head northeast from Palm Springs to this preserve. It has a system of sand dunes and several palm oases that were formed because the San Andreas Fault lines here allow water flowing underground to rise to the surface. A mile-long walk along Thousand Palms Oasis reveals pools supporting the tiny endangered desert pupfish and more than 183 bird species. Families like the relatively flat trail that is mostly shaded. The preserve has a visitor center, nature and equestrian trails, restrooms, and picnic facilities. Guided hikes are offered October–March. ■ **TIP→ Be aware that it's exceptionally hot in summer here.** ✉ *29200 Thousand Palms Canyon Rd., Thousand Palms* ☎ *760/343–1234* 🌐 *www.cnlm.org/portfolio_page/coachella-valley* 🎟 *Free* ⏲ *Visitor center closed May–Sept. Parking lot and hiking closed Aug.*

Shields Date Garden and Café

STORE/MALL | Sample, select, and take home some of Shields's locally grown dates. Ten varieties are available, including the giant supersweet royal medjools, along with specialty date products such as date crystals, stuffed dates, confections, and local honey. At the Shields Date Garden Café you can try an iconic date shake, dig into date pancakes, or go exotic with a date burger. Breakfast and lunch are served daily. ✉ *80–225 Hwy. 111* ☎ *760/347–0996* 🌐 *www.shieldsdategarden.com* ⏲ *No dinner.*

🍴 Restaurants

Ciro's Ristorante and Pizzeria

$ | **SICILIAN** | Serving pizza and pasta since the 1960s, this popular restaurant has a few unusual pies on the menu, including cashew with three cheeses. The decor is classic pizza joint, with checkered tablecloths and bentwood chairs. **Known for:** daily pasta specials; classic Italian dishes; house-made, hand-tossed pizza dough. [$] *Average main: $16* ✉ *81–963 Hwy. 111* ☎ *760/347–6503* ⏲ *No lunch weekends.*

Performing Arts

MUSIC FESTIVALS

★ **Coachella Valley Music and Arts Festival**
FESTIVALS | Among Southern California's
biggest parties, the festival draws hundreds of thousands of rock music fans to
Indio each April for two weekends of live
concerts. Headliners have included acts
such as Lady Gaga, Childish Gambino,
Ariana Grande, Tame Impala, Kendrick
Lamar, Jack Johnson, and Radiohead.
Many attendees camp on-site, but to
give your ears a rest postconcert you
might want to stay at a nearby hotel.
■ **TIP→ The festival sells out before the
lineup is announced, so expect to pay big
bucks if you haven't purchased tickets by
late fall.** ⊠ *Empire Polo Club, 81–800 Ave.
51* ⊕ *www.coachella.com.*

Borrego Springs

66 miles southwest of Indio.

The permanent population of Borrego
Springs, set squarely in the middle of
Anza-Borrego Desert State Park, hovers
around 2,500. From September through
June, when temperatures stay in the
'80s and '90s, you can engage in outdoor
activities such as hiking, nature study,
golfing, tennis, horseback riding, and
mountain biking. If winter rains cooper-
ate, Borrego Springs puts on some of
the best wildflower displays in the low
desert. In some years, the desert floor
is carpeted with color: yellow dandelions
and sunflowers, pink primrose, purple
sand verbena, and blue wild heliotrope.
The bloom generally lasts from late
February through April. For current
information on wildflowers around
Borrego Springs, call Anza-Borrego
Desert State Park's wildflower hotline
(☎ *760/767–4684*).

GETTING HERE AND AROUND

You can access Anza Borrego by taking
the Highway 86 exit from I–10, south
of Indio. Highway 86 passes through
Coachella and along the western shore
of the Salton Sea. Turn west on Highway
S22 at Salton City and follow it to Peg
Leg Road, where you turn south until you
reach Palm Canyon Drive. Turn west, and
the road leads to the center of Borrego
Springs, Christmas Circle, where most
major roads come together. Well-marked
roads radiating from the circle will take
you to the most popular sites in the
state park. If coming from the San Diego
area, drive east on I–8 to the Cuyamaca
Mountains, exit at Highway 79, and enjoy
the lovely 23-mile drive through the
mountains until you reach Julian; head
east on Highway 78 and follow signs to
Borrego Springs.

ESSENTIALS

**VISITOR INFORMATION Borrego Springs
Chamber of Commerce & Visitors Bureau.**
⊠ *786 Palm Canyon Dr.* ☎ *760/767–5555,
800/559–5524* ⊕ *www.borregosprings-
chamber.com.*

Sights

★ **Anza-Borrego Desert State Park**
NATIONAL/STATE PARK | One of the richest
living natural-history museums in the
nation, this state park is a vast, nearly
uninhabited wilderness where you can
step through a field of wildflowers, cool
off in a palm-shaded oasis, count zillions
of stars in the black night sky, and listen
to coyotes howl at dusk. The landscape,
largely undisturbed by humans, reveals a
rich natural history. There's evidence of a
vast inland sea in the piles of oyster beds
near Split Mountain and of the power of
natural forces such as earthquakes and
flash floods. In addition, recent scientific
work has confirmed that the Borrego
Badlands, with more than 6,000 meters
of exposed fossil-bearing sediments, is
likely the richest such deposit in North
America, telling the story of 7 million

years of climate change, upheaval, and prehistoric animals. Evidence has been unearthed of saber-toothed cats, flamingos, zebras, and the largest flying bird in the northern hemisphere beneath the now-parched sand.

Today the desert's most treasured inhabitants are the herds of elusive and endangered native bighorn sheep, or borrego, for which the park is named. Among the strange desert plants you may observe are the gnarly elephant trees. As these are endangered, rangers don't encourage visitors to seek out the secluded grove at Fish Creek, but there are a few examples at the visitor center garden. After a wet winter you can see a short-lived but stunning display of cacti, succulents, and desert wildflowers in bloom.

The park is unusually accessible to visitors. Admission to the park is free, and few areas are off-limits. There are two developed campgrounds, but you can camp anywhere; just follow the trails and pitch a tent wherever you like. There are more than 500 miles of dirt roads, two huge wilderness areas, and 110 miles of riding and hiking trails. Many sites can be seen from paved roads, but some require driving on dirt roads, for which rangers recommend you use a four-wheel-drive vehicle. When you do leave the pavement, carry the appropriate supplies: a cell phone (which may be unreliable in some areas), a shovel and other tools, flares, blankets, and plenty of water. The canyons are susceptible to flash flooding, so inquire about weather conditions (even on sunny days) before entering. **■ TIP→ Borrego resorts, restaurants, and the state park have Wi-Fi, but the service is spotty at best. If you need to talk to someone in the area, it's best to find a phone with a landline.**

Stop by the **visitor center** to get oriented, to pick up a park map, and to learn about weather, road, and wildlife conditions. Designed to keep cool during the desert's blazing-hot summers, the center is built underground, beneath a demonstration desert garden containing examples of most of the native flora and a little pupfish pond. Displays inside the center illustrate the natural history of the area. Picnic tables are scattered throughout, making this a good place to linger and enjoy the view. ✉ *Visitor Center, 200 Palm Canyon Dr., Hwy. S22* ☎ *760/767–4205, 760/767–4684 wildflower hotline* 🌐 *www.parks.ca.gov* 🎫 *Free; day-use parking in campground areas $10* ☞ *Make a campground reservation at: reservecalifornia.com.*

★ Galleta Meadows

PUBLIC ART | FAMILY | At Galleta Meadows, camels, llamas, saber-toothed tigers, tortoises, and monumental gomphotherium (a sort of ancient elephant) appear to roam the Earth again. These life-size bronze figures are of prehistoric animals whose fossils can be found in the Borrego Badlands. The collection of more than 130 sculptures, created by Ricardo Breceda, was commissioned by the late Dennis Avery, who installed the works of art on property he owned for the entertainment of locals and visitors. Maps are available from Borrego Springs Chamber of Commerce. ✉ *Borrego Springs Rd., from Christmas Circle to Henderson Canyon* ☎ *760/767–5555* 🎫 *Free.*

🍴 Restaurants

The Arches

$$$ | MODERN AMERICAN | On the edge of the Borrego Springs Resort's golf course, set beneath a canopy of grapefruit trees, The Arches is a pleasant place to eat. For breakfast you'll find burritos alongside French toast, omelets, and eggs Benedict; lunch (best enjoyed on the patio) and dinner options include sandwiches and salads, as well as hearty pasta, seafood, grilled meats, and fish entrées. **Known for:** light fare; nightly specials; popular happy hour. [$] *Average main: $27* ✉ *1112 Tilting T Dr.* ☎ *760/767–5700*

🌐 *www.borregospringsresort.com/dining.asp* 🕑 *Summer hrs vary; call ahead.*

Carlee's Place

$$ | AMERICAN | Sooner or later most visitors to Borrego Springs wind up at Carlee's Place for a drink and a bite to eat, drawn by an extra-long menu with everything from burgers, salads, and sandwiches to seafood dishes and prime rib. It's an all-American place, where your server might call you "honey" while setting a huge steak in front of you, and fellow diners might play pool and dance to jukebox music. **Known for:** down-home atmosphere; martinis and classic cocktails; everything made from scratch. [$] *Average main: $25* ✉ *660 Palm Canyon Dr.* ☎ *760/767–3262* 🌐 *www.carleesplace.com.*

Carmelita's Mexican Grill and Cantina

$ | MEXICAN | A friendly, family-run eatery tucked into a back corner of what is called "The Mall," Carmelita's draws diners all day, whether it's for a hearty breakfast, a cooked-to-order enchilada or burrito, or just a brew or margarita at the bar. The menu lists typical combination plates (enchiladas, burritos, tamales, and tacos). **Known for:** dog-friendly patio; house-made masa dough and salsas; full bar with sports TVs. [$] *Average main: $15* ✉ *575 Palm Canyon Dr.* ☎ *760/767–5666* 🌐 *www.facebook.com/carmelitasborrego.*

Coyote Steakhouse

$$$ | MODERN AMERICAN | This upscale restaurant at the Palms at Indian Head hotel caters to those who want a fancy dinner, particularly hunks of filet mignon or rack of lamb served at candlelit tables with white tablecloths overlooking the pool. Pet owners will appreciate the canine menu, whose treats include house-made peanut-butter dog cookies. **Known for:** romantic candlelit dining room; pork tenderloin and prime rib; classic mid-century setting. [$] *Average main: $30* ✉ *2220 Hoberg Rd.* ☎ *760/767–7788* 🌐 *www.thepalmsatindianhead.com* 🕑 *No breakfast or lunch.*

Los Jilberto's Taco Shop

$ | MEXICAN | A casual local favorite for affordable Mexican dishes, Jilberto's serves up big burritos and meaty enchiladas. **Known for:** authentic Mexican dishes cooked to order; all-day breakfast menu; reasonable prices. [$] *Average main: $12* ✉ *655 Palm Canyon Dr.* ☎ *760/767–1008* 🌐 *www.losjilbertostacoshop.com* 💳 *No credit cards.*

Hotels

Borrego Springs Resort & Spa

$$ | RESORT | The large rooms at this quiet resort are set around a swimming pool and come with either a shaded balcony or a patio with desert views. **Pros:** tennis courts and bikes available; good desert views from most rooms; close to sculpture gardens. **Cons:** rooms slightly dated; average service; breakfast not included. [$] *Rooms from: $209* ✉ *1112 Tilting T Dr.* ☎ *760/767–5700, 888/826–7734* 🌐 *www.borregospringsresort.com* 🔑 *100 rooms* 🍴 *No meals.*

★ **Borrego Valley Inn**

$$$ | B&B/INN | Those looking for desert landscapes and some stargazing—guests must be 21 or older—may enjoy the adobe Southwestern-style buildings here that house spacious rooms, which boasts plenty of natural light, original art, pine beds, and corner fireplaces. **Pros:** swim under the stars in the clothing-optional pool; exquisite desert gardens; breakfast included. **Cons:** no kids and no pets; rooms could use sprucing up; service inconsistent. [$] *Rooms from: $285* ✉ *405 Palm Canyon Dr.* ☎ *760/767–0311, 800/333–5810* 🌐 *www.borregovalleyinn.com* 🔑 *15 rooms* 🍴 *Free breakfast.*

★ **La Casa Del Zorro**

$$ | RESORT | FAMILY | The draws at this desert hideaway a short drive from Anza Borrego State Park include three guest-only pools, a hot tub, five night-lit tennis courts and two pickleball courts, a yoga studio, a spa, a restaurant, and the lively Fox Den Bar. The 42-acre property pays tribute to its surroundings with a cactus garden, a firepit, and two tall, welded-metal animal sculptures by local artist Ricardo Breceda. **Pros:** private pool or hot tub in many casitas; 26 pools (including a 25-meter lap pool) and 14 water features; on-site spa, bar, and restaurant. **Cons:** service can be spotty; remote desert location; occasional strong desert winds sweep sand across the property. [$] *Rooms from: $189* ✉ *3845 Yaqui Pass Rd.* ☎ *760/767–0100* 🌐 *www.lacasadelzorro.com* 🛏 *63 units* 🍴 *No meals.*

Activities

GOLF

★ Rams Hill Golf Club

GOLF | Originally an exclusive, private course that fell into disrepair, the Tom Fazio–designed Rams Hill was resurrected and reopened in 2014. It's now consistently ranked as one of the top courses in California, with exceptional height variations, streams, waterfalls, and expansive views from its hilltop perch to the desert below. ✉ *1881 Rams Hill Rd.* ☎ *760/767–3500* 🌐 *www.ramshill.com* ⛳ *18 holes, 7232 yds, par 72* ☞ *From $120. Closed June–Oct.*

Shopping

Borrego Outfitters

CONVENIENCE/GENERAL STORES | This contemporary general store stocks high-end outdoor gear, hiking essentials, personal care items from Burt's Bees, footwear from Teva and Merrill, swimsuits, and tabletop items. You can browse through racks of clothing and piles of hats, all suited to the desert climate. ✉ *579 Palm Canyon Dr.* ☎ *760/767–3502* 🌐 *www.borregooutfitters.com.*

Salton Sea

29 miles east of Borrego Springs; 30 miles southeast of Indio.

The Salton Sea, one of the largest inland seas on Earth, is the product of both natural and artificial forces. The sea occupies the Salton Basin, a remnant of prehistoric Lake Cahuilla. Over the centuries, the Colorado River flooded the basin, and the water drained into the Gulf of California. In 1905, a flood once again filled the Salton Basin, but the exit to the gulf was blocked by sediment. The floodwaters remained in the basin, creating a saline lake 228 feet below sea level and about 35 miles long and 15 miles wide, with a surface area of nearly 380 square miles. The sea, which lies along the Pacific Flyway, supports 400 species of birds. Fishing for tilapia, boating, camping, and bird-watching are popular activities year-round.

GETTING HERE AND AROUND

Salton Sea State Recreation Area includes about 14 miles of coastline on the northeastern shore of the sea, about 30 miles south of Indio via Highway 111. The Sonny Bono Salton Sea National Wildlife Refuge fills the southernmost tip of the sea's shore. To reach it from the recreation area, continue south about 60 miles to Niland; continue south to Sinclair Road, and turn west following the road to the Refuge Headquarters.

Sights

Salton Sea State Recreation Area

NATIONAL/STATE PARK | **FAMILY** | This huge recreation area on the sea's north shore draws thousands each year to its playgrounds, hiking trails, fishing spots, and boat launches. Ranger-guided bird walks take place on Saturday; you'll see migrating and native birds including Canada geese, pelicans, and shorebirds. ✉ *100–225 State Park Rd., North Shore*

☏ 760/393–3059, 760/393–3810 visitor center ⊕ www.parks.ca.gov 🖾 $7.

Sonny Bono Salton Sea National Wildlife Refuge

NATURE PRESERVE | The 2,200-acre wildlife refuge here, on the Pacific Flyway, is a wonderful spot for viewing migratory birds. There's an observation deck where you can watch Canada geese, and along the trails you might view eared grebes, burrowing owls, great blue herons, ospreys, and yellow-footed gulls. ⚠ **Though the scenery is beautiful, the waters here give off an unpleasant odor, and the New River, which empties into the sea, is quite toxic.** ✉ 906 W. Sinclair Rd., Calipatria ☏ 760/348–5278 ⊕ www.fws.gov/refuge/sonny_bono_salton_sea/ 🖾 Free ⊘ Closed weekends Mar.–Oct.

Desert Hot Springs

9 miles north of Palm Springs.

Desert Hot Springs's famous mineral waters, thought by some to have curative powers, bubble up at temperatures of 90°F to 148°F and flow into the wells of more than 40 hotel spas.

GETTING HERE AND AROUND

Desert Hot Springs lies due north of Palm Springs. Take Gene Autry Trail north to I–10, where the street name changes to Palm. Continue north to Pierson Boulevard, the town's center.

Sights

Cabot's Pueblo Museum

MUSEUM | Cabot Yerxa, the man who found the spring that made Desert Hot Springs famous, built a quirky, four-story, 35-room pueblo between 1939 and his death in 1965. Now a museum run by the city, the Hopi-inspired adobe structure is filled with memorabilia of Yerxa's time as a homesteader; his encounters with Hollywood celebrities at the nearby Bar-H Ranch; his expedition to the Alaskan gold

rush; and many other events. The home, much of it crafted out of materials Yerxa recycled from the desert, can only be seen on hour-long tours. Outside, walk the grounds to a lookout with amazing desert views. ✉ 67–616 E. Desert View Ave., at Eliseo Rd. ☏ 760/329–7610 ⊕ www.cabotsmuseum.org 🖾 Grounds-only ticket $5, pueblo-tour ticket $13 ⊘ Closed Sun.–Wed. ☞ Tours every ½-hr 9–11:30 and 1:30–2:30.

Hotels

Two Bunch Palms

$$$ | **RESORT** | This adults-only hotel on a gorgeous, 72-acre property with stunning views of Mt. San Jacinto provides a luxurious and relaxing experience, with access to natural hot springs. **Pros:** on-site restaurant serves breakfast, lunch, and dinner; fresh juice bar open all day; full-service spa, popular since the 1940s. **Cons:** some rooms have no TV; no pets allowed; minimum age 18. 💲 Rooms from: $349 ✉ 67425 Two Bunch Palms Trail ☏ 760/676–5000 ⊕ twobunchpalms.com ➷ 68 rooms ⧦ No meals.

Yucca Valley

21 miles northeast of Desert Hot Springs.

One of the high desert's fastest-growing cities, Yucca Valley is emerging as a bedroom community for people who work as far away as Ontario, 85 miles to the west. Here, you can shop for necessities, get your car serviced, grab coffee, purchase vintage furnishings, and chow down at fast-food outlets. Just up Pioneertown Road, you'll find the most-talked-about dining establishment in the desert: Pappy & Harriet's, the famed performance venue that hosts big-name talent.

GETTING HERE AND AROUND

The drive to Yucca Valley on Highway 62/Twentynine Palms Highway passes through the Painted Hills and drops down into a valley. Take Pioneertown Road north to the Old West outpost.

ESSENTIALS

VISITOR INFORMATION California Welcome Center Yucca Valley. ✉ *56711 Twentynine Palms Hwy.* ☎ *760/365–5464* 🌐 *www.californiawelcomecenter.com.* **Yucca Valley Chamber of Commerce.** ✉ *56711 Twentynine Palms Hwy.* ☎ *760/365–6323* 🌐 *www.yuccavalley.org.*

Sights

Hi-Desert Nature Museum

MUSEUM | **FAMILY** | Natural and cultural history of the Morongo Basis and High Desert are the focus here. A small live-animal display includes scorpions, snakes, lizards, and small mammals. You'll also find gems and minerals, fossils from the Paleozoic era, taxidermy, and Native American artifacts. There's also a children's area and art exhibits. ✉ *Yucca Valley Community Center, 57090 Twentynine Palms Hwy.* ☎ *760/369–7212* 🌐 *hidesertnaturemuseum.org* 🎟 *Free* 🕒 *Closed Sun.–Tues.*

Pioneertown

TOWN | In 1946, Roy Rogers, Gene Autry, the Sons of the Pioneers (the music group for which the town is named), and Russ Hayden built Pioneertown, an 1880s-style Wild West movie set complete with hitching posts, a saloon, and an OK Corral. You can stroll past wooden and adobe storefronts and feel like you're back in the Old West. Pappy & Harriet's Pioneertown Palace, now the town's top draw, has evolved into a hip venue for indie and mainstream performers such as Dengue Fever, Neko Case, and Robert Plant. ✉ *53688 Pioneertown Rd., Pioneertown* ✣ *4 miles north of Yucca Valley* 🌐 *pappyandharriets.com.*

Restaurants

Frontier Café

$ | **CAFÉ** | A cozy coffeehouse with a counterculture vibe, Frontier is a good place to stop before heading into the park or up to Pioneertown. Fill up on a breakfast bagel or fresh-baked muffin paired with a coffee drink, and pick up a salad, hot or cold sandwich, and dessert for lunch. **Known for:** fresh bakery items; vegan, veggie, and gluten-free options; daily specials. [$] *Average main: $12* ✉ *55844 Twentynine Palms Hwy.* ☎ *760/820–1360* 🌐 *www.cafefrontier.com* 🕒 *No dinner.*

★ Pappy & Harriet's Pioneertown Palace

$$ | **AMERICAN** | **FAMILY** | Smack in the middle of what looks like the set of a Western is this cozy saloon where you can have dinner, relax over a drink at the bar, and catch some great indie bands or legendary artists—Leon Russell, Lorde, Paul McCartney, and Robert Plant have all played here. Pappy & Harriet's may be in the middle of nowhere, but you'll need reservations for dinner on weekends. **Known for:** live music several days/nights a week; Tex-Mex, Santa Maria–style barbecue; fun and lively atmosphere. [$] *Average main: $25* ✉ *53688 Pioneertown Rd., Pioneertown* ☎ *760/365–5956* 🌐 *www.pappyandharriets.com* 🕒 *Closed Tues. and Wed.*

Hotels

Pioneertown Motel

$$ | **HOTEL** | Built in 1946 as a bunkhouse for Western film stars shooting in Pioneertown, this motel sticks close to its roots: its clean rooms are rustic and modern, with Western-style accents and exposed-wood-beam ceilings. **Pros:** Western movie time warp; great stargazing; surrounded by mesas and protected land. **Cons:** no frills; small rooms; hot in summer. [$] *Rooms from: $180* ✉ *5040 Curtis Rd., Pioneertown* ☎ *760/365–7001* 🌐 *www.pioneertown-motel.com* 🔑 *19 rooms* 🍴 *No meals.*

Chapter 8

JOSHUA TREE NATIONAL PARK

8

Updated by
Cheryl Crabtree

⛺ Camping	🛏 Hotels	🏃 Activities	👁 Scenery	👥 Crowds
★★★★★	★★★★☆	★★★★★	★★★★★	★★★★☆

WELCOME TO JOSHUA TREE NATIONAL PARK

TOP REASONS TO GO

★ **Rock climbing:** Joshua Tree is a world-class site with challenges for climbers of just about every skill level.

★ **Peace and quiet:** Roughly two hours from Los Angeles, this great wilderness is the ultimate escape from technology.

★ **Stargazing:** You'll be mesmerized by the Milky Way flowing across the summer sky. For spectacular natural fireworks, visit in mid-August during the Perseid meteor shower and watch shooting stars streak overhead.

★ **Wildflowers:** In spring, the hillsides explode in a patchwork of yellow, blue, pink, and white.

★ **Sunsets:** Twilight is a magical time here, especially during the winter, when the setting sun casts a golden glow on the mountains.

1 Park Boulevard. Drive the paved loop road between the west and north entrances to explore many of the park's main sights. Crawl between the big rocks at Hidden Valley, and you'll understand why this boulder-strewn area near the park's west entrance was once a cattle rustlers' hideout.

2 Keys View Road. Keys View is the park's most dramatic overlook—on clear days you can see Signal Mountain in Mexico.

3 Highway 62. Spot wildlife at Black Rock and Indian Cove (you might spy a desert tortoise). Near the park's north entrance, walk the nature trail around Oasis of Mara, which the first settlers, the Serrano, dubbed "the place of little springs and much grass."

4 Pinto Basin Road. Pull out binoculars at Cottonwood Spring, one of the best birding spots in the park. Come to Cholla Cactus Garden in the late afternoon, when the spiky stalks of the bigelow (jumping) cholla cactus are backlit against an intense blue sky.

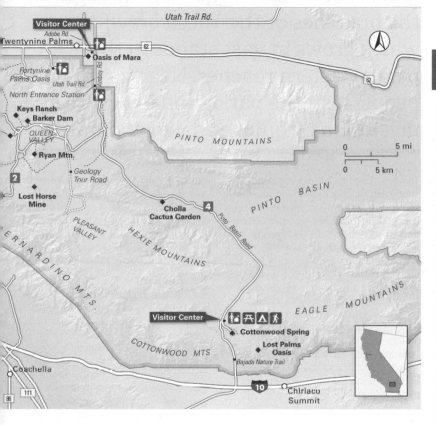

Joshua Tree teems with fascinating landscapes and life-forms, including its namesake trees. Dagger-like tufts grace the branches of the *Yucca brevifolia*, which grows in vast stands in the park's western reaches. Nearly 3 million people visit the park annually, but it's mysteriously quiet at dawn and dusk.

The park occupies a remote area in southeastern California, where two distinct ecosystems meet: the arid Mojave Desert and the sparsely vegetated Colorado Desert—part of the Sonoran Desert, which stretches across California, Arizona, and northern Mexico. Humans have inhabited the area for at least 5,000 years, starting with the Pinto and other Native American cultures. Cattlemen, miners, and homesteaders arrived in the 1800s and early 1900s. By the 1920s, new roads lured developers and others. Pasadena resident and plant enthusiast Minerva Hoyt visited the desert often and witnessed reckless poaching and pillaging of cacti and other plants. She spearheaded studies to prove the value of regional plants and wildlife. Thanks to her dedicated efforts, Joshua Tree National Monument (825,000 acres) was established in 1936.

The 29 Palms Corporation deeded part of the historic Oasis of Mara to the National Park Service in 1950, and the monument became an official national park on October 31, 1994. Today the park encompasses about 800,000 acres (nearly 600,000 is designated wilderness). Elevation ranges from 536 feet to the peak of 5,814-foot Quail Mountain. The diverse habitats within the park protect more than 800 plant, 250 bird, and 57 mammal species, including the desert bighorn sheep and 46 reptile species, such as the endangered desert tortoise. The park also preserves numerous archaeological sites and historic structures.

You can experience Joshua Tree National Park on several levels. Even on a short excursion along Park Boulevard between the Joshua Tree entrance station and Oasis of Mara, you'll see the essence of North American desert scenery—including a staggering abundance of flora along a dozen self-guided nature trails. You'll also see remnants of homesteads from a century ago, now mostly abandoned and wind-worn. If rock climbing is your passion, this is the place for you: boulder-strewn mountaintops and slopes beckon. Nightfall brings opportunities for stellar stargazing—Joshua Tree was designated an official International Dark Sky Park in 2017. Though trails are closed after sunset, you can park at any of the road pullouts and check out the sparkling shows above. Joshua Tree National Park is a pristine wilderness where you can enjoy a solitary stroll along a trail and commune with nature. Be sure to take some time to explore on your own and enjoy the peace and quiet.

AVERAGE HIGH/LOW TEMPERATURES					
JAN.	**FEB.**	**MAR.**	**APR.**	**MAY**	**JUNE**
62/32	65/37	72/40	80/50	90/55	100/65
JULY	**AUG.**	**SEPT.**	**OCT.**	**NOV.**	**DEC.**
105/70	101/78	96/62	85/55	72/40	62/31

Planning

When to Go

October through May, when the desert is cooler, is when most visitors arrive. Daytime temperatures range from the mid-70s in December and January to mid-90s in October and May. Lows can dip to near freezing in midwinter, and you may even encounter snow at the higher elevations. Summers can be torrid, with daytime temperatures reaching 110°F.

Getting Here and Around

AIR

Palm Springs International Airport is the closest major air gateway to Joshua Tree National Park. It's about 45 miles from the park. The drive from Los Angeles International Airport to Joshua Tree takes about two to three hours.

CAR

An isolated island of pristine wilderness—a rarity these days—Joshua Tree National Park is within a short drive of 11 million Southern California residents. Most visitors, in fact, make the two- to three-hour drive from the Los Angeles area to enjoy a weekend of solitude in 792,726 acres of untouched desert. The urban sprawl of Palm Springs (home to the nearest airport) is 45 miles away, but gateway towns Joshua Tree, Yucca Valley, and Twentynine Palms are just north of the park. If you're staying in the Palm Springs area, you can enjoy the highlights of the park in one day, including a stop for a picnic at a scenic spot. Within the

park, passenger cars are fine for paved areas, but you'll need four-wheel drive for many of the rugged backcountry roadways. At the park's most popular sites, parking is limited. Joshua Tree does not have public transportation.

■ TIP➔ If you'd prefer not to drive, most Palm Springs area hotels can arrange a half- or full-day tour that hits the highlights of Joshua Tree National Park. But you'll need to spend two or three days camping here to truly experience the quiet beauty of the desert.

Park Essentials

ACCESSIBILITY

Black Rock Canyon and Jumbo Rocks campgrounds have one accessible campsite each. Nature trails at Oasis of Mara, Bajada, Keys View, and Cap Rock are accessible. Some trails at roadside viewpoints can be negotiated by those with limited mobility.

PARK FEES AND PERMITS

Park admission is $30 per car; $15 per person on foot, bicycle, or horse; and $25 per person by motorcycle. The Joshua Tree Pass, good for one year, is $55.

PARK HOURS

The park is open every day, around the clock, but visitor centers are staffed from approximately 8 am to 5 pm. The park is in the Pacific time one.

CELL PHONE RECEPTION

Cell phones don't work in most areas of the park, and there are no telephones in its interior.

Joshua Tree in One Day

After stocking up on water, snacks, and lunch in Yucca Valley or Joshua Tree (you won't find any supplies inside the park), begin your visit at the **Joshua Tree Visitor Center**, where you can pick up maps and peruse exhibits to get acquainted with what awaits you. Enter the park itself at the nearby **West Entrance Station**, and continue driving along the highly scenic and well-maintained **Park Boulevard**. Stop first at **Hidden Valley** to relax at the picnic area or hike the easy, mile-long loop trail. After a few more miles, turn left onto the spur road to the trailhead for the **Barker Dam Nature Trail**. Walk the easy 1.1-mile loop to view a water tank ranchers built to quench their cattle's thirst; along the way, you'll spot birds and a handful of cactus varieties. Return to Park Boulevard and head south; you'll soon leave the main road again for the drive to **Keys View**. The easy loop trail here is only ¼ mile, but the views extend for miles in every direction—look for the San Andreas Fault, the Salton Sea, and nearby mountains. Return to Park Boulevard, where you'll find **Cap Rock**, another short loop trail winding amid rock formations and Joshua trees.

Continuing along Park Boulevard, the start of the 18-mile self-guided **Geology Tour Road** will soon appear on your right. A brochure outlining its 16 stops is available at visitor centers; note that the round-trip will take about two hours, and high-clearance, four-wheel-drive vehicles are recommended after stop 9. ■ TIP➜ Do not attempt if it has recently rained. Back on Park Boulevard, you'll soon arrive at the aptly named **Skull Rock**. This downright spooky formation is next to the parking lot; a nearby trailhead marks the beginning of a 1.7-mile nature trail. End your day with a stop at the **Visitor Center** in Twentynine Palms, where you can stroll through the historic **Oasis of Mara**, popular with area settlers. ■ TIP➜ Reverse the itinerary to avoid long lines of cars at the Joshua Tree entrance on weekends and anytime during high season. The 29 Palms entrance is just 15 miles east, and is usually less crowded, so precious parking spots are more likely to be available.

Hotels

Area lodging choices are limited to a few motels, chain hotels, vacation rentals, and several upscale establishments in the gateway towns. In general, most offer few amenities and are modestly priced. For a more extensive range of lodging options, you'll need to head to Palm Springs and the surrounding desert resort communities. Book ahead for the spring wildflower season—reservations may be difficult to obtain then.

Restaurants

Dining options in the gateway towns around the park are extremely limited—you'll mostly find fast-food outlets and a few casual eateries in Yucca Valley and Twentynine Palms. The exception is the restaurant at 29 Palms Inn, which has an interesting California-cuisine menu that features lots of veggies. For the most part, though, plan on traveling to the Palm Springs desert resort area for a fine-dining experience.

Hotel and restaurant reviews have been shortened. For full information visit Fodors.com. Hotel prices are the lowest cost of a standard double room in high season. Restaurant prices are the average cost of a main course at dinner, or if dinner is not served, at lunch.

What It Costs

	$	$$	$$$	$$$$
RESTAURANTS				
	under $17	$17–$26	$27–$36	over $36
HOTELS				
	under $150	$150–$250	$251–$350	over $350

Tours

Big Wheel Tours

EXCURSIONS | Based in Palm Desert, Big Wheel Tours offers van excursions, jeep tours, and hiking trips through the park. Bicycle tours (road and mountain bike) are available outside the park boundary. Pickups are available at Palm Springs area hotels. ⊠ *41625 Eclectic St., Suite O-1, Palm Desert* ☎ *760/779-1837* ⊕ *www.bwbtours.com* ☎ *From $169.*

Joshua Tree Adventures

GUIDED TOURS | A local family operates this well-respected tour company, which offers a range of customized private outings, from hikes and scenic tours to full- and multiday hike-and-climb combinations. ⊠ *61622 El Cajon Dr., Joshua Tree* ☎ *802/673-4385* ⊕ *jtreeadventures. com* ☎ *From $70.*

★ Keys Ranch Tour

GUIDED TOURS | A guide takes you through the former home of a family that homesteaded here for 60 years. In addition to the ranch, a workshop, store, and schoolhouse are still standing, and the grounds are strewn with vehicles and mining equipment. The 90-minute tour, which begins at the Keys Ranch gate,

tells the history of the family that built the ranch. Tickets are $10, and reservations are required. ⊠ *Keys Ranch gate* ☎ *760/367-5522* ⊕ *www.nps.gov/jotr.*

Mojave Guides

SPECIAL-INTEREST | Led by resident and certified climbing instructor Seth Pettit, a team of expert guides provides customized half-, full-, and multiday technical rock-climbing courses for everyone from beginners to experts. ⊠ *Joshua Tree* ☎ *760/820-2806* ⊕ *www.mojaveguides. com* ☎ *From $100.*

Twentynine Palms Astronomy Club

SPECIAL-INTEREST | Book a private night sky experience for 2 to 10 people led by astrophotographer Steve Caron and others who have a passion for sharing the night sky. They bring high-powered telescopes and other equipment to a location of your choice in the Morongo Basin—from Morongo Valley in the west to Wonder Valley in the east, plus Pioneertown and Landers. ⊠ *Twentynine Palms* ☎ *760/401-3004* ⊕ *www.29palmsastronomy.org* ☎ *From $250 for a 2-hr session.*

Visitor Information

CONTACTS Joshua Tree National Park. ⊠ *74485 National Park Dr., Twentynine Palms* ☎ *760/367-5522* ⊕ *www.nps.gov/jotr.*

Park Boulevard

Well-paved Park Boulevard—the park's main artery—loops between the west entrance near the town of Joshua Tree and the north entrance just south of Twentynine Palms. If you have time only for a short visit, driving Park Boulevard is your best choice. It traverses the most scenic portions of Joshua Tree in the park's high-desert section. Along with some sweeping desert views, you'll see jumbles of splendid boulder formations, stands of Joshua trees, and Hidden Valley and Barker Dam, remnants of the area's wild and woolly past. From the Oasis Visitor Center, drive south. After about 5 miles, the road forks; turn right and head west toward Jumbo Rocks (clearly marked with a road sign).

Sights

HISTORIC SIGHTS
Hidden Valley
NATURE SITE | FAMILY | This legendary cattle-rustlers' hideout is set among big boulders along a 1-mile loop trail. Kids love to scramble on and around the rocks. There are shaded picnic tables here. *⊠ Park Blvd. ⊹ 14 miles south of west entrance.*

★ Keys Ranch
HOUSE | This 150-acre ranch, which once belonged to William and Frances Keys and is now on the National Historic Register, illustrates one of the area's most successful attempts at homesteading. The couple raised five children under extreme desert conditions. Most of the original buildings, including the house, school, store, and workshop, have been restored to the way they were when William died in 1969. The only way to see the ranch is on one of the 90-minute walking tours, usually offered Friday–Sunday, October–May and weekends in summer; reservations are required. *⊠ Joshua Tree National Park ⊹ 2 miles north of Barker Dam Rd. ☎ 877/444–6777 ⊕ www.nps.gov/jotr/planyourvisit/ranch-tour.htm ⊠ $10, reservations through recreation.gov.*

SCENIC STOPS
Barker Dam
DAM | Built around 1900 by ranchers and miners to hold water for cattle and mining operations, the dam now collects rainwater and is a good place to spot wildlife such as the elusive bighorn

sheep. *⊠ Barker Dam Rd. ⊹ Off Park Blvd., 10 miles south of west entrance.*

TRAILS
Hidden Valley Trail
TRAIL | FAMILY | Crawl through the rocks surrounding Hidden Valley to see where cattle rustlers supposedly hung out on this 1-mile loop. *Easy. ⊠ Joshua Tree National Park ⊹ Trailhead: At Hidden Valley Picnic Area.*

★ Ryan Mountain Trail
TRAIL | The payoff for hiking to the top of 5,461-foot Ryan Mountain is one of the best panoramic views of Joshua Tree. From here, you can see Mt. San Jacinto, Mt. San Gorgonio, Lost Horse Valley, and the Pinto Basin. You'll need two to three hours to complete the 3-mile round-trip with 1,000-plus feet of elevation gain. *Moderate. ⊠ Joshua Tree National Park ⊹ Trailhead: At Ryan Mountain parking area, 13 miles southeast of park's west entrance, or Sheep Pass, 16 miles southwest of Oasis Visitor Center.*

Skull Rock Trail
TRAIL | The 1.7-mile loop guides hikers through boulder piles, desert washes, and a rocky alley. It's named for what is perhaps the park's most famous rock formation, which resembles the eye sockets and nasal cavity of a human skull. Access the trail from within Jumbo Rocks Campground or from a small parking area on the highway just east of the campground. *Easy. ⊠ Joshua Tree National Park ⊹ Trailhead: At Jumbo Rocks Campground.*

Split Rock Loop Trail
TRAIL | Experience rocks, trees, and geological wonders along this 2½-mile loop trail (including a short spur to Face Rock) through boulder fields and oak and pine woodlands up to Joshua tree stands. *Moderate. ⊠ Joshua Tree National Park ⊹ Trailhead: Along dirt road off main Park Blvd. (signs point the way).*

VISITOR CENTERS
Joshua Tree Visitor Center
INFO CENTER | This visitor center has maps and interesting exhibits illustrating park geology, cultural and historic sites, and hiking and rock-climbing activities. There's also a small bookstore and café. Restrooms with flush toilets are on the premises. ⊠ *6554 Park Blvd., Joshua Tree* ☎ *760/366–1855* ⊕ *www.nps.gov/jotr.*

Keys View Road

Keys View Road travels south from Park Boulevard from Cap Rock up to Keys View, the best vista point in the park. If you plan to hike up to historic Lost Horse Mine, you'll find the trailhead along the way.

Sights

HISTORIC SIGHTS
Lost Horse Mine

MINE | This historic mine, which produced 10,000 ounces of gold and 16,000 ounces of silver between 1894 and 1931, was among Southern California's most productive mines. The 10-stamp mill is considered one of the best preserved of its type in the park system. The site is accessed via a fairly strenuous, 4-mile, round-trip hike. Mind the park warnings, and don't enter any mine in Joshua Tree. ⊠ *Keys View Rd.* ✛ *About 15 miles south of west entrance.*

SCENIC STOPS
★ Keys View

VIEWPOINT | At 5,185 feet, this point affords a sweeping view of the Santa Rosa Mountains and Coachella Valley, the San Andreas Fault, the peak of 11,500-foot Mt. San Gorgonio, the shimmering surface of Salton Sea, and—on a rare clear day—Signal Mountain in Mexico. Sunrise and sunset are magical times, when the light throws rocks and trees into high relief before bathing the hills in brilliant shades of red, orange, and gold. ⊠ *Keys View Rd.* ✛ *16 miles south of park's west entrance.*

TRAILS
Cap Rock

TRAIL | This ½-mile, wheelchair-accessible loop—named after a boulder that sits atop a huge rock formation like a cap—winds through other fascinating rock formations and has signs that explain the geology of the Mojave Desert. *Easy.* ⊠ *Joshua Tree National Park* ✛ *Trailhead: Keys View Rd. near junction with Park Blvd.*

Highway 62

Highway 62 stretches along the northern border of the park, from Yucca Valley in the West and Twentynine Palms in the east. Visitors can access the Black Rock, Indian Cove, Fortynine Palms, and Oasis of Mara sections of the park off this road, as well as the main visitor centers and park entrances in Joshua Tree and Twentynine Palms.

Sights

SCENIC STOPS
Fortynine Palms Oasis

NATIVE SITE | A short drive off Highway 62, this site is a bit of a preview of what the park's interior has to offer: stands of fan palms, interesting petroglyphs, and evidence of fires built by early Native Americans. Because animals frequent this area, you may spot a coyote, bobcat, or roadrunner. ⊠ *End of Canyon Rd.* ✛ *4 miles west of Twentynine Palms.*

Indian Cove

RESTAURANT—SIGHT | The view from here is of rock formations that draw thousands of climbers to the park each year. This isolated area is reached via Twentynine Palms Highway. ⊠ *End of Indian Cove Rd.*

Did You Know?

Found only in Arizona, California, Nevada, and Utah, the Joshua tree (*Yucca brevifolia*) is actually a member of the agave family. Native Americans used the Joshua tree's hearty foliage like leather, forming it into everyday items like baskets and shoes. Later, early settlers used its core and limbs for building fences to contain their livestock.

TRAILS
Hi-View Nature Trail
TRAIL | This 1.3-mile loop climbs nearly to the top of 4,500-foot Summit Peak. The views of nearby Mt. San Gorgonio (snow-capped in winter) make the moderately steep journey worth the effort. You can pick up a pamphlet describing the vegetation you'll see along the way at any visitor center. *Moderate.* ⊠ *Joshua Tree National Park* ✛ *Trailhead: ½ mile west of Black Rock Canyon Campground.*

Indian Cove Trail
TRAIL | Look for lizards and roadrunners along this ½-mile loop that follows a desert wash. A walk along this well-signed trail reveals signs of Native American habitation, animals, and flora such as desert willow and yucca. *Easy.* ⊠ *Joshua Tree National Park* ✛ *Trailhead: At west end of Indian Cove Campground.*

Oasis of Mara Trail
TRAIL | A stroll along this short, wheel-chair-accessible trail, located just outside the visitor center, reveals how early settlers took advantage of this oasis, which was first settled by the Serrano tribe. *Mara* means "place of little springs and much grass" in their language. The Serrano, who farmed the oasis until the mid-1850s, planted one palm tree for each male baby born during the first year of the settlement. *Easy.* ⊠ *Joshua Tree National Park* ✛ *Trailhead: At Oasis Visitor Center.*

VISITOR CENTERS
Oasis Visitor Center
INFO CENTER | Exhibits here illustrate how Joshua Tree was formed, reveal the differences between the park's two types of desert, and demonstrate how plants and animals eke out an existence in this arid climate. Take the ½-mile nature walk through the nearby Oasis of Mara, which is alive with palm trees and mesquite shrubs. Facilities include picnic tables, restrooms, and a bookstore. ⊠ *74485 National Park Dr., Twentynine Palms* ☎ *760/367–5500* ⊕ *www.nps.gov/jotr.*

Pinto Basin Road

This paved road takes you from high Mojave desert to low Colorado desert. A long, slow drive, the route runs from the main part of the park to Interstate 10; it can add as much as an hour to and from Palm Springs (round-trip), but the views and roadside exhibits make it worth the extra time. From the Oasis Visitor Center, drive south. After about 5 miles, the road forks; take a left, and continue another 9 miles to the Cholla Cactus Garden, where the sun fills the cactus needles with light. Past that is the Ocotillo Patch, filled with spindly plants bearing razor-sharp thorns and, after a rain, bright green leaves and brilliant red flowers. Side trips from this route require a 4X4.

Sights

SCENIC DRIVES
Geology Tour Road
SCENIC DRIVE | Some of the park's most fascinating landscapes can be observed from this 18-mile dirt road. Parts of the journey are rough; a 4X4 vehicle is required after mile marker 9. Sights to see include a 100-year-old stone dam called Squaw Tank, defunct mines, and a large plain with an abundance of Joshua trees. There are 16 stops along the way, so give yourself about two hours to complete the round-trip trek. ⊠ *South of Park Blvd., west of Jumbo Rocks.*

SCENIC STOPS
Cholla Cactus Garden
GARDEN | This stand of bigelow cholla (sometimes called jumping cholla, because its hooked spines seem to jump at you) is best seen and photographed in late afternoon, when the backlit spiky stalks stand out against a colorful sky. ⊠ *Pinto Basin Rd.* ✛ *20 miles north of Cottonwood Visitor Center.*

Cottonwood Spring
NATIVE SITE | Home to the native Cahuilla people for centuries, this spring provided

water for travelers and early prospectors. The area, which supports a large stand of fan palms and cottonwood trees, is one of the best stops for bird-watching, as migrating birds (and bighorn sheep) rely on the water as well. A number of gold mines were located here, and the area still has some remains, including concrete pillars. ⊠ *Cottonwood Visitor Center*.

Lost Palms Oasis

TRAIL | More than 100 fan palms comprise the largest group of the exotic plants in the park. A spring bubbles from between the rocks but disappears into the sandy, boulder-strewn canyon. The 7½-mile, round-trip hike is not for everyone, and not recommended during summer months. Bring plenty of water! ⊠ *Cottonwood Visitor Center*.

Ocotillo Patch

GARDEN | Stop here for a roadside exhibit on the dramatic display made by the red-tipped succulent after even the shortest rain shower. ⊠ *Pinto Basin Rd.* ✛ *About 3 miles east of Cholla Cactus Gardens*.

TRAILS
Bajada

TRAIL | Learn all about what plants do to survive in the Colorado Desert on this ¼-mile loop. *Easy.* ⊠ *Joshua Tree National Park* ✛ *Trailhead: South of Cottonwood Visitor Center, ½ mile from park entrance*.

Mastodon Peak Trail

TRAIL | Some boulder scrambling is optional on this 3-mile hike that loops up to the 3,371-foot Mastodon Peak, and the journey rewards you with stunning views of the Salton Sea. The trail passes through a region where gold was mined from 1919 to 1932, so be on the lookout for open mines. The peak draws its name from a large rock formation that early miners believed looked like the head of a prehistoric behemoth. *Moderate.* ⊠ *Joshua Tree National Park* ✛ *Trailhead: At Cottonwood Spring Oasis*.

VISITOR CENTERS
Cottonwood Visitor Center

INFO CENTER | The south entrance is the closest to Interstate 10, the east–west highway from Los Angeles to Phoenix. Exhibits in this small center, staffed by rangers and volunteers, illustrate the region's natural history. The center also has restrooms with flush toilets. ⊠ *Cottonwood Spring, Pinto Basin Rd.* ⊕ *www.nps.gov/jotr*.

 Activities

BIKING
Covington Flats

BICYCLING | This 4-mile route takes you past impressive Joshua trees as well as pinyon pines, junipers, and areas of lush desert vegetation. It's tough going toward the end, but once you reach 5,518-foot Eureka Peak you'll have great views of Palm Springs, the Morongo Basin, and the surrounding mountains. ⊠ *Joshua Tree National Park* ✛ *Trailhead: At Covington Flats picnic area, La Contenta Rd., 10 miles south of Rte. 62.*

Pinkham Canyon and Thermal Canyon Roads

BICYCLING | This challenging 20-mile route begins at the Cottonwood Visitor Center and loops through the Cottonwood Mountains. The unpaved trail follows Smoke Tree Wash through Pinkham Canyon, rounds Thermal Canyon, and loops back to the beginning. Rough and narrow in places, the road travels through soft sand and rocky floodplains. ⊠ *Joshua Tree National Park* ✛ *Trailhead: At Cottonwood Visitor Center.*

Queen Valley

BICYCLING | This 13.4-mile network of mostly level roads winds through one of the park's most impressive groves of Joshua trees. You can also leave your bike at one of the racks placed in the area and explore on foot. ⊠ *Joshua Tree National Park* ✛ *Trailhead: At Hidden Valley Campground, and accessible opposite Geology Tour Rd. at Big Horn Pass.*

BIRD-WATCHING

Joshua Tree, located on the inland portion of the Pacific Flyway, hosts about 250 species of birds, and the park is a popular seasonal location for bird-watching. During the fall migration, which runs mid-September through mid-October, there are several reliable sighting areas. At Barker Dam you might spot white-throated swifts, several types of swallows, or red-tailed hawks. Lucy's warblers, flycatchers, and Anna's hummingbirds cruise around Cottonwood Spring, a serene palm-shaded setting; occasional ducks, herons, and egrets, as well as migrating rufous and calliope hummingbirds, wintering prairie falcons, and a resident barn owl could show up. Black Rock Canyon sees pinyon jays, while Covington Flats reliably gets mountain quail, and you may see La Conte's thrashers, ruby-crowned kinglets, and warbling vireos at either locale. Rufous hummingbirds, Pacific slope flycatchers, and various warblers are frequent visitors to Indian Cove. Lists of birds found in the park, as well as information on recent sightings, are available at visitor centers.

CAMPING

Park campgrounds, set at elevations from 3,000 to 4,500 feet, have only primitive facilities; few have drinking water. Most accept reservations up to six months in advance but only for October through Memorial Day. Campsites at Belle, Hidden Valley, and White Tank are first-come, first-served. Belle and White Tank campgrounds, and parts of Black Rock Canyon, Cottonwood, and Indian Cove campgrounds, are closed from the day after Memorial Day to September. ■TIP➔ Campgrounds fill quickly, so reserve well in advance. Also, the park may soon require reservations at all campgrounds.

Belle Campground. This small campground is popular with families as there are a number of boulders kids can scramble over and around. ⊠ *9 miles south of Oasis of Mara* ☎ *760/367–5500* ⊕ *www. nps.gov/jotr.*

Black Rock Canyon Campground. Set among juniper bushes, cholla cacti, and other desert shrubs, Black Rock Canyon is one of the park's prettiest campgrounds. ⊠ *Joshua La., south of Hwy. 62 and Hwy. 247* ☎ *877/444–6777* ⊕ *www. recreation.gov.*

Cottonwood Campground. In spring, this campground, the southernmost one in the park (and therefore often the last to fill up), is surrounded by some of the desert's finest wildflowers and is a great spot to watch the night sky. ⊠ *Pinto Basin Rd., 32 miles south of North Entrance Station* ☎ *877/444–6777* ⊕ *www.nps.gov/jotr.*

Hidden Valley Campground. This campground is a favorite with rock climbers, who make their way up valley formations that have names like the Blob, Old Woman, and Chimney Rock. ⊠ *Off Park Blvd., 20 miles southwest of Oasis of Mara* ☎ *760/367-5500* ⊕ *www.nps.gov/jotr.*

Indian Cove Campground. This is a sought-after spot for rock climbers, primarily because it lies among the 50 square miles of rugged terrain at the Wonderland of Rocks. ⊠ *Indian Cove Rd., south of Hwy. 62* ☎ *877/444–6777* ⊕ *www.nps.gov/jotr.*

Jumbo Rocks. Each campsite at this well-regarded campground tucked among giant boulders has a bit of privacy. It's a good home base for visiting many of Joshua Tree's attractions. ⊠ *Park Blvd., 11 miles from Oasis of Mara* ☎ *877/444–6777* ⊕ *www.nps.gov/jotr.*

Learn about the park's flora and fauna by attending the ranger programs.

White Tank. This small, quiet campground is popular with families because a nearby trail leads to a natural arch. ✉ *Pinto Basin Rd., 11 miles south of Oasis of Mara* ☎ *760/367–5500* ⊕ *www.nps.gov/jotr.*

EDUCATIONAL PROGRAMS

The Desert Institute at Joshua Tree National Park

COLLEGE | The nonprofit educational partner of the park offers a full schedule of lectures, classes, and hikes. Class topics include basket making, painting, and photography, while field trips include workshops on cultural history, natural science, and how to survive in the desert. ✉ *74485 National Park Dr., Twentynine Palms* ☎ *760/367–5535* ⊕ *www.joshuatree.org.*

Stargazing

COLLEGE | At Joshua Tree National Park, designated an International Dark Sky Park in 2017, you can tour the Milky Way on summer evenings using binoculars. Rangers also offer programs on some evenings when the moon isn't visible. Browse the schedule online. The park also partners with Sky's the Limit Observatory on the Utah Trail in Twentynine Palms (⊕ *www.skysthelimit29.org*); check the website for current offerings. ✉ *Cottonwood Campground Amphitheater, Oasis Visitor Center, Sky's the Limit Observatory* ⊕ *www.nps.gov/jotr/planyourvisit/calendar.htm.*

RANGER PROGRAMS

Evening Programs

TOUR—SIGHT | Rangers present 45-minute-long programs, often on Friday or Saturday evening, at Cottonwood Amphitheater, Indian Cove Amphitheater, and Jumbo Rocks Campground. Topics range from natural history to local lore. As times and days for such offerings aren't fixed, it's best to check the online schedule. ✉ *Joshua Tree National Park* 🎟 *Free.*

HIKING

There are more than 190 miles of hiking trails in Joshua Tree, ranging from ¼-mile nature trails to 35-mile treks. Some connect with each other, so you can design your own desert maze. Remember that drinking water is hard to come by—you won't find it in the park except at the entrances. Bring along at least a gallon per person for all but the shortest hikes, more if the weather is hot.

Before striking out on a hike or apparent nature trail, check out the signage. Roadside signage identifies hiking- and rock-climbing routes.

ROCK CLIMBING

With an abundance of weathered igneous boulder outcroppings, Joshua Tree is one of the nation's top winter-climbing destinations. There are more than 4,500 established routes offering a full menu of climbing experiences—from bouldering for beginners in the Wonderland of Rocks to multiple-pitch climbs at Echo Rock and Saddle Rock. The best-known climb in the park is Hidden Valley's Sports Challenge Rock. A map inside the *Joshua Tree Guide* shows locations of selected wilderness and nonwilderness climbs.

Joshua Tree Rock Climbing School

CLIMBING/MOUNTAINEERING | The school offers several programs, from one-day introductory classes to multiday programs for experienced climbers, and provides all needed equipment. Beginning classes, offered year-round on most weekends, are limited to six people age eight or older. ⊠ *Joshua Tree National Park* ☎ *760/366–4745* ⊕ *www.joshuatreerockclimbing.com* ⊠ *From $195.*

Vertical Adventures Rock Climbing School

CLIMBING/MOUNTAINEERING | About 1,000 climbers each year learn the sport in Joshua Tree National Park through this school. Classes, offered September–May, meet at a designated location in the park, and all equipment is provided. ⊠ *Joshua Tree National Park* ☎ *800/514–8785 office, 949/322–6108 mobile/text* ⊕ *www.vertical-adventures.com* ⊠ *From $165.*

What's Nearby

Joshua Tree

12 miles east of Yucca Valley.

Artists and renegades have long found solace in the small upcountry desert town of Joshua Tree, home to artsy vintage shops, cafés, and B&Bs and a gateway to Joshua Tree National Park. Those who zip through town might wonder what all the hype is about, but if you slow down and spend time chatting with the folks in this funky community, you'll find much to love.

GETTING HERE AND AROUND

Highway 62 is the main route to and through Joshua Tree. Most businesses are here or along Park Boulevard as it heads toward the park.

👁 Sights

★ Noah Purifoy Desert Art Museum of Assemblage Art

ARTS VENUE | This vast, 10-acre art installation full of "assemblage art" on a sandy tract of land in the town of Joshua Tree honors the work of artist Noah Purifoy. The sculptures blend with the spare desert in an almost postapocalyptic way. Purifoy lived most of his life in this desert until his death is 2004. He used found materials to make commentary on social issues. His art has been showcased at LACMA, J. Paul Getty Museum, MOCA, and many more. ⊠ *63030 Blair La.* ⊕ *www.noahpurifoy.com* ⊠ *Free* 🕐 *Closes at sunset.*

🍴 Restaurants

Crossroads Cafe

$$ | AMERICAN | Mexican breakfasts, chicken-cilantro soup, and hearty sandwiches are among the draws at this Joshua Tree institution for prehike breakfasts, birthday lunches, and early dinners. Taxidermied animals and beer-can lights hint at the

Did You Know?

Joshua Tree is one of the world's most popular rock-climbing and bouldering destinations, with more than 400 climbing formations (including Frigid Tower, pictured here) and 4,500 routes.

community's consciousness, while the tattooed waitresses and slew of veggie options make it clear that the Crossroads is unlike anywhere else in San Bernardino County. **Known for:** rustic wooden interior and bar; hearty and affordable meals; vegetarian and vegan dishes. [$] *Average main: $12* ✉ *61715 Twentynine Palms Hwy.* ☎ *760/366–5414* 🌐 *crossroadscafe-jtree.com.*

Twentynine Palms

12 miles east of Joshua Tree.

The main gateway town to Joshua Tree National Park, Twentynine Palms is also the location of the U.S. Marine Air Ground Task Force Training Center. You can find services, supplies, and lodging in town.

GETTING HERE AND AROUND

Highway 62 is the main route to and through Twentynine Palms. Most businesses here center on Highway 62 and Utah Trail, 3 miles north of Joshua Tree's entrance.

ESSENTIALS

VISITOR INFORMATION Twentynine Palms Visitor Center and Gallery. ✉ *73484 Twentynine Palms Hwy.* 🌐 *www.visit29.org.*

Sights

Oasis of Murals

PUBLIC ART | Twenty-six murals painted on the sides of buildings depict the history, wildlife, and landscape of Twentynine Palms. You can't miss the art on a drive around town, but you can also pick up a free map from the visitor center. ✉ *Twentynine Palms* 🌐 *www.action29palmsmurals.com.*

Sky's the Limit Observatory & Nature Center

OBSERVATORY | Run by a dedicated, local nonprofit, this 15-acre park near the northern entrance to Joshua Tree National Park educates visitors on the region's celestial and terrestial attributes. It has an observatory dome with a 14-inch telescope, nature trails that feature desert plants, a meditation garden, and an orrery (a scaled rendition of what's happening in the night sky). The public is invited to free star parties every Saturday night (except when the moon is full) and to join classes, clinics, and special programs. ✉ *9697 Utah Trail* ☎ *760/490–9561* 🌐 *www.skysthelimit29.org.*

29 Palms Art Gallery

MUSEUM | This gallery features work by local painters, sculptors, and jewelry makers inspired by the desert landscape. If you find yourself inspired as well, sign up for one of the day-long art workshops. ✉ *74055 Cottonwood Dr.* ☎ *760/367–7819* 🌐 *www.29palmsartgallery.com* 🕒 *Closed Mon.–Wed. Also closed Thurs. in summer.*

🍴 Restaurants

Campbell Hill Bakery

$ | **BAKERY** | Prepare to wait in line to order from the counter at this tiny but exceedingly popular eatery, owned and operated by professionals in the bakery business who escaped from New York City to the California high desert. Delectable loaves of bread, scones, muffins, and other sweet and savory treats take center stage, but you can also pick up sandwiches and various entrées—from beef pot pie and flatbreads to pizza and lasagna. **Known for:** hefty Cubano, Philly cheesesteak, and Italian subs; daily specials; good place to pick up food before touring the park. [$] *Average main: $12* ✉ *73491 Twentynine Palms Hwy.* ☎ *760/401–8284* 🌐 *campbellhillbakery.com* 🕒 *No dinner. Closed Sun.*

Kitchen in the Desert

$ | **AMERICAN** | This popular spot in a renovated courtyard complex with murals and mining artifacts serves comfort food with a Caribbean flair. The chef, who hails from Trinidad, creates artful dishes derived from family recipes with dashes of American and global influences—for

example, Trinidadian doubles (curried chickpeas with dahl bread, cucumbers, and tamarind sauce), Dan Dan noodles (cumin-spiced pork and soba noodles with tahini), bacon burgers, and fried Oreos and donuts for dessert. **Known for:** convenient location near the junction of Highway 62 and National Park Drive; meats grilled or smoked outdoors over a mesquite fire; vegetarian and gluten-free dishes. Ⓢ *Average main: $15* ✉ *6427 Mesquite Ave.* ☎ *760/865–0245* ⊕ *kitcheninthedesert.com* ⊘ *No lunch.*

Hotels

Campbell House

$$ | **B&B/INN** | To the wealthy pioneer who erected the stone mansion now occupied by this bed-and-breakfast, expense was no object, which is evident in the 50-foot-long, planked-maple floor in the great room, the intricate carpentry, and the huge stone fireplaces that warm the house on the rare cold night. **Pros:** elegant rooms and public spaces; access to amenities at sister property, 29 Palms Inn; great horned owls on property. **Cons:** somewhat isolated location; three-story main building doesn't have an elevator; no TVs or refrigerators in some rooms. Ⓢ *Rooms from: $165* ✉ *74744 Joe Davis Dr.* ☎ *760/367–3238* ⊕ *www.campbellhouse29palms.com* ⟿ *12 units* ⦿ *Free breakfast.*

Harmony Motel

$ | **HOTEL** | In 1987, the rock band U2 stayed at the roadside Harmony Motel—set on two acres of natural desert with onubstructed views of the mountains of Joshua Tree National Park—while posing for images to adorn their legendary album *U2: The Joshua Tree.* **Pros:** cactus gardens and nature trail; outdoor pool and hot tub; close to Fortynine Palms Oasis and Indian Cove. **Cons:** small property that books quickly; not close to restaurants or entertainment; on a busy highway. Ⓢ *Rooms from: $95* ✉ *71161 Twentynine Palms Hwy.* ☎ *760/367–3351* ⊕ *www.harmonymotel.com* ⟿ *11 units* ⦿ *No meals.*

Sunnyvale Garden Suites

$ | **HOTEL** | Bay Area retirees transformed this former 1990s condominium complex into an all-suite hotel with paths that meander through carefully tended desert gardens that have sitting areas. **Pros:** outdoor hot tub, game room, community patio with fire pit, exercise room; close to national park entrance and military base; personal attention from owners and staff. **Cons:** noise can travel through thin walls and ceilings; no breakfast included; 3 miles to nearest grocery store. Ⓢ *Rooms from: $111* ✉ *73843 Sunnyvale Dr.* ☎ *760/361–3939* ⊕ *sunnyvalesuites.com* ⟿ *21 suites* ⦿ *No meals.*

★ 29 Palms Inn

$$ | **B&B/INN** | **FAMILY** | The closest lodging to the entrance to Joshua Tree National Park, the funky 29 Palms Inn scatters a collection of adobe and wood-frame cottages, some dating back to the 1920s and 1930s, over 70 acres of grounds that include the ancient Oasis of Mara, a popular destination for birds and bird-watchers year-round. **Pros:** gracious hospitality; exceptional bird-watching; art gallery, pool, and on-site restaurant. **Cons:** rustic accommodations; limited amenities; no in-room Wi-Fi. Ⓢ *Rooms from: $140* ✉ *73950 Inn Ave.* ☎ *760/367–3505* ⊕ *www.29palmsinn.com* ⟿ *24 units* ⦿ *Free breakfast.*

Chapter 9

MOJAVE DESERT

Updated by
Cheryl Crabtree

⊙ Sights	🍴 Restaurants	🛏 Hotels	🛍 Shopping	🍸 Nightlife
★★★★★	★★☆☆☆	★☆☆☆☆	★☆☆☆☆	★☆☆☆☆

WELCOME TO MOJAVE DESERT

TOP REASONS TO GO

★ **Nostalgia:** Old neon signs, historic motels, and restored (or neglected but still striking) rail stations abound across this desert landscape. Don't miss the classic eateries along the way, including Emma Jean's Holland Burger Cafe in Victorville.

★ **Great ghost towns:** California's gold rush brought miners to the Mojave, and the towns they left behind have their own unique charms.

★ **Desert flora and fauna:** Explore the Mojave National Preserve to view Joshua trees, volcanic cinder cones, huge sand dunes, desert tortoises, and other natural wonders. Combine a visit to the Mojave with one to Death Valley to experience still more of the region's unique desert terrain.

★ **Explore ancient history:** The Mojave Desert is replete with rare petroglyphs, some dating back almost 16,000 years.

1 Lancaster. Poppies and aerospace tech (including Edwards Air Force Base) thrive in and near this western Mojave hub.

2 Red Rock Canyon State Park. Colorful formations, Native American heritage, and mining history converge in an eerily gorgeous setting.

3 Ridgecrest. A gateway to Death Valley, the northern Mojave's largest town is a welcome oasis near Trona Pinnacles and Petroglyph Canyons.

4 Randsburg. Wander the well-preserved streets of a historic mining town.

5 Victorville. Experience the Mother Road at the California Route 66 Museum.

6 Barstow. Visit the Mojave's "capital" to explore museums (many in the restored Harvey House depot) and Calico Ghost town.

7 Mojave National Preserve. Ancient lava beds, rare plants and animals, and towering dunes are among this 1.6-million-acre sanctuary's sights.

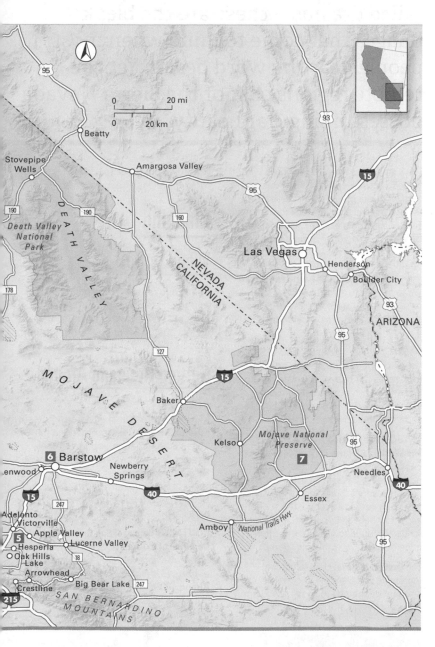

Dust and desolation, tumbleweeds and rattlesnakes, barren landscapes and failed dreams—these are the bleak images that come to mind when most people hear the word *desert*. Yet the remote regions east of the Sierra Nevada possess a singular beauty.

The vast spaces here are peppered with creosite bushes, spiky Joshua trees and cacti, undulating sand dunes, faulted mountains, and dramatic rock formations. The topography is extreme: the Mojave Desert, once part of an ancient inland sea, is one of the largest swaths of open land in Southern California, with elevations ranging from 3,000 to 5,000 feet, while Death Valley, to the north, drops to almost 300 feet below sea level and contains the lowest (and hottest) spot in North America.

Access to the Mojave is via I–40 and I–15, Highways 14 and 95, and U.S. 395. As abandoned homesteads can attest, the area is not heavily populated, with just a few communities separated by expanses in which visitors can both lose and find themselves.

MAJOR REGIONS

The Western Mojave. Lancaster, Red Rock Canyon State Park, Ridgecrest, and Randsburg are all in this vast area, where wildflowers bloom in spring and snow caps the mountain peaks year-round. The scenery is especially beautiful along U.S. 395, which runs north up to towns at the western edge of Death Valley National Park.

The Eastern Mojave. Here you'll find Victorville and Barstow, the main hubs of a region defined by majestic, wide-open spaces and one of the state's most rewarding but demanding destinations: Mojave National Preserve.

Planning

When to Go

Spring and fall are the best seasons to tour the desert. Winters are generally mild, but summers can be cruel. If you're on a budget, be aware that room rates drop as the temperatures rise.

Getting Here and Around

AIR

McCarran International (slated to be renamed Harry Reid International) in Las Vegas is the nearest airport to many eastern Mojave destinations. Hollywood Burbank is the largest and closest airport to the western Mojave region. Barstow and Inyokern airports serve small, private planes.

CONTACTS County of San Bernardino Department of Airports. ✉ *For Needles and Barstow-Daggett* ⊕ *cms.sbcounty.gov/ airports/Home.aspx.* **Hollywood Burbank Airport.** ✉ *2627 N. Hollywood Way, Burbank* ☎ *818/840–8840* ⊕ *hollywoodburbankairport.com.* **Inyokern Airport.** ✉ *1669*

Airport Rd., off Hwy. 178, 9 miles west of Ridgecrest, Inyokern ☎ *760/377–5844* ⊕ *www.inyokernairport.com.* **McCarran International Airport.** ✉ *5757 Wayne Newton Blvd., Las Vegas* ☎ *702/261–5211* ⊕ *www.mccarran.com.*

BUS

Greyhound provides bus service to Barstow and Victorville; check with the chambers of commerce about local bus service, which is generally more useful to residents than to tourists.

CAR

The major north–south route through the western Mojave is U.S. 395, which intersects with I–15 between Cajon Pass and Victorville. Farther west, Highway 14 runs north–south between Inyokern (near Ridgecrest) and Lancaster. Two major east–west routes travel through the Mojave: to the north, I–15 to Las Vegas, Nevada; to the south, I–40 to the Mojave National Preserve. At the intersection of the two interstates, in Barstow, I–15 veers south toward Victorville and Los Angeles, and I–40 gives way to Highway 58 west toward Bakersfield.

■ TIP→ **For the latest Mojave traffic and weather, tune in to the Highway Stations (98.1 FM near Barstow, 98.9 FM near Essex, and 99.7 FM near Baker).** Traffic can be especially troublesome Friday through Sunday, when thousands of Angelenos head to Las Vegas for a bit of R&R.

TRAIN

Amtrak trains traveling east and west stop in Victorville and Barstow, but the stations aren't staffed, so you'll have to purchase tickets in advance and handle your own baggage. The Barstow station is served daily by Amtrak California motor coaches that stop in Los Angeles, Bakersfield, Las Vegas, and elsewhere. Amtrak buses also stop in Lancaster and Mojave. Metrolink's Antelope Valley line travels from Los Angeles Union Station north to Burbank Airport, Palmdale, and Lancaster.

CONTACTS Metrolink. ☎ *800/371–5465* ⊕ *metrolinktrains.com.*

Restaurants

Throughout the desert, dining is a fairly simple affair. There are chain establishments in Ridgecrest, Lancaster, Victorville, and Barstow, as well as some ethnic eateries.

Hotels

Chain hotel properties and roadside motels are the desert's primary lodging options. The tourist season runs from late May through September. Reservations are rarely a problem, but it's still wise to make them.

Restaurant and hotel reviews have been shortened. For full information, visit Fodors.com. Restaurant prices are the average cost of a main course at dinner, or if dinner is not served, at lunch. Hotel prices are the lowest cost of a standard double room in high season.

What It Costs			
$	$$	$$$	$$$$
RESTAURANTS			
under $17	$17–$26	$27–$36	over $36
HOTELS			
under $150	$150–$250	$251–$350	over $350

Tours

Sierra Club

SPECIAL-INTEREST | The San Gorgonio Chapter of the Sierra Club and the chapter's Mojave Group conduct interesting field trips and desert excursions. Activities are often volunteer-run and free, but participants are sometimes required to cover parking and other expenses.

☎ 951/684–6203 ⊕ sangorgonio2.sierra-club.org ☜ Some free; fee tour prices vary.

Visitor Information

CONTACTS Bureau of Land Management. ☒ California Desert District Office, 22835 Calle San Juan De Los Lagos, Moreno Valley ☎ 951/697–5200, 760/833–7100 ⊕ www.blm.gov/office/california-desert-district-office. **California Welcome Center Barstow.** ☒ 2796 Tanger Way, Suite 100, Barstow ⊹ off Lenwood Rd. ☎ 760/253–4782 ⊕ www.visitcalifornia.com/experience/california-welcome-center-barstow/.

Lancaster

70 miles north of Los Angeles.

Points of interest around Lancaster include a state poppy reserve that bursts to life in the spring and Edwards Air Force Base, which many consider the birthplace of supersonic flight. Lancaster was founded in 1876, when the Southern Pacific Railroad arrived. Before that, several Native American tribes, some of whose descendants still live in the surrounding mountains, inhabited it. The adjacent town of Palmdale (often included with Lancaster as part of the Antelope Valley region) evolved from a sleepy agricultural community into an aerospace and defense capital when Edwards Air Force Base and U.S. Air Force Plant 42 were established after World War II.

GETTING HERE AND AROUND
From the Los Angeles basin, take Highway 14, which proceeds north to Mojave and Highway 58, a link between Bakersfield and Barstow. Regional Metrolink trains serve Lancaster from the Los Angeles area. Local transit exists, but a car is the best way to experience this area.

ESSENTIALS
VISITOR INFORMATION Antelope Valley Chambers of Commerce. ☒ 554 W. Lancaster Blvd. ☎ 661/948–4518 ⊕ www.avchambers.org. **Destination Lancaster.** ☒ 554 W. Lancaster Blvd. ☎ 661/400–0342 ⊕ www.destinationlancasterca.org.

Sights

Antelope Valley California Poppy Reserve
NATIONAL/STATE PARK | The California poppy, the state flower, can be spotted throughout the state, but this quiet park holds the densest concentration. Eight miles of trails wind through 1,745 acres of hills carpeted with poppies and other wildflowers, including a paved section that allows wheelchair access. Keep in mind that poppy flowers will curl up their petals if it's too windy or cold, so plan accordingly. Heed the rules and stay on the official trails when taking photos.
■ TIP→ **Blooming season is usually March through May.** On a clear day at any time of year, you'll be treated to sweeping views of Antelope Valley. Visit the website or call the wildflower hotline for the current bloom status. ☒ 15101 Lancaster Rd., west off Hwy. 14, Ave. I Exit ☎ 661/724–1180 wildflower hotline, 661/946–6092 administration ⊕ www.parks.ca.gov/poppyreserve ☜ $10 per vehicle ⊙ Visitor center closed mid-May–Feb.

Antelope Valley Indian Museum
MUSEUM | FAMILY | This museum got its start as a private collection of American Indian antiquities gathered in the 1920s by artist and amateur naturalist Howard Arden Edwards. Today, his Swiss chalet–style home is a state museum known for one-of-a-kind artifacts from California, Southwest, and Great Basin native cultures, including ancient tools, artwork, basketry, and rugs. To get here, exit north off Highway 138 at 165th Street East and follow the signs, or take the Avenue K exit off Highway 14. ☒ 15701 E. Ave. M ☎ 661/946–3055 ⊕ www.avim.parks.ca.gov ☜ $3 ⊙ Closed weekdays.

Antelope Valley Winery/Donato Family Vineyard

STORE/MALL | Cyndee and Frank Donato purchased the Los Angeles–based McLester Winery in 1990 and moved it to Lancaster, where the high-desert sun and nighttime chill work their magic on wine grapes such as Merlot, Zinfandel, and Sangiovese. In addition to tastings, the winery hosts a Saturday farmers' market (from May through November between 9 and noon) and sells grass-fed buffalo and other game and exotic meats such as venison, pheasant, and wild boar. ✉ *42041 20th St. W, at Ave. M* ☎ *661/722–0145, 888/282–8332* ⊕ *www.avwinery.com* ✉ *Winery free, tastings from $12* ⊙ *Closed Mon. and Tues.*

The BLVD

ARTS VENUE | Lancaster's downtown arts and culture district and social hub, The BLVD, stretches for nine blocks along West Lancaster Boulevard from 10th Street West to Sierra Highway. Boeing Plaza anchors the east end and marks the start of the Aerospace Walk of Honor—a series of murals and monuments lauding 100 legendary figures, including Neil Armstrong and Chuck Yeager. The district is also home to the Lancaster Performing Arts Center, the Lancaster Museum of Art & History, galleries, restaurants, boutiques, coffee and tea shops, craft breweries, and entertainment venues. ✉ *W. Lancaster Blvd.* ⊹ *10th St. W to Sierra Hwy. and Jackman to Milling Sts.* ☎ *661/723–6078* ⊕ *www.theblvdlancaster.com.*

Exotic Feline Breeding Compound's Feline Conservation Center

ZOO | About two dozen species of wild cats, from the unusual, weasel-size jaguarundi to leopards, tigers, and jaguars, inhabit this small, orderly facility. You can see the cats up close (behind barrier fences) in the parklike public zoo and research center, and docents are available to answer questions. ✉ *Rhyolite Ave. off Mojave-Tropico Rd., Rosamond* ☎ *661/256–3793* ⊕ *www.wildcatzoo.org* ✉ *$10* ⊙ *Closed Wed. and Sun.*

St. Andrew's Abbeys

RELIGIOUS SITE | Nestled in the foothills of the Antelope Valley, this peaceful enclave is both Benedictine monastery and restful retreat for those wanting to get away from the bustle of everyday life. Day visitors can walk the lush tree-lined grounds, including a large, shaded pond teeming with ducks and red-eared turtles, or browse the well-stocked gift shop for religious keepsakes. An extensive collection of ceramic tiles in the image of saints and angels by Father Maur van Doorslaer, a Belgian monk whose work U.S. and Canadian collectors favor, are among the items sold here to help sustain the monastery and its good works. ✉ *31001 N. Valyermo Rd., south of Hwy. 138, Valyermo* ☎ *661/944–2178 ceramics studio* ⊕ *www.saintandrewsabbey.com* ✉ *Free.*

Red Rock Canyon State Park

48 miles north of Lancaster.

On the stretch of Highway 14 that slices through Red Rock Canyon State Park, it's easy to become caught up in the momentum of rushing to your "real" destination. But it would be a shame not to stop for this deeply beautiful canyon, with its rich, layered colors and Native American heritage.

GETTING HERE AND AROUND

The only practical way to get here is by car, taking Highway 14 north from the Palmdale-Lancaster area or south from Ridgecrest.

Did You Know?

Movies like *Jurassic Park* have been shot in Red Rock Canyon State Park in the Mojave Desert.

⊙ Sights

Red Rock Canyon State Park
NATIONAL/STATE PARK | A geological feast for the eyes with its layers of pink, white, red, and brown rock, this remote canyon is also a region of fascinating biological diversity—the ecosystems of the Sierra Nevada, the Mojave Desert, and the Basin Range all converge here. Native Americans known as the Kawaiisu lived here some 20,000 years ago; later, Mojave Indians roamed the land for centuries. You can still see remains of gold mining operations in the park, and movies such as *Jurassic Park* have been shot here. For a quiet nature trail a little off the beaten path try the 0.75-mile loop at Red Cliffs Natural Preserve on Highway 14, across from the entrance to the Ricardo Campground. ✉ *Visitor Center, 37749 Abbott Dr., off Hwy. 14, Cantil* ☎ *661/946–6092* ⊕ *www.parks.ca.gov* 💲 *$6 per vehicle.*

Ridgecrest

28 miles northeast of Red Rock Canyon State Park, 77 miles south of Lone Pine.

A military town that serves the U.S. Naval Weapons Center to its north, Ridgecrest has scores of stores, restaurants, and hotels. With about 29,000 residents, it's the last city of any significant size you'll encounter as you head northeast toward Death Valley National Park. It's a good base for visiting regional attractions such as the Trona Pinnacles and Petroglyph Canyons.

GETTING HERE AND AROUND
Arrive here by car via U.S. 395 or, from the Los Angeles area, Highway 14.

ESSENTIALS
VISITOR INFORMATION Ridgecrest Area Convention and Visitors Bureau. ✉ *643 N. China Lake Blvd.* ☎ *760/375–8202, 800/847–4830* ⊕ *goridgecrest.com.*

⊙ Sights

Indian Wells Brewing Company
WINERY/DISTILLERY | After driving through the hot desert, you'll surely appreciate a cold one at Indian Wells Brewing Company, where master brewer Rick Lovett lovingly crafts his Lobotomy Bock, Amnesia I.P.A., and Lunatic Lemonade, among others. If you have the kids along, grab a six-pack of his specialty root beer, black cherry, orange, or cream soda. ✉ *2565 N. Hwy. 14, 2 miles west of U.S. 395, Inyokern* ☎ *760/377–5989* ⊕ *www.mojavered.com.*

Maturango Museum
CANYON | FAMILY | The museum contains interesting exhibits that survey the Upper Mojave Desert area's art, history, and geology, and sponsors tours of the amazing rock drawings in Petroglyph Canyons. ✉ *100 E. Las Flores Ave., at Hwy. 178* ☎ *760/375–6900* ⊕ *www.maturango.org* 💲 *$5.*

★ Petroglyph Canyons
CANYON | FAMILY | Thousands of well-preserved images of animals and humans are scratched or pecked into dark basaltic rocks at Big Petroglyph and Little Petroglyph canyons in the Coso Mountain range, the largest concentration of ancient rock art in the Northern Hemisphere. The canyons lie within the million-acre U.S. Naval Weapons Center at China Lake. Only the drawings of Little Petroglyph can be visited, and only on a guided tour arranged in advance through the Maturango Museum. Tour participants must be U.S. citizens over 10 years of age, and fill out an online application to obtain security clearance. Detailed information about the spring and fall tours, which fill up fast, is provided on the museum's website. ✉ *100 E. Las Flores Ave.* ☎ *760/375–6900* ⊕ *www.maturango.org* 💲 *$60* ⊗ *Closed Dec.–Feb. and June–mid-Sept.*

Trona Pinnacles National Natural Landmark

ARCHAEOLOGICAL SITE | Fantastic-looking formations of calcium carbonate, known as tufa, were formed underwater along fault lines in the bed of what is now Searles Dry Lake. Some of the more than 500 spires stand as tall as 140 feet, creating a landscape so surreal that it doubled for outer-space terrain in the film *Star Trek V.* An easy-to-walk ½-mile trail allows you to see the tufa up close, but wear sturdy shoes—tufa cuts like coral. The best road to the area can be impassable after a rainstorm. ⊠ *Pinnacle Rd.* ✛ *5 miles south of Hwy. 178, 18 miles east of Ridgecrest* ☎ *760/384–5400 Ridgecrest BLM office* ⊕ *www.blm.gov/visit/trona-pinnacles.*

 Hotels

Hampton Inn & Suites Ridgecrest

$$ | **HOTEL** | Clean and reliable, the Hampton has a well-equipped exercise room, pool, spotless Internet service, and complimentary breakfast. **Pros:** attentive, friendly service; good breakfast; big rooms. **Cons:** a rather strong chain vibe; thin walls; basic breakfast. $ *Rooms from: $159* ⊠ *104 E. Sydnor Ave.* ☎ *760/446–1968* ⊕ *hamptoninn3.hilton.com* ⇆ *93 rooms* ⦿ *Free breakfast.*

Randsburg

21 miles south of Ridgecrest, 26 miles east of Red Rock Canyon State Park.

Randsburg and nearby Red Mountain and Johannesburg make up the Rand Mining District, which first boomed with the discovery of gold in the Rand Mountains in 1895. Rich tungsten ore, used in World War I to make steel alloy, was discovered in 1907, and silver was found in 1919. The boom has gone bust, but the area still has some residents, a few antiques shops, and plenty of character. Butte Avenue is the main drag in Randsburg, whose tiny city jail, just

off Butte, is among the original buildings still standing. An archetypal Old West cemetery perched on a hillside looms over Johannesburg.

GETTING HERE AND AROUND

Arriving by car is the best transportation option. From Red Rock Canyon, drive east on Redrock Randsburg Road. From Ridgecrest, drive south on South China Lake Road and U.S. 395.

 Sights

Desert Tortoise Natural Area

NATURE PRESERVE | It may not always be easy to spot the elusive desert tortoise in this peaceful protected habitat but the approximately 40-square-mile area often blazes with wildflowers in the spring and early summer. It is also a great spot to see desert kit fox, red-tailed hawks, cactus wrens, and Mojave rattlesnakes; walking paths and a small interpretive center are part of the experience. ⊠ *8 miles northeast of California City via Randsburg Mojave Rd.* ☎ *442/294–4258* ⊕ *www.tortoise-tracks.org* ⦿ *Free.*

General Store

RESTAURANT—SIGHT | Built as Randsburg's Drug Store in 1896, the General Store is one of the area's few surviving ghost-town buildings with an original tin ceiling, light fixtures, and 1904-era marble-and-stained-glass soda fountain. You can still enjoy a phosphate soda from that same fountain, or a lunch of burgers, hot dogs, and chili. ⊠ *35 Butte Ave.* ☎ *760/374–2143* ⊕ *www.randsburggeneralstore.com* ⦿ *Closed Tues. and Wed.*

Victorville

87 miles south of Ridgecrest.

At the southwest corner of the Mojave is sprawling Victorville, a town with a rich Route 66 heritage and a museum dedicated to the Mother Road. Victorville was named for Santa Fe Railroad pioneer

Jacob Nash Victor, who drove the first locomotive through the Cajon Pass here in 1885. Once home to Native Americans, the town later became a rest stop for Mormons and missionaries. In 1941, George Air Force Base, now an airport and storage area, brought scores of military families to the area, many of which have stayed on to raise families of their own.

GETTING HERE AND AROUND

Drive here on I–15 from Los Angeles or Las Vegas, or from the north via U.S. 395. Amtrak and Greyhound also serve the town. There are local buses, but touring by car is more practical.

Sights

California Route 66 Museum

MUSEUM | Visitors from around the world still think of Historic Route 66 as one of the best ways to see the real America and this 4,500-square-foot museum is chock-full of memorabilia such as maps and postcards, photographs, paintings, and nostalgic displays that bring the iconic highway's history to life. Friendly museum volunteers are more than happy to answer questions and take your picture inside the flower-painted VW Love Bus. ✉ *16825 S. D St., between 5th and 6th Sts.* ☎ *760/951–0436* 🌐 *califrt66museum.org* 🎟 *Free* 🕒 *Closed Tues. and Wed.*

Mojave Narrows Regional Park

CITY PARK | **FAMILY** | This 840-acre park is one of the few spots where the Mojave River flows aboveground, and the result is open pastures, wetlands, and two lakes surrounded by cottonwoods and cattails. Amenities include camping, fishing, equestrian/walking trails, and a large playground with water park. ✉ *18000 Yates Rd., north on Ridgecrest Rd. off Bear Valley Rd.* ☎ *760/245–2226* 🌐 *cms.sbcounty.gov/parks* 🎟 *From $8* 🕒 *Closed Tues. and Wed.*

Restaurants

Emma Jean's Holland Burger Cafe

$ | **DINER** | The short-order cook and his grill are literally center stage in this tiny, family-owned restaurant along Historic Route 66, which has changed little since it first opened in 1947. It's the peach cobbler, Brian burger, and fried chicken that keep locals lining up at the door, but anyone wanting a glimpse of 20th-century Americana can get their kicks here, too. **Known for:** Route 66 memorabilia; historical diner; hearty breakfasts. [$] *Average main: $12* ✉ *17143 N. D St., at Water Power Housing Dr.* ☎ *760/243–9938* 🌐 *www.hollandburger.com* 💳 *No credit cards* 🕒 *Closed Sun. No dinner.*

Molly Brown's Country Cafe

$ | **AMERICAN** | **FAMILY** | There's no mystery why this place is a locals' favorite—the cozy eatery offers a mouthwatering breakfast menu that includes everything from chicken fried steak to a sizzling garden skillet brimming with fresh vegetables. Lunch includes sandwiches, salads, and hot plates such as meat loaf with potatoes, veggies, and corn bread. **Known for:** hearty breakfasts; locals' favorite; homemade breads. [$] *Average main: $13* ✉ *15775 Mojave Dr.* ☎ *760/241–4900* 🌐 *www.mollybrownscountrycafe.com.*

Hotels

Courtyard Marriott Victorville Hesperia

$$ | **HOTEL** | **FAMILY** | Rooms are spacious and contemporary, and there is both an indoor pool and large outdoor patio and pool area ideal for large groups. **Pros:** convenient location off I–15; some rooms with desert views; two pools. **Cons:** breakfast only with certain room rates; bistro menu options limited; some rooms close to freeway noise. [$] *Rooms from: $168* ✉ *9619 Mariposa Rd., Hesperia* ☎ *760/956–3876* 🌐 *www.marriott.com* 🔑 *131 rooms* 🍴 *No meals.*

Many of the buildings in the popular Calico Ghost Town are authentic.

Barstow

32 miles northeast of Victorville.

Barstow was born in 1886, when a subsidiary of the Atchison, Topeka, and Santa Fe Railway began construction of a Harvey House depot and hotel here. The depot has been restored and includes two free museums; the family-friendly Calico Ghost Town is just north of town, and there are well-known chain motels and restaurants right off I–15 if you need a rest and refuel before the next stop.

GETTING HERE AND AROUND

Driving here on I–15 from Los Angeles or Las Vegas is the best option, although you can reach Barstow via Amtrak or Greyhound. The local bus service is helpful for sights downtown.

ESSENTIALS

TRANSPORTATION INFORMATION Barstow Area Transit/Victor Valley Transit. ☎ *760/948–3030* ⊕ *vvta.org.*

VISITOR INFORMATION Barstow Area Chamber of Commerce and Visitors Bureau. ✉ *229 E. Main St.* ☎ *760/256–8617* ⊕ *www.barstowchamber.com.* **California Welcome Center Barstow.** ✉ *2796 Tanger Way, Suite 100, off Lenwood Rd.* ☎ *760/253–4782* ⊕ *www.visitcalifornia.com/experience/california-welcome-center-barstow.* **Mojave National Preserve Headquarters.** ✉ *2701 Barstow Rd.* ☎ *760/252–6100* ⊕ *www.nps.gov/moja/planyourvisit/visitorcenters.htm.*

Sights

Afton Canyon

CANYON | Because of its colorful, steep walls, Afton Canyon is often called the Grand Canyon of the Mojave. It was carved over thousands of years by the rushing waters of the Mojave River, which makes one of its few aboveground appearances here. The dirt road that leads to the canyon is ungraded in spots, so it is best to explore it in an all-terrain vehicle. ✉ *Off Afton Rd., 36 miles northeast of Barstow via I–15* ⊕ *www.recreation.gov.*

Bagdad Café

RESTAURANT—SIGHT | Tourists from all over the world flock to this Route 66 eatery, built in the 1940s and where the 1987 film of the same name was shot. The divey café's walls are crammed with memorabilia donated by visitors famous and otherwise. The very limited bill of fare includes the Bagdad omelet and a buffalo burger with fries, but this place is really about soaking up the Route 66-Americana vibe. ⊠ *46548 National Trails Hwy., at Nopal La., Newberry Springs* ☎ *760/257–3101.*

★ Calico Ghost Town

GHOST TOWN | FAMILY | This former silver-mining boom town was founded in 1881, and, within a few years, it boasted 500 mines and 22 saloons. Its reconstruction by Walter Knott of Knott's Berry Farm makes it more about G-rated family entertainment than the town's gritty past, but that doesn't seem to take away from the fun of panning for (fool's) gold, touring the original tunnels of Maggie Mine, or taking a leisurely ride on the Calico Odessa Railroad. Five of the original buildings are still standing, such as the impressive Lane's General Store, and its setting among the stark beauty of the Calico Hills can make a stroll along this once-bustling Main Street downright peaceful. ■TIP➔ **Calico also has ghost tours and regular events such as the yearly bluegrass festival on Mother's Day weekend.** ⊠ *36600 Ghost Town Rd., off I–15, Yermo* ☎ *760/254–1123* ⊕ *parks. sbcounty.gov/park/calico-ghost-town-regional-park* ⊡ *$8.*

Casa Del Desierto Harvey House

HISTORIC SITE | This historic train depot was built around 1911 (the original 1885 structure was destroyed by fire) and was one of the original Harvey Houses, providing dining and lodging for weary travelers along the rail lines. Waitresses at the depots were popularized in movies such as *The Harvey Girls* with Judy Garland. It now houses offices and two museums:

the Western American Railroad and Route 66 Mother Road, but you can still walk along the porticos of the impressive Spanish Renaissance Classical building, or stroll into the restored lobby where you'll find the original staircase, terrazzo floor, and copper chandeliers. ⊠ *681 N. 1st Ave., near Riverside Dr.* ☎ *760/818–4400* ⊕ *www.barstowharveyhouse.com* ⊡ *Free* ⊗ *Closed Sun.*

Desert Discovery Center

MUSEUM | FAMILY | The center's main attraction is Old Woman Meteorite, the second-largest such celestial object ever found in the United States. It was discovered in 1976 about 50 miles from Barstow. The center also has exhibits of fossils, plants, and local animals. Environmental education, history, and the arts are among the topics of workshops and presentations the center hosts. Follow the outdoor desert nature trail with interpretive signs on desert plants and early man's relationship with native plants for shelter, medicine, clothing, food, and weaponry. ■TIP➔ **Reserve a spot in advance for the Stone Age to Space Age tour, offered the first Saturday of the month at 10 am (about 1½ hours, donations appreciated). It begins with a Route 66 history presentation at the Desert Discovery Center, followed by visits to the Main Street Murals and the NASA Goldstone Visitor Center.** ⊠ *831 Barstow Rd.* ☎ *760/252–6060* ⊕ *www.desertdiscoverycenter.com* ⊡ *Free* ⊗ *Closed Sun. and Mon.*

★ Goldstone Deep Space Communications Complex

MUSEUM | FAMILY | Friendly and enthusiastic staffers conduct guided tours of this 53-square-mile complex at Fort Irwin Military Base, 35 miles north of Barstow. Tours start at the Goldstone Museum, where exhibits detail past and present space missions and Deep Space Network history. From there, you'll drive out to see the massive concave antennas, starting with those used for early manned space flights and culminating with the 24-story-tall "listening" device. This is one of only three complexes in the world that make up the Deep Space Network, tracking and communicating with spacecraft throughout our solar system. Appointments are required; contact the complex to reserve a slot. ⊠ *NASA Goldstone Visitor Center, 681 N. 1st Ave.* 🕾 *760/255–8688* ⊕ *www.gdscc.nasa.gov* 🎟 *Free* ⊗ *Closed Sun.*

Main Street Murals

PUBLIC ART | FAMILY | More than two dozen hand-painted murals in downtown Barstow depict the town's history, from prehistoric times and early explorers to pioneer caravans, mining eras, and Route 66. Walking tour guides are available at the Barstow Chamber of Commerce and the public library. Contact the Desert Discovery Center for more details on the murals and monthly guided tours. ⊠ *E. Main St.* ✛ *Between 1st and 7th Sts.* 🕾 *760/252–6060* ⊕ *www.mainstreetmurals.com.*

Mojave River Valley Museum

MUSEUM | FAMILY | The floor-to-ceiling collection of local history, both quirky and conventional, includes Ice Age fossils such as a giant mammoth tusk dug up in 2006, Native American artifacts, 19th-century handmade quilts, and displays on early settlers. Entrance is free and there's a little gift shop with a nice collection of books about the area. ■**TIP➜ The story about Possum Trot and its population of folk-art dolls is not to be missed.** ⊠ *270 E. Virginia Way, at Barstow Rd.* 🕾 *760/256–5452* ⊕ *www.mojaverivervalleymuseum.org* 🎟 *Free.*

Rainbow Basin National Natural Landmark

NATIONAL/STATE PARK | Many science-fiction movies set on Mars have been filmed at this landmark 8 miles north of Barstow. Huge slabs of red, orange, white, and green stone tilt at crazy angles like ships about to capsize and traces of ancient beasts such as mastodons and bear-dogs, which roamed the basin up to 16 million years ago have been discovered in its fossil beds. The dirt road around the basin is narrow and bumpy so vehicles with higher clearance are recommended and rain can quickly turn the road to mud; at times, only four-wheel-drive vehicles are permitted. ⊠ *Fossil Bed Rd., 3 miles west of Fort Irwin Rd. (head north from I–15)* 🕾 *760/252–6000* ⊕ *www.blm.gov/visit/rainbow-basin-natural-area.*

Skyline Drive-In Theatre

ARTS VENUE | Check out a bit of surviving Americana at this dusty drive-in, where you can watch the latest Hollywood flicks among the Joshua trees and starry night sky. Keep in mind the old-time speakers are no more; sound is tuned in via car radio. ⊠ *31175 Old Hwy. 58* 🕾 *760/256–3333* 🎟 *$10 per person* ⊗ *Closed early Dec.–early Mar.*

Western America Railroad Museum

MUSEUM | FAMILY | You can almost hear the murmur of passengers and rhythmic, metal-on-metal clatter as you stroll past the old cabooses, railcars and engines, such as Sante Fe number 95, that are on display outside the historic Barstow station where this museum is located. The next stop is the indoor portion of the collection, including a train simulator, rail equipment, model railroad display, and other memorabilia. A handful of artifacts from the depot's Harvey House days are on display, as well as period dining-car china from railways around the country. ⊠ *Casa Del Desierto, 685 N. 1st Ave., near Riverside Dr.* 🕾 *760/256–9276* ⊕ *barstowharveyhouse.com* 🎟 *Free* ⊗ *Closed Mon.–Thurs.*

Restaurants

Peggy Sue's 50s Diner

$ | **AMERICAN** | **FAMILY** | Checkerboard floors and life-size versions of Elvis and Marilyn Monroe greet you at this funky '50s coffee shop and pizza parlor in the middle of the Mojave. The fare is basic American—fries, onion rings, burgers, pork chops—with some fun surprises such as pineapple pie and deep-fried dill pickles. **Known for:** movie, TV memorabilia; over-the-top '50s vibe; gift shop, jukebox, soda fountain, duck pond. Ⓢ *Average main: $14* ✉ *35654 W. Yermo Rd., at Daggett-Yermo Rd., Yermo* ☎ *760/254–3370* ⊕ *www.peggysuesdiner.com.*

🛏 Hotels

Ayres Hotel Barstow

$ | **HOTEL** | **FAMILY** | In a sea of chain hotels this one has a few homespun touches up its sleeves, such as fresh-baked cookies in the cozy lobby lounge every evening. **Pros:** clean rooms, engaged management; entirely nonsmoking; Tesla charging stations. **Cons:** pricey for Barstow; near freeway; shared parking lot with other businesses. Ⓢ *Rooms from: $139* ✉ *2812 Lenwood Rd.* ☎ *760/307–3121* ⊕ *www.ayreshotels.com/ayres-hotel-barstow* ⇌ *92 rooms* ❘◎❘ *Free breakfast.*

Mojave National Preserve

Visitor center 118 miles east of Barstow, 58 miles west of Needles.

The 1.6 million acres of the Mojave National Preserve hold a surprising abundance of plant and animal life—especially considering their elevation (nearly 8,000 feet in some areas). There are traces of human history here as well, including abandoned army posts and vestiges of mining and ranching towns. The Cinder Cone Lava Beds area holds 75 inactive volcanoes; the youngest is 11,500 years old. North Cima Road passes a significant Joshua tree forest. Mojave National Preserve rangers also oversee the adjacent 20,920-acre Castle Mountains National Monument, created in 2016.

GETTING HERE AND AROUND

A car is the best way to access the preserve, which lies between I–15 and I–40. Kelbaker Road bisects the park from north to south; northbound from I–40, Essex Road gets you to Hole-in-the-Wall on pavement but is graveled beyond there.

Sights

Hole-in-the-Wall

NATURE SITE | Created millions of years ago by volcanic activity, Hole-in-the-Wall formed when gases were trapped between layers of deposited ash, rock, and lava; the gas bubbles left holes in the solidified material. You will encounter one of California's most distinctive hiking experiences here. Proceeding clockwise from a small visitor center, you walk gently down and around a craggy hill, past cacti and fading petroglyphs to Banshee Canyon, whose pockmarked walls resemble Swiss cheese. From there you head back out of the canyon, supporting yourself with widely spaced iron rings (some of which wiggle precariously from their rock moorings) as you ascend a 50-foot incline that deposits you back near the visitor center. The one-hour adventure can be challenging but wholly entertaining. ▪**TIP**➜ **There are no services (gas or food) nearby; be sure to fill your tank and pack some snacks before heading out here.** ✉ *Mojave National Preserve* ☎ *760/252–6104* ⊕ *www.nps.gov/moja* 💲 *Free.*

★ Kelso Dunes

NATURE SITE | As you enter the preserve from the south, you'll pass miles of open scrub brush, Joshua trees, and beautiful red-black cinder cones before encountering the Kelso Dunes. These golden, fine-sand slopes cover 70 square miles, reaching heights of 600 feet. You can reach them via a short walk from the main parking area, but be prepared for a serious workout. When you reach the top of a dune, kick a little bit of sand down the lee side and listen to the sand "sing." North of the dunes, in the town of Kelso, is the Mission revival–style **Kelso Depot Visitor Center.** The striking building, which dates from 1923, contains several rooms of desert- and train-theme exhibits.

✉ *For Kelso Depot Visitor Center, take Kelbaker Rd. exit from I–15 (head south 34 miles) or I–40 (head north 22 miles)* ☎ *760/252–6100, 760/252–6108* ⊕ *www. nps.gov/moja* 🖼 *Free* ☉ *Kelso Depot visitor center closed Tues. and Wed.*

Chapter 10

DEATH VALLEY NATIONAL PARK

10

Updated by
Cheryl Crabtree

🏕 **Camping**
★★★☆☆

🛏 **Hotels**
★★★★☆

🏃 **Activities**
★★★☆☆

👁 **Scenery**
★★★★★

👥 **Crowds**
★★☆☆☆

WELCOME TO DEATH VALLEY NATIONAL PARK

TOP REASONS TO GO

★ **Roving rocks:** Death Valley's Racetrack is home to moving boulders, a rare phenomenon that until recently had scientists baffled.

★ **Lowest spot on the continent:** Stand on the lowest spot on the continent at Badwater, 282 feet below sea level.

★ **Wildflower explosion:** In spring, this desert landscape is ablaze with greenery and colorful flowers, especially between Badwater and Ashford Mill.

★ **Ghost towns:** Death Valley is renowned for its Wild West heritage and is home to dozens of crumbling settlements including Chloride City, Greenwater, Harrisburg, Keeler, Leadfield, Panamint City, and Skidoo, as well as nearby Ballarat and Rhyolite.

★ **Naturally amazing:** From canyons to sand dunes to salt flats and dry lake beds, Death Valley serves up plenty of geological treasures.

1 Central Death Valley. Furnace Creek sits in the heart of Death Valley—if you have only a short time in the park, head here. You can visit gorgeous Golden Canyon, Zabriskie Point, the Salt Creek Interpretive Trail, and Artists Drive, among other popular points of interest.

2 Northern Death Valley. This region is uphill from Furnace Creek, which means marginally cooler temperatures. Be sure to stop by Rhyolite Ghost Town on Highway 374 before entering the park and exploring colorful Titus Canyon and jaw-dropping Ubehebe Crater.

3 Southern Death Valley. This is a desolate area, but there are plenty of sights that help convey Death Valley's rich history. Don't miss the Dublin Gulch Caves.

4 Western Death Valley. Panamint Springs Resort is a nice place to grab a meal and get your bearings before moving on to quaint Darwin Falls, smooth rolling sand dunes, beehive-shape Wildrose Charcoal Kilns, and historic Stovepipe Wells Village.

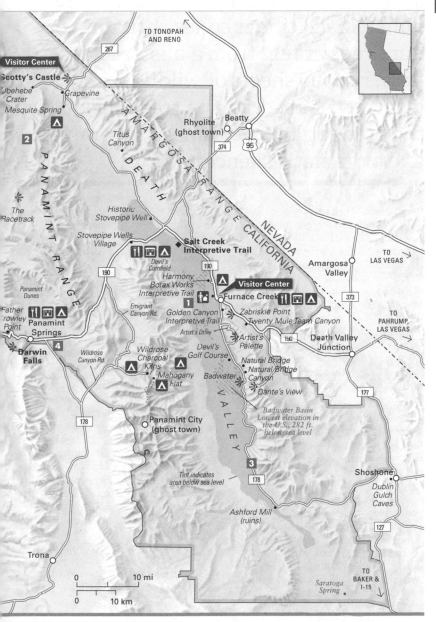

TO TONOPAH
AND RENO

267

Visitor Center
Scotty's Castle
Ubehebe
Crater
Mesquite Spring

2

Grapevine

Titus
Canyon

Rhyolite
(ghost town)

Beatty

374

95

NEVADA
CALIFORNIA

TO
LAS VEGAS

Amargosa
Valley

P A N A M I N T   R A N G E

The
Racetrack

Historic
Stovepipe Well

Stovepipe Wells
Village

Salt Creek
Interpretive Trail

190

Devil's
Cornfield

Harmony
Borax Works
Interpretive Trail

190

Visitor Center

Furnace Creek

373

TO
PAHRUMP,
LAS VEGAS

Panamint
Dunes

Emigrant
Canyon Rd.

Golden Canyon
Interpretive Trail

Zabriskie Point
Twenty Mule Team Canyon

Death Valley
Junction

Father
Crowley
Point

Panamint
Springs

4

Artist's Drive

Artist's
Palette

190

Darwin
Falls

Wildrose
Canyon Rd.

Wildrose
Charcoal
Kilns

Mahogany
Flat

Devil's
Golf Course

Badwater

Natural Bridge
Natural Bridge
Canyon

Dante's View

127

178

Panamint City
(ghost town)

Badwater Basin
Lowest elevation in
the U.S., 282 ft.
below sea level

Tint indicates
area below sea level

3

178

D E A T H   V A L L E Y

Shoshone

Dublin
Gulch
Caves

Ashford Mill
(ruins)

127

Trona

0   10 mi

0   10 km

Saratoga
Spring

TO
BAKER &
I-15

A M A R G O S A   R A N G E

The natural riches of Death Valley—the largest national park outside Alaska—are overwhelming: rolling waves of sand dunes, black cinder cones thrusting up hundreds of feet from a blistered desert floor, riotous sheets of wildflowers, bizarrely shaped Joshua trees basking in the orange glow of a sunset, tiny pupfish, and a dramatic silence.

This is a land of extremes of climate (hottest and driest) and geography. The park centers on Death Valley, which extends 156 miles from north to south and includes Badwater Basin, the lowest point in the USA (282 feet below sea level). Two mountain ranges border the valley: the Panamint on the west, where Telescope Peak juts more than 11,000 feet up from the valley floor, and the Amargosa in the east. Salt basins, spring-fed oases, sand dunes, deep canyons, and more than a thousand miles of paved and dirt roads punctuate the barren landscapes.

Humans first roamed this once-lush region around 10,000 years ago. The Timbisha Shoshone have lived here for more than a thousand years, originally along the shores of a 30-foot-deep lake. They called the area Timbisha for the red-hued rocks in the hillsides. Gold-rush pioneers looking for a shortcut to California traversed the barren expanse in 1849; some met their demise in the harsh environment, and those who survived named the place Death Valley. Silver and borax mining companies soon arrived on the scene. They didn't last long (most had stopped operations by 1910), but they left ghost towns and ramshackle mines as evidence of their dreams.

In 1933, President Herbert Hoover proclaimed the area a national monument to protect both its natural beauty and its scientific importance. In 1994, Congress passed the California Desert Protection Act, adding 1.3 million acres and designating the region a national park. Today, Death Valley National Park encompasses nearly 3.5 million acres, 93% of which is designated wilderness.

Despite its moniker, Death Valley teems with life. More than a million visitors a year come here to view plants and animals that reveal remarkable adaptations to the desert environment, hike through deep canyons and up mountain trails, gaze at planets and stars in a vast night sky, and follow in the footsteps of ancient cultures and pioneers. They come to explore an outstanding, exceptionally diverse outdoor natural history museum, filled with excellent examples of the planet's geological history. Most of all, they come to experience peace, quiet, and solitude in a stark, surreal landscape found nowhere else on Earth.

Death Valley in One Day

If you begin the day in Furnace Creek, you can see several sights without doing much driving. Bring plenty of water with you and some food, too. Rise early and drive the 20 miles on Badwater Road to **Badwater**, which looks out on the lowest point in the Western Hemisphere and is a dramatic place to watch the sunrise. Returning north, stop at **Natural Bridge**, a medium-size conglomerate rock formation that has been hollowed at its base to form a span across the canyon, and then at the **Devil's Golf Course**, so named because of the large pinnacles of salt present here. Detour to the right onto **Artists Drive**, a 9-mile one-way, northbound route

that passes **Artists Palette.** The reds, yellows, oranges, and greens come from minerals in the rocks and the earth. Four miles north of Artists Drive is the **Golden Canyon Interpretive Trail**, a 2-mile round-trip that winds through a canyon with colorful rock walls. Just before Furnace Creek, take Highway 190 3 miles east to **Zabriskie Point**, overlooking dramatic, furrowed red-brown hills and the **Twenty Mule Team Canyon.** Return to Furnace Creek, where you can grab a meal and visit the museum at the Furnace Creek Visitor Center. Heading north from Furnace Creek, pull off the highway and take a look at the historic **Harmony Borax Works.**

AVERAGE HIGH/LOW TEMPERATURES					
JAN.	FEB.	MAR.	APR.	MAY	JUNE
65/39	72/46	80/53	90/62	99/71	109/80
JULY	AUG.	SEPT.	OCT.	NOV.	DEC.
115/88	113/85	106/75	92/62	76/48	65/39

Planning

When to Go

Most of the park's 1.7 million annual visitors come between late fall and early spring, taking advantage of moderate temperatures and the lack of rainfall. During these cooler months, you will need to book a room in advance, but don't worry: the park never feels crowded. If you visit in summer, believe everything you've ever heard about desert heat—it can be brutal, with temperatures often topping 120°F. The dry air wicks moisture from the body without causing a sweat, so drink plenty of water. Bring sunglasses,

a hat, and sufficient clothing to block the sun's rays and the wind. Flash floods are fairly common; sections of roadway can be flooded or washed away, as they were after a major flood in 2015. The wettest month is February, when the park receives an average of 0.3 inch of rain.

Getting Here and Around

AIR
The closest airport to the park with commercial service, Las Vegas McCarran (slated to be renamed Harry Reid) International Airport, is 130 miles away, so you'll still need to drive a couple of hours to reach the park. Roughly 160 miles to the west, Burbank's Bob Hope Airport is the second-closest airport.

CAR

It can take more than three hours to cross from one side of the park to another, so it's important to choose an entrance point that makes sense for what you want to see. If you're driving from Los Angeles, enter through the western portion along Highway 395; from Las Vegas, enter from the north at Beatty, Nevada, or via the central entrance at Death Valley Junction. Travelers from Orange County, San Diego, and the Inland Empire should access the park via Interstate 15 North at Baker.

Distances can be deceiving: what seems close can be very far away. Much of the park can be viewed on regularly scheduled bus tours, but these often don't allow time for hikes to sites not seen from the road, such as Salt Creek, Golden Canyon, and Natural Bridge. The best option is to drive to a number of the sites, get out of the car, and walk.

When driving in Death Valley, reliable maps are important, as signage is often limited or, in a few places, nonexistent. Bring a phone, but don't rely on cell coverage exclusively in every remote area, and pack plenty of food and water (3 gallons per person per day is recommended). Cars, especially in summer, should be prepared for the hot, dry weather, too. Some of the park's most spectacular canyons are accessible only via four-wheel-drive vehicles, but make sure the trip is well planned and use a backcountry map. Be aware of possible winter closures or driving restrictions because of snow. The National Park Service's website (⊕ nps.gov/deva) stays up-to-date on road closures during the wet (and popular) months. ⚠ **One of the park's signature landmarks, Scotty's Castle, and the 8-mile road connecting it to the park border may be closed until 2022 due to damage from a 2015 flood.**

CONTACTS California Highway Patrol. ☏ 800/427–7623 recorded info from CalTrans, 760/872–5900 live dispatcher at Bishop Communications Center ⊕ www.chp.ca.gov. **California State Department of Transportation Hotline** ☏ 800/427–7623 ⊕ www.dot.ca.gov.

Park Essentials

ACCESSIBILITY

All of Death Valley's visitor centers, contact stations, and museums are accessible to all visitors. The campgrounds at Furnace Creek, Sunset, and Stovepipe Wells have wheelchair-accessible sites. Highway 190, Badwater Road, and paved roads to Dante's View and Wildrose provide access to the major scenic viewpoints and historic points of interest.

PARK FEES AND PERMITS

The entrance fee is $30 per vehicle, $25 for motorcycles, and $15 for those entering on foot or bike. The payment, valid for seven consecutive days, is collected at the park's ranger stations, self-serve fee stations, and the visitor center at Furnace Creek. Annual park passes, valid only at Death Valley, are $55.

A permit is not required for groups of 14 or fewer, but if you're planning an overnight visit to the backcountry, complete a registration form at the Furnace Creek Visitor Center. Backcountry camping is allowed in areas that are at least 2 miles from maintained campgrounds and the main paved or unpaved roads and ¼ mile from water sources. Most abandoned mining areas are restricted to day use.

PARK HOURS

The park is open day or night year-round. Most facilities operate daily 8–6.

CELL PHONE RECEPTION

Results vary, but in general you should be able to get fairly good reception on the valley floor. In the surrounding mountains, however, don't count on it.

Hotels

It's difficult to find lodging anywhere in Death Valley that doesn't have breathtaking views of the park and surrounding mountains. Most accommodations, aside from the Inn at Death Valley, are homey and rustic. Rooms fill up quickly during the fall and spring seasons, and reservations are required about three months in advance for the prime weekends.

Restaurants

Inside the park, if you're looking for a special evening out, head to the Inn at Death Valley Dining Room, which is also a great spot to start the day with a hearty gourmet breakfast. Most other eateries within the park are mom-and-pop-type places with basic American fare.

Hotel and restaurant reviews have been shortened. For full information visit Fodors.com. Hotel prices are the lowest cost of a standard double room in high season. Restaurant prices are the average cost of a main course at dinner, or it dinner is not served, at lunch.

What It Costs			
$	$$	$$$	$$$$
RESTAURANTS			
under $17	$17–$26	$27–$36	over $36
HOTELS			
under $150	$150–$250	$251–$350	over $350

Tours

Furnace Creek Visitor Center Programs
GUIDED TOURS | This center has many programs, including ranger-led hikes that explore natural wonders such as Golden Canyon, nighttime stargazing parties with telescopes, and evening ranger talks. ⊠ *Furnace Creek Visitor Center, Rte. 190, 30 miles northwest of Death Valley Junction, Death Valley* ☎ *760/786–2331* ⊕ *www.nps.gov/deva/planyourvisit/tours. htm* 🎟 *Free.*

Visitor Information

CONTACTS Death Valley National Park.
☎ *760/786–3200* ⊕ *www.nps.gov/deva.*

Central Death Valley

12 miles west of the Death Valley National Park Highway 190 entrance.

Furnace Creek village (194 feet below sea level) was once the center of mining operations for the Pacific Coast Borax Company. Today, it's the hub of Death Valley National Park, home to park headquarters and visitor center; the Timbisha Indian Village; and the Oasis at Death Valley hotels, golf course, restaurants, and market. Many major park sites are a short drive from here, including Artists Drive, Badwater Basin, Dante's View, and Zabriskie Point. Stovepipe Wells Village (where you will want to fill up at the gas station) lies 25 miles northwest of Furnace Creek.

◉ Sights

HISTORIC SIGHTS
Harmony Borax Works
HISTORIC SITE | Death Valley's mule teams hauled borax from here to the railroad town of Mojave, 165 miles away. The teams plied the route until 1889, when the railroad finally arrived in Zabriskie.

Constructed in 1883, one of the oldest buildings in Death Valley houses the Borax Museum, 2 miles south of the borax works at the Ranch at the Oasis at Death Valley (between the restaurants and the post office). Originally a miners' bunkhouse, the building once stood in Twenty Mule Team Canyon. Now it displays mining machinery and historical exhibits. The adjacent structure is the original mule-team barn. ⊠ *Harmony Borax Works Rd., west of Hwy. 190 at Ranch at Death Valley* ⊕ *www.nps.gov/ deva/historyculture/harmony.htm.*

SCENIC DRIVE
Artists Drive
SCENIC DRIVE | This 9-mile, one-way route skirts the foothills of the Black Mountains and provides intimate views of the changing landscape. Once inside the palette, the valley's expanses are replaced by the small-scale natural beauty of pigments created by volcanic deposits or sedimentary layers. It's a quiet, lonely drive, and shouldn't be rushed. Reach Artists Palette by heading south on Badwater Road from its intersection with Route 190. ⊠ *Death Valley National Park.*

SCENIC STOPS
Artists Palette
NATURE SITE | So called for the contrasting colors of its volcanic deposits and sedimentary layers, this is one of the signature sights of Death Valley. Artists Drive, the approach to the area, is one-way heading north off Badwater Road, so if you're visiting Badwater from Furnace Creek, come here on the way back. The drive winds through foothills of sedimentary and volcanic rocks. About 4 miles along, a short side road veers right to a parking lot that's a few hundred feet before the "palette," whose natural colors include shades of green, gold, and pink. ⊠ *Off Badwater Rd., Death Valley* ⊕ *11 miles south of Furnace Creek.*

Badwater Basin
NATURE SITE | At 282 feet below sea level, Badwater is the lowest spot of land in North America—and also one of the hottest. Stairs and wheelchair ramps descend from the parking lot to a wooden platform that overlooks a sodium chloride pool, a small but remarkably persistent reminder that the valley floor used to contain a lake. You can continue past the platform on a broad, white path that peters out after a ½ mile or so. Badwater is one of the most popular and easily accessible sites within the park. From this lowest point, be sure to look across to Telescope Peak, which towers more than 2 miles above the valley floor. ⊠ *Badwater Rd., Death Valley* ⊕ *19 miles south of Furnace Creek.*

Devil's Golf Course
NATURE SITE | Thousands of miniature salt pinnacles carved into surreal shapes by the desert wind dot this wildly varied landscape. The salt was pushed up to the surface by pressure created as underground salt- and water-bearing gravel crystallized. Get out of your vehicle and take a closer look; you may see perfectly round holes descending into the ground. ⊠ *Badwater Rd., Death Valley* ⊕ *13 miles south of Furnace Creek. Turn right onto dirt road and drive 1 mile.*

Golden Canyon
NATURE SITE | Just south of Furnace Creek, these glimmering mountains are perhaps best known for their role in the original *Star Wars.* The canyon is also a fine hiking spot, with gorgeous views of the Panamint Mountains, ancient dry lake beds, and alluvial fans. ⊠ *Hwy. 178, Death Valley* ⊕ *From Furnace Creek Visitor Center, drive 2 miles south on Hwy. 190, then 2 miles south on Hwy. 178 to parking area; the lot has kiosk with trail guides.*

The Mesquite Flat Sand Dunes

Mesquite Flat Sand Dunes

NATURE SITE | These dunes, made up of minute pieces of quartz and other rock, are ever-changing products of the wind-rippled hills, with curving crests and a sun-bleached hue. The dunes are the most photographed destination in the park, and you can see them at their best at sunrise and sunset. Keep your eyes open for animal tracks—you may even spot a coyote or fox. Bring plenty of water, and note where you parked your car: it's easy to become disoriented in this ocean of sand. If you lose your bearings, climb to the top of a dune, and scan the horizon for the parking lot. ⊠ *Death Valley ⊹ 19 miles north of Hwy. 190, northeast of Stovepipe Wells Village.*

Zabriskie Point

VIEWPOINT | Although only about 710 feet in elevation, this is one of the park's most scenic spots, overlooking a striking panorama of wrinkled, multicolor hills. It's a great place to watch the sunrise, but it can be bustling any time of day. Pair it with a drive out to magnificent Dante's

View. ⊠ *Hwy. 190, Death Valley ⊹ 5 miles south of Furnace Creek.*

TRAILS

Keane Wonder Mine Trail

TRAIL | This fascinating relic of Death Valley's gold-mining past, built in 1907, reopened in November 2017 after nine years of repair work. Its most unique feature is the mile-long tramway that descends 1,000 vertical feet, which once carried gold ore and still has the original cables attached. From here, a network of trails leads to other old mines. A climb to the uppermost tramway terminal is rewarded by expansive views of the valley. ⊠ *Access road off Beatty Cutoff Rd., 17½ miles north of Furnace Creek, Death Valley.*

Mosaic Canyon Trail

TRAIL | FAMILY | A gradual uphill trail (4 miles round-trip) winds through the smoothly polished, marbleized limestone walls of this narrow canyon. There are dry falls to climb at the upper end. *Moderate.* ⊠ *Death Valley ⊹ Trailhead: Access road off Hwy. 190, ½ mile west of Stovepipe Wells Village.*

Natural Bridge Canyon Trail

TRAIL | A rough 2-mile access road from Badwater Road leads to a trailhead. From there, set off to see interesting geological features in addition to the bridge, which is a ½ mile away. The one-way trail continues for a few hundred yards, but scenic returns diminish quickly, and eventually you're confronted with climbing boulders. *Easy.* ✉ *Death Valley* ✣ *Trailhead: Access road off Badwater Rd., 15 miles south of Furnace Creek.*

Salt Creek Interpretive Trail

TRAIL | **FAMILY** | This trail, a ½-mile boardwalk circuit, loops through a spring-fed wash. The nearby hills are brown and gray, but the floor of the wash is alive with aquatic plants such as pickleweed and salt grass. The stream and ponds here are among the few places in the park to see the rare pupfish, the only native fish species in Death Valley. They're most easily seen during their spawning season in February and March. Animals such as bobcats, foxes, coyotes, and snakes visit the spring, and you may also see ravens, common snipes, killdeer, and great blue herons. *Easy.* ✉ *Death Valley* ✣ *Trailhead: Off Hwy. 190, 14 miles north of Furnace Creek.*

VISITOR CENTERS

Furnace Creek Visitor Center and Museum

INFO CENTER | The exhibits and artifacts here provide a broad overview of how Death Valley formed; you can pick up maps at the bookstore run by the Death Valley Natural History Association. This is also the place to find out about ranger programs (available November through April) or check out a live presentation about the valley's cultural and natural history. The helpful center offers regular showings of a 20-minute film about the park, and this is the place for children to get their free Junior Ranger booklet, packed with games and information about the park and its critters. ✉ *Hwy. 190, Death Valley* ✣ *30 miles northwest of Death Valley Junction* ☎ *760/786–3200* 🌐 *www.nps.gov/deva.*

🍴 Restaurants

★ Inn at the Oasis at Death Valley Dining Room

$$$$ | **AMERICAN** | Fireplaces, beamed ceilings, and spectacular views provide a visual feast to match this fine-dining restaurant's ambitious menu. Dinner entrées include salmon, free-range chicken, and filet mignon, and there's a seasonal menu of vegetarian dishes. **Known for:** views of surrounding desert; old-school charm; can be pricey. [$] *Average main: $42* ✉ *Inn at the Oasis at Death Valley, Hwy. 190, Furnace Creek* ☎ *760/786–3385* 🌐 *www.oasisatdeathvalley.com.*

Last Kind Words Saloon

$$$ | **AMERICAN** | Swing through wooden doors into a spacious dining room that re-creates an authentic Old West saloon, decked out with a wooden bar and furniture, mounted animal heads, fugitive wanted fliers, film posters, and other memorabilia. The traditional steak house menu also includes crab cakes and other seafood, along with pastas, flatbreads, and vegan and gluten-free options. **Known for:** hefty steaks, ribs, and seasonal game dishes; extensive drinks menu, from local craft beer to whiskeys and wines; outdoor patio with fireplace. [$] *Average main: $29* ✉ *The Ranch at the Oasis at Death Valley, Hwy. 190, Furnace Creek* ☎ *760/786–3335* 🌐 *www.oasisatdeathvalley.com/dine/last-kind-words-saloon.*

🛏 Hotels

★ The Inn at the Oasis at Death Valley

$$$$ | **HOTEL** | Built in 1927, this adobe-brick-and-stone lodge in one of the park's greenest oases reopened in 2018 after a $100 million renovation, offering Death Valley's most luxurious accommodations, including 22 brand-new one- and two-bedroom casitas. **Pros:** refined; comfortable; great views. **Cons:** services reduced during low season (July and August); expensive; resort fee. [$] *Rooms*

from: $499 ✉ *Furnace Creek Village, near intersection of Hwy. 190 and Badwater Rd., Death Valley* ☎ *760/786–2345* 🌐 *www.oasisatdeathvalley.com* 🛏 *88 rooms* 🍴 *No meals.*

The Ranch at the Oasis at Death Valley
$$$ | **RESORT** | **FAMILY** | Originally the crew headquarters for the Pacific Coast Borax Company, the four buildings here have motel-style rooms that are a great option for families. **Pros:** good family atmosphere; central location; walk to the golf course. **Cons:** rooms can get hot in summer despite A/C; resort fee; thin walls and ceilings in some rooms. [$] *Rooms from: $279* ✉ *Hwy. 190, Furnace Creek* ☎ *760/786–2345* 🌐 *www.oasisatdeathvalley.com* 🛏 *224 rooms* 🍴 *No meals.*

Stovepipe Wells Village Hotel
$ | **HOTEL** | If you prefer quiet nights and an unfettered view of the night sky and nearby Mesquite Flat Sand Dunes and Mosaic Canyon, this property is for you. **Pros:** intimate, relaxed; no big-time partying; authentic desert-community ambience. **Cons:** isolated; cheapest patio rooms very small; limited Wi-Fi access. [$] *Rooms from: $144* ✉ *51880 Hwy. 190, Stovepipe Wells* ☎ *760/786–7090* 🌐 *www.deathvalleyhotels.com* 🛏 *83 rooms* 🍴 *No meals.*

Northern Death Valley

6 miles west of Beatty, Nevada, via Nevada Hwy. 374, and 54 miles north of Furnace Creek via Hwy. 190 and Scotty's Castle Rd.

Venture into the remote northern region of the park to travel along the 27-mile Titus Canyon scenic drive, visit Racetrack and Ubehebe Crater, and hike along Fall Canyon and Titus Canyon Trails. Scotty's Castle, one of the park's main sights, and the 8-mile road that connects it to the park border, is currently closed to repair damage from a 2015 flood; it's expected to reopen in 2022. Check the park website for updates before you visit.

👁 Sights

SCENIC DRIVES

Titus Canyon
SCENIC DRIVE | This popular, one-way, 27-mile drive starts at Nevada Highway 374 (Daylight Pass Road), 2 miles from the park's boundary. Highlights include the Leadville Ghost Town and the spectacular limestone and dolomite narrows. Toward the end, a two-way section of gravel road leads you into the mouth of the canyon from Scotty's Castle Road (closed until at least 2022). This drive is steep, bumpy, and narrow. High-clearance vehicles are strongly recommended. ✉ *Death Valley National Park* ✥ *Access road off Nevada Hwy. 374, 6 miles west of Beatty, NV.*

SCENIC STOPS

Racetrack
NATURE SITE | Getting here involves a 28-mile journey over a washboard dirt road, but the reward is well worth the trip. Where else in the world do rocks move on their own? This mysterious phenomenon, which baffled scientists for years, now appears to have been "settled." Research has shown that the movement merely involves a rare confluence of conditions: rain and then cold to create a layer of ice that becomes a sail, thus enabling gusty winds to readily push the rocks along—sometimes for several hundred yards. When the mud dries, a telltale trail remains. The trek to the Racetrack can be made in a truck or SUV with thick tires (including spares) and high clearance; other types of vehicles aren't recommended as sharp rocks can slash tires. ✉ *Death Valley* ✥ *27 miles west of Ubehebe Crater via rough dirt road.*

Ubehebe Crater
VOLCANO | At 500 feet deep and ½ mile across, this crater resulted from underground steam and gas explosions, some as recently as 300 years ago. Volcanic ash spreads out over most of the area, and the cinders lie as deep as 150 feet near

the crater's rim. Trek down to the crater's floor or walk around it on a fairly level path. Either way, you need about an hour and will be treated to fantastic views. The hike from the floor can be strenuous. ⊠ *N. Death Valley Hwy., Death Valley* ⊕ *8 miles northwest of Scotty's Castle.*

TRAILS
Fall Canyon Trail
TRAIL | This is a 3-mile, one-way hike from the Titus canyon parking area. First, walk ½ mile north along the base of the mountains to a large wash, then go 2½ miles up the canyon to a 35-foot dry fall. You can continue by climbing around to the falls on the south side. *Moderate.* ⊠ *Death Valley National Park* ⊕ *Trailhead: Access road off Scotty's Castle Rd., 33 miles northwest of Furnace Creek.*

Titus Canyon Trail
TRAIL | The narrow floor of Titus Canyon is made of hard-packed gravel and dirt, and it's a constant, moderate, uphill walk (3-mile round-trip is the trail's most popular tack). Klare Spring and some petroglyphs are 5½ miles from the western mouth of the canyon, but you can get a feeling for the area on a shorter walk. *Easy.* ⊠ *Death Valley National Park.*

Southern Death Valley

Entrance on Hwy. 178, 1 mile west of Shoshone and 73 miles southeast of Furnace Creek.

Highway 178 traverses Death Valley from its southern border near Shoshone, through Badwater Basin, and up to Furnace Creek.

Sights
SCENIC STOPS
★ Dante's View
VIEWPOINT | This lookout is 5,450 feet above sea level in the Black Mountains. In the dry desert air you can see across most of 160-mile-long Death Valley. The

view is astounding. Take a 10-minute, mildly strenuous walk from the parking lot toward a series of rocky overlooks, where, with binoculars, you can spot some signature sites. A few interpretive signs point out the highlights below in the valley and across in the Sierra. Getting here from Furnace Creek takes about an hour—time well invested. ⊠ *Dante's View Rd., Death Valley* ⊕ *Off Hwy. 190, 35 miles from Badwater, 20 miles south of Twenty Mule Team Canyon.*

Western Death Valley

Panamint Springs is on Hwy. 190, 30 miles southwest of Stovepipe Wells and 50 miles east of Lone Pine and Hwy. 395.

Panamint Springs, a tiny burg with a rustic resort, market, and gas station, anchors the western portion of the park and is a good base for hiking several trails. Pull over at Father Crowley Vista Point for exceptional views of the Panamint Valley and the high Sierra on Highway 190 if you're traveling between Lone Pine and Panamint Springs.

Sights
SCENIC STOPS
Father Crowley Vista Point
VIEWPOINT | Pull off Highway 190 in Western Death Valley into the vista point parking lot to gaze at the remnants of eerie volcanic flows down to Rainbow Canyon. Stroll a short distance to catch a sweeping overview of northern Panamint Valley. This is also an excellent site for stargazing. ⊠ *Death Valley National Park.*

TRAILS
★ Darwin Falls
TRAIL | **FAMILY** | This lovely, 2-mile round-trip hike rewards you with a refreshing year-round waterfall surrounded by thick vegetation and a rocky gorge. No swimming or bathing is allowed, but it's a

beautiful place for a picnic. Adventurous hikers can scramble higher toward more rewarding views of the falls. ⚠ **Some sections of the trail are not passable for those with mobility issues.** *Easy.* ✉ *Death Valley National Park* ✣ *Trailhead: Access the 2-mile graded dirt road and parking area off Hwy. 190, 1 mile west of Panamint Springs Resort.*

★ Telescope Peak Trail

TRAIL | The 14-mile round-trip (with 3,000 feet of elevation gain) trail begins at Mahogany Flat Campground, which is accessible by a rough dirt road. The steep and at some points treacherous trail winds through pinyon, juniper, and bristlecone pines, with excellent views of Death Valley and Panamint Valley. Ice axes and crampons may be necessary in winter—check at the Furnace Creek Visitor Center. It takes a minimum of six grueling hours to hike to the top of the 11,049-foot peak and then return. *Difficult.* ✉ *Death Valley* ✣ *Trailhead: Off Wildrose Rd., south of Charcoal Kilns.*

🍴 Restaurants

Panamint Springs Resort Restaurant

$ | **AMERICAN** | This is a great place for steak and a beer—choose from more than 150 different beers and ales—or pasta and a salad. In summer, evening meals are served outdoors on the porch, which has spectacular views of Panamint Valley. **Known for:** good burgers; extensive beer selection; great views from the porch. [$] *Average main: $15* ✉ *Hwy. 190, Death Valley* ✣ *31 miles west of Stovepipe Wells* ☎ *775/482–7680* 🌐 *www.panamintsprings.com/services/dining-bar.*

Activities

BIKING

Mountain biking is permitted on any of the back roads and roadways open to the public (bikes aren't permitted on hiking trails). Visit 🌐 *www.nps.gov/deva/planyourvisit/bikingandmtbiking.htm* for a list of suggested routes for all levels of ability.

Escape Adventures

BICYCLING | Ride into the heart of Death Valley on the Death Valley & Red Rock Mountain Bike Tour, a five-day trip through the national park. A customizable two-day journey (on single-track trails and jeep roads) includes accommodations (both camping and inns). Bikes, tents, and other gear may be rented for an additional price. Tours are available February–April and October only. ✉ *Death Valley National Park* ☎ *800/596–2953, 702/596–2953* 🌐 *www.escapeadventures.com* 🎟 *From $1950.*

BIRD-WATCHING

Approximately 350 bird species have been identified in Death Valley. You can download a complete park bird checklist, divided by season, at 🌐 *www.nps.gov/deva/learn/nature/upload/death-valley-bird-checklist.pdf.* Rangers at Furnace Creek Visitor Center often lead birding walks through various locations between November and March.

CAMPING

Camping is prohibited in historic sites and day-use spots. You'll need a high-clearance or 4X4 vehicle to reach campgrounds. For backcountry camping information, visit 🌐 *www.nps.gov/deva/planyourvisit/camping.htm.*

Fires are permitted only in metal grates and may be restricted in summer. Wood gathering is prohibited at all campgrounds, and it's best to bring your own. Firewood is expensive and limited in supply at general stores in Furnace Creek and Stovepipe Wells.

Furnace Creek. This campground, 196 feet below sea level, has some shaded tent sites and is open all year. ✉ *Hwy. 190, Furnace Creek* ☎ *760/786–2441.*

Mahogany Flat. If you have a four-wheel-drive vehicle and want to scale Telescope Peak, the park's highest mountain, you might want to sleep at one of the few shaded spots in Death Valley, at a cool 8,133 feet. ⊠ *Off Wildrose Rd., south of Charcoal Kilns* ☎ *No phone.*

Panamint Springs Resort. Part of a complex that includes a motel and cabin, this campground is surrounded by cottonwoods. The daily fee includes use of the showers and restrooms. ⊠ *Hwy. 190, 28 miles west of Stovepipe Wells* ☎ *775/482–7680.*

Sunset Campground. This first-come, first-served campground is a gravel-and-asphalt RV city. Closed mid-April to mid-October. ⊠ *Sunset Campground Rd., 1 mile north of Furnace Creek* ☎ *800/365–2267.*

Texas Spring. This campsite south of the Furnace Creek Visitor Center has good views and facilities and is a few dollars cheaper than Furnace Creek. It's closed mid-May to mid-October. ⊠ *Off Badwater Rd., south of Furnace Creek Visitor Center* ☎ *800/365–2267.*

EDUCATIONAL PROGRAMS
Junior Ranger Program
TOUR—SIGHT | FAMILY | Children can pick up a workbook and complete activities to earn a souvenir badge. ⊠ *Death Valley National Park.*

FOUR-WHEELING
Butte Valley
TOUR—SPORTS | A high-clearance, four-wheel-drive vehicle and nerves of steel are required to tackle this 21-mile road in the southwest part of the park. It climbs from 200 feet below sea level to an elevation of 4,700 feet, and the geological formations along the way reveal the development of Death Valley. It also travels through Butte Valley, passing the Warm Springs talc mine, to Geologist's Cabin, a charming and cheery little structure where you can spend the night, if nobody else beats you to it. The cabin, which sits under a cottonwood tree, has a fireplace, table and chairs, and a sink. Farther up the road, Stella's Cabin and Russell Camp are also open for public

use. Keep the historic cabins clean, and restock any items that you use. The road is even rougher if you continue over Mengel Pass. Check road conditions before heading out. ⊠ *Trailhead on Warm Spring Canyon Rd., Death Valley* ✛ *50 miles south of Furnace Creek Visitor Center.*

GOLF
Furnace Creek Golf Course at the Oasis at Death Valley
GOLF | Golfers rave about how their drives carry at altitude, so what happens on the lowest golf course in the world (214 feet below sea level)? Its improbably green fairways are lined with date palms and tamarisk trees, and its level of difficulty is rated surprisingly high. You can rent clubs and carts, and there are golf packages available for resort guests. In fall and winter, reservations are essential. ⊠ *Hwy. 190, Furnace Creek* ☎ *760/786–3373* ⊕ *www.oasisatdeathvalley.com* ✑ *From $48* ⅄. *18 holes, 6215 yards, par 70.*

HIKING
Plan to hike before or after midday in the spring, summer, or fall, unless you're in the mood for a masochistic baking. Carry plenty of water, wear protective clothing, and keep an eye out for black widows, scorpions, snakes, and other potentially dangerous creatures.

HORSEBACK AND CARRIAGE RIDES
Furnace Creek Stables
HORSEBACK RIDING | FAMILY | Set off on a one- or two-hour guided horseback, carriage, or hay wagon ride from Furnace Creek Stables. The rides traverse trails with views of the surrounding mountains, where multicolor volcanic rock and alluvial fans form a background for date palms and other vegetation. Evening carriage rides take passengers around the golf course and the Ranch at Death Valley. The stables are open October–May only. ⊠ *Hwy. 190, Furnace Creek* ☎ *760/614–1018* ⊕ *www.oasisatdeathvalley.com/plan/horseback-wagon-rides* ✑ *From $60.*

What's Nearby

Beatty

7 miles east of Death Valley National Park Devil's Gate entrance.

The tiny Old West town of Beatty, a northeastern gateway to Death Valley National Park, has a well-preserved historic downtown district that's worth exploring. It's also a good place to relax and refresh thanks to its cluster of hotels, restaurants, and other services. Hundreds of hiking, biking, and off-highway vehicle roads stretch out from here in all directions. Beatty is also home to the Death Valley Nut and Candy Company, Nevada's largest candy store, and the Rhyolite Ghost Town is just 5 miles west of downtown.

ESSENTIALS

VISITOR INFORMATION Beatty Chamber of Commerce. ✉ *119 E. Main St., Beatty* ☎ *775/553–2424* 🌐 *www.beattynevada.org.*

Sights

Rhyolite

GHOST TOWN | FAMILY | Though it's not within the boundary of Death Valley National Park, this Nevada ghost town, named for the silica volcanic rock nearby, is still a big draw. Around 1904, Rhyolite's Montgomery Shoshone Mine caused a financial boom, and fancy buildings sprung up all over town. Today you can still explore many of the crumbling edifices. The Bottle House, built by miner Tom Kelly out of almost 50,000 Adolphus Busch beer bottles, is a must-see. ✉ *Hwy. 374* ✣ *35 miles north of Furnace Creek Visitor Center and 5 miles west of Beatty* 🌐 *www.nps.gov/deva/learn/historyculture/rhyolite-ghost-town.htm.*

Restaurants

Smokin J's BBQ

$$ | BARBECUE | A local favorite, this central Texas–style barbecue joint slow cooks brisket, pulled pork, ribs, and chicken on an oak-fired grill and serves them in baskets heaping with fries, onion rings, and other sides. Pick up meats by the pound to feast on at your lodgings later on. **Known for:** smoked-meat sandwiches; brisket chili bowls; great-value combo plates and meals. [$] *Average main: $17* ✉ *107 W. Main St., Beatty* ☎ *775/553–5160* 🌐 *www.facebook.com/Smokinjsbarbecue.*

Shoshone

1 mile from Death Valley National Park's Badwater entrance.

A prospector founded this tiny burg in 1910, hoping to build businesses around a new rail stop. He and his family eventually developed the town, and his descendents still run Shoshone Village, which encompasses a hotel, general store, gas station, museum, spring-fed swimming pool, restaurant, campground, and RV park. Nearby nature trails wind through wetlands, pupfish ponds, and bird and endangered-species habitats.

ESSENTIALS

VISITOR INFORMATION Shoshone Museum Visitor Center. ✉ *Rte. 127, Shoshone* ☎ *760/852–4524* 🌐 *shoshonevillage.com/shoshone-museum.html.*

Sights

Dublin Gulch

CAVE | FAMILY | A series of caves, carved into the caliche soil by miners during the 1920s, is a great spot for exploring and is a hit with kids. Among its more famous residents were Shorty Harris and Death Valley Scotty, who spent many nights weaving tales of strikes and adventures to entertain fellow miners. You aren't allowed to walk inside, but you can view the cells—with their stone walls, sleeping platforms, and metal chimneys—from the exterior. ✉ *Shoshone* ✥ *0.3 miles southwest of Shoshone Village off Hwy. 127* 🌐 *www.shoshonevillage.com/explore-shoshone.*

Marta Becket's Amargosa Opera House

PERFORMANCE VENUE | An artist and dancer from New York, Marta Becket first visited the former railway town of Death Valley Junction while on tour in 1967. Later that year, she returned to town and leased a boarded-up social hall that sat amid a group of rundown mock Spanish–colonial buildings. The nonprofit she formed in the early 1970s eventually purchased the property, where she performed for nearly 50 years. To compensate for the sparse audiences in the early days, Becket painted a Renaissance-era Spanish crowd on the walls and ceiling, turning the theater into a trompe-l'oeil masterpiece. A hotel and café still operate on-site, and the opera house presents performances from October to May. Guided tours are available year-round for a suggested $5 donation per person. ✉ *Rte. 127, Death Valley Junction* ✥ *27 miles north of Shoshone* ☎ *760/852–4441* 🌐 *www.amargosaoperahouse.org* 🎟 *Varies.*

Shoshone Museum

MUSEUM | This museum chronicles the local history of Death Valley and houses a unique collection of period items and minerals and rocks from the area. ✉ *Rte. 127, Shoshone* ☎ *760/852–4524* 🌐 *www.shoshonevillage.com/shoshone-museum.html* 🎟 *Free.*

🍴 Restaurants

Crowbar Café and Saloon

$ | **AMERICAN** | **FAMILY** | In an old wooden building where antique photos adorn the walls and mining equipment stands in the corners, the Crowbar serves enormous helpings of regional dishes such as steak and taco salads. Home-baked fruit pies make fine desserts, and frosty beers are surefire thirst quenchers. **Known for:** home-baked fruit pies; rattlesnake chili; great breakfast spot. [$] *Average main: $15* ✉ *Rte. 127, Shoshone* ☎ *760/852–4123* 🌐 *www.shoshonevillage.com/shoshone-crowbar-cafe-saloon.html.*

🛏 Hotels

Shoshone Inn

$ | **HOTEL** | Built in 1956, the rustic Shoshone Inn has simple, cozy rooms surrounding a motor court and a warm spring-fed swimming pool built into the foothills. **Pros:** walk to market, restaurant, museum; courtyard with firepit; peaceful retreat. **Cons:** an hour's drive to main park sights; certain rooms and beds too small for some; no room phones, spotty cell service. [$] *Rooms from: $135* ✉ *Hwy. 127, Shoshone* ☎ *760/852–4335* 🌐 *www.shoshonevillage.com/death-valley-lodging-shoshone-inn* 🛏 *18 units* 🍽 *No meals.*

Chapter 11

THE CENTRAL COAST

11

FROM VENTURA TO BIG SUR WITH CHANNEL ISLANDS NATIONAL PARK

Updated by
Cheryl Crabtree

 Sights
★★★★★

 Restaurants
★★★★☆

 Hotels
★★★★★

 Shopping
★★☆☆☆

 Nightlife
★☆☆☆☆

WELCOME TO THE CENTRAL COAST

TOP REASONS TO GO

★ **Incredible nature:** The wild and wonderful Central Coast is home to Channel Islands National Park, two national marine sanctuaries, state parks and beaches, and the rugged Los Padres National Forest.

★ **Edible bounty:** Land and sea provide enough fresh regional foods to satisfy the most sophisticated foodies. Get your fill at countless farmers' markets, wineries, and restaurants.

★ **Outdoor activities:** Kick back and revel in the California lifestyle. Surf, golf, kayak, hike, play tennis—or just hang out and enjoy the gorgeous scenery.

★ **Small-town charm, big-city culture:** With all the amazing cultural opportunities—museums, theater, music, and festivals—you might start thinking you're in L.A. or San Francisco.

★ **Wine tasting:** Central Coast wines earn high critical praise. Sample them in urban tasting rooms, dusty crossroads towns, and at high- and low-tech rural wineries.

1 Ventura. A walkable city with miles of beaches.

2 Channel Islands National Park. North America's Galapagos.

3 Ojai. Lush site of the film *Lost Horizon.*

4 Santa Barbara. The American Riviera.

5 Santa Ynez. An 1880s frontier town preserved.

6 Los Olivos. Has tasting rooms galore.

7 Solvang. America's "Little Denmark."

8 Buellton. Gateway to Santa Barbara wine country.

9 Pismo Beach. Classic California coastal city.

10 Avila Beach. A tiny village in a sunny cove.

11 San Luis Obispo. A busy university town.

12 Paso Robles. A small city amid a booming wine region.

13 Morro Bay. Outdoor activities reign here.

14 Cambria. A historic village with scenic shores and towering pines.

15 San Simeon. Home to Hearst Castle.

16 Big Sur Coast. A bucket-list road trip.

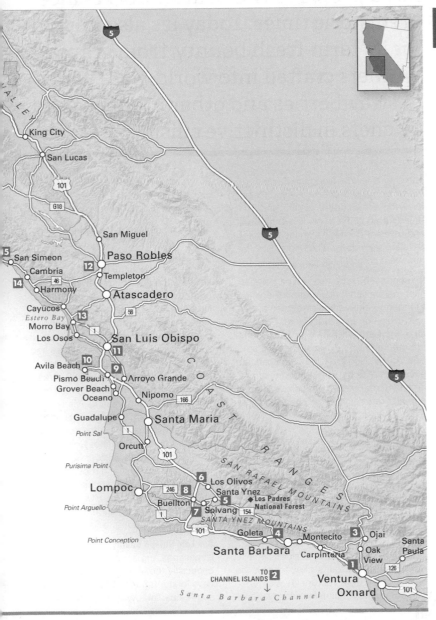

Balmy weather, glorious beaches, crystal-clear air, and serene landscapes have lured people to the Central Coast since prehistoric times. Today it's also known for its farm-fresh bounty, from grapes vintners crafted into world-class wines, to strawberries and other produce used by chefs in distinctive cuisine.

The scenic variety along the Pacific coast is equally impressive—you'll see everything from dramatic cliffs and grass-tufted bluffs to wildlife estuaries and miles of dunes. It's an ideal place to relax, slow down, and appreciate the abundant natural beauty.

Offshore, a pristine national park and a vast marine sanctuary protect the wild, wonderful underwater resources of this incredible corner of the planet. But not all of the Central Coast's top attractions are natural: Ventura, Santa Barbara, and San Luis Obispo are filled with sparkling examples of Spanish-Mediterranean architecture, bustling shopping districts, and first-rate restaurants showcasing regional foods and wines.

MAJOR REGIONS

Ventura County. Ventura County was first settled by the Chumash Indians. Spanish missionaries were the first Europeans to arrive, followed by Americans and other Europeans, who established towns, transportation networks, and farms. Since the 1920s, agriculture has been steadily replaced as the area's main industry—first by the oil business and more recently by tourism. Accessible via boat or plane from Ventura (as well as Santa Barbara), Channel Islands National Park consists of five protected islands just 11 miles offshore where hiking, kayaking, and wildlife viewing abound.

Santa Barbara County. The Santa Ynez Mountains divide the county geographically; U.S. 101 passes through a mountain tunnel leading inland. The South Coast includes the city of Santa Barbara and other coastal towns and small cities. Northern Santa Barbara County, which includes the communities of Buellton, Solvang, Santa Ynez, and Los Olivos, used to be known for sprawling ranches and strawberry and broccoli fields. Today, its nearly 300 wineries and 15,000 acres of vineyards stretch from the Santa Ynez Valley in the south to Santa Maria in the north. More than 70 grape varietals grow here, but over half the vineyards are planted with Chardonnay, Pinot Noir, and Syrah. Two-lane Highway 154 over San Marcos Pass is the shortest and most scenic route from Santa Barbara into the Santa Ynez Valley. Alternatively, U.S. 101 travels north 43 miles to Buellton, then 7 miles east through Solvang to Santa Ynez.

San Luis Obispo County. The area's pristine landscapes and abundant wildlife areas, especially those around Morro Bay, have long attracted nature lovers. In the south, coastal towns like Pismo Beach have great sand and surf. An inland wine region stretches from the Edna, Arroyo Grande, and Avila valleys and Nipomo in the south to Paso Robles in the north. A good way to explore the county is to follow the 101-mile Highway 1 Discovery Route (⊕ *highway1discoveryroute. com*), which travels off the beaten track through 10 small communities, from to Oceano/Nipomo, Arroyo Grande, Avila Beach, and Edna Valley in the south to Los Osos/Baywood Park, Cayucos, Cambria, San Simeon, and Ragged Point in the north.

Big Sur Coast. Long a retreat of artists and writers, Big Sur is a place of ancient forests and rugged shores that stretch 90 miles from San Simeon to Carmel. Residents have protected it from over-development, and much of the region lies within state parks and the more than 165,000-acre Ventana Wilderness, itself part of the Los Padres National Forest.

Planning

When to Go

The Central Coast climate is mild year-round. If you like to swim in warmer (if still nippy) ocean waters, July and August are the best months to visit. Be aware that this is also high season. Fog often rolls in along the coastal areas in early summer; you'll need a jacket, especially after sunset, close to the shore. It usually rains from December through March. From April to early June and early fall the weather is almost as fine as in high season, and the pace is less hectic.

FESTIVALS AND EVENTS

Old Spanish Days Fiesta. Santa Barbara celebrates its Spanish, Mexican, and Chumash heritage in early August with music, dancing, an all-equestrian parade, a carnival, and a rodeo. ⊕ *www. sbfiesta.org*.

Paso Robles Wine Festival. Most local wineries pour at this mid-May outdoor festival with winery open houses, winemaker dinners, live bands, and food vendors. ⊕ *pasowine.com*.

Santa Barbara International Film Festival. The 11-day festival in February or early March attracts film enthusiasts and major stars to downtown venues for screenings, panels, and tributes. ⊕ *sbiff.org*.

Summer Solstice Celebration. More than 100,000 revelers celebrate the arts at this mid-June Santa Barbara event featuring a parade of costumed participants who dance, drum, and ride people-powered floats up State Street. ⊕ *www. solsticeparade.com*.

Getting Here and Around

AIR

Alaska Air, American, Contour, Delta, Frontier, Southwest, and United fly to Santa Barbara Airport (SBA), 9 miles from downtown. United, Alaska, and American provide service to San Luis Obispo County Regional Airport (SBP), 3 miles from downtown San Luis Obispo.

Santa Barbara Airbus shuttles travelers between Santa Barbara and Los Angeles for $60 one-way and $110 round-trip. The Santa Barbara Metropolitan Transit District Bus 11 ($1.75) runs every 30 minutes from the airport to the downtown transit center. A taxi between the airport and the hotel districts costs between $22 and $40.

AIRPORT CONTACTS San Luis Obispo County Regional Airport. (*SBP*) ✉ *901 Airport Dr., off Hwy. 227, San Luis Obispo* ☎ *805/781–5205* ⊕ *sloairport.com*. **Santa Barbara Airbus.** ☎ *805/964–7759, 800/423–1618* ⊕ *www.sbairbus.com*. **Santa Barbara Airport.** (*SBA*) ✉ *500 Fowler Rd., off U.S. 101 Exit 104B, Santa Barbara* ☎ *805/683–4011* ⊕ *www.flysba.santabarbaraca.gov*.

BUS

Greyhound provides service from Los Angeles and San Francisco to San Luis Obispo, Ventura, and Santa Barbara. In addition to serving these three cities, several local transit companies provide regional service, including Gold Coast Transit (Ventura and Ojai); Santa Barbara Metropolitan Transit District (the city and the county's south coast, from Goleta in the west to Carpinteria in the east); Santa Ynez Valley Transit (Santa Ynez, Los Olivos, Ballard, Solvang, and Buellton); and San Luis Obispo Regional Transit Authority (SLORTA; San Luis Obispo, Paso Robles, and Pismo Beach and other coastal towns).

BUS CONTACTS Gold Coast Transit. ☎ 805/487–4222 ⊕ goldcoasttransit.org. **San Luis Obispo Regional Transit Authority.** ☎ 805/541–2228 ⊕ www.slorta.org. **Santa Barbara Metropolitan Transit District.** ☎ 805/963–3366 ⊕ sbmtd.gov. **Santa Ynez Valley Transit.** ☎ 805/688–5452 ⊕ www.syvt.com.

CAR

Driving is the easiest way to experience the Central Coast. The main north–south routes to and through the Central Coast from Los Angeles and San Francisco are U.S. 101, which travels inland, and highly scenic Highway 1, which hugs the coast. ■TIP→ **A great way to see the region is by following the Highway 1 Discovery Route, a 101-mile designated road trip that takes you off the beaten track through 10 small towns and cities.** Note that, between Ventura County and northern Santa Barbara County, U.S. 101 and Highway 1 are the same road. Highway 1 separates from U.S. 101 north of Gaviota, rejoining it again at Pismo Beach. Along any stretch where these two highways are separate, U.S. 101 is the quicker route.

The most dramatic section of the Central Coast is the 70 miles between San Simeon and Big Sur. The road is narrow and twisting, with a single lane in each direction. In fog or rain the drive can be downright nerve-racking; in wet seasons mudslides can close portions of the road. Other routes into the Central Coast include Highway 46 and Highway 33, which head, respectively, west and south from I–5 near Bakersfield.

CONTACTS California Highway 1 Discovery Route. ⊕ highway1discoveryroute.com.

TRAIN

The Amtrak *Coast Starlight*, which runs between Los Angeles and Seattle via Oakland, stops in Paso Robles, San Luis Obispo, Santa Barbara, and Oxnard. Amtrak also runs several *Pacific Surfliner* trains and buses daily between San Luis Obispo, Santa Barbara, Los Angeles, and San Diego. Metrolink Regional Rail Service trains connect Ventura and Oxnard with Los Angeles and points between.

TRAIN CONTACTS Metrolink. ☎ 800/371–5465 ⊕ metrolinktrains.com.

Restaurants

The cuisine in Ventura and Santa Barbara is every bit as eclectic as it is in California's bigger cities; fresh seafood is a standout. A foodie renaissance has overtaken the entire region from Ventura to Paso Robles, spawning dozens of restaurants touting locavore cuisine made with fresh organic produce and meats. Dining attire on the Central Coast is generally casual, though slightly dressy casual wear is the custom at pricier restaurants.

Hotels

Expect to pay top dollar for rooms along the shore, especially in summer. Moderately priced hotels and motels do exist—most just a short drive inland from their higher-price counterparts. Make your reservations as early as possible, and take advantage of midweek specials to get the best rates. It's common for lodgings to require two-day minimum stays on holidays and some weekends, especially in summer, and to double rates during festivals and other events.

Restaurant and hotel reviews have been shortened. For full information, visit Fodors.com. Restaurant prices are the average cost of a main course at dinner, or if dinner is not served, at lunch. Hotel prices are the lowest cost of a standard double room in high season.

What It Costs

	$	$$	$$$	$$$$
RESTAURANTS				
	under $17	$17–$26	$27–$36	over $36
HOTELS				
	under $150	$150–$250	$251–$350	over $350

Tours

Many tour companies will pick you up at your hotel or central locations; ask about this when booking.

Central Coast Food Tours
SPECIAL-INTEREST | Food and wine destinations are the focus of this outfit's walking tours of shops, restaurants, wineries, and other spots in San Luis Obispo, Paso Robles, and elsewhere. ☎ 844/337–1686 ⊕ centralcoastfoodtours.com ✉ From $94.

Cloud Climbers Jeep and Wine Tours
SPECIAL-INTEREST | This outfit conducts trips in open-air, six-passenger jeeps to the Santa Barbara/Santa Ynez mountains and Wine Country. Tour options include wine tasting, mountain, sunset, and a discovery adventure for families. The company also offers a four-hour All Around Ojai Tour and arranges horseback riding and trap-shooting tours. ☎ 805/646–3200 ⊕ ccjeeps.com ✉ From $400 for exclusive jeep tour w/ driver guide.

Grapeline Wine Tours
SPECIAL-INTEREST | Wine and vineyard picnic tours in Paso Robles and the Santa Ynez Valley are Grapeline's specialty. ☎ 951/693–5755 ⊕ gogrape.com ✉ From $139.

Santa Barbara Adventure Company
SPECIAL-INTEREST | This outfit provides coastal kayak tours, bike tours, and surf and SUP lessons. Sister company Santa Barbara Wine Country Tours shuttles guests on tasting adventures in the Santa Ynez Valley. ✉ 32 E. Haley St., Santa Barbara ☎ 805/824–9283 ⊕ www.sbadventureco.com.

Santa Barbara Wine Country Cycling Tours
BICYCLE TOURS | The company leads half- and full-day tours of the Santa Ynez wine region, conducts hiking and cycling tours, and rents bicycles and e-bikes. ☎ 888/557–8687, 805/686–9490 ⊕ winecountrycycling.com ✉ From $125.

Stagecoach Co. Wine Tours
SPECIAL-INTEREST | Locally owned and operated, Stagecoach runs daily wine-tasting excursions and group and private tours to smaller boutique wineries through the Santa Ynez Valley in Sprinter vans or a minicoach. ✉ Solvang ☎ 805/686–8347 ⊕ winetourssantaynez.com ✉ From $183.

Sustainable Vine Wine Tours
SPECIAL-INTEREST | This green-minded company specializes in eco-friendly Santa Ynez Valley wine tours in luxury vans and Tesla SUVs. Trips include tastings at limited-production wineries committed to sustainable practices. An organic picnic lunch is served. ☎ 805/698–3911 ⊕ sustainablevine.com ✉ From $185.

TOAST Tours
SPECIAL-INTEREST | Owned and operated by a sommelier couple with extensive guiding experience in Europe, Napa and Sonoma before relocating to Paso Robles, TOAST leads small-group tours to Central Coast wineries tasting rooms and Hearst Castle. They also offer three-day

tours from either Los Angeles or San Francisco to Central Coast wineries and Hearst Castle, as well as private tours, charters, and transportation. ☎ *805/400–3141* ⊕ *www.toasttours.com* ✉ *From $139.*

Visitor Information

CONTACTS Central Coast Tourism Council. ⊕ *centralcoast-tourism.com.* **Santa Barbara Vintners.** ☎ *805/688–0881* ⊕ *www.sbcountywines.com.* **SLO Coast Wine.** ☎ *805/550–2506* ⊕ *slocoastwine.com.* **Visit Santa Barbara.** ⊕ *www.santabaraca.com.* **Visit the Santa Ynez Valley.** ⊕ *www.visitsyv.com.* **Visit SLO CAL.** ☎ *805/541–8000* ⊕ *slocal.com.*

Ventura

60 miles north of Los Angeles.

Ventura Harbor is home to myriad fishing boats, restaurants, and water-activity centers where you can rent boats and take harbor cruises. The city is also very walkable. If you drive here, park your car in one of the city's free 24-hour parking lots, and explore on foot.

The most popular outdoor activities in Ventura are beach-going and whale-watching. California gray whales migrate offshore through the Santa Barbara Channel from late December through March; giant blue and humpback whales feed here from mid-June through September. The channel teems with marine life year-round, so tours, which depart from Ventura Harbor, include more than just whale sightings. The harbor is also home to the Channel Islands National Park visitor center and to Island Packers, which transports visitors to the park's islands.

GETTING HERE AND AROUND
U.S. 101 is the north–south main route into town, but for a scenic drive, take Highway 1 north from Santa Monica. The highway merges with U.S. 101 just south of Ventura. ■**TIP→ Traveling north to Ventura from Los Angeles on weekdays, it's best to depart before 6 am, between 10 and 2, or after 7 pm, or you'll get caught in the extended rush-hour traffic. Coming south from Santa Barbara, depart before 1 or after 6 pm.** On weekends, traffic is generally fine except southbound on U.S. 101 between Santa Barbara and Ventura on Sunday late afternoon and early evening.

ESSENTIALS
VISITOR INFORMATION Ventura Visitors and Convention Bureau. ✉ *Downtown Visitor Center, 101 S. California St.* ☎ *805/641–1400* ⊕ *visitventuraca.com.*

 # Sights

Mission San Buenaventura
HISTORIC SITE | The ninth of the 21 California missions, Mission San Buenaventura was established in 1782, and the current church was rebuilt and rededicated in 1809. A self-guided tour takes you through a small museum, a quiet courtyard, and a chapel with 250-year-old paintings. ✉ *211 E. Main St., at Figueroa St.* ☎ *805/648–4496 gift shop* ⊕ *www.sanbuenaventuramission.org* ✉ *$5.*

Museum of Ventura County
MUSEUM | Exhibits in a contemporary complex of galleries and a sunny courtyard plaza tell the story of Ventura County from prehistoric times to the present. A highlight is the gallery that contains Ojai artist George Stuart's historical figures, dressed in exceptionally detailed, custom-made clothing reflecting their particular eras. In the courtyard, eight panels made with 45,000 pieces of cut glass form a history time line. ✉ *100 E. Main St., at S. Ventura Ave.* ☎ *805/653–0323* ⊕ *www.venturamuseum.org* ✉ *$5* ⊘ *Closed Mon.–Wed.*

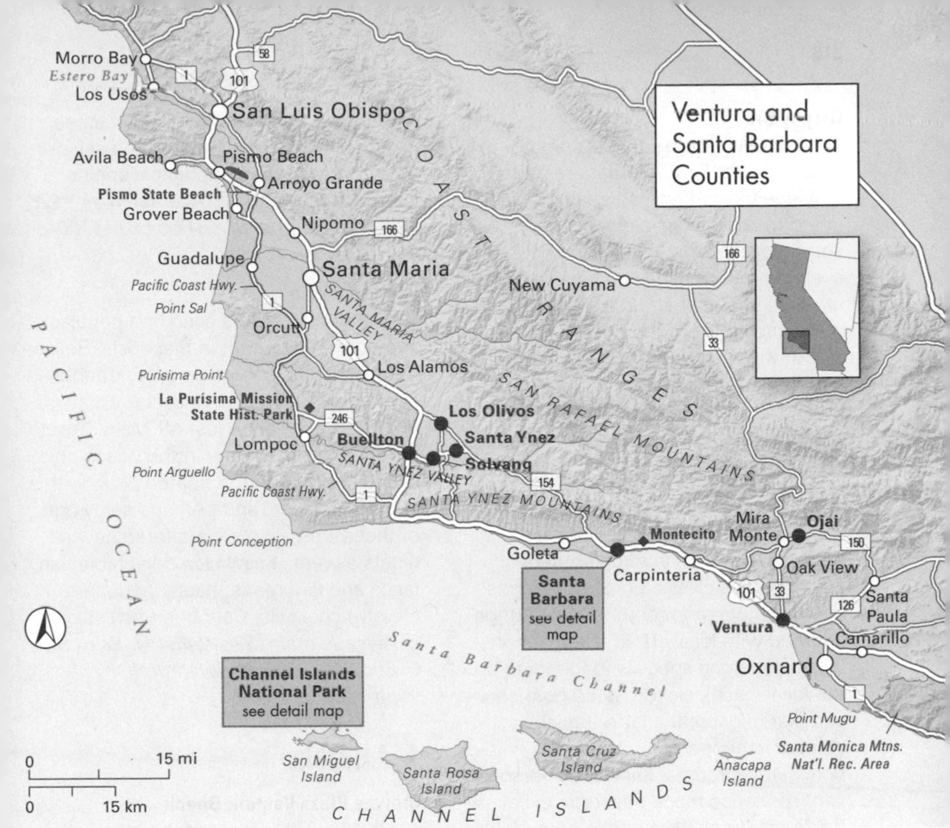

★ Ventura Oceanfront

PROMENADE | Four miles of gorgeous coastline stretch from the county fairgrounds at the northern border of the city of San Buenaventura, through San Buenaventura State Beach, down to Ventura Harbor Village in the south. The main attraction here is the San Buenaventura City Pier, a landmark built in 1872 and restored in 1993. Surfers rip the waves just north of the pier, and sunbathers relax on white-sand beaches on either side. The mile-long promenade and the Omer Rains Bike Trail north of the pier attract scores of joggers, surrey cyclers, and bikers throughout the year. ✉ *California St., at ocean's edge.*

🍴 Restaurants

Andria's Seafood

$$ | **SEAFOOD** | The specialties at this casual, family-oriented restaurant in Ventura Harbor Village are fresh fish-and-chips and homemade clam chowder. After placing your order at the counter, you can sit outside on the patio and enjoy the view of the harbor and marina. **Known for:** harbor views; plates with locally caught grilled fish; wide-ranging menu of salads, burgers, chicken, and sides. [$] *Average main: $18* ✉ *1449 Spinnaker Dr., Suite A* ☎ *805/654–0546* 🌐 *andriasseafood.com.*

Brophy Bros

$$ | **SEAFOOD** | The Ventura outpost of the wildly popular Santa Barbara restaurant provides the same fresh seafood-oriented meals in a spacious second-story setting overlooking the harbor. Feast on everything from fish-and-chips and crab cakes to chowder and delectable fish—often straight from the boats moored below. **Known for:** lively atmosphere; harbor views; killer clam bar. [$] *Average main: $26* ✉ *1559 Spinnaker Dr., in Ventura Harbor Village* ☎ *805/639–0865* 🌐 *brophybros.com.*

★ Café Zack

$$$ | **AMERICAN** | A local favorite for anniversaries and other celebrations, Zack's serves classic European dishes in an intimate, two-room 1930s cottage adorned with local art. Entrées of note include seafood specials (depending on the local catch), slow-roasted boar shank, and filet mignon, the latter typically crusted in peppercorns or topped with porcini mushrooms. **Known for:** personal service; house-made desserts; excellent California wines. [$] *Average main: $32* ✉ *1095 E. Thompson Blvd., at S. Ann St.* ☎ *805/643–9445* 🌐 *cafezack.com* 🕒 *Closed Sun. No lunch Sat.*

Harbor Cove Café

$ | **CAFÉ** | Waterfront views (from beside the Channel Islands National Park Robert J. Lagomarsino Visitor Center), hearty, cooked-to-order meals, and boxed picnic lunches make this casual dockside eatery a popular spot for island travelers and beachgoers. **Known for:** hearty breakfasts; harbor views; seafood tacos. [$] *Average main: $15* ✉ *1867 Spinnaker Dr.* ☎ *805/658–1639* 🕒 *No dinner.*

Lure Fish House

$$ | **SEAFOOD** | Fresh, sustainably caught seafood charbroiled over a mesquite grill, a well-stocked oyster bar, specialty cocktails, and a wine list heavy on local vintages lure diners into this slick, nautical-theme space downtown. The menu, which emphasizes the use of organic vegetables alongside the local catches, includes tacos, sandwiches, and salads. **Known for:** shrimp-and-chips; cioppino; charbroiled oysters. [$] *Average main: $25* ✉ *60 S. California St.* ☎ *805/567–4400* 🌐 *lurefishhouse.com.*

Rumfish y Vino

$$ | **CARIBBEAN** | The sibling of a popular namesake restaurant in Placencia, Belize, Rumfish y Vino serves up zesty Caribbean fare with a California Wine Country twist in a courtyard venue just off Main Street near the mission. Dine in the beach-chic dining room or on the heated patio with a roaring fireplace, and perhaps enjoy one of the live music shows offered several nights a week. **Known for:** delectable fish tacos and flatbreads; happy hour and creative cocktails; Caribbean fish stew. [$] *Average main: $26* ✉ *434 N. Palm St.* ☎ *805/667–9288* 🌐 *www.rumfishyvino-ventura.com.*

🛏 Hotels

Crowne Plaza Ventura Beach

$$ | **HOTEL** | A 12-story hotel with an enviable location on the beach and next to a historic pier, the Crowne Plaza is within walking distance of downtown restaurants and nightlife. **Pros:** on the beach; near downtown; steps from waterfront. **Cons:** early-morning train noise; waterfront crowded in summer; self parking is in an adjacent public lot. [$] *Rooms from: $200* ✉ *450 E. Harbor Blvd.* ☎ *800/842–0800, 805/648–2100* 🌐 *cpventura.com* 🛏 *235 rooms* 🍴 *No meals.*

Four Points by Sheraton Ventura Harbor Resort

$$ | **RESORT** | An on-site restaurant, spacious rooms, and a slew of amenities make this 17-acre property—which includes sister hotel Holiday Inn Express—a popular and practical choice for Channel Islands visitors. **Pros:** close to island transportation; quiet location; short drive to historic downtown. **Cons:** not in the heart of downtown; noisy seagulls

sometimes congregate nearby; service can be spotty. $ Rooms from: $199 ✉ 1050 Schooner Dr. ☎ 805/658–1212, 800/368–7764 ⊕ fourpoints.com/ventura ⇱ 106 rooms ⦿ No meals.

Holiday Inn Express Ventura Harbor
$$ | HOTEL | A favorite among Channel Islands visitors, this quiet, comfortable, lodge-inspired property sits right at the Ventura Harbor entrance. **Pros:** quiet at night; easy access to harbor restaurants and activities; five-minute drive to downtown. **Cons:** busy area on weekends; complaints of erratic service; fee for parking. $ Rooms from: $189 ✉ 1080 Navigator Dr. ☎ 805/856–9533, 888/233–9450 ⊕ hiexpress.com ⇱ 109 rooms ⦿ Free breakfast.

Ventura Beach Marriott
$$ | HOTEL | Spacious, contemporary rooms, a peaceful location just steps from San Buenaventura State Beach, and easy access to downtown arts and culture make the Marriott a popular choice. **Pros:** walk to beach, biking/jogging trails, and restaurants; a block from historic pier; great value for location. **Cons:** close to highway; near busy intersection; special event noise some evenings. $ Rooms from: $239 ✉ 2055 E. Harbor Blvd. ☎ 805/643–6000, 888/236–2427 ⊕ marriottventurabeach.com ⇱ 285 rooms ⦿ No meals.

Waypoint Ventura
$$ | HOTEL | Stay in a meticulousy restored vintage Airstream or Spartan trailer in a landscaped park on a bluff overlooking Ventura State Beach. **Pros:** a block from Ventura Pier and a short walk to downtown; free access to fire pits, barbecues, lawn games, and house bikes; walk to craft brewery (sister business). **Cons:** near the train tracks; can be difficult to find; near several ongoing construction sites. $ Rooms from: $209 ✉ 398 S. Ash St., Unit E ☎ 805/888–5750 ⊕ www.waypointventura.com ⇱ 19 vintage trailers ⦿ No meals.

Channel Islands National Park

Via boat, Santa Cruz Island is 32 miles southwest of Ventura Harbor and 28 miles south of Santa Barbara.

On crystal-clear days the craggy peaks of the Channel Islands are easy to see from the mainland, jutting from the Pacific in such sharp detail it seems you could reach out and touch them. The islands are not too far away—a high-speed boat will whisk you to the closest ones in less than an hour—yet very few people ever visit them. Those who do venture out to the islands will experience one of the most splendid land-and-sea wilderness areas on the planet. Camping is your only lodging choice on the islands, but it's a fantastic way to experience the natural beauty and isolation of the park. Campsites are primitive, with no water (except on Santa Rosa and Santa Cruz) or electricity. Campsites are $15 per night; you must arrange your transportation before you reserve your site (☎ 877/444–6777) or online (⊕ www.recreation.gov) up to five months in advance.

Channel Islands National Park includes five of the eight Channel Islands and the one nautical mile of ocean that surrounds them. Six nautical miles of surrounding channel waters are designated a National Marine Sanctuary and are teeming with life, including giant kelp forests, 345 fish species, dolphins, whales, seals, sea lions, and seabirds. To maintain the integrity of their habitats, pets are not allowed in the park.

GETTING HERE AND AROUND
Most visitors access the Channel Islands via an Island Packers boat from Ventura Harbor. To reach the harbor by car, exit U.S. 101 in Ventura at Seaward Boulevard or Victoria Avenue and follow the signs to Ventura Harbor/Spinnaker Drive. An Island Packers boat heads to Anacapa

Channel Islands

Santa Barbara Channel

Goleta
Goleta Point
Santa Barbara
Santa Barbara Harbor
Montecito
Carpinteria
El Rio
Oxnard
Ventura
Visitor Center
Ventura Harbor
Point Mugu
Channel Islands Harbor

SANTA YNEZ MOUNTAINS

101 154 126 33 150 1

Santa Cruz Island
Visitor Center
Scorpion Ranch
Prisoners Harbor
Main Ranch
Painted Cave
West Point
Mount Diablo 2,450 ft
Central Valley
CINP East Santa Cruz
Smugglers Cove
West Santa Cruz: The Nature Conservancy
Morse Point
San Pedro Point
Anacapa Passage

Anacapa Island
Summit Peak 936 ft
Light Station & Museum

Santa Rosa Island
Carrington Point
Bechers Bay
Torrey Pines
East Point
Johnsons Lee
South Point
Vail & Vickers Ranch
Soledad Peak 1,574 ft
Santa Cruz Channel

San Miguel Island
Harris Point
Point Bennett
Cuyler Harbor
Tyler Bight
Cabrillo Monument
Lester Ranch site
Sandy Point
San Miguel Passage

PACIFIC OCEAN

Santa Barbara Island is approximately 52 miles southeast of Santa Cruz Island
Santa Barbara Island Light Beacon
Santa Barbara Island

0   10 mi
0   10 km

Island from Oxnard's Channel Islands Harbor, which you can reach from Ventura Harbor by following Harbor Boulevard south about 6 miles and continuing south on Victoria Avenue. Private vehicles are not permitted on the islands.

BOAT TOURS
Channel Islands Expeditions

EXCURSIONS | Channel Islands Expeditions runs kayaking, paddleboarding, hiking, snorkeling, and scuba excursions to the National Marine Sanctuary and Channel Islands National Park. Boats depart from Santa Barbara Harbor and Channel Islands Harbor in Oxnard, south of Ventura. ⊠ *Santa Barbara Harbor* ☎ *805/899–4925* ⊕ *explorechannelislands.com.*

Island Packers

BOAT TOURS | FAMILY | Sailing on high-speed catamarans from Ventura or a monohull vessel from Oxnard, Island Packers goes to Santa Cruz Island daily most of the year, weather permitting. The boats also go to Anacapa several days a week and to the outer islands from April through November. They also cruise along Anacapa's north shore on three-hour wildlife tours (no disembarking) several times a week. Rates start at $40 for whale-watching and wildlife cruises; other types of trips start at $63. ⊠ *1691 Spinnaker Dr., Ventura* ☎ *805/642–1393* ⊕ *islandpackers.com.*

Sights

Anacapa Island

ISLAND | Most people think of Anacapa as an island, but it's actually comprised of three narrow islets. Although the tips of these volcanic formations nearly touch, the islets are inaccessible from one another except by boat. All three have towering cliffs, isolated sea caves, and natural bridges; Arch Rock, on East Anacapa, is one of the best-known symbols of Channel Islands National Park.

Wildlife viewing is the main activity on East Anacapa, particularly in summer when seagull chicks are newly hatched and sea lions and seals lounge on the beaches. Exhibits at East Anacapa's compact **museum** include the original lead-crystal Fresnel lens from the 1932 lighthouse.

On West Anacapa, depending on the season and the number of desirable species lurking about here, boats travel to **Frenchy's Cove.** On a voyage here you might see anemones, limpets, barnacles, mussel beds, and colorful marine algae in the pristine tide pools. The rest of West Anacapa is closed to protect nesting brown pelicans. ⊠ *Channel Islands National Park.*

Channel Islands National Park Robert J. Lagomarsino Visitor Center

INFO CENTER | The park's visitor center has a three-story observation tower with telescopes, a bookstore, and a museum. A 24-minute film, *Treasure in the Sea,* provides an engaging overview of the islands, and, in the marine life exhibit, sea stars cling to rocks, and a brilliant orange Garibaldi darts around. Also on display are full-size reproductions of a male northern elephant seal and the pygmy mammoth skeleton unearthed on Santa Rosa Island in 1994.

On weekends and holidays at 11 am and 3 pm, rangers lead various free public programs describing park resources, and, from Wednesday through Saturday in summer, the center screens live ranger broadcasts of hikes and dives on Anacapa Island. Webcam images of bald eagles and other land and sea creatures are also shown at the center and on the park's website. ⊠ *1901 Spinnaker Dr., Ventura* ☎ *805/658–5730* ⊕ *www.nps.gov/chis.*

San Miguel Island

ISLAND | The westernmost of the Channel Islands, San Miguel Island is frequently battered by storms sweeping across the North Pacific. The 15-square-mile island's wild windswept landscape is lush with vegetation. Point Bennett, at the western tip, offers one of the world's most spectacular wildlife displays when more than 30,000 pinnipeds hit its beach. Explorer Juan Rodríguez Cabrillo was the first European to visit this island; he claimed it for Spain in 1542. Legend holds that Cabrillo died on one of the Channel Islands—no one knows where he's buried, but there's a memorial to him on a bluff above Cuyler Harbor. ⊠ *Channel Islands National Park.*

Santa Barbara Island

ISLAND | At about 1 square mile, Santa Barbara Island is the smallest of the Channel Islands and nearly 35 miles south of the others. Triangular in shape, Santa Barbara's steep cliffs—which offer a perfect nesting spot for the Scripps's murrelet, a rare seabird—are topped by twin peaks. In spring you can enjoy a brilliant display of yellow coreopsis. Learn about the wildlife on and around the islands at the island's small museum. ⊠ *Channel Islands National Park.*

★ Santa Cruz Island

ISLAND | Five miles west of Anacapa, 96-square-mile Santa Cruz Island is the largest of the Channel Islands. The National Park Service manages the easternmost 24% of the island; the rest is owned by the Nature Conservancy, which requires a permit to land. When your boat drops you off on a portion of the 70 miles of craggy coastline, you see two rugged mountain ranges with peaks soaring to 2,500 feet and deep canyons traversed by streams. This landscape is the habitat of a remarkable variety of flora and fauna—more than 600 types of plants, 140 kinds of land birds, 11 mammal species, five varieties of reptiles, and three amphibian species live here. Bird-watchers may want to look for the endemic island scrub jay, which is found nowhere else in the world.

One of the largest and deepest sea caves in the world, **Painted Cave** lies along the northwest coast of Santa Cruz. Named for the colorful lichen and algae that cover its walls, Painted Cave is nearly ¼ mile long and 100 feet wide. In spring a waterfall cascades over the entrance. Kayakers may encounter seals or sea lions cruising alongside their boats inside the cave. The Channel Islands hold some of the richest archaeological resources in North America; all artifacts are protected within the park. Remnants of a dozen Chumash villages can be seen on the island. The largest of these villages, at the eastern end, occupied the area now called **Scorpion Ranch.** The Chumash mined extensive chert deposits on the island for tools to produce shell-bead money, which they traded with people on the mainland. You can learn about Chumash history and view artifacts, tools, and exhibits on native plant and wildlife at the interpretive visitor center near the landing dock. Visitors can also explore remnants of the early-1900s ranching era in the restored historic adobe and outbuildings. ⊠ *Channel Islands National Park.*

Santa Rosa Island

ISLAND | Between Santa Cruz and San Miguel, Santa Rosa is the second largest of the Channel Islands. The terrain along the coast varies from broad, sandy beaches to sheer cliffs—a central mountain range, rising to 1,589 feet, breaks the island's relatively low profile. Santa Rosa is home to about 500 species of plants, including the rare Torrey pine, and three unusual mammals, the island fox, the spotted skunk, and the deer mouse. They hardly compare, though, to their predecessors: a nearly complete skeleton of a 6-foot-tall pygmy mammoth was unearthed in 1994.

From 1901 to 1998, cattle were raised at the island's **Vail & Vickers Ranch.** The route from Santa Rosa's landing dock to the campground passes by the historic ranch buildings, barns, equipment, and the wooden pier where cattle were brought onto the island. ⊠ *Channel Islands National Park.*

🏃 Activities

Channel Islands Adventure Company leads guided sea cave kayak and snorkel tours at Scorpion Anchorage in Channel Island National Park. Snorkel equipment is also available for rent on the island. Various concessionaires at Ventura Harbor Village (☎ 805-477-0470 ⊕ www.venturaharborvillage.com) arrange diving, paddling, kayaking, and other Channel Islands excursions out of Ventura. Island Packers provides public transportation to the islands and conducts whale-watching and wildlife cruises.

DIVING

Some of the best snorkeling and diving in the world can be found in the cool waters surrounding the Channel Islands. In the relatively warm water around Anacapa and eastern Santa Cruz, photographers can get great shots of rarely seen giant black bass swimming among the kelp forests. Here you also find a reef covered with red brittle starfish. If you're an experienced diver, you might swim among five species of seals and sea lions, or try your hand at spearing rockfish or halibut near San Miguel and Santa Rosa. The best time to scuba dive is in summer and fall, when the water is often clear up to a 100-foot depth.

KAYAKING

The most remote parts of the Channel Islands are accessible only by a sea kayak. Some of the best kayaking in the park can be found on Anacapa, Santa Barbara, and the eastern tip of Santa Cruz. It's too far to kayak from the mainland out to the islands, but outfitters have tours that take you to the islands. Tours are offered year-round, but high seas may cause trip cancellations between December and March. ⚠ **Channel waters can be unpredictable and challenging. Guided trips are highly recommended.**

WHALE-WATCHING

About a third of the world's cetacean species (27 to be exact) can be seen in the Santa Barbara Channel. In July and August, humpback and blue whales feed off the north shore of Santa Rosa. From late December through March, up to 10,000 gray whales pass through the Santa Barbara Channel on their way from Alaska to Mexico and back again; if you go on a whale-watching trip during this time frame you're likely to spot one or more of them. Other types of whales, but lower in number, swim the channel from June through August.

Ojai

15 miles north of Ventura.

The Ojai Valley, which director Frank Capra used as a backdrop for his 1936 film *Lost Horizon,* sizzles in the summer when temperatures routinely reach 90°F. The acres of orange and avocado groves here evoke postcard images of long-ago agricultural Southern California. Many artists and celebrities have sought refuge from life in the fast lane in lush Ojai.

GETTING HERE AND AROUND

From northern Ventura, Highway 33 veers east from U.S. 101 and climbs inland to Ojai. From Santa Barbara, exit U.S. 101 at Highway 150 in Carpinteria, then travel east 20 miles on a twisting, two-lane road that is not recommended at night or during poor weather. You can also access Ojai by heading west from I–5 on Highway 126. Exit at Santa Paula and follow Highway 150 north for 16 miles to Ojai.

Ojai can be easily explored on foot; you can also hop on the Ojai Trolley ($1.50, or $4 day pass), which, until about 5 pm, follows two routes around Ojai and neighboring Miramonte on weekdays and one route on weekends. Tell the driver you're visiting, and you'll get an informal guided tour.

ESSENTIALS

BUS CONTACTS Ojai Trolley. ☎ *805/646–5581* 🌐 *ojaitrolley.com.*

VISITOR INFORMATION Ojai Visitors Bureau. 🌐 *ojaivisitors.com.*

👁 Sights

Ojai Art Center

ARTS VENUE | California's oldest nonprofit, multipurpose arts center exhibits visual art from various disciplines and presents theater, dance, and other performances. ✉ *113 S. Montgomery St., near E. Ojai Ave.* ☎ *805/646–0117* 🌐 *www.ojaiart-center.org* 🕒 *Closed Mon.*

Ojai Avenue

NEIGHBORHOOD | The work of local artists is displayed in the Spanish-style shopping arcade along the avenue downtown. On Sunday between 9 and 1, organic and specialty growers sell their produce at the outdoor market behind the arcade.

Ojai Valley Museum

MUSEUM | **FAMILY** | The museum collects, preserves, and presents exhibits about the art, history, and culture of Ojai and Ojai Valley. Walking tours of Ojai depart from here. ✉ *130 W. Ojai Ave.* ☎ *805/640–1390* 🌐 *ojaivalleymuseum.org* 🎟 *Museum $5, walking tours from $7* 🕒 *Closed Mon.–Thurs.*

Ojai Valley Trail

TRAIL | The 18-mile trail is open to pedestrians, joggers, equestrians, bikers, and others on nonmotorized vehicles. You can access it anywhere along its route. ✉ *Parallel to Hwy. 33 from Soule Park in Ojai to ocean in Ventura* ☎ *888/652–4669* 🌐 *ojaivisitors.com.*

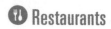

🍴 Restaurants

Boccali's

$ | **ITALIAN** | Edging a ranch, citrus groves, and a seasonal garden that provides produce for menu items, the modest but cheery Boccali's attracts many loyal fans. When it's warm, you can dine alfresco in the oak-shaded patio and lawn area and sometimes listen to live music. **Known for:** family-run operation; hand-rolled pizzas and home-style pastas; seasonal strawberry shortcake. [$] *Average main: $16* ✉ *3277 Ojai Ave., about 2 miles east of downtown* ☎ *805/646–6116* 🌐 *bocca-lis.com* 🕒 *No lunch Mon. and Tues.*

Farmer and the Cook

$ | **AMERICAN** | An organic farmer and his chef-wife run this funky café/bakery/market in Meiners Oaks, just a few miles west of downtown Ojai. Fill up at the soup and salad bar, order a wood-fired pizza, bento box, sandwich, or a daily special, then grab a table indoors or out on the patio. **Known for:** many veggie, vegan, and gluten-free options; grab-and-go meals; Mexican-focused menu. [$] *Average main: $16* ✉ *339 W. El Roblar* ☎ *805/640–9608* 🌐 *www.farmerandcook.com.*

★ Nocciola

$$$ | **ITALIAN** | Authentic northern Italian dishes with a California twist, a cozy fire-place dining room in a century-old Crafts-man-style house, and a covered patio amid the oaks draw locals and visitors alike to this popular eatery, owned by an Italian chef and his American wife (the family lives upstairs). The menu changes seasonally, but regular stars include seared sea scallops with Parmesan fondue and truffle shavings, homemade pastas made with organic egg yolks, and *pappardelle* with slow-roasted wild boar. **Known for:** great wild fish and game; Moment Pink signature cocktail; five-course tasting menu. [$] *Average main:*

$35 ✉ *314 El Paseo Rd.* ☎ *805/640–1648* 🌐 *nocciolaojai.com* 🕑 *No lunch.*

Hotels

The Iguana Inns of Ojai
$$ | **B&B/INN** | Artists own and operate these two bohemian-chic inns: The Blue Iguana, a cozy Southwestern-style hotel about 2 miles west of downtown, and the Emerald Iguana, which has art nouveau rooms, suites, and cottages in a secluded residential setting near downtown Ojai. **Pros:** colorful art everywhere; secluded; pet-friendly (Blue Iguana). **Cons:** 2 miles from downtown; on a highway; no children under 14 (or pets) at Emerald Iguana. [$] *Rooms from: $189* ✉ *11794 N. Ventura Ave.* ☎ *805/646–5277* 🌐 *iguanainnsofojai.com* 🛏 *20 units* 🍴 *Free breakfast.*

Ojai Rancho Inn
$$ | **HOTEL** | A collection of one-story buildings and cottages tucked between Ojai Avenue and the bike trail, this ranch-style motel attracts hipsters and those who appreciate a rustic getaway with modern comforts and a laid-back vintage vibe. **Pros:** free loaner cruiser bikes; small on-site bar; nice pool area with lounge chairs. **Cons:** not fancy or luxurious; rooms could use soundproofing; some road noise in rooms close to the road. [$] *Rooms from: $209* ✉ *615 W. Ojai Ave.* ☎ *805/646–1434* 🌐 *ojairanchoinn.com* 🛏 *17 rooms* 🍴 *No meals.*

★ Ojai Valley Inn & Spa
$$$$ | **RESORT** | This outdoorsy, golf-oriented resort and spa is set on 220 beautifully landscaped, oak-studded acres, with hillside views in nearly all directions. **Pros:** championship golf course, separate family and adult swimming pools, exceptional outdoor activities; on-site spa with 24 treatment rooms and two pools; multiple on-site restaurants serving regional cuisine. **Cons:** high room rates for the region; areas near restaurants can be noisy; not near downtown Ojai or Ventura. [$] *Rooms from: $500* ✉ *905 Country Club Rd.* ☎ *855/697–8780* 🌐 *ojairesort.com* 🛏 *303 rooms* 🍴 *No meals.*

Su Nido Inn
$$ | **B&B/INN** | A short walk from downtown Ojai sights and restaurants, this posh Mission Revival–style inn sits in a quiet neighborhood a few blocks from Libbey Park. **Pros:** walking distance from downtown; homey feel; soaking tubs and private patios or balconies in some rooms. **Cons:** no pool (and can get hot in summer); too quiet for some; 2-night minimum stay on weekends. [$] *Rooms from: $229* ✉ *301 N. Montgomery St.* ☎ *805/754–3513, 866/646–7080* 🌐 *www.sunidoinn.com* 🛏 *12 rooms* 🍴 *No meals.*

Santa Barbara

27 miles northwest of Ventura and 29 miles west of Ojai.

Santa Barbara has long been an oasis for Los Angelenos seeking respite from big-city life. The attractions begin at the ocean and end in the foothills of the Santa Ynez Mountains. The waterfront here is beautiful, with palm-studded promenades and plenty of sand.

In the few miles between the beaches and the hills are downtown, Mission Santa Barbara, and the Santa Barbara Botanic Garden. For spectacular views of the city and the Santa Barbara Channel, drive along Alameda Padre Serra, a hillside road that begins near the mission and continues to Montecito.

GETTING HERE AND AROUND

U.S. 101 is the main route into Santa Barbara. If you're staying in town, a car is handy but not essential; the beaches and downtown are easily explored by bicycle or on foot. Visit the Santa Barbara Car Free website for bike-route and walking-tour maps, suggestions for car-free vacations, and transportation discounts.

Santa Barbara Metropolitan Transit District's Line 22 bus serves major tourist sights. Several bus lines connect with the very convenient electric shuttles that cruise the waterfront every 10 to 15 minutes (50¢ each way, $1 day pass).

CONTACTS Santa Barbara Car Free.
☎ 805/696–1100 ⊕ santabarbaracarfree.org.

TOURS
Land and Sea Tours
SPECIAL-INTEREST | This outfit conducts 90-minute narrated tours in an amphibious 49-passenger vehicle nicknamed the Land Shark. The adventure begins with a drive through the city, followed by a plunge into the harbor for a cruise along the coast. ✉ 10 E. Cabrillo Blvd., at Stearns Wharf ☎ 805/683–7600 ⊕ out-2seesb.com ☑ From $40.

Santa Barbara Trolley Company
SPECIAL-INTEREST | Loop past major hotels, shopping areas, and attractions on a 90-minute tour ($25) aboard a motorized, San Francisco–style cable car. The company sometimes offers a hop-on-hop-off option, but days when this option is offered vary, so check ahead. ☎ 805/965–0353 ⊕ www.sbtrolley.com.

ESSENTIALS
VISITOR INFORMATION Garden Street Visitor Center. ✉ 1 Garden St., at Cabrillo Blvd. ☎ 805/965–3021 ⊕ www.sbchamber.org. **State Street Visitor Center.** ✉ 120 State St. ☎ 805/869–2632 ⊕ sbchamber.org.

 Sights

Andree Clark Bird Refuge
NATURE PRESERVE | This peaceful lagoon and its gardens sit north of East Beach. Bike trails and footpaths, punctuated by signs identifying native and migratory birds, skirt the lagoon. ✉ 1400 E. Cabrillo Blvd., near the zoo ☑ Free.

Carriage and Western Art Museum
MUSEUM | **FAMILY** | The country's largest collection of old horse-drawn vehicles—painstakingly restored—is exhibited here, everything from polished hearses to police buggies to old stagecoaches and circus vehicles. In August the Old Spanish Days Fiesta borrows many of the vehicles for a jaunt around town. Docents lead free tours from 1 to 4 pm the third Sunday of the month. ✉ Pershing Park, 129 Castillo St. ☎ 805/962–2353 ⊕ carriagemuseum.org ☑ Free ⊗ Closed weekends.

El Presidio State Historic Park
MILITARY SITE | **FAMILY** | Founded in 1782, El Presidio was one of four military strongholds established by the Spanish along the coast of California. The park encompasses much of the original site in the heart of downtown. El Cuartel, the adobe guardhouse, is the oldest building in Santa Barbara and the second oldest in California. ✉ 123 E. Canon Perdido St., at Anacapa St. ☎ 805/965–0093 ⊕ www.sbthp.org ☑ $5.

Funk Zone
NEIGHBORHOOD | A formerly run-down industrial neighborhood near the waterfront and train station, the Funk Zone has evolved into a hip hangout filled with wine-tasting rooms, arts-and-crafts studios, murals, breweries, distilleries, restaurants, and small shops. It's fun to poke around the three-square-block district. ■TIP→ **Street parking is limited, so leave your car in a nearby city lot and cruise up and down the alleys on foot.** ✉ Between State and Garden Sts. and Cabrillo Blvd. and U.S. 101 ⊕ funkzone.net.

★ Lotusland
GARDEN | **FAMILY** | The 37-acre estate called Lotusland—often ranked among the world's 10 best gardens—once belonged to the Polish opera singer Ganna Walska, who purchased it in 1941 and lived here until her death in 1984. Many of the exotic trees and other subtropical flora were planted in 1882 by

horticulturist R. Kinton Stevens. On the self-guided tour—the only option for visiting unless you're a member (reserve well ahead in summer)—you'll see an outdoor theater, a topiary garden, a lotus pond, and a huge collection of rare cycads, an unusual plant genus that has been around since the time of the dinosaurs. ⊠ *695 Ashley Rd., off Sycamore Canyon Rd. (Hwy. 192), Montecito* ✦ *Visitor entrance gate is on Cold Spring Rd. at Sycamore Canyon Rd.* ☎ *805/969–9990* ⊕ *lotusland.org* ⊠ *$50* ⊘ *Closed mid-Nov.–mid-Feb. No tours Sun.–Tues., except every 3rd Sun. of month.*

Montecito

TOWN | Since the late 1800s, the tree-studded hills and valleys of this town have attracted the rich and famous: Hollywood icons, business tycoons, tech moguls, and old money families who installed themselves years ago. Shady roads wind through the community, which consists mostly of gated estates. Swank boutiques line **Coast Village Road**, where well-heeled residents such as Oprah Winfrey, Katy Perry, and Prince Harry and Meghan Markle find peaceful refuge from the paparazzi. Residents also hang out in the Upper Village, a chic shopping area with restaurants and cafés at the intersection of San Ysidro and East Valley roads.

★ MOXI–The Wolf Museum of Exploration and Innovation

MUSEUM | FAMILY | It took more than two decades of unrelenting community advocacy to develop this exceptional science hub, which opened in early 2017 in a three-story, Spanish-Mediterranean building next to the train station and a block from Stearns Wharf and the beach. The 70-plus interactive exhibits—devoted to science, technology, engineering, arts, and mathematics (STEAM)—are integrated so curious visitors of all ages can explore seven themed areas (called tracks). In the Speed Track, build a model car and race it against two others on a test track—then use the collected data to reconfigure your car for improved performance. In the Fantastic Forces space, construct a contraption to send on a test flight in a wind column. Other sections include the Light, Tech, and Sound Tracks, plus the Innovation Workshop maker space and the Interactive Media Track, which hosts temporary exhibits. On the rooftop Sky Garden, which has terrific downtown panoramas, make music with wind- and solar-powered instruments, splash around in the interactive White-water feature, and peer down through glass floor windows to view the happy faces of explorers below. ⊠ *125 State St.* ☎ *805/770–5000* ⊕ *moxi.org* ⊠ *$16.*

★ Old Mission Santa Barbara

RELIGIOUS SITE | FAMILY | Dating from 1786 and widely referred to as the "Queen of Missions," this is one of the most beautiful and frequently photographed buildings in coastal California. The architecture evolved from adobe-brick buildings with thatch roofs to more permanent edifices as the mission's population burgeoned. An 1812 earthquake destroyed the third church built on the site. Its replacement, the present structure, is still a functioning Catholic church. Old Mission Santa Barbara has a splendid Spanish/Mexican colonial art collection, as well as Chumash sculptures and the only Native American–made altar and tabernacle left in the California missions. ⊠ *2201 Laguna St., at E. Los Olivos St.* ☎ *805/682–4149 gift shop, 805/682–4713 tours* ⊕ *www.santabarbara-mission.org* ⊠ *$15 self-guided tour.*

Santa Barbara Botanic Garden

GARDEN | FAMILY | Five miles of scenic trails meander through the garden's 78 acres of native plants. The Mission Dam, built in 1806, stands just beyond the redwood grove and above the restored aqueduct that once carried water to the Old Mission Santa Barbara. More than a thousand plant species thrive in various themed sections, including mountains, deserts, meadows, redwoods, and

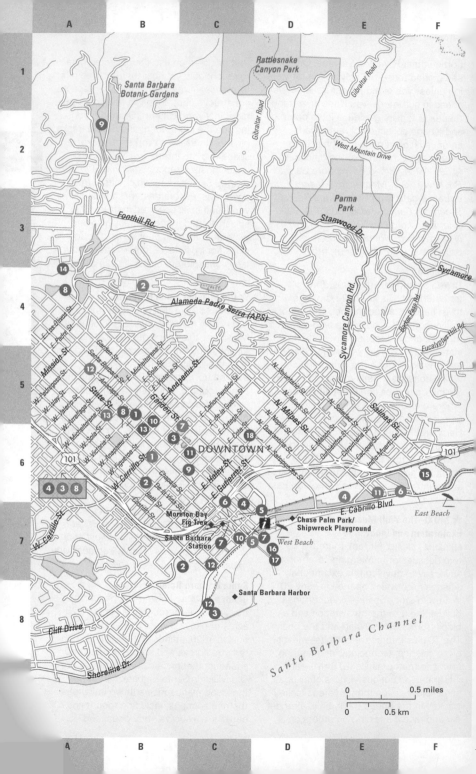

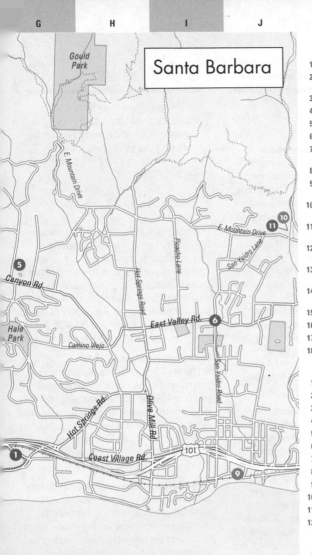

Santa Barbara

Sights ▼

Restaurants ▼

Hotels ▼

KEY

1 *Exploring Sights*

1 *Restaurants*

1 *Hotels*

i *Tourist information*

Channel Islands. ■TIP→ A conservation center dedicated to rare and endangered plant species presents rotating exhibitions. ✉ *1212 Mission Canyon Rd., north of Foothill Rd. (Hwy. 192)* ☎ *805/682–4726* ⊕ *www.sbbg.org* ☞ *$16.*

★ Santa Barbara County Courthouse

GOVERNMENT BUILDING | Hand-painted tiles and a spiral staircase infuse the courthouse, a national historic landmark, with the grandeur of a Moorish palace. This magnificent building was completed in 1929. An elevator rises to an arched observation area in the tower that provides a panoramic view of the city. Before or after you take in the view, you can (if it's open) visit an engaging gallery devoted to the workings of the tower's original, still operational Seth Thomas clock. The murals in the second-floor ceremonial chambers were painted by an artist who did backdrops for some of Cecil B. DeMille's films. ✉ *1100 Anacapa St., at E. Anapamu St.* ☎ *805/962–6464* ⊕ *sbcourthouse.org.*

Santa Barbara Historical Museum

MUSEUM | The historical society's museum exhibits decorative and fine arts, furniture, costumes, and documents from the town's past. Adjacent to it is the Gledhill Library, a collection of books, photographs, maps, and manuscripts. Tours are by appointment only. Admission is free for anyone under 18. ✉ *136 E. De La Guerra St., at Santa Barbara St.* ☎ *805/966–1601* ⊕ *www.sbhistorical.org* ☞ *Museum $7; library from $2 per hr for research* ☉ *Closed Mon.*

Santa Barbara Maritime Museum

MUSEUM | **FAMILY** | California's seafaring history is the focus here. High-tech, hands-on exhibits, such as a virtual sportfishing activity that lets participants haul in a "big one" and a local surfing history retrospective, make this a fun stop for families. In 2018, the museum introduced a fascinating History of Oil in the Santa Barbara Channel exhibit that traces the Chumash Indians' use of natural seeps to

Best Views

Drive along Alameda Padre Serra, a hillside road that begins near the mission and continues to Montecito, to feast your eyes on spectacular views of the city and the Santa Barbara Channel.

the infamous 1969 oil spill that spawned the modern environmental movement. The museum's shining star is a rare, 17-foot-tall Fresnel lens from the historic Point Conception Lighthouse. Ride the elevator to the fourth-floor observation area for great harbor views. ✉ *113 Harbor Way, off Shoreline Dr.* ☎ *805/962–8404* ⊕ *sbmm.org* ☞ *$8* ☉ *Closed Mon.–Wed.*

Santa Barbara Museum of Art

MUSEUM | The highlights of this museum's permanent collection include ancient sculpture, Asian art, impressionist paintings, contemporary art, photography, and American works in several mediums. ✉ *1130 State St., at E. Anapamu St.* ☎ *805/963–4364* ⊕ *sbma.net* ☞ *$10, free Thurs. 5–8* ☉ *Closed Mon.*

Santa Barbara Museum of Natural History

MUSEUM | **FAMILY** | A gigantic blue whale skeleton greets you at the entrance to this 17-acre complex, whose major draws include its planetarium, paleo and marine life exhibits, and gem and mineral displays. Startlingly alive-looking stuffed specimens in the Mammal and Bird Halls include a smiling grizzly bear and nesting California condors. A room of dioramas illustrates Chumash Indian history and culture while a Santa Barbara Gallery showcases the region's unique biodiversity. Outdoors, nature trails wind through the serene oak woodlands and a summer butterfly pavilion. ✉ *2559 Puesta del Sol Rd., off Mission Canyon Rd.* ☎ *805/682–4711* ⊕ *sbnature. org* ☞ *$17; free one Sun. of month Sept.– Apr.* ☉ *Closed Mon. and Tues.*

California's Missions

California history changed forever in the 18th century when Spanish explorers founded a series of missions along the Pacific coast. Believing they were following God's will, they wanted to spread the gospel and convert as many natives as possible. The process produced a collision between the Hispanic and California Indian cultures, resulting in one of the most striking legacies of Old California: the Spanish mission churches. Rising like mirages in the middle of desert plains and rolling hills, these historic sites transport you back to the days of the Spanish colonial period.

Father of the Missions

Father Junípero Serra is an icon of the Spanish colonial period. At the behest of the Spanish government, the diminutive padre—then well into his fifties, and despite a chronic leg infection—started out on foot from Baja California to search for suitable mission sites, with a goal of reaching Monterey. In 1769 he helped establish Alta California's first mission in San Diego and continued his travels until his death in 1784, by which time he had founded eight more missions.

El Camino Real

The system ended about a decade after the Mexican government took control of Alta California in the early 1820s and began to secularize the missions. In 1848, the Americans assumed control of the territory, and California became part of the United States. Today, all 21 of these missions stand as extraordinary monuments to their colorful past. Many are found on or near the "King's Road"—El Camino Real—which linked these mission outposts. At the height of the mission system the trail was approximately 600 miles long, eventually extending from San Diego to Sonoma. Today the road is commemorated on portions of Routes 101 and 82 in the form of roadside bell markers erected by CalTrans every 1 to 2 miles between San Diego and San Francisco.

Mission Architecture

Mission architecture reflects a gorgeous blend of European and New World influences. While naves followed the simple forms of Franciscan Gothic, cloisters (with beautiful arcades) adopted aspects of the Romanesque style, and ornamental touches of the Spanish Renaissance—including red-tiled roofs and wrought-iron grilles—added even more elegance. In the 20th century, the Mission Revival Style had a huge impact on architecture and design in California, as seen in examples ranging from San Diego's Union Station to Stanford University's main quadrangle. For information on California's missions, see ⊕ *california-missionsfoundation.org*.

11

The Central Coast SANTA BARBARA

Santa Barbara Zoo

ZOO | FAMILY | This compact zoo's gorgeous grounds shelter elephants, gorillas, Australian wildlife, exotic birds, and big cats, and has many exhibits that educate visitors on conservation efforts to save endangered species like the California condor and the red-legged frog. For small children, there's a scenic railroad and barnyard area where they can feed domestic sheep. Three high-tech dinosaurs and an 8-foot-tall grizzly bear puppet perform in live stage shows (free with admission), daily in summer and on weekends the rest of the year. Kids especially love feeding the giraffes from a view deck overlooking the beach. ■TIP→ **The palm-studded lawns on a hilltop overlooking the beach are perfect spots for family picnics.** ✉ *500 Niños Dr., off El Cabrillo Blvd.* ☎ *805/962–5339 main line, 805/962–6310 info line* ⊕ *santabarbarazoo.org* ✆ *Zoo $20, parking $11.*

Sea Center

ZOO | FAMILY | A branch of the Santa Barbara Museum of Natural History, the center specializes in Santa Barbara Channel marine life and conservation. Though small compared to aquariums in Monterey and Long Beach, this is a fascinating, hands-on marine science laboratory that lets you participate in experiments, projects, and exhibits, including touch pools. The two-story glass walls here open to stunning ocean, mountain, and city views. ✉ *211 Stearns Wharf* ☎ *805/962–2526* ⊕ *sbnature.org* ✆ *$10.*

Stearns Wharf

MARINA | Built in 1872, Stearns Wharf is Santa Barbara's most visited landmark. Expansive views of the mountains, cityscape, and harbor unfold from every vantage point on the three-block-long pier. Although it's a nice walk from the Cabrillo Boulevard parking areas, you can also park on the pier and then wander through the shops and stop for a meal at one of the wharf's restaurants. ✉ *Cabrillo Blvd. and State St.* ⊕ *stearnswharf.org.*

Urban Wine Trail

WINERY/DISTILLERY | More than 30 winery tasting rooms in six neighborhoods form the Urban Wine Trail. Most are within walking distance of the waterfront and the lower State Street shopping and restaurant district. **Santa Barbara Winery** (202 Anacapa St.), **The Valley Project** (116 E. Yanonali St.), and **Grassini Family Vineyards** (813 Anacapa St.) are good places to start your oenological trek. ✉ *Santa Barbara* ⊕ *urbanwinetrailsb.com.*

Santa Barbara Style

After a 1925 earthquake demolished many buildings, the city seized a golden opportunity to assume a Spanish-Mediterranean style. It established an architectural board of review, which, along with city commissions, created strict building codes for the downtown district: red-tile roofs, earth-tone facades, arches, wrought-iron embellishments, and height restrictions (about four stories).

⚓ Beaches

Arroyo Burro Beach

BEACH—SIGHT | FAMILY | The beach's usually gentle surf makes it ideal for families with young children. It's a local favorite because you can walk for miles in both directions when tides are low. Leashed dogs are allowed on the main stretch of beach and westward; they are allowed to romp off-leash east of the slough at the beach entrance. The parking lots fill early on weekends and throughout the summer, but the park is relatively quiet at other times. Walk along the beach just a few hundreds yards away from the main steps at the entrance to escape crowds on warm-weather days. Surfers, swimmers, stand-up paddlers, and boogie boarders regularly ply the waves, and photographers come often to catch the vivid sunsets. **Amenities:** food and drink; lifeguard in summer; parking; showers; toilets. **Best for:** sunset; surfing; swimming; walking. ✉ *Cliff Dr. and Las Positas Rd.* ⊕ *countyofsb.org/parks.*

★ East Beach

BEACH—SIGHT | FAMILY | The wide swath of sand at the east end of Cabrillo Boulevard is a great spot for people-watching. East Beach has sand volleyball courts,

Be sure to visit Santa Barbara's beautiful—and usually uncrowded—beaches.

summertime lifeguard and sports competitions, and arts-and-crafts shows on Sundays and holidays. You can use showers, a weight room, and lockers (bring your own towel) and rent umbrellas and boogie boards at the Cabrillo Bathhouse. Next door, there's an elaborate jungle-gym play area for kids. Hotels line the boulevard across from the beach. **Amenities:** food and drink; lifeguards in summer; parking (fee); showers; toilets; water sports. **Best for:** walking; swimming; surfing. ✉ *1118 Cabrillo Blvd., at Ninos Dr.* ☎ *805/897–2680.*

🍴 Restaurants

Arigato Sushi

$$$ | JAPANESE | You might have to wait for a table at this two-story restaurant and sushi bar—locals line up early for the wildly creative combination rolls and other delectables (first come, first served). Fans of authentic Japanese food sometimes disagree about the quality of the seafood, but all dishes are fresh and artfully presented. **Known for:** innovative creations; lively atmosphere; patio and second-floor balcony seating. [$] *Average main: $30* ✉ *1225 State St., near W. Victoria St.* ☎ *805/965–6074* 🌐 *www.arigatosb.com* 🕒 *No lunch.*

Barbareño

$$$ | MODERN AMERICAN | Determined to push the boundaries of farm-to-table, college friends who worked at the same Los Angeles eatery banded together in 2014 to launch Barbareño. They churn their own butter, bake their own breads, make condiments from scratch, and forage mushrooms, eucalyptus leaves, and other ingredients from the wild. **Known for:** youthful, sophisticated vibe; chef's sampler plate; monthly seasonal menu. [$] *Average main: $31* ✉ *205 W. Canon Perdido St., at De La Vina St.* ☎ *805/963–9591* 🌐 *barbareno.com* 🕒 *Closed Mon. and Tues. No lunch.*

Brophy Bros

$$ | SEAFOOD | The outdoor tables at this casual harborside restaurant have perfect views of the marina and mountains. Staffers serve enormous, exceptionally fresh fish dishes and will text you when your table's ready so you can stroll along the breakwater and explore the harbor while you wait. **Known for:** seafood salad and chowder; stellar clam bar; long wait times. [$] *Average main: $26* ✉ *119 Harbor Way, off Shoreline Dr.* ☎ *805/966–4418* 🌐 *brophybros.com.*

Jeannine's

$ | AMERICAN | Take a break from waterfront and State Street explorations at Jeannine's, revered locally for its wholesome sandwiches, salads, and baked goods, made from scratch with organic and natural ingredients. Dine in the expansive dining room or patio, or pick up a turkey cranberry or chicken pesto sandwich to go, and picnic on the beach or nearby Chase Palm Park. Jeannine's also has outlets in Montecito, Uptown, and Goleta. **Known for:** fantastic pastries; hearty, healthful breakfasts; turkey roasted or smoked in-house. [$] *Average main: $16* ✉ *1 State St., at Cabrillo Blvd.* ☎ *805/687–8701* 🌐 *jeannines.com* ⏲ *No dinner.*

★ The Lark

$$$ | MODERN AMERICAN | Shared dining—small plates and larger—and a seasonal menu showcasing local ingredients are the focus at this urban-chic restaurant named for an overnight all-Pullman train that chugged into the nearby railroad station for six decades. Sit at the 24-seat communal table set atop vintage radiators, or at tables and booths crafted from antique Spanish church pews and other repurposed or recycled materials. **Known for:** social environment; wines curated by a master sommelier; handcrafted locavore cocktails. [$] *Average main: $35* ✉ *131 Anacapa St., at E. Yanonali St.* ☎ *805/284–0370* 🌐 *www.thelarksb.com* ⏲ *No lunch.*

Loquita

$$$ | SPANISH | In a cozy space on a prime corner at the gateway to the Funk Zone near Stearns Wharf, Loquita honors Santa Barbara's Spanish heritage by serving up authentic Spanish dishes, wines, and cocktails made with fresh, sustainably sourced local ingredients. The menu covers all bases, from tapas to wood-fired seafood and grilled meats to Spanish wines, vermouth, gin and tonics, and sangria. **Known for:** multiple types of paella; counter and takeaway items; great gin and tonic. [$] *Average main: $31* ✉ *202 State St.* ☎ *805/880–3380* 🌐 *www.loquitasb.com.*

Oku

$$$ | MODERN ASIAN | Locals and visitors alike flock to this sleek, Asian-inspired restaurant across from Stearns Wharf and East Beach (reserve a second-story table for killer views). The eclectic menu focuses mostly on small plates meant for sharing and includes classic dishes like sushi, sashimi, yakisoba, ramen soup with pork belly, and black garlic filet mignon, but also creative surprises like the halibut-crab-avocado "lollipop" and lobster-tempura-wagyu beef roll. **Known for:** two cocktail bars and a sushi bar; crispy Korean cauliflower with yuzu-shiso aioli, kalbi-style short ribs; craft cocktails, extensive wine and sake list. [$] *Average main: $28* ✉ *29 E. Cabrillo Blvd.* ☎ *805/690–1650* 🌐 *www.okurestaurant.com.*

Take the Kids

Two fun playgrounds provide welcome interludes for the young set. Children love tooling around **Kids' World** (✉ *Garden and Micheltorena Sts.*), a public playground with a castle-shaped maze of climbing structures, slides, and tunnels. At **Shipwreck Playground** (✉ *Chase Palm Park, E. Cabrillo Blvd., east of Garden St.*), parents take as much pleasure in the waterfront views as the kids do in the nautical-theme diversions.

Olio e Limone

$$$ | ITALIAN | Sophisticated Italian cuisine with an emphasis on Sicily is served at this restaurant near the Arlington. The juicy veal chop is popular, but surprises abound here; be sure to try unusual dishes such as ribbon pasta with quail and sausage in a mushroom ragout, or the duck ravioli. **Known for:** grilled veal and lamb chops; cozy white-tablecloth dining room; adjacent raw bar and casual pizzeria. ⓢ *Average main: $32 ⊠ 17 W. Victoria St., at State St. ☏ 805/899–2699 ⊕ www. olioelimone.com ⊘ No lunch Sun.*

Palace Grill

$$$ | SOUTHERN | Mardi Gras energy, team-style service, lively music, and great Cajun, creole, and Caribbean food have made the Palace a Santa Barbara icon. Be prepared to wait for a table on Friday and Saturday nights, though the live entertainment and free appetizers, sent out front when the line is long, will whet your appetite for the feast to come. **Known for:** blackened fish and meats; Louisiana bread pudding soufflé; Cajun martini served in a mason jar. ⓢ *Average main: $32 ⊠ 8 E. Cota St., at State St. ☏ 805/963–5000 ⊕ palacegrill.com.*

Santo Mezcal

$$$ | MODERN MEXICAN | Authentic flavors of coastal Mexico and fresh local ingredients make for packed indoor and outdoor tables at this popular eatery a block from the train station. For breakfast, fill up on huevos rancheros or chilaquiles; for lunch or dinner feast on seafood ceviches, grilled chicken breast with authentic mole poblano, or Mexican shrimp in a creamy mezcal sauce. **Known for:** weekday happy hour; fresh crab enchiladas and quesadillas; grilled rib-eye tacos; good selection of tequila, mezcal, cocktails. ⓢ *Average main: $28 ⊠ 119 State St. ☏ 805/883–3593 ⊕ www.santomezcalsb.com.*

★ The Stonehouse

$$$$ | AMERICAN | The elegant Stonehouse—consistently lauded as one of the nation's top restaurants—is inside a century-old granite former farmhouse at the San Ysidro Ranch resort. The menu changes constantly, but might include pan-seared abalone or classic steak Diane flambéed table-side. **Known for:** ingredients from on-site garden; heated ocean-view deck with fireplace; elegant dining room. ⓢ *Average main: $63 ⊠ 900 San Ysidro La., off San Ysidro Rd., Montecito ☏ 805/565–1720 ⊕ www. sanysidroranch.com.*

★ Toma

$$$ | ITALIAN | Seasonal, locally sourced ingredients and softly lit muted-yellow walls evoke the flavors and charms of Tuscany and the Mediterranean at this rustic-romantic restaurant across from the harbor and West Beach. Ahi sashimi tucked in a crisp sesame cone is a popular appetizer, after which you can proceed to a house-made pasta dish or rock shrimp gnocchi. **Known for:** house-made pastas and gnocchi; wines from Italy and California's Central Coast; romantic waterfront setting. ⓢ *Average main: $34 ⊠ 324 W. Cabrillo Blvd., near Castillo St. ☏ 805/962–0777 ⊕ www.tomarestaurant.com ⊘ No lunch.*

🛏 Hotels

Canary Hotel

$$$$ | HOTEL | A full-service hotel in the heart of downtown, this Kimpton property blends a casual, beach-getaway feel with contemporary California style. **Pros:** upscale local cuisine at on-site Finch & Fork restaurant; rooms come with candles, yoga mats, and binoculars (for touring); adjacent fitness center. **Cons:** across from transit center; a mile from the beach; some rooms on the small side. ⓢ *Rooms from: $515 ⊠ 31 W. Carrillo St. ☏ 805/884–0300, 855/546–7866 ⊕ www.canarysantabarbara.com ⇥ 97 rooms ⦿ No meals.*

★ El Encanto, a Belmond Hotel

$$$$ | HOTEL | Built in 1915 and following more than a $100 million of extensive renovations a century later, this Santa Barbara icon lives on to thrill a new generation of guests with its relaxed-luxe bungalow rooms, lush gardens, and personalized service. **Pros:** dining terrace with panoramic city and ocean views; stellar spa facility; infinity pool with ocean views. **Cons:** long walk to downtown; pricey; guests staying for more than a few days may find the restaurant menus limited. $ *Rooms from: $990* ✉ *800 Alvarado Pl.* ☎ *805/845–5800, 800/393–5315* ⊕ *www.belmond.com* 🛏 *92 rooms* ❍| *No meals.*

The Goodland

$$$ | HOTEL | A vintage Woody car, a silver Airstream trailer, and a lobby record shop are among the elements that bring 1960s California surf culture to life at this Kimpton hotel in Goleta. **Pros:** cool and casual vibe; live music or DJs several evenings a week; complimentary wine-and-beer social hour and s'mores by the fireside. **Cons:** not close to downtown Santa Barbara; some rooms on the small side; thin walls allow for noise transfer from neighboring rooms. $ *Rooms from: $284* ✉ *5650 Calle Real, Goleta* ☎ *877/480–1465, 805/964–6241* ⊕ *www.thegoodland.com* 🛏 *158 rooms* ❍| *No meals.*

Hilton Santa Barbara Beachfront Resort

$$$$ | RESORT | A full-scale resort with seven buildings spread over 24 landscaped acres across from East Beach, this hotel was founded by the late TV actor Fess Parker, best known for playing Davy Crockett and Daniel Boone. **Pros:** numerous amenities; right across from the beach; free shuttle to train station and airport. **Cons:** train noise filters into some rooms; too spread out for some; pricey. $ *Rooms from: $475* ✉ *633 E. Cabrillo Blvd.* ☎ *800/879–2929, 805/564–4333* ⊕ *www.hiltonsantabarbarabeachfrontresort.com* 🛏 *360 rooms* ❍| *No meals.*

★ Hotel Californian

$$$$ | HOTEL | A sprawling collection of Spanish-Moorish buildings that opened in 2017 at the site of the historic 1925 Hotel Californian, this sophisticated hotel with a hip youthful vibe occupies nearly three full blocks just steps from Stearns Wharf and the harbor. **Pros:** steps from the waterfront, Funk Zone, MOXI, and beaches; resort-style amenities; on-site parking. **Cons:** area gets crowded in summer and holiday weekends; must walk or bike to downtown attractions; train whistle noise in rooms close to station. $ *Rooms from: $699* ✉ *36 State St.* ☎ *805/882–0100* ⊕ *www.thehotelcalifornian.com* 🛏 *121 rooms* ❍| *No meals.*

Mar Monte Hotel

$$$$ | HOTEL | A complex of five buildings on 3 landscaped acres across from East Beach, the historic Mar Monte, part of the Hyatt family of properties, completed a $27 million renovation in 2020 and is an appealing lodging option. **Pros:** steps from the beach; many room types and rates; on-site restaurant, pool, bar/café. **Cons:** not in the heart of downtown; busy area in summer; no on-site self-parking, only valet service (fee). $ *Rooms from: $429* ✉ *1111 E. Cabrillo Blvd.* ☎ *805/882–1234, 800/643–1994* ⊕ *www.hyatt.com* 🛏 *174 rooms* ❍| *No meals.*

Palihouse Santa Barbara

$$$$ | HOTEL | A ½ block from the Presidio in the heart of downtown, this secluded retreat celebrates Santa Barbara style and design, from the Spanish-Mediterranean exterior with wrought-iron balconies to the interior's Palisociety signature hipster interpretation of local character (e.g., bright colors throughout, a custom playlist that sets an upbeat mood, a bowl of bright yellow tennis balls in the lobby lounge). **Pros:** walk to downtown shops, restaurants, sights; indoor parking beneath the hotel; spacious rooms. **Cons:** resort fee (includes parking); not on the waterfront; too small and serene for those who prefer a lively setting.

Ⓢ *Rooms from: $475* ✉ *915 Garden St.*
☎ *805/564–4700* ⊕ *www.palisociety.
com/hotels/santa-barbara* ⇲ *24 rooms*
⦿ *No meals.*

★ The Ritz-Carlton Bacara, Santa Barbara

$$$$ | RESORT | A luxury resort with four
restaurants and a 42,000-square-foot
spa and fitness center with 36 treatment
rooms, the Ritz-Carlton Bacara provides
a gorgeous setting for relaxing retreats.
Pros: many diversions including hiking
and stargazing; three zero-edge pools;
three golf courses nearby. **Cons:** pricey;
not close to downtown; sand on beach
not pristine enough for some. Ⓢ *Rooms
from: $499* ✉ *8301 Hollister Ave., Goleta*
☎ *805/968–0100* ⊕ *www.ritzcarlton.com/
en/hotels/california/santa-barbara* ⇲ *358
rooms* ⦿ *Free breakfast.*

★ Rosewood Miramar Beach

$$$$ | RESORT | This luxury resort, opened
in 2019, sprawls across 16 lush acres
on one of the area's most scenic and
exclusive beaches. **Pros:** two cabana-lined
pools; six restaurants and bars; steps to
the beach. **Cons:** too expensive for some;
next to a busy freeway and train tracks;
popular weekend wedding site with lively
partiers. Ⓢ *Rooms from: $1650* ✉ *1759
S. Jameson La., Montecito* ☎ *805/900–
8388* ⊕ *www.rosewoodhotels.com/en/
miramar-beach-montecito* ⇲ *160 rooms*
⦿ *No meals.*

★ Santa Barbara Inn

$$$$ | HOTEL | This full-service, fami-
ly-owned, Spanish-Mediterranean hotel
occupies a prime waterfront corner
across from East Beach. **Pros:** many
rooms have ocean views; suites come
with whirlpool tubs; delicious on-site restaurant Convivo. **Cons:** on a busy boulevard; limited street parking; not within
easy walking distance of downtown.
Ⓢ *Rooms from: $399* ✉ *901 E. Cabrillo
Blvd.* ✛ *At Milpas St.* ☎ *800/231–0431,
805/966–2285* ⊕ *www.santabarbarainn.
com* ⇲ *70 rooms* ⦿ *No meals.*

★ San Ysidro Ranch

$$$$ | RESORT | At this romantic hideaway
on a historic property in the Montecito
foothills—where John and Jackie Ken-
nedy spent their honeymoon and Oprah
sends her out-of-town visitors—guest
cottages are scattered among groves
of orange trees and flower beds. **Pros:**
rooms come with private outdoor spas;
17 miles of hiking trails nearby; Plow &
Angel Bistro and Stonehouse restaurants
on-site are Santa Barbara institutions.
Cons: very expensive; too remote for
some; noise from nearby bridal parties
travels to some suites. Ⓢ *Rooms from:
$1895* ✉ *900 San Ysidro La., Montecito*
☎ *805/565–1700* ⊕ *www.sanysidroranch.
com* ⇲ *38 units* ⦿ *All-inclusive* ⌖ *2-day
minimum stay on weekends, 3 days on
holiday weekends.*

★ Simpson House Inn

$$$ | B&B/INN | If you're a fan of traditional
bed-and-breakfast inns, this property,
with its beautifully appointed Victorian
main house and acre of lush gardens, is
for you. **Pros:** elegant furnishings; impeccable landscaping; within walking distance of downtown. **Cons:** some rooms
in main building are small; two-night minimum stay on weekends May–October;
no pets allowed. Ⓢ *Rooms from: $339*
✉ *121 E. Arrellaga St.* ☎ *805/963–7067*
⊕ *www.simpsonhouseinn.com* ⇲ *15
rooms* ⦿ *Free breakfast.*

The Upham

$$$ | B&B/INN | Built in 1871, this Victorian
in the downtown arts and culture district
has been restored as a full-service hotel.
Pros: 1-acre garden; easy walk to theaters; excellent on-site restaurant. **Cons:**
some rooms are small; not near beach or
waterfront; no in-room safes. Ⓢ *Rooms
from: $285* ✉ *1404 De la Vina St.*
☎ *805/962–0058* ⊕ *www.uphamhotel.
com* ⇲ *50 rooms* ⦿ *No meals* ⌖ *2-night
minimum stay on weekends.*

Nightlife

The bar, club, and live music scene centers on lower State Street, between the 300 and 800 blocks.

Draughtsmen Aleworks

BREWPUBS/BEER GARDENS | A low-key taproom with board and card games for entertainment, Draughtsmen pours its own craft beer, wine, cider, and hop tea. At the main taproom in Goleta, you can view the brewing facilities and sometimes take a tour. ✉ *1131 State St., in Mosaic Locale* ☎ *805/259–4356* ⊕ *www. draughtsmenaleworks.com.*

The Good Lion

BARS/PUBS | The cocktail menu at this intimate neighborhood bar near The Granada Theatre changes weekly, depending on the fresh organic bounty available at the markets. All juices are organic and squeezed fresh daily, and all syrups are made in house with organic produce and sweeteners. ✉ *1212 State St.* ☎ *805/845–8754* ⊕ *www.goodlion-cocktails.com.*

Joe's Cafe

BARS/PUBS | Steins of beer and stiff cocktails accompany hearty bar food at Joe's. It's a fun, if occasionally rowdy, collegiate scene. ✉ *536 State St., at E. Cota St.* ☎ *805/966–4638* ⊕ *joescafesb.com.*

Lucky's

BARS/PUBS | A slick sports bar attached to an upscale steak house owned by the maker of Lucky Brand dungarees, this place attracts hip patrons hoping to see and be seen. ✉ *1279 Coast Village Rd., near Olive Mill Rd., Montecito* ☎ *805/565–7540* ⊕ *luckys-steakhouse.com.*

M. Special Brewing Company

BREWPUBS/BEER GARDENS | A favorite stop on the local beer trail, this lively taproom has more than a dozen craft beers and live music on weekends. A second taproom (and the main brewery) is in Goleta, near UCSB. ✉ *634 State St.* ☎ *805/968–6500* ⊕ *www.mspecialbrewco.com.*

Milk & Honey

BARS/PUBS | Artfully prepared tapas, mango mojitos, and exotic cocktails lure trendy crowds to swank M&H, despite high prices and a reputation for inattentive service. ✉ *30 W. Anapamu St., at State St.* ☎ *805/275–4232* ⊕ *www. milknhoneytapas.com.*

SOhO

MUSIC CLUBS | A lively restaurant, bar, and music venue, SOhO books all kinds of musical acts, from jazz to blues to rock. ✉ *1221 State St., at W. Victoria St.* ☎ *805/962–7776* ⊕ *www.sohosb.com.*

✪ Performing Arts

The arts district, with theaters, restaurants, and cafés, starts around the 900 block of State and continues north to the 1300 block. To see what's scheduled around town, pick up the free weekly *Santa Barbara Independent* newspaper or visit its website, ⊕ *www.independent. com.*

Arlington Theatre

ARTS CENTERS | This Moorish-style auditorium presents touring performers and films throughout the year. ✉ *1317 State St., at Arlington Ave.* ☎ *805/963–4408* ⊕ *thearlingtontheatre.com.*

Center Stage Theatre

ARTS CENTERS | This venue hosts plays, music, dance, and readings. ✉ *Paseo Nuevo Center, Chapala and De la Guerra Sts., 2nd fl.* ☎ *805/963–0408* ⊕ *www. centerstagetheater.org.*

Ensemble Theatre Company (ETC)

THEATER | The company stages classic and contemporary comedies, musicals, and dramas. ✉ *33 W. Victoria St., at Chapala St.* ☎ *805/965–5400* ⊕ *www.etcsb.org.*

The Granada Theatre

THEATER | A restored, modernized landmark that dates from 1924, the Granada hosts Broadway touring shows and dance, music, and other cultural events.

✉ 1214 State St., at E. Anapamu St.
☎ 805/899–2222 ⊕ granadasb.org.

Lobero Theatre

THEATER | A state landmark, the Lobero hosts community theater groups and touring professionals. ✉ 33 E. Canon Perdido St., at Anacapa St. ☎ 805/963–0761 ⊕ www.lobero.com.

🍽 Shopping

BOOKS

Book Den

BOOKS/STATIONERY | Bibliophiles have browsed for new, used, and out-of-print books at this independent shop since 1933. ✉ 15 E. Anapamu St., at State St. ☎ 805/962–3321 ⊕ bookden.com.

Chaucer's Bookstore

BOOKS/STATIONERY | This well-stocked independent shop is a favorite of many locals. ✉ Loreto Plaza, 3321 State St., at Los Positas Rd. ☎ 805/682–6787 ⊕ www.chaucersbooks.com.

CLOTHING

Channel Islands Surfboards

CLOTHING | Come here for top-of-the-line surfboards and the latest in California beachwear, sandals, and accessories. ✉ 36 Anacapa St., at E. Mason St. ☎ 805/966–7213 ⊕ www.cisurfboards.com.

DIANI

CLOTHING | This upscale, European-style women's boutique dresses clients in designer clothing from around the world. Sibling shoe and home-and-garden shops are nearby. ✉ 1324 State St., at Arlington Ave. ☎ 805/966–3114, 805/966–7175 shoe shop ⊕ dianiboutique.com.

SeaVees

SHOES/LUGGAGE/LEATHER GOODS | Santa Barbara–based SeaVees makes and sells casual, comfortable, '60s-style California sneakers that have a classy, dressed-up flair. ✉ 24 E. Mason St. ☎ 805/774–1964 ⊙ Closed Tues.

Surf N Wear's Beach House

CLOTHING | This shop carries surf clothing, gear, and collectibles; it's also the home of Santa Barbara Surf Shop and the exclusive local dealer of Surfboards by Yater. ✉ 10 State St., at Cabrillo Blvd. ☎ 805/963–1281 ⊕ www.surfnwear.com.

Wendy Foster

CLOTHING | This store sells casual-chic women's fashions at its flagship store downtown and four other outlets around the county. ✉ 1220 State St., at E. Victoria St. ☎ 805/966–2276 ⊕ wendyfoster.com.

FOOD AND WINE

Santa Barbara Public Market

FOOD/CANDY | A dozen food and beverage vendors occupy this spacious arts district galleria. Stock up on gourmet goodies; sip on handcrafted wines and beers while watching sports events; and nosh on noodle bowls, sushi, artisanal ice cream, and savory street tacos. ✉ 38 W. Victoria St., at Chapala St. ☎ 805/770–7702 ⊕ sbpublicmarket.com.

SHOPPING AREAS

★ El Paseo

SHOPPING NEIGHBORHOODS | Wine-tasting rooms, shops, art galleries, and studios share the courtyard and gardens of this historic arcade. ✉ Canon Perdido St., between State and Anacapa Sts.

★ State Street

SHOPPING NEIGHBORHOODS | Between Cabrillo Boulevard and Sola Street, State Street is a shopper's paradise. Chic malls, quirky storefronts, antiques emporia, elegant boutiques, and funky thrift shops abound. Numerous community activities take place at **Paseo Nuevo,** an open-air mall in the 700 block. Shops, restaurants, galleries, and fountains line the tiled walkways of **La Arcada,** a small complex of landscaped courtyards in the 1100 block designed by architect Myron Hunt in 1926.

Summerland

SHOPPING NEIGHBORHOODS | Serious antiques hunters head southeast of Santa Barbara to Summerland, which is full of shops and markets. Several good ones are along Lillie Avenue and Ortega Hill Road. ⊠ *Summerland.*

Activities

BIKING

Cabrillo Bike Path

BICYCLING | The level, two-lane, 3-mile Cabrillo Bike Path passes the Santa Barbara Zoo, the Andree Clark Bird Refuge, beaches, and the harbor. Stop for a meal at one of the restaurants along the way, or for a picnic along the palm-lined path looking out on the Pacific.

Mad Dogs & Englishmen

BICYCLING | Tucked in a storefront near Butterfly Beach, Andree Clark Bird Refuge, and miles of bike lanes, Mad Dogs & Englishmen rents and sells premium e-bikes and custom sidecars (great for kids and pets). It also provides self-guided, private, and guided cycling tours in Santa Barbara and at sister shops in downtown Carmel, Monterey, and Mill Valley. ⊠ *1080 Coast Village Rd.* ☏ *805/837–0033* ⊕ *maddogsenglishmen. com.*

Wheel Fun Rentals

BICYCLING | You can rent bikes (electric, cruiser, and regular), quadricycles, electric vehicles, and skates here. ⊠ *24 E. Mason St.* ☏ *805/966–2282* ⊕ *wheelfunrentalssb.com.*

BOATS AND CHARTERS

★ *Condor Express*

BOATING | From SEA Landing, the *Condor Express,* a 75-foot, high-speed catamaran, whisks up to 149 passengers toward the Channel Islands on whale-watching excursions and sunset and dinner cruises. ⊠ *301 W. Cabrillo Blvd.* ☏ *805/882–0088, 888/779–4253* ⊕ *condorexpress. com.*

Earth Day

In 1969, 200,000 gallons of crude oil spilled into the Santa Barbara Channel, causing an immediate outcry from residents. The day after the spill, Get Oil Out (GOO) was established; the group helped lead the successful fight for legislation to limit and regulate offshore drilling in California. The Santa Barbara spill also spawned Earth Day, which is still celebrated across the nation today.

Paddle Sports Center

WATER SPORTS | This full-service center in the harbor rents kayaks, stand-up paddleboards, surfboards, boogie boards, and water-sports gear. ⊠ *117 B Harbor Way, off Shoreline Dr.* ☏ *805/617–3425 rentals* ⊕ *www.paddlesportsca.com.*

Santa Barbara Sailing Center

BOATING | The center offers sailing instruction, rents and charters sailboats, kayaks, and stand-up paddleboards, and organizes dinner and sunset champagne cruises, island excursions, and whale-watching trips. ⊠ *Santa Barbara Harbor launching ramp* ☏ *805/962–2826* ⊕ *sbsail.com.*

Santa Barbara Water Taxi

BOATING | FAMILY | Children beg to ride *Lil' Toot,* a cheery yellow water taxi that cruises from the harbor to Stearns Wharf and back again. The fare for kids is $2 each way. ⊠ *Santa Barbara Harbor and Stearns Wharf* ☏ *805/465–6676* ⊕ *www. celebrationsantabarbara.com/* 🖅 *$5 one-way.*

SEA Landing

BOATING | This outfit operates surface and deep-sea fishing charters year-round. ⊠ *Cabrillo Blvd., at Bath St., and breakwater in Santa Barbara Harbor* ☏ *805/963–3564* ⊕ *sealanding.net.*

TENNIS

City of Santa Barbara Parks and Recreation Department

TENNIS | The City of Santa Barbara Parks and Recreation Department oversees the Municipal Tennis Center, which has hard courts (9 tennis and 12 pickleball) in an enclosed stadium. The department also operates public outdoor courts throughout town with lighted play until 9 pm weekdays. You can purchase day permits ($5) at the courts or by calling the rec department. ☎ *805/564–5573* 🌐 *santabarbaraca.gov/tennis.*

Santa Ynez

31 miles northeast of Santa Barbara.

Founded in 1882, the tiny town of Santa Ynez still has many of its original frontier buildings. You can walk through its three-block downtown in a few minutes, shop for antiques, and hang around the old-time saloon. At some of the Santa Ynez Valley's best restaurants, you just might bump into one of the celebrities who own nearby ranches.

GETTING HERE AND AROUND

Take Highway 154 over San Marcos Pass or U.S. 101 north 43 miles to Buellton, then 7 miles east.

Sights

Gainey Vineyard

WINERY/DISTILLERY | The 1,800-acre Gainey Ranch, straddling the banks of the Santa Ynez River, includes about 100 acres of organic vineyards: Sauvignon Blanc, Merlot, Cabernet Sauvignon, and Cabernet Franc. The winery also makes wines from Chardonnay, Pinot Noir, and Syrah grapes from the Santa Rita Hills. You can taste the latest releases—the estate Pinot Noir is especially good—in a Spanish-style hacienda overlooking the ranch. ✉ *3950 E. Hwy. 246* ☎ *805/688–0558* 🌐 *www.gaineyvineyard.com* 🎟 *Tastings from $20, jeep tour and barn tasting $25.*

Restaurants

S.Y. Kitchen

$$$ | **ITALIAN** | The owners of Toscana, a popular eatery in L.A.'s Brentwood neighborhood, run this rustic-chic restaurant with an Italy-meets-California Wine Country vibe. Chef and co-owner Luca Crestanelli, a native of Verona, Italy, typically offers multiple seasonal daily specials. **Known for:** wood-fired pizzas and oak-grilled entrées; creative craft cocktails; gelatos and "not-so-classic" tiramisu. [$] *Average main: $28* ✉ *1110 Faraday St., at Sagunto St.* ☎ *805/691–9794* 🌐 *www.sykitchen.com.*

Hotels

ForFriends Inn

$$ | **B&B/INN** | Close friends own and operate this luxury B&B, designed as a social place where friends gather to enjoy good wine, food, and music in a casual backyard setting. **Pros:** three-course breakfast, evening wine and appetizers included; friendly innkeepers; "Friendship Pass" provides perks and savings at restaurants and wineries. **Cons:** not suitable for children; no pets allowed; must climb stairs to second-floor rooms. [$] *Rooms from: $245* ✉ *1121 Edison St.* ☎ *805/693–0303* 🌐 *www.forfriendsinn.com* 🛏 *7 units* 🍴 *Free breakfast.*

Activities

Cloud Nine Glider Rides

FLYING/SKYDIVING/SOARING | The outfit's scenic glider rides last from 10 to 50 minutes. Tour options include the Santa Ynez Valley, coastal mountains and the Channel Islands, and celebrity homes. ✉ *Santa Ynez Airport, 900 Airport Rd.* ☎ *805/602–6620* 🌐 *cloud9gliderrides.com* 🎟 *From $185.*

Los Olivos

4 miles north of Santa Ynez.

This pretty village was once on Spanish-built El Camino Real (Royal Road) and later a stop on major stagecoach and rail routes. Tasting rooms, art galleries, antiques stores, and country markets line Grand Avenue and intersecting streets for several blocks.

GETTING HERE AND AROUND

From U.S. 101 north or south, exit at Highway 154 and drive east about 8 miles. From Santa Barbara, travel 30 miles northwest on Highway 154.

Sights

Blair Fox Cellars

WINERY/DISTILLERY | Blair Fox, a Santa Barbara native, crafts small-lot Rhône-style wines made from organic grapes. The bar in his rustic Los Olivos tasting room, where you can sample exceptional vineyard-designated Syrahs and other wines, was hewn from Australian white oak reclaimed from an old Tasmanian schoolhouse. ✉ *2477 Alamo Pintado Ave.* ☎ *805/691–1678* 🌐 *www.blairfoxcellars.com* 🎟 *Tastings $15* 🕒 *Closed Tues. and Wed.*

Coquelicot Estate Vineyard

WINERY/DISTILLERY | Named for the vivid red poppy flowers that blanket the French countryside and appear on all its labels, this limited-production winery focuses on handcrafted Bordeaux wines made from grapes at its certified organic 58-acre Santa Ynez Valley vineyard. Don't miss samples of the flagship wines: Sixer (a Syrah and Viogner blend), Mon Amour (a Bordeaux blend), and the estate Sauvignon Blanc and Rosé. ✉ *2884 Grand Ave.* ☎ *805/688–1500* 🌐 *www.coquelicotwines.com* 🎟 *Tastings from $18.*

Firestone Vineyard

WINERY/DISTILLERY | Heirs to the Firestone tire fortune developed (but no longer own) this winery known for Chardonnay, Gewürztraminer, Cabernet Sauvignon, and Syrah—and for the fantastic valley views from its tasting room (reservations required) and picnic area. The walking tour here is highly informative. ✉ *5017 Zaca Station Rd., off U.S. 101* ☎ *805/688–3940* 🌐 *www.firestonewine.com* 🎟 *Tastings from $20, tour $25.*

Restaurants

Los Olivos Wine Merchant Cafe

$$ | **AMERICAN** | Part wine store and part social hub, this café focuses on wine-friendly fish, pasta, and meat dishes, plus salads, pizzas, and burgers. Don't miss the brie baked in cinnamon puff pastry or the homemade focaccia bread and dipping oil. **Known for:** nearly everything made in-house; ingredients from own organic café farm; wines from own estate winery. [$] *Average main: $24* ✉ *2879 Grand Ave.* ☎ *805/688–7265* 🌐 *www.winemerchantcafe.com* 🕒 *No breakfast.*

Hotels

★ Ballard Inn & The Gathering Table

$$$ | **B&B/INN** | Set among orchards and vineyards in the tiny town of Ballard, 2 miles south of Los Olivos, this inn makes an elegant Wine Country escape. **Pros:** exceptional food; attentive staff; secluded setting. **Cons:** some baths could use updating; restaurant noise sometimes travels upstairs; no in-room phones or TVs. [$] *Rooms from: $329* ✉ *2436 Baseline Ave., Ballard* ☎ *805/688–7770, 800/638–2466* 🌐 *ballardinn.com* 🛏 *15 rooms* 🍴 *Free breakfast.*

Fess Parker's Wine Country Inn

$$$$ | **B&B/INN** | This luxury inn includes an elegant, tree-shaded French country–style main building and an equally attractive annex across the street with a pool and day spa. **Pros:** convenient wine-touring base; walking distance from restaurants and galleries; Nella restaurant on-site. **Cons:** pricey for the area; not pet-friendly; thin walls between some rooms. $ *Rooms from: $395* ✉ *2860 Grand Ave.* ☎ *805/688–7788, 800/446–2455* ⊕ *www.fessparkerinn.com* ⇌ *19 rooms* ⦿ *Free breakfast.*

Solvang

5 miles south of Los Olivos.

You'll know you've reached the town of Solvang when the architecture suddenly changes to half-timber buildings and windmills. Danish educators settled the town in 1911—the flatlands and rolling green hills reminded them of home. Solvang has attracted tourists for decades, but it's lately become more sophisticated, with smorgasbords giving way to galleries, upscale restaurants, and wine-tasting rooms by day and wine bars by night.

GETTING HERE AND AROUND

Highway 246 West (Mission Drive) traverses Solvang, connecting with U.S. 101 to the west and Highway 154 to the east. Alamo Pintado Road connects Solvang with Ballard and Los Olivos to the north. Park your car in one of the free public lots and stroll the town. Or take the bus: Santa Ynez Valley Transit shuttles run between Solvang and nearby towns.

ESSENTIALS

VISITOR INFORMATION Solvang Visitors Center. ✉ *1639 Copenhagen Dr., at 2nd St.* ☎ *805/688–6144* ⊕ *www.solvangusa.com.*

Sights

Buttonwood Farm Winery & Vineyard
WINERY/DISTILLERY | Winemaker Karen Steinwachs transforms Bordeaux and Rhône varietals grown on Buttonwood Farm's 42-acre, sustainably farmed estate vineyard into delicious, value-laden wines. The flagship wines—Sauvignon Blanc, Cabernet Franc, and Cabernet Sauvignon—are distributed regionally, but many are small-lot specialty wines and blends available only at the winery. Steinwachs also crafts Chardonnay and

Pinot Noir wines with grapes from a vineyard in the cool-climate Sta. Rita Hills AVA 25 miles to the west. Sign up in advance for the hour-long Vineyard Walk (daily at 10 am) followed by a reserve tasting. ✉ *1500 Alamo Pintado Rd.* ☎ *805/688–3032* ⊕ *www.buttonwoodwinery.com* ⛿ *Tasting $15, walk and reserve tasting $35.*

Mission Santa Inés
RELIGIOUS SITE | The mission holds an impressive collection of paintings, statuary, vestments, and Chumash and Spanish artifacts in a serene bluff-top setting. You can tour the museum, sanctuary, and gardens. ✉ *1760 Mission Dr., at Alisal Rd.* ☎ *805/688–4815* ⊕ *missionsantaines.org* ⛿ *$6.*

 Restaurants

★ First & Oak

$$$$ | **AMERICAN** | Create your own custom tasting menu by choosing among five different groups of eclectic California–French dishes paired with local wines at this elegant farm-to-table restaurant inside the Mirabelle Inn. The seasonal menu changes constantly, but regulars include smoked sweet-and-spicy duck wings, truffle-roasted cauliflower, local spot prawns, short rib bourguignonne, and pears poached in red wine from the sommelier-owner's organic Coceliquot Estate Vineyard. **Known for:** intimate fine-dining setting; sommelier-owner selected wine list; complex dishes and presentation. $ *Average main: $37* ✉ *409 1st St.* ✛ *At Oak St.* ☎ *805/688–1703* ⊕ *www.firstandoak.com.*

peasants FEAST

$$ | **MODERN AMERICAN** | **FAMILY** | This low-key, family-friendly eatery in the heart of town serves up fresh-as-it-gets, made-from-scratch dishes that showcase seasonal local bounty sourced from trusted fishers and farmers. Feast on soups, beef-and-cheese smash burgers, and various salads and sandwiches in the

casual interior or in the cozy brick patio. **Known for:** tacos with rockfish, gourmet mushrooms, or slow-cooked pork; house-cured and smoked bacon, pickled organic veggies, pastrami-smoked salmon; house-made ice cream and desserts. [$] *Average main: $17* ✉ *487 Atterdag Rd.* ☎ *805/686–4555* 🌐 *www.peasantsfeast.com* ⏲ *Closed Mon. and Tues.*

★ Sear Steakhouse

$$$$ | **STEAKHOUSE** | This true farm-to-table restaurant (most ingredients come from the owners' organic farm, planted with more than 100 varieties of fruits, veggies, and herbs) serves classic steak house dishes that have a regional flair. Steaks come from high-end purveyors in Colorado and local ranches; seafood from regional waters; and other dishes like watermelon gazpacho, creamed spinach, and sauteed mushrooms showcase seasonal bounty. **Known for:** lively bar scene with dining until 2 am; classic and modern cocktails; culinary feasts on the farm (check website for schedule). [$] *Average main: $43* ✉ *478 4th Place* ☎ *805/245–9564* 🌐 *www.searsteakhouse.com* ⏲ *Closed Mon. No lunch.*

Succulent Café

$$$ | **AMERICAN** | Locals flock to this cozy café for its comfort cuisine and regional wines and craft beers. Order at the counter, and staffers will deliver your meal to the interior dining areas or the sunny outdoor patio. **Known for:** artisanal charcuterie plates; pet-friendly patio; homemade biscuits and gravy, house-roasted turkey. [$] *Average main: $28* ✉ *1555 Mission Dr., at 4th Pl.* ☎ *805/691–9444* 🌐 *succulentcafe.com* ⏲ *Closed Tues.*

Hotels

★ Alisal Guest Ranch and Resort

$$$$ | **RESORT** | Since 1946 celebrities and plain folk alike have come to this 10,000-acre ranch to join in a slew of activities, including horseback riding, tennis, golf, archery, boating, and fishing. **Pros:** Old West atmosphere; breakfast and dinner included in the rate; free Wi-Fi. **Cons:** no in-room phones or TVs; not close to downtown; jacket required for dinner. [$] *Rooms from: $735* ✉ *1054 Alisal Rd.* ☎ *805/688–6411, 800/425–4725* 🌐 *alisal.com* 🛏 *73 rooms* 🍴 *All-inclusive.*

★ Hotel Corque

$$ | **HOTEL** | Owned by the Santa Ynez Band of Chumash Indians, the stunning three-story "Corque" provides a full slate of upscale amenities. **Pros:** friendly, professional staff; short walk to shops, tasting rooms and restaurants; free Wi-Fi. **Cons:** no kitchenettes or laundry facilities; some rooms need updating; not pet-friendly. [$] *Rooms from: $239* ✉ *400 Alisal Rd.* ☎ *805/688–8000* 🌐 *hotelcorque.com* 🛏 *132 rooms* 🍴 *No meals.*

The Landsby

$$$ | **B&B/INN** | New owners remodeled the former old-world-style Petersen Village Inn and transformed it into a cozy, contemporary Scandinavian retreat that feels like a residence in downtown Copenhagen. **Pros:** in the heart of Solvang; easy parking; courtyard with fire pits. **Cons:** on highway; unusual hallway configuration can be confusing; thin walls in some rooms. [$] *Rooms from: $279* ✉ *1576 Mission Dr.* ☎ *805/688–3121* 🌐 *thelandsby.com* 🛏 *51 rooms* 🍴 *No meals.*

★ Mirabelle Inn

$$$ | **B&B/INN** | French, Danish, and American flags at the entrance and crystal chandeliers, soaring ceilings, and skylights in the lobby set the tone from the get-go in this elegant four-story inn a few blocks from the main tourist hub. **Pros:** excellent farm-to-table restaurant (dinner only); on-site concierge and sommelier; away from noisy crowds. **Cons:** some rooms on the small side; not in the heart of town; restaurant noise travels to nearby rooms. [$] *Rooms from: $260* ✉ *409 1st St.* ✣ *At Oak St.* ☎ *805/688–1703, 800/786–7925* 🌐 *mirabelleinn.com* 🛏 *12 rooms* 🍴 *No meals.*

🎭 Performing Arts

Solvang Festival Theater

THEATER | Pacific Conservatory of the Performing Arts presents crowd-pleasing musicals like *A Gentleman's Guide to Love and Murder* and *Million Dollar Quartet*, as well as Oscar Wilde's *The Importance of Being Earnest*, and contemporary plays at this 700-seat outdoor amphitheater. ⊠ *420 2nd St., at Molle Way* ☎ *805/922–8313* ⊕ *pcpa.org* ☞ *Performances June–Oct.*

Buellton

3 miles west of Solvang.

A crossroads town at the intersection of U.S. 101 and Highway 246, Buellton has evolved from a sleepy gas and coffee stop into an enclave of wine-tasting rooms, beer gardens, and restaurants. It's also a gateway to the Santa Rita Hills Wine Trail to the west and to Solvang, Santa Ynez, and Los Olivos to the east.

GETTING HERE AND AROUND

Driving is the easiest way to get to Buellton. From Santa Barbara, follow U.S. 101 north to the Highway 246 exit. Santa Ynez Valley Transit serves Buellton with shuttle buses from Solvang and nearby towns.

ESSENTIALS

VISITOR INFORMATION Discover Buellton. ⊠ *597 Ave. of the Flags, No. 101* ☎ *805/688–7829* ⊕ *discoverbuellton.com.* **Santa Rita Hills Wine Trail.** ⊕ *santaritahillswinetrail.com.*

👁 Sights

Alma Rosa Winery

WINERY/DISTILLERY | Winemaker Richard Sanford helped put Santa Barbara County on the international wine map with a 1989 Pinot Noir. For Alma Rosa, started in 2005, he crafts wines from grapes grown on 100-plus acres of certified organic vineyards in the Santa Rita Hills. The Pinot Noirs and Chardonnays are exceptional. Vineyard tours and tastings are available by appointment. ⊠ *181 C Industrial Way, off Hwy. 246, west of U.S. 101* ☎ *805/688–9090* ⊕ *almarosawinery.com* ⊡ *Tastings $20.*

Industrial Way

NEIGHBORHOOD | A half mile west of U.S. 101, head south from Highway 246 on Industrial Way to explore a hip and happening collection of food and drink destinations. Top stops include **Industrial Eats** (a craft butcher shop and restaurant), **Figueroa Mountain Brewing Kitchen,** the **Alma Rosa Winery** tasting room, and **McClain Cellars.** ⊠ *Industrial Way, off Hwy. 246* ⊕ *www.industrialwaysbc.com.*

Lafond Winery and Vineyards

WINERY/DISTILLERY | A rich, concentrated Pinot Noir is the main attention-getter at this winery that also produces noteworthy Chardonnays and Syrahs. Bottles with Lafond's SRH (Santa Rita Hills) label are an especially good value. The winery also has a tasting room at 111 East Yanonali Street in Santa Barbara's Funk Zone. ⊠ *6855 Santa Rosa Rd., west of U.S. 101 Exit 139* ☎ *805/688–7921* ⊕ *lafondwinery.com* ⊡ *Tastings $15.*

La Purísima Mission State Historic Park

RELIGIOUS SITE | **FAMILY** | The state's most fully restored mission, founded in 1787, stands in a stark and still remote location that powerfully evokes the lives and isolation of California's Spanish settlers. Docents lead tours Wednesday to Sunday (daily June to August), and vivid displays illustrate the secular and religious activities that formed mission life. ⊠ *2295 Purisima Rd., off Hwy. 246, 14 miles west of Buellton, Lompoc* ☎ *805/733–3713* ⊕ *www.lapurisimamission.org* ⊡ *$6 per vehicle.*

Los Alamos

HISTORIC SITE | A tiny stagecoach town founded in 1876, Los Alamos is a fun, Old West stopover when driving along Highway 101. Many of its original structures, including the 1880 Union Hotel, still line several blocks of Bell Street, the main drag. In recent years Los Alamos has evolved into a hip food-and-wine destination with first-rate tasting rooms and restaurants within the western-style buildings. Standouts include **Pico Los Alamos, Bob's Well Bread,** and **Casa Dumetz Wines.** ✉ *On Hwy. 101, 15 miles north of Buellton* 🌐 *www.visitsyv.com/discover-syv/los-alamos.*

🍴 Restaurants

The Hitching Post II

$$$$ | **AMERICAN** | You'll find everything from grilled artichokes to quail at this casual eatery, but most people come for the smoky Santa Maria–style barbecue. Be sure to try a glass of owner-chef-winemaker Frank Ostini's signature Highliner Pinot Noir, a star in the film *Sideways.* **Known for:** entrées grilled over local red oak; chef-owner makes his own wines; classic cocktails. [$] *Average main: $38* ✉ *406 E. Hwy. 246, off U.S. 101* ☎ *805/688–0676* 🌐 *www.hitchingpost2.com* 🕒 *No lunch.*

🛏 Hotels

Inn at Zaca Creek

$$$$ | **HOTEL** | Originally built by descendants of Buellton's founding family and reinvented as a rustic luxury resort after decades of dormancy, this elegant collection of suites, a restaurant, and secluded, multitiered spaces on 3 tree-studded acres pays homage to the land's historic roots and pastoral setting. **Pros:** on-site fine-dining restaurant and bar; secluded site near ranches and a residential area; attentive and personal service and hospitality. **Cons:** next to Highway 101; popular wedding venue with lively guests; not in the heart of town. [$] *Rooms from: $360* ✉ *1297 Jonata Park Rd.* ☎ *805/688–2412* 🌐 *za-ca-creek.com* 🛏 *6 suites* 🍽 *No meals.*

Volcanoes?

Those eye-catching sawed-off peaks along the drive from Pismo Beach to Morro Bay are called the Nine Sisters—a series of ancient volcanic plugs. Morro Rock, the northernmost sibling and a state historic monument, is the most famous and photographed of the clan.

Pismo Beach

51 miles northwest of Buellton.

About 20 miles of sandy shoreline—nicknamed the Bakersfield Riviera for the throngs of vacationers who come here from the Central Valley—begins at the town of Pismo Beach. The southern end of town runs along sand dunes, some of which are open to cars and off-road vehicles. Sheltered by the dunes, a grove of eucalyptus trees attracts thousands of migrating monarch butterflies from November through February. A long, broad beach fronts the center of town, where a municipal pier extends into the sea at the foot of shop-lined Pomeroy Street. To the north, hotels and homes perch atop chalky oceanfront cliffs. Fewer than 10,000 people live in this quintessential surfer haven, but Pismo Beach has a slew of hotels and restaurants with great views of the Pacific Ocean.

GETTING HERE AND AROUND

Pismo Beach straddles both sides of U.S. 101. If you're coming from the south and have time for a scenic drive, exit U.S. 101 in Santa Maria and take Highway 166 west for 8 miles to Guadalupe and follow Highway 1 north 16 miles to

Pismo Beach. South County Area Transit (SCAT; 🌐 *www.slorta.org*) buses run throughout San Luis Obispo and connect the city with nearby towns. On summer weekends, the free Avila Trolley extends service to Pismo Beach.

ESSENTIALS

VISITOR INFORMATION California Welcome Center. ✉ *333 5 Cities Dr.* ☎ *805/688–7354* 🌐 *www.visitcalifornia.com/experience/california-welcome-center-pismo-beach.* **Pismo Beach Visitor Information Center.** ✉ *Dolliver St./Hwy. 1 , at Hinds Ave.* ☎ *800/443–7778, 805/556–7397* 🌐 *classiccalifornia.com.*

Beaches

★ Oceano Dunes State Vehicular Recreation Area

BEACH—SIGHT | Part of the spectacular Guadalupe-Nipomo Dunes, this 3,600-acre coastal playground is one of the few places in California where you can drive or ride off-highway vehicles on the beach and sand dunes. Hike, ride horses, kiteboard, join a Hummer tour, or rent an ATV or a dune buggy and cruise up the white-sand peaks for spectacular views. At **Oso Flaco Lake Nature Area**—3 miles west of Highway 1 on Oso Flaco Road—a 1½-mile boardwalk over the lake leads to a platform with views up and down the coast. Leashed dogs are allowed in much of the park except Oso Flaco and Pismo Dunes Natural Reserve. **Amenities:** food and drink; lifeguards (seasonal); parking (fee); showers; toilets; water sports. **Best for:** sunset; surfing; swimming; walking. ✉ *West end of Pier Ave., off Hwy. 1, Oceano* ☎ *805/773–7170* 🌐 *www.parks.ca.gov* 🎟 *$5 per vehicle.*

Pismo State Beach

BEACH—SIGHT | Hike, surf, ride horses, swim, fish in a lagoon or off the pier, and dig for Pismo clams at this busy state beach. One of the day-use parking areas is off Highway 1 near the **Monarch Butterfly Grove,** where from November through February monarch butterflies nest in eucalyptus and Monterey pines. The other parking area is about 1½ miles south at Pier Avenue. **Amenities:** food and drink; lifeguards (seasonal); parking (fee); showers; toilets; water sports. **Best for:** sunset; surfing; swimming; walking. ✉ *555 Pier Ave., off Hwy. 1, 3 miles south of downtown Pismo Beach, Oceano* ☎ *805/473–7220* 🌐 *www.parks.ca.gov* 🎟 *Day-use $10 per vehicle if parking at beach.*

Restaurants

Cracked Crab

$$$ | **SEAFOOD** | This traditional New England–style crab shack imports fresh seafood daily from Australia, Alaska, and the East Coast. Fish is line-caught, much of the produce is organic, and everything is made from scratch. **Known for:** shellfish meals in a bucket, dumped on the table; casual setting; menu changes daily. [$] *Average main: $32* ✉ *751 Price St., near Main St.* ☎ *805/773–2722* 🌐 *www.crackedcrab.com.*

★ Ember

$$$ | **MODERN AMERICAN** | A barn-style restaurant with high ceilings and an open kitchen, Ember enjoys a red-hot reputation for Italian-inflected dishes prepared in an authentic Tuscan fireplace or a wood-burning oven. Chef-owner Brian Collins, a native of Arroyo Grande, the town bordering Pismo Beach, honed his culinary skills at Berkeley's legendary Chez Panisse Restaurant. **Known for:** seasonal menu changes monthly; wood-fired flatbread pizzas; long lines during prime time (no reservations). [$] *Average main: $34* ✉ *1200 E. Grand Ave., at Brisco Rd., Arroyo Grande* ☎ *805/474–7700* 🌐 *www.emberwoodfire.com* 🕒 *Closed Mon. and Tues. No lunch.*

Giuseppe's Cucina Italiana

$$$ | **ITALIAN** | The classic flavors of southern Italy are highlighted at this lively downtown spot. Most recipes originate from Bari, a seaport on the Adriatic; the menu includes breads and pizzas baked in the wood-burning oven, hearty dishes such as dry-aged steak and rack of lamb, and homemade pastas. **Known for:** lively family-style atmosphere; daily specials; most fruits and veggies come from owner's 12-acre farm. $ *Average main: $28* ⊠ *891 Price St., at Pismo Ave.* ☎ *805/773–2870* ⊕ *giuseppesrestaurant. com* ⊙ *No lunch weekdays.*

Splash Café

$ | **SEAFOOD** | Folks stand in line down the block for clam chowder served in a sourdough bread bowl at this wildly popular seafood stand. You can also order beach food such as fresh steamed clams, burgers, and fried calamari at the counter (no table service) here and at Splash's second location in San Luis Obispo, which has an on-site bakery and additional menu items. **Known for:** famous clam chowder; sourdough bread bowls baked in-house; cheery hole-in-the-wall. $ *Average main: $12* ⊠ *197 Pomeroy St., at Cypress St.* ☎ *805/773–4653* ⊕ *splashcafe.com.*

The Spoon Trade

$$ | **AMERICAN** | A silver spoon display at the entrance reflects this casual eatery's mission to "spoon food and trade stories" with diners who indulge in traditional American comfort food with a modern twist. Perennial menu faves include tri-tip tartare, deviled eggs, meat loaf Stroganoff, and fried chicken with sourdough waffles; save room for a root beer float or brown sugar pot de creme for dessert. **Known for:** pet-friendly patio; house-made pastas; lively dining room with open kitchen. $ *Average main: $25* ⊠ *295 W. Grand Ave.* ☎ *805/904–6773* ⊕ *www.thespoontrade.com* ⊙ *Closed Mon. and Tues. No lunch weekdays.*

Ventana Grill

$$$ | **FUSION** | Perched on a bluff at the northern edge of Pismo Beach, Ventana Grill offers ocean views from nearly every table, unusual seafood-centered Latin American–California fusion dishes, and more than 50 tequilas plus craft cocktails at the bar. Reservations are essential—this place is almost always packed, especially during the weekday happy hour. **Known for:** happy hour with sunset views; salsas and sauces made from scratch; more than 50 tequila selections. $ *Average main: $28* ⊠ *2575 Price St.* ☎ *805/773–0000* ⊕ *ventanagrill.com.*

Hotels

The Cliffs Hotel & Spa

$$ | **RESORT** | Lawns and palm trees surround this full-service resort that perches dramatically on an oceanfront cliff. **Pros:** beach access via short downhill path; oceanfront restaurant and lounge; bluff-top walking trail. **Cons:** not close to downtown; rooms near service areas and elevator can be noisy; resort fee. $ *Rooms from: $239* ⊠ *2757 Shell Beach Rd.* ☎ *805/773–5000, 800/826–7827* ⊕ *www.cliffsresort.com* ⟿ *160 rooms* ⑪ *No meals.*

Dolphin Bay Resort & Spa

$$$$ | **RESORT** | On grass-covered bluffs overlooking Shell Beach, this luxury resort looks and feels like an exclusive community of villas; choose among sprawling one- or two-bedroom suites, each with a gourmet kitchen, laundry room with washer and dryer, and contemporary furnishings. **Pros:** lavish apartment units; Lido farm-to-table restaurant; many suites have ocean views. **Cons:** hefty price tag; vibe too uppercrust for some; not close to downtown. $ *Rooms from: $489* ⊠ *2727 Shell Beach Rd.* ☎ *805/773–4300, 800/516–0112 reservations, 805/773–8900 restaurant* ⊕ *www.thedolphinbay.com* ⟿ *60 suites* ⑪ *No meals.*

Inn at the Pier

$$$$ | **HOTEL** | The luxe Inn at the Pier opened in winter 2017, covering a prime city block just steps from the sand and across from the pier. **Pros:** walk to downtown restaurants, sights, shops; fitness

San Luis Obispo County and Big Sur Coast

center and cruiser bike rentals; new building. **Cons:** daily resort fee; valet parking only; bar noise travels to some rooms. $ *Rooms from: $359* ✉ *601 Cypress St.* ☎ *805/295–5565* ⊕ *www.theinnatthepier. com* ⇄ *104 rooms* ⦿ *No meals.*

Pismo Lighthouse Suites

$$$ | HOTEL | Each of the well-appointed two-room, two-bath suites at this oceanfront resort has a private balcony or patio. **Pros:** sport court features life-size chess game; nautical-style furnishings; nice pool area. **Cons:** not easy to walk to main attractions; some units are next to busy road; first-floor units can hear footsteps from suites above. $ *Rooms from: $269* ✉ *2411 Price St.* ☎ *805/773– 2411, 800/245–2411* ⊕ *www.pismolight- housesuites.com* ⇄ *70 suites* ⦿ *Free breakfast.*

SeaVenture Beach Hotel & Restaurant

$$$ | HOTEL | The bright, homey rooms at this hotel all have fireplaces and feather- beds; most have balconies with private hot tubs, and some have beautiful ocean views. **Pros:** on the beach; excellent food; romantic rooms. **Cons:** touristy area; some rooms and facilities dated; dark hallways. $ *Rooms from: $279* ✉ *100 Ocean View Ave.* ☎ *805/773–4994* ⊕ *www.seaventure. com* ⇄ *50 rooms* ⦿ *No meals.*

Avila Beach

4 miles north of Pismo Beach.

Because the village of Avila Beach and the sandy, cove-front shoreline for which it's named face south into the Pacific Ocean, they get more sun and less fog than any other stretch of coast in the area. With its fortuitous climate and protected waters, Avila's public beach draws sunbathers and families; summer weekends are very busy. Downtown Avila Beach has a lively seaside promenade and some shops and hotels, but for real local color, head to the far end of the cove and watch the commercial fishers off-load their catch on the old Port San Luis wharf. On Friday from mid-April through mid-September, a fish and farmers' market livens up the beach area with music, fresh local produce and seafood, and children's activities.

GETTING HERE AND AROUND

Exit U.S. 101 at Avila Beach Drive and head 3 miles west to reach the beach. The free Avila Trolley operates weekends year-round, plus Friday afternoon and evening from April to September. The minibuses connect Avila Beach and Port San Luis to Shell Beach, with multiple stops along the way. Service extends to Pismo Beach in summer.

ESSENTIALS

VISITOR INFORMATION Avila Beach Tourism Alliance. 🌐 *visitavilabeach.com.*

Sights

Avila Valley Barn

RESTAURANT—SIGHT | FAMILY | An old-fashioned, family-friendly country store jam-packed with local fruits and vegetables, prepared foods, and gifts, Avila Valley Barn also gives visitors a chance to experience rural American traditions. You can pet farm animals and savor homemade ice cream and pies daily, and on weekends ride a hay wagon out to the fields to pick your own produce. ✉ *560 Avila Beach Dr., San Luis Obispo* ☎ *805/595–2816* 🌐 *www.avilavalleybarn.com* 🕒 *Closed Tues. and Wed. Jan.–Mar.*

Point San Luis Lighthouse

LIGHTHOUSE | FAMILY | Docents lead hikes along scenic Pecho Coast Trail (3½ miles round-trip) to see the historic 1890 lighthouse and its rare Fresnel lens. ■ **TIP→ If you'd prefer a lift out to the lighthouse, join a shuttle tour. Hikes and tours require reservations.** ✉ *Point San Luis, 1¾ miles west of Harford Pier, Port San Luis* ☎ *805/540–5771* 🌐 *www.pointsanluislighthouse.org* 🎫 *Shuttle tours $25; hikes free ($10 to enter lighthouse).*

Beaches

Avila City Beach

BEACH—SIGHT | FAMILY | At the edge of a sunny cove next to downtown shops and restaurants, Avila's ½-mile stretch of white sand is especially family-friendly, with a playground, barbecue and picnic tables, volleyball and basketball courts, and lifeguards on watch in summer and on many holiday weekends. The free beachfront parking fills up fast, but there's a nearby pay lot ($6 for the day, $2 after 4 pm). Dogs aren't allowed on the beach from 10 to 5. **Amenities:** food and drink; lifeguards (seasonal); parking; showers; toilets; water sports. **Best for:** sunset; surfing; swimming; walking. ✉ *Avila Beach Dr., at 1st St.* 🌐 *www.visitavilabeach.com* 🎫 *Free.*

Restaurants

Mersea's

$ | SEAFOOD | Walk down the pier to this casual crab shack where you can order at the counter, grab a drink at the bar, and find a seat on the deck or in the casual indoor dining area to gaze at spectacular Avila Bay views while you dine. The menu includes chowder bowls, burgers, sandwiches, seafood, and salads, plus bowls of fish, shrimp, or chicken served over rice pilaf and veggies. **Known for:** clam chowder in sourdough bread bowls; fish tacos; fresh local ingredients. [$] *Average main: $16* ✉ *3985 Port San Luis Pier* ✥ *At Port San Luis* ☎ *805/548–2290* 🌐 *www.merseas.com.*

Ocean Grill

$$$ | SEAFOOD | Across from the promenade, beach, and pier, Ocean Grill serves up fresh seafood to diners who typically arrive before sunset to enjoy the views. Boats anchored in the bay provide much of the seafood, which pairs well with the mostly regional wines on the list. **Known for:** fantastic ocean views; wood-fired pizzas; gluten-free and vegetarian options. $ *Average main: $29* ⊠ *268 Front St.* ☎ *805/595–4050* ⊕ *www.oceangrillavila. com* ☉ *No lunch Mon.–Thurs.*

 ## Hotels

Avila La Fonda

$$$ | **HOTEL** | Modeled after a village in early California's Mexican period, Avila La Fonda surrounds guests with rich jewel tones, fountains, and upscale comfort; its facade replicates eight different casitas, including several famous historic homes in Mexico. **Pros:** one-of-a-kind theme and artwork; flexible room combinations; a block from the beach. **Cons:** pricey for the area; most rooms don't have an ocean view; spotty Wi-Fi. $ *Rooms from: $329* ⊠ *101 San Miguel St.* ☎ *805/595–1700* ⊕ *www.avilalafondahotel.com* ⊅ *28 rooms* ⦿ *No meals.*

Avila Lighthouse Suites

$$$$ | **HOTEL** | Families, honeymooners, and business travelers all find respite at this two-story, all-suites luxury hotel. **Pros:** directly across from beach; easy walk to restaurants and shops; free underground parking. **Cons:** noise from passersby can be heard in room; some ocean-view rooms have limited vistas; basic breakfast. $ *Rooms from: $359* ⊠ *550 Front St.* ☎ *805/627–1900, 800/372–8452* ⊕ *www.avilalighthousesuites.com* ⊅ *54 suites* ⦿ *Free breakfast.*

Sycamore Mineral Springs Resort & Spa

$$$ | **RESORT** | This wellness resort's hot mineral springs bubble up into private outdoor tubs on an oak-and-sycamore-forest hillside. **Pros:** great place to rejuvenate; nice hiking nearby; incredible spa with yoga classes, integrative healing arts, and many treatments. **Cons:** rooms vary in quality; 2½ miles from the beach; road noise can travel to certain areas of property. $ *Rooms from: $259* ⊠ *1215 Avila Beach Dr., San Luis Obispo* ☎ *805/595–7302* ⊕ *www.sycamoresprings.com* ⊅ *72 rooms* ⦿ *No meals.*

San Luis Obispo

8 miles north of Avila Beach.

About halfway between San Francisco and Los Angeles, San Luis Obispo spreads out below gentle hills and rocky extinct volcanoes. Its main appeal lies in its architecturally diverse, pedestrian-friendly downtown, which bustles with shoppers, restaurant goers, and students from California Polytechnic State University, known as Cal Poly. On Thursday evening from 6 to 9 the city's famed farmers' market fills Higuera Street with local produce, entertainment, and food stalls.

San Luis Obispo is the commercial center of a wine region whose appellations (Edna Valley, Arroyo Grande Valley) stretch west toward the coast and east toward the inland mountains. Many of the nearly 30 wineries here line Highway 227 and connecting roads. The region is known for Chardonnay and Pinot Noir, although many wineries experiment with other varietals and blends. Wine-touring maps are available around San Luis Obispo. Many wineries charge a small tasting fee; most tasting rooms close at 5.

GETTING HERE AND AROUND

U.S. 101/Highway 1 traverses the city for several miles. From the north, Highway 1 merges with U.S. 101 when it reaches the city limits. The wineries of the Edna Valley and Arroyo Grande Valley wine regions lie south of town off Highway 227, the parallel (to the east) Orcutt Road, and connecting roads.

SLO City Transit buses operate daily. The Downtown Trolley provides evening service to the city's hub every Thursday, on Friday from June to early September, and Saturday from April through October.

ESSENTIALS

VISITOR INFORMATION San Luis Obispo Chamber of Commerce. ⊠ *895 Monterey St.* ☎ *805/781–2777* ⊕ *slochamber.org.* **San Luis Obispo City Visitor Information.** ☎ *877/756–8696* ⊕ *visitslo.com.*

Sights

Biddle Ranch Vineyard

WINERY/DISTILLERY | Glass doors and walls in a converted dairy barn fill the Biddle Ranch Vineyard tasting room with light and sweeping valley, mountain, and vineyard views. The small-production winery focuses on estate Chardonnay (the adjacent 17-acre vineyard is planted exclusively to the grape), plus Pinot Noir and various red blends. ⊠ *2050 Biddle Ranch Rd.* ✛ *At Hwy. 227* ☎ *805/543– 2399* ⊕ *www.biddleranch.com* 🍷 *Tastings $25 (reservations required)* ⊘ *Closed Tues. and Wed.*

Claiborne & Churchill

WINERY/DISTILLERY | An eco-friendly winery built from straw bales, C&C makes small lots of aromatic Alsatian-style wines such as dry Riesling and Gewürztraminer, plus Pinot Noir blends, Syrah, and Chardonnay. ⊠ *2649 Carpenter Canyon Rd., at Price Canyon Rd.* ☎ *805/544–4066* ⊕ *www.claibornechurchill.com* 🍷 *Tastings $22.*

Mission San Luis Obispo de Tolosa

RELIGIOUS SITE | Sun-dappled Mission Plaza fronts the fifth mission established in 1772 by Franciscan friars. A small museum exhibits artifacts of the Chumash Indians and early Spanish settlers. ⊠ *751 Palm St., at Chorro St.* ☎ *805/543–6850* ⊕ *www.missionsanluisobispo.org* 🍷 *$3.*

Old Edna

TOWN | This peaceful, 2-acre site once *was* the town of Edna. Nowadays you can peek at the vintage 1897 and 1908

Deep Roots

Way back in the 1700s, the Spanish padres who accompanied Father Junípero Serra planted grapevines from Mexico along California's Central Coast and began using European wine-making techniques to turn the grapes into delectable vintages.

farmhouse cottages, taste Sextant wines, pick up sandwiches at the gourmet deli, and stroll along Old Edna Lane. ⊠ *1653 Old Maxwellton Rd., at Hwy. 227* ☎ *805/710–3701 Old Edna Townsite, 805/542–0133 tasting room and deli* ⊕ *oldedna.com.*

San Luis Obispo Children's Museum

MUSEUM | **FAMILY** | Activities at this facility geared to kids under age 10 include an "imagination-powered" elevator that transports visitors to a series of underground caverns. Elsewhere, simulated lava and steam sputter from an active volcano. Kids can pick rubber fruit at a farmers' market and race in a fire engine to fight a fire. ⊠ *1010 Nipomo St., at Monterey St.* ☎ *805/544–5437* ⊕ *www.slocm.org* 🍷 *$8* ⊘ *Closed Tues. Closed nonholiday Mon. Sept.–Apr.*

Talley Vineyards

WINERY/DISTILLERY | Acres of Chardonnay and Pinot Noir, plus smaller parcels of Sauvignon Blanc, Syrah, and other varietals blanket Talley's mountain-ringed dell in the Arroyo Grande Valley. Enjoy stunning estate views in the sleek interior and on the adjacent patio, where all tastings are seated (no tasting bar) and require an appointment. Standout wines include the single-vineyard Rosemary's Pinot Noir and Chardonnay. ⊠ *3031 Lopez Dr., off Orcutt Rd., Arroyo Grande* ☎ *805/489–0446* ⊕ *www.talleyvineyards. com* 🍷 *Tastings from $30.*

Wolff Vineyards
WINERY/DISTILLERY | Syrah, Petite Sirah, and Riesling join the expected Pinot Noir and Chardonnay as the stars at this family-run winery 6 miles south of downtown. The pourers are friendly, and you'll often meet one of the owners or their children in the tasting room. With its hillside views, the outdoor patio is a great place to enjoy an afternoon picnic. ✉ *6238 Orcutt Rd., near Biddle Ranch Rd.* ☎ *805/781–0448* 🌐 *www.wolffvineyards.com* 🎫 *Tastings $15.*

🍴 Restaurants

Big Sky Café
$$ | **ECLECTIC** | Family-friendly Big Sky turns local and organically grown ingredients into global dishes, starting with breakfast. Just pick your continent: braised Argentinian lamb shanks, Southeast Asian noodle bowls, Middle Eastern lamb burger, Maryland crab cakes. **Known for:** artsy, creative vibe; ample choices for vegetarians; locavore pioneer. [$] *Average main: $21* ✉ *1121 Broad St., at Higuera St.* ☎ *805/545–5401* 🌐 *bigskycafe.com.*

★ Giuseppe's Cucina Rustica
$$$ | **ITALIAN** | The younger sibling of the hugely popular Guiseppe's restaurant in Pismo Beach, this lively downtown eatery serves up authentic southern Italian fare in the historic Sinsheimer Bros. building, originally constructed in 1884. Dine in the spacious main restaurant amid high ceilings, fireplaces, and bar, or in the courtyard beneath strings of twinkling lights. **Known for:** bread, sauce, pasta, gelato and other desserts made in-house; organic ingredients from the owner's 12-acre farm or sourced from local purveyors; historic ambience. [$] *Average main: $27* ✉ *849 Monterey St.* ☎ *805/541–9922* 🌐 *www.giuseppesrestaurant.com.*

Luna Red
$$$ | **INTERNATIONAL** | A spacious, contemporary space with a festive outdoor patio, this restaurant near Mission Plaza serves creative tapas and cocktails. The small plates include birria-braised beef tacos, avocado-tuna ceviche, and empanadas stuffed with squash and goat cheese. **Known for:** excellent traditional Valencian paellas; craft cocktails; lively music scene. [$] *Average main: $27* ✉ *1023 Chorro St., at Monterey St.* ☎ *805/540–5243* 🌐 *www.lunaredslo.com.*

Mo's Smokehouse BBQ
$ | **SOUTHERN** | Barbecue joints abound on the Central Coast, but this one excels. Various Southern-style sauces season tender hickory-smoked ribs and shredded-meat sandwiches, and sides such as baked beans, coleslaw, homemade potato chips, and garlic bread extend the pleasure. **Known for:** barbecue sampler with ribs, pork, and chicken; barbecue chicken and other fresh salads; house-made potato chips, garlic fries, and other sides. [$] *Average main: $16* ✉ *1005 Monterey St., at Osos St.* ☎ *805/544–6193* 🌐 *smokinmosbbq.com.*

Novo Restaurant & Lounge
$$ | **ECLECTIC** | In the colorful dining room or on the large creek-side deck, this animated downtown eatery will take you on a culinary world tour. The salads, small plates, and entrées come from nearly every continent. **Known for:** value-laden happy hour from 3 to 6; savory curry and noodle dishes; local farmers' market ingredients. [$] *Average main: $25* ✉ *726 Higuera St., at Broad St.* ☎ *805/543–3986* 🌐 *www.novorestaurant.com.*

SLO Provisions
$ | **AMERICAN** | Stop at this casual café/market in the Upper Monterey neighborhood for a sit-down or take-away meal all day. Apart from full meals, order specialty sandwiches, farm-fresh salads, and baked goods, or hang out and taste wine or beer at the casual tasting bar. **Known for:** house-roasted rotisserie meats; family-style dinners; daily specials. [$] *Average main: $16* ✉ *1255 Monterey St.* ☎ *805/439–4298* 🌐 *www.sloprovisions.com* 🕓 *Closed Sun.*

Hotels

Garden Street Inn

$$ | **B&B/INN** | From this restored 1887 Italianate Queen Anne downtown, you can walk to many restaurants and attractions; uniquely decorated rooms, each with private bath, are filled with antiques, and some rooms have stained-glass windows, fireplaces, and decks. **Pros:** lavish homemade breakfast; convenient location; complementary wine-and-cheese reception. **Cons:** city noise filters into some rooms; not great for families; no elevator. [$] *Rooms from: $249* ✉ *1212 Garden St.* ☎ *805/545–9802* 🌐 *www.gardenstreetinn.com* 🛏 *13 rooms* 🍴 *Free breakfast.*

Granada Hotel & Bistro

$$$ | **HOTEL** | Built in 1922 in the heart of downtown and sparkling again after 2012 renovations, the two-story Granada is a vintage-style retreat with hardwood floors, redbrick walls, and antique rugs. **Pros:** one of a few full-service hotels in the heart of downtown; easy walk to restaurants, shops, and sights; farm-to-table Granada Bistro and Nightcap cocktail bar, and grab-and-go restaurant on-site. **Cons:** some rooms are tiny; sometimes noisy near restaurant kitchen; late-night bar noise travels to some rooms. [$] *Rooms from: $279* ✉ *1126 Morro St.* ☎ *805/544–9100* 🌐 *www.granadahotelandbistro.com* 🛏 *17 rooms* 🍴 *No meals.*

★ Hotel Cerro

$$$ | **HOTEL** | San Luis Obispo's Chumash, mission, and 19th-century industrial eras blend with urban sophistication in this eco-friendly, four-story complex, which opened in summer 2019. **Pros:** on-site restaurant, café, and lobby lounge; tree-lined outdoor terrace; designed and built to meet LEED Silver status. **Cons:** in the heart of the downtown bar scene; limited on-site valet parking only; room designs not ideal for families with small children. [$] *Rooms from: $275* ✉ *1125 Garden St.* ☎ *805/548–1000* 🌐 *www.hotelcerro.com* 🛏 *65 rooms* 🍴 *No meals.*

Hotel San Luis Obispo

$$$$ | **HOTEL** | Completed in 2019, the sleek, three-story Hotel San Luis Obispo offers a full range of services and upscale amenities, just a block from the mission and steps from restaurants, shops, and nightlife. **Pros:** in the heart of the downtown historic district; park the car and walk to most attractions; new building. **Cons:** valet parking only; some rooms overlook a parking garage; too pet-friendly for some guests. [$] *Rooms from: $459* ✉ *877 Palm St.* ☎ *805/235–0700* 🌐 *hotel-slo.com* 🛏 *78 rooms* 🍴 *No meals.*

The Kinney San Luis Obispo

$$ | **HOTEL** | The Kinney celebrates nearby Cal Poly's culture and history in fun, hipster fashion, with local photos, college sports equipment displays, and hanging wicker swings and vintage games and books in the lobby lounge. **Pros:** close to Cal Poly campus; heated pool and sundeck; free parking and Wi-Fi. **Cons:** A/C less than adequate in some rooms; tiny fitness center; motel vibe. [$] *Rooms from: $175* ✉ *1800 Monterey St.* ☎ *805/544–8600* 🌐 *www.thekinneyslo.com* 🛏 *100 rooms* 🍴 *Free breakfast.*

★ Madonna Inn

$$ | **HOTEL** | From its rococo bathrooms to its pink-on-pink froufrou steak house, the Madonna Inn is fabulous or tacky, depending on your taste. **Pros:** fun, one-of-a-kind experience; infinity pool, exercise room, and day spa; each room has its own distinct identity, for example, Safari Room. **Cons:** rooms vary widely; must appreciate kitsch; no elevator. [$] *Rooms from: $229* ✉ *100 Madonna Rd.* ☎ *805/543–3000, 800/543–9666* 🌐 *www.madonnainn.com* 🛏 *110 rooms* 🍴 *No meals.*

Petit Soleil

$$ | **B&B/INN** | A cobblestone courtyard, country-French custom furnishings, and Gallic music piped through the halls evoke a Provençal mood at this cheery inn. **Pros:** includes wine and appetizers at cocktail hour; includes scrumptious

breakfasts; cozy rooms with luxury touches. **Cons:** sits on a busy avenue; cramped parking; some rooms are tiny. $ *Rooms from: $189* ✉ *1473 Monterey St.* ☎ *805/549–0321, 800/676–1588* ⊕ *www.psslo.com* ↪ *16 rooms* ⦿ *Free breakfast.*

ⓨ Nightlife

SLO's club scene is centered on Higuera Street, off Monterey Street.

Koberl at Blue

BARS/PUBS | A trendy crowd hangs out at this upscale restaurant's slick bar to sip on exotic martinis and the many local and imported beers and wines. ✉ *998 Monterey St., at Osos St.* ☎ *805/783–1135* ⊕ *www.epkoberl.com.*

The Libertine Brewing Company

BREWPUBS/BEER GARDENS | Come to Libertine to savor 76 craft beers and wines on tap, house-made brews of kombucha and cold brew coffee, and pub food infused with the brewery's own wild ales. ✉ *1234 Broad St.* ☎ *805/548–2337* ⊕ *www.libertinebrewing.com/san-luis-obispo.*

Nightcap

BARS/PUBS | Indulge in craft and vintage cocktails at the Granada Hotel's artsy cocktail lounge, decked out in pink- and rose-colored velvet, mirrored ceilings, and marble tables and countertops. ✉ *1130 Morro St.* ☎ *805/544–9100.*

🎟 Performing Arts

Performing Arts Center, San Luis Obispo

ARTS CENTERS | A truly great performance space, the center hosts live theater, dance, and music. ✉ *Cal Poly, 1 Grand Ave., off U.S. 101* ☎ *805/756–4849* ⊕ *www.calpolyarts.org.*

San Luis Obispo Repertory Theatre

THEATER | SLO County's only nonprofit, fully professional theater group presents dramas, musicals, readings, and other performances year-round. ✉ *888 Morro St.* ☎ *805/706–2440 box office* ⊕ *www.slolittletheatre.org.*

Shopping

Higuera Street

SHOPPING NEIGHBORHOODS | Many of San Luis Obispo's locally owned and operated shops cluster around downtown's Higuera Street in the blocks east of the mission. Also head up Monterey Street just north of the mission to find more small stores with one-of-a-kind treasures. ✉ *San Luis Obispo.*

Paso Robles

30 miles north of San Luis Obispo, 25 miles northwest of Morro Bay.

In the 1860s, tourists began flocking to this ranching outpost to "take the cure" in a bathhouse fed by underground mineral hot springs. An Old West town emerged, and grand Victorian homes went up, followed in the 20th century by Craftsman bungalows. These days, the wooded hills of Paso Robles west of U.S. 101 and the flatter, more open land to the freeway's east hold more than 250 wineries, many with tasting rooms. Hot summer days, cool nights, and varied soils and microclimates allow growers to cultivate an impressive array of Bordeaux, Rhône, and other grape types.

Cabernet Sauvignon grows well in the Paso Robles AVA—40,000 of its 600,000-plus acres are planted to grapes—as do Petit Verdot, Grenache, Syrah, Viognier, and Zinfandel. In recognition of the diverse growing conditions, the AVA was divided into 11 subappellations in 2014. Pick up a wine-touring map at lodgings, wineries, and attractions around town. The fee at most tasting rooms is between $10 and $25; many lodgings pass out discount coupons.

Upmarket restaurants, bars, antiques stores, and little shops fill the streets around oak-shaded City Park, where special events of all kinds—custom car shows, an olive festival, Friday-night summer concerts—take place on many weekends. Despite its increasing sophistication, Paso (as the locals call it) retains a small-town vibe. The city celebrates its cowboy roots in late July and early August with the two-week California Mid-State Fair, complete with livestock auctions, carnival rides, and corn dogs.

GETTING HERE AND AROUND

U.S. 101 runs north–south through Paso Robles. Highway 46 West links Paso Robles to Highway 1 and Cambria on the coast. Highway 46 East connects Paso Robles with I–5 and the San Joaquin Valley. Public transit is not convenient for wine touring and sightseeing.

ESSENTIALS

VISITOR INFORMATION Paso Robles CAB Collective. ☎ 805/543–2288 ⊕ pasoroblescab.com. **Paso Robles Wine Country Alliance.** ☎ 805/239–8463 ⊕ pasowine. com. **Paso Robles Visitor Center.** ⊠ 1225 Park St., near 12th St. ☎ 805/238–0506 ⊕ travelpaso.com. **Rhone Rangers/Paso Robles.** ⊕ www.rhonerangers.org.

 Sights

Brecon Estate

WINERY/DISTILLERY | Small-batch super-premium wines sold exclusively in the tasting room are the main focus of this much-lauded, 40-acre, Westside estate winery. Specialties include Albariño, Cabernet Franc, and Rhone blends. Brecon also crafts Bordeaux varietals, including the reserve Old Vine Cabernet Sauvignon, with estate grapes from one of the oldest vines in Paso Robles. Taste wines within the urban-chic cedar barn, which combines Scandinavian and Australian design elements, or at tables on the shady patio. ⊠ 7450 Vineyard Dr. ☎ 805/239–2200 ⊕ breconestate.com ☒ Tastings $20.

★ Calcareous Vineyard

WINERY/DISTILLERY | Elegant wines, a stylish tasting room, and knockout hilltop views make for a winning experience at this winery along winding Peachy Canyon Road. Cabernet Sauvignon, Syrah, and Zinfandel grapes thrive in the summer heat and limestone soils of the two vineyards near the tasting room; and a third vineyard on cooler York Mountain produces Pinot Noir, Chardonnay, and a Cabernet with a completely different character from the Peachy Canyon edition. ■TIP→ **The picnic area's expansive eastward views invite lingering.** ⊠ 3430 Peachy Canyon Rd. ☎ 805/239–0289 ⊕ calcareous.com ☒ Tastings $20; tour and tasting (reservations required) from $35.

Denner Vineyards

WINERY/DISTILLERY | The sloping roof of this winery's tasting room and production facility mimics the gently rolling, limestone-laden landscape it occupies. The respect for the terrain that the architecture exhibits repeats itself in the farming and cellar techniques used to create Denner's mostly Rhône-style wines, which—along with Zinfandel, Cabernet Sauvignon, and a few other reds—routinely receive mid-90s scores from major critics. Appointment-only tastings indoors or out take advantage of hilltop views of Willow Creek District trees, vines, and pastures. ⊠ 5414 Vineyard Dr. ☎ 805/239–4287 ⊕ www.dennervineyards.com ☒ Tastings $25.

Eberle Winery

WINERY/DISTILLERY | Even if you don't drink wine, stop here for a tour (reservations essential) of the huge wine caves beneath the vineyards. Eberle produces wines from Bordeaux, Rhône, and Italian varietals and makes intriguing blends including Côte-du-Rôbles Blanc and Rouge and Cabernet Sauvignon–Syrah. ⊠ 3810 Hwy. 46 E, 3½ miles east of U.S. 101 ☎ 805/238–9607 ⊕ www. eberlewinery.com ☒ Basic tasting free ($10 reservation fee for up to 6 people), *private tour and tasting (up to 6 people) $50 by appointment.*

Firestone Walker Brewing Company

WINERY/DISTILLERY | At this working craft brewery you can sample medal-winners such as the Double Barrel Ale and learn about the beer-making process on 45-minute guided tours of the brewhouse and cellar. ⊠ *1400 Ramada Dr., east side of U.S. 101; exit at Hwy. 46 W/ Cambria, but head east* ☎ *805/296–7454 visitor center* ⊕ *www.firestonebeer.com* 🥤 *Tastings from $2 per sample, tour $12 (includes 4 samples).*

Halter Ranch Vineyard

WINERY/DISTILLERY | A good place to learn about contemporary Paso Robles wine making, this ultramodern operation produces high-quality wines from estate-grown Bordeaux and Rhône grapes grown in sustainably farmed vineyards. The gravity-flow winery, which you can view on tours, is a marvel of efficiency. Ancestor, the flagship wine, a potent Bordeaux-style blend of Cabernet Sauvignon, Petit Verdot, and Malbec, is named for the ranch's huge centuries-old coast oak tree. ⊠ *8910 Adelaida Rd., at Vineyard Dr.* ☎ *888/367–9977* ⊕ *www.halterranch. com* 🥤 *Tastings from $35.*

JUSTIN Vineyards & Winery

WINERY/DISTILLERY | This suave winery built its reputation on Isosceles, a hearty Bordeaux blend, usually of Cabernet Sauvignon, Cabernet Franc, and Merlot. JUSTIN's Cabernet Sauvignon is also well regarded, as is the Right Angle blend of Cab and three other varietals. Tastings here take place in an expansive room whose equally expansive windows provide views of the hillside vineyards. ⊠ *11680 Chimney Rock Rd., 15 miles west of U.S. 101's Hwy 46 E exit; take 24th St. west and follow road (name changes along the way) to Chimney Rock Rd.* ☎ *805/238–6932* ⊕ *justinwine. com* 🥤 *Tastings $40, tour and tasting $65* ↻ *Tours 10 and 2:30 (reservations recommended).*

★ Niner Wine Estate

WINERY/DISTILLERY | A family-owned winery in the Willow Creek district, Niner is known equally for its range of estate wines (especially powerful reds) and its farm-fresh lunches designed to complement wine tasting flights. For a special treat, sign up for the Fog Catcher flight, which focuses on components of its Bordeaux blend. The option to order lunch is available with tasting reservations, which are required. ⊠ *2400 Hwy. 46 W* ☎ *805/239–2233* ⊕ *www.ninerwine.com* 🥤 *Tastings $30, Fog Catcher flight $50.*

Opolo

WINERY/DISTILLERY | Opolo means "fun" in Greek, an apt name for a crowd-pleasing winery that effectively combines casual food, accessible wines, and peppy service—plus regular events that often inspire spontaneous singing and dancing. Wine-tasting flights at the westside vineyard include Opolo's flagship wine, Mountain Zinfandel, and specialty single varietals. The on-site Willow Creek Distillery produces nearly a dozen types of brandies and whiskeys; the $10 tasting flight is a good introduction to spirits. ⊠ *7110 Vineyard Dr.* ☎ *805/238–9593.*

Paso Robles Market Walk

MARKET | Taste wine and craft beer, feast on ramen bowls, burgers, and sweet treats, and shop for one-of-a-kind gifts in this upscale public market in a residential area six blocks north of City Park. The eclectic collection of purveyors showcases the products of local chefs, vintners, and makers—all committed to sustainable business practices. ■**TIP→ Book a room in one of the six luxury lofts on the market's second floor for convenient dining and shopping before or after wine touring.** ⊠ *1803 Spring St.* ☎ *805/720–1255* ⊕ *www.pasomarketwalk.com.*

★ Pasolivo

WINERY/DISTILLERY | While touring the idyllic west side of Paso Robles, take a break from wine tasting by stopping at Pasolivo. Find out how the artisans here make their Tuscan-style olive oils on a high-tech Italian press, and test the acclaimed results. If you're in downtown Paso Robles, stop by Pasolivo's urban tasting room at 1229 Park Street. ✉ *8530 Vineyard Dr., west off U.S. 101 (Exit 224) or Hwy. 46 W (Exit 228)* ☎ *805/227–0186* ⊕ *www.pasolivo.com* ✉ *Tastings $5.*

Re:Find Handcrafted Spirits

WINERY/DISTILLERY | The owners of Villacana Winery in west Paso Robles launched the first local distillery in 2011, aiming to repurpose the saignee (free-run juice) that's typically tossed out during the wine-making process. They ferment and distill the leftover high-quality juices into premium spirits, thus reclaiming about 60 acres of premium wine grapes. Taste vodka, gin, whiskey, bourbon, limoncello, and kumquat liqueurs in the tiny barrel-room tasting space or outdoors under the oaks. ✉ *2725 Adelaida Rd.* ☎ *805/239–9456* ⊕ *refinddistillery.com* ✉ *Tastings $20* ⊘ *Closed Mon. and Tues.*

River Oaks Hot Springs & Spa

SPA—SIGHT | The lakeside spa, on 240 hilly acres near the intersection of U.S. 101 and Highway 46 East, is a great place to relax after wine tasting or festival-going. Soak in a private indoor or outdoor hot tub fed by natural mineral springs, or indulge in a massage or facial. ✉ *800 Clubhouse Dr., off River Oaks Dr., just north of River Oaks Golf Course* ☎ *805/238–4600* ⊕ *riveroakshotsprings. com* ✉ *From $16 per hr.*

★ Sensorio

PUBLIC ART | This 386-acre interactive garden engages the senses; honors the natural topography; and offers a wide range of amusing, mystical, and kinetic experiences. It launched in 2019 with internationally renowned artist Bruce Munro's solar-powered, 15-acre, walk-through installation, *Field of Light,* an array of 58,800 fiber-optic illuminated stemmed spheres that subtly morph into undulating colors. In 2021, Sensorio added *Light Towers,* a stunning collection of 69 colorful, fiber-optic-lit towers composed of more than 17,000 wine bottles that ripple to a custom musical score. A visit begins in the pre-dusk hours to capture the changing light of the landscape and the installation as darkness descends. A hospitality area offers live entertainment by local musicians, snacks, meals, beer, and wine. Sign up for the VIP Experience to gain exclusive access to an Airstream bar, private tables, and firepits on a terrace overlooking *Field of Light.* Reserve your timed-entry space well in advance: Sensorio is phenomenally popular. ✉ *4380 E. Hwy. 46* ☎ *805/226–4287* ⊕ *sensoriopaso.com* ✉ *General admission $32, VIP Experience $81* ⊘ *Closed Mon.–Wed.*

★ Sixmilebridge Vineyards

WINERY/DISTILLERY | In a cutting-edge facility on a 95-acre Westside estate, Sixmilebridge (named for the owner's ancestral home in Ireland), produces limited-production Cabernet Sauvignon and Bordeaux blends crafted mostly from organically grown estate fruit. A spacious terrace surrounding a 150-year-old coastal oak tree is reserved for those who purchase a glass or bottle of wine (picnics welcome). ✉ *5120 Peachy Canyon Rd.* ☎ *805/239–5844* ⊕ *sixmilebridge.com* ✉ *Tastings from $30.*

SummerWood Winery

WINERY/DISTILLERY | Rhône varietals do well in the Paso Robles AVA, where many wineries, including this one, produce "GSM" (Grenache, Syrah, Mourvèdre) red blends, along with whites such as Viognier, Marsanne, and Grenache Blanc. Winemaker Mauricio Marchant displays a subtle touch with Rhône whites and reds, as well as Sentio, a Petit Verdot–heavy Bordeaux red blend. Tastings here are relaxed and informal, and there's a patio from which you can enjoy the vineyard views. ✉ *2175 Arbor Rd., off Hwy. 46W* ☎ *805/227–1365* ⊕ *summerwoodwine.com* ✉ *Tastings $20, reserve $40.*

Tablas Creek Vineyard

WINERY/DISTILLERY | Tucked in the western hills of Paso Robles, Tablas Creek is known for its blends of certified biodynamically grown, hand-harvested Rhône varietals. Roussanne and Viognier are the standout whites; the Mourvèdre-heavy blend called Panoplie (it also includes Grenache and Syrah) has received high praise in recent years. ■ **TIP→ There's a fine picnic area here.** ✉ *9339 Adelaida Rd., west of Vineyard Dr.* ☎ *805/237–1231* 🌐 *www.tablascreek.com* 🎫 *Tastings from $20 (reserve $45 by appointment), tour free.*

★ Tin City

WINERY/DISTILLERY | This industrial park on the southern border of Paso Robles houses a collection of wineries, craft breweries, distilleries, and specialty shops where you can pick up sheep's milk ice cream, fresh pasta, and other local wares. Good places to start your explorations include Giornata Winery, Levo Winery, and TinCity Cider Co. Dine casually at McPhee's Canteen restaurant or upscale (dinner only) at Six Test Kitchen. ✉ *Limestone Way* ✥ *East of Ramada Dr. via Marquita Ave.* 🌐 *www.tincitypaso.com.*

🍴 Restaurants

BL Brasserie

$$$ | **FRENCH** | Owner-chef Laurent Grangien's handsome, welcoming French bistro occupies an 1890s brick building across from City Park. He focuses on traditional dishes such as duck confit, rack of lamb, and onion soup, but always prepares a few au courant daily specials as well. **Known for:** classic French dishes made with local ingredients; good selection of local and international wines; four-tasting menu Thurs. [$] *Average main: $34* ✉ *1202 Pine St., at 12th St.* ☎ *805/226–8191* 🌐 *www.blbrasserie.com* 🕒 *Closed Mon. No lunch Sun.*

SIP Certification

Many wineries in Paso Robles take pride in being SIP (Sustainability in Practice) Certified, for which they undergo a rigorous third-party audit of their entire operations. Water and energy conservation practices are reviewed, along with pest management and other aspects of farming. Also considered are the wages, benefits, and working conditions of the employees, and the steps taken to mitigate the impact of grape growing and wine production on area habitats.

The Hatch

$$ | **AMERICAN** | A wood-fired rotisserie in an open kitchen, simple but tasty comfort foods and a lively bar scene attract locals and visitors alike to this cozy, casual space in an historic brick building a block north from the main square. Fuel up body and soul with menu favorites like meat loaf, shrimp and grits, bacon burgers, pies, cakes, and sundaes. **Known for:** house-made sauces, house-pickled fruits and veggies, house-cured ham; craft cocktails and small-batch whiskies; daily rotisserie specials: chicken, ribs, lamb, tri-tip. [$] *Average main: $22* ✉ *835 13th St.* ☎ *805/221–5727* 🌐 *hatchpasorobles.com* 🕒 *No lunch.*

Il Cortile

$$$$ | **MODERN ITALIAN** | One of two Paso establishments owned by chef Santos MacDonal and his wife, Carole, this Italian restaurant entices diners with complex flavors and a contemporary space with art-deco overtones. Consistent crowd-pleasers often on the menu include beef carpaccio with white truffle cream sauce and shaved black truffles and pappardelle with wild boar ragu. **Known for:** house-made pastas; excellent wine pairings; ingredients from chef's garden. $ *Average main: $38* ✉ *608 12th St., near Spring St.* ☎ *805/226–0300* ⊕ *www.ilcortileristorante.com* ☾ *Closed Mon. and Tues. No lunch.*

Jeffry's Wine Country BBQ

$ | **AMERICAN** | Award-winning local chef Jeff Wiesinger and his wife Kathleen opened this casual eatery, tucked in a hidden courtyard a block from downtown City Park. Feast indoors or out on made-to-order sandwiches, hearty mac-and-cheese bowls, house-made potato chips, fresh salads, craft beer, and local wines while listening to throwback soundtracks from the '60s and '70s. **Known for:** delectable mac-and-cheese dishes; smoked tri-tip and other meats; savory paella. $ *Average main: $16* ✉ *819 12th St., Suite B* ⊹ *In alley between 12th and 13th Sts.* ☎ *805/ 369–2132* ⊕ *jeffryswinecountrybbq.com* ☾ *Closed Wed.*

La Cosecha

$$$ | **SOUTH AMERICAN** | At barlike, tin-ceilinged La Cosecha (Spanish for "the harvest"), Honduran-born chef Santos MacDonal faithfully re-creates dishes from Spain and South America. Noteworthy starters include *pastelitos catracho*, Honduran-style empanadas in a light tomato sauce served with *queso fresco* (fresh cheese) and micro cilantro. **Known for:** fusion of Latin spices and fresh local fare; daily paella special; artisanal cocktails. $ *Average main: $34* ✉ *835 12th St., near Pine St.* ☎ *805/237–0019* ⊕ *www.lacosechabr.com* ☾ *Closed Mon. Closed Tues. Jan. and Feb.*

McPhee's Grill

$$$$ | **AMERICAN** | Just south of Paso Robles in tiny Templeton, this casual chophouse in an 1860s wood-frame storefront serves sophisticated, contemporary versions of traditional Western fare such as oak-grilled filet mignon and fresh seafood tostadas. The house-label wines, made especially for the restaurant, are quite good. **Known for:** meats grilled over red oak; local seasonal menu; excellent wine selections. $ *Average main: $39* ✉ *416 S. Main St., at 5th St., Templeton* ☎ *805/434–3204* ⊕ *mcpheesgrill.com* ☾ *Closed Mon. and Tues. No lunch.*

 Hotels

★ Allegretto

$$$ | **RESORT** | This swank, 20-acre Tuscan-style resort amid estate vineyards is also a private museum where owner Douglas Ayres displays hundreds of artworks and artifacts collected on his world travels: ancient Indian river stones and statues; a massive cross section from a giant sequoia; Russian and California impressionist paintings; mandalas; and more (nonguests are welcome to walk around). **Pros:** yoga in medieval abbey; full-service restaurant Cello and spa; bocce ball, firepit, and other diversions. **Cons:** not close to downtown square; pricey; some rooms close to courtyard music. $ *Rooms from: $349* ✉ *2700 Buena Vista Dr.* ☎ *805/369–2500* ⊕ *www.allegrettoresort.com* ⇆ *171 rooms* ⏚ *No meals.*

★ Hotel Cheval

$$$$ | **HOTEL** | Equestrian themes surface throughout this intimate European-style boutique hotel a half block from the main square and near some of Paso's best restaurants. **Pros:** most rooms have fireplaces; sip wine and champagne at the on-site Pony Club and zinc bar; extremely personalized service. **Cons:** views aren't great; no pool or hot tub; no elevator. $ *Rooms from: $410* ✉ *1021 Pine St.* ☎ *805/226–9995, 866/522–6999* ⊕ *www.hotelcheval.com* ⇆ *16 rooms* ⏚ *Free breakfast.*

JUST Inn

$$$$ | **B&B/INN** | Fine wines, a destination restaurant, and a vineyard's-edge setting make a stay at Justin winery's on-site inn an exercise in sophisticated seclusion. **Pros:** amazing night skies; vineyard views; destination restaurant. **Cons:** half-hour drive to town; location may be too secluded for some; spotty cell service.

$ *Rooms from: $620* ✉ *11680 Chimney Rock Rd.* ☎ *805/238–6932, 800/726–0049* ⊕ *www.justinwine.com* ⤴ *4 suites* ⎜◯⎜ *Free breakfast.*

La Quinta Inn & Suites

$$ | HOTEL | A good value for Paso Robles, this three-story chain property attracts heavy repeat business with its upbeat staff and slew of perks. **Pros:** apartment-style suites in separate building; free happy hour with local wines and appetizers; good for leisure or business travelers. **Cons:** conventional decor; not downtown; basic breakfast. $ *Rooms from: $189* ✉ *2615 Buena Vista Dr.* ☎ *805/239–3004, 800/753–3757* ⊕ *www.laquintapasorobles.com* ⤴ *101 rooms* ⎜◯⎜ *Free breakfast.*

Paso Robles Inn

$$ | HOTEL | On the site of an old spa hotel of the same name, the various buildings at this historic inn cluster around a lush, shaded garden with a pool. **Pros:** private hot tubs in many rooms; special touches like unique photography in each room; across from town square. **Cons:** fronts a busy street; rooms vary in size and amenities; some areas could use an upgrade. $ *Rooms from: $189* ✉ *1103 Spring St.* ☎ *805/238–2660, 800/676–1713* ⊕ *www.pasoroblesinn.com* ⤴ *122 rooms* ⎜◯⎜ *No meals.*

★ SummerWood Inn

$$$ | B&B/INN | Easygoing hospitality, vineyard-view rooms, and elaborate breakfasts make this inn a mile west of U.S. 101 worth seeking out. **Pros:** convenient wine-touring base; elaborate breakfasts; complimentary tastings at associated winery. **Cons:** some noise from nearby highway during the day; no elevator; not close to downtown restaurants. $ *Rooms from: $340* ✉ *2130 Arbor Rd., 1 mile west of U.S. 101, at Hwy. 46W* ☎ *805/227–1111* ⊕ *www.summerwoodwine.com/inn* ⤴ *9 rooms* ⎜◯⎜ *Free breakfast.*

Nightlife

1122 Speakeasy

BARS/PUBS | Press the doorbell and request permission to enter this elegant, 1930s-era cocktail lounge and speakeasy on the back patio of Pappy McGregor's Pub on the main square. It has just 28 seats, so be prepared to wait in line on weekend nights. ✉ *1122 Pine St.* ⊕ *Entrance on Railroad St. or walk through pub* ☎ *805/238–4141* ⊕ *www.eleven-twentytwo.com* ⌖ *Closed Mon. and Tues.*

 Performing Arts

Vina Robles Amphitheatre

CONCERTS | At this 3,300-seat, Mission-style venue with good food, wine, and sight lines, you can enjoy acclaimed musicians in concert. ✉ *Vina Robles winery, 3800 Mill Rd., off Hwy. 46* ☎ *805/286–3680* ⊕ *www.vinarobles-amphitheatre.com* ⌖ *Performances Apr.–Nov.*

Morro Bay

30 miles southwest of Paso Robles, 14 miles north of San Luis Obispo.

Commercial fishermen slog around Morro Bay in galoshes, and beat-up fishing boats bob in the bay's protected waters. Nature-oriented activities take center stage here: kayaking, hiking, biking, fishing, and wildlife-watching around the bay and national marine estuary and along the state beach.

GETTING HERE AND AROUND

From U.S. 101 south or north, exit at Highway 1 in San Luis Obispo and head west. Scenic Highway 1 passes through the eastern edge of town. From Atascadero, two-lane Highway 41 West treks over the mountains to Morro Bay. San Luis Obispo RTA Route 12 buses travel year-round between Morro Bay, San Luis

Obispo, Cayucos, Cambria, San Simeon, and Hearst Castle. The Morro Bay Shuttle picks up riders throughout the town from Friday through Monday in summer ($1.25 one-way, $3 day pass).

ESSENTIALS

VISITOR INFORMATION Morro Bay Tourism. ✉ *695 Harbor St., at Napa Ave.* 🌐 *www.morrobay.org.*

Sights

Embarcadero

NEIGHBORHOOD | The center of Morro Bay action on land is the Embarcadero, where vacationers pour in and out of souvenir shops and seafood restaurants and stroll or bike along the scenic half-mile Harborwalk to Morro Rock. From here, you can get out on the bay in a kayak or tour boat. ✉ *On waterfront from Beach St. to Tidelands Park.*

Montaña de Oro State Park

NATIONAL/STATE PARK | West of San Luis Obispo, Los Osos Valley Road winds past farms and ranches to this state park whose miles of nature trails traverse rocky shoreline, wild beaches, and hills overlooking dramatic scenery. Check out the tide pools, watch the waves roll into the bluffs, and picnic in the eucalyptus groves. From Montaña de Oro you can reach Morro Bay by following the coastline along South Bay Boulevard 8 miles through the quaint residential villages of Los Osos and Baywood Park. ✉ *West about 13 miles from downtown San Luis Obispo on Madonna Rd., to Los Osos Valley Rd., to Pecho Valley Rd.; to continue on to Morro Bay, backtrack east to Los Osos Valley Rd., then head north on S. Bay Blvd., and west on State Park Rd., San Luis Obispo* ☎ *805/772–6101* 🌐 *www.parks.ca.gov.*

Morro Bay State Park Museum of Natural History

MUSEUM | **FAMILY** | The museum's entertaining interactive exhibits explain the natural environment and how to preserve it—in the bay and estuary and on the rest of the planet. **■TIP→ Kids age 16 and under are admitted free.** ✉ *20 State Park Rd., south of downtown* ☎ *805/772–2694* 🌐 *centralcoastparks.org* 🎟 *$3.*

Morro Rock

NATURE PRESERVE | At the mouth of Morro Bay stands 576-foot-high Morro Rock, one of nine small volcanic peaks, or morros, in the area. A short walk leads to a breakwater, with the harbor on one side and crashing ocean waves on the other. You may not climb the rock, where endangered falcons and other birds nest. Sea lions and otters often play in the water below the rock. ✉ *Northern end of Embarcadero.*

Restaurants

Dorn's Original Breakers Cafe

$$ | **SEAFOOD** | This restaurant overlooking the harbor has satisfied local appetites since 1942 and serves straight-ahead dishes such as cod or shrimp fish-and-chips or calamari tubes sautéed in butter and wine. **Known for:** sweeping views of Morro Rock and the bay; fresh local seafood; friendly, efficient service. [$] *Average main: $23* ✉ *801 Market Ave., at Morro Bay Blvd.* ☎ *805/772–4415* 🌐 *www.dornscafe.com.*

Taco Temple

$ | **SOUTHWESTERN** | This family-run diner serves some of the freshest food around. The seafood-heavy menu includes salmon burritos, superb fish tacos with mango salsa, and other dishes hailing from somewhere between California and Mexico. **Known for:** fresh seafood and salsa bar; hefty portions; daily specials. [$] *Average main: $16* ✉ *2680 Main St., at Elena St.,* *just north of Hwy. 1/Hwy. 41 junction* ☎ *805/772–4965* 🌐 *tacotemple.com.*

★ **Tognazzini's Dockside**

$$ | **SEAFOOD** | Captain Mark Tognazzini catches seasonal seafood and delivers the bounty to his family's collection of down-home, no-frills enterprises in the harbor: a fish market with patio dining and up-close views of Morro Rock (Dockside Too), and the original Dockside restaurant. Local musicians play live music nearly every day at the outdoor patio at Dockside Too. **Known for:** fresh-as-it-gets local seafood; live music nearly every day year-round; front-row seats to Morro Rock views. [$] *Average main: $20* ✉ *1245 Embarcadero* ☎ *805/772–8100 restaurant, 805/772–8120 fish market and patio dining* 🌐 *www.morrobaydockside.com.*

Windows on the Water

$$$$ | **SEAFOOD** | Diners at this second-floor restaurant view the sunset through giant picture windows. Meanwhile, fresh fish and other dishes based on local ingredients emerge from the wood-fired oven in the open kitchen, and oysters on the half shell beckon from the raw bar. **Known for:** sustainably sourced seafood; 20-plus wines by the glass; menu changes nightly. [$] *Average main: $39* ✉ *699 Embarcadero, at Pacific St.* ☎ *805/772–0677* 🌐 *www.windowsmb.com* 🕒 *Closed Sun. and Mon. No lunch.*

Hotels

★ **Anderson Inn**

$$$ | **B&B/INN** | Friendly, personalized service and an oceanfront setting keep loyal patrons returning to this Embarcadero inn, which features well-appointed rooms with state-of-the-art tiled bathrooms and cozy comforters atop king beds. **Pros:** walk to restaurants and sights; spacious rooms; oceanfront rooms have fireplaces and private balconies. **Cons:** not low-budget; waterfront area can get crowded; need to book well in advance—fills quickly. [$] *Rooms from: $285* ✉ *897 Embarcadero* ☎ *805/772–3434, 866/950–3434 toll-free reservations* 🌐 *andersoninnmorrobay.com* 🛏 *8 rooms* 🍴 *No meals.*

The Inn at Morro Bay

$$ | **RESORT** | Surrounded by eucalyptus trees, this inn abuts a heron rookery and Morro Bay State Park. **Pros:** great for wildlife lovers; stellar views from restaurant and some rooms; nearby golf course, wellness center on-site. **Cons:** some rooms on the small side; birds and seals can wake you early; remote location, not close to the Embarcadero. [$] *Rooms from: $189* ✉ *60 State Park Rd.* ☎ *805/772–5651* 🌐 *innatmorrobay.com* 🛏 *98 rooms* 🍴 *No meals.*

Activities

Lost Isle Adventures

BOATING | Offerings include 45-minute jaunts around Morro Bay ($20) or adults-only sunset cruises ($25) aboard a tiki-themed boat. A faster adventure boat is used for 90-minute whale-watching excursions ($85). ✉ *Giovanni's Fish Market, 1001 Front St., on the Embarcadero* ☎ *805/440–8170* 🌐 *morrobaytikiboat.com.*

Sub-Sea Tours & Kayaks

BOATING | You can view sea life aboard this outfit's glass-bottom boat, watch whales from its catamaran, or rent a kayak, canoe, or stand-up paddleboard. ✉ *699 Embarcadero* ☎ *805/772–9463* 🌐 *subseatours.com.*

Virg's Landing

FISHING | Virg's conducts deep-sea-fishing and whale-watching trips. ✉ *1169 Market Ave.* ☎ *805/772–1222* 🌐 *virgslanding.com.*

Cambria

28 miles west of Paso Robles, 20 miles north of Morro Bay.

Cambria, set on piney hills above the sea, was settled by Welsh miners in the 1890s. In the 1970s the isolated setting attracted artists and other independent types; the town now caters to tourists, but it still bears the imprint of its bohemian past. Both of Cambria's downtowns, the original East Village and the newer West Village, are packed with art and crafts galleries, antiques shops, cafés, restaurants, and B&Bs.

Two diverting detours lie between Morro Bay and Cambria. In the laid-back beach town of Cayucos, 4 miles north of Morro Bay, you can stroll the long pier, feast on chowder (at Duckie's), and sample the namesake delicacies of the Brown Butter Cookie Co. Over in Harmony, a quaint former dairy town 7 miles south of Cambria (population 18), you can take in the glassworks, pottery, and other artsy enterprises.

GETTING HERE AND AROUND

Highway 1 leads to Cambria from the north and south. Highway 246 West curves from U.S. 101 through the mountains to Cambria. San Luis Obispo RTA Route 12 buses stop in Cambria (and Hearst Castle).

ESSENTIALS

VISITOR INFORMATION Cambria Chamber of Commerce. ⊠ *767 Main St.* ☎ *805/927–3624* ⊕ *www.cambriachamber.org.*

 Sights

Covell Ranch Clydesdale Horses

NATURE PRESERVE | Come to the 2,000-acre Covell Ranch to see one of the world's largest private stands of endangered Monterey pines and witness herds of gentle Clydesdales roaming the range. Much of the ranch is in a conservation easement that will never be developed.

The 1½-hour guided vehicle tours take you through pastures and historic pine groves to the barn. The ranch also offers trail rides. ⊠ *5694 Bridge St.* ☎ *805/975–7332* ⊕ *www.covellsclydesdaleranch. com* ✉ *Tours $200 for up to 5 persons* ⊙ *Tours and trail rides by appointment only.*

Fiscalini Ranch Preserve

NATURE PRESERVE | Walk down a mile-long coastal bluff trail to spot migrating whales, otters, and shorebirds at this 450-acre public space. Miles of additional scenic trails crisscross the protected habitats of rare and endangered species of flora and fauna, including a Monterey pine forest, western pond turtles, monarch butterflies, and burrowing owls. Dogs are permitted on-leash everywhere and off-leash on all trails except the bluff. ⊠ *Hwy. 1, between Cambria Rd. and Main St. to the north, and Burton Dr. and Warren Rd. to the south; access either end of bluff trail off Windsor Blvd.* ☎ *805/927–2856* ⊕ *www.fiscaliniranch-preserve.org.*

Leffingwell Landing

CITY PARK | A state picnic ground, the landing is a good place for examining tidal pools and watching otters as they frolic in the surf. ⊠ *North end of Moonstone Beach Dr.* ☎ *805/927–2070.*

Moonstone Beach Drive

SCENIC DRIVE | The drive runs along a bluff above the ocean, paralleled by a 3-mile boardwalk that winds along the beach. On this photogenic walk you might glimpse sea lions and sea otters, and perhaps a gray whale during winter and spring. Year-round, birds fly about, and tiny creatures scurry amid the tidepools. ⊠ *Off Hwy. 1.*

★ Stolo Family Vineyards

WINERY/DISTILLERY | Just 3 miles from the ocean and a short drive from Cambria's East Village, the 52-acre Stolo estate produces about 4,000 cases of premium wine each year. The estate Syrahs consistently win top awards; sample these and other estate wines, including Pinot Noir, dry Gewurztraminer, Sauvignon Blanc, and Chardonnays, in the hilltop tasting room on the site of a former dairy farm. If the weather's nice, sit out on the sprawling lawn near a 1920s barn and 1895 farmhouse. ⊠ *3776 Santa Rosa Creek Rd.* ☎ *805/924–3131* ⊕ *stolofamily-vineyards.com.*

 Restaurants

Linn's Restaurant

$$ | **AMERICAN** | **FAMILY** | Homemade olallieberry pies, soups, potpies, and other farmhouse comfort foods share the menu at this spacious East Village restaurant with fancier farm-to-table dishes such as organic, free-range chicken topped with raspberry-orange-cranberry sauce. Also on-site are a bakery, a café serving more casual fare (take-out available), and a gift shop that sells gourmet foods. **Known for:** olallieberry pie; numerous gluten-free and vegan options; family-owned and-operated for decades. $ *Average main: $25* ⊠ *2277 Main St., at Wall St.* ☎ *805/927–0371* ⊕ *www.linns-fruitbin.com.*

★ Madeline's

$$$ | **FRENCH FUSION** | Dine on stellar French-American delights at a romantic, candlit table in this tiny restaurant within a tasting room and wineshop in Cambria's West Village. The menu changes seasonally, but you might start with diver scallops or stuffed quail, then move on to Louisiana seafood gumbo or Long Island duck breast, and bananas foster or crème brûlée for dessert. **Known for:** lamb osso buco, octopus, and other unusual dishes; excellent selection of local wines; bread pudding and other house-made desserts. $ *Average main: $33* ⊠ *788 Main St.* ☎ *805/927–4175* ⊕ *www.madelinescambria.com.*

Robin's

$$$ | **ECLECTIC** | An international, vegetarian-friendly dining experience awaits you at this cozy East Village cottage. Dinner choices include chicken enchiladas, grilled Skuna Bay salmon, lamb curry, and short ribs. **Known for:** savory curries; top-notch salmon bisque; secluded (heated) garden patio. $ *Average main: $28* ⊠ *4095 Burton Dr., at Center St.* ☎ *805/927–5007* ⊕ *robinsrestaurant.com.*

★ Sea Chest Oyster Bar and Restaurant

$$$ | **SEAFOOD** | Cambria's best place for seafood fills up soon after it opens at 5:30 (no reservations taken). Those in the know grab seats at the oyster bar and take in spectacular sunsets while watching the chefs broil fresh halibut, steam garlicky clams, and fry crispy calamari steaks; if you arrive to a wait, play cribbage or checkers in the game room. **Known for:** New England chowder house vibe; savory cioppino; waiting areas in wine bar, game room, and patio with firepit. $ *Average main: $35* ⊠ *6216 Moonstone Beach Dr., near Weymouth St.* ☎ *805/927–4514* ⊕ *seachestoysterbar.com* ▭ *No credit cards* ☽ *Closed Tues. mid-Sept.–May. No lunch.*

Hotels

Cambria Pines Lodge

$$ | **RESORT** | This 25-acre retreat up the hill from the East Village is a good choice for families; accommodations range from basic fireplace cabins to motel-style standard rooms to large fireplace suites and deluxe suites with spa tubs. **Pros:** short walk from downtown; live music nightly in the lounge; verdant gardens. **Cons:** service and housekeeping not always top-quality; some units need updating; thin walls in some units. $ *Rooms from: $169* ⊠ *2905 Burton Dr.* ☎ *805/927–4200, 800/966–6490* ⊕ *www.cambriapineslodge.com* ⇴ *152 rooms* ⦿ *Free breakfast.*

Moonstone Landing
$$ | **HOTEL** | This up-to-date motel's amenities, reasonable rates, and accommodating staff make it a Moonstone Beach winner. **Pros:** sleek furnishings; across from the beach; cheery lounge. **Cons:** narrow property; some rooms overlook a parking lot; noise occasionally travels from next-door restaurant machinery. [$] *Rooms from: $189* ✉ *6240 Moonstone Beach Dr.* ☎ *805/927–0012, 800/830–4540* 🌐 *www.moonstonelanding.com* 🛏 *29 rooms* 🍴 *Free breakfast.*

★ **Olallieberry Inn**
$$ | **B&B/INN** | The second-oldest home in Cambria (built in 1875) and a national historic monument, this painstakingly restored B&B inn offers luxurious creature comforts in a pristine English garden setting on the banks of Santa Rosa Creek. **Pros:** gourmet three-course breakfast; wine hour with homemade appetizers; walk to East Village restaurants and shops. **Cons:** no elevator; no children under 12; some rooms front busy road. [$] *Rooms from: $225* ✉ *2476 Main St.* ☎ *805/927–3222* 🌐 *www.olallieberry.com* 🛏 *9 rooms* 🍴 *Free breakfast.*

★ **White Water Cambria**
$$$$ | **HOTEL** | A fascinating design that blends beach-boho 1970s California with Scandinavian modern elements (clean lines, light woods, natural accents), an inviting lobby lounge with sweeping ocean views, and cozy rooms that evoke unfussy luxury make White Water stand out among Moonstone Beach lodgings. **Pros:** lobby lounge with small bites and shared plates, cocktails, wine, and craft beer; steps to the beach and walking trails; fleet of complimentary Linus bikes. **Cons:** not in downtown Cambria; some rooms on the small side; fog sometimes obscures ocean views. [$] *Rooms from: $399* ✉ *6736 Moonstone Beach Dr.* ☎ *805/927–1066* 🌐 *whitewatercambria.com* 🛏 *25 rooms* 🍴 *Free breakfast.*

San Simeon

9 miles north of Cambria, 65 miles south of Big Sur.

Whalers founded San Simeon in the 1850s, but had virtually abandoned it by 1865, when Senator George Hearst began purchasing most of the surrounding ranch land. Hearst turned San Simeon into a bustling port, and his son, William Randolph Hearst, further developed the area while erecting Hearst Castle (one of the many remarkable stops you'll encounter when driving along Highway 1). Today San Simeon is basically a strip of unremarkable gift shops and so-so motels that straddle Highway 1 about 4 miles south of the castle's entrance, but Old San Simeon, right across from the entrance, is worth a peek. Julia Morgan, William Randolph Hearst's architect, designed some of the village's Mission Revival–style buildings.

GETTING HERE AND AROUND

Highway 1 is the only way to reach San Simeon. Connect with the highway off U.S. 101 directly or via rural routes such as Highway 41 West (Atascadero to Morro Bay) and Highway 46 West (Paso Robles to Cambria).

ESSENTIALS

VISITOR INFORMATION San Simeon Chamber of Commerce Visitor Center. ✉ *250 San Simeon Ave.* ☎ *805/927–3500* 🌐 *www.visitsansimeonca.com.*

Sights

★ **Hearst Castle**
CASTLE/PALACE | Officially known as "Hearst San Simeon State Historical Monument," Hearst Castle sits in solitary splendor atop La Cuesta Encantada (the Enchanted Hill). Its buildings and gardens spread over 127 acres that were the heart of newspaper magnate William Randolph Hearst's 250,000-acre ranch. Hearst commissioned renowned

California architect Julia Morgan to design the estate, but he was very much involved with the final product, a blend of Italian, Spanish, and Moorish styles. The 115-room main structure and three huge "cottages" are connected by terraces and staircases and surrounded by pools, gardens, and statuary. In its heyday the castle, whose buildings hold about 22,000 works of fine and decorative art, was a playground for Hearst and his guests—Hollywood celebrities, political leaders, scientists, and other well-known figures. Construction began in 1919 and was never officially completed. Work was halted in 1947 when Hearst had to leave San Simeon because of failing health. The Hearst Corporation donated the property to the State of California in 1958, and it is now part of the state park system.

Access to the castle is through the visitor center at the foot of the hill, where you can view educational exhibits and a 40-minute film about Hearst's life and the castle's construction. Buses from the center zigzag up to the hilltop estate, where guides conduct four daytime tours, each with a different focus: Grand Rooms, Upstairs Suites, Designing the Dream, and Cottages and Kitchen. These tours take about three hours and include a movie screening, and time at the end to explore the castle's exterior and gardens. In spring and fall, docents in period costume portray Hearst's guests and staff for the Evening Tour, which begins around sunset. Reservations are recommended for all tours, which include a ½-mile walk and between 150 and 400 stairs. ■ TIP→ **Be sure to check the website in advance of your visit for any updates and to make tour reservations.** ⊠ *San Simeon State Park, 750 Hearst Castle Rd.* ☎ *800/444–4445, 518/218–5078 international reservations* ⊕ *www.hearstcastle.org* ☝ *Daytime tours from $25, evening tours $36.*

Hearst Ranch Winery

WINERY/DISTILLERY | Old whaling equipment and Hearst Ranch and Hearst Castle memorabilia decorate this winery's casual Old San Simeon outpost. The tasting room occupies a historic warehouse building with a gift shop, deli, and an outdoor deck and umbrella-shaded tables overlooking San Simeon Cove. The flagship wines include a Bordeaux-style red blend with Petite Sirah added to round out the flavor, and Rhône-style white and red blends. Malbec and Tempranillo are two other strong suits. ⊠ *442 SLO San Simeon Rd., off Hwy. 1* ☎ *805/927–4100* ⊕ *www.hearstranchwinery.com* ☝ *Tastings from $25.*

Piedras Blancas Elephant Seal Rookery

NATURE PRESERVE | **FAMILY** | A large colony of elephant seals (at last count 25,000) gathers every year at Piedras Blancas Elephant Seal Rookery, on the beaches near Piedras Blancas Lighthouse. The huge males with their pendulous, trunklike noses typically start appearing on shore in late November, and the females begin to arrive in December to give birth—most babies are born in the last two weeks of January. The newborn pups spend about four weeks nursing before their mothers head out to sea, leaving them on their own; the "weaners" leave the rookery when they are about 3½ months old. The seals return in the spring and summer months to molt or rest, but not en masse as in winter. You can watch them from a boardwalk along the bluffs just a few feet above the beach; do not attempt to approach them as they are wild animals. The nonprofit Friends of the Elephant Seal runs a small visitor center and gift shop (*250 San Simeon Ave.*) in San Simeon. ⊠ *Off Hwy. 1, 4½ miles north of Hearst Castle, just south of Piedras Blancas Lighthouse* ☎ *805/924–1628* ⊕ *www.elephantseal.org.*

Piedras Blancas Light Station

TOUR—SIGHT | If you think traversing craggy, twisting Highway 1 is tough, imagine trying to navigate a boat up the rocky coastline (*piedras blancas* means "white rocks" in Spanish) near San Simeon before lighthouses were built. Captains must have cheered wildly when the beam began to shine here in 1875. Try to time a visit to include the 9:45 am tour held on Tuesday, Thursday, and Saturday year-round, as well as on Monday and Friday in summer. ■TIP➔ **Do not meet your guide at the gate to the lighthouse—you'll miss the tour. Meet instead at the former Piedras Blancas Motel, 1½ miles north of the light station.** ⊠ *San Simeon* ☎ *877/444–6777* ⊕ *www. piedrasblancas.org* ✑ *$10, advance reservations and online ticket purchase required* ☞ *No pets allowed.*

🌞 Beaches

William Randolph Hearst Memorial Beach
BEACH—SIGHT | This wide, sandy beach edges a protected cove on both sides of San Simeon Pier. Fish from the pier or from a charter boat, picnic and barbecue on the bluffs, or boogie board or bodysurf the relatively gentle waves. In summer you can rent a kayak and paddle out into the bay for close encounters with marine life and sea caves. The NOAA Coastal Discovery Center, next to the parking lot, has interactive exhibits and hosts educational activities and events. **Amenities:** food and drink; parking; toilets; water sports. **Best for:** sunset; swimming; walking. ⊠ *750 Hearst Castle Rd., off Hwy. 1, west of Hearst Castle entrance* ☎ *805/927–2035* ⊕ *www.parks.ca.gov /?page_id=589* ✑ *Free.*

Big Sur Coast

76 miles north along Hwy. 1 from San Simeon to Bixby Creek Bridge.

The countercultural spirit of Big Sur—a loose string of coast-hugging properties along Highway 1—is alive and well. Its few residents include the very wealthy, the enthusiastically outdoorsy, and the utterly evolved: since the 1960s, the Esalen Institute, a center for alternative

education and East–West philosophical study, has attracted seekers of higher consciousness and devotees of the property's hot springs. Today, posh and rustic resorts amid the redwoods cater to visitors drawn by the scenery and the serenity. Southern Big Sur, the 52-mile stretch between San Simeon and Julia Pfeiffer Burns State Park, is especially rugged—a rocky world of mountains, cliffs, and beaches.

GETTING HERE AND AROUND

To explore Southern Big Sur from the south, access Highway 1 from U.S. 101 in San Luis Obispo; from the north, take rural route Highway 46 West (Paso Robles to Cambria) or Highway 41 West (Atascadero to Morro Bay). Nacimiento-to-Fergusson Road snakes from mountains and forest from U.S. 101 at Jolon about 25 miles to Highway 1 at Kirk Creek, about 4 miles south of Lucia; this curving, sometimes precipitous road is a motorcyclist favorite, not recommended for the faint of heart or during inclement weather.

To reach Central Big Sur, head north from Julia Pfeiffer Burns State Park on Highway 1 or follow Highway 1 south out of Carmel. Monterey-Salinas Transit runs the Line 22 Big Sur bus from Monterey and Carmel to Central Big Sur (last stop is Nepenthe) daily from late May to early September and on weekends the rest of the year.

BUS CONTACT Monterey-Salinas Transit. ☎ *888/678–2871* ⊕ *www.mst.org.*

ESSENTIALS
Stop by Big Sur Station to talk to staff, get information on activities and road conditions, and take advantage of public restrooms and fairly reliable cell service.

VISITOR INFORMATION Big Sur Chamber of Commerce. ☎ *831/667–2100* ⊕ *bigsur-california.org.* **Big Sur Station.** ⊠ *47555 California Hwy. 1, ¼ mile south of Pfeiffer Big Sur State Park entrance, Big Sur* ☎ *831/667–2315.*

Sights

Bixby Creek Bridge
BRIDGE/TUNNEL | The graceful arc of Bixby Creek Bridge is a photographer's dream. Built in 1932, the bridge spans a deep canyon, more than 100 feet wide at the bottom. From the north-side parking area you can admire the view or walk the 550-foot structure. ⊠ *Hwy. 1, 6 miles north of Point Sur State Historic Park, 13 miles south of Carmel, Big Sur.*

★ Highway 1
SCENIC DRIVE | One of California's most spectacular drives snakes up the coast north of San Simeon. Numerous pullouts offer tremendous views and photo ops. On some beaches, huge elephant seals lounge nonchalantly, seemingly oblivious to the attention of rubberneckers. Heavy rain can cause mudslides that block the highway north and south of Big Sur. ⚠ **Sections of Highway 1 are sometimes closed for general maintenance or repairs. Before traveling, visit bigsurcalifornia.org and click on the Highway 1 Conditions and Information link.** ⊕ *www.dot.ca.gov.*

Julia Pfeiffer Burns State Park
NATIONAL/STATE PARK | The park provides fine hiking, from an easy ½-mile stroll with marvelous coastal views to a strenuous 6-mile trek through redwoods. The big draw here, an 80-foot waterfall that drops into the ocean, gets crowded in summer; still, it's an astounding place to contemplate nature. Migrating whales, harbor seals, and sea lions can sometimes be spotted just offshore. ⚠ **Trails east of Highway 1 and beach access to McWay Falls were closed in 2021 due to fire and slide damage; check website for current status.** ⊠ *Hwy. 1, 15 miles north of Lucia* ☎ *831/667–1112* ⊕ *www.parks. ca.gov* ⊠ *$10.*

Pfeiffer Big Sur State Park
NATIONAL/STATE PARK | Among the many hiking trails at Pfeiffer Big Sur, a short route through a redwood-filled valley leads to a waterfall. You can double back or continue on the more difficult trail along the valley wall for views over miles of treetops to the sea. ⊠ *47231 Hwy. 1, Big Sur* ☎ *831/667–2315* ⊕ *www.parks. ca.gov* ⊠ *$10 per vehicle.*

★ Pfeiffer Canyon Bridge
BRIDGE/TUNNEL | In February 2017, heavy winter rains caused an old concrete bridge built in 1968 to crack and slip downhill at Pfeiffer Canyon, in the heart of Big Sur. Engineers deemed the old bridge irreparable, and auto and pedestrian access to Highway 1 south of the bridge was cut off indefinitely. CalTrans quickly made plans to construct a new, $24-million bridge to span the deep canyon. Normally, such a massive project would take at least seven years, but CalTrans accelerated the project and completed it in less than a year. The new bridge—a 21st-century engineering marvel—stretches 310 feet across the ravine without the need for column support. It's made of 15 steel girders, each weighing 62 tons and connected by steel plates holding 14,000 bolts. ⊠ *Hwy. 1, Big Sur* ✛ *0.7 mile south of Big Sur Station.*

Point Sur State Historic Park
NATIONAL/STATE PARK | An 1889 lighthouse at this state park still stands watch from atop a large volcanic rock. Four lighthouse keepers lived here with their families until 1974, when the light station became automated. Their homes and working spaces are open to the public only on three-hour ranger-led tours. Considerable walking, including up two stairways, is involved. Strollers are not allowed. ⊠ *Hwy. 1, 7 miles north of Pfeiffer Big Sur State Park, Big Sur* ☎ *831/625–4419* ⊕ *www. pointsur.org* ⊠ *$15* ☞ *Call or visit website for current tour schedule.*

Beaches

Pfeiffer Beach
BEACH—SIGHT | Through a hole in one of the gigantic boulders at secluded Pfeiffer Beach, you can watch the waves break

first on the seaside and then on the beach side. Keep a sharp eye out for the unsigned, nongated road to the beach: it branches west of Highway 1 between the post office and Pfeiffer Big Sur State Park. The 2-mile, one-lane road descends sharply. **Amenities:** parking (fee); toilets. **Best for:** solitude; sunset. ✉ *Off Hwy. 1, 1 mile south of Pfeiffer Big Sur State Park, Big Sur* 🎟 *$12 per vehicle.*

🍴 Restaurants

★ Deetjen's Big Sur Inn

$$$ | **AMERICAN** | The candle-lighted, creaky-floor restaurant in the main house at the historic inn of the same name is a Big Sur institution. It serves spicy seafood paella, grass-fed filet mignon, and rack of lamb for dinner and flavorful eggs Benedict for breakfast. **Known for:** rustic, romantic setting; ingredients from sustainable purveyors; stellar weekend breakfast. [$] *Average main: $32* ✉ *Hwy. 1, 3½ miles south of Pfeiffer Big Sur State Park, Big Sur* ☎ *831/667–2378* 🌐 *www.deetjens.com* 🕑 *Closed Weds. and Thurs. No lunch.*

★ Nepenthe

$$$$ | **AMERICAN** | It may be that no other restaurant between San Francisco and Los Angeles has a better coastal view than Nepenthe, named for an opiate mentioned in Greek literature that would induce a state of "no sorrow." For the real show, settle on the terraced deck in the late afternoon, order a glass from the extensive wine list, and watch the sun slip into the Pacific Ocean. **Known for:** ambrosia burger, fresh fish, hormone-free steaks; multiple view decks; brunch and lunch at casual outdoor Café Kevah. [$] *Average main: $39* ✉ *48510 Hwy. 1, 2½ miles south of Big Sur Station, Big Sur* ☎ *831/667–2345* 🌐 *nepenthebigsur.com.*

★ Sierra Mar

$$$$ | **AMERICAN** | At cliff's edge 1,200 feet above the Pacific at the ultrachic Post Ranch Inn, Sierra Mar serves cutting-edge American cuisine made from mostly organic, seasonal ingredients, some from the on-site chef's garden. The four-course prix-fixe option always shines. **Known for:** stunning panoramic ocean views; one of the nation's most extensive wine lists; iconic Big Sur farm-to-table experience. [$] *Average main: $145* ✉ *Hwy. 1, 1½ miles south of Pfeiffer Big Sur State Park, Big Sur* ☎ *831/667–2800* 🌐 *www.postranchinn.com/dining.*

🛏 Hotels

Big Sur Lodge

$$$ | **HOTEL** | The lodge's modern, motel-style cottages with Mission-style furnishings and vaulted ceilings sit in a meadow surrounded by redwood trees and flowering shrubbery. **Pros:** secluded setting near trailheads; good camping alternative; rates include state parks pass. **Cons:** basic rooms; walk to main lodge; thin common walls in some units. [$] *Rooms from: $279* ✉ *Pfeiffer Big Sur State Park, 47225 Hwy. 1, Big Sur* ☎ *855/238–6950 reservations* 🌐 *www.bigsurlodge.com* 🛏 *62 rooms* 🍽 *No meals.*

Big Sur River Inn

$$$ | **B&B/INN** | During summer at this rustic property you can sip drinks beside—or in—the Big Sur River fronted by the inn's wooded grounds; if you're here on a Sunday afternoon between May and September you can enjoy live music on the restaurant's deck. **Pros:** riverside setting complete with outdoor pool; next to a restaurant and small market; recently renovated baths. **Cons:** standard motel rooms across the road; no phone in rooms; fronts busy road. [$] *Rooms from: $295* ✉ *Hwy. 1, 2 miles north of Pfeiffer Big Sur State Park, Big Sur* ☎ *831/667–2700, 831/667–2743, 800/548–3610* 🌐 *www.bigsurriverinn.com* 🛏 *22 rooms* 🍽 *No meals.*

Deetjen's Big Sur Inn
$$$ | **B&B/INN** | This historic 1930s Norwegian-style property is endearingly rustic, with its village of cabins nestled in the redwoods; many of the very individual rooms have their own fireplaces. **Pros:** tons of character; wooded grounds; excellent food and wine in on-site restaurant. **Cons:** thin walls; some rooms don't have private baths; no TVs or Wi-Fi, limited cell service. [$] *Rooms from: $250* ✉ *Hwy. 1, 3½ miles south of Pfeiffer Big Sur State Park, Big Sur* ☎ *831/667–2377* 🌐 *www.deetjens.com* 🛏 *20 rooms, 15 with bath* 🍴 *No meals* ☞ *2-night minimum stay on weekends.*

Glen Oaks Big Sur
$$$ | **HOTEL** | At this rustic-modern cluster of adobe-and-redwood buildings, you can choose between motel-style rooms, cabins, and cottages in the woods. **Pros:** in the heart of town; natural river-rock radiant-heated tiles; restaurant across the street. **Cons:** near busy road and parking lot; no TVs; some cabins tiny. [$] *Rooms from: $320* ✉ *Hwy. 1, 1 mile north of Pfeiffer Big Sur State Park, Big Sur* ☎ *831/667–2105* 🌐 *www.glenoaksbigsur.com* 🛏 *29 units* 🍴 *No meals.*

★ **Post Ranch Inn**
$$$$ | **RESORT** | This luxurious retreat is perfect for getaways; the redwood guesthouses, all of which have views of the sea or the mountains, blend almost invisibly into a wooded cliff 1,200 feet above the ocean. **Pros:** units come with fireplaces and private decks; on-site activities like yoga and stargazing; gorgeous property with hiking trails and spectacular views. **Cons:** expensive; austere design; not a good choice if you're afraid of heights. [$] *Rooms from: $1425* ✉ *Hwy. 1, 1½ miles south of Pfeiffer Big Sur State Park, Big Sur* ☎ *831/667–2200, 800/527–2200* 🌐 *www.postranchinn.com* 🛏 *41 units* 🍴 *Free breakfast.*

Ragged Point Inn
$$ | **HOTEL** | At this cliff-top resort—the only inn and restaurant for miles around—glass walls in most rooms open to awesome ocean views. **Pros:** on the cliffs; good burgers and locally made ice cream; idyllic views. **Cons:** busy road stop during the day; often booked for weekend weddings; spotty cell phone service. [$] *Rooms from: $239* ✉ *19019 Hwy. 1, 15 miles north of San Simeon, Ragged Point* ☎ *805/927–4502, 805/927–5708 restaurant, 888/584–6374* 🌐 *www.raggedpointinn.com* 🛏 *39 rooms* 🍴 *No meals.*

Treebones Resort
$$$$ | **RESORT** | Perched on a hilltop surrounded by national forest and stunning, unobstructed ocean views, this yurt resort provides a stellar back-to-nature experience along with creature comforts. **Pros:** luxury yurts with cozy beds; lodge with fireplace and games; local food at Wild Coast Restaurant and decked sushi bar. **Cons:** steep paths; no private bathrooms; not good for families with young children. [$] *Rooms from: $390* ✉ *71895 Hwy. 1, Willow Creek Rd., 32 miles north of San Simeon, 1 mile north of Gorda* ☎ *805/927–2390, 877/424–4787* 🌐 *www.treebonesresort.com* 🛏 *23 camping options* 🍴 *Free breakfast* ☞ *2-night minimum.*

★ **Ventana Big Sur**
$$$$ | **HOTEL** | Hundreds of celebrities have escaped to Ventana Big Sur, a romantic resort on 160 tranquil acres 1,200 feet above the Pacific. **Pros:** secluded; nature trails everywhere; rates include daily guided hike, yoga, wine and cheese hour. **Cons:** expensive; some rooms lack an ocean view; not family-friendly. [$] *Rooms from: $1500* ✉ *Hwy. 1, almost 1 mile south of Pfeiffer Big Sur State Park, Big Sur* ☎ *831/667–2331, 800/628–6500* 🌐 *www.ventanabigsur.com* 🛏 *74 units* 🍴 *All-inclusive.*

Chapter 12

MONTEREY BAY AREA

FROM CARMEL TO SANTA CRUZ

12

Updated by
Cheryl Crabtree

👁 Sights	🍴 Restaurants	🛏 Hotels	🛍 Shopping	🍸 Nightlife
★★★★★	★★★★☆	★★★★★	★★☆☆☆	★☆☆☆☆

WELCOME TO THE MONTEREY BAY AREA

TOP REASONS TO GO

★ **Marine life:** Monterey Bay is the location of the world's third-largest marine sanctuary, home to whales, otters, and other underwater creatures.

★ **Getaway central:** For more than a century, urbanites have come to the Monterey Bay area to unwind, relax, and have fun. It's a great place to browse unique shops and galleries, ride a giant roller coaster, or play a round of golf on a world-class course.

★ **Nature preserves:** More than the sea is protected here: the region boasts nearly 30 state parks, beaches, and preserves—fantastic places for walking, jogging, hiking, and biking.

★ **Wine and dine:** The area's rich agricultural bounty translates into abundant fresh produce, great wines, and fabulous dining. It's no wonder more than 300 culinary events take place here every year.

★ **Small-town vibes:** Even the cities here are friendly, walkable places where you'll feel like a local.

1 Carmel-by-the-Sea. Galleries and cobblestone streets are among its charms.

2 Carmel Valley. An esteemed wine region marks this celebrity enclave.

3 Pebble Beach. This world-class golf destination also has the stunning 17-Mile Drive.

4 Pacific Grove. A picturesque city known for its migrating butterflies.

5 Monterey. The state's first capital is rich in history and marine life.

6 Salinas. The heart of Steinbeck country is also known for its fruits and veggies.

7 Pinnacles National Park. A volcano with jagged spires and caves.

8 Moss Landing. This tiny fishing port is near marine preserves.

9 Aptos. A charming village that edges redwood forests and stellar beaches.

10 Capitola and Soquel. Seaside gateways to mountain wine country.

11 Santa Cruz. World-famous surf and a university are among its draws.

0		5 mi
0		5 km

North of Big Sur, the coastline softens into lower bluffs, windswept dunes, pristine estuaries, and long, sandy beaches bordering one of the world's most amazing marine environments— Monterey Bay.

The bay itself is protected by the Monterey Bay National Marine Sanctuary, which holds the nation's largest undersea canyon—bigger and deeper than the Grand Canyon. Sunny coastal communities such as Aptos, Capitola, Soquel, and Santa Cruz offer miles of sand and surf. On-the-water activities abound, from whale-watching and kayaking to sailing and surfing. Bay cruises from Monterey and Moss Landing almost always encounter other enchanting sea creatures, among them sea otters, sea lions, and porpoises.

Land-based activities include hiking, ziplining in the redwood canopy, and wine tasting along urban and rural trails. Golf has been an integral part of the Monterey Peninsula's social and recreational scene since the Del Monte Golf Course opened in 1897. Today, Pebble Beach's championship courses host prestigious tournaments. Quaint, walkable towns such as Carmel-by-the-Sea and Carmel Valley Village are dotted with smart restaurants and galleries that encourage culinary and cultural immersion. Monterey's well-preserved waterfront invites historical exploration. Of course, whatever activity you pursue, natural splendor appears at every turn.

MAJOR REGIONS
The Monterey Peninsula. On the peninsula at the bay's southern end are Carmel-by-the-Sea—a good jumping-off point for the Carmel Valley wine region—Pebble Beach, Pacific Grove, and Monterey itself, home to a world-famous aquarium.

East and North of the Monterey Peninsula. Inland from the bay, amid a rich agricultural area that many refer to as Steinbeck Country, is Salinas, with Pinnacles National Park farther to the southeast. North of Monterey, Highway 1 cruises along the bay's curving coastline, passing windswept beaches piled high with dunes, as well as wetlands and artichoke and strawberry fields. Here you'll find Moss Landing, where otters and seals play; classic seaside villages such as Aptos, Soquel, and Capitola; and Santa Cruz, home of surf legends, a historic boardwalk, and UC Santa Cruz.

Planning

When to Go

Summer is peak season; mild weather brings in big crowds. In this coastal region a cool breeze generally blows and fog often rolls in from offshore; you will frequently need a sweater or windbreaker. Off-season, from November through April, fewer people visit and the mood is mellower. Rainfall is heaviest in January and February. Fall and spring days are often clearer than those in summer.

FESTIVALS AND EVENTS

Carmel Bach Festival. This three-week, mid-July festival has presented the works of Johann Sebastian Bach and his contemporaries since 1935. ⊕ *bachfestival.org*

Jazz Bash by the Bay. Bands play early jazz, big band, swing, ragtime, blues, zydeco, and gypsy jazz at waterfront venues during this festival, held on the first full weekend of March. ⊕ *jazzbashmonterey.com.*

Monterey International Blues Festival. This event on the last weekend in June draws blues fans to the Monterey Fairgrounds. ⊕ *montereyinternationalbluesfestival.com.*

Monterey Jazz Festival. The world's oldest jazz festival, held the third full weekend in September, attracts top-name performers and their fans to the Monterey Fairgrounds. ⊕ *montereyjazzfestival.org.*

Getting Here and Around

AIR

Monterey Regional Airport, 3 miles east of downtown Monterey off Highway 68, is served by Alaska, Allegiant, American, Avelo, JSX, and United. Taxi service costs from $14 to $16 to downtown, and from $23 to $25 to Carmel. Monterey Airbus service between the region and the San Jose and San Francisco airports starts at $42; the Early Bird Airport Shuttle costs from $100 to $235 ($250 from Oakland).

AIRPORT CONTACTS Monterey Regional Airport. (*MRY*) ✉ *200 Fred Kane Dr., at Olmsted Rd., off Hwy. 68, Monterey* ☎ *831/648–7000* ⊕ *www.montereyairport.com.*

GROUND TRANSPORTATION Central Coast Cab Company. ☎ *831/626–3333* ⊕ *www.centralcoastcabcompany.com.* **Early Bird Airport Shuttle.** ☎ *831/462–3933* ⊕ *www.earlybirdairportshuttle.com.* **Monterey Airbus.** ☎ *831/373–7777* ⊕ *www.montereyairbus.com.* **Yellow Cab.** ☎ *831/333–1234* ⊕ *www.yellowcab1234.com.*

BUS

Greyhound serves Santa Cruz and Salinas from San Francisco (3 hours) and San Jose (4½ hours). Monterey-Salinas Transit (MST) provides frequent service in Monterey County (from $2.50 to $3.50; day pass $10), and Santa Cruz METRO ($2; day pass from $6 to $14) buses operate throughout Santa Cruz County. You can switch between the lines in Watsonville.

BUS CONTACTS Monterey-Salinas Transit. ☎ *888/678–2871* ⊕ *mst.org.* **Santa Cruz METRO.** ☎ *831/425–8600* ⊕ *scmtd.com.*

CAR

Highway 1 runs south–north along the coast, linking the towns of Carmel-by-the-Sea, Monterey, and Santa Cruz; some sections have only two lanes. The freeway, U.S. 101, lies to the east, roughly parallel to Highway 1. The two roads are connected by Highway 68 from Pacific Grove to Salinas; Highway 156 from Castroville to Prunedale; Highway 152 from Watsonville to Gilroy; and Highway 17 from Santa Cruz to San Jose.

■TIP➔ **Traffic near Santa Cruz can crawl to a standstill during commuter hours. Avoid traveling between 7 and 9 am and between 4 and 7 pm.**

The drive south from San Francisco to Monterey can be made comfortably in three hours or less. The most scenic way is to follow Highway 1 down the coast. A generally faster route is I–280 south to Highway 85 to Highway 17 to Highway 1. The drive from the Los Angeles area takes five or six hours. Take U.S. 101 to Salinas, and head west on Highway 68. You can also follow Highway 1 up the coast.

TRAIN

Amtrak's *Coast Starlight* runs between Los Angeles, Oakland, and Seattle. You can also take the *Pacific Surfliner* to San Luis Obispo and connect to Amtrak buses to Salinas or San Jose. From the train station in Salinas you can connect with buses serving Carmel and Monterey, and from the train station in San Jose with buses to Santa Cruz.

Restaurants

The Monterey Bay area is a culinary paradise. The surrounding waters are full of fish, wild game roams the foothills, and the inland valleys are some of the most fertile in the country—local chefs draw on this bounty for their fresh, truly Californian cuisine. Except at beachside stands and inexpensive eateries, where anything goes, casual but neat dress is the norm.

Hotels

Accommodations in the Monterey area range from no-frills motels to luxurious hotels. Pacific Grove, amply endowed with ornate Victorian houses, is the region's bed-and-breakfast capital; Carmel also has charming inns. Lavish resorts cluster in exclusive Pebble Beach and pastoral Carmel Valley.

High season runs from May through October. Rates in winter, especially at the larger hotels, may drop by 50% or more, and smaller inns often offer midweek specials. Whatever the month, some properties require a two-night stay on weekends. ■TIP→ Many of the fancier accommodations aren't suitable for children; if you're traveling with kids, ask before you book.

Restaurant and hotel reviews have been shortened. For full information, visit Fodors.com. Restaurant prices are the average cost of a main course at dinner, or if dinner is not served, at lunch. Hotel prices are the lowest cost of a standard double room in high season

What It Costs

	$	$$	$$$	$$$$
RESTAURANTS				
	under $17	$17–$26	$27–$36	over $36
HOTELS				
	under $150	$150–$250	$251–$350	over $350

Tours

Ag Venture Tours & Consulting
GUIDED TOURS | Crowd-pleasing half- and full-day wine tasting, sightseeing, walking, and agricultural tours are Ag Venture's specialty. Tastings are at Monterey and Santa Cruz Mountains wineries; sightseeing opportunities include the Monterey Peninsula, Big Sur, and Santa Cruz; and the agricultural forays take in the Salinas and Pajaro valleys. Customized itineraries can be arranged. ☎ 831/761–8463 ⊕ agventuretours.com 🏷 From $55 (half-day) and $110 (full day).

Monterey Guided Wine Tours
SPECIAL-INTEREST | The company's guides lead customized wine tours in Monterey, Carmel, and Carmel Valley, along with the Santa Lucia Highlands, the Santa Cruz Mountains, and the Paso Robles area. Tours, which typically last from four to six hours, take place in a town car, a stretch limo, or a party bus. ☎ 831/920–2792 ⊕ montereyguidedwinetours.com 🏷 From $175.

Visitor Information

CONTACTS **Monterey County Convention & Visitors Bureau.** ☎ 888/221–1010 ⊕ www.seemonterey.com. **Monterey Wine Country.** ☎ 831/375–9400 ⊕ www. montereywines.org. **Santa Cruz Mountains Winegrowers Association.** ✉ 335 Spreckels Dr., #B, Aptos ☎ 831/685–8463 ⊕ winesofthesantacruzmountains.com. **Visit Santa Cruz County.** ✉ 303 Water St.,

12

Monterey Bay Area CARMEL-BY-THE-SEA

No. 100, Santa Cruz ☎ 831/425–1234, 800/833–3494 ⊕ visitsantacruz.org.

Carmel-by-the-Sea

26 miles north of Big Sur.

Even when its population quadruples with tourists on weekends and in summer, Carmel-by-the-Sea, commonly referred to as Carmel, retains its identity as a quaint village. Self-consciously charming, the town is populated by many celebrities, major and minor, and has its share of quirky ordinances. For instance, women wearing high heels do not have the right to pursue legal action if they trip and fall on the cobblestone streets, and drivers who hit a tree and leave the scene are charged with hit-and-run.

Buildings have no street numbers—street names are written on discreet white posts—and consequently no mail delivery. One way to commune with the locals: head to the post office. Artists started this community, and their legacy is evident in the numerous galleries.

GETTING HERE AND AROUND

From north or south follow Highway 1 to Carmel. Head west at Ocean Avenue to reach the main village hub.

TOURS

Carmel Food Tours

WALKING TOURS | Taste your way through Carmel-by-the-Sea culinary delights on this guided walking tour to restaurants and shops that serve small portions of standout offerings, from empanadas and ribs to honey and chocolate. Along the way, guides share colorful tales about local culture, history, and architecture. The Classic Tour (which departs from the Sunset Cultural Center) includes seven tasting stops and lasts three hours. The five-hour Bikes, Bites, & Bevs Tour combines a morning e-bike tour through Carmel to Point Lobos with four food and wine/cocktail destinations in the

afternoon. Tickets must be purchased in advance. ✉ *Sunset Cultural Center, 9th Ave. at San Carlos St., Carmel* ☎ *831/256–3007, 831/216–8533 tickets* ⊕ *www.carmelfoodtour.com* 🎫 *From $94.*

Carmel Walks

WALKING TOURS | For insight into Carmel's history and culture, join one of these guided two-hour ambles through hidden courtyards, gardens, and pathways. Tours depart from the Pine Inn courtyard, on Lincoln Street. Call to reserve a spot. ✉ *Lincoln St. at 6th Ave., Carmel* ☎ *831/223–4399* ⊕ *carmelwalks.com* 🎫 *From $30.*

ESSENTIALS

VISITOR INFORMATION Carmel Chamber of Commerce. ✉ *Visitor center, in Carmel Plaza, Ocean Ave. between Junipero and Mission Sts., Carmel* ☎ *831/624–2522, 800/550–4333* ⊕ *carmelchamber.org.*

 Sights

Carmel Mission

RELIGIOUS SITE | Long before it became a shopping and browsing destination, Carmel was an important religious center during the establishment of Spanish California. That heritage is preserved in the Mission San Carlos Borroméo del Rio Carmelo, more commonly known as the Carmel Mission. Founded in 1771, it served as headquarters for the mission system in California under Father Junípero Serra. Adjoining the stone church is a tranquil garden planted with California poppies. Museum rooms at the mission include an early kitchen, Serra's spartan sleeping quarters and burial shrine, and the first college library in California. ✉ *3080 Rio Rd., at Lasuen Dr., Carmel* ☎ *831/624–1271* ⊕ *carmelmission.org* 🎫 *$10* ☉ *Closed Mon. and Tues.*

★ Ocean Avenue

NEIGHBORHOOD | Downtown Carmel's chief lure is shopping, especially along its main street, Ocean Avenue, between

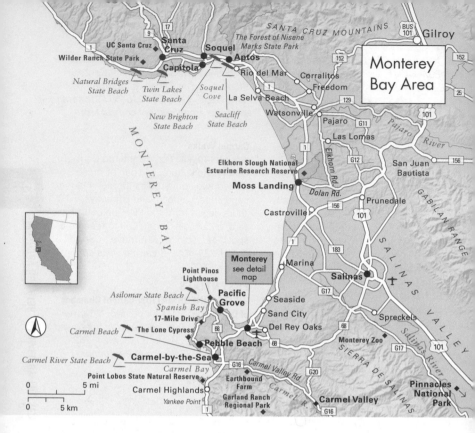

Monterey Bay Area

Junipero Avenue and Camino Real. The architecture here is a mishmash of ersatz Tudor, Mediterranean, and other styles. ⊠ *Carmel*.

★ Point Lobos State Natural Reserve

NATIONAL/STATE PARK | A 350-acre headland harboring a wealth of marine life, the reserve lies a few miles south of Carmel. The best way to explore here is to walk along one of the many trails. The Cypress Grove Trail leads through a forest of Monterey cypress (one of only two natural groves remaining) that clings to the rocks above an emerald-green cove. Sea Lion Point Trail is a good place to view sea lions. From those and other trails, you might also spot otters, harbor seals, and (in winter and spring) migrating whales. An additional 750 acres of the reserve is an undersea marine park open to qualified scuba divers. No pets are allowed. ■**TIP→ Arrive early (or in late afternoon) to avoid crowds; the parking lots fill up.** ⊠ *Hwy. 1, Carmel* 🕾 *831/624–4909* ⊕ *www.pointlobos.org* ⊠ *$10 per vehicle.*

Tor House

HOUSE | Scattered throughout the pines of Carmel-by-the-Sea are houses and cottages originally built for the writers, artists, and photographers who discovered the area decades ago. Among the most impressive dwellings is Tor House, a stone cottage built in 1919 by poet Robinson Jeffers on a craggy knoll overlooking the sea. Portraits, books, and unusual art objects fill the low-ceilinged rooms. The highlight of the small estate is Hawk Tower, a detached edifice set with stones from the Carmel coastline—as well as one from the Great Wall of China. The docents who lead tours (six people maximum) are well informed about the poet's work and life. Reservations are required. Call the reservation line or click on the reservation link on the website. ✉ *26304 Ocean View Ave., Carmel* ☎ *831/624–1813 direct docent office line, Mon., Tues., and Thurs. only* 🌐 *www.torhouse.org* 🎟 *$12* ☞ *No children under 12.*

Beaches

Carmel Beach

BEACH—SIGHT | Carmel-by-the-Sea's greatest attraction is its rugged coastline, with pine and cypress forests and countless inlets. Carmel Beach, an easy walk from downtown shops, has sparkling white sands and magnificent sunsets. ■ **TIP→ Dogs are allowed to romp off-leash here. Amenities:** parking (no fee); toilets. **Best for:** sunset; surfing; walking. ✉ *End of Ocean Ave., Carmel.*

Carmel River State Beach

NATURE PRESERVE | This sugar-white beach, stretching 106 acres along Carmel Bay, is adjacent to a bird sanctuary, where you might spot pelicans, kingfishers, hawks, and sandpipers. Dogs are allowed on leash. **Amenities:** parking (no fee); toilets. **Best for:** sunrise; sunset; walking. ✉ *Off Scenic Rd., south of Carmel Beach, Carmel* ☎ *831/649–2836* 🌐 *www.parks.ca.gov* 🎟 *Free.*

Restaurants

Anton and Michel

$$$ | **AMERICAN** | Carefully prepared California cuisine is the draw at this airy restaurant. The rack of lamb is carved at the table, the grilled halloumi cheese and tomatoes are meticulously stacked and served with basil and Kalamata olive tapenade, and the desserts are set aflame before your eyes. **Known for:** romantic courtyard with fountain; elegant interior with fireplace lounge; flambé desserts. [$] *Average main: $35* ✉ *Mission St. and 7th Ave., Carmel* ☎ *831/624–2406* 🌐 *antonandmichel.com.*

★ Aubergine

$$$$ | **AMERICAN** | To eat and sleep at luxe L'Auberge Carmel is an experience in itself, but even those staying elsewhere can splurge at the inn's intimate restaurant, which was awarded a Michelin star in 2019. Chef Justin Cogley's nine-course prix-fixe tasting menu (your only option at dinner, $205 per person) is a gastronomical experience unrivaled in the region. **Known for:** exceptional chef's choice tasting menu; expert wine pairings; intimate nine-table dining room. [$] *Average main: $185* ✉ *Monte Verde at 7th Ave., Carmel* ☎ *831/624–8578* 🌐 *auberginecarmel.com* 🕒 *No lunch.*

★ Basil

$$ | **MODERN AMERICAN** | Eco-friendly Basil was Monterey County's first restaurant to achieve a green-dining certification, recognition of its commitment to using organic, sustainably cultivated ingredients in creative dishes such as black squid linguine with sea urchin sauce, charred octopus, and smoked venison and other house-made charcuterie. **Known for:** organic ingredients; creative cocktails; year-round patio dining. [$] *Average main: $25* ✉ *Paseo Square, San Carlos St., between Ocean Ave. and 7th Ave., Carmel* ☎ *831/626–8226* 🌐 *basilcarmel.com*

Casanova

$$$ | **MEDITERRANEAN** | This restaurant inspires European-style celebration and romance in an intimate French-country setting. Feast on authentic dishes from southern France and northern Italy—think beef tartare and escargot. **Known for:** house-made pastas and gnocchi; private dining at antique Van Gogh's table; romantic candlelight dining room and outdoor patio. [$] *Average main: $34* ✉ *5th Ave., between San Carlos and Mission Sts., Carmel* ☎ *831/625–0501* 🌐 *www.casanovacarmel.com.*

The Cottage Restaurant

$$ | **AMERICAN** | This family-friendly spot serves sandwiches, pizzas, and homemade soups at lunch, but the best meal

Point Lobos State Natural Reserve offers stunning vistas of sea and sky.

is breakfast (good thing it's served all day). The menu offers six variations on eggs Benedict and all kinds of sweet and savory crepes. **Known for:** artichoke soup; eggs Benedict and crepes; daily specials. [$] *Average main: $17* ✉ *Lincoln St. between Ocean and 7th Aves., Carmel* ☎ *831/625–6260* 🌐 *cottagerestaurant.com* ⏲ *No dinner.*

Flying Fish Grill

$$$ | SEAFOOD | Simple in appearance yet bold with its flavors, this Japanese–California seafood restaurant is one of Carmel's most inventive eateries. The warm, wood-lined dining room is broken up into very private booths. **Known for:** almond-crusted sea bass served with Chinese cabbage and rock shrimp stir-fry; clay pot dinners for two cooked at the table; authentic Asian decor. [$] *Average main: $30* ✉ *Carmel Plaza, Mission St. between Ocean and 7th Aves., Carmel* ☎ *831/625–1962* 🌐 *flyingfishgrill.com* ⏲ *No lunch.*

Grasing's Coastal Cuisine

$$$$ | AMERICAN | Chef Kurt Grasing draws from fresh Carmel Coast and Central Valley ingredients to whip up contemporary adaptations of European-provincial and American dishes. Longtime menu favorites include duck with fresh cherries in a red wine sauce, a savory sausage and seafood paella, and grilled steaks and chops. **Known for:** artichoke-heart lasagna; grilled steaks; bar, patio lounge, and rooftop deck. [$] *Average main: $39* ✉ *6th Ave. and Mission St., Carmel* ☎ *831/624–6562* 🌐 *grasings.com.*

L'Escargot

$$$ | FRENCH | Chef-owner Kericos Loutas personally sees to each plate of food served at this romantic, unpretentious French restaurant. Order the pan-roasted duck breast or the veal medallions with wild mushrooms or white wine sauce; or, if you can't decide, choose the three-course prix-fixe dinner. **Known for:** authentic French-country dishes; prix-fixe dinner option; locally sourced ingredients. [$] *Average main: $36* ✉ *Mission* *and 4th Ave., Carmel* ☎ *831/620–1942* 🌐 *escargot-carmel.com* 🕒 *Closed Mon. and Tues.*

★ The Pocket

$$ | MODERN ITALIAN | In surf lingo, "the pocket" is a perfect riding spot within a barrel-shape wave, and this Italian–Californian restaurant is likewise a perfect (casual and unfussy) gathering spot for those who seek first-rate food, wine, and cocktails. The co-owners—a chef and sommelier with years of experience running restaurants in Pebble Beach and around the world—craft seasonal menus that focus on seafood, fresh pastas, curries, steaks, and braised meats. **Known for:** sleek marble, wood, and slate dining room and bar, spacious garden seating; full bar, extensive list of more than 400 wines; lively atmosphere, especially during the daily happy hour. [$] *Average main: $32* ✉ *Lincoln St., between 5th and 6th Ave., Carmel* ☎ *831/626–8000* 🌐 *www.thepocketcarmel.com.*

Vesuvio

$$$ | ITALIAN | Chef and restaurateur Rich Pèpe heats up the night with this lively trattoria downstairs and swinging rooftop terrace, the Starlight Lounge 65°. Pèpe's elegant take on traditional Italian cuisine yields dishes such as wild-boar Bolognese pappardelle, lobster ravioli, and velvety limoncello mousse cake. **Known for:** traditional cuisine of Campania, Italy; two bars with pizzas and small plates; live music on rooftop terrace in summer. [$] *Average main: $30* ✉ *6th and Junipero Aves., Carmel* ☎ *831/625–1766* 🌐 *vesuviocarmel.com* 🕒 *No lunch.*

Hotels

Cypress Inn

$$$ | B&B/INN | This luxurious inn has a fresh, Mediterranean ambience with Moroccan touches. **Pros:** luxury without snobbery; popular lounge and restaurant; British-style afternoon tea on Saturdays. **Cons:** not for the pet-phobic; some rooms and baths are tiny; basic amenities. [$] *Rooms from: $279* ✉ *Lincoln St. and 7th Ave., Carmel* ☎ *831/624–3871, 800/443–7443* 🌐 *cypress-inn.com* 🛏 *44 rooms* 🍴 *Free breakfast.*

The Hideaway

$$$ | HOTEL | On a quiet street with a residential vibe, The Hideaway is a peaceful haven for those seeking stylish comfort in the heart of town. **Pros:** easy walk to shops, restaurants, galleries; short walk to Carmel Beach; pet-friendly amenities. **Cons:** street parking only; no pool or hot tub; some rooms are tiny. [$] *Rooms from: $295* ✉ *Junipero St. at 8th Ave., Carmel* ☎ *888/565–1420* 🌐 *hideawaycarmel.com* 🛏 *24 rooms* 🍴 *Free breakfast.*

Hyatt Carmel Highlands

$$$$ | HOTEL | High on a hill overlooking the Pacific, this place has superb views and accommodations that include king rooms with fireplaces, suites with personal Jacuzzis, and full town houses with many perks. **Pros:** killer views; romantic getaway; great food. **Cons:** thin walls; must drive to the center of town; some rooms and buildings need update. [$] *Rooms from: $499* ✉ *120 Highlands Dr., Carmel* ☎ *831/620–1234* 🌐 *www.hyatt.com* 🛏 *48 rooms* 🍴 *No meals.*

La Playa Carmel

$$$$ | HOTEL | A historic complex of lush gardens and Mediterranean-style buildings, La Playa has light and airy interiors done in Carmel Bay beach-cottage style. **Pros:** historic restaurant and bar; manicured gardens; two blocks from the beach. **Cons:** four stories (no elevator); busy lobby; some rooms are on the small side. [$] *Rooms from: $449* ✉ *Camino Real at 8th Ave., Carmel* ☎ *800/582–8900, 831/293–6100* 🌐 *laplayahotel.com* 🛏 *75 rooms* 🍴 *Free breakfast.*

★ L'Auberge Carmel

$$$$ | B&B/INN | Stepping through the doors of this elegant inn is like being transported to a little European village. **Pros:** in town but off the main drag; four blocks from the beach; full-service luxury. **Cons:** touristy area; not a good choice for families; no A/C. $ *Rooms from: $485* ✉ *Monte Verde at 7th Ave., Carmel* ☎ *831/624–8578* 🌐 *www.laubergecarmel.com* 🛏 *20 rooms* 🍴 *Free breakfast.*

Mission Ranch

$$ | HOTEL | Movie star Clint Eastwood owns this sprawling property whose accommodations include rooms in a converted barn, and several cottages, some with fireplaces. **Pros:** farm setting; pastoral views; great for tennis buffs. **Cons:** busy parking lot; must drive to the heart of town; old buildings. $ *Rooms from: $175* ✉ *26270 Dolores St., Carmel* ☎ *831/624–6436, 800/538–8221, 831/625–9040 restaurant* 🌐 *www.missionranchcarmel.com* 🛏 *31 rooms* 🍴 *Free breakfast.*

Pine Inn

$$ | HOTEL | A favorite with generations of visitors, the Pine Inn is four blocks from the beach and has Victorian-style furnishings, complete with a grandfather clock, padded fabric wall panels, antique tapestries, and marble tabletops. **Pros:** elegant; close to shopping and dining; full breakfast included weekdays. **Cons:** on the town's busiest street; public areas a bit dark; limited parking. $ *Rooms from: $189* ✉ *Ocean Ave. and Monte Verde St., Carmel* ☎ *831/624–3851, 800/228–3851* 🌐 *pineinn.com* 🛏 *49 rooms* 🍴 *Free breakfast.*

Tally Ho Inn

$$ | B&B/INN | This inn is nearly all suites, many of which have fireplaces and floor-to-ceiling glass walls that open onto ocean-view patios. **Pros:** within walking distance of shops, restaurants, beach; free parking; spacious rooms. **Cons:** small property; busy area; basic breakfast. $ *Rooms from: $229* ✉ *Monte Verde St. and 6th Ave., Carmel* ☎ *831/624–2232, 800/652–2632* 🌐 *tallyho-inn.com* 🛏 *12 rooms* 🍴 *Free breakfast.*

Tickle Pink Inn

$$$$ | B&B/INN | Atop a towering cliff, this inn has views of the Big Sur coastline, which you can contemplate from your private balcony. **Pros:** close to great hiking; intimate; dramatic views. **Cons:** close to a big hotel; lots of traffic during the day; basic breakfast. $ *Rooms from: $389* ✉ *155 Highland Dr., Carmel* ☎ *831/624–1244, 800/635–4774* 🌐 *ticklepink.com* 🛏 *34 units* 🍴 *Free breakfast.*

Nightlife

BARS AND PUBS

Barmel

BARS/PUBS | Al Capone and other Prohibition-era legends once sidled up to this hip nightspot's carved wooden bar. Rock to DJ music and sit indoors, or head out to the pet-friendly patio. Some menu items pay homage to California's early days, and you can order Baja-style dishes from the adjacent Pescadero restaurant, which is under the same ownership. ✉ *San Carlos St., between Ocean and 7th Aves., Carmel* ☎ *831/626–2095* 🌐 *www.facebook.com/BarmelByTheSea.*

Mulligan Public House

BARS/PUBS | A sports bar with seven TV screens, 12 beers on tap, and extensive menu packed with hearty American pub food, Mulligan usually stays open until midnight. ✉ *5 Dolores St., at Ocean* ☎ *831/250–5910* 🌐 *mulliganspublichouse.com.*

Shopping

ART GALLERIES

Carmel Art Association

ART GALLERIES | Carmel's oldest gallery, established in 1927, exhibits original paintings and sculptures by local artists. ✉ *Dolores St., between 5th and 6th Aves., Carmel* ☎ *831/624–6176* 🌐 *carmelart.org* 🕒 *Closed Tues. and Wed.*

Dawson Cole Fine Art

ART GALLERIES | Amazing images of dancers, athletes, and other humans in motion come to life in this gallery that is devoted to the artworks of Monterey Bay resident Richard MacDonald, one of the most famed figurative sculptors of our time. ✉ *Lincoln St., at 6th Ave., Carmel* ☎ *831/624–8200* ⊕ *dawsoncolefineart. com* ⬛ *Free.*

Galerie Plein Aire

ART GALLERIES | The gallery showcases the oil paintings (mostly large-format seascapes and landscapes) of local artists Cyndra Bradford and Jeff Daniel Smith. ✉ *3663 The Barnyard, Carmel* ☎ *831/277–6165* ⊕ *galeriepleinaire.com* ☾ *Closed Tues. and Wed.*

Gallery Sur

ART GALLERIES | Fine art photography of the Big Sur Coast and the Monterey Peninsula, including scenic shots and golf images, is the focus here. ✉ *6th Ave., between Dolores and Lincoln Sts., Carmel* ☎ *831/626–2615* ⊕ *gallerysur.com.*

★ Weston Gallery

ART GALLERIES | Run by the family of the late Edward Weston, this is hands down the best photography gallery around, with contemporary color photography and classic black-and-whites. ✉ *6th Ave., between Dolores and Lincoln Sts., Carmel* ☎ *831/624–4453* ⊕ *westongallery. com.*

MALLS

Carmel Plaza

SHOPPING CENTERS/MALLS | Tiffany & Co. and Anthropologie are among the name brands doing business at this mall on Carmel's east side, but what makes it worth a stop are homegrown enterprises such as Carmel Honey Company for local honey; Madrigal for women's fashion; and J. Lawrence Khaki's for debonair menswear. Flying Fish Grill and several other restaurants are here, along with the Wrath Wines tasting room (Chardonnay and Pinot Noir). The Carmel Chamber of Commerce Visitor Center (open daily) is on the second floor. ✉ *Ocean Ave. and Mission St., Carmel* ☎ *831/624–1385* ⊕ *carmelplaza.com.*

SPECIALTY SHOPS

Bittner

SPECIALTY STORES | The shop carries collectible and vintage pens from around the world. ✉ *Ocean Ave., between Mission and San Carlos Sts., Carmel* ☎ *831/626–8828* ⊕ *bittner.com.*

elizabethW

GIFTS/SOUVENIRS | Named after the designer and owner's pioneering great-grandmother, elizabethW handcrafts fragrances, essential oils, candles, silk eye pillows, and other soul-soothing goods for bath, body, and home. ✉ *Ocean Ave., between Monte Verde and Lincoln, Carmel* ☎ *831/626–3892* ⊕ *elizabethw.com.*

Foxy Couture

CLOTHING | Shop for one-of-a-kind treasures at this curated collection of gently used luxury couture and vintage clothes and accessories—think Chanel, Hermes, and Gucci—without paying a hefty price tag. ✉ *San Carlos St., in Vanervort Court, between Ocean and 7th Aves., Carmel* ☎ *831/625–9995* ⊕ *foxycouturecarmel. com* ☾ *Closed Tues. and Wed.*

Intima

SPECIALTY STORES | The European lingerie ranges from lacy to racy. ✉ *San Carlos St., between Ocean and 6th Aves., Carmel* ☎ *831/625–0599* ⊕ *www.intimacarmel.com.*

Jan de Luz

SPECIALTY STORES | This shop monograms and embroiders fine linens (including bathrobes) while you wait. ✉ *Dolores St., at 6th Ave. NE, Carmel* ☎ *831/622–7621* ⊕ *jandeluzlinens.com.*

Carmel Valley

10 miles east of Carmel.

Carmel Valley Road, which heads inland from Highway 1 south of Carmel, is the main thoroughfare through this valley, a secluded enclave of horse ranchers and other well-heeled residents who prefer the area's sunny climate to coastal fog and wind. Once thick with dairy farms, the valley has evolved into an esteemed wine appellation. Carmel Valley Village has crafts shops, art galleries, and the tasting rooms of numerous local wineries.

GETTING HERE AND AROUND

From U.S. 101 north or south, exit at Highway 68 and head west toward the coast. Scenic, two-lane Laureles Grade winds west over the mountains to Carmel Valley Road north of the village.

TOURS

Carmel Valley Grapevine Express

BUS TOURS | An incredible bargain, the express—aka MST's Bus 24—travels between downtown Monterey and Carmel Valley Village, with stops near wineries, restaurants, and shopping centers. ☎ *888/678–2871* ⊕ *mst.org* 🎫 *$10 all-day pass.*

 Sights

Bernardus Tasting Room

WINERY/DISTILLERY | At the tasting room of Bernardus, known for its Bordeaux-style red blend, called Marinus, and Chardonnays, you can sample current releases and library and reserve wines. ⊠ *5 W. Carmel Valley Rd., at El Caminito Rd.* ☎ *831/298–8021, 800/223–2533* ⊕ *bernardus.com* 🎫 *Tastings from $15.*

Cowgirl Winery

WINERY/DISTILLERY | Cowgirl chic prevails in the main tasting building here, and it's just plain rustic at the outdoor tables, set amid chickens, a tractor, and a flatbed truck. The wines include Chardonnay, Cabernet Sauvignon, Malbec, Pinot Noir, Rosé, and some blends. ⊠ *25 Pilot Rd., off W. Carmel Valley Rd.* ☎ *831/298–7030* ⊕ *cowgirlwinery.com* 🎫 *Tastings from $20.*

Earthbound Farm

FARM/RANCH | FAMILY | Pick up fresh vegetables, ready-to-eat meals, gourmet groceries, flowers, and gifts at Earthbound Farm, the world's largest grower of organic produce. You can also take a romp in the kids' garden, cut your own herbs, and stroll through the chamomile aromatherapy labyrinth. Special events, on Saturday from April through December, include bug walks and garlic-braiding workshops. ⊠ *7250 Carmel Valley Rd., Carmel* ☎ *831/625–6219* ⊕ *www.ebfarm.com* 🎫 *Free.*

★ Folktale Winery & Vineyards

WINERY/DISTILLERY | The expansive winery on a 15-acre estate (formerly Chateau Julienne) offers daily tastings, live music on weekends (plus Friday in summer and fall), and special events and programs such as Saturday yoga in the vineyard. Best-known wines include the estate Pinot Noir, Sparkling Rosé, and Le Mistral Joseph's Blend. Chefs in the on-site restaurant cook up small plates with wine pairing suggestions. Tours of the winery and organically farmed vineyards are available by appointment. ⊠ *8940 Carmel Valley Rd.* ✛ *At Schetter Rd.* ☎ *831/293–7500* ⊕ *folktalewinery.com* 🎫 *Tastings from $20; tours $40 (includes tasting)* ⊗ *Closed Mon.–Wed.*

Garland Ranch Regional Park

NATIONAL/STATE PARK | Hiking trails stretch across much of this park's 4,500 acres of meadows, forested hillsides, and creeks. ⊠ *700 W. Carmel Valley Rd., 9 miles east of Carmel-by-the-Sea* ☎ *831/372–3196* ⊕ *www.mprpd.org.*

★ Holman Ranch Vineyards Tasting Room

WINERY/DISTILLERY | Estate-grown Chardonnay and Pinot Noir are among the standout wines made by Holman Ranch, which pours samples in its chic tasting room and on two patios in the historic Will's Fargo tavern building. The 15-acre ranch itself is just up the road, set amid rolling hills that were once part of the Carmel mission's land grant. You can book winery and vineyard tours by appointment ⊠ *18 W. Carmel Valley Rd.* ☎ *831/601–8761* ⊕ *holmanranch.com* ⊠ *Tastings from $35* ☉ *Closed Tues. and Wed.*

Restaurants

Café Rustica

$$ | **EUROPEAN** | European country cooking is the focus at this lively roadhouse, where specialties include roasted meats, seafood, pastas, and thin-crust pizzas from the wood-fired oven. It can get noisy inside; for a quieter meal, request a table outside. **Known for:** Tuscan-flavored dishes from Alsace; open kitchen with wood-fired oven; outdoor patio seating. $ *Average main: $26* ⊠ *10 Delfino Pl., at Pilot Rd., off Carmel Valley Rd.* ☎ *831/659–4444* ⊕ *caferusticavillage.com* ☉ *Closed Mon. No lunch Tues. and Wed.*

Corkscrew Café

$$ | **MODERN AMERICAN** | Farm-fresh food is the specialty of this casual, Old Monterey–style bistro. Herbs and seasonal produce come from the Corkscrew's own organic gardens, the catch of the day comes from local waters, and the meats are hormone-free. **Known for:** wood-fired pizzas; fantastic regional wine list; garden patio. $ *Average main: $22* ⊠ *55 W. Carmel Valley Rd.* ☎ *831/659–8888* ⊕ *www.corkscrewcafe.com* ☉ *Closed Jan.*

Roux

$$$ | **MODERN FRENCH** | Chef Fabrice Roux, who hails from France, worked at lauded Parisian restaurants for more than a decade before coming to Carmel Valley to wow diners with his contemporary takes on traditional French-Mediterranean cuisine. The eclectic menu, with mostly small and large plates meant for sharing, focuses on local ingredients procured

that week: perhaps crispy duck leg confit, tuna tartare, or braised wild-boar bourguignon. **Known for:** expert food and wine pairings; European-style cottage with private room for dining and tastings; extensive wine list with more than 400 labels. $ *Average main: $33* ⊠ *6 Pilot Rd.* ☎ *831/659–5020* ⊕ *rouxcarmel.com* ☉ *Closed Tues. No lunch Wed. and Thurs.* ⊟ *No credit cards.*

Wagon Wheel Coffee Shop

$ | **AMERICAN** | This local hangout—decorated with wagon wheels, cowboy hats, and lassos—serves terrific hearty breakfasts, including oatmeal and banana pancakes, eggs Benedict, and biscuits and gravy. The lunch menu includes a dozen different burgers and other sandwiches. **Known for:** traditional American breakfast; cowboy-theme setting; lively local clientele. $ *Average main: $15* ⊠ *Valley Hill Center, 7156 Carmel Valley Rd., next to Quail Lodge, Carmel* ☎ *831/624–8878* ⊟ *No credit cards* ☉ *No dinner.*

🛌 Hotels

★ Bernardus Lodge & Spa

$$$$ | **RESORT** | The spacious guest rooms at this luxury spa resort have vaulted ceilings, French oak floors, featherbeds, fireplaces, patios, and bathrooms with heated-tile floors and soaking tubs for two. **Pros:** exceptional personal service; outstanding food and wine; serene, cushy full-service spa. **Cons:** hefty rates; can feel a little snooty; resort fee. $ *Rooms from: $445* ⊠ *415 W. Carmel Valley Rd.* ☎ *831/658–3400* ⊕ *www.bernarduslodge.com* ⊅ *73 rooms* ⫶◎⫶ *No meals.*

★ Carmel Valley Ranch

$$$$ | **RESORT** | The activity options at this luxury ranch are so varied that the resort provides a program director to guide you through them. **Pros:** stunning natural setting; tons of activities; River Ranch center with a pool, splash zone, boccie courts, and fitness center. **Cons:** must

drive several miles to shops and nightlife; high rates; footsteps from neighboring rooms easy to hear in some buildings. [$] *Rooms from: $699* ✉ *1 Old Ranch Rd., Carmel* ☎ *831/625–9500, 855/687–7262 toll-free reservations* 🌐 *carmelvalleyranch.com* 🛏 *181 suites* 🍴 *No meals.*

Quail Lodge & Golf Club

$$$$ | **HOTEL** | **FAMILY** | A sprawling collection of ranch-style buildings on 850 acres of meadows, fairways, and lakes, Quail Lodge offers luxury rooms and outdoor activities at surprisingly affordable rates. **Pros:** on the golf course; on-site restaurant; spacious rooms. **Cons:** service sometimes spotty; 5 miles from the beach and Carmel Valley Village; basic amenities. [$] *Rooms from: $395* ✉ *8205 Valley Greens Dr., Carmel* ☎ *866/675–1101 reservations, 831/624–2888* 🌐 *www.quaillodge.com* 🛏 *93 rooms* 🍴 *No meals.*

★ Stonepine Estate

$$$$ | **RESORT** | Set on 330 pastoral acres, the former estate of the Crocker banking family has been converted to a luxurious inn. **Pros:** supremely exclusive; close to Carmel Valley Village; attentive, personalized service. **Cons:** difficult to get a reservation; far from the coast; expensive rates. [$] *Rooms from: $500* ✉ *150 E. Carmel Valley Rd.* ☎ *831/659–2245* 🌐 *www.stonepineestate.com* 🛏 *13 units* 🍴 *No meals.*

Activities

GOLF

Quail Lodge & Golf Club

GOLF | Robert Muir Graves designed this championship semiprivate 18-hole course next to Quail Lodge that provides challenging play for golfers of all skill levels. The scenic course, which incorporates five lakes and edges the Carmel River, was completely renovated in 2015 by golf architect Todd Eckenrode to add extra challenge to the golf experience, white sand bunkers, and other enhancements. For the most part flat, the walkable course is well maintained, with stunning views, lush fairways, and ultrasmooth greens. ✉ *8000 Valley Greens Dr., Carmel* ☎ *831/620–8808 golf shop, 831/620–8866 club concierge* 🌐 *www.quaillodge.com* 🎫 *$196* ⛳ *18 holes, 6500 yards, par 71.*

SPAS

★ Refuge

FITNESS/HEALTH CLUBS | At this co-ed, European-style center on 2 serene acres you can recharge without breaking the bank. Heat up in the eucalyptus steam room or cedar sauna, plunge into cold pools, and relax indoors in zero-gravity chairs or outdoors in Adirondack chairs around firepits. Repeat the cycle a few times, then lounge around the thermal waterfall pools. Talk is not allowed, and bathing suits are required. ✉ *27300 Rancho San Carlos Rd., south off Carmel Valley Rd., Carmel* ☎ *831/620–7360* 🌐 *refuge.com* 🎫 *$44* ☞ *$52 admission; $155 50-min massage (includes Refuge admission), $12 robe rental, hot tubs (outdoor), sauna, steam room. Services: aromatherapy, hydrotherapy, massage.*

Pebble Beach

Off North San Antonio Ave. in Carmel-by-the-Sea or off Sunset Dr. in Pacific Grove.

In 1919 the Pacific Improvement Company acquired 18,000 acres of prime land on the Monterey Peninsula, including the entire Pebble Beach coastal region and much of Pacific Grove. Pebble Beach Golf Links and The Lodge at Pebble Beach opened the same year, and the private enclave evolved into a world-class golf destination with three posh lodges, five golf courses, hiking and riding trails, and some of the West Coast's ritziest homes. Pebble Beach has hosted major international golf tournaments, including the U.S. Open in 2019. The annual Pebble Beach Food & Wine, a four-day event in late April with 100 celebrity chefs, is one of the West Coast's premier culinary festivals.

GETTING HERE AND AROUND

If you drive south from Monterey on Highway 1, exit at 17-Mile Drive/Sunset Drive in Pacific Grove to find the northern entrance gate. Coming from Carmel, exit at Ocean Avenue and follow the road almost to the beach; turn right on North San Antonio Avenue to the Carmel Gate. You can also enter through the Highway 1 Gate off Highway 68. Monterey–Salinas Transit buses provide regular service in and around Pebble Beach.

Sights

★ The Lone Cypress

FOREST | The most-photographed tree along 17-Mile Drive is the weather-sculpted Lone Cypress, which grows out of a precipitous outcropping above the waves about 1½ miles up the road from Pebble Beach Golf Links. You can't walk out to the tree, but you can stop for a view of it at a small parking area off the road.

★ 17-Mile Drive

SCENIC DRIVE | Primordial nature resides in quiet harmony with palatial, mostly Spanish Mission–style estates along 17-Mile Drive, which winds through an 8,400-acre microcosm of the Pebble Beach coastal landscape. Dotting the drive are rare Monterey cypresses, trees so gnarled and twisted that Robert Louis Stevenson described them as "ghosts fleeing before the wind." The most famous of these is the **Lone Cypress**. Other highlights include **Bird Rock** and **Seal Rock,** home to harbor seals, sea lions, cormorants, and pelicans and other sea creatures and birds, and the **Crocker Marble Palace,** inspired by a Byzantine castle and easily identifiable by its dozens of marble arches.

■ TIP→ **If you spend $35 or more on dining in Pebble Beach and show a receipt upon exiting, you'll receive a refund off the drive's $10.75 per-car fee.** ⊠ *Hwy. 1 Gate, 17-Mile Dr., at Hwy. 68* 🎫 *$11 per car, free for bicyclists.*

Hotels

★ Casa Palmero

$$$$ | RESORT | This exclusive boutique hotel evokes a stately Mediterranean villa. **Pros:** ultimate in pampering; sumptuous decor; more private than sister resorts. **Cons:** rates out of reach for most visitors; not the best views compared to sister lodges; some showers on the small side. 💲 *Rooms from: $1150* ⊠ *1518 Cypress Dr.* 📞 *831/622–6650, 800/877–0597 reservations* ⊕ *www.pebblebeach. com* 🛏 *24 rooms* ¡⊙¡ *Free breakfast.*

The Inn at Spanish Bay

$$$$ | RESORT | This resort sprawls along a breathtaking stretch of shoreline and has plush, 600-square-foot rooms. **Pros:** attentive service; many amenities; spectacular views. **Cons:** huge hotel; 4 miles from other Pebble Beach Resorts facilities; atmosphere too snobbish for some. 💲 *Rooms from: $870* ⊠ *2700 17-Mile Dr.* 📞 *831/647–7500, 800/877–0597* ⊕ *www.pebblebeach. com* 🛏 *269 rooms* ¡⊙¡ *No meals.*

The Lodge at Pebble Beach

$$$$ | RESORT | Most rooms have wood-burning fireplaces and many have wonderful ocean views at this circa-1919 resort, which was expanded to include the 38-room Fairway One complex in 2017. **Pros:** world-class golf; borders the ocean and fairways; fabulous facilities. **Cons:** some rooms are on the small side; very pricey; not many activities if you don't golf. 💲 *Rooms from: $990* ⊠ *1700 17-Mile Dr.* 📞 *831/624–3811, 800/877–0597* ⊕ *www.pebblebeach.com* 🛏 *199 rooms* ¡⊙¡ *No meals.*

Activities

GOLF
The Hay

GOLF | The only 9-hole, par-3 course on the Monterey Peninsula open to the public, Peter Hay attracts golfers of all skill levels. It's an ideal place for warm-ups, practicing short games, and for those

Did You Know?

The Lone Cypress has stood on this rock for more than 250 years. The tree is the official symbol of the Pebble Beach Company.

who don't have time to play 18 holes. ✉ *17-Mile Dr. and Portola Rd.* ☎ *800/877–0597* ⊕ *www.pebblebeach.com* ✉ *$65* ⛳ *9 holes, 725 yards, par 27.*

Links at Spanish Bay

GOLF | This course, which hugs a choice stretch of shoreline, was designed by Robert Trent Jones Jr., Tom Watson, and Sandy Tatum in the rugged manner of traditional Scottish links, with sand dunes and coastal marshes interspersed among the greens. A bagpiper signals the course's closing each day. ■**TIP→** **Nonguests of the Pebble Beach Resorts can reserve tee times up to two months in advance.** ✉ *17-Mile Dr., north end* ☎ *800/877–0597* ⊕ *www.pebblebeach.com* ✉ *$295* ⛳ *18 holes, 6821 yards, par 72.*

★ Pebble Beach Golf Links

GOLF | Each February, show-business celebrities and golf pros team up at this course, the main site of the glamorous AT&T Pebble Beach National Pro-Am tournament. On most days the rest of the year, tee times are available to guests of the Pebble Beach Resorts who book a minimum two-night stay. Nonguests can reserve a tee time only one day in advance on a space-available basis; resort guests can reserve up to 18 months in advance. ✉ *17-Mile Dr., near The Lodge at Pebble Beach* ☎ *800/877–0597* ⊕ *www.pebblebeach.com* ✉ *$575* ⛳ *18 holes, 6828 yards, par 72.*

Poppy Hills

GOLF | An 18-hole course designed in 1986 by Robert Trent Jones Jr., Poppy Hills reopened in 2014 after a yearlong renovation that Jones supervised. Each hole has been restored to its natural elevation along the forest floor, and all 18 greens have been rebuilt with bent grass. Individuals may reserve up to a month in advance. ■**TIP→** **Poppy Hills, owned by a golfing nonprofit, represents good value for this area.** ✉ *3200 Lopez Rd., at 17-Mile Dr.* ☎ *831/622–8239* ⊕ *poppyhillsgolf.com* ✉ *$250* ⛳ *18 holes, 7002 yards, par 73.5.*

Spyglass Hill

GOLF | With three holes rated among the toughest on the PGA tour, Spyglass Hill, designed by Robert Trent Jones Sr. and Jr., challenges golfers with its varied terrain but rewards them with glorious views. The first 5 holes border the Pacific, and the other 13 reach deep into the Del Monte Forest. Reservations are essential and may be made up to one month in advance (18 months for resort guests). ✉ *Stevenson Dr. and Spyglass Hill Rd.* ☎ *800/877–0597* ⊕ *www.pebblebeach.com* ✉ *$415* ⛳ *18 holes, 6960 yards, par 72.*

Pacific Grove

3 miles north of Carmel-by-the-Sea.

This picturesque town, which began as a summer retreat for church groups more than a century ago, recalls its prim and proper Victorian heritage in its host of tiny board-and-batten cottages and stately mansions. However, long before the church groups flocked here the area received thousands of annual pilgrims—in the form of bright orange-and-black monarch butterflies. They still come, migrating south from Canada and the Pacific Northwest to take residence in pine and eucalyptus groves from October through March. In Butterfly Town USA, as Pacific Grove is known, the sight of a mass of butterflies hanging from the branches like a long, fluttering veil is unforgettable.

A prime way to enjoy Pacific Grove is to walk or bicycle the 3 miles of city-owned shoreline along Ocean View Boulevard, a cliff-top area landscaped with native plants and dotted with benches meant for sitting and gazing at the sea. You can spot many types of birds here, including the web-footed cormorants that crowd the massive rocks rising out of the surf. Two Victorians of note along Ocean View are the Queen Anne–style Green Gables, at No. 301—erected in 1888, it's now an inn—and the 1909 Pryor House, at No. 429, a massive, shingled, private residence with a leaded- and beveled-glass doorway.

GETTING HERE AND AROUND

Reach Pacific Grove via Highway 68 off Highway 1, just south of Monterey. From Cannery Row in Monterey, head north until the road merges with Ocean Boulevard and follow it along the coast. MST buses travel within Pacific Grove and surrounding towns.

Sights

Lovers Point Park

CITY PARK | FAMILY | The coastal views are gorgeous from this waterfront park whose sheltered beach has a children's pool and a picnic area. The main lawn has a volleyball court and a snack bar. ✉ *Ocean View Blvd. northwest of Forest Ave.* 🌐 *www.cityofpacificgrove.org/living/recreation/parks/lovers-point-park.*

Monarch Grove Sanctuary

NATURE PRESERVE | FAMILY | The sanctuary is a reliable spot for viewing monarch butterflies between November and February. **■ TIP→ The best time to visit is between noon and 3 pm.** ✉ *250 Ridge Rd., off Lighthouse Ave.* 🌐 *www.pgmuseum.org/monarch-viewing.*

Pacific Grove Museum of Natural History

MUSEUM | The museum, a good source for the latest information about monarch butterflies, has permanent exhibitions about the butterflies, birds of Monterey County, biodiversity, and plants. There's a native plant garden, and a display documents life in Pacific Grove's 19th-century Chinese fishing village. ✉ *165 Forest Ave., at Central Ave.* ☎ *831/648–5716* 🌐 *pgmuseum.org* 🎫 *$9* 🕒 *Closed Mon.*

Point Pinos Lighthouse

LIGHTHOUSE | FAMILY | At this 1855 structure, the West Coast's oldest continuously operating lighthouse, you can learn about the lighting and foghorn operations and wander through a small museum containing U.S. Coast Guard memorabilia. ✉ *Asilomar Ave., between Lighthouse Ave. and Del Monte Blvd.* ☎ *831/648–5722* 🌐 *cityofpg.org/lighthouse* 🎫 *$5* 🕒 *Closed weekdays some months; visit website for current schedule.*

Beaches

Asilomar State Beach

BEACH—SIGHT | A beautiful coastal area, Asilomar State Beach stretches between Point Pinos and the Del Monte Forest. The 100 acres of dunes, tidal pools, and pocket-size beaches form one of the region's richest areas for marine life—including surfers, who migrate here most winter mornings. Leashed dogs are allowed on the beach. **Amenities:** none. **Best for:** sunrise; sunset; surfing; walking. ✉ *Sunset Dr. and Asilomar Ave.* ☎ *831/646–6440* 🌐 *www.parks.ca.gov.*

Restaurants

Beach House

$$$ | MODERN AMERICAN | Patrons of this bluff-top perch sip classic cocktails, sample California fare, and watch the otters frolic on Lovers Point Beach below. The sunset discounts between 4 and 5:30 (reservations recommended) are a great value. **Known for:** sweeping bluff-top views; heated patio; seafood and organic pastas. [$] *Average main: $28* ✉ *620 Ocean View Blvd.* ☎ *831/375–2345* 🌐 *beachhousepg.com* 🕒 *No lunch.*

★ Fandango

$$$ | MEDITERRANEAN | The menu here is mostly Mediterranean and southern French, with such dishes as osso buco and paella. The decor follows suit: stone walls and country furniture lend the restaurant the earthy feel of a European farmhouse. **Known for:** wood-fire-grilled rack of lamb, seafood, and beef; convivial residential vibe; traditional European flavors. [$] *Average main: $36* ✉ *223 17th*

St., south of Lighthouse Ave. ☎ *831/372–3456* ⊕ *fandangorestaurant.com.*

Fishwife

$$ | **SEAFOOD** | Fresh fish with a Latin accent makes this a favorite of locals for lunch or a casual dinner. Standards are the sea garden salads—topped with your choice of fish—and the fried seafood plates. **Known for:** fisherman's bowls with fresh local seafood; house-made desserts; crab cakes and New Zealand mussels. $ *Average main: $22* ⊠ *1996½ Sunset Dr., at Asilomar Blvd.* ☎ *831/375–7107* ⊕ *fishwife.com.*

Jennini Kitchen + Wine Bar

$$ | **MEDITERRANEAN** | Sommelier Thamin Saleh, who named his lively restaurant and wine bar after his hometown in Palestine, designed a seasonally changing menu of small plates and entrées that showcases the cuisine of the eastern Mediterranean and southern Spain. Dishes might include chicken and merguez tagine, crispy lamb shanks, hummus and baba ghanoush, and filone bread with goat butter. **Known for:** Sunday night paella (order 24 hours in advance other nights); eclectic, value-driven wine list with 180 selections; creative twists on classic dishes. $ *Average main: $25* ⊠ *542 Lighthouse Ave.* ☎ *831/920–2662* ⊕ *www.jeninni.com* ☉ *No lunch. Closed Tues. and Wed.*

★ Passionfish

$$$ | **MODERN AMERICAN** | South American artwork and artifacts decorate Passionfish, and Latin and Asian flavors infuse the dishes. The chef shops at local farmers' markets several times a week to find the best produce, fish, and meat available, then pairs it with creative sauces like a caper, raisin, and walnut relish. **Known for:** sustainably sourced seafood and organic ingredients; reasonably priced wine list that supports small producers; slow-cooked meats. $ *Average main: $28* ⊠ *701 Lighthouse Ave.* ☎ *831/655–3311* ⊕ *www.passionfish.net* ☉ *No lunch.*

Peppers Mexicali Cafe

$$ | **MEXICAN** | This cheerful, white-walled storefront serves traditional dishes from Mexico and Latin America, with an emphasis on fresh seafood. Excellent red and green salsas are made throughout the day, and there's a large selection of beers, along with fresh lime margaritas. **Known for:** traditional Latin American dishes; fresh lime margaritas; daily specials. $ *Average main: $20* ⊠ *170 Forest Ave., between Lighthouse and Central Aves.* ☎ *831/373–6892* ⊕ *peppersmexicalicafe. com* ☉ *Closed Tues. No lunch Sun.*

Red House Café

$$ | **AMERICAN** | When it's nice out, sun pours through the big windows of this cozy restaurant and across tables on the porch; when fog rolls in, the fireplace is lit. The American menu changes with the seasons, but grilled lamb chops atop mashed potatoes are often on offer for dinner, and a grilled calamari steak might be served for lunch, either in a salad or as part of a sandwich. **Known for:** cozy homelike dining areas; comfort food; stellar breakfast and brunch. $ *Average main: $22* ⊠ *662 Lighthouse Ave., at 19th St.* ☎ *831/643–1060* ⊕ *redhousecafe.com* ☉ *No dinner Mon.*

Hotels

Gosby House Inn

$$ | **B&B/INN** | Though in the town center, this turreted butter-yellow Queen Anne Victorian has an informal feel. **Pros:** peaceful; homey; within walking distance of shops and restaurants. **Cons:** too frilly for some; area is busy during the day; limited parking. $ *Rooms from: $165* ⊠ *643 Lighthouse Ave.* ☎ *831/375–1287* ⊕ *gosbyhouseinn.com* ⇱ *22 rooms* ⏚ *Free breakfast.*

★ Green Gables Inn

$$ | **B&B/INN** | Stained-glass windows and ornate interior details compete with spectacular ocean views at this Queen Anne–style mansion. **Pros:** exceptional views; impeccable attention to historic detail; afternoon wine and cheese served in the parlor. **Cons:** some rooms are small; thin walls; breakfast room can be crowded. [$] *Rooms from: $179* ✉ *301 Ocean View Blvd.* ☎ *831/375–2095* 🌐 *www.greengablesinnpg.com* 🛏 *11 rooms* 🍴 *Free breakfast.*

Martine Inn

$$$ | **B&B/INN** | The glassed-in parlor and many guest rooms at this 1899 Mediterranean-style villa have stunning ocean views. **Pros:** romantic; exquisite antiques; ocean views. **Cons:** not child-friendly; sits on a busy thoroughfare; inconvenient parking. [$] *Rooms from: $259* ✉ *255 Ocean View Blvd.* ☎ *831/373–3388* 🌐 *martineinn.com* 🛏 *25 rooms* 🍴 *Free breakfast.*

Monterey

2 miles southeast of Pacific Grove, 2 miles north of Carmel.

Monterey is a scenic city filled with early California history: adobe buildings from the 1700s, Colton Hall, where California's first constitution was drafted in 1849, and Cannery Row, made famous by author John Steinbeck. Thousands of visitors come each year to mingle with otters and other sea creatures at the world-famous Monterey Bay Aquarium and in the protected waters of the national marine sanctuary that hugs the shoreline.

GETTING HERE AND AROUND

From San Jose or San Francisco, take U.S. 101 south to Highway 156 West at Prunedale. Head west about 8 miles to Highway 1 and follow it about 15 miles south. From San Luis Obispo, take U.S. 101 north to Salinas and drive west on Highway 68 about 20 miles.

Many MST bus lines connect at the Monterey Transit Center, at Pearl Street and Munras Avenue. In summer (daily from 10 until at least 7) and on weekends and holidays the rest of the year, the free MST Monterey Trolley travels from downtown Monterey along Cannery Row to the Aquarium and back.

TOURS

Old Monterey Walking Tour

WALKING TOURS | Learn all about Monterey's storied past by joining a guided walking tour through the historic district. Tours begin at the Custom House in Custom House Plaza, across from Fisherman's Wharf and are typically offered Thursday through Sunday at 11, 1, and 3. **■ TIP→ Tours are free for everyone on the last Sunday of the month.** ✉ *Monterey* 🌐 *www.parks.ca.gov/?page_id=951* 🎟 *Tours $10.*

The Original Monterey Walking Tours

WALKING TOURS | Learn more about Monterey's past, primarily the Mexican period until California statehood, on a guided tour through downtown Monterey. You can also join a guided walking tour of Cannery Row in the morning. Tours last 1½ to 2 hours and are offered Thursday–Sunday at 10 am and 2. Reservations are essential. ✉ *Monterey* ☎ *831/521–4884* 🌐 *www.walkmonterey.com* 🎟 *From $25.*

ESSENTIALS

VISITOR INFORMATION Visit Monterey. ✉ *401 Camino El Estero* ☎ *888/221–1010* 🌐 *www.seemonterey.com.*

👁 Sights

A Taste of Monterey

WINERY/DISTILLERY | Without driving the back roads, you can taste the wines of nearly 100 area vintners (craft beers, too) while taking in fantastic bay views. Bottles are available for purchase, and food is served from 11:30 until closing. ✉ *700 Cannery Row, Suite KK* ☎ *831/646–5446* 🌐 *atasteofmonterey.com* 🎟 *Tastings $20.*

Cannery Row

NEIGHBORHOOD | When John Steinbeck published the novel *Cannery Row* in 1945, he immortalized a place of rough-edged working people. The waterfront street, edging a mile of gorgeous coastline, once was crowded with sardine canneries processing, at their peak, nearly 200,000 tons of the smelly silver fish a year. During the mid-1940s, however, the sardines disappeared from the bay, causing the canneries to close. Through the years the old tin-roof canneries have been converted into restaurants, art galleries, and malls with shops selling T-shirts, fudge, and plastic sea otters. Recent tourist development along the row has been more tasteful, however, and includes stylish inns and hotels, wine tasting rooms, and upscale specialty shops. ⊠ *Cannery Row, between Reeside and David Aves.* ⊕ *canneryrow.com.*

Colton Hall

MUSEUM | A convention of delegates met here in 1849 to draft the first state constitution. The stone building, which has served as a school, a courthouse, and the county seat, is a city-run museum furnished as it was during the constitutional convention. The extensive grounds outside the hall surround the Old Monterey Jail. ⊠ *570 Pacific St., between Madison and Jefferson Sts.* ☎ *831/646–3933* ⊕ *www.monterey.org/museums* ⌾ *Free.*

Fisherman's Wharf

PEDESTRIAN MALL | **FAMILY** | The mournful barking of sea lions provides a steady soundtrack all along Monterey's waterfront, but the best way to actually view the whiskered marine mammals is to walk along one of the two piers across from Custom House Plaza. Lined with souvenir shops, the wharf is undeniably touristy, but it's lively and entertaining. At Wharf No. 2, a working municipal pier, you can see the day's catch being unloaded from fishing boats on one side and fishermen casting their lines into the water on the other. The pier has a couple of low-key restaurants, from whose seats lucky customers might spot otters and

harbor seals. ⊠ *At end of Calle Principal* ⊕ *www.montereywharf.com.*

Fort Ord National Monument

NATIONAL/STATE PARK | Scenic beauty, biodiversity, and miles of trails make this former U.S. Army training grounds a haven for nature lovers and outdoor enthusiasts. The 7,200-acre park, which stretches east over the hills between Monterey and Salinas, is also protected habitat for 35 species of rare and endangered plants and animals. There are 86 miles of single-track, dirt, and paved trails for hiking, biking, and horseback riding. The main trailheads are the Creekside, off Creekside Terrace near Portola Road, and Badger Hills, off Highway 68 in Salinas. Maps are available at the various trail-access points and on the park's website. ∎ **TIP→ Dogs are permitted on trails, but should be leashed when other people are nearby.** ⊠ *Bordered by Hwy. 68 and Gen. Jim Moore and Reservation Rds.* ☎ *831/582–2200* ⊕ *www.blm.gov/programs/national-conservation-lands/california/fort-ord-national-monument* ⌾ *Free.*

★ Monterey Bay Aquarium

ZOO | **FAMILY** | Playful otters and other sea creatures surround you the minute you enter this extraordinary facility, where all the exhibits convey what it's like to be in the water with the animals. Leopard sharks swim in a three-story, sunlit kelp forest exhibit; sardines swim around your head in a circular tank; and jellyfish drift in and out of view in dramatically lighted spaces that suggest the ocean depths. A petting pool puts you literally in touch with bat rays, and the million-gallon Open Seas exhibit illustrates the variety of creatures—from hammerhead sharks to placid-looking turtles—that live in the eastern Pacific. Splash Zone's 45, interactive, bilingual exhibits let kids commune with African penguins, clownfish, and other marine life. The only drawback to the aquarium experience is that it must be shared with the throngs that congregate

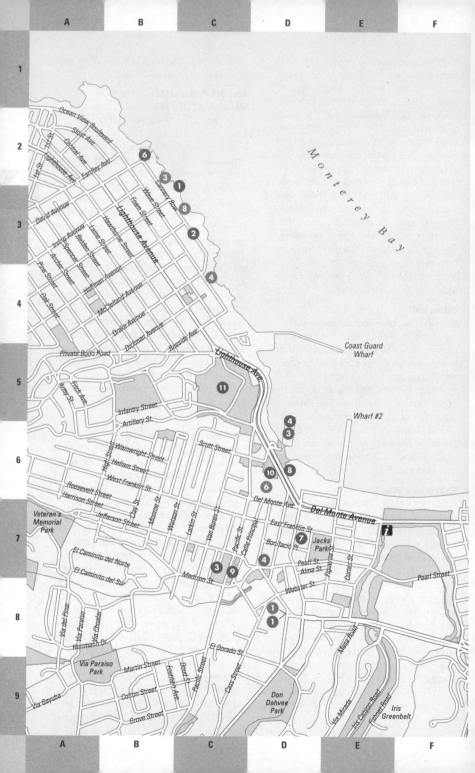

Monterey

KEY

1 *Exploring Sights*

1 *Restaurants*

1 *Hotels*

i *Tourist information*

Monterey
Municipal Beach

Del Monte Avenue

Del Monte Avenue

1st St.
2nd St.
3rd Street
4th Street
5th Street
6th Street
Park Avenue
7th Street
8th Street

Sloat Avenue

Cunningham Rd.
Stone Road

Lake Drive

East Road

Helvic Ave.
Portola Ave.
Palo Verde Ave.
Encina Ave.

University Way
Gabrilla Highway

Mark Thomas Dr.

Fairground Road

Monterey Salinas Hwy.

daily, but most visitors think it's worth it. ⊠ *886 Cannery Row* ☎ *831/648–4800 info, 866/963–9645 for advance tickets* ⊕ *www.montereybayaquarium.org* 🎫 *$50.*

Monterey County Youth Museum (*MY Museum*)

MUSEUM | FAMILY | Monterey Bay comes to life from a child's perspective in this fun-filled, interactive indoor exploration center. The seven exhibit galleries showcase the science and nature of the Big Sur coast, theater arts, Pebble Beach golf, and beaches. Also here are a live performance theater, a creation station, a hospital emergency room, and an agriculture corner where kids follow artichokes, strawberries, and other fruits and veggies on their evolution from sprout to harvest to farmers' markets. ⊠ *425 Washington St., between E. Franklin St. and Bonifacio Pl.* ☎ *831/649–6444* ⊕ *mymuseum.org* 🎫 *$8* ⊗ *Closed Mon.*

Monterey History and Art Association Salvador Dali Exposition

MUSEUM | Whether you're a fan of surrealist art or not, come to The Dali Expo to gain rare insight into the life and work of famed Spanish artist Salvador Dali, who lived in Monterey in the 1940s. The permanent exhibition houses nearly 600 artworks in various media, including 400 Dali originals. The museum's name reflects Dali's ties to nearby 17-Mile Drive, where he lived, worked, and hosted parties that included Andy Warhol, Walt Disney, Bob Hope, and other celebrities. ⊠ *5 Custom House Plaza* ☎ *831/372–2608* ⊕ *www.mhaadali. com* 🎫 *$20.*

Monterey Museum of Art at Pacific Street

MUSEUM | Photographs by Ansel Adams and Edward Weston and works by other artists who have spent time on the peninsula are on display here, along with international folk art, from Kentucky hearth brooms to Tibetan prayer wheels. ⊠ *559 Pacific St., across from Colton*

Steinbeck's Cannery Row

"Cannery Row in Monterey in California is a poem, a stink, a grating noise, a quality of light, a tone, a habit, a nostalgia, a dream. Cannery Row is the gathered and scattered, tin and iron and rust and splintered wood, chipped pavement and weedy lots and junk heaps, sardine canneries of corrugated iron, honky tonks, restaurants and whore houses, and little crowded groceries, and laboratories and flophouses." —John Steinbeck, *Cannery Row*

Hall ☎ *831/372–5477* ⊕ *montereyart.org* 🎫 *$15* ⊗ *Closed Sun.–Wed.*

★ Monterey State Historic Park

NATIONAL/STATE PARK | You can glimpse Monterey's early history in several well-preserved adobe buildings in Custom House Plaza and the downtown area. Although most are only open via guided tours (check ahead for details), some also have beautiful gardens to explore. Set in what was once a hotel and saloon, the **Pacific House Museum** now houses a visitor center and exhibits of gold-rush relics; photographs of old Monterey; and Native American baskets, pottery, and other artifacts. The adjacent **Custom House,** built by the Mexican government in 1827 and now California's oldest standing public building, was the first stop for sea traders whose goods were subject to duties. (In 1846 Commodore John Sloat raised the American flag over this adobe structure and claimed California for the United States.)

Exhibits at **Casa Soberanes** (1842), once a customs-house guard's residence, survey Monterey life from Mexican rule to the present. A veranda encircles the second

California sea lions are intelligent, social animals that live (and sleep) close together in groups.

floor of **Larkin House** (1835), whose namesake, an early California statesman, brought many of the antique furnishings inside from New Hampshire. **Stevenson House** was named in honor of author Robert Louis Stevenson, who boarded here briefly in a tiny upstairs room that's now furnished with items from his family's estate. Other rooms include a gallery of memorabilia and a children's nursery with Victorian toys. **■TIP→ If the buildings are closed, you can access a cell-phone tour 24/7 (☎ *831/998–9458*) or download an app.** ✉ *Pacific House Museum visitor center, 10 Custom House Plaza* ☎ *831/649–2907* 🌐 *www.parks.ca.gov/mshp* 🎟 *Free–$5, 1-hr history walk $10.*

Presidio of Monterey Museum

MUSEUM | This spot has been significant for centuries. Its first incarnation was as a Native American village for the Rumsien tribe. The Spanish explorer Sebastián Vizcaíno landed here in 1602, and Father Junípero Serra arrived in 1770. Notable battles fought here include the 1818 skirmish in which the corsair Hipólito Bruchard conquered the Spanish garrison that stood on this site and claimed part of California for Argentina. The indoor museum tells the stories; plaques mark the outdoor sites. ✉ *Presidio of Monterey, Corporal Ewing Rd., off Lighthouse Ave.* ☎ *831/646–3456* 🌐 *www.monterey.org/museums* 🎟 *Free* 🕒 *Closed Tues. and Wed.*

🍴 Restaurants

Estéban Restaurant

$$$ | **SPANISH** | In a festive fireplace dining room at Casa Munras hotel, Estéban serves modern and classic versions of Spanish cuisine: empanadas, Moorish chickpea stew, and three types of paella. Midweek specials abound: on Tuesday nights, feast on a four-course prix-fixe paella dinner ($38 per person), bottles of wine are half off on Monday, and Wednesday wine flights are just $16 for three tastes. **Known for:** daily tapas happy hour from 4:30 to 6; patio with firepit; special menus for kids and pups. [$] *Average main: $30* ✉ *700 Munras Ave.*

☎ 831/375–0176 🌐 *www.estebanrestaurant.com* ⏲ *No lunch.*

Monterey's Fish House

$$ | **SEAFOOD** | Casual yet stylish and always packed, this seafood restaurant is removed from the hubbub of the wharf. The bartenders and waitstaff will gladly advise you on the perfect wine to go with your poached, blackened, or oak-grilled seafood. **Known for:** seafood, steaks, house-made pasta; festive atmosphere; oyster bar. [$] *Average main: $22* ✉ *2114 Del Monte Ave., at Dela Vina Ave.* ☎ *831/373–4647* 🌐 *montereyfishhouse.com* ⏲ *No lunch weekends.*

Old Fisherman's Grotto

$$$ | **SEAFOOD** | Otters and seals frolic in the water just below this nautical-theme Fisherman's Wharf restaurant famous for its creamy clam chowder. Seafood paella, sand dabs, filet mignon, teriyaki chicken, and several pastas are among the many entrée options. **Known for:** Monterey-style clam chowder and calamari; bay views; full bar and carefully curated wine list. [$] *Average main: $29* ✉ *39 Fisherman's Wharf* ☎ *831/375–4604* 🌐 *oldfishermansgrotto.com.*

Old Monterey Café

$ | **AMERICAN** | Breakfast here gets constant local raves—its fame rests on familiar favorites: a dozen kinds of omelets, and pancakes from blueberry to cinnamon-raisin-pecan. For lunch are good soups, salads, and sandwiches. **Known for:** seven types of eggs Benedict; upbeat, team-style service; all meals cooked to order. [$] *Average main: $15* ✉ *489 Alvarado St., at Munras Ave.* ☎ *831/646–1021* 🌐 *oldmontereycafeca.com* ⏲ *No dinner.*

Tarpy's Roadhouse

$$$ | **AMERICAN** | Fun, dressed-up American favorites—a little something for everyone—are served in this renovated early-1900s stone farmhouse several miles east of town. The kitchen cranks out everything from Cajun-spiced prawns to meat loaf with marsala–mushroom gravy to grilled ribs and steaks. **Known for:** American comfort food with a California twist; rustic dining: indoor fireplace or garden courtyard; generous portions. [$] *Average main: $29* ✉ *2999 Monterey–Salinas Hwy., Hwy. 68* ☎ *831/647–1444* 🌐 *tarpys.com.*

🛏 Hotels

Casa Munras Garden Hotel & Spa

$$ | **HOTEL** | **FAMILY** | A cluster of Spanish-themed buildings in the heart of downtown, Casa Munras pays homage to Monterey's roots and the legacy of Spanish diplomat Don Estéban Munras, who built a residence on the site in 1824. **Pros:** full-service spa, heated swimming pool, hot tub, and fitness room; excellent on-site tapas restaurant; walk to downtown sights and restaurants. **Cons:** $15 parking fee; pool area can get noisy; thin walls. [$] *Rooms from: $199* ✉ *700 Munras Ave.* ☎ *831/375–2411, 800/222–2446* 🌐 *www.hotelcasamunras.com* 🛏 *163 rooms* 🍴 *No meals.*

Hyatt Regency Monterey

$$ | **RESORT** | **FAMILY** | A 22-acre resort amid cypress forests on the Del Monte Golf Course, the Hyatt Regency Monterey is a good choice for business travelers and families (especially those with pets) seeking relatively affordable lodgings with numerous on-site services. **Pros:** half the rooms overlook the golf course; six tennis courts, firepits, two pools and hot tubs, hammocks, swings on property; on-site restaurant with live weekend entertainment. **Cons:** not in heart of downtown; sprawling resort that can seem packed during busy seasons; not ideal for pet-phobic guests. [$] *Rooms from: $179* ✉ *1 Old Golf Course Rd.* ☎ *831/372–1234* 🌐 *www.hyatt.com* 🛏 *560 rooms* 🍴 *No meals.*

InterContinental the Clement Monterey

$$$ | **HOTEL** | **FAMILY** | Spectacular bay views, upscale amenities, assiduous service, and a superb location next to the

The Monterey Bay National Marine Sanctuary

Although Monterey's coastal landscapes are stunning, their beauty is more than equaled by the wonders that lie offshore. The Monterey Bay National Marine Sanctuary—which stretches 276 miles, from north of San Francisco almost down to Santa Barbara—teems with abundant life, and has topography as diverse as that aboveground.

The preserve's 5,322 square miles include vast submarine canyons, which reach down 10,663 feet at their deepest point. They also encompass dense forests of giant kelp—a kind of seaweed that can grow more than a hundred feet from its roots on the ocean floor. These kelp forests are especially robust off Monterey.

The sanctuary was established in 1992 to protect the habitat of the many species that thrive in the bay. Some animals can be seen quite easily from land. In summer and winter you might glimpse the offshore spray of gray whales as they migrate between their summer feeding grounds in Alaska and their breeding grounds in Baja. Clouds of marine birds—including white-faced ibis, three types of albatross, and more than 15 types of gull—skim the waves, or roost in the rock islands along 17-Mile Drive. Sea otters dart and gambol in the calmer waters of the bay; and of course, you can watch the sea lions—and hear their round-the-clock barking—on the wharves in Santa Cruz and Monterey.

The sanctuary supports many other creatures, however, that remain unseen by most on-land visitors. Some of these are enormous, such as the giant blue whales that arrive to feed on plankton in summer; others, like the more than 22 species of red algae in these waters, are microscopic. So whether you choose to visit the Monterey Bay Aquarium, take a whale-watch trip, or look out to sea with your binoculars, remember you're seeing just a small part of a vibrant underwater kingdom.

aquarium propelled this luxury hotel to immediate stardom. **Pros:** a block from the aquarium; fantastic waterfront views from some rooms; great for families. **Cons:** a tad formal; not budget; Cannery Row crowds everywhere on busy weekends and holidays. ⓢ *Rooms from: $305* ✉ *750 Cannery Row* ☎ *831/375–4500* ⊕ *www.ictheclementmonterey.com* ⥂ *208 rooms* ⦿ *No meals.*

Monterey Plaza Hotel & Spa

$$$ | HOTEL | Guests at this Cannery Row hotel can see frolicking sea otters from its wide outdoor patio and many room balconies. **Pros:** on the ocean; many amenities; attentive service. **Cons:** touristy area; heavy traffic; resort fee. ⓢ *Rooms from: $306* ✉ *400 Cannery Row* ☎ *831/920–6710* ⊕ *www.montereyplaza-hotel.com* ⥂ *290 rooms* ⦿ *No meals.*

Monterey Tides

$$ | RESORT | One of the area's best values, this hotel has a great waterfront location—2 miles north of Monterey, with views of the bay and the city skyline—and offers a surprising array of amenities. **Pros:** on the beach; great value; family-friendly. **Cons:** several miles from major attractions; big-box mall neighborhood; most rooms on the small side. ⓢ *Rooms from: $206* ✉ *2600 Sand Dunes Dr.* ☎ *831/394–3321, 800/242–8627* ⊕ *montereytides.com* ⥂ *196 rooms* ⦿ *No meals.*

Portola Hotel & Spa at Monterey Bay
$$$ | **HOTEL** | One of Monterey's largest hotels, and locally owned and operated for more than 40 years, the coastal-themed Portola anchors a prime city block between Custom House Plaza and the Monterey Conference Center. **Pros:** walk to sights and downtown restaurants and shops; three on-site restaurants and coffee shop; pet- and family-friendly. **Cons:** crowded when conferences convene; no limit on dog size; parking fee. [$] *Rooms from: $269* ✉ *2 Portola Plaza* ☎ *831/649–4511, 888/222–5851* 🌐 *www.portolahotel.com* 🛏 *379 rooms* 🍴 *No meals.*

The Sanctuary Beach Resort
$$$$ | **HOTEL** | **FAMILY** | Walk to the sand from spacious, luxurious bungalows furnished in contemporary, ocean-themed style at this 19-acre, wellness-centered resort next to Marina Dunes Preserve and a secluded stretch of Marina State Beach. **Pros:** easy access to hiking and biking trails; heated pool, on-site spa services; each bungalow has two rooms that can combine for families and groups. **Cons:** not in the heart of town; parking lot relatively far from rooms; area weather is often cooler than other parts of the bay. [$] *Rooms from: $399* ✉ *3295 Dunes Dr., Seaside* ☎ *855/693–6583* 🌐 *www.thesanctuarybeachresort.com* 🛏 *60 rooms* 🍴 *No meals.*

Spindrift Inn
$$$ | **HOTEL** | This boutique hotel on Cannery Row has beach access and a rooftop garden that overlooks the water. **Pros:** close to aquarium; steps from the beach; friendly staff. **Cons:** throngs of visitors outside; can be noisy; not good for families. [$] *Rooms from: $279* ✉ *652 Cannery Row* ☎ *831/646–8900, 800/841–1879* 🌐 *www.spindriftinn.com* 🛏 *45 rooms* 🍴 *Free breakfast.*

Former Capital of California

In 1602 Spanish explorer Sebastián Vizcaíno stepped ashore on a remote California peninsula. He named it after the viceroy of New Spain—Count de Monte Rey. Soon the Spanish built a military outpost, and the site was the capital of California until the state came under American rule.

Nightlife

BARS

Alvarado Street Brewery & Grill
BREWPUBS/BEER GARDENS | Housed in an historic Beaux Arts building that dates back to 1916, this craft brewery lures locals and visitors alike with a full bar and 20 craft beers on tap, decent gastropub menu, beer garden, and shaded sidewalk patio. The company also has a brewery, bistro, and wine bar in Carmel Plaza in Carmel-by-the-Sea. ✉ *426 Alvarado St.* ☎ *831/655–2337* 🌐 *www.alvaradostreetbrewery.com.*

Cibo
MUSIC CLUBS | An Italian restaurant and event venue with a big bar area, Cibo brings live jazz and other music to downtown from Tuesday through Sunday. ✉ *301 Alvarado St., at Del Monte Ave.* ☎ *831/649–8151* 🌐 *cibo.com.*

Crown & Anchor
BARS/PUBS | An authentic British pub, downtown Crown & Anchor has 20 beers on tap, classic cocktails, and a full menu, including 18 daily specials available in the restaurant and heated patio until midnight. ✉ *150 W. Franklin St.* ☎ *831/649–6496* 🌐 *crownandanchor.net.*

Peter B's Brewpub

BREWPUBS/BEER GARDENS | House-made beers, 18 HDTVs, a decent pub menu, and a pet-friendly patio ensure lively crowds at this craft brewery in back of the Portola Hotel & Spa. ⊠ *2 Portola Plaza* ☎ *831/649–2699* ⊕ *www.peterbsbrewpub.com.*

Turn 12 Bar & Grill

BARS/PUBS | The motorcycles and vintage photographs at this downtown watering hole pay homage to nearby 11-turn Laguna Seca Raceway. The large-screen TVs, heated outdoor patio, happy-hour specials, and live entertainment keep the place jumpin' into the wee hours. ⊠ *400 Tyler St., at E. Franklin St.* ☎ *831/372–8876* ⊕ *turn12barandgrill.com.*

 # Shopping

Alvarado and nearby downtown streets are good places to start a Monterey shopping spree, especially if you're interested in antiques and collectibles.

Cannery Row Antique Mall

ANTIQUES/COLLECTIBLES | Bargain hunters can sometimes find little treasures at the mall, which houses more than 100 local vendors under one roof. ⊠ *471 Wave St.* ☎ *831/655–0264* ⊕ *canneryrowantiquemall.com.*

The Custom House Gift Shop

SPECIALTY STORES | This store sells 1800s-theme items such as toys, as well as books related to Monterey and California heritage. ⊠ *Custom House Plaza, in the Custom House bldg.* ☎ *831/649–7111.*

Old Monterey Book Co.

BOOKS/STATIONERY | Antiquarian books and prints are this shop's specialties. ⊠ *136 Bonifacio Pl., off Alvarado St.* ☎ *831/372–3111* ☽ *Closed Mon.*

 # Activities

Monterey Bay waters never warm to the temperatures of their Southern California counterparts—the warmest they get is the low 60s. That's one reason why the marine life here is so diverse, which in turn brings out the fishers, kayakers, and whale-watchers. During the rainy winter, the waves grow larger, and surfers flock to the water. On land pretty much year-round, bikers find opportunities to ride, and walkers have plenty of waterfront to stroll.

BIKING
Adventures by the Sea

BICYCLING | You can rent surreys plus tandem, standard, and electric bicycles from this outfit that also conducts bike and kayak tours, and rents kayaks and stand-up paddleboards. There are multiple locations along Cannery Row and Custom House Plaza as well as branches at Lovers Point in Pacific Grove and 17-Mile Drive in Pebble Beach. ⊠ *299 Cannery Row* ☎ *831/372–1807, 800/979–3370 reservations* ⊕ *adventuresbythesea.com.*

FISHING
J&M Sport Fishing

FISHING | This outfit takes beginning and experienced fishers out to sea to catch rock cod, ling cod, sand dabs, mackerel, halibut, salmon (in season), albacore, squid, Dungeness crab, and other species. ⊠ *66 Fisherman's Wharf* ☎ *831/372–7440* ⊕ *jmsportfishing.com.*

HIKING
Monterey Bay Coastal Recreation Trail

HIKING/WALKING | From Custom House Plaza, you can walk along the coast in either direction on this 29-mile-long trail and take in spectacular views of the sea. The trail runs from north of Monterey in Castroville south to Pacific Grove, with sections continuing around Pebble Beach. Much of the path follows an old Southern Pacific Railroad route. ☎ *888/221–1010* ⊕ *seemonterey.com/things-to-do/parks/coastal-trail.*

KAYAKING

★ Monterey Bay Kayaks

KAYAKING | For many visitors the best way to see the bay is by kayak. This company rents equipment and conducts classes and natural-history tours. ⊠ *693 Del Monte Ave.* ☏ *831/373–5357* ⊕ *www. montereybaykayaks.com.*

WHALE-WATCHING

Thousands of gray whales pass close by the Monterey Coast on their annual migration between the Bering Sea and Baja California, and a whale-watching cruise is the best way to see these magnificent mammals close up. The migration south takes place from December through March; January is prime viewing time. The whales migrate north from March through June. Blue whales and humpbacks also pass the coast; they're most easily spotted in late summer and early fall.

Fast Raft Ocean Safaris

TOUR—SPORTS | Naturalists lead whale-watching and sightseeing tours of Monterey Bay aboard the 33-foot *Ranger,* a six-passenger, rigid-hull, inflatable boat. The speedy craft slips into coves inaccessible to larger vessels, and its quiet engines enable intimate marine experiences without disturbing wildlife. Children ages eight and older are welcome to participate. From April to November, the boat departs from Moss Landing Harbor North Boat Launching Ramp. ⊠ *32 Cannery Row, Suite F2* ☏ *408/659–3900* ⊕ *www.fastraft.com* ⊠ *From $185.*

Monterey Bay Whale Watch

WHALE-WATCHING | The marine biologists here lead three- to five-hour whale-watching tours. ⊠ *84 Fisherman's Wharf* ☏ *831/375–4658* ⊕ *montereybaywhalewatch.com.*

Princess Monterey Whale Watching

WHALE-WATCHING | Tours are offered daily on a 100-passenger high-speed cruiser and a large 100-foot boat. ⊠ *96 Fisherman's Wharf* ☏ *831/372–2203* ⊕ *montereywhalewatching.com.*

Salinas

17 miles east of Monterey on Hwy. 68.

Salinas, a hardworking city surrounded by vineyards and fruit and vegetable fields, honors the memory and literary legacy of John Steinbeck, its most famous native, with the National Steinbeck Center. The facility is in Old Town Salinas, where renovated turn-of-the-20th-century stone buildings house shops and restaurants.

ESSENTIALS

VISITOR INFORMATION California Welcome Center. ⊠ *1213 N. Davis Rd.* ☏ *831/757–8687* ⊕ *www.visitcalifornia. com.*

Sights

Monterey Zoo

ZOO | **FAMILY** | Exotic animals, many of them retired from film, television, and live production work or rescued from less-than-ideal environments, find sanctuary here. The zoo offers daily tours (1 pm and 3 pm June–August, 1 pm September–May), but for an in-depth experience, stay in a safari bungalow on-site at Vision Quest Safari B&B, where guests can join the elephants in their enclosures for breakfast. The inn's room rate includes a complimentary zoo tour. ⊠ *400 River Rd.* ☏ *831/455–1901* ⊕ *www.montereyzoo. com* ⊠ *$35.*

★ National Steinbeck Center

MUSEUM | The center's exhibits document the life of Pulitzer- and Nobel-prize winner John Steinbeck and the history of the nearby communities that inspired novels such as *East of Eden.* Highlights include reproductions of the green pickup-camper from *Travels with Charley* and the bunk room from *Of Mice and Men.*
Steinbeck House, the author's Victorian birthplace, at 132 Central Avenue, is two blocks from the center. Now a popular (lunch-only) restaurant and gift shop with docent-led tours, it displays memorabilia.

✉ *1 Main St.* ☎ *831/775–4721* ⊕ *www. steinbeck.org* 🖾 *$15.*

San Juan Bautista State Historic Park
HISTORIC SITE | With the low-slung, colonnaded **Mission San Juan Bautista** as its drawing card, this park 20 miles northeast of Salinas is about as close to early-19th-century California as you can get. Historic buildings ring the wide green plaza, among them an adobe home furnished with Spanish-colonial antiques, a hotel frozen in the 1860s, a blacksmith shop, a pioneer cabin, and a jailhouse. The mission's cemetery contains the unmarked graves of more than 4,300 Native American converts. ■TIP➔ On **the first Saturday of the month, costumed volunteers engage in quilting bees, tortilla making, and other frontier activities, and sarsaparilla and other nonalcoholic drinks are served in the saloon.** ✉ *19 Franklin St., San Juan Bautista* ☎ *831/623–4881* ⊕ *www.parks.ca.gov* 🖾 *$3 park, $4 mission.*

Pinnacles National Park

38 miles southeast of Salinas.

It was Teddy Roosevelt who recognized the uniqueness of this ancient volcano—its jagged spires and monoliths thrusting upward from chaparral-covered mountains—when he made it a national monument in 1908. Though only about two hours from the bustling Bay Area, the outside world seems to recede even before you reach the park's gates.

GETTING HERE AND AROUND
One of the first things you need to decide when visiting Pinnacles is which entrance—east or west—you'll use, because there's no road connecting the two rugged peaks separating them. Entering from Highway 25 on the east is straightforward. The gate is only a mile or so from the turnoff. From the west, once you head east out of Soledad on Highway 146, the road quickly becomes narrow and hilly, with many blind curves. Drive slowly and cautiously along the 10 miles or so before you reach the west entrance.

ESSENTIALS
VISITOR INFORMATION
Pinnacles Visitor Center
INFO CENTER | At the park's main visitor center, near the eastern entrance, you'll find a helpful selection of maps, books, and gifts. The adjacent campground store sells light snacks. ✉ *5000 Hwy. 146, Paicines* ☎ *831/389–4485* ⊕ *www.nps.gov/pinn.*

West Pinnacles Visitor Contact Station
INFO CENTER | This small ranger station is just past the park's western entrance, about 10 miles east of Soledad. Here you can get maps and information, watch a 13-minute film about Pinnacles, and view interpretive exhibits. No food or drink is available here. ✉ *Hwy. 146, Soledad* ☎ *831/389–4427* ⊕ *www.nps.gov/pinn.*

Sights

Pinnacles National Park
NATIONAL/STATE PARK | FAMILY | The many attractions at Pinnacles include talus caves, 30 miles of hiking trails, and hundreds of rock-climbing routes. A mosaic of diverse habitats supports an amazing variety of wildlife species: 160 birds, 48 mammals, 70 butterflies, and nearly 400 bees. The park is also home to some of the world's remaining few hundred condors in captivity and release areas. Fourteen of California's 25 bat species live in caves and other habitats in the park. President Theodore Roosevelt declared this remarkable 26,000-acre geologic and wildlife preserve a national monument in 1908. President Barack Obama officially designated it a national park in 2013.

The pinnacles are believed to have been created when two major tectonic plates collided and pushed a smaller plate down beneath the earth's crust, spawning volcanoes in what's now called the Gabilan Mountains, southeast of Salinas and

Monterey. After the eruptions ceased, the San Andreas Fault split the volcanic field in two, carrying part of it northward to what is now Pinnacles National Park. Millions of years of erosion left a rugged landscape of rocky spires and crags, or pinnacles. Boulders fell into canyons and valleys, creating talus caves and a paradise for modern-day rock climbers. Spring is the most popular time to visit, when colorful wildflowers blanket the meadows; the light and scenery can be striking in fall and winter; the summer heat is often brutal. The park has two entrances—east and west—but they are not connected. The Pinnacles Visitor Center, Bear Gulch Nature Center, Park Headquarters, the Pinnacles Campground, and the Bear Gulch Cave and Reservoir are on the east side. The Chaparral Parking Area is on the west side, where you can feast on fantastic views of the Pinnacles High Peaks from the parking area. Dogs are not allowed on hiking trails. ■ TIP→ **The east entrance is 32 miles southeast of Hollister via Highway 25. The west entrance is about 12 miles east of Soledad via Highway 146.** ⊠ *5000 Hwy. 146, Paicines* ☎ *831/389–4486* ⊕ *www. nps.gov/pinn* ⊠ *$30 per vehicle, $15 per visitor if biking or walking.*

Activities

HIKING

Hiking is the most popular activity at Pinnacles, with more than 30 miles of trails for every interest and level of fitness. Because there isn't a road through the park, hiking is also the only way to experience its interior, including the High Peaks, the talus caves, and the reservoir.

★ Balconies Cliffs–Cave Loop

TRAIL | FAMILY | Grab your flashlight before heading out from the Chaparral Trailhead parking lot for this 2.4-mile loop that takes you through the Balconies Caves. This trail is especially beautiful in spring, when wildflowers carpet the canyon floor. About 0.6 mile from the start of the

trail, turn left to begin ascending the Balconies Cliffs Trail, where you'll be rewarded with close-up views of Machete Ridge and other steep, vertical formations; you may run across rock climbers testing their skills before rounding the loop and descending back through the cave. *Easy– Moderate.* ⊠ *Pinnacles National Park* ⊹ *Trailhead: Chaparral Parking Area.*

★ Bear Gulch Cave–Moses Spring–Rim Trail Loop

TRAIL | FAMILY | Perhaps the most popular hike at Pinnacles, this relatively short (2.2-mile) loop trail is fun for kids and adults. It leads to the Bear Gulch cave system, and if your timing is right, you'll pass by several seasonal waterfalls inside the caves (flashlights are required). If it's been raining, check with a ranger, as the caves can flood. The upper side of the cave is usually closed in spring and early summer to protect the Townsend's big-ear bats and their pups. *Easy.* ⊹ *Trailhead: Bear Gulch Day Use Area.*

Moss Landing

12 miles north of Salinas.

Moss Landing is not much more than a couple of blocks of cafés and restaurants, art galleries, and studios, plus a busy fishing port, but therein lies its charm. It's a fine place to overnight or stop for a meal and get a dose of nature.

GETTING HERE AND AROUND

From Highway 1 north or south, exit at Moss Landing Road on the ocean side. MST buses serve Moss Landing.

TOURS

Elkhorn Slough Safari Nature Boat Tours

BOAT TOURS | This outfit's naturalists lead two-hour tours of Elkhorn Sough aboard a 27-foot pontoon boat. Reservations are required. ⊠ *Moss Landing Harbor* ☎ *831/633–5555* ⊕ *elkhornslough.com* ⊠ *$43.*

ESSENTIALS

VISITOR INFORMATION Moss Landing Chamber of Commerce. ☎ *831/633–4501* 🌐 *mosslandingchamber.com.*

Sights

Elkhorn Slough National Estuarine Research Reserve

NATURE PRESERVE | The reserve's 1,700 acres of tidal flats and salt marshes form a complex environment that supports some 300 species of birds. A walk along the meandering waterways and wetlands can reveal hawks, white-tailed kites, owls, herons, and egrets. Also living or visiting here are sea otters, sharks, rays, and many other animals. ✉ *1700 Elkhorn Rd., Watsonville* ☎ *831/728–2822* 🌐 *elkhornslough.org* 🕒 *Closed Mon. and Tues.*

Restaurants

Haute Enchilada

$$ | **SOUTH AMERICAN** | Part of a complex that includes art galleries and an events venue, the Haute adds bohemian character to the seafaring village of Moss Landing. The inventive Latin American–inspired dishes include shrimp and black corn enchiladas topped with a citrus cilantro cream sauce, and roasted *pasilla* chilies stuffed with mashed plantains and caramelized onions. **Known for:** extensive cocktail and wine list; many vegan and gluten-free options; artsy atmosphere. [$] *Average main: $26* ✉ *7902 Moss Landing Rd.* ☎ *831/633–5843* 🌐 *hauteenchilada.com* 🕒 *Closed Tues. and Wed.*

Phil's Fish Market & Eatery

$$ | **SEAFOOD** | Exquisitely fresh, simply prepared seafood (try the cioppino) is on the menu at this warehouselike restaurant on the harbor; all kinds of glistening fish are for sale at the market in the front. **Known for:** cioppino; clam chowder; myriad artichoke dishes. [$] *Average main: $22* ✉ *7600 Sandholdt Rd.* ☎ *831/633–2152* 🌐 *philsfishmarket.com.*

Hotels

Captain's Inn

$$ | **B&B/INN** | Commune with nature and pamper yourself with upscale creature comforts at this green-certified complex in the heart of town. **Pros:** walk to restaurants and shops; tranquil natural setting; closest Monterey Bay hotel to Pinnacles National Park. **Cons:** rooms in historic building don't have water views; far from urban amenities; not appropriate for young children. [$] *Rooms from: $189* ✉ *8122 Moss Landing Rd.* ☎ *831/633–5550* 🌐 *www.captainsinn.com* 🛏 *10 rooms* 🍴 *Free breakfast.*

Activities

KAYAKING

Monterey Bay Kayaks

KAYAKING | Rent a kayak to paddle out into Elkhorn Slough for up-close wildlife encounters. ✉ *2390 Hwy. 1, at North Harbor* ☎ *831/373–5357* 🌐 *montereybaykayaks.com.*

Aptos

17 miles north of Moss Landing.

Backed by a redwood forest and facing the sea, downtown Aptos—known as Aptos Village—is a place of wooden walkways and false-fronted shops. Antiques dealers cluster along Trout Gulch Road, off Soquel Drive east of Highway 1.

GETTING HERE AND AROUND

Use Highway 1 to reach Aptos from Santa Cruz or Monterey. Exit at State Park Drive to reach the main shopping hub and Aptos Village. You can also exit at Freedom Boulevard or Rio del Mar. Soquel Drive is the main artery through town.

ESSENTIALS

VISITOR INFORMATION Aptos Chamber of Commerce. ✉ *7605–A Old Dominion Ct.* ☎ *831/688–1467* 🌐 *aptoschamber.com.*

Beaches

★ Seacliff State Beach

BEACH—SIGHT | FAMILY | Sandstone bluffs tower above this popular beach with a long fishing pier. The 1.5-mile walk north to adjacent New Brighton State Beach in Capitola is one of the nicest on the bay. Leashed dogs are allowed on the beach. **Amenities:** food and drink; lifeguards; parking (fee); showers; toilets. **Best for:** sunset; swimming; walking. ⊠ *201 State Park Dr.* ☎ *831/685–6500* ⊕ *www.parks. ca.gov* ⊠ *$10 per vehicle.*

 Restaurants

Bittersweet Bistro

$$$ | MEDITERRANEAN | A large old tavern with cathedral ceilings houses this popular bistro, where the Mediterranean–California menu changes seasonally, but regular highlights include paella, seafood puttanesca, and pepper-crusted rib-eye steak with Cabernet demi-glace. **Known for:** value-laden happy hour; seafood specials; house-made desserts. $ *Average main: $29* ⊠ *787 Rio Del Mar Blvd., off Hwy. 1* ☎ *831/662–9799* ⊕ *www.bittersweetbistro.com* ☉ *Closed Mon. and Tues.*

Hotels

Seascape Beach Resort

$$$$ | RESORT | FAMILY | It's easy to unwind at this full-fledged resort on a bluff overlooking Monterey Bay. The spacious suites sleep from two to eight people. **Pros:** time share–style apartments; access to miles of beachfront; superb views. **Cons:** far from city life; most bathrooms are small; some rooms need updating. $ *Rooms from: $387* ⊠ *1 Seascape Resort Dr.* ☎ *831/662–7171, 866/867–0976* ⊕ *seascaperesort.com* ⇌ *285 suites* ⚫ *No meals.*

Capitola and Soquel

4 miles northwest of Aptos.

On the National Register of Historic places as California's first seaside resort town, the village of Capitola has been in a holiday mood since the late 1800s. Casual eateries, surf shops, and ice cream parlors pack its walkable downtown. Inland, across Highway 1, antiques shops line Soquel Drive in the town of Soquel. Wineries dot the Santa Cruz Mountains beyond.

GETTING HERE AND AROUND

From Santa Cruz or Monterey, follow Highway 1 to the Capitola/Soquel (Bay Avenue) exit about 7 miles south of Santa Cruz and head west to reach Capitola and east to access Soquel Village. On summer weekends, park for free in the lot behind the Crossroads Center, a block west of the freeway, and hop aboard the free Capitola Shuttle to the village.

ESSENTIALS

VISITOR INFORMATION Capitola-Soquel Chamber of Commerce. ⊠ *716-G Capitola Ave., Capitola* ☎ *831/475–6522* ⊕ *capitolachamber.com.*

Beaches

★ New Brighton State Beach

BEACH—SIGHT | FAMILY | Once the site of a Chinese fishing village, New Brighton is now a popular surfing and camping spot. Its Pacific Migrations Visitor Center traces the history of the Chinese and other peoples who settled around Monterey Bay. It also documents the migratory patterns of the area's wildlife, such as monarch butterflies and gray whales. Leashed dogs are allowed in the park. New Brighton connects with Seacliff Beach, and at low tide you can walk or run along this scenic stretch of sand for nearly 16 miles south (though you might have to wade through a few creeks). ■ **TIP→ The 1½-mile stroll from**

New Brighton to Seacliff's concrete ship is a local favorite. Amenities: parking (fee); showers; toilets. **Best for:** sunset; swimming; walking. ✉ *1500 State Park Dr., off Hwy. 1, Capitola* ☎ *831/464–6329* 🌐 *www.parks.ca.gov* 🎟 *$10 per vehicle.*

🍴 Restaurants

Carpo's

$ | **SEAFOOD** | **FAMILY** | Locals love this casual counter where seafood predominates, but you can also order burgers, salads, and steaks. Baskets of battered snapper are among the favorites, along with calamari, prawns, seafood kebabs, fish-and-chips, and homemade olallieberry pie. **Known for:** large portions of healthy comfort food; lots of options under $12; soup and salad bar. [$] *Average main: $14* ✉ *2400 Porter St., at Hwy. 1, Soquel* ☎ *831/476–6260* 🌐 *carposrestaurant.com.*

Gayle's Bakery & Rosticceria

$$ | **CAFÉ** | **FAMILY** | Whether you're in the mood for an orange-olallieberry muffin, a wild rice and chicken salad, or tri-tip on garlic toast, this bakery-deli's varied menu is likely to satisfy. Munch on your lemon meringue tartlet or chocolate brownie on the shady patio, or dig into the daily blue-plate dinner—teriyaki grilled skirt steak with edamame–shiitake sticky rice, perhaps, or roast turkey breast with Chardonnay gravy—amid the whirl of activity inside. **Known for:** prepared meals to go; on-site bakery and rosticceria; deli and espresso bar. [$] *Average main: $17* ✉ *504 Bay Ave., Capitola* ☎ *831/462–1200* 🌐 *www.gaylesbakery.com.*

Shadowbrook

$$$$ | **EUROPEAN** | To get to this romantic spot overlooking Soquel Creek, you can take a cable car or walk the stairs down a steep, fern-lined bank beside a running waterfall. Dining room options include the rooftop Redwood Room, the wood-paneled Wine Cellar, the creek-side, glass-enclosed Greenhouse, the Fireplace Room, and the airy Garden Room. **Known for:** romantic creek-side setting; prime rib and grilled seafood; local special-occasion favorite for nearly 70 years. [$] *Average main: $36* ✉ *1750 Wharf Rd., at Lincoln Ave., Capitola* ☎ *831/475–1511* 🌐 *www.shadowbrook-capitola.com.*

California's Oldest Resort Town

As far as anyone knows for certain, Capitola is the Pacific coast's oldest seaside resort town. In 1856, a pioneer acquired Soquel Landing, the picturesque lagoon and beach where Soquel Creek empties into the bay, and built a wharf. Another man opened a campground along the shore, and his daughter named it Capitola after a heroine in a novel series. After the train came to town in the 1870s, thousands of vacationers began arriving to bask in the sun on the glorious beach.

🛏 Hotels

Inn at Depot Hill

$$$ | **B&B/INN** | This inventively designed B&B in a former rail depot views itself as a link to the era of luxury train travel. **Pros:** short walk to beach and village; historic charm; excellent service. **Cons:** fills quickly; hot-tub conversation audible in some rooms; rooms need updating. [$] *Rooms from: $309* ✉ *250 Monterey Ave., Capitola* ☎ *831/462–3376, 800/572–2632* 🌐 *www.innatdepothill.com* 🛏 *13 rooms* 🍴 *Free breakfast.*

Santa Cruz

5 miles west of Capitola, 48 miles north of Monterey.

The big city on this stretch of the California coast, Santa Cruz (pop. 63,364) is less manicured than Carmel or Monterey. Long known for its surfing and its amusement-filled beach boardwalk, the town is an eclectic mix of grand Victorian-era homes, beachside inns, and multimillion dollar compounds owned by tech gurus. The opening of the University of California campus in the 1960s swung the town sharply to the left politically, and the counterculture more or less lives on here. At the same time, a revitalized downtown and an insane real-estate market reflect the city's proximity to Silicon Valley, which is just a 30-minute drive to the north, and to a growing wine region in the surrounding mountains.

Amble around downtown's Santa Cruz Farmers' Market (Wednesday afternoons year-round) to experience the local culture, which derives much of its character from close connections to food and farming. The market covers a city block and includes not just the expected organic produce, but also live music and booths with local crafts and prepared food.

GETTING HERE AND AROUND
From the San Francisco Bay area, take Highway 17 south over the mountains to Santa Cruz, where it merges with Highway 1. Use Highway 1 to get around the area. The Santa Cruz Transit Center is at 920 Pacific Avenue, at Front Street, a short walk from the wharf and boardwalk, with connections to public transit throughout the Monterey Bay and San Francisco Bay areas. You can purchase day passes for Santa Cruz METRO buses here.

ESSENTIALS
VISITOR INFORMATION Visit Santa Cruz County. ⊠ *303 Water St., Suite 100* ☎ *831/425–1234, 800/833–3494* ⊕ *www. visitsantacruz.org.*

Sights

Monterey Bay National Marine Sanctuary Exploration Center
INFO CENTER | FAMILY | The interactive and multimedia exhibits at this fascinating interpretive center reveal and explain the treasures of the nation's largest marine sanctuary. The two-story building, across from the main beach and municipal wharf, has films and exhibits about migratory species, watersheds, underwater canyons, kelp forests, and intertidal zones. The second-floor deck has stellar ocean views and an interactive station that provides real-time weather, surf, and buoy reports. ⊠ *35 Pacific Ave., near Beach St.* ☎ *831/421–9993* ⊕ *montereybay.noaa.gov/vc/sec* ⊠ *Free* ⊗ *Closed Mon. and Tues.*

Mystery Spot
LOCAL INTEREST | Hokey tourist trap or genuine scientific enigma? Since 1940, curious throngs baffled by the Mystery Spot have made it one of the most visited attractions in Santa Cruz. The laws of gravity and physics don't appear to apply in this tiny patch of redwood forest, where balls roll uphill and people stand on a slant. ■**TIP→ On weekends and holidays, it's wise to purchase tickets online in advance.** ⊠ *465 Mystery Spot Rd., off Branciforte Dr. (north off Hwy. 1)* ☎ *831/423–8897* ⊕ *mysteryspot.com* ⊠ *$8, parking $5.*

Pacific Avenue
NEIGHBORHOOD | When you've had your fill of the city's beaches and waters, take a stroll in downtown Santa Cruz, especially on Pacific Avenue between Laurel and Water streets. Vintage boutiques and mountain-sports stores, sushi bars, and Mexican restaurants, day spas, and nightclubs keep the main drag and the surrounding streets hopping from midmorning until late evening.

★ Santa Cruz Beach Boardwalk

CAROUSEL | FAMILY | Santa Cruz has been a seaside resort since the mid-19th century. Along one end of the broad, south-facing beach, the boardwalk has entertained holidaymakers for more than a century. Its Looff carousel and classic wooden Giant Dipper roller coaster, both dating from the early 1900s, are surrounded by high-tech thrill rides and easygoing kiddie rides with ocean views. Video and arcade games, a minigolf course, and a laser-tag arena pack one gigantic building, which is open daily even if the rides aren't running. You have to pay to play, but you can wander the entire boardwalk for free while sampling carnival fare such as corn dogs and garlic fries. ⊠ *Along Beach St.* ☎ *831/423–5590 info line* ⊕ *beachboardwalk.com* ⊡ *$40 day pass for unlimited rides, or pay per ride* ⊙ *Some rides closed Sept.–May.*

Santa Cruz Municipal Wharf

MARINA | FAMILY | Jutting half a mile into the ocean near one end of the boardwalk, the century-old Municipal Wharf is lined with seafood restaurants, a wine bar, souvenir shops, and outfitters offering bay cruises, fishing trips, and boat rentals. A salty soundtrack drifts up from under the wharf, where barking sea lions lounge in heaps on the crossbeams. ⊠ *Beach St. and Pacific Ave.* ☎ *831/459–3800* ⊕ *www.santacruzwharf.com.*

Santa Cruz Surfing Museum

MUSEUM | This museum inside the Mark Abbott Memorial Lighthouse chronicles local surfing history. Photographs show old-time surfers, and a display of boards includes rarities such as a heavy redwood plank predating the fiberglass era and the remains of a modern board chomped by a great white shark. Surfer docents reminisce about the good old days. ⊠ *Lighthouse Point Park, 701 W. Cliff Dr. near Pelton Ave.* ☎ *831/420–6289* ⊡ *$2 suggested donation* ⊙ *Closed Tues. and Wed. except open Tues. July–early Sept.*

Seymour Marine Discovery Center

ZOO | FAMILY | Part of the Long Marine Laboratory at the University of California Santa Cruz's Institute of Marine Sciences, the center looks more like a research facility than a slick aquarium. Interactive exhibits demonstrate how scientists study the ocean, and the aquarium displays creatures of interest to marine biologists. The 87-foot blue whale skeleton is one of the world's largest. ■TIP➔ **General tours take place in the afternoon, and there's an abbreviated tour at 11 am for families with small children.** ⊠ *100 Shaffer Rd., end of Delaware Ave., west of Natural Bridges State Beach* ☎ *831/459–3800* ⊕ *seymourcenter.ucsc.edu* ⊡ *$10* ⊙ *Closed Mon.*

Surf City Vintners

WINERY/DISTILLERY | A dozen tasting rooms of limited-production wineries occupy renovated warehouse spaces west of the beach. MJA, Sones Cellars, Santa Cruz Mountain Vineyard, and Equinox are good places to start. Also here are the Santa Cruz Mountain Brewing Company and El Salchichero, popular for its homemade sausages, jams, and pickled and candied vegetables. ⊠ *Swift Street Courtyard, 334 Ingalls St., at Swift St., off Hwy. 1 (Mission St.)* ⊕ *surfcityvintners.com.*

UC Santa Cruz

COLLEGE | The 2,000-acre University of California Santa Cruz campus nestles in the forested hills above town. Its sylvan setting, ocean vistas, and redwood architecture make the university worth a visit, as does its **arboretum** ($5, open daily from 9 to 5), whose walking path leads through areas dedicated to the plants of California, Australia, New Zealand, and South Africa. ■TIP➔ **Free shuttles help students and visitors get around campus, and you can join a guided tour (online reservation required).** ⊠ *Main entrance at Bay and High Sts. (turn left on High for arboretum)* ☎ *831/459–0111* ⊕ *www.ucsc.edu/visit.*

★ West Cliff Drive

SCENIC DRIVE | The road that winds along an oceanfront bluff from the municipal wharf to Natural Bridges State Beach makes for a spectacular drive, but it's even more fun to walk or bike the paved path that parallels the road. Surfers bob and swoosh in Monterey Bay at several points near the foot of the bluff, especially at a break known as **Steamer Lane.** Named for a surfer who died here in 1965, the nearby Mark Abbott Memorial Lighthouse stands at Point Santa Cruz, the cliff's major promontory. From here you can watch pinnipeds hang out, sunbathe, and frolic on Seal Rock. ✉ *Santa Cruz.*

Wilder Ranch State Park

NATIONAL/STATE PARK | In this park's Cultural Preserve you can visit the homes, barns, workshops, and bunkhouse of a 19th-century dairy farm. Nature has reclaimed most of the ranch land, and native plants and wildlife have returned to the 7,000 acres of forest, grassland, canyons, estuaries, and beaches. Hike, bike, or ride horseback on miles of ocean-view trails. Dogs aren't allowed at Wilder Ranch. ✉ *Hwy. 1, 1 mile north of Santa Cruz* ☎ *831/426–0505 Interpretive Center, 831/423–9703 trail information* 🌐 *www.parks.ca.gov* 🎟 *$10 per car* ⏲ *Interpretive center closed Mon.–Wed.*

Beaches

Natural Bridges State Beach

BEACH—SIGHT | **FAMILY** | At the end of West Cliff Drive lies this stretch of soft sand edged with tide pools and sea-sculpted rock bridges. ■ **TIP→ From September to early January a colony of monarch butterflies roosts in the eucalyptus grove. Amenities:** lifeguards; parking (fee); toilets. **Best for:** sunrise; sunset; surfing; swimming. ✉ *2531 W. Cliff Dr.* ☎ *831/423–4609* 🌐 *www.parks.ca.gov* 🎟 *Beach free, parking $10.*

Twin Lakes State Beach

BEACH—SIGHT | **FAMILY** | Stretching a half mile along the coast on both sides of the small-craft jetties, Twin Lakes is one of Monterey Bay's sunniest beaches. It encompasses Seabright State Beach (with access in a residential neighborhood on the upcoast side) and Black's Beach on the downcoast side. Families often come here to sunbathe, picnic, and hike the nature trail around adjacent Schwann Lake. Parking is tricky from May through September—you need to pay for an $8 day-use permit at a kiosk and the lot fills quickly—but you can park all day in the harbor pay lot and walk here. Leashed dogs are allowed. **Amenities:** food and drink; lifeguards (seasonal); parking; showers; toilets; water sports (seasonal). **Best for:** sunset; surfing; swimming; walking. ✉ *7th Ave., at East Cliff Dr.* ☎ *831/427–4868* 🌐 *www.parks.ca.gov.*

🍴 Restaurants

Crow's Nest

$$$ | **SEAFOOD** | **FAMILY** | Vintage surfboards and local surf photography line the walls and nearly every table overlooks sand and surf at this restaurant on the Santa Cruz Harbor. For sweeping ocean views and fish tacos, burgers, and other casual fare, head upstairs to the Breakwater Bar & Grill. **Known for:** house-smoked salmon and calamari apps; crab-cake eggs Benedict and olallieberry pancakes; on-site market with pizzas, sandwiches, soups, and salads. [$] *Average main: $27* ✉ *2218 E. Cliff Dr., west of 7th Ave.* ☎ *831/476–4560* 🌐 *crowsnest-santacruz.com.*

★ Laili Restaurant

$$ | **MEDITERRANEAN** | Exotic Mediterranean flavors with an Afghan twist take center stage at this artsy, stylish space with soaring ceilings. In the evening, locals come to relax over wine and soft jazz at the blue-concrete bar, on the heated patio with twinkly lights, or at a communal table near the open kitchen.

Known for: house-made pastas and numerous vegetarian and vegan options; fresh naan, chutneys, and dips with every meal; traditional dishes like pomegranate eggplant and maushawa soup. [$] *Average main: $24* ✉ *101–B Cooper St., near Pacific Ave.* ☎ *831/423–4545* 🌐 *lailirestaurant.com.*

La Posta Via

$$ | ITALIAN | Authentic Italian fare made with fresh local produce lures diners into cozy, modern-rustic La Posta. Nearly everything is made in-house, from the pizzas and breads baked in the brick oven to the pasta and the vanilla-bean gelato. **Known for:** seasonal wild-nettle lasagna; braised lamb shank; in the heart of the Seabright neighborhood. [$] *Average main: $24* ✉ *538 Seabright Ave., at Logan St.* ☎ *831/457–2782* 🌐 *lapostarestaurant.com* 🕒 *Closed Mon. No lunch.*

Oswald

$$$$ | EUROPEAN | Sophisticated yet unpretentious European-inspired California cooking is the order of the day at this intimate and stylish bistro with a seasonal menu, which might include such items as seafood risotto or crispy duck breast in a pomegranate reduction sauce. The creative concoctions poured at the slick marble bar include whiskey mixed with apple and lemon juice, and tequila with celery juice and lime. **Known for:** house-made pork sausage; craft cocktails; local art displays that change monthly. [$] *Average main: $34* ✉ *121 Soquel Ave., at Front St.* ☎ *831/423–7427* 🌐 *oswaldrestaurant.com* 🕒 *Closed Sun.–Tues.*

★ Soif

$$$ | MEDITERRANEAN | Wine reigns at this sleek bistro and wineshop that takes its name from the French word for thirst—the selections come from near and far, and you can order many of them by the taste or glass. Mediterranean-inspired small plates and entrées are served at the copper-top bar, the big communal table, and private tables. **Known for:** Mediterranean-style dishes; diverse, interesting wine selection; jazz combo or solo pianist plays on some evenings. [$] *Average main: $27* ✉ *105 Walnut Ave.* ☎ *831/423–2020* 🌐 *www.soifwine.com* 🕒 *Closed Mon. and Tues. No lunch.*

Zachary's

$ | AMERICAN | This noisy café filled with students and families defines the funky essence of Santa Cruz. It also dishes up great breakfasts: stay simple with sourdough pancakes, or go for Mike's Mess—eggs scrambled with bacon, mushrooms, and home fries, then topped with sour cream, melted cheese, and fresh tomatoes. **Known for:** nearly everything made in-house; "Mike's Mess" egg dishes; local organic ingredients. [$] *Average main: $15* ✉ *819 Pacific Ave.* ☎ *831/427–0646* 🌐 *www.zacharyssantacruz.com* 🕒 *Closed Mon. No dinner.*

🛏 Hotels

Babbling Brook Inn

$$$ | B&B/INN | Though it's in the middle of Santa Cruz, this B&B has lush gardens, a running stream, and tall trees that make you feel like you're in a secluded wood. **Pros:** close to UCSC; within walking distance of downtown shops; woodsy feel. **Cons:** near a high school; some rooms close to a busy street; many stairs and no elevator. [$] *Rooms from: $280* ✉ *1025 Laurel St.* ☎ *831/427–2437, 800/866–1131* 🌐 *babblingbrookinn.com* 🛏 *13 rooms* 🍴 *Free breakfast.*

Carousel Beach Inn

$$ | HOTEL | This basic but comfy motel, decorated in bold, retro, seaside style and across the street from the boardwalk, is ideal for travelers who want easy access to the sand and the amusement park rides without spending a fortune. **Pros:** steps from Santa Cruz Main Beach; affordable lodging rates and ride packages; free parking and Wi-Fi. **Cons:** no pool or spa; no exercise room; not pet-friendly. [$] *Rooms from: $159* ✉ *110 Riverside Ave.* ☎ *831/425–7090*

🌐 *carousel-beach-inn.com* 🛏 *34 rooms* 🍴 *Free breakfast.*

★ Chaminade Resort & Spa

$$$ | **RESORT** | **FAMILY** | Secluded on 300 hilltop acres of redwood and eucalyptus forest laced with hiking trails, this Mission-style complex also features a lovely terrace restaurant with expansive views of Monterey Bay. Guest rooms are furnished in an eclectic, bohemian style that pays homage to the artsy local community and the city's industrial past. **Pros:** peaceful, verdant setting; full-service spa and large pool; ideal spot for romance and rejuvenation. **Cons:** not within walking distance of downtown; not near the ocean; resort fee. [$] *Rooms from: $279* ✉ *1 Chaminade La.* ☎ *800/283–6569, 831/475–5600* 🌐 *www.chaminade.com* 🛏 *156 rooms* 🍴 *No meals.*

Dream Inn Santa Cruz

$$$$ | **HOTEL** | A short stroll from the boardwalk and wharf, this full-service luxury hotel is the only lodging in Santa Cruz directly on the beach, and its rooms all have private balconies or patios overlooking Monterey Bay. Accommodations have contemporary furnishings, bold colors, and upscale linens, but the main draw here is having the ocean at your doorstep. **Pros:** restaurant with sweeping views of Monterey Bay; cool mid-century modern design; walk to boardwalk and downtown. **Cons:** expensive; area gets congested on summer weekends; pool area and hallways can be noisy. [$] *Rooms from: $324* ✉ *175 W. Cliff Dr.* ☎ *831/740–8069* 🌐 *www.dreaminnsantacruz.com* 🛏 *165 rooms* 🍴 *No meals.*

Hotel Paradox

$$$ | **HOTEL** | About a mile from the ocean and two blocks from Pacific Avenue, this stylish, forest-theme complex (part of the Marriott Autograph Collection) is among the few full-service hotels in town. **Pros:** close to downtown and main beach; spacious pool area with cabanas, firepits, hot tub, and dining and cocktail service; on-site farm-to-table restaurant. **Cons:** pool area can get crowded on warm-weather days; some rooms on the small side; thin walls. [$] *Rooms from: $279* ✉ *611 Ocean St.* ☎ *831/425–7100, 855/425–7200* 🌐 *hotelparadox.com* 🛏 *172 rooms* 🍴 *No meals.*

Hyatt Place Santa Cruz

$$ | **HOTEL** | Vintage surfboards and local art grace the walls of the spacious, ocean-theme lobby at this downtown hotel. **Pros:** close to restaurants and shops; outdoor pool and hot tub and 24-hour fitness center; on-site restaurant and bar. **Cons:** not on the beach; valet parking only; fronts busy road. [$] *Rooms from: $219* ✉ *407 Broadway* ☎ *831/226–2304* 🌐 *hyattplace.com* 🛏 *106 rooms* 🍴 *No meals.*

Pacific Blue Inn

$$ | **B&B/INN** | Green themes predominate in this three-story, eco-friendly inn on a sliver of prime downtown real estate. **Pros:** free parking; free bicycles; downtown location. **Cons:** tiny property; not suitable for children; parking lot is a block away. [$] *Rooms from: $189* ✉ *636 Pacific Ave.* ☎ *831/600–8880* 🌐 *pacificblueinn.com* 🛏 *9 rooms* 🍴 *No meals.*

Sea & Sand Inn

$$ | **HOTEL** | Location is the main appeal of this motel atop a waterfront bluff, where all rooms have an ocean view and the boardwalk is just down the street. **Pros:** beach is steps away; friendly staff; tidy landscaping. **Cons:** tight parking lot; fronts a busy road; can be noisy. [$] *Rooms from: $249* ✉ *201 W. Cliff Dr.* ☎ *831/427–3400* 🌐 *seaandsandinn.com* 🛏 *22 units* 🍴 *Free breakfast.*

★ West Cliff Inn

$$$ | **B&B/INN** | On bluffs across from Cowell Beach, this three-story, Italianate property, built in 1877, exudes classic California beach style. **Pros:** killer bay and boardwalk views; walking distance of the beach; close to downtown. **Cons:** boardwalk noise; street traffic. [$] *Rooms from: $299* ✉ *174 West Cliff Dr.*

☎ *831/457–2200* ⊕ *www.westcliffinn. com* ⇄ *9 units* ⦿ *Free breakfast.*

Nightlife

Catalyst
DANCE CLUBS | This huge, grimy, and fun club books rock, indie rock, punk, death-metal, reggae, and other acts. ✉ *1011 Pacific Ave.* ☎ *877/987–6487* ⊕ *catalystclub.com.*

Kuumbwa Jazz Center
MUSIC CLUBS | The center draws top performers such as Lee Ritenour, Chris Potter, and the Dave Holland Trio. A café serves meals an hour before most shows. ✉ *320–2 Cedar St.* ☎ *831/427–2227* ⊕ *kuumbwajazz.org.*

Moe's Alley
MUSIC CLUBS | Blues, salsa, reggae, funk: delightfully casual Moe's presents it all (and more). ✉ *1535 Commercial Way* ☎ *831/479–1854* ⊕ *moesalley.com* ⊘ *Closed Mon.*

🎬 Performing Arts

Tannery Arts Center
ARTS CENTERS | The former Salz Tannery now contains nearly 30 studios and live-work spaces for artists whose disciplines range from ceramics and glass to film and digital media; most have public hours of operation. Performances also take place at the on-site Colligan Theater, and the center hosts assorted arts events on weekends and, occasionally, on week-days. ✉ *1060 River St., at intersection of Hwys. 1 and 9* ⊕ *tanneryartscenter.org.*

💼 Shopping

Bookshop Santa Cruz
BOOKS/STATIONERY | In 2021, the town's best and most beloved independent bookstore celebrated its 55th anniversary of selling new, used, and remaindered titles. The children's section is especially comprehensive, and the shop's special events calendar is packed with readings, social mixers, book signings, and discussions. ✉ *1520 Pacific Ave.* ☎ *831/423–0900* ⊕ *bookshopsantacruz.com.*

O'Neill Surf Shop
SPORTING GOODS | Local surfers get their wetties (wet suits) and other gear at this O'Neill store or the one in Capitola, at 1115 41st Avenue. There's also a satellite shop on the Santa Cruz Boardwalk. ✉ *110 Cooper St.* ☎ *831/469–4377* ⊕ *www. oneill.com.*

Santa Cruz Downtown Farmers' Market
OUTDOOR/FLEA/GREEN MARKETS | **FAMILY** Santa Cruz is famous for its long tradition of organic growing and sustainable living, and its downtown market (one of five countywide) reflects the incredible diversity and quality of local agriculture and the synergistic daily life of commu-nity-minded residents. The busy market, which always has live music, happens every Wednesday from 1 to 6, rain or shine. The stalls cover much of an entire city block near Pacific Avenue and include fresh produce plus everything from oysters, beer, bread, and charcuterie to arts and crafts to prepared foods made from ingredients sourced from on-site vendors. ✉ *Cedar St. at Lincoln St.* ☎ *831/454–0566* ⊕ *www.santacruzfarm-ersmarket.org.*

🏃 Activities

BICYCLING
Another Bike Shop
BICYCLING | Mountain bikers should head here for tips on the best area trails and to browse cutting-edge gear made and test-ed locally. ✉ *2361 Mission St., at King St.* ☎ *831/427–2232* ⊕ *www.anotherbike-shop.com.*

BOATS AND CHARTERS
Chardonnay II Sailing Charters
BOATING | The 70-foot *Chardonnay II* departs year-round from Santa Cruz yacht harbor on whale-watching, sunset, and other cruises around Monterey Bay. Most

O'Neill: A Santa Cruz Icon

O'Neill wet suits and beachwear weren't exactly born in Santa Cruz, but as far as most of the world is concerned, the O'Neill brand is synonymous with Santa Cruz and surfing legend.

The O'Neill wet-suit story began in 1952, when Jack O'Neill and his brother, Robert, opened their first surf shop in a garage across from San Francisco's Ocean Beach. While shaping balsa surfboards and selling accessories, the O'Neills experimented with solutions to a common surfer problem: frigid waters. Tired of being forced back to shore, blue-lipped and shivering after just 20 or 30 minutes riding the waves, they played with various materials and eventually designed a neoprene vest.

In 1959, Jack moved his shop 90 miles south to Cowell's Beach in Santa Cruz. It quickly became a popular surf hangout, and O'Neill's new wet suits began to sell like hotcakes. In the early 1960s, the company opened a warehouse for manufacturing on a larger scale. Santa Cruz soon became a major surf city, attracting wave riders to prime breaks at Steamer Lane, Pleasure Point, and the Hook. In 1965, O'Neill pioneered the first wet-suit boots, and, in 1971, Jack's son invented the surf leash. By 1980, O'Neill stood at the top of the world wet-suit market. On June 2, 2017, Jack O'Neill passed away at the age of 94, in his longtime Pleasure Point residence overlooking the surf.

12

Monterey Bay Area SANTA CRUZ

regularly scheduled excursions cost $70; food and drink are served on many of them. Reservations are essential. ✉ *Santa Cruz West Harbor, 790 Mariner Park Way* ☎ *831/423–1213* ⊕ *chardonnay.com.*

Stagnaro Sport Fishing, Charters & Whale Watching Cruises

BOATING | Stagnaro (aka Santa Cruz Whale Watching) offers salmon, albacore, and rock-cod fishing expeditions (fees include bait) as well as whale-watching, dolphin, and sea-life cruises year-round. ✉ *1718 Brommer St., near Santa Cruz Harbor* ☎ *831/427–0230* ⊕ *stagnaros.com* ✆ *From $61.*

GOLF

DeLaveaga Golf Course

GOLF | Woodsy DeLaveaga, a public course set in a hilly park, overlooks Santa Cruz and the bay. With its canyons, tree-lined fairways, and notoriously difficult par-5, dogleg 10th hole, the course challenges novices and seasoned golfers. ✉ *401 Upper Park Rd.* ☎ *831/423–7214* ⊕ *www.delaveagagolf.com* ✆ *$60 weekdays, $80 weekends/holidays* 🏌 *18 holes, 5700 yards, par 70.*

Pasatiempo Golf Club

GOLF | Designed by famed golf architect Dr. Alister MacKenzie in 1929, this semiprivate course, set amid undulating hills just above the city, is among the nation's top championship courses. Golfers rave about the spectacular views and challenging terrain. According to the club, MacKenzie, who designed Pebble Beach's exclusive Cypress Point course and Augusta National in Georgia, the home of the Masters Golf Tournament, declared this his favorite layout. ✉ *20 Clubhouse Rd.* ☎ *831/459–9155* ⊕ *www. pasatiempo.com* ✆ *From $325* 🏌 *18 holes, 6125 yards, par 72.*

KAYAKING
Kayak Connection
KAYAKING | From March through May, participants in this outfit's tours mingle with gray whales and their calves on their northward journey to Alaska. Throughout the year, the company rents kayaks and paddleboards and conducts tours of Natural Bridges State Beach, Capitola, and Elkhorn Slough. ✉ *Santa Cruz Harbor, 413 Lake Ave., No. 3* ☎ *831/479–1121* ⊕ *kayakconnection.com* 🖃 *From $65 for scheduled tours.*

Venture Quest Kayaking
KAYAKING | Explore hidden coves and kelp forests on guided two-hour kayak tours that depart from Santa Cruz Wharf. The tours include a kayaking lesson. Venture Quest also rents kayaks (and wet suits and gear), and arranges tours at other Monterey Bay destinations, including Elkhorn Slough. ✉ *2 Santa Cruz Wharf* ☎ *831/427–2267 kayak hotline, 831/425–8445 rental office* ⊕ *kayaksantacruz.com* 🖃 *From $35 for rentals, $60 for tours.*

SURFING
Club-Ed Surf School and Camps
SURFING | Find out what all the fun is about at Club-Ed. Your first private or group lesson ($100 and up) includes all equipment. ✉ *Cowell's Beach, at Dream Inn Santa Cruz* ☎ *831/464–0177* ⊕ *club-ed.com.*

Cowell's Surf Shop
SURFING | This shop sells gear, clothing, and swimwear; rents surfboards, stand-up paddleboards, and wet suits; and offers lessons. ✉ *30 Front St.* ☎ *831/427–2355* ⊕ *www.facebook.com/cowellssurfshop.*

Richard Schmidt Surf School
SURFING | Since 1978, Richard Schmidt has shared the stoke of surfing and the importance of ocean awareness and conservation with legions of students of all ages. Today, the outfit offers surfing and stand-up paddleboard lessons (equipment provided) as well as marine adventure tours in Santa Cruz and elsewhere on the bay. Locations depend on where the waves are breaking or the wind's a'blowing, but outings typically convene at Cowell's Beach or Pleasure Point. ✉ *Santa Cruz* ☎ *831/423–0928* ⊕ *www.richardschmidt.com* 🖃 *From $100.*

ZIP-LINING
Mount Hermon Adventures
TOUR—SPORTS | Zip line through the redwoods at this adventure center in the Santa Cruz Mountains. On some summer weekends there's an aerial adventure course with obstacles and challenges in the redwoods. ■**TIP➔ To participate (reservations essential), you must be at least 10 years old and at least 54 inches tall, and weigh between 75 and 250 pounds.** ✉ *17 Conference Dr., 9 miles north of downtown Santa Cruz near Felton, Mount Hermon* ☎ *831/430–4357* ⊕ *mounthermonadventures.com* 🖃 *From $79.*

Index

428

Photo Credits

Front Cover: Ron Thomas/iStockphoto [Description: Beach and breaking surf of Laguna Beach, California. Flowers and palms fill the foreground.]. **Back cover, from left to right:** Valhalla/Design & Conquer, Kimberly Beck Rubio/iStockphoto, Salvador Ceja/Dreamstime. **Spine:** Ken Wolter/Shutterstock. **Interior, from left to right:** Daniel Sanchez/istockphoto (1). Frank DeBonis/istockphoto (2-3). Jose Angel Astor Rocha/Shutterstock (5). **Chapter 1: Experience Southern California:** Sean Xu/shutterstock (6-7). choness/istockphoto (8-9). Jill Krueger (9). Charlie Blacker/istockphoto (9). Brian Flaigmore/Dreamstime (10). Melanie Stocker/Courtesy sandiego.org (10). Chris Martin/Dreamstime (10). Hamilton Pytluk/Universal Studios Hollywood (10). rpac78/shutterstock (11). Courtesy sandiego.org (11). Visit California/Bongo (12). Sergey Didenko/Shutterstock. (12). Kelly vanDellen/istockphoto (12). Jose Angel Astor Rocha/Shutterstock (12). Lisa Field/Courtesy sandiego.org (13). Michele Kemper/Dreamstime (13). Visit California/thatgirlproductions.com/Jamie Williams (14). Visit California/Robert Holmes (14). Briana Edwards/Paramount studios (14). Visit California/Blaise (14). Visit California/Blaise (15). nisimo/shutterstock (20). Christian Heinz/shutterstock (21). Joseph S Giacalone/Alamy (22). Dancestrokes/Shutterstock (22). Sebastien Burel/Shutterstock (22). Marcel Fuentes/Shutterstock (23). Julia Hiebaum/Alamy (23). travelview/Shutterstock (24). Pinz Bowling Center (24). www.nicholasnicholas.com (24). LMWH/Shutterstock (24). Chateau Marmont (25). Toscana Resturant/Rob Stark (25). Henry Hargreaves (25). Catch Hospitality Group (25). **Chapter 3: Southern California's Best Road Trips:** PauloZimmermann/istockphoto (37). **Chapter 4: San Diego:** Sierralara/shutterstock (49). Americanspirit/Dreamstime (75). alisafarov/Shutterstock (75). Robert Holmes (76). Steve Snodgrass [CC BY 2.0]/Flickr (77). Lequint/Dreamstime (78). Edward Fielding/Shutterstock (78). fPat [CC BY 2.0]/Flickr (78). fPat [CC BY 2.0]/Flickr (78). Chris Gotz/Shutterstock (78). Jose Angel Astor Rocha/Shutterstock (79). Howard Sandler/iStockphoto (92). **Chapter 5: Disneyland and Orange County:** Beach Media/shutterstock (103). Eric Castro [CC BY-NC-SA 2.0]/Flickr (114). Robert Holmes (124). f00sion/iStockphoto (127). www.rwongphoto.com/Alamy (130). Brett Shoaf/Artistic Visuals Photography (134). Lowe Llaguno/Shutterstock (137). Steve Heap/shutterstock.com (142). **Chapter 6: Los Angeles:** Jill Krueger (147). Paper Cat/shutterstock (155). Carl Yu (171). Adam Latham (182). **Chapter 7: Palm Springs:** Carol M. Highsmith/Visit California (221). Danielschreurs/Dreamstime (230). David Falk/iStockphoto (241). **Chapter 8: Joshua Tree National Park:** Eric Foltz/iStockphoto (257). Dennis Silvas/shutterstock (266). miroslav_1/istockphoto (270). Greg Epperson/shutterstock (272). **Chapter 9: Mojave Desert:** Sierralara/shutterstock (275). mlgb/Fodors.com Member (281). DebsG/shutterstock (284). Maksershov/Dreamstime (288). **Chapter 10: Death Valley National Park:** Bryan Brazil/Shutterstock (293). kavram/shutterstock (301). **Chapter 11: The Central Coast:** jamesh1977/istockphoto (309). Davidmschrader/Dreamstime (333). Aimee M Lee/Shutterstock (367). lucky-photographer/istockphoto (370-371). **Chapter 12: Monterey Bay Area:** haveseen/shutterstock (375). Nadezhdasarkisian/Dreamstime (384). Artyart/Shutterstock (392). Wolterk/Dreamstime (401). Mike Brake/Dreamstime (411). **About Our Writers:** All photos are courtesy of the writers.

*Every effort has been made to trace the copyright holders, and we apologize in advance for any accidental errors. We would be happy to apply the corrections in the following edition of this publication.